New Voyages and Travels: Originals and Translations Ed. by Sir R. Phillips.

by New Voyages

Address:
HardPress
8345 NW 66TH ST #2561
MIAMI FL 33166-2626
USA
Email: info@hardpress.net

NEW

VOYAGES

AND

T R A V E L S;

CONSISTING OF

ORIGINALS AND TRANSLATIONS.

VOL. IX.

WITH FOUR ENGRAVINGS.

LONDON:

PRINTED FOR SIR RICHARD PHILLIPS AND Co.

BRIDE-COURT, BRIDGE-STREET; AND TO BE HAD OF ALL BOOKSELLERS.

Price 21s. Half-bound.

D. Sidney and Co. Printers,
Northumberland Street, Strand.

CONTENTS TO VOL. IX.

———

ENGRAVINGS IN THIS VOLUME.

Tour over the Alps.

Recollections in Sicily.

Russian Missions into the Interior of Asia.

TRAVELS

ON THE

CONTINENT

AND IN

ENGLAND.

BY DR. A. H. NIEMEYER.

Translated from the German.

London:

ICHARD PHILLIPS AND Co.

T, BRIDGE-STREET.

1823.

* Volume Eight is now on sale, as well as all the former Volumes and Numbers, and they may be had of all the Booksellers.

G. Sidney, Printer,
Northumberland-street, Strand.

TRANSLATOR'S PREFACE.

It is amusing and instructive to see ourselves, as in a glass, in the accounts of foreigners. Persons cannot see themselves so well as they are seen by others. No nation has a higher opinion of itself than the English. Foreigners, however, take the liberty to speak of us as we do of them—as they find us; and though it may not in all cases be gratifying to hear what they say of us, it is always amusing, and often affords a valuable lesson.

Stephen Perlin, a French ecclesiastic, who was in England in the reign of Edward VI., and who wrote with all the prejudices of his countrymen, is extremely scurrilous :—"One may observe of the English," says he, "that they are neither valiant in war, nor faithful in peace, which is apparent by experience; for although they are placed in a good soil, and a good country, they are wicked, and so extremely fickle, that at one moment they will adore a prince, and the next moment they would kill or crucify him. They have a mortal enmity to the French, whom they conceive to be their ancient enemies, and in common call us French dogs—but they hate all sorts of strangers. It displeases me that these villains, in their own country, spit in our faces, although, when they are in France, we treat them like divinities. But herein the French demonstrate themselves to be of a noble and generous spirit." He afterwards tempers his abuse with some compliments, particularly to our females :—"The men are large, handsome, and ruddy, with flaxen hair, being in a northern latitude; the *women*, of any estimation, are the greatest beauties in the world, and as fair as alabaster, without offence to those of Italy, Flanders, and Germany be it spoken ; they are also cheerful and courteous, and of a good address." Of the country he says, " In this kingdom are so many beautiful *ships*, so handsome are hardly to be seen elsewhere in the whole world. Here are also many fine islands and plenty of pasture, with such quantities of game, that in these islands (which are all surrounded with woods and thick hedges) it is not uncustomary to see at one time more than one hundred rabbits running about in one meadow." He speaks, perhaps, in just terms, of what was a great fault in our national character then, and is even too much so now—our fondness for drinking. " The English are great drunkards. In drinking or eating they will say to you a hundred times, ' *I drink to you*,' and you should answer them in their language, ' *I pledge you*.' When they are drunk, they will swear blood and death that you shall drink all that is in your cup. But it is to be noted, as I have before said, that in this excellent kingdom there is no kind of order, for the people are reprobates, and thorough enemies to good manners and letters, and know not whether they belong to God or the devil."

Hentzner, the German traveller, who was here in the reign of queen Elizabeth, is far more candid, and rather laughs at, than censures us. He says, " The English are serious, like the Germans, and lovers of show : they excel in dancing and music, for they are active and lively, though of a thicker make than the French ; they cut their hair close on the middle of the head, letting it grow on either side ; they are good sailors and better pirates, cunning, treacherous, and thievish ; about three hundred are said to be hanged annually at London ; they give the wall as the place of honour ; hawking is the general sport of the gentry ; they are more polite in eating than the *French*, devouring less bread but more meat, which they roast in perfection ; they put a deal of sugar in their drink ; their beds are covered with tapestry, even those of the farmers ; they are often molested with scurvy, said to have first crept into *England* with the *Norman* conquest. In the field they are powerful, successful against their enemies, impatient of any thing like slavery; vastly fond of great noises that fill the air, such as the firing of cannon, drums, and the ringing of bells; so that it is common for a number of them, that have got a glass in their heads, to go up in some belfry and ring the bells for hours together, for the sake of exercise. If they see a foreigner very well made or particularly handsome, they will say *it is a pity he is not an* ENGLISHMAN."

Le Serre, who attended Mary de Medicis to England, when she visited her daughter Henrietta Maria, the queen of Charles I., and who partook of all the hospitalities of the English court, (whatever he might think) speaks of us in the most enthusiastic terms. Our ladies he describes as positive divinities, and the country and inhabitants generally, as worthy the highest admiration. To be sure, he was writing the description of a most splendid spectacle, of which he was the witness, where the people were all dressed in their holiday clothes, and as the same kind of ceremony attended the queen's mother, all the way from her landing at Dover, he may be said to have only seen the best side of us.

Jorevin de Rochford, another French traveller in the time of Charles II., says—" This nation is tolerably polite, in which they, in a great measure, resemble the French, whose modes and fashions they study and imitate. They are in general large, fair, pretty well made, and have good faces. They are good warriors on the land, but more particularly so on the sea: they are dexterous and courageous, proper to engage in a field of battle, where they are not afraid of blows. And the honour of understanding the art of ship-building beyond all the other nations of Europe, must be allowed to the English. Strangers in general are not liked in London, even the Irish and Scots, who are the subjects of the same king. They have a great respect for their women, whom they court with all imaginable civility. They always sit at the head of the table, and dispose

of what is placed on it by helping every one, entertaining the
company with some pleasant conceit or agreeable story. In
fine, they are respected as mistresses, whom every one is desirous of obeying, so that to speak with truth, England is the
paradise of women, as Spain and Italy is their purgatory."

The above travellers, it will be recollected, are describing
our forefathers, and drawing a picture which, in some respects,
is as new to us as it was to them. The next is a traveller of
comparatively modern days—a man of information, and apparently good nature. He speaks, as indeed almost all foreigners do, of the same extreme rudeness of the lower orders of
English, but bestows every praise on the higher ranks, as well
as on the country generally. The person we allude to is *M.
Grossly*, who wrote his Tour in the year 1772.—Our custom
of shaking hands, he describes very ludicrously :—"To take a
man by the arm," says he, " and shake it until his shoulder is
almost dislocated, is one of the grand testimonies of friendship
which the English give each other, when they happen to meet.
This they do very coolly ; there is no expression of friendship
in their countenances, yet the whole soul enters into the arm
which gives the shake ; and this supplies the place of the embraces and salutes of the French."

The following sketches of London were drawn by Mr. Ka-
ramsin, a Russian traveller, who visited England about the
year 1798 :—

" I sent for a barber, and they brought me a thick phlegma-
tic Englishman, who, having first unmercifully flayed my face,
plastered my head with flour and tallow. ' Alas, I am no
longer in Paris,' I said to myself, with a sigh, ' where the
powder-puff of the ingenious lively Rulet played like a gentle
zephyr around my head, and strewed it with a resplendent
white aromatic rime.' To my complaints that he was flaying
me, that his pomatum stunk, and that his hair-powder was
only coarse flour, the unpolished English barber sullenly answered, ' I don't understand you, Sir !'

" I put on my Parisian frock, bethought me of dear France

with a sigh, and walked out in a very melancholy mood. But the cloud that darkened my soul soon vanished at the sight of the beautiful illumination, which presented itself to my wondering eyes.—Though the sun was scarcely set, all the lamps in the streets were lighted up. There are thousands of them, and which ever way I turn I behold a fiery string, as it were, extended through the air; I had never before seen any thing similar to it, and I no longer wondered at the mistake of a German prince, who on making his entry into London, imagined that it was an illumination provided on purpose to welcome him with peculiar marks of honour. The English are fond of light, and they spend millions to supply, by artificial, the want of the solar rays—an indubitable proof of the national wealth.

" Whoever calls London noisy must either never have seen it, or must have no correct idea of what a noisy city is. London is populous it is true; but, compared with Paris, and even with Moscow, it is extraordinarily quiet. The inhabitants of London seem to be either half asleep, or overcome with lassitude from their excessive activity and exertion. If the rattling of the carriages did not, from time to time, shake the auditory nerve, a stranger might frequently suppose he had become deaf, while passing along some of the most populous and most frequented streets. I stepped into several coffee-houses, where I found from twenty to thirty persons reading the newspapers, and drinking their port; while the profoundest silence reigned in the room, except that perhaps every quarter of an hour, one hears a solitary ' *Your health, Gentlemen !*' Can it then excite wonder, that the English are such deep thinkers, and that their parliamentary orators know not when to leave off, when once they have begun to speak ? it would seem as if they were tired of, and willing to make amends for their usual taciturnity.

" But if my ears thus enjoy rest and quiet, my eyes are the more busily engaged. In London, too, the women are very handsome, and they dress with tasteful simplicity; they are all without either powder or paint, and wear hats, which seem to have been invented by the Graces themselves; they seem rather to fly than to walk; their neat little feet, which peep out from under their snow-white muslin robe, scarcely touch the pavement. Over their white corset an Indian shawl is spread, on which their fair hair descends in charming ringlets: for to me, at least, it seems that the greater part of the English women have fair hair: the most beautiful of them, however, are brunettes. The physiognomies of the men may be arranged under three classes; they are either surly, good-natured, or brutish. I can safely swear, that in no other country have I seen so many brutish faces as here; and I am now convinced that Hogarth drew from nature.—Such physiognomies are, it is true, [only to be met with among the populace; but then there is so much variety, so much characteristic expression in them, that ten Lavaters would scarcely be able to point out the bad qualities and propensities which they indicate."

Besides these, we have had Dr. WENDEBORN's view of England; a very flattering and well-tempered account of our manners, characters, and institutions, in the middle of the reign of George the third. Afterwards, M. Von ARCHENTOLTZ drew a picture of England: he praised the nation, and held it up as an example to others. But, during the last war, one PILLET, a Frenchman, published a most disgusting portrait of England, caricatured and libelled our women, and represented the men as universal and habitual drunkards.

The last severe strictures were those of a New Englandman, of which we gave the substance in a late number of this work.

In every respect it is useful, as a means of improvement, and as a corrector of vanity, to read and study these notions of foreigners. Like English travellers in other countries, they make their own habits the standards of perfection: but their criticisms enable us to make comparisons, and rub off the rust of our own prejudices.

The veteran traveller, Dr. Niemeyer, will neither be found to play the critic or eulogist. He describes honestly what he saw, and, as a book of facts, his work merits respect and attention.

TRAVELS

IN

GERMANY, THE NETHERLANDS,

AND

ENGLAND.

———————

An opportunity of furnishing this first Volume of my general Travels was afforded me by my Journey to England in the year 1819. The public anxiety evinced for the work, and the participation taken in my feelings, were alike pleasing and affecting to me. Still, the request made to me, that I would furnish the world with something to read upon *this Country*, gave rise to very serious reflection, and greatly encouraged my own inclinations; for it is far easier to expect, than it is possible to furnish, much matter, at least during the short stay I made in so remarkable a country; and the observations and reflections which strike every one, even during the shortest sojourn, are already known to most people.

However, as every person considers the objects with his own eyes, and as these objects may receive an appropriate character, even from the time in which they are contemplated, what is already known may be repeated, and even the contrast of the different views and ideas formed of them may afford an interest to their treatment. This *individuality*, as it were, of consideration, attended me in my contemplations, and I have endeavoured to lay the same before the public in a representation of all that I saw and heard in England. A simple description of the objects, a precise topography, and detailed narration of all that either was or was not remarkable, formed much less my plan, than the communication of those particular ideas and sentiments which the objects produced in me. Every man, without having stirred even from his own dwelling, may write and fill whole volumes with reflections, and may be enabled to complete a tenth work from the refuse of *nine* more ancient ones. But, by following this manner, it easily happens to the reader, like the young traveller in Italy, who, indeed, in order to remain true to his plan of travels, left nothing unseen, and wrote every evening in his journal how many churches and galleries he had gone through, and always ended with a *" God be praised."*—A certain dull and tedious uniformity is invariably inseparable from a detailed description of buildings, picture galleries, museums, country seats, and gardens. This is frequently carried so far as to obliterate even the wish of being present ourselves, either at the periods or situations referred to.

After this preface, simple historical relations will not be expected in the following sheets, but attempts rather to connect more general considerations with the individual ones, to bring the past to the present, and, upon the brilliant theatre of events, to introduce recollections of those persons who have moved, acted, and played their part, perhaps, even centuries ago. This has introduced here and there some historical episodes, which certainly may possess but little interest for many of our readers ; but still, perhaps, as they are taken from the fountains, will contain *something* new, and at any rate must become newly interesting, by the history they afford, of our own time. In representing the impressions made by single objects, it is, moreover, impossible to avoid speaking of one's self. But is not almost every description of travel a journal of our own biography ?

The report spread in various places, that these Travels had been undertaken by high appointment, for particular purposes, and even at the public expense, with reference partly to the system of English universities and schools, I positively refute. I am ready to pay the merited compliment to the excellence which all Europe have acknowledged in the customary tribute to the English constitution. Much, however, as is certainly excellent in it, greatly I fear a great part of it is not applicable to the situation of my own country. But when the grand effects of public spirit, and of unrestrained energy of every kind, which the government affords to the citizen in that relation, are compared with other constitutions, where so frequently every remedy is expected from narrow proposals, little-minded formalities, and a mistrustful watchfulness, which only lame and oppress, it becomes difficult to forego the wish, that we approach not nearer the British public spirit.

It was my rule to give an impartial representation of every thing I found in Oxford, Cambridge, and Eton. Notwithstanding, however, the above assertion, I am just as far from giving my unconditional disapprobation of every thing to be found in those places, as to agree with the eulogiums upon them, made by some of my own countrymen, who were certainly influenced rather by the deception which the appearance of perfect order and morality occasions, than by a profound acquaintance with the whole regulations of the interior.

The religious and church institutions were certainly a principal object of my observation ; and I have endeavoured, as far as it was possible, to touch upon their various parties. Most of the works which have appeared in England and Germany upon them, have been hitherto little satisfactory ; it is, however, difficult, in forming a comparison of so many opposite ways of thinking, not to incline, in our judgment, somewhat more to the one than the other, according as we ourselves, in the one or the other, think we discover more satisfaction to our own religious views. The point of union, however, is highly remarkable, which, in our days, thousands of the members of all these churches and spiritual corporations have discovered, and have extended, by their united endeavours, the empire of Christianity throughout the world.

From early youth no foreign country possessed so high an interest in my mind as England. Many circumstances conspired to awaken and to cherish this favourable predilection.

My first education was formed at a period when, notwithstanding the continually augmenting number of German classics, translations from British poets and prose writers, appertained to the most approved productions, and gained thereby a very considerable influence over the taste and the ton of many dispositions. In the collection of works belonging to the Belles Lettres, from which we were allowed every week at school to select one book, were to be found by the side of Bodmer, Haller, Klopstock, Kleist, &c., the works of Milton, Thomson, and Glover; the English Spectator, Harvey and Richardson ; together with the first German translation of Shakspeare by Wieland ; and, above all, Young, whose dignified melancholy imparted itself to all young people of both sexes, who were at all inclined to serious consideration. Foreign writers, in fact, were more frequently sought after than those of our own country. Successful, indeed, as many translations into the German have been, I panted still more after the original, and the more tasteless I found the French literature at that time, from not being acquainted with the best works in that language, the more zealously I cultivated the English.

I found every opportunity of speaking and writing the English language in the society of Mr. Samuel Thornton, at that time a young Englishman who was studying with me at the school, and whom, exactly 50 years after our first school acquaintance, I again met with as the first Bank Director of London.   Whenever I wrote small notes to him, he gave himself the trouble to correct them, and supplied me occasionally with the lecture of those periodical works, &c. which he was in the habit of receiving from England.   Thus my inclination towards every thing which came across the channel found much food in the years I passed at the University from 1771 to 1776 ; added to which two young people from Calcutta, who were to return to their native country, were given over to my care, in order that I might freshen their memory with the remembrance of their native language, which they had entirely forgotten.   Moreover, a young Gentleman of the name of Meyer, from London, who studied at the University, and was frequently my companion, contributed no little to my improvement in the English language ; as in his frequent walks with me, it was his delight to speak of his native country, of the life he had led in England, and the friend his heart had left behind, in preference to study and sciences : and this conversation took place in English.

The interest I took in the constitution of Great Britain, and the History of the Nation, was increased by the reading of the Public Papers, and still more by that of the English Historians, Burnett and Hume.   None of the Histories of modern States attracted my notice so much.   To me it appeared, particularly in many of its periods, like a great drama which offers inexhaustible matter to the reflection, presents new views to the sentiments, and which, precisely on this account, can be continually read over and over again without tiring.   By this repetition I became also so well acquainted with the particular circumstances that had occurred in that period, that I only wanted to gaze on the local picture, upon which once the principal characters, partly so noble and so heroic, and partly so dreadful and horrible, had figured, until they either terminated their career in the Tower, or found their tranquillity in Westminster Abbey.

Still, however, my longing after that Theatre of great events, and the Pantheon of immortal Britons, could only be satisfied in the years which are better devoted to repose than to new wanderings.   Every other plan of Travels appeared to me more easily to be carried into execution, than a flight over the sea. No inducement offered from companions who were equally inclined ; exaggerated representations of the indispensable expenditure of time and money ; even the idea which had easily influenced me, that, in order not to be received coolly, it was necessary to be a *perfect* master of the language—all this moderated my wishes, and weakened my expectations.

My hopes, all of a sudden, received new life in the dreadful years of war, in which the sight of the endless misery of the thousands who had gained the victory by their death and wounds, on the neighbouring plains of battle around Leipsic, scarce left us the feeling or sentiment arising from a deliverance. It is well known what England then contributed towards those families in Germany who were become wretched. It became my agreeable commission to be the Agent and Letter Writer for this Committee. As our Orphan-house, at that time a large Hospital of more than 2500 sick and wounded, was deprived of almost all its resources, I renewed the connexion with my old school-fellow, of whom I have already spoken, and was happy enough, through his influence, and that of other excellent men, such as Dr. Steinkopf, Messieurs Schwabe and Ackermann, to meet with the most ardent support, which proved alike a blessing to the town and the orphans.

The respect I had always borne towards a noble nation, which wished to appropriate to herself, by a great liberality, at once the fortune and the misery of a war, which set the continent in flames, and which she only viewed from afar upon her secure island, was now augmented by a *warm sense of gratitude.* This I had been enabled to express to one of those persons most actively employed for the relief of Germany, the celebrated artist, Mr. Ackermann, upon the occasion of his visiting his native country in the year 1818, when I shewed him the benevolent institutions which had been also assisted through his influence in the years of the greatest misery. Much conversation upon England followed ; and the assurance I received from him of a friendly reception, and that, according to his avowal, even an imperfect acquaintance with the language would be sufficient, gave greater weight to his pressing invitation.

A year later the long wished for company offered itself quite unexpectedly in the person of a gentleman who had been long established in the Bookselling business in London, Mr. Bohte, who was returning to England from the Eastern Fair of Leipsic. What could have been more welcome to me, to whose companionship could my anxious friends have better entrusted me, than to one who had experienced so much in his Travels, both by sea and land, who was moreover in full possession of the language, and who united the most pleasing, the most urbane, and social disposition, with a thorough knowledge of the country and its manners ?

Our journey took the direction of Halberstadt, Brunswick,

Hanover, Bremen, Oldenburg, and a part of East Friesland. As far as Hanover all was new to me; this heightened the interest. But it was of importance to us all to stop no where for any considerable time, and to attain the end of our journey as quickly as possible. "What," might I say with Goethe in his Travels to Italy, "what did I not leave unseen, both on right "and left, in order to carry into execution the *one* intention, "which had almost grown too old in my soul."

We left Halle on the 26th of May. Where is the man who does not feel some anxiety upon quitting his home, his friends, and his office, for a considerable period? Nothing so much recompenses us at such a moment, as a fine sky, good roads, and expeditious travelling. On the enjoyment of all these we had to congratulate ourselves. Nature every where surrounded us with the nuptial ornaments of Spring. No cloud on the horizon predicted any interruption. The most magnificent sunset followed one of the most serene days, and the evening refreshed us with its fragrance and coolness.

Brunswick, 28th May.

In the year 1770, I first greeted the old town of the Guelphs. To what men had not the youth to look up at that time? Ebert, the translator of Young, Zachariah, Gærtner, Schmidt. The young Eschenburg was then in the bloom of youth, alike elegant in person and mind, possessing a high sounding pathos in his declamation, and surrounded by all the superb works of British art. To him Germany was indebted for her acquaintance with English Literature. His Translation of Shakspeare has only been rivalled by the later one of Schlegel.

Five and forty years after our first acquaintance, I now availed myself of the opportunity which the interval of preparation for our further progress afforded, to find him out, and to solicit his blessings for the country with which he was so well acquainted. It was surprising to me that, so well versed in the English language, and connected with so many Englishmen living in his house, he should never have seen the country, and even scarce knew where to give an address to an acquaintance. "But so it comes to pass," said he, "when we continually put "off what appears easy to carry into execution. And at last "the summons to our last journey hurries us on." And so it has happened. He died on the 29th February, 1820, and though he did not belong to the original genius, Germany acknowledges how much she is indebted to him for the liberal participation he afforded her in the rich treasures of his literary acquirements.

Hanover, 29th May.

No traveller, and least of all the young, ought to neglect an opportunity of making acquaintance with respectable veterans in the service of science or the state, whose spiritual being may remain alive and powerful, when all that is temporal cannot remain untouched by the hand of destroying time. This conviction came forcibly upon me, when, the day after my meeting again with Eschenburg, I still found the father of German philosophers and pedagogues, J. G. H. Feder, alive, from whose compendium I had first learnt to set logic and metaphysics in scientific order, and had held my first lecture thereon in the year 1777. He was eighty years old. But still joy and satisfaction beamed from his wan countenance, animated by his expressive eye,—what moderation in judgment,—what tranquil contentment with the present,—what quiet expectation of the future ! In his discourse there was no trace of the irremediable fragilities of age ;—he pressed me warmly to his breast, when telling me, should I touch Hanover upon my return from England, I might probably meet with him again !

Bremen, 30th, 31st May, 1st June.

The Museum, which rose from a small beginning to an excellent institution, is an eternal monument of patriotism, not merely mercantile, but of patriotism directed towards a generally enlightened education. A single work, the Hawksworth Collection of later Travels round the World, which some friends, panting after knowledge, procured at their mutual expense, first gave rise to the idea of a reading society. This reading society gave rise to the establishment of a small library. Hence became associated the idea of an union of physiology and natural history ; afterwards the formation of a cabinet of natural productions, of instruments, models ; which has since become daily more important by continued purchases and presents, under the excellent superintendence of Professor Merten, who is distinguished by the great variety of his acquirements. The Museum is publicly opened for this purpose three times a week. Immediately regular meetings were formed for conversation and information, until, at last, the plan came to full perfection for an institution calculated for the advancement and refinement of the inhabitants of Bremen, of both sexes. At the present the rooms of the Museum are only opened to those who wish to make themselves acquainted with the literature and information of the day, from the most important domestic and foreign periodical publications. There is also a general Library for the use of all who wish to extend their knowledge to any department of science. This Library appears to me to realize the ideas in great measure which a truly patriotic member, Professor Rump, in three lectures he held before the museum, has developed "regarding a public collection of books for the national improvement."

The lectures too, which are read every Monday, upon generally interesting and important objects in nature, history, and literature, contribute no less to the advantage of both sexes who thirst after knowledge. The effects produced in the female circles will materially differ than when this life consists only in an interchange of housekeeping with the toilette, the gaming table or the ball room ; or, when reading finds any place, it is only that of the corrupt stock of common circulating libraries, which has no tendency to elevate the taste for a higher order of literature.

Of what importance such institutions are for large *trading cities,* will be visible to whoever has had an opportunity of observing how frequently a narrow intellect characterizes the man, who is no more than a merchant, and who displays an ignorant as well as high-minded indifference towards every advantage which is not connected with pecuniary gain ; whilst, at the same time, he evinces a rude contempt for learning and science in the midst of his respect for large capitalists, or at least allows himself the most confidently asserted opinions upon works of talent and spirit, particularly when the payment of coin at once authorizes him to pass his judgment.

If Bremen be thus honourably distinguished above many other great trading towns, she is just as little behind hand in the warm participation on the two most important methods of forming the mind, which are connected with all classes of the citizens, viz. education and religion. The liveliest interest has been particularly evinced in the last few years for school learning, and the new organization of the higher, the middling, and elementary institutions, promise the most magnificent fruits.

If the zealous participation of all ranks in the christian places of meeting did not only assure us of the outward respect and attachment shewn to accustomed ceremonies, but at the same time prove the interest the heart takes in religion, and the lively effect of the same, the sight at least of the thronged churches, although service is performed three times a day, must give rise to the most favourable opinion.

The two subterraneous curiosities of Bremen, which all the geographical descriptions remind the traveller of, must not be passed over without a visit.

The Lead Cellar (Bleykeller) is a large vault under the choir of the cathedral. In former times, the lead with which part of the roof was covered was melted in it, and thence it took its name. For centuries ago it was the custom to place persons of rank here, who accidentally died in Bremen upon their travels; and, probably, the discovery was made just as accidentally, that instead of rotting, they dried up, and were changed into a kind of mummy. Thus the English Countess Stanhope has been preserved more than two hundred years: a Swedish General with his Aid-de-Camp, and a Swedish Countess, since the period of the thirty years' war; the remains of an unfortunate tiler, together with similar mummies of dead cats, birds, &c. &c. The appearance is certainly more common than is believed, and just as frequently to be explained from the constitution of the bodies themselves, as from the dryness and sharp draught of air felt in the vaults.

From these friendless tombs, where even the slow destruction of what was once animated makes the picture of death only more dreadful, we went immediately into the justly-prized subterraneous vaults over which the Town-house *(Rathhous)* and the Exchange are built. What a contrast! From the stillness of death to the cheerfulness of active life. When the business of the day is over, the citizens of the town assemble here, form groups in smaller or larger boxes, which are erected for the purpose, in confidential conversation, and forget, over glasses filled with the juice of the finest grape their cares and troubles, at least for a few hours.

Oldenburgh, 2d June;—Leer, 3d;—Aurich, 4th.

The road to Oldenburg, which is frequently very tedious, leads partly through the Bremen, and partly through the Hanoverian, territories. We arrived there, however, soon enough to get a good view of the town, the rich ducal nursery garden, and the pleasing disposal of the grounds and environs of the palace.

Where the territory of Oldenburg ends, that of East Friesland begins, a small province, but distinguished by a variety of peculiarities. Besieged towards the west and north by the waves of an ocean, what an immense application of human industry must it not have cost, from early times, to snatch it from the reach of the most dreadful of elements, or to secure it against the same by means of immeasurable dikes; or, when from time to time the flood, in reparation of its theft, places new land upon it, by mounding it, to form Polder and Groden. The tract of land through which our road led us formed the most agreeable contrast with the sandy heaths through which we had passed.   We found ourselves surprised with the luxuriant vegetation of the fertile soil, surrounded with smiling meadows, animated by the well-known flocks of Friesland. The villages, with their cheerful houses, built of tiles, became more friendly and cleanly.   A refreshing coolness blew upon us from the thickest part of the plantations, and thus we arrived at Leer about evening.   Geography makes this place only a market-town; but, from the elegance of many of its houses, and more from the activity in the streets, it presents the idea of a very small, indeed, but wealthy city.   What makes it also still more animated is the Lede, which empties itself into the Ems, and with it flows towards the North Sea, and thus gives life to shipping and ship-building.

The straight road to Holland would have been through Emden. A particular interest, however, attracted me to Aurich, the capital and former seat of the court of the principality.   The hours passed too swiftly at Aurich.   For a moment I saw the former house of the family Wurmbs, now belonging to the Bachmeisters, and the amiable inhabitants pardoned the annoyance of a grateful man, who wished to pay homage to the manes of his benefactress in her native place.

The Trechschyt (so the boat is called) brought us to Emden earlier than we expected.   The remaining hours of the evening, and a few in the morning, afforded us at least time enough for a general view of the town and port, in which the vessels were just now getting ready for a cruise upon the herring fishery, which is the principal source of subsistence of the inhabitants.

5th June.

In the morning, about nine o'clock, we left Emden; and about noon saluted the coasts of Holland in Delfziel. The large lake, known under the name of the Dollart, which we passed over, afforded rich matter for contemplation, by the remembrance of the former ages which here lay buried. Here, where restless floods are now streaming, stood, 500 years ago, and, partly, somewhat later, upwards of fifty flourishing towns and villages, large churches, and rich cloisters. Here, according to the old chronicles, were market-towns which could reckon 180 mothers of families, who wore massive golden bucklers upon their breasts, according to the dress then in fashion.   Of all this nothing remains but the name.   Even the last tops of the steeples and of the walls, which, for a considerable time, were seen topping out at the ebb tide, all sunk without a trace.   Over former fat pastures now sail richly-laden vessels, and fishing is followed where, formerly, the sowing of the best corn, and the most luxuriant wheat, produced an harvest of one hundred fold. The present *Reiderland,* celebrated for the particular abundance of its vegetation, for its Groden and Polder, is only a remaining part of the once so important tract of country which connected East Friesland with Groningen. The larger part is formed into a bay. Words can ill describe the great deluge which first broke in at midnight, just as the people were preparing themselves for Christmas morning, drove down the dams or mounds, and scattered death and destruction in every direction. Our vessel was thus floating over an immense grave of billows, over which the lake, with the pleasing rays of the morning dawn, spread itself out like a refulgent silver coverlid. But reflection drew the eye down into the deep. It might have been able to look down into the dreadful abysses in which so many productions of laborious diligence, so many works of inventive art, so many energetic bodies, lay sunk in ruins ; for more than 50,000 souls, of every class, sex, and age, who once, like ourselves, rejoiced in life, were sent on that dreadful night, in a few minutes, to their long and peaceful abode ; the Christmas gladness of happy children was turned into the cry of anxiety and horror ; and the chaunts of the mass preachers and the holy cloistered nuns, were converted into an eternal silence. And still, as many accounts say, the blind element would scarcely have been able to effect such inroads, had not hostile elements raged in the breasts of many of the principal persons ; had not hatred and envy separated those through whose serviceable labours of mounding and mending, the rage of the sea could have been quelled, and the country secured. So, like upon a thousand fields of battle, here too lay innumerable innocent sacrifices of the passions and follies of a few. Who can find out the exit from this labyrinth of human fate !

Holland, 6th, 12th June.

The Trechschyt goes regularly at certain hours from Delfziel to Groningen. We passed down the canals of the province of this name in the company of some well-informed men, from whom much was to be learnt. The journey continued till late in the evening, and only one hour remained to wander by moonlight through one of the finest towns of Holland, together with its fine university, and to return the visit of the naturalist, Mr. Professor Swindern. I found him accidentally in the circle of young East Friesland students, around a table richly provided with the natural productions of the country.

It is necessary to leave Groningen very early in the morning, and take a good carriage, in order, by passing rapidly through Friesland, to arrive at a certain hour before evening in Lemmer, a small lively town, where the packet boat leaves for Amsterdam. This time too the Sunday had animated the roads, the villages, and the pleasing little towns, like Nordyk, where we took our dinner. Sun-set imparted a magnificence to the evening upon the Sudersee beyond all description. We soon came in sight of the Islands of Lydan and Monnekendyk ; but the wind was not favourable, and the rocking of the vessel had a disagreeable effect upon many of the passengers, and gave all of us an idea of what we had to expect in the open sea. Before noon we were in sight of Amsterdam, which was continually rising more visibly from behind a wood of masts. At getting out, one boat followed us upon another, contending which should conduct us through the canals of the city to our quarters. We arrived about dinner time. The journey through Holland was indeed only a passage, but nevertheless, I did not feel disposed to lose the few days in which we made it. I had remained longer in this country, so highly interesting in many respects, in the year 1806.

With regard to literary institutions, much more appears to have been done for the *lower* than the *higher* schools. The French preacher, Monsieur Teissedre L'Ange, to whom *my maxims of education* are indebted for a Dutch translation made with great judgment and knowledge of the language, was just now as actively employed for the good of the poor schools in Amsterdam, as he had been formerly in Haerlem. In the latter city I missed the superintendant of the united Belgian national and citizen schools, but I overtook him in his journey at Rotterdam. He was going to Brussels and the other French provinces of the Netherlands, in order, if possible, to spread the same good spirit which had gained him such high merit in the Dutch ; for few laboured as he had done, in the spirit and to the purposes of the highly respectable Nieuwen Heysen, founder of Maatshappytot nut van't Algemeen. There were very few points upon which we did not agree in our conversation, in a long walk we took in the delightful environs of Rotterdam. As historical information it deserves to be remarked, that even at the period when Holland had Buonaparte for a king, the course of education was not at all impeded, and the French commissaries, whom Napoleon sent into the Netherlands and the Hanse Towns, in order to give an account of the condition in which school education was found, could hardly say enough in praise of the high perfection which the national school (Lager Schooler) had attained in Holland.

In Leyden, a new picture was offered me of the dreadful power of two destructive elements. On the 12th January, 1807, a large ship, laden with 40,000 pounds of powder, in seventy barrels, which was destined for Delft, and lay in the middle of the canal, blew up, (no one has ever discovered by what accident) with a dreadful explosion. The effects of the shock were felt at a still further distance, at the Hague, at Amsterdam, at Utrecht, and at Zwolt. In the town itself it appeared as if the earth had opened, the heavens were on flames, and the end of the world arrived. Almost all the houses situated in the Rappenburg, the most beautiful part of Leyden, fell down at one instant; a still greater number, upwards of 800, were considerably damaged; even in distant parts of the town no tiles were to be found upon many of the roofs, no window remained uninjured, and no door upon its hinges. In many families they had just sat down to dinner. At the next moment, every thing in the palaces of the rich, and in the habitations of the poor, lay in ruins. Of two large boarding establishment, and a poor school, very few persons could be saved. Whoever was struck in the street by the blow, was carried into the air, either fell wounded if not dead, to the ground, or if he remained alive, on seeking his home he no longer found any shelter. For two or three days nothing was heard but lamentation out of the holes under ground, which were shut up from the efforts of the workmen by huge masses of stone. There was scarce any considerable house which had not to lament the loss of a friend or relation. Still the number of the dead was less than at first believed. Many had been preserved almost by a miracle. Of many, however, not the smallest remains were any longer to be found. Lacerated and disfigured bodies were continually brought to the Town-house, that their relatives might discover who they were. Many a family was wholly extirpated with all its branches.

Thus I found whole streets and quarters, in which at my first visit, in the year 1806, I had wandered amongst sumptuous buildings, at present converted into empty squares, covered with grass and planted with young trees; and had it not been for the celebrated Doctor of Law, Professor Tydeman, who honoured me with being my guide, I should hardly have found my way in this *new Leyden.* A secret shudder overcame me, when I placed myself as a stranger in Leyden during these dreadful days. If they had happened four months earlier, I might have met with the fate which befel many a stranger, whose business had carried him thither, and of whom no one could tell on what spot he had found his grave.

Still, as time heals all wounds, these scenes of horror were forgotten. Less was said about them, than I expected. People too were already accustomed to the deserted quarters, and had partly given them a very pleasing appearance.

Rotterdam, 11th June.

The only day which remained for me to view this extensive and interesting town, as celebrated for its considerable trade as for its delightful situation on the banks of the Maese, was passed too quickly in conversation with M. Van dem Ende, and in the benevolent hospitality of an old friend, Mr. Goede, one of the most diligent translators and preservers of translations of German writings.

It was vacation at the flourishing institution of education of Mr. de Raadt, and the master of the house was absent. Willingly would I in person have imparted to him the hopes which his worthy son, who during two years was my intimate companion, and one of the most zealous in the study of the theory and history of instruction, had excited in us, and who, as might be expected, transplanted much of what he saw here, and every where upon his travels, successfully upon the soil of his native country. Certainly it will have become very clear to him, how high the well-organised schools in Germany stand above the best private institutions, where the superintendant feels himself always tied by a certain dependence upon under teachers, whom he cannot do well without.

The following morning we hastened to the vessel which always goes away on the days when the packet-boat in Helvoetsluys weighs anchor for England. In Nieuwesluis we alighted, and found a carriage in readiness to conduct persons and baggage to Helvoetsluys. We reached there at noon. As we arrived, the captain of the Packet in rotation to sail, received us in uniform. As the packet generally, unless there is a total want of wind, goes out in the afternoon, no time is to be lost in getting passports reviewed at the neighbouring office, and settling for the passage, which amounted to about 15 or 16 dollars of our money.

On Saturday forenoon at four o'clock, we received an invitation to come on board. At five o'clock all was in order. The wind was throughout contrary; but tacking and cruizing soon removed us from the sight of the Dutch coast. The continent gradually disappeared as we sailed over the wide expanse of sea, whilst we took an anxious survey of our native shore.

Our voyage lasted from the 12th to 15th of June, when we landed at Harwich. The joy at landing, the comfortable prospect before me of clean inns, and convenient stage coaches, the latter so great a novelty to all strangers unacquainted with the mechanical elegance and even refinement to which they have arrived in England, perfectly enraptured me, and I could not avoid giving vent to the grateful feelings excited, by praises as flattering as they were just. How grateful was the impression produced by contemplating this rich country teeming with the highest cultivation, and now in all the pride of magnificent bloom! Every where traces of agricultural industry meet the eye. I imagined I was arriving in beautiful and wealthy *cities*, while I was only in a *village*. I thought I was beholding the most magnificent country seats, and still they were only the habitations of the farmers or merchants. The houses in the cities or market towns are indeed usually small and narrow—but how friendly an appearance do they not afford by their windows as bright as looking glass, by the pretty hedges, and the small flower gardens through which a clean path conducts you to the house door. And how the mercantile life begins even in the country! I drove by from one shop to another. Behind the high windows of beautiful crown glass, which form the lower story, all kinds of wares are artfully laid out to view. And what cleanliness and neatness in the dress of most people we met with, who, full of curiosity, advanced to the door or window, when the coach passed by, expecting friends or relations, and helping them down from the roof of the carriage. As if borne by the almost indescribable crowd of passengers in carriages and on horseback, which begins particularly after Rumford, two German miles distant from London, where the road is already lined on both sides with dwellings, I arrived, as all travellers have denominated it, in the town (die Stadt); so London is plainly called, as formerly Rome in Italy —but without knowing rightly where it begins, as there is not the least appearance of gates. It was already dark, but the illumination, which begins very early, displayed every object to my view. The impression which the grandeur and extent of the town cannot fail to make upon every beholder is truly astonishing. The sumptuous buildings, the constantly moving scene, are striking peculiarities and features which far surpass those of Amsterdam, Paris, Copenhagen, Vienna, and Venice, and impress every person who for the first time steps into this *little world*, at present inhabited by at least 1,200,000 souls. It is indeed a mixture of astonishment and anxiety.

Residence in England.

I will now candidly and honestly impart, as it appeared to me, whatever I have seen, observed, and experienced in the very limited time to which I was confined. Others have seen many things quite otherwise, and judged of them accordingly. My own opinion, which had been previously formed from the earliest works upon England, has often become quite changed by ocular inspection. I have generally found that writers have been too hasty to see well; too prejudiced in order to judge impartially; too inclined to believe every thing in order to examine with care; and frequently sacrifice the rigid truth to a witty conceit or striking representation.

Amongst the older works Alberti is become tolerably out of use. Volkman remains still a good guide, and has at least registered all that is to be seen with diligence, although he is frequently most laconic where details might have been expected. Others, such as Faugas, S. Fond, Nemnich, Young, Gilpin, had rather the economical, the picturesque, a natural history in view, which lay out of my plan. Moritz, without satisfying is interesting from the truth of narration, during the short stay he made. Archenholz indeed, on the contrary, furnishes far more, although much that he says can be considered only as a sketch. I have found the well-informed Kuttner, Wendeborn, and Goede, by far the most serviceable writers. Madame Schopenhaver, in her English journey, possesses the talent of making fine observation, which, however, deviates here and there into an unreasonable severity, arising from what she personally experienced; whilst she, however, retains a lively representation of all that she saw. In the Gallo American, Mr. Simond, it is impossible not to perceive the liveliness which distinguishes the French character, although he lived more than twenty years in America. It is tempered, however, by that earnest and love of truth which mark the half nationalized Englishman. Professor Spieker's, by far the best topographical description, has appeared only lately.

I have formed to myself no particular plans and purposes in making this visit, and still less have I been entrusted, as it has been here and there hinted, with particular commissions. The end of my endeavours was to get acquainted with this remarkable country, in all its various points of view, as far as it was possible in the short two months I resided in it, and with uninterrupted enjoyment of good health and careful employment of every hour, I have succeeded far beyond my own expectations, both in seeing much and in gaining a variety of useful intelligence. I was naturally attracted towards every thing that concerned the *spiritual* and *religious* education of the nation. I think I am enabled, therefore, to give a more exact description of every thing of this kind than other travellers, who either hasten over it too quickly, or do not touch upon it at all.

Many of the travellers who were making the journey for the first time, had been already consulting with each other what *curiosities* of London they should first see. But when the end of our journey was attained, every thing appeared, to me at least, quite different. In considering the immense *whole, particularities* disappear. Here is no time to think upon what is *distant*, because what is *near* already chains the attention. It is well known too, that the great specimens of magnificence, Westminster Abbey, St. Paul's Cathedral, the Exchange, the Bank, and the Harbour, &c. will not escape observation.

All travellers have very properly observed that, whilst other capital cities create an impression by the magnificence of the style of architecture in which their *houses* and *palaces* are built, even when the towns are as quiet and depopulated as *Potsdam*, or even *Berlin* is in some quarters, this impression is far from being produced in *London*. Of *palaces*, properly so called, there is no trace, as in the above cities, in Prague, Vienna, Paris, or in the sumptuous, although smaller Italian capitals. Even the dwellings of royalty bear the name only of *Houses*, (the insignificant St. James's Palace excepted) for example, Buckingham House, where George the Third and his Queen used to reside, Carlton House, where the present King resided when he was still Prince Regent, Somerset House, &c. &c. &c. All the magnificence of which they can boast must be sought for in the interior of the chambers, and not in the exterior. The whole of London is built of a reddish and white grey bricks, and these are very rarely covered over with stucco. Stone is met with only in a very few modern buildings. From the *smoke of the sea coal*, which, particularly at the end of autumn and winter, envelopes the whole of London, all the houses soon receive a black appearance, which is only somewhat compensated for by the shining looking glass of which the windows are composed. Most of the houses are perfectly like each other, generally very narrow.

Were we, therefore, to imagine to ourselves London, even in its most beautiful and most modern quarters, depopulated and without trade, it would become, indeed, particularly in the frequently narrow streets of the city, a black melancholy mass of houses, to live amongst which would create only ennui and disgust. But how totally different does it appear, when *life* and activity commence at the dawn of morning, and only terminate towards midnight, and not only the *moving* stream of people, but also the *immoveable* piles of goods which are presented to the eye in countless shapes, in the production of an industry, directed to a thousand employments, every where rivets the attention.

If these magazines and shops afford by *day* the most interesting sight to the stranger, and fixes his attention at every step he takes, the effect becomes far superior in the *evening*. The *illumination of the streets of London* has always been celebrated. It is at present greatly augmented by the use of *Gas-lights*. This pure light, which burns in the lanterns of the streets as well as in the shops, as soon as it becomes dusk, throws such a magic splendour over every thing, that we may imagine ourselves wandering amongst enchanted castles. As *looking glasses* are made use of in many extensive shops, every thing is reflected in a double and threefold degree. The costly silk stuffs of the most burning colours, laid in picturesque order by the side of and over each other; the East India shawls, the works in glass, the rarest fruits of all countries piled up pyramidically, the natural and artificial flowers appear as beautiful again as at day time. Between them the large round flasks and vases of the Chymists, as the Apothecaries are called, make a brilliant display. They are filled with clear red, blue, green, and yellow waters, and appear as if rubies, sapphires, topazes, and emeralds were shining in them. At a distance they raise an idea of a festive illumination, but these appearances are those of every day. It cannot be denied that the streets of London, in this respect, offer to the passenger every evening an extraordinary and singular sight.

And still, after all the magnificence and riches, the most surprising object of contemplation for the foreigner, consists in the hundred thousands of *people* who are continually moving up and down in this vast panorama.

The endless stream of people who, in following their business, particularly in the principal streets, are every where moving, like the ebb and flow of a tide, would render walking in the highest degree troublesome, were the passenger not secured from all danger of being injured by the continually rolling carriages, by the *trottoirs*, or foot pavements, raised a little above the street by the sides of the houses.

All the foot passengers, I met with in the large streets bore almost without exception the appearance of being in *easy circumstances*. Poverty and filth, which are not wanting even in London, are to be found far more generally in the smaller streets of the city. In the larger streets, on the contrary, almost every one is well dressed; the men usually wear black, and always very white linen, for the latter is indispensable in order to appear as a gentleman; the women, without exception, wear hats, and are very elegantly attired. It is related that nothing struck even the Emperor of Russia so much in London, as the great number of well-dressed men and women whom he every where encountered; generally speaking, too, the physiognomist and observer of mankind finds no where such food for his reflection as here; for where does he meet with bright intellect and stupid torpidity; bashful modesty and proud ignorance; idleness and indefatigable activity; the ugly and the beautiful, (the latter however is here really predominant in both sexes,) in such varied forms? Where does he find more opportunity for making reflections upon the varied application and misapplication of human abilities?

A similar throng and mass of people is to be seen, indeed, at certain hours, in all large cities, and every where, where there is something to be gazed upon. The *peculiarity* of London, however, is, that it never leaves off. A foreigner, who arrived at night, and towards noon came out of his lodging, which was situated in a principal street, stood still at the street-door, when he saw this stream of people flowing in every direction around him, in order, as he himself afterwards related, *to let the people first pass by!* Hour passed after hour, till finally a friend met with him, and assured him, he might wait till the evening, and that it would only cease towards night-time. He had, in fact, seriously thought that some sight, or execution, had been the occasion of this immense throng and the motion of so vast a crowd. Certainly, when *hanging-day* arrives, which is frequent enough, the *pressure* is, indeed, indescribable.

Manners, and way of Living, in England.

My stay in the country was too short to enable me to consider the prevailing manners and ways of living in all the various shapes they offer to the traveller. I have, indeed, given myself every trouble to come in contact with persons of different and manifold dispositions and employments, and, in this respect, I have succeeded. I have neither neglected to visit the poor miserable districts in the City, Southwark, and St. Giles's, where the lowest classes dwell, nor the most sumptuous quarters, the abode of affluence. By far too many figures, however, present themselves to me, that I could execute and give a proper finish to so great a picture. For this purpose, too, it would be necessary to possess the talent of the noblest historical painters, of a West, an Angelica; and to unite, that of a Tenier with those of the masters of caricatures, Hogarth and Rowlandson.

The *difference of classes* constitutes here, as every where, the principal difference in the manners. It is, however, certainly more difficult in England, than in other countries, to ascertain this difference from external appearances. This arises from the manner of *dress.* The men's costume displays the greatest simplicity. The quality of the articles worn is, indeed, various; but, whatever meets the eye, whether in the street, or in company, whether worn by the minister of state, the opulent lord, the merchant, the wealthy mechanic, the clerk in the counting-house, is, throughout, the same; and, in the usual intercourse of social life, the court gala alone excepted, no exception is made therein. In the most populous streets I have never noticed any person who was to be distinguished by any external mark, particular uniform, the decoration of an order, or anything similar. What in Germany becomes a kind of duty to wear, would here create surprize, and, probably, would expose the wearer only to the insults and ridicule of the populace.

It is in no respect different with regard to the dress of the *women.* The real worth and costliness of the articles, not the particular manner of dress, constitutes the difference. In certain parts of the town, I thought I perceived only persons of rank, however they may vary in situation of life and property, because, in ordinary life, the humblest chambermaid wears her hat and muslin dress, as well as the richest lady; and, upon occasions, only of court ceremony, sumptuous festivals, or upon her visits to the *Italian Opera,* does the latter display all the magnificence and expense of dress.

In many establishments the *late hour of tea-time* concludes the arrangement of meals. A simple but cold supper is, nevertheless, to be met with sometimes, when the dinner hour happens between four and five o'clock. This supper takes place between the hours of nine and ten. It is natural, however, to imagine, from the way of life led by the great, that when we read of the supper commencing at four or five o'clock in the morning, that the same bears a proportion to a dinner at seven or eight in the evening, the natural consequence of which is, that in such houses, the hours of rising correspond almost with our dinner hour.

This is to be attributed partly to the immense size of the town, and to the course of business. The courts of justice and of law, the offices, the counting-houses the members, of which are frequently obliged to make a journey of several miles, cannot be shut so soon, opened again, and the business terminated, as in smaller places. To which may be added, that all the mails take their departure after midnight, and that a letter is certain of being forwarded, if delivered, even at the office, a short time before twelve o'clock. Thus, in this great emporium of the trade of the world, the merchant frequently avails himself of the last moment he is allowed to wait, to forward any fresh intelligence that may transpire.

The Sunday in England.

Almost all travellers complain that they found nothing more melancholy than the British manner of keeping the Sunday. They assure us that on that day all nature appears expired, and that every tone of joy is hushed in sorrow. They pity the people who are thus denied every lawful enjoyment, and consider our laws far more happy, which are strangers to this constraint. I frankly assert that the Sunday has not appeared to me so gloomy and joyless, and that I reckon many of the Sundays I passed in England amongst the most pleasing days of my recollection, and cannot even suppress the wish that we at least might see a little more of that practised in Germany which is found in the highly respectable families of that country, both with respect to character and religious education. I am not here meaning to speak of those who, imbued with a stern religious melancholy, consider it a sin to divert themselves with the most innocent recreations, such as playing upon an instrument, or the reading of any book the contents of which treat not of religious subjects, and think themselves obliged to keep the sabbath holy, more in a sense of the old testament than in a christian one; but I mean to speak of those who could not but wish, that a certain uniform sentiment were introduced also into Germany in keeping the hours of Sunday.—

I think, however, that whoever does not consider the theatre, balls, and gambling, as indispensable in order to be amused or to get rid of his ennui, whoever has not lost all taste for the great beauties of nature and the joys of a noble and cheerful sociability in the family circle, cannot fail in being merry both within and without London, even on the Sunday.

First impression made by the National Character, the Social Life, and the ton of Intercourse.

What first presents itself to the traveller in foreign countries, and which he encounters at almost every step he takes, is the peculiarity in the customs, manners, and habits of social life, with which, in order not to appear singular, he must necessarily make himself acquainted. Nevertheless, we become nearly as soon accustomed thereto as the eye to new objects. After a few weeks residence we begin to pass rapidly over what at the beginning was wont to fix our attention for several days, and which we thought we should never grow tired of considering.—Just as easily we accommodate ourselves to the established manner of arranging the day and plan of life.

I had heard and read so much of the coldness, reserve, and even of the pride of the English, who contemn every thing foreign, that it would but little have astonished me had I found this generally so. I will however not deny that single occurrences of this kind have come before me, and that, for example, in my travels during the voyage, in the post coaches, I have made many an acquaintance, which left not the slightest wish in my mind to continue them. In places particularly where many people meet together, for example, in coffee houses and inns, there is opportunity to perceive the unusual *taciturnity*, and love of silence which prevails; as frequently persons who have been long and intimately acquainted with each other, can sit for hours by the side of the fire without uttering one word; nay, they seem to wonder if, according to our German social manner which inclines so much to discourse, you endeavour to address it to them. In the domestic circles I found, particularly the younger unmarried ladies, for the most part very still, and always purposely shy. Persons, who have long lived amongst the English, assert also, that in family circles and friendly meetings it is not rarely the case, that a long pause follows after a long conversation. It remains to be decided therefore by the feelings of each individual, whether this has not more charms for the man who knows how to employ himself within the resources of his own mind, than an endless chatter about *nothings*, and the tiresome endeavours of many companions, male or female, never to let the conversation drop, and who, that they may only speak, are continually making the most common-place questions.

Speaking, however, from my own experience, I cannot at all agree in the complaint which has been made of a *thorough* cold or repulsive conduct. First of all, I must praise the great politeness with which the stranger is set right by those who are altogether unacquainted with him. As I never had a *Laquais de place*, even in the first weeks of my stay, in order that I might find my own way by myself the more readily, I have been frequently exposed to the necessity of troubling persons I met with questions; and I have tried this purposely with people of all conditions of life. Never has an unfriendly word put me to the blush; generally speaking, however, a polite manner in putting people into the right road, is a tolerable common virtue, which may have suffered here and there a little by incomprehensible or even troublesome questions made by the foreigner. The nature of man inclines him to participation; and even the feeling, that we know something better than another who may be our superior, is often an agreeable one.

In the society of the *better-informed classes* you indeed expect in vain that formal ceremony, those low reverences, and established usages of outward politeness upon arrival and taking leave, to which formerly at least people were accustomed in Germany, although they are daily losing their ground. On the other hand, however, true politeness reigns in England, together with the noblest *simplicity of manner*; consisting more in facts than in words. The hand is given to the person of the highest rank, as well as to the equal, and you are certain of a friendly return. The *lord*, as well as your *friend*, is saluted with a *good morning*, and leave taken of them, with a *good evening*, or a *good night*. *Embracing and kissing*, amongst men, appear to the English as unnatural, and the man would be exposed to insult even, should he be seen following the German custom in the street. This, indeed, may be carried too far; but we must still allow, that the fine token of *love* and *inward friendship*, is sacrificed by us too much to unnecessary ceremony; and we must rejoice rather, that what had become a frequently burthensome, and wherewithal a repugnant custom, is disappearing more and more from the circles of the men; for example, that of offering, after any great social entertainment, 30 or 40 embraces, twice or three times as many kisses, and, as formerly was the custom, of kissing the hand of every lady. Amongst the English women, I have never noticed this latter custom at coming and going, but frequently in families, amongst affectionate parents, children, brothers and sisters.

The strong exterior contrast of ranks, so common in our country, appears less frequent in England, and in this respect too, one of the finest peculiarities of British life is indisputably displayed. Every one feels in that country, that he is *free born,* that, by the constitution of the country, as well as by his natural liberty, he is a protected man, and that all, in the eye of the law, have an equal right. He knows that, either personally, or by his representative, he has a voice in the great concerns of the nation; that, if he commits a crime, his equals will judge him, that he is secured from the *oppressions* of overbearance, whether of the *nobles, the military,* or *the clergy,* so long as he confines himself only within the bounds of the laws. Attempts are not wanting, even in England, of individual members of these classes, to elevate themselves above the others. But as every house proprietor thinks his house is his castle, so every citizen of state considers the principles of the constitution as the bulwark of his liberty. Much of this, indeed, may consist

in *imagination,* but this, of itself, frequently makes us contented and happy.   This spirit is cherished from early youth; it
grows up with the boy and the young man. Parents themselves
treat their sons, sacred as the paternal power is, in this spirit;
and the *domestic* education is, in the highest degree, liberal.
Hence arises the unconstrained manner of intercourse of all
ranks amongst each other; hence the facility, as soon as a
person is only decently attired, of getting access to the first
houses without much ceremony; hence the candour in opposing in public meetings and assemblies of the people, the Duke
and the Earl, as well as a brewer of beer, if they should happen not to be of the same opinion. Of this the debates in
parliament are the best proof.   But as these debates are public,
they are known to and read by all ranks, and form the public
spirit.

This public spirit is not a little cherished and promoted by all
public events, mutually serviceable enterprizes, and institutions
forming the most usual topic of conversation. In Germany,
even men of superior education can find delight for hours in
the petty novelties of the day, in the miserable prattle about
what other men say, how they dress themselves, receive visits,
or go out ; and frequently the most insipid jokes, which, on
account of their being so continually repeated, are called
stereotypes, are preferred to the most scientific subjects. Such
things are not suited, as many impartial observers who have
lived in England many years assure me, to the taste of well-
educated company in that country.   Politics and trade are indeed the principal theme of discourse. But an interest is
also evinced for what is *generally serviceable to mankind,* and
many matters of this nature are frequently treated of with the
greatest earnestness over a glass of porter or wine.

From this kind of conversation, a certain seriousness must
naturally accompany social life ; and the loud and frequently
noisy behaviour, as well as the shout of any individual, would
appear as a failure in good manners.   But this is the reason
of a large mass of sound ideas, of a perspicuity in opinion,
and an ability in expression, being extended in all classes of
people ; in which respect it cannot be denied that *Life* forms
the Englishman far more than the *School.* That *public spirit,* as
far as it consists in the participation in the general concerns
of the nation, sometimes displays itself in a manner which
would excite any thing but respect, or a wish that it might so
exist amongst us, is already sufficiently known from the events
which have lately occurred. If popular meetings, like the
last in London and Manchester; if at sometimes earnest, and
at others laughable speeches, proclamations and actions, astonish

less there, and probably occasion less harm than they would with us ; this must be attributed to the constitution, which affords security in such manifold ways ; although the reflecting and the reasonable part of the nation are not perfectly easy at such scenes, and think of measures to ward off the storm, well knowing how much evil generally ensues, when the poorer classes of people wish to effect by force, that change which can only be the work of deep reflection, and a profound insight into the real situation of things.

But there are *finer effects* of this *public spirit*, which, although less taken notice of in German publications, and on that account too little known out of England, merit far more our respect and consideration. Through that spirit, *institutions, coalitions,* and *foundations,* have been brought about, partly in the capital, partly in the whole country and the most distant colonies, which, both in the excellence of their appointment, as well as in the grandeur of their plans, hardly have their equal.

Two principal motives have certainly operated to this effect, in an equal degree : on the one hand, it might almost be said, that the disposition is inherent in the nation for every thing which appertains to the *public weal* and *national instruction,* were the latter only to be effected by the most rigid application of human powers; on the other hand, the *religious spirit,* which, whether more or less pure, is still indisputably extended *amongst all ranks* in England more than elsewhere. Both have had a very great share in very many of the important *institutions* and *coalitions* of modern times, which, as soon as we are better acquainted with them, exceed almost all expectation and imagination. If the *first* idea of these originated with a large number of enterprizing men, animated with a religious spirit, and an high zeal for maintaining and extending the doctrines of Christianity, they found also, from those who probably participated not in that spirit with them, or were even unbelievers or indifferent, the most powerful support. They are animated at least by a lively spirit for every thing which the *human weal, liberty,* and *industry* demands, or which can contribute any thing to the honour and renown of the nation. On this account it is that we see princes, dukes, and many other members of the highest classes, who enjoy not altogether the reputation of a particular religious feeling, or austerity of morals, still connect themselves willingly and frequently with all assemblies or institutions, the end of which is directed to mutually useful enterprizes or the highest concerns of humanity; and protect and advance them by a patronage which they willingly under-

take. How far vanity may find a place therein is their concern. The general good gains always by their interest and
influence.

Westminster Abbey.

In the year 1807 I stood in St. Deny's, upon the ruined
vaults of the rulers of France, and contemplated the building
of the marble hall, in which *Napoleon* formerly intended to
repose with his dynasty. Still earlier, in the year 1798, I saw the
magnificent Sarcophagus of *Denmark's* Kings in the Cathedral
of *Rothschild.* In the year 1811, a poor capuchin conducted
me, with a single taper in his hand, down into the damp vaults,
where a narrow space contained the coffins of the rulers of
the Austrian Empire. The remembrance of all these and
other sumptuous abodes of death was awakened in me, as I
wandered in London, amongst the lofty vaults of Westminster
Abbey.

Shakspeare's monument, the model of which is not unknown to us, in plaster and cuts, from the editions of his
works, first attracted my attention. He stands thoughtful, in
a free position, leaning upon a pedestal, and points to a roll
of parchment, upon which some lines, taken from one of his
plays, are read ; which may be considered as the most applicable inscription to the entrance of this abode of so many of
the powerful, who once stood upon the greatest terrestrial
height to which humanity can aspire.

An attractive feeling towards my native country drew me
from Shakspeare's monument to the place of repose of two
great German artists, whose merits even proud Britain has
not disdained to do homage to ; that of the great painter
Kneller, in the reigns of Charles II., James II., William III.,
and George I, and of the equally great musician, G. F. Handel.

Kneller's monument is simple ; but far more majestic that
of the immortal composer of so many oratorios, which are still
admired in Germany, and who still enjoys in England, down
to this moment, the most unlimited admiration. The genial
artist stands upright, noble alike in shape as in intellect, with
his left arm supported upon musical instruments. Highly
expressive is the erection of his head in order to pay attention
to the tones of a harp, with which an angel descends from the
clouds. His inscription is simple. I in vain looked, however,
for an intimation that he was a German, and *Halle* his place
of birth.

If, indeed, some of these monuments are deserving of attention with respect to the art, it still bears reference only to the smaller number of them, particularly the modern. It is not in fine arts that the English generally distinguish themselves. In Westminster also many of those which possess merit are the works of *foreigners.* Among those which even the British prize the most, are the works of *Ruysbrack* and *Roubillac.* But the former was a *Dutchman*, the latter a *Frenchman.* At present they possess an artist in John Flaxman, who is honoured in foreign countries, and who has given an example of the high talent he possesses in the monuments to Lord Mansfield, and the great naval hero Lord Nelson, in St. Paul's Cathedral.

Westminster Abbey approaches nearest, as a royal burying-place, to the cathedral in Rothschild, near Copenhagen, and that of St. Deny's.

I have however not been able to suppress the wish, which has been expressed by so many travellers, that, in a country of the greatest cleanliness and elegance, a place which is so much visited, might be kept cleaner, and secured from dust and cob-webs ; and I have just as little been able to withhold my opinion that the dressed wax figures of the Queens Elizabeth, Mary, Ann, as well as of William Pitt, Chatham, and Nelson, which stand here in niches in some of the chapels, would be far more appropriately placed in any collection of curiosities, or in the British Museum.

The Royal Residence, Carlton House.

I have had an opportunity of making myself acquainted with this residence.

It is necessary to have particular recommendations to see the interior of Carlton House. The *Armoury* fills four rooms on the second story, near which the Prince himself resides. To a military visitor it must be in the highest degree interesting and instructing to view the whole of the different arms borne by all nations, from the Prussian Grenadier, or Chasseur, to the Seapoy, the Chinese, Japanese, and the Body Guard of the Great Mogul; and to be enabled to make observations upon the progress of the art of war, and even of taste in the preparation of all these instruments of death. The riches which these four rooms contain in single and precious articles, in the noblest metals, in jewels and pearls, with which the sumptuous sabres, daggers, turbans, and helmets are adorned, is indeed incalculable. Above all, as might easily be expected, what has been brought from the East Indies, that is to say, much of the incalculable treasures which became a booty of the English, in the year 1792 after the taking of Seringapatam where Tippoo Saib lost both his life and empire, hold a distinguished place. The Chair of the Golden Throne of the last King of Candy, Rajah Sindah, forms a large sun with innumerable rays broken by jewels of a very rare size. His throne is shewn as the most modern monument of British conquests in India.

When I see myself surrounded here by all these trophies, which a spiritual, far more than a physical superiority, but still more an unbounded lust of possession and controul, than any just pretension, has here collected, how is it possible not to be induced to ask what gave Europeans, or, to speak more accurately, what gave a trading company the right of overturning kingdoms in a foreign part of the world; and subjecting nations to their sway, who certainly would never have thought of disturbing the tranquillity of a distant insular empire?

The private dwelling rooms of the present king, in Carlton House, are not visible to foreigners. But the state rooms and the halls in the lower story, afford by their appropriate magnificence, modern taste, and incalculable riches, far more entertainment than we are usually wont to find, when we are obliged to pass through, by the side of tiresome conductors, all the apartments of royal residences. The connoisseur in the fine arts, finds excellent pictures of the old and modern schools, together with busts of Fox, Lady Hastings, &c.—In the library the literati, and particularly the friend of elegant editions and rarities of every kind, would willingly pass many days.

The Prisons,—King's Bench, Newgate, and Mill Bank.

It is a melancholy consideration that, together with the moral excellence to be found in England, at the same time so great a degree of corruption displays itself in all possible shapes, that scarcely can sufficient room be found to prevent the malefactors of every description from being injurious to society by separating them from it. This, indeed, would occasion little surprize in London, which resembles a little world; and where, consequently, no appearance either of bad or of good can be unexpected; but unfortunately, there is hardly a large town, or one even of the middle class, in which the same observation might not be made. To this depravity the necessities of the lower classes have probably the most contributed.

The complaint, however, is nearly as general, that the usual institutions of chastisement and improvement are become, to many, the school of complete depravity; and numbers of these persons lose in them, at once, both their physical and moral character. It is well known that many excellent men, both in Germany and in England, have been deeply sensible of this ; that Howard particularly has advised and done much, in order to effect a radical reform in the prisons ; and we can only be the more astonished, that in the native country of this rare friend to humanity, the effects of his active mind are not more generally visible. The nation has not denied him his merit, a proof of which is to be found in the monument, which is erected to him in St. Paul's Cathedral. But every where, indeed, the most magnificent ideas meet with endless difficulties, even where a good will to carry them into execution is not wanting.

A glance into the benevolent Institutions of London.

It would be necessary either to write an entire book, or repeat what has been already written, were I only to confine myself to the representation of those humane Institutions and Establishments which are collected in London ; and it would be indispensable to pass a whole year, and not merely a few months, in order to become intimately acquainted with them.

I have purposely visited only some of the most important establishments, because the man who wishes to see every thing, seldom sees any thing rightly, and leaves the objects he visits rather fatigued than informed. I would not even venture to give a decided character to those I have visited, because I well know that great discrimination is necessary, in order to enter into the spirit of great Institutions, that we may neither become partial nor unjust. If they are not wholly in decay, the *fine* side alone appears to the casual visitor, either because this only is shewn to him, or because the defects, according to their nature, are more secret and concealed.

A part of these Institutions is to be traced from early times, when religious Institutions were met with every where in Catholic countries, and were raised by that religious spirit, which certainly may have had its origin more from the erroneous opinion of gaining a blessed life, or of making amends for old sins, than from pure love of God and humanity. It cannot be denied, that the zeal for them has very soon been lost, together with the belief that works of this kind possessed the power of affording a blessed life, which the reformers contended against. But no where has this been the case less than in England. Public spirit, and with many also, the spirit of christian love, has maintained itself throughout the later centuries, and still displays itself in new undertakings. A great part of the most magnificent Institutions, the hospital of St. Luke, for 300 persons, the Foundling, which provides for 400 children, the Insurance Institutions, for life and property, the great *National* and *Sunday Schools*, for which annually half a million of dollars are collected by Voluntary Subscription, belong, like the Institutions for fallen girls, to the last century, and partly even to more modern times.

Respecting Christ's Hospital I have to offer the following reflections: as in England generally the preservation of what is ancient in manners and customs is much attended to, this attention is also to be remarked in the *dress* of the *pupils* of the above Institution. At first sight, indeed, it appears something very singular. Represent to yourself young people, some of 12, 16, or 17 years of age, in a dark blue coat, perfectly similar to our *children's frocks*, falling down to the feet; under the chin there is a small white facing, like the cape of our clergy; a small red stripe, or girdle, buckled round the body, yellow stockings, and the head covered with a small blue cap, with a tassel. Notwithstanding this strange uniform, which can never be taken for any other, we look with the greatest pleasure and satisfaction upon the 6 or 700 boys who are assembled in the house. The greatest cleanliness is observed in all of them. Hereto their peculiar washing establishment greatly contributes. They bathe daily in a large room, with long benches placed before the reservoir of water, 50 and 50 at a time; head, hands, and feet are plunged into running water, partly cold and partly tepid, and they dry themselves with towels hanging upon rollers. The most perfect health and cheerfulness are visible upon every countenance. I was present at one of their meals, which was animated by a joyful behaviour, was simple, but wholesome and abundant. The great Hall called forcibly to my remembrance the dining-room in the Orphan House at Halle, where frequently 700 persons have been also counted at table. The Prayer before and after the meal, was said with much expression and reverence by some of the pupils, and always finished with an *Amen* from the whole assemblage. Stately matrons, well paid, belonging to the house, distributed the soup and meat. Every table has its superintendant, taken from the circle of the pupils. The Steward, Mr. Huggin, superintended the whole at a table placed in the middle. I was much struck at seeing upon this table all kinds of articles, such as keys, buttons, small money, buckles, &c.; but the superintendent informed me that a strict account was observed of giving back every thing, even the smallest trifle, be it ever so insignificant, to the person who had lost it. Generally speaking, these *Blue-coat boys*, as they are universally called, enjoy a very good character. They are, indeed, treated and educated according to strict rules, but very liberally. They are allowed to go out by two and two, as soon as they conduct themselves well; and I have been assured that there has hardly ever been an instance of these youths allowing themselves to commit any irregularity in the street; in which respect they deserve to be held up for imitation by the youth in many of our large and small German towns.

St. Bartholomew's Hospital, and St. Luke's.

I observed these great Institutions with attention. Even had I only taken a peep into the few Institutions I have described, I should entirely participate in the feeling which is pronounced of them in a dignified and animated manner, by a celebrated writer.

" In what other country in Europe," says Goede, at the conclusion of his Description of St. Luke's, " is only a *single* institution of this extent to be found, which has maintained itself flourishing, without any legislative controul, for half a century, by free *charitable donations.* Yet what is this single institution in comparison with more than two hundred others, which continue uninterruptedly to flourish in London by mere acts of free benevolence! In speaking of institutions, I understood by that name permanent foundations, not those voluntary provisions for the poor and sick, which are not to be numbered in London; not those societies which are united for charitable purposes for certain monthly contributions (the friendly societies), and of which, a few years back, more than 680 were reckoned. If we compare, however, the immense number of charitable foundations of this kind, which are scattered throughout the kingdom, with the amount of all the benevolent institutions of London, we find the former far surpass them in number, grandeur, and riches; and the whole great picture of the patriotic benevolence of the English nation, displays itself before us in so moving a magnificence, that in the tranquil consideration of it, every better, holy, and religious feeling, becomes heightened, strengthened, and extended."

FIRST VIEW OF THE INSTITUTIONS FOR THE EXTENSION AND ADVANCEMENT OF RELIGION.

General View.

Amongst all the public undertakings in Great Britain, none are of so great an extent, none awaken so general a participation amongst persons of all classes, sects, and parties, at home and abroad, than those institutions which have for their object the *diffusion of the Bible amongst all the nations of the earth, and the communication of Christianity amongst unchristian people.*

In these endeavours, which are forwarded by so many thousands in all countries, partly by the most charitable contributions, to which regents on their thrones, as well as the poor in their huts, offer either large sums or humble mites, a greater part of the Christian world, view the *finest character of the times,* the commencement of the fulfilment of the command of Christ,—"There shall be but one shepherd, and but one flock." But they are attended, in England as well as with us, not only by *good,* but also by *bad* consequences. To the man to whom religion and Christianity is all a dream and nonsense, to the unbeliever, they are only vexation and folly; the indifferent man, to whom the transition from one religion to another appears only an exchange of errors, considers them as an useless waste of important powers, for vain enterprizes. But many too, who have the highest respect for religion and the holy Book, are tempted at times to doubt of the purity of the intent, and to think they only wish to move God thereby to bless men, temporally, who do so much for his honour : at times they are uncertain whether rude nations by civilization gain any thing in happiness and morality, or at least, whether, by *this way* and by *this means,* the end can be best attained, viz. that of making knowledge and virtue more general.

Who would deny his respect to that man who makes it the business of his life *to bring light into the understanding, and tranquillity into the heart of his fellow creatures,* however different he may think of his person, his direct, or indirect calling, and the means he chooses to produce that effect? In truth, the most inimical incredulity, and the most immoral neglect of religion, can alone disavow the holy Being after whose name we are called, whilst the modest doubter at least allows him the merit of an honest enthusiasm, highly honourable to him, from the greatness of his plan, and the sanctity of his purpose. Let persons therefore decide for themselves whether their reproach, of such large sums being dedicated to this purpose, is just. If it is considered munificent in a sovereign to devote half a million to the decoration of his palace, to sumptuous edifices, to play-houses, shall it be called less munificent in a nation which applies similar, and far larger sums, to human improvement, and the felicity of mankind ?

But abstracting ourselves from the influence of religion, and the Bible as its document upon the superior illumination, instruction, and the consolation of the human heart, is not the simple *civilization* of rude nations, and the salvation of the same from heathen unbelief, from the most cruel and revolting customs, something highly benevolent? and which even the wisdom of the Bramins in India, among whom there are certainly many learned and very respectable persons, cannot or will not destroy. But what an important step is already gained as soon as we succeed in making even the elements of all higher knowledge more general amongst them. *Ulphilas,* bishop of the Goths in the fourth century, lives continually in the respectful remembrance of all succeeding ages, because he it was who translated the New Testament into his language for his rude tribe, and taught them at the same time to know and *read* the alphabet. Through the zeal of the English Bible Society, the Bible however becomes a book which, from the great variety of its contents, and whilst it represents man in all the degrees of his civilization, gives the translator so much opportunity for the formation and enrichment of language, since it is given in the tongues of twenty-five Asiatic nations, and as many in North America, who never had the least idea of *writing* and *letters.* In Serampore, too, the greatest activity reigns in this branch of literature. Moreover, the higher cultivation of the mind has always been in close connexion with the culture of languages.

We may, therefore, well ask the bitter reproachers and mockers of the Missionary and Bible Societies, whether they should not highly prize every attempt to extend the empire of human knowledge, and to make rude nations by degrees susceptible of it, as it cannot be unknown to them, that *those* nations also, amongst whom arts, knowledge, and learning have attained the highest point, were originally rude barbarians; and that the holy Bonifacius found our German forefathers quite upon a lower scale of civilization than, thanks to God, we stand upon at present? Or are they really so little disposed to be citizens of the world, that they can only grant light to a small part of the inhabitants of the earth; and give themselves no concern whether or not an innumerable host of rational beings, who are as susceptible as themselves of spiritual improvement and moral dignity, wander for ever in darkness, and are sacrificed to all the errors and degeneration produced by their rude and beastial inclination to sensuality? Have they no sense of the raptures of the friend of humanity and the true christian, when he reflects that, by his participation in the union of religious persons, one tribe after another, enlightened and improved by a truly humane religion like our own, not only abrogate the foolish and senseless, but also the murderous part of idolatry; no longer kneel before altars which reek with the blood of innocent children, youths, and maidens; no longer consider the millions born to slavery as only half human, over whom power is given to be free?

Or is this picture somewhat exaggerated? Let those who probably think so read what Mr. Bowdich has detailed to us, who, in the year 1817, visited the State of Ashantee, upon the gold-coast of Africa, as English ambassador. He was eye-witness, at the death of one of their princesses, of three young girls, and immediately after them of 13 men, who had their arms and heads slowly taken off, in order to send a train after the princess. "Infinitely greater cruelties," says he, "occur at the death of a king, as every family then must repeat the human sacrifices for those who died under his government. The orans, or gentlemen of the chamber, to the amount of more than one hundred, are sacrificed together upon his grave, besides a large number of women. At the funeral celebration of the mother of the present king, her son offered up only *three thousand* human sacrifices, among which were *two thousand* prisoners. The large towns sent each 100, the smaller 10 persons, to slaughter."

If we rejoiced generally that, upon the appearance of the Saviour of the world, light was spread over the nations to which we belong; if we have rejoiced at the spirit of reformation, that the night which had obscured it was obliged to give place to the day,—shall we not wish success and the happiest consequences to that enterprise whereby the same blessing may be extended to nations which now wander in darkness?

Much time will still be necessary before the religious wishes for a general civilization and moralization of the human race, as they are now promised in a number of writings, which have issued forth in England and her colonies, can be fulfilled. We may, however, cherish more ardent hopes, since at no period has so much been done in a spirit at once so dignified and forbearing as in ours, (resembling the endeavours made by the Roman propaganda) both by the Bible Societies and the Missionaries.

The British and Foreign Bible Society.

It is well known that, since the year 1804, another society has connected itself with those which have long existed in England, for the advancement of the knowledge of christianity, both in Great Britain as well as in the whole of Europe, and the most remote parts of the world, the principal endeavours of which are almost exclusively directed to the extension of the Holy Scriptures. As together with many English, who were warmed with the interests of religion, both of secular and ecclesiastical conditions, foreigners living in London, and amongst them particularly the preacher at the German congregation in the Savoy, Dr. Steinkopf, participated in the interest, the same soon became extended on the continent, and there is scarce a province at present of any importance, wherein Sister Societies, which stand in the closest connexion with the British, are not to be found.   The society is of the persuasion that, as the Holy Scriptures have ever been one of the principal means of extending the true knowledge of God and devotion amongst mankind, this religious disposition can be animated amongst christians by nothing better than by assisting all in the use of the Bible, nay, that even amongst heathen nations, nothing can so certainly open the road to christianity, as by making it possible to deliver the holy document to each of them in their native language.

The centre of this society, from which, in the whole of England, Scotland, and Ireland, as well as in all celebrated countries of the old and modern world, similar societies have arisen, is in London.   Perhaps in no empire of the world are so many religious parties to be found as in Great Britain, which differ so greatly in their opinions and views, and a part of which are very disinclined, even one towards the other.   It is, therefore, the more remarkable, that almost all are united in the advancement of this purpose.   The Bible Societies, like the Missionary, reckon among them both Evangelical and Presbyterians, Dissenters, Methodists and Quakers, and I heard even the little party of the Unitarians, which departs from the church in some of its principal doctrines, speak with respect of the endeavours which had been made, although they did not approve of all the measures which were taken.   Even this speaks of the goodness of the purpose, for whatever is acknowledged by so many parties to be salutary, and against which even party-spirit has nothing to declaim, must certainly possess an intrinsic merit and value.

So great an undertaking could not be supported without various *economical* and *technical* arrangements, and soon formed itself into a large mercantile establishment.   With regard to the house in Essex Street, purchased for this purpose, the regulation and general order deserve my highest praise.—I looked with astonishment upon the vast supplies, and thespaces which are daily exhausted and filled up again.   The attention is not less riveted by the superb mechanism whereby the bales and boxes, destined for all the countries of the earth, are carefully packed, weighed, bound and unbound, for their journey through one half of the world. The number of hands daily employed in the manufacture of paper, in printing, &c. &c. are incalculable, and the happy effects, produced by the employment of so many workmen of every kind, are indescribable.

On the 5th July I was introduced to the weekly assemblage of the Society. A place was offered me, (as is usual with strangers,) by the side of the President, Lord Teignmouth. This highly respectable veteran, who was many years Governor-General in India, introduced, at the same time with me, a Supreme Judge to the assemblage, Mr. Harrison, who had just arrived from Calcutta, and had been at the head of the Bible Society of that country. This gentleman gave an account of the astonishing progress the same made in Bengal. One of the British Secretaries, Mr. Owen, afterwards communicated Letters he had received from Switzerland and France, upon the same subject, and which countries he had shortly before travelled through. I was now formally addressed, and requested by Dr. Steinkopf, Secretary for the Society in Foreign parts, to give an account of the progress of the Bible Society of Halle, the founders of which, Canstein and Franke, belong to the few persons of my native country whose names are well known, and even celebrated, in certain circles. Although I was not entirely ignorant of the language, still I was not a little surprised at the commission; nevertheless, my courage increased during the address, by a benevolent participation taken in my feelings, and even when I wanted the proper term of expression, I was assisted by the friendly assistance of the surrounding assemblage. I then endeavoured to satisfy them as well as I was able. When I reported that the Canstein Bible press had increased in modern times from 6 to 12 presses; that these presses daily issued at least 12,000 sheets, printed on both sides, and were, at the same time, unable to answer the demand; that the great augmentation in the price of paper, and all materials for the press, and even the high duties upon paper, made it almost impossible to continue the old price of sale, without loss;—when I reported all this, the words *Hear, Hear!* failed not to fall from their lips, which is a token, with the English, of any thing which appears to them important. This gave me greater courage, partly to solicit the support from this Institution, by a press of *English manufacture*, as some of our own were grown very old; and partly to propose that copies of all the bibles hitherto printed in foreign languages, might be sent to our Library.

I cannot reflect without emotion upon those solemn hours, and particularly upon the excellent replies with which Mr. Owen, one of the most animated speakers I have heard in England, replied to my wishes, which were, indeed, not uttered without diffidence. "We have perceived," said he, "with great participation, that the work continues to prosper and take effect, through the means employed by the highly respected gentlemen, Canstein and Franke. Only," said he, with a fine application of feeling, "Only, I may be allowed to regret that they have *solicited*, where they had a right to *demand*. Nay, it is our duty to support every undertaking connected with our purposes. We are only the housekeepers, and receive the rich gifts, in order to assist those who are in want of our assistance. We will give whatever we are able, and let it be the tribute of our high respect for an Institution which, long since, has been a pattern to our own activity."

And the Society has indeed kept its word! Through its liberality the Canstein Institution is not only in possession of two of these presses, above 1000 dollars in value, but a present has been made to it, by order of that Committee, of stereotype plates, necessary to a perfect edition of the bible.

This Institution is indisputably one of the greatest which have ever existed for religious purposes; the yearly expenditure thereof already amounts to nearly 500,000 dollars, without mentioning what is expended directly by the sister Societies in all parts of the world.

It has been asked whether a part of this large sum could not be better employed in the appointment of enlightened teachers and explainers of the scriptures, who are capable of handling the contents of the holy book, as prudent fathers of families; since it can hardly be denied that the bible must not remain a secret to a number of persons without education, and who even possess not the least mechanical ability in reading?

The *British Bible Society*, however, is governed by the maxim, that, in order to attain a great end, its activity must not be divided. *Preaching of the word*, or *teaching*, is the duty of the *Missionary Societies*. The Bible Society has made it its principal object to sacrifice every thing in order that the most important means of instruction, the holy Scriptures, may be wanting nowhere. On this account it is, that the Society wishes to diffuse the bible without any assistance or impediment, without remarks and explanations, in order that the editions may not be exposed to the suspicion of being subject to wilful changes, and that nothing may disturb the simplicity of the endeavour, and that the insight into the understanding and the use of the holy book may be more free to every one.

It is hardly possible to represent, in few words, what has been already done by the united endeavours of so many thousand members of this Society, both in and out of Britain. It would be necessary to have read the annual accounts which have appeared upon the subject, and, together with the *Sum-*

mary Review, at the same time to have received the detached Reports from all parts of the world, in order to have any idea of it. The chief Society contains, alone, in the British empire, about 500 assistant Societies. The most brilliant idea, however, is presented to us of the grandeur of its effect, by knowing, for example, that in the first ten years alone, (from 1804 to 1814,) the same were placed in condition, by voluntary contributions, of devoting the sum of £299,287 sterling, to these purposes ; and that in the year 1818 alone, the outgoings, which were fully covered by the amount received, amounted to 500,000 dollars; that these sums only comprehended those which, *directly* or *indirectly,* came into their treasury, and not what was collected in other countries, upon the example of England. Above 100 Editions of the Holy Scriptures, and of the New Testament, have already been made in England, Germany, Russia, and the East Indies, in the various European, Asiatic, African, and American languages and dialects, and millions of copies of the holy Book have been scattered throughout the world.

The Thames Bridges.

A very correct notion is acquired of the increase of the metropolis of England, which even surpasses every representation which has been made of it, and of the extension of the environs in all directions, by a comparison of the old plans of London with the modern ones.

As in England, generally, they never omit to mention how much every thing that is shewn may have cost, the descriptions of London give circumstantial details of the expenses of all the bold works to be seen in the metropolis, and inform you, for example, how much stone and iron work may have been employed upon the Bridges, according to measure and weight ; nay, calculations have even been made of the number of persons, horses, and carriages, which may be received as the daily average of the passengers to and fro. According thereto, on one Sunday, 89,640 foot-passengers, and 1240 coaches passed the London Bridge, and every thing in respective proportion.

The general impression which the view of this unique mercantile traffic produced in me, and must, indeed, produce in the breast of every unprejudiced observer, was the effect of a variety of, and contrast between, opposite feelings. On the one hand, that restless endeavour after wealth, which belongs only to this world, which appears to exclude every other consideration, and to which wealth, sooner or later, even the possessor must become indifferent, and, finally, can easily do without ; which, moreover, even in the plenitude of possession, seldom affords what is so earnestly sought after, a contented and happy life, free from care, appears rather to excite our regret than to add to our satisfaction. On the other hand, the tranquil philosopher, who, unobserved by the world, or only known by some select friends, strives to obtain those imperishable goods which make the loss of all others so easy, appears not only to stand much higher in a moral character than the milionary and the nabob, almost sinking under the weight of India's gold, but he appears to be, in fact, by far the happiest man. Who is there, who is not acquainted with many a rich speculator, in his native country, who, however he may assist and be useful to others by his activity, still derives the least enjoyment himself, from the uneasy restlessness, the night-watchings, the anxious dreams, to which he is exposed, and from his increasing money coffers? if, indeed, he is not fool enough, as many of them are, to starve by the side of the latter.

On the other hand it cannot, and it must not, be denied, that the height upon which a large trading state stands, is not throughout the work of physical, as well as of spiritual, powers. The endeavour to appropriate and employ every thing to one's self, in a thousand ways, which the earth conceals in her bosom, or which her bosom produces, has either given the first impulse to many a science, or affords it the great means of assistance, without which the world would hardly have attained that degree of perfection at which we now behold it. The fewest number of my readers will require to be remembered, how far we should have remained behind, without the art of navigation, in the knowledge of the firmament, and the laws of the universe. And, would *navigation* have existed without *trade?*

The great and well-informed merchant may be said to have attained that summit of knowledge of the world, upon which alone views are to be formed of the generality of mankind, whether ignorant or learned, as well as of the connexions between the most distant nations, which lead him to enterprizes so rich in their consequences, and which are hardly possible to be effected in a lower scale of view. But there is something still more sublime, which lies beyond every thing that is earthly. If he leave not the latter out of sight, and is able to preserve in himself the feeling of a higher destination of man, he belongs, indisputably, to the most respectable, as well as the most active and serviceable, member of human society.

The British Museum.—Lord Elgin's Antiquities.

Time only allowed me to visit occasionally this celebrated
collection of curiosities of every kind. The connoisseur alone,
too, is enabled to place a just estimation upon whatever
appertains therein to nature and art; but, in order to avail
one's self of the treasures in the library, it is necessary to have
leisure, and some decided purposes. As, however, I must
conclude, from many questions which have been made to me,
that my readers expect me to say something upon this subject
also, I will endeavour at least to set right many improper
representations which appear to be made of this, as the name
indicates, National Institution, and to give a general view of
the same.

First, let it be remarked, that the better part of the collection was a legacy, made in the middle of the foregoing century,
by Hans Sloane, a private individual, a physician and natural
historian, and became the property of the nation for a moderate sum of money; and was, very soon afterwards, so much
augmented and extended by the possession of Cotton's and
Harley's Manuscripts, by presents, and the purchase of private
collections, as well as by the patriotic zeal manifested by the
trustees, and, finally, by the interest which Parliament took in
the institution, that the room even in the very large palace
which formerly belonged to the Duke of Montague, is daily
becoming too small to contain the collection.

On that account it has been long since desirable that a
national building should be erected, which should properly
correspond to the value of the treasures here collected, and
render, at the same time, the inspection of the same more
convenient. But, even the very important augmentation of
value it has received in Lord Elgin's Grecian acquisitions, has
not been hitherto sufficient to satisfy this general expectation
of the nation.

I can offer no opinion of the value of the collection of
natural productions, of the purpose of their exhibition and
classification, of their relative comparison with other collections; as, for example, the Museum of Natural History, in
the Jardin des Plantes, at Paris. The endless variety, the
public display of the inexhaustible riches of nature, afford,
however, the non-connoisseur a delightful enjoyment.

As man generally feels interested most in all that concerns
his own nature, we feel a desire to spend a considerable time
in the apartments which contain the dress, tools, arms, and
works of art, belonging to the most opposite nations. Where,

indeed, is a richer supply of these articles to be expected than in a country whose seamen touch all parts of the habitable world, and are become so well acquainted, either by force of arms or by trade, with the means of making the possession of them their own ? What an addition alone has been made by the great discoveries by sea? Any foreigner, of whatever part of the globe, continent, or islands, may be certain to find something here which has once either clothed, armed, given pleasure to, terrified, amused, or adorned, men of *his* cast.

One of the most distinguished ornaments of the Museum, is the valuable collection of Mr. Hamilton, who, it is well known, when he was Ambassador at Naples, employed all his diligence upon the study of antiquity, and took so great a part in the excavations which were made in the two towns of Pompeii and Herculaneum, which disappeared more than 1700 years ago. Who does not know that we are indebted almost to him alone for the knowledge of the ancient Etrurian vase pictures, and that a new territory, as it were, has been gained thereby in the map of antiquity ? The whole treasure of his gains in Italy was brought back with him to England, and, in the year 1772, was given over to the Museum for the sum of 48,000 dollars. Here we behold, at present, the originals of thousands of successful imitations, which at present adorn the castles and houses of the inhabitants of taste in all countries.

The greatest, at least the most invaluable treasure of the Museum, is the library. A learned man, Sir Robert Cotton in the seventeenth century, dedicated his life to make a particular collection of old manuscript documents, and numberless original letters, both of his own time and of antiquity, the catalogue of which alone fills an entire folio volume. What secrets of the most retired family life, what documents of human passions may not here lie before us, and still are secured from all discovery. Enveloped in dark leather covers, with short inscriptions or numbers, they may be said to remain there like grey antiquity herself. Any person who had time only to find out the interesting parts of them, which have never been made use of, for the enriching of history, would not repent the trouble he has taken. In the midst of these manuscript antiquities, the fragment of the original Magna Charta, which John was obliged to sign in 1215, reposes in its own desk, under frames and glass, like a holy relic of the palladium of British liberty. Some unknown accident had conveyed that original into the workshop of a tailor, who was about to cut out measures from it, when a connoisseur, acquainted with ancient writing, happened to step in, and saved it from total destruction.

The Harleian collection of manuscripts, the catalogue of which contains 8000 numbers, is still more copious: this is considered almost as the greatest treasure of the kind in England. A similar collection bears the name of *royal.*

The *printed works* are contained in sixteen halls and rooms in the lower story. The Librarian, Dr. Baber, who is as polite as he is learned, made me acquainted with the regulation and order of the library. As the greater part thereof has arisen from legacies and presents, whereby it was frequently requested that every collection should be preserved together, containing its own works, the partitions, on this account, bear the name of their original possessors. The proper *Royal Library,* which was formerly concealed in the dark corners of Westminster Abbey, has now been placed in a beautiful and light situation. The most costly of sumptuous works, which printing and literature can show, appear to be here united. A copy must be delivered of every thing which appears in London, and you are carefully informed of the enormous prices of many capital works.

The present King, when he was Prince Regent, granted an unusual large sum (my memory has not clearly retained to what amount), in order to represent, in print, a perfect facsimile of one of the most celebrated of all manuscripts of holy writing, the Codex Alexandrinus. Some of the letters have been cast entirely after the traits of the original. Only a moderate number of copies is struck off, and they are rather made a present of, than sold, by the government. The commencement that has already been made, under Mr. Baber's direction, awakens the best expectations of the undertaking. This venerable document, which is at least twelve hundred years old, of a religious industry, brings to lively remembrance great names, who once were, and are still, dear to science.

The Gallery, in which the works of art of antiquity are exposed in fourteen partitions, has been lately extended by a very light, and, it is to be hoped, only temporary, erection, for the Elgin collection. A sight of these ancient and modern treasures of the Museum, must afford every connoisseur a high treat, although Italy and France, particularly when the latter possessed the property of all countries, may have been richer. We wander here, indeed, amongst many lamentable ruins, and must, probably, bring with us as much power of imagination as love of the arts, in order to give a perfection to what is wanting by analogy, and to find particular parts, crippled as they are beautiful. But what has no longer charms for the eye, may still be instructive to the artist ; and thus it is that we must allow the zeal and animation of the antiquarian to reverence every fragment of a period, which appears before his eyes as the Golden Age. He must only allow those who are uninformed in these matters, but whom he may probably find more natural in their observations than those who affect to be connoisseurs in the arts, to pass their time more willingly by the side of a pleasing imitation in plaster, than by that of the most celebrated Torso, the value of which they are not able to comprehend.

Yet above all the ancient works of art which the British Museum possesses, scarce any thing rivets the attention more than the modern acquisition made by the collection of Lord Elgin, or the Elgin marbles, as they are generally called.

Like Hamilton had done in Italy, Lord Elgin, a Scotchman, who was from the year 1799 ambassador at the Ottoman Porte, availed himself of his high situation, in order to perfect a plan which he had already formed in England, and which he had deliberated upon with friends of the art, viz. to collect not only accurate drawings of the remains of ancient Grecian architecture and sculpture, but casts in plaster, and thus to snatch from entire destruction every thing that had escaped the ravages of time, and the barbarity of conquerors. Attended by six artists, whom he had particularly associated with himself, at his own expense, in Rome, he came to Constantinople, and after many difficulties, which he overcame by prudence and perseverance, finally received permission from the Turkish government to send his attendants to Athens, in order to commence the work. Indefatigable as they were, still three years were consumed before all the monuments in Athens, and partly beyond its territory, were measured, drawn, and cast off. Still, however, a nearer acquaintance with the situation in which they were found, furnished him with a further conviction that the continual injuries done to them by the Turks, the mouldering of whole statues, and their being crushed to mortar, would shortly leave no trace of them behind. On that account, every thing was now sacrificed to save what still could be saved, and they succeeded so well therein, that a *Firman* was delivered to the senior officer of Athens, by which Lord Elgin was justified, not only to make casts of every thing, but also to carry away, to order to be packed up and shipped, whatever he might find serviceable to his views. Thus he returned to England with a rare booty of preserved remains of the magnificent period of Grecian art.

Are we to complain of him in the present situation of

affairs in Greece ?   Are those acquisitions to be called an unworthy theft ?   There is no doubt, that in order to enjoy to the full the magnificent works of art, it is necessary to tread on the soil and neighbourhood in which they have arisen ; that in a mixed collection they are only laid out to the view of the curious, and never produce the same effect; on that account I have seen many a noble Frank, proud indeed at the victory of his nation, still wander in mournful melancholy amongst the statues, which he had earlier admired as property of the Vatican, in the Belvidere, or in the Medicean palaces of Italy. But does that man deserve blame and reproach, who probably avails himself of the only moment left, in order to prevent the creations of masterly hands from being broken by the hammers of barbarians, and the pestle of the mortar crushing the marble which represented god-like forms ?   Or is the Briton to suffer himself to be outdone by the Frenchman, who has long sighed after the possession of these treasures ?

Greatly as every thing may deserve the attention of the connoisseur, which belongs to those times when the arts flourished in Athens, still we feel ourselves most penetrated and captivated, when, on the sides of the gallery, we view the remains of those celebrated reliefs which formed the frieze of the temple of Minerva, the greatest architectural work with which Pericles adorned Athens.   Little as this celebrated Parthenon, executed in white marble, remained like its original form, still the hand, or direction, of the great Grecian master could not be concealed, neither in the magnificent statues of Theseus and Ilyssus, nor in the *friese*, originally 600 feet long, which went over the Doric row of pillars, on both sides of the temple.   For Plutarch and Pausanias leave us in no doubt that we here behold the works of that Phidias whose high sense of the beautiful in the art, first conceived, and whose chisel has executed, or at least perfected them.

No description can be expected here of these costly works " of such powerful effect by their grandeur, inimitable in their grace and beauty."   Such, after what Hamilton, Millin, Bottiger, and Thiersch, have said upon them, would prove only very deficient, and would be moreover beyond the limits of this work.   Even the extent of the value which they possess as one whole and separately, for the arts and for students, can only be properly prized by a connoisseur living amidst these archæological studies, and who is well versed in the secrets of the same. Still, however, the unpractised eye could not avoid noticing what filled such competent judges as Viconti and Canova with astonishment—that variety and truth in the movement of so many figures, particularly in the treatment of the *Battle of the Centaurs,* which adorned the entrance of the temple over the colonnade, and still more of the *great train at the festival of the Panathenaon,* which was represented in the frieze of the proper temple in a long row of half-size statues.   What grandeur of design in the horses and animals, what richness and taste in the drapery, what beauty in the positions adapted to the purest models !

What, however, more than all overpowered me was, the reflection upon the *wonderful vicissitudes of time,* which are brought so lively to our remembrance upon beholding these treasures of *Athens* transported to *London !*

What was Britain when these statues first came out of the workshops of Phidias ? when that temple of Minerva first stood perfected in all its magnificence before the astonished Athenians ?   A distant island, for the most part only known to a few Phœnician sailors for its copper mines, the name of which was hardly uttered by any Grecian lip, in the most highly polished and elegant city of the former world.   And now this same elegant city, the abode of sciences and arts, without which Rome in her intellectual acquirements would scarcely have become what she did become, at whose sources of learning the noblest spirits of all centuries have drank—what is this Athens in these days ?   A melancholy heap of ashes and of ruins, towards which the metropolis of then unknown Britain, which has risen like a colossus, has stretched forth her saving hand, of that metropolis more than double as large in number of inhabitants as the whole territory of the republic of Attica, in order that whatever still remained possible to be preserved, might not become a prey to those barbarians, at the sight of whom the Muses have long since fled.   They have taken their flight over the sea, and what once flourished under an Ionian sky, has found its asylum in the cold north.

" Is it, then, really so"—said I often to myself—as frequently as I wandered amongst and under these treasures, " or is it illusion? Has Pericles once stood before these marble statues directing how they should be divided in the temple ?   Did Socrates, Plato, Sophocles, Euripides, and Pindar, once pass musing by the same ?   Under these metopes on the frontispiece of the entrance, did the stately Pompa once move, at the festival of the Parthenon, into the interior of the sanctuary, to the statue of the goddess carrying the holy veil, woven by the noblest ladies of quality, as an offering of incense ?"

Since I was considering the Elgin marbles amidst such monologues, the history of our days has attracted the attention irresistibly to the country whence they are derived.   Greece is under arms from the streams of Epirus to the banks of the

Danube; Macedonia, Peloponnesus, the coast of Asia Minor, even Athens, are in contest, not with centaurs and statues, but with a dreadful tyranny, destructive of all the rights of humanity and of religion. Has the counsel of the Omnipotent determined, every earnest reflecting man enquires, that ancient Hellas should awaken anew, and the long-expired phœnix again lift its head above the ashes? May not, probably, many of these marble statues, like a banished foreigner, again return to their liberated native land?

Who can dare to look into the book of Providence? But if victory should crown the oppressed, and if a real Liberty, under the protection of the Laws, put an end, too, to its own degeneration, what an unexpected catastrophe would not attend all that is great, which the history of our times has to hand over to posterity!

The age of Phidias and Praxiteles, for the arts, may then once more return, which may be connected too closely with that *mythological world,* and those *old gods,* which no one can wish back again, who possesses not, what a well-known writing of Winkelman calls, an heathen nature. That Plato whom the ancients called the *godly,* drove even poets from his republic, who had imputed every human passion and folly to the godhead, and had induced them to all the errors of a degenerate humanity. There is something higher than art, although the talent of art belongs to the *godly,* which lies in the spirit of man. The *addressing the godhead in spirit,* is a more majestic idea than any imagination which can float before the mind of a Phidias, or a Raphael.

May then that truly classic soil become again the seat of free, happy, and as it is to be wished, of far better men than the mass of those *ancient Hellenians* were, and probably could be at that time. May the resurrection of Greece, Heathen or Mahomedan bigotry, give place to Christian superstition. May the God, unknown to the ancient Athenians, whom an apostle announced upon the Areopagus, be adored; and a religion thus be exalted which is more than a sensual culture, and from which moral maxims are inseparable; then may the nation return to the enjoyment of a more *real humanity* than antiquity was acquainted with, and much of that superstition which belonged only to the time, and which was obliged to conform itself to that period, and deserved to perish with it, will never return. We shall the more joyfully celebrate the victory of justice over oppression, and reckon it amongst the events of our times which gladden the heart, that we have survived such a period.

Visits to the Bell and Lancastrian Schools.

A method of instruction according to which many millions of children are taught at present not only in *England* but also in *France, Switzerland, Denmark, Russia,* the *East and West Indies,* and even in *Hayti* and *St. Domingo,* which, however it may be looked upon by many as a *dead, spiritless,* and merely *mechanical discipline,* is also encouraged by many intelligent men of the most opposite parties, alike interested however for the education of youth. Such a plan of instruction must naturally contain something in it which produces the most blessed effects. We hardly find any thing similar to it in modern days in the whole history of scholastic instruction. If, indeed, it were only a benevolent institution for those countries, provinces, or towns, which still suffer from a want of *instructors and means of assistance,* it still deserves, nevertheless, as long as this deficiency is assisted, the greatest attention of the friends of humanity, and particularly of the friends of youth; and if only something valuable is preserved therein by experience, it would be unjust to leave the good unregarded on account of what may be faulty.

Much as I had read upon the subject from my calling, and from being early appointed *Foreign Member of the British and Foreign School Society,* had come into the possession of the information which has appeared upon the subject, still the immediate personal contemplation of it surpassed all description. I must, however, first assure my readers, that I have visited and observed the Bell and Lancastrian Schools without any prejudice in favour of their method, and rather with a preconceived opinion against them; and that I am even very far at present from wishing their *unconditional* adoption and imitation in Germany; that certainly, however, the view of their Institutions, and of all that is effected by them, has convinced me, that much therein is founded upon just, although not entirely new, methodical maxims; and that in a short time they are able to produce much, with small means, for *certain ends.* When we compare therewith, how badly *elementary knowledge* and mechanical rudiments are imparted in innumerable towns and country schools of our native land, on account of the unserviceableness, torpidity, or poverty of the instructors, much as has been written upon the improvement of the education of youth, and effected by benevolent governments, we may well be induced to endeavour to remedy many evils by this method.

Foundation of the Schools.

The name of Bell and Lancastrian Schools, brings us back immediately to the *founders*.

Dr. BELL is a Clergyman still living. He was first called as a preacher to Madras, and, in the year 1789, appointed one of the Directors of the Society, founded there for the education of children who were for the most part born of Indian mothers, and were not only grown up without having received any education, but were even frequently sold for purposes of vice. He directed the Institution, refusing the salary of some thousand dollars, which was offered him ; introduced many methods already in use amongst the Malabars, for example, the painting of letters on sand, formed some able boys to be teachers of the younger, and released himself thereby from unserviceable older teachers, who every where conspired against him. For seven years he executed this office, when his health obliged him to return to England. He left behind him, however, perfect rules for instruction, and soon after his arrival in London, gave out his work,—" System, or Trial of Education, according to which a Scholar or grown up Person may educate himself, under the superintendence of a Teacher or Father." When he offered the manuscript to the bookseller, he said,—" I shall be called an enthusiast : should we, however, live a thousand years, we shall see the methods herein described followed by the whole world." And, in truth, some schools, although slowly, began to be instituted in England after this method.

Bell now withdrew himself into solitude, and came forward again only when the Lancastrian Schools displeased the *Evangelical Church*, and the latter formed a *National Society* for the support of the schools: since that time Bell is become again an active member. The more the zeal between the two institutions has increased, the more he is taken notice of by the predominant church; and in the year 1819, he was upon his travels, and gave me an opportunity of making his personal acquaintance.

JOSEPH LANCASTER opened, when only twenty years of age, in the year 1798, a school for poor persons in a suburb of London, for a trifling school charge. It soon increased to many hundreds of children, a great part of whom paid nothing. He too contrived to select ushers or under teachers from the children, and thereby to save expenses. Of Bell at first he had read nothing.· Both however came near to each other in their ideas; the school began to gain respect. Subscriptions were opened for the support of the man who had shewn himself so zealous for the education of so many entirely neglected children. The rich Duke of Bedford was at the head of it. In the year 1804 the school had increased to 800, and soon afterwards to 1000 children, and therewith two sisters educated 200 girls according to the plan of their brother. For *these thousand children, Lancaster* was *the only schoolmaster.* The encouragements given by money daily increased. The King and the whole of the Royal Family interested themselves for it, and Lancaster henceforward named his method the *Royal Lancastrian system of Education.* But he was a quaker, and explained not the catechism of the English church.—This displeased the high church, and very repectable men, for example, Bishop Marsh, considered it their duty to warn even preachers against his system. It has been related to me, that clergymen of influence felt it to be their duty to represent Lancaster's undertaking to the King as dangerous to the Church; but the latter replied, "I have supported him and I will support him."

In the meantime the contributions in money decreased during this party contest, and Bell's school continually gained ground.

Still this animated Lancaster's enthusiasm only the more. He continued his school, making the greatest sacrifices, and employing a restless activity; travelled frequently, in order to gain proselytes to his system, which appeared to him the concern of humanity. He succeeded, too, in this. Wherever he came a mass of people came forth to hear his Lectures, as he was not deficient in a certain natural talent of oratory. He was also convinced, as Bell had been before, that all the world would gradually follow his system. The exclamation was read in many of his Letters,—"I am only the instrument; God has given me a trumpet in my hand, and it must be sounded throughout the whole country. The poor of Britain, the poor of Europe, like the poor of the *whole world*, shall receive education, and no human power shall prevent it." Of what a different kind is such an enthusiasm, were it even not wholly void of a certain esteem of himself, to the miserable, contemptible fanaticisms of a Southcott and others, who would endeavour, by their devotional nothingness, to introduce the kingdom of God. Certainly, religious fanatics too are capable of great sacrifices. But having no clear idea of what they propose to themselves to obtain, they attach themselves to the most indirect means, and leave a well-ordered and regular plan of action to common men, above whom they consider themselves so greatly elevated.

Soon, however, even with Lancaster's actions, it was the

business, for which an interest was shown, rather than his person. Although he wanted not money, he understood nothing less than how to employ it. He soon fell into debt; and, according to the English laws, into the greatest danger of losing his liberty. The noble spirit, however, evinced by some persons, who were animated for the business of education of the poor, and were free from all spirit of party, again saved him.

A society was gradually formed, under the title of the *United British and Foreign School Association,* through the restless activity of which, which produced great effects, the method became very soon extended to many schools. The centre school remained in London. At first, Lancaster was the first teacher. But, accustomed to act independently, and being himself of a very restless character, he separated at last, commenced an institution on his own account, and lives at present, suffering almost want, in Manchester, personally sunk in the public opinion, whilst his institution has obtained an extension which is hardly to be calculated.

Organization of the Bell and Lancastrian School Institutions in London, and their extension in and out of England.

Thus two men, by their participating ideas, have produced an effect, with which all that has been done in Germany, by similar methodical teachers, such as Basedow and Pestalozzi, cannot at all be compared. Schools have been appointed upon the most comprehensive scale, where schools never existed. Children out of number have been educated according to fixed maxims. Little as may be thought of what has been brought about, a large part of these children are still snatched thereby from utter ignorance and depravity. This effect has not been confined to Great Britain: it has penetrated into all the neighbouring, and partly into the most distant, countries; to people of the most opposite religions, and the most different manners. It is, in our times, just as much a pedagogical phenomenon, as the expansion of the Bible Societies in the province of religion. In England alone, two great Societies are the two centre points whence every thing emanates, and the members of which are represented by presidents, secretaries, treasurers, and other officers as their organs.

Both of these Unions or Societies have, entirely independent of, and almost in opposition to, each other, founded schools throughout the whole of England, in all the possessions, and in the East and West Indies. Those which the high church takes under its protection, and have obtained, since the year 1817, a charter of incorporation, are called National Schools;

the remainder are the Lancastrian, or schools of the British and Foreign School Society.

Both have the *same tendency*—the greatest possible advancement of education amongst all, particularly the poorer classes of citizens, by the least possible expense in teachers and means of instruction.

They are, throughout, similar; not only in the plan of teaching, but in the whole nature of their appointment, even in the local. The sexes only, and not the classes, are separated in the London schools. However great the number of the scholars, male and female, may be, they are all collected in one large hall. In the two great central schools of the metropolis, of which that of Bell lies in the heart of the City, the other on the other side of the Thames, in the Borough Road, in Southwark; these halls, or rooms, are lighted from above by obliquely-placed windows (something similar to those in large hot-houses), so that almost the whole roof is of glass, whereby a clear and equal light is spread over all the seats of the children. The Lancastrian school-buildings are entirely new built; and, when I saw them, every thing was far neater, more agreeable, and convenient, than in the National School in Baldwin's Gardens.

In the school-room the upper teacher stands upon an elevation before a table, and directs the whole by certain signs of command. The children sit before small writing-desks, which I, however, almost wholly missed in the National School, upon benches which are still narrower, standing parallel with the breadth of the room. Between the benches and the side walls is a free passage, six feet broad. Half-circles of iron are laid in the ground in this passage, and denote the places upon which the children, the little under-teacher in the middle, must form a half-circle of twelve or sixteen, in order to repeat the exercise tables of *letters, syllables, words, lines,* and *calculations,* which hang upon the side walls. The different classes are pointed out by a glass telegraph on the bench where the new class begins. The foremost small tables have borders somewhat raised, between which fine sand is strewed, wherein the first attempts at writing are made. All who are present receive instruction *at the same time.* I confess that it far surpassed my expectations, to find that, in spite of four or five hundred children, who make such an unavoidable noise, the instruction is not at all disturbed or distracted. The children were clothed very poorly, but were, withal, very cleanly both in face and hands.

The only important difference is to be found in what respects *religious education.* In the national schools, the Church Catechism is considered as a fundamental point according to the thirty-nine Articles. In the Lancaster schools, they confine themselves only to the Bible and religious hymns. Instructive writings for young persons, many of which particularly appear in Ireland, are given into the hands of the children. The clergy blame this, because the predominant religion of the country is not planted in their youthful hearts ; but, on the other hand, the friends of Lancaster grant admittance to children of all parties, leave the choice of the system of instruction to riper years, and only wish *religion*, and not *theology*, to be taught in the schools. It is on this account that, in the directing society, members are to be found of all religious parties.

The extension and effect which hitherto the schools of both societies have enjoyed and produced, may be nearly equal. Above one thousand schools are connected with the two London central schools. In these, upper teachers, male and females, are continually formed and sent into all the provinces. According to the last accounts, lying before me, of the year 1819, the number of children educated in England, according to the Bell and Lancastrian method, amounts to above 200,000.

Since the year 1814, France has begun also to take the liveliest interest in these kinds of national education, and highly-distinguished individuals, such as the Baron Gerando and Count Lasterie, placed themselves at the head of it. These schools multiply every year, both in and out of Paris. The Emperor Alexander sent young men to England, from the Pedagogical Institution at Petersburg, in order to learn the method, and the most perfect work, which we hitherto possess upon this subject, has also been given out by the desire of this Monarch, by the Russian Imperial Counsellor, in the German, French, and Russian languages. M. von Karazay assures us, too, in his work, which appeared in Casan in the year 1819, that in this manner 200,000 Russian soldiers, and other grown up persons, have learnt to read, to reckon, and write, during the years 1817 and 1818. In Sweden, Denmark, and Naples, this method has also been followed. The superintendents of the *national schools* confine themselves particularly to England. The society for Britain and Foreign parts, however, according to the Lancastrian methods, are in close correspondence with all countries. I was presented to the meeting by Dr. Schwabe, the worthy Secretary of the same for the exterior, and was received in the most welcome manner, as a foreign member. One of the most meritorious superintendents, Mr. Allen, was absent. A Quaker held the chair.

Letters were read, from all parts, of the successful progress that had been made.

A man, like Dr. Schwabe, to whom German pedagogical maxims and plan of instruction are not unknown, would, indisputably, be best adapted to controul them.

Of the principal Maxims contained in the Institutions of these Schools, and the most important Plan of Instruction which they follow.

In order that we may not form an erroneous opinion of these institutions, which have been so greatly extended, it is necessary, first of all, to know how badly off the poorer classes of people were for education, and partly still are, in England and Ireland (but less so in Scotland). The Sunday-schools, which have been already introduced into these countries, since the year 1784, are a proof that innumerable poor were not at all provided with daily schools, since the children of the poor, in order to gain their bread, were often obliged to work, from the tenderest infancy, in the manufactories, from early in the morning till late in the evening. Thousands and thousands have grown up without having received the least instruction, or have, at most, received the most wretched of all, from travelling school-masters, who travelled about the country, in a circumference of about thirty miles. Although the subject has been sometimes brought before parliament, it has still either been very soon dropped, or it has been found a subject of hesitation to make a certain knowledge and acquirements general property, and, therefore, it has been strenuously opposed. England, in this respect, cannot be compared with Germany, where there is scarcely any place, however small, in which something of a school, be the same ever so miserable, is not to be met with.

Whatever wishes the friend of humanity may still entertain for the fulfilment of a better plan of instruction and improvement of the rising generation, they tend rather to the interior melioration of our school education, whilst Bell, Lancaster, and the members of the school societies, are labouring only to the end, that instruction may be generally imparted, and the schools increased, according to the increase of the population.

If in Germany the system of improvement in the education of youth has a tendency not only to confine his knowledge to the principal and most necessary elements, but, as the poorest child is just as capable of instruction, nay, often more so, than the richest, to form every one as perfect as possible, and to make all, if not learned, at least enlightened; it is, on the other hand, considered in England as a great object gained, if only the hundred thousand of children, who are running about either in total ignorance, or miserably educated, are brought into some *discipline and order*, and the most simple means of further formation of the mind imparted to them.

Still, only even to attain this end, sums which could not have been raised would have been necessary, to pay and appoint a number of teachers, according to the comparison with the number of scholars. That, however, one teacher alone could employ hundreds for a continuance, without soon sinking under the weight of the duty, was considered as impossible. The idea was therefore embraced, of proceeding in the schools as in manufacturing establishments, to appoint masters, workmen, and apprentices, to make use of the more able scholars for the education of the incompetent, and, at the same time, to let them learn and teach, and again, even by teaching, improve themselves.

It was, therefore, well understood, that even able scholars could not be fitted for teaching or instruction, in the higher sense of the word. But they were found perfectly sufficient for rendering assistance, and promoting discipline. This was considered sufficient for the first years. As in England, generally, the formation and practice of the powers of thought are effected rather in *the school of life*, than in *that of instruction*, it was considered proper to leave the higher developement of the understanding to later times. It was difficult, therefore, to convince persons of the utility of our *thinking exercises*, so called, particularly as their use is certainly much *perverted* in many schools.

As the poorest of the people were to participate in the instruction, attention was paid to the greatest simplicity in the method of imparting the same, and as the time of those persons, in which they can visit the school, is generally very prescribed, it became a matter of necessity that in the shortest time possible, whatever is most important to all should be carried on in a steady order without either leaving off, distractions of any kind, or interference of other matters. The connexion of one thing with another is, indeed, the greatest advantage in manufactures. Where was this better known than in England? This appeared to be applicable also to school instruction.

If it be asked how far the ends, which are prescribed by this institution, are attained by all these regulations and methods, since I have visited both the two large central schools in London, as well as others in the small towns, for example in Harwich, and have attended the instruction, I venture to offer the following impartial opinion.

The children afforded in every class whatever was the intention of that class. They read audibly and properly; in the upper class, even with expression. They wrote upon their little boards of slate (in the national schools even without having a table, standing upon the hand) whatever was dictated to them, very clearly, and mostly orthographically right; and many could already write a fine hand. Their memory was certain. The young monitors executed their office with great punctuality, and a severity which gave their countenance and voice almost the character of austerity. I could form no opinion, however, how far the children are advanced in the formation of intellect; for every thing which I saw and heard of was taught them. This, however, I know for certain, that we may go into many of our country schools, and those of our small towns, wherein the children will not be found half so practised in the acquirements I have mentioned, which constitute, in Germany also, the principal part of the elementary instruction. I know also that the spirit of order and punctuality which distinguishes those institutions must be wished for in every school, as well as an obedience to command; and, finally, that the citizens of all towns would take as great an interest in the concern of popular instruction as is met with in England.

As in these institutions, moreover, the teachers are requested to make the most rigid observation of, and pay attention to every thing which the regulations prescribe, and nothing is entirely left to their option, upon the whole they have appeared perfectly adequate to the attainment of the principal object, since the introduction of the system; and departures therefrom have only been allowed in some particular points.

Idle children were placed in a cradle. If they ran from their places they were enclosed, like young fowls, in a hanging basket. A paper crown, or fool's cap, was placed upon the heads of the obstinate, and thus they were carried about in the school; and two boys, who went before them, cried out the faults they had committed. Those who would not learn were bound with ropes, knotted in a coverlet, and at times were suffered to sleep a whole night upon the ground. A wooden yoke was also fixed upon the obstinate, who were sometimes coupled together. Those who were resolutely bad, had an iron hung about their necks of the weight of four or six pounds. Little faults were noted by punishment marks upon which the fault was written, such as a babbler, disturber. The rewards consisted, for the most part, in small presents, partly in marks of honour and higher places.

Generally speaking, the school discipline of Bell appears to have had, from the commencement, a milder character. I thought I discovered softness and mildness in the treatment of the children, particularly in the teachers, male and female, and in the monitors of the national school, under the direction of Mr. Johnson.   However, a more humane spirit begins to reign in the Lancastrian schools also, and corporeal punishments and ill treatments are no longer heard of.

Be this as it may, this plan of education, which has been instituted and extended with such particular success, has produced the most blessed consequences to Great Britain and many other countries, and, at the same time, has immediately advanced the higher purpose which the Bible Societies have in view.   For it may be asserted that, by this manner, millions of children have at least laid the ground-work of knowledge and acquirements, to which they would have remained strangers for ever.   The yearly accounts, too, which come in from so many towns, prove the beneficial influence which this has had upon the manners and the conduct of the children.   Order, cleanliness, and more quiet behaviour, have taken place of what was always found the most contrary thereto—the greatest dissipation in youth.   The old remark, too, has hereby been again confirmed, that good schools have a benevolent influence upon the parents, and that, from what the children bring back to their homes, the former even may be induced to reflection.   The new appearance of the light, kindled in the schools, has often penetrated into the most obscure hut.   I shall impart only a few facts here, from many which I have collected upon this head.

In many places, where schools had been instituted with apparent success, grown-up persons became sensible how greatly their children surpassed them, and made known their own ardent desire to learn to read and write.   In North Wales, a clever preacher, Mr. Charles, immediately made a beginning with them.   The education began with eighteen persons ; after three months, however, the school contained more than eighty ; and the example was imitated by the whole surrounding country.   A sermon, which he gave, produced the consequence, that, in a short time, no *spectacles* were any longer to be found in the shops of the adjoining villages, as all the old men and women had procured themselves a pair, in order to learn therewith to read.   Many of them made a very rapid progress.   Just as active was Mr. Smith, in Bristol.   Attended by two friends, he went throughout an entire parish, from house to house, and wrote down the names of those, who declared themselves willing to learn to read.   The first man who was registered was William Wood, sixty-three years of age ; and the first woman, Jane Burrace, forty years old.   Two rooms, free from rent and taxes, were given over to Mr.

Smith ; books were lent him, and two persons willingly offered their services as teachers. Both schools were opened on the 8th of March, 1812, one with eleven men, the other with ten women ; and they very soon saw, with pleasure, that the progress made surpassed all expectation ; the beneficent influence which the school visit had upon their plan of life, was also striking. The desire of learning to read extended itself from one quarter to another. Smith, encouraged thereby, gave all his attention to the work. Although he had only a salary of eighteen shillings a week, he paid three to another man, who was obliged to neglect part of his own duties, in order that he might the more zealously devote himself to his new and delightful employment. A place was assigned to him wherein he held his schools, and books were given him for his use therein. The inhabitants of Bristol directed their attention to its success ; and a few weeks afterwards, a society was formed for the instruction of the grown-up poor in the reading of the Holy Scriptures. Dr. Pole, a Quaker, and member of this society, drew up an appeal to the public, wherein he challenged them to make similar institutions. He addressed himself particularly to the members of the different Bible Societies, and made them observe, that the end of these societies could never be attained, if the persons to whom they made presents of the Bible could not read them ; and that the utility of the schools, for grown-up persons, must not be confined to them, but extended to their children. This appeal to the public, of which nearly a thousand copies were distributed, occasioned a rapid augmentation of similar schools and school societies in other places. In the year 1816, the number of the Bristol schools, for men, amounted to twenty-four ; those for women, to thirty-one ; and 3321 persons had already enjoyed education in them. On the 11th June, 1815, a society, similar to the Bristol, was formed in the city of London, under the superintendance of the Lord Mayor ; a year after, a similar one was instituted in the suburb of Southwark. Almost all the towns in the kingdom followed the example ; and it is now thought, in some places, that few, and perhaps not a single individual, are to be found who cannot read.

Very interesting proofs have been given that very old persons are capable of learning to read. In a school at Bath there were, at one time, five old women, whose united ages amounted to two hundred and eighty years : these persons, when they began to go to school, were scarcely acquainted with the alphabet ; but at the end of the year they were capable of reading very well in the bible. At Bristol, a woman eighty-five years of age, learnt to read well in eight weeks ;

many caricatures of the younger part of the world, have disappeared.

In the institutions for boys, the education is confined, for the
most part, to elementary knowledge, although many of them
boast and talk loudly of the various acquirements which are to
be learnt in them.   We should think, the almost marketing
annunciations which appear in the daily Journals, would rather
deter parents from sending their offspring to them.   But still
these annunciations cannot fail in obtaining their end, since
they are always repeated.   As it is at the option, moreover, of
every one who knows not what plan of life to commence, to
announce himself as a teacher, and the higher authorities give
themselves no concern about his qualifications, we may easily
suppose how badly such pupils are instructed in the house of
such a person, and how little they learn.   There are still, however, particular establishments, which have been very much
applauded.   Many country clergymen, particularly, are said to
form a very happy exception, who, whilst they are not, however, without paying regard to the improvement of their confined situation, devote themselves to the undertaking with zeal,
earnestness, and dignity, and produce a very beneficent effect
upon those who are confided to them.   Adult foreigners too, who
wish to learn the English language, often spend half a year with
such men, and live like one of the family, not without improvement, in their quiet and respectable family circle.

As the boarding and private institutions, as well as the higher schools, have their fixed holydays, which are tolerably long,
the bond between parents and children becomes again fastened,
and those weeks wherein the children return home, are devoted to family festivals.   I was in London exactly at one of
these holyday times, and had, therefore, an opportunity of
being a frequent witness to the happiness the parents felt, in
their house being rendered more lively by the presence of their
children, and the sons not less so, who being liberated from
the rigorous rules imposed upon them in the schools, could
enjoy themselves at the tables of the mothers, who never
omitted to indemnify them for the long deprivation they had
endured.

GRAMMAR SCHOOLS.

Visit to Eton.

It is a very difficult matter to get well acquainted with the
interior of the British institutions for education.   I was even
disadvised to make attempts, in London, to gain admission
either into Westminster school or any other school of the me-

tropolis. I hardly expected to have succeeded so far as I did in Eton, the most celebrated institution in the neighbourhood of London.

The College, or the School of Eton, consists of two courts, which are surrounded on all sides by buildings, and which are close on each other. The entire middle wing, which separates the courts, forms the dwelling of the Provost, &c. &c.

As it is not so easy to get acquainted with the system of instruction, as it is imparted in Eton and the other learned schools in and without London, every stranger cannot find access to the public hours of teaching, and I could not, therefore, be present even at one of them; it is, nevertheless, not difficult to obtain some knowledge of the course of education, from the descriptions given by the scholars and teachers.

We shall be enabled to judge how far every thing, even in the *exterior form*, differs from the arrangements of our schools, from the whole quire containing only *two large Classes*. In the Westminster School even, all the seven classes were held in a single smoky room. Formerly, says Wedderburn, a curtain divided the hall into two parts. But this has been long since torn away. In Eton three or four pulpits in each of the two rooms, stand at some distance apart, upon which the different divisions, without interfering with each other, are educated at the same time. Hence it becomes clear to me at once in what manner the Bell and Lancastrian method in England, which also brings together so many hundred children into one space, was far less stranger than it would have been in Germany. Amongst the peculiarities, moreover, are the hours of instruction, which are continually interchanged with the free hours, and that much is *recited* and *repeated* in the classes, but hardly any thing is written down. The teachers have a fixed plan of instruction, and they rarely find it necessary to prepare themselves much beforehand, as they perfectly answer the purposes of their calling by making propositions, by examining what they have learnt by heart, and correcting their labours.

The education is confined chiefly to the two ancient classic languages, and in these, indubitably, the greatest advancement is made. How far other branches of knowledge, that is to say, geographical, historical, and natural historical acquirements, are inferior to the instruction imparted in our schools, as an acquaintance with foreign literature is not at all thought of; how cold and meagre the religious part of instruction is, is partly proved from the books of education which are in use, and partly from the repeated conversations I have held upon the subject, both with teachers and pupils. In the instruction in the classic languages they appear only to have in view to bring the scholars so far, that they may read the Greeks and Romans without difficulty, in order to become acquainted with their contents and spirit, and to acquire a certain facility in their own use of the language. For this purpose, frequent Latin and Greek poetical exercises, as formerly were in use in our own schools, particularly the Saxon, are considered the best, and in which individuals, as the Musée Etonienses prove, make a considerable progress. Little care is bestowed, in the hours of instruction, upon extensive interpretation or finer criticism, because it is not the intention to form mere philologists; but this is left rather to their own study, or to the private instruction of particular tutors or under-teachers, when able heads can be found to undertake it. But a certain *general classic instruction*, imparted through the language and the beautiful forms of the old authors, is certainly principally aimed at. I am almost of opinion, that a more proper method is followed, in this respect, than that which is pursued by many teachers in our own learned institutions, who already frequently, in the lower and middle classes, embitter the learning of languages by too difficult linguistical, grammatical, critical, and metrical subtilities, and by frequently bringing only their own learning to view, never stir from one particular spot, but neglect what ought to be first considered, a certain readiness in analysing, construing, and cursory reading. The consequence of all this is, that the majority, after the school-hours, retain only a bitter remembrance of the oppressive moments of teaching; and, frequently, a total oblivion or neglect of these studies ensues. It is an indisputable advantage, in the English schools, that most is left to private diligence; that the scholar must read and work much by himself; and, thereby, can act more freely, instead of being deafened by perpetual catechising. Many, certainly, acquire thereby a greater activity, ability, and love of study. The consequences thereof are seen in the great respect continually shown for classic literature, which is proved by the libraries of statesmen, and even of such persons who have devoted themselves to no learned profession, as well as in the frequent quotations of appropriate passages from the ancient writers, which are made in parliamentary speeches and upon other occasions. How very different is this, with few exceptions, in Germany. How rarely men of business, nay, even clergymen, who, when they have made a considerable progress at school in the classics, either devote to them, occasionally, their hours of leisure, or even remain in the possession of the most preferable authors. Must we not be discontented, therefore, if an entire separation ensues, from all that is scientific, and the whole life is divided between the employment of the calling and sensual enjoyments.

AN EVENING AT SIR JOSEPH BANKS'S.

The people of England have been long accustomed to associate the recollections of the highly-venerated King George the Third, and the memory of those veterans, Dr. Herschel and Sir Joseph Banks, who were not only his equals in age, bu· were distinguished by his particular confidence, and enjoyeu the frequent hospitalities of royalty. All three of this rare society were still living, when I visited England. The astronomer is the only one living at present.

I hardly ventured to indulge a hope of making a personal acquaintance with him however, as in Germany it was reported that, on account of his old age, he was altogether inaccessible. But I found exactly the contrary. On the 2d of June, I was introduced into the company which usually assembles every Sunday evening around him.

Only the elder part of my readers may remember the lively interest the great voyage round the world awakened in Germany. This voyage was ordered to be undertaken exactly 50 years ago, by the English government, and we are indebted to it for so important a part of the nearer acquaintance we possess with the new quarter of the globe. That part of my readers alone will remember with what curiosity the Hawkesworth collection, as soon as the translation of it appeared, was read. Then too we got acquainted, for the first time, with this learned naturalist, who made the first South Sea voyage with Captain Cook (like the two Fosters a few years later, the second) and who, after surmounting dangers in the sea and in those islands, which before then had been trodden by no European foot, returned with a booty so valuable for the sciences. Foreign parts too did honour to his restless endeavours to extend the limits of human knowledge, and to bring to a certainty what the earlier voyages of discovery of *Magellan*, and various *Spanish and Belgian navigators;* and, since the middle of the foregoing century, a *Byron, Wallis, Carteret,* and *Bourgainville,* had made only probable.

In the possession of a large fortune, treated by his King as a friend, invested with all the honourable tokens of merit, unfettered by public business, he has lived almost half a century in an indefatigable devotion to the purposes of science. His house, which contains the treasures of a library almost unique, particularly in natural history, notwithstanding the many presents he has made to the British Museum, of many botanical and other curiosities of natural history, was open every day to all the learned. Every forenoon they were allowed to make use of the chambers of the same for reading, investigation, and inspection, and they were certain of finding every interesting pamphlet, or any other literary novelty, ready upon the table for their information.

On Sunday evening Banks's residence was properly the place of resort of no inconsiderable number of natural historians, chemists, and other well informed travellers, who came there both to impart to the proprietor any thing that had appeared to them remarkable in the different districts of knowledge and science, and to maintain a scientific correspondence amongst themselves.

I found the veteran in his middle library room, dressed in splendid attire, with the broad ribbon of his order over his shoulder and breast, just as he was accustomed to appear, as president, at the sittings of the Royal Society for the extension of natural science, to which we are indebted, since the year 1766, for those valuable philosophical transactions. He sat, as he was lame in the feet, upon an arm chair which moved with rollers, supporting his left arm upon a table which was standing by him. It was, indeed, scarce any thing more than the outward form and cover of a spirit which was formerly so animated; his sense and memory were weak; but still his countenance bespoke the expression of a friendly participation in the feelings of all around him. Every foreigner was at least mentioned to him, and whoever had any thing to offer, omitted not to lay it before him. I had also the pleasure of meeting here with our Lichtenstein, whose acquaintance I had frequently failed in making in Berlin, who was also so good as to give me the names of the most important persons, who were here assembled from the most remote countries. The eye, however, always returned to the celebrated person with rapture, and we rejoiced at contemplating him, at least, as a holy ruin.

Few have, without at the same time shining as an author, laboured so long, so actively, and so powerfully, in the advancement of natural knowledge, as he has done. Well might Cuvier, with the greatest justice, boast of him in the eulogy he read not long ago to the French Academy of Sciences. "Every where, where a useful undertaking has been brought about, he has co-operated by the advice he has given and the services he has performed; wherever he has met with a worthy scholar, or learned man, he has opened to them the treasures of nature with the greatest liberality." How many have not borrowed largely from his treasures? and thus has his uncommon rich fund of observations and collections been imparted for the greatest part to the world, although he himself has made but little of them known. On the sea voyage he was, what with respect to a man of Cook's character was not easy to accomplish, at all times the mediator and peace-maker. He has richly scattered, in those islands, the seeds of the European world, and from them again brought a number of seeds with him to Europe, and liberally imparted them to all the great nursery gardens. He proved himself also a benefactor to Iceland, which he visited a few years after his voyage round the world; for he sent whole ships laden with provisions at his own expense to the inhabitants of that island, who were suffering want upon occasion of a famine.

In the long and sanguinary war between France and England, wherein many of the rights of mankind and nations were violated, he proved himself always the noble-minded protector of learned men and travellers, as well as of all the scientific enterprizes undertaken by hostile France. To him alone are the English literati, who were made prisoners, indebted for the interest he evinced for them at the National Institution in Paris. During Cook's voyage, Banks instigated the British government, notwithstanding the reciprocal enmities which prevailed, to suffer the Frenchman, La Perouse, to sail peaceably in all seas. He availed himself of his extensive correspondence to obtain information of the unsuccessful result. When the considerable collection of natural curiosities, which Labilladiere had sent to France upon his voyage, fell into the hands of English cruisers, and thus became the property of the government, Banks, with a noble mind, again employed all his influence, and the boxes, without being opened, were sent untouched to France. In this way men act, in whose opinion that man stands above the citizen of any individual state, who makes the empire of science of more importance than the changeable empires of the earth.

It is now more than a year that his remains repose in the bosom of that earth which he once sailed around, and with the produce and manufactures of which he had made himself better acquainted and enquired into, more than most have done.

VISIT TO A QUAKER'S MEETING, WITH RECOLLECTIONS OF THE ORIGIN AND CONSTITUTION OF THE SOCIETY.

The great merits which Mrs. Fry has gained by the improvement she has introduced into the jails, are well known. She belongs to the sect which bears the name of Quakers. The more this church society distinguishes itself in so remarkable a manner, both by its maxims and constitution, and the peculiarity of its worship, the more curious I became to attend one of its Sunday meetings.

The founder of the society, George Fox, (born in 1624) was the son of a poor weaver. He enjoyed only the education which a small school afforded ; was, from childhood, of an earnest and quiet disposition, was put apprentice to a shoemaker, but was obliged, however, as his master traded also in wool and sheep, frequently to watch over the flocks. This monotonous employment separating him from intercourse with mankind, he became only more confined within himself, continually making reflections upon religious objects, looking with horror upon the corruptions of the great crowd, and often breaking out when grown up a young man, and perceiving the immorality which surrounded him, into exclamations which had correction for their tendency. The lively fancy, however, with which he was endowed, found much food in solitude, and his mind was continually raised to the contemplation of the Deity. God beholds him in nature, since he cannot find him in the desert, romantic life of his fellow-creatures. Thus he stands at one time, when 19 years of age, upon an high mountain, surrounded with God in prayer, and begs that he will shew him the way to holy salvation. There the man lost in religious adoration thinks he hears the voice of God, which makes known to him the corruption of the world, but at the same time the prospect is held out that God's work may be promoted by pure zeal. "Towards the north," so Penn relates of him, "he thinks he beholds great nations, thickly thronged on each other, like mists of the sun, which shall be brought to the Lord, in order that, at last, they may become one flock guided by one shepherd." He holds himself called to be a moralist. The church life affords him no satisfaction. How could this have been possible at that time, when the parties of the Evangelical, Independents, and Puritans were employed in the wildest dispute ; when the one persecuted the other with rage, and all spirit of true Christianity appeared to be lost ?

The enthusiasm which has attacked him, leads him in the meantime, by degrees, to highly romantic imaginations. He thinks wicked spirits have taken an oath that they are able to cure diseases. He preaches repentance in towns and villages, without art indeed, without rule, simple, frequently breaking off, and speaking ungrammatically, but still so eloquent and heart-touching, that his own imagination even imparts itself to the hearers. They think as he does on the inward light, which is participated to him, and that what he teaches will be beneficial to every man who seeks it, and guide them safer than any written education, or than, as he loudly asserts, the altogether corrupted church condition of instruction, which on that account can be easily dispensed with. His wife, Margaret Fell, co-operates zealously with him, since, according to his doctrine, inward illumination cannot be confined to one sex. Thus she teaches and preaches as he does, as often as the spirit moves her.

The effects of his doctrine,—the continually increasing boldness with which he even interrupted the preachers in the church, attracted the attention of the magistrates. He was nine times carried into prison, but was always liberated, as he could not be convicted of any crime. Persecution, however, only increases his zeal. He travels through the greater part of England, visits America, Holland, and Germany, and sees his followers becoming daily more numerous; by degrees, however, he got rid of the wanderings and extravagancies of fanaticism, particularly in the intercourse he carried on with such excellent men as William Penn and Robert Barclay. At last he lived in London, and looking back with great pleasure upon his work, and still exhorting them, in the written Address he left behind him, to peace and unity in spirit, he died, in full possession of his faculties, in the year 1691.

If Fox and (as this is generally the case,) many of his still more zealous followers were more warm, and made many alterations; if their zeal for their occupation sometimes led them even into the commission of punishable crime; we must not forget, that almost the whole at first consisted of persons of the lowest class, who, partly out of want of knowledge, and partly doubtful, by the bloody contentions existing between the reigning church parties, of what they ought to believe, and how they were to serve God, attached themselves to men who boldly contradicted these errors, and who at least kept themselves free from the many vices predominant in other clergy, from avarice and intemperance. These persons, however, found that the learning of which the latter boasted produced little; and that frequently the most uncultivated men, soldiers, women, children, prayed more devoutly, and preached more powerfully, than the learned hirelings, who, living little according to the spirit of the gospel, still called themselves clergy.

In all this there was much truth. Many persecuted persons made so great an impression by becoming martyrs to their constancy, that frequently even the judges were disarmed, by the natural eloquence of the accused. By degrees, also, excellent, well educated, and truly religious men, began to separate the gold from the dross; and many religious, and wherewithal free-thinking minds, thought they saw the business of christianity consist, not in scholastical logical terms; not in modes ofinstruction, which even went beyond the holy scriptures; but in that pure devotion to God, and real belief, which is unattended by caprice of any kind. Hence we have an explanation of the rapid and wide extension made by this Society, which purified itself always more from excrescences, became continually more mild and temperate thereby, however, because it suffered itself to be led astray by no persecutions, which followed it every where, but remained faithful to its maxims, manners, and customs. Thus this Society attained, at last, the permission of acting as it chose, and the most perfect liberty of religion was allowed it.

In England the Quakers cannot fail in obtaining the public respect, as they are amongst the most active promoters of all benevolent and generally useful institutions and undertakings; and have gained themselves great merit, particularly in the improvement of hospitals, schools, and prisons. That they are to be distinguished by their honesty and purity of manners, may certainly partly be the consequences of the severe discipline, or church rules, to which they are subjected, and the continual controul of morals over the members. With all this, however, the effects of a certain religious principle are not to be denied.

From this picture of their manners, it may be well expected that the method of their worship distinguishes itself from the regulations of the other church parties in many points. As the business of religion is, for them, altogether internal, they are, therefore, disinclined to all outward demonstrations of the same. They consider it, indeed, salutary and fitted to the spirit of the Apostolic church, to meet at certain times, and choose for this purpose the Sunday. But they have neither churches, nor any kind of holy customs. There are six meeting places, in the different quarters of London. I visited one, tolerably large, in St. Martin's Lane, and found a large room, with two rows of benches, for men and women, the one behind the other, which were separated only by a passage. On the wall at the end of the room, in view of the meeting, there is a raised seat for the eldest person. There is no pulpit nor altar, no organ nor painting; nor the most trifling decoration upon the white walls.

The members assembled at a certain hour, were not even summoned by a bell, and sat themselves down, quietly, wrapt up in themselves, with their heads covered, and countenances fixed upon the ground. There was no chant, no sound of a human voice. They were silent and obstinate, until an inward impulse was capable of animating any member among the men or the women, of exciting them, and encouraging them to loud discourse. I passed an hour and a half in this dead stillness, which was only at times interrupted by a gentle sickly cough, or a deep sigh. I still had hopes that the mouth would be opened; but in vain. It is not, however, always so. If any member feels himself moved and encouraged by the spirit to speak, he rises up from his place and speaks; sometimes only a few words, at times more at length, either praying, instructing, encouraging, or admonishing; at other times he discourses, either upon words of the bible, or at his own liberty, and unconstrained. This time the spirit prevailed over no one. I left, indeed, before the conclusion of the meeting, in order not to miss another object I had in view. But an acquaintance who had waited till the end, told me that the assembly soon broke up in silence. Well acquainted with the Society, he assured me that this quiet meeting, this temporal liberation from all worldly affairs, this self-contemplation, this life in what is above the sensual, this proper hour of devotion, was very honourable to many, and had a beneficent influence upon them. The more the body reposes, the more active is the spirit: the less foreign influence disturbs the soul, the more active and more appropriate becomes reflection, the more deep the feeling. If any speech was made, there were individuals who spoke well, generally very tediously, but at all times audibly and intelligibly.

That the Quakers think themselves enabled to do without learned preachers ordained by the church, is partly founded in the opinion, that the Christian religion was, at the beginning, extended in the world by religious persons, but not by schoolmen; and what may be necessary for all to know, is also intelligible in the holy Scriptures, without learning; and partly upon their disinclination to all systematical treatment of the doctrine of religion, whereby nothing is gained. The prescription of the Baptism, and ceremony of the Supper, they do not explain literally, but imaginary, from an inward new life, and purifying of the heart, and by a spiritual enjoyment of the Redeemer. Marriage is fulfilled without any interference of a Priest, as a contract before witnesses, and is therefore inviolable. Burials take place without any ceremony, and no tomb-stone, which the English consider so much, point out their graves.

A GLANCE INTO THE COURTS OF JUSTICE.

*Corruption of the lower Class of People—Effects of Publicity—
Trial by Jury.*

I would very willingly have made myself acquainted with
the English constitution, with regard to its judicial proceedings, by a more frequent attendance at the public sittings.
An irresistible wish frequently arises even upon the reading of
the daily papers, wherein so accurate an account is given of
all that passes, to be an ocular witness thereof. Time, however, failed me. For there is no difficulty, since from the
perfect publicity of the trials, access is free to every one, and
only a very strong influx of the curious, (as the narrowness of
the local situation frequently makes it difficult to get in, even
when you have finally paved yourself a road by a small piece of
money,) renders a long stay therein very troublesome.

This is always the case in the upper house of Parliament.
Here, it is well known, is the seat of *the highest* law authority.
It extends only over the first dignitaries of the empire, and
we know from history that, more than once, crowned
heads were obliged to appear before it as impeached persons.
We have ourselves survived to see a Queen before the bar.
The Lord High Chancellor, the third man after the King, is at
the head of the session. Generally his speech is short, and
sounds like the voice of an oracle. Lord Eldon, who is at
present invested with this distinguished office, appeared to me
to enjoy general respect.

He sits not in Parliament only, but in the high Court of
Chancery, which assembles in the environs of Lincoln's Inn
Fields, as the only judge. He hears the advocates who have
every thing prepared in writing, and pronounces sentence, from
which there is no appeal but to Parliament. When the written law appears too severe for any single case, he is allowed
to decide according to reason and the internal judgment of his
conscience. As every court is held in the name of the King, and
the Lord Chancellor has the great seal in his possession, they
have therefore given him the name of the Keeper of the King's
Conscience.

In earlier times indeed the kings themselves were wont to
sit at justice at the tribunal, which was always in the neighbourhood of the court, but has been held for several centuries
in Westminster. On this account this court of justice received
the name of the King's Bench. Under the empty places of
the king sit the judges. But even in these, notwithstanding

the large room of Westminster hall which is so near, the space is so narrow, the number of spectators frequently so great, that without having understood any thing clearly I was glad to squeeze myself out again, although a longer view of the various physiognomies of the judges and lawyers, peeping out of their large perukes, even without understanding them, would have been very interesting to me.

Besides these courts of justice, there are many others according to the difference of the objects, amongst which it is well known, that that which bears the name of Doctors' Commons, is at the same time the school for those who choose to devote themselves to civil law.

It is easy to suppose that these numerous courts of justice must be in constant activity in a town like London, where such a mass of people are thronged together, even were we less acquainted with the moral condition of the lower classes of people particularly, and with the experience of those who have long made observations thereon. It is impossible to read the well known work of Colquhoun upon the London Police, without being seized with the most painful feelings. To the dreadful view of all the secret and public misdeeds and crimes, which are committed daily, is added the [mournful experience which he assures us he has made upon the little effect produced by the laws and punishments, which, in many cases, are carried to a severity almost draconic.

Indeed, when we walk around the principal environs of London; when, on Sundays particularly, we see ourselves surrounded with such a number of people, in whose countenances and deportment, health, ease, spiritual cultivation, honesty, security in feeling of liberty, nobility of mind and contentment, are so visibly imprinted, scarcely can we be induced to believe that, in the circumference of the *very same* town, a countless number of the most despicable human beings, a depraved class of people, are to be met with, in whom even the last traces of all sense of morality are extinguished. But at the same time we cannot suppress a deep feeling of compassion, in observing how many of them, without it being their own fault, appear to have been devoted to crime from their birth, ere they could sink so deeply. Colquhoun thinks that the great moral corruption, into which so many thousands sink yearly, both publickly and in secret, is particularly to be explained by two reasons; partly from the immeasurable trade of the metropolis, which indeed raises the state to an extraordinary summit of riches, but at the same time introduces an endless number of temptations to excesses of every kind; partly from the love of gambling, which is become predominant beyond all representation, and to which, time, fortune, conscience, and frequently even life itself, are made a sacrifice.

Indeed, the greater part of the judicial proceedings arise from fraud, theft, murder, and particularly the most unpardonable of all crimes, forgery, or issuing of false bank notes. Wherever the latter is proved, neither youth, sex, inexperience, nor seduction, are capable of averting the most severe judgment. This severity has very frequently, in modern times, been called into question, and on that account a reform of the criminal code has been brought forward in parliament, particularly since Colquhoun has proved, even to ocular demonstration, how little that severity has hitherto either prevented, or lessened crimes.

If this severity in England appear, moreover, justified, from the consideration that in a trading state, fidelity and credit, and the most unconditional respect for the property of others, are objects of the highest interest; and that the severity of the law in this case possesses indisputably something very warning and deterring; still, at least, our feelings cannot accustom themselves to behold the obstinate adherence to the syllable and words of the law, which just as often absolves the guilty, as it condemns the less so, although it is not to be denied that the accused may not calculate upon the greatest mildness, and that not the smallest circumstance is overlooked which might save him. Still the decisions must appear to us frequently very strange. When a person is declared innocent of the charge of having adulterated port wine, because he can prove that, in the mixture, there has not been a drop of *pure port wine;* when convicted coiners of false money get off, because the stamp was not fully perfect; when the smallest oversight in the form of the proceedings, carries the greatest culprits through; when children of 14 or 15 years of age are condemned to death, because death stands written upon theft; when search after gold and silver coin is not allowed, because the law speaks of copper coin,—we can hardly comprehend how the spirit of the laws can be so entirely sacrificed to the letter and the words. This has, however, found its protectors, even amongst German writers. They are, however, far more unanimous in the praises they bestow upon the publicity given to judicial proceedings and the trial by Jury. Hume, Montesquieu, De Lolme, and almost all travellers and authors who have written upon England, consider the Jury particularly, which moreover they are indebted to the Saxons for, as the most perfect institution of a Constitution of justice, particularly against the preponderance of the monarch, and as the true palladium of English liberty. No wonder that this judgment is so general, as this kind of administration of law appears to gain the public favour, the sentiment, and even the fancy, in an equal degree.

Who can deny that even the sight of a solemn assembly of justice, in the antique costume, by commanding respect, possesses not something imposing, as well as attractive, by the participation it awakens in the high-raised expectation, whether death or life shall be decided by one word. Hardly can the mere reading, even, of the most interesting criminal trials, produce a similar effect. Here the person of the defendant stands opposite to the plaintiff, the plaintiff to the advocate, and all stand before the Chief Judge, with his assistants. We see how attentive and thoughtful the twelve of the Jury are, how tranquilly they take up all that passes before them, until the moment arrives in which the last decision will be demanded from them. Like a *narration* bears reference to the *representation* of a drama, so this public mode of justice stands with respect to our written processes, or to an inquisitorial proceeding carried on with closed doors. If the action passes not exactly before our eyes, we still see the actor before us. If curiosity excites all people as often as the person, who has attempted or attempts any thing horrid, is taken up and brought to prison, what a far greater satisfaction does this curiosity derive from beholding and considering him for hours. Where would the physiognomist, or the observer of mankind, find more matter for his contemplation? All the contradictions and oppositions of feelings, of circumstances, of passions in the human mind, come forward in undeniable signs, looks, behaviour, and words. The coolness of the judge, who, because he is accustomed almost to see nothing around him but the guilty, is not terrified by the exposition of any crime; the warmth of the advocate who offers every thing to save, if possible, even the heavily accused; then again the manifold guilt, which sometimes expresses itself in confidence and choaked sorrow, sometimes in anxiety and repentance, at times between fear and hope, and yet in tranquil resignation—all this rushes forcibly before our view at every public trial.

What rich matter a visit to these public judicial proceedings furnished me with, for contemplation upon all that I had seen and heard, and particularly for a comparison with our constitution. The repeated challenges made by a German acquaintance, " still to allow that the English method of administration of justice affords quite another security to the citizen, than ours, and that in this publicity the nation possesses one means more to form a right sense in the people of their rights and duties," carried me frequently back to the subject. We had also, in the period of the French Westphalian dominion, had similar constitutions, and thereby earned our own experience.

Still, where men of deep insight into the study of law, and who are thereby not merely observers themselves, but who are also accurately acquainted with every thing which history and the experience of the advantages and faults of the different kinds of administration, particularly of criminal justice, have taught; where writers like Montesquieu, of France, Feuerbach, of Germany, have given their voices, the laymen ought reasonably to withdraw in silence.   However, it may still be allowed him to impart the reflections which he opposed to that unconditional defender of the English court of justice, and whereby he at last might offer something of his own observations, although made in quite other views, and the experience which he was enabled to make himself.

First of all I must indeed allow what my worthy friend, the upper president Vincke, has already made me attentive to, that by the publicity of the administration of justice, as well as every one being judged by his equal, man becomes influenced with a feeling for his dignity as a man, and the citizen with public spirit, and that has a powerful effect also upon the political character of the nation.   I must also allow that both by the attention given to, as well as the reading of, the whole trial in the public papers, the people in many respects become enlightened upon their laws, and become better acquainted with the consequences of acts, than could be attained in Germany, even after the introduction of the proposition that has been made, of submitting to the schools an extract from the laws of the country.   On the other hand, it might also be asked, whether the effects of the expected morality appear in England so visibly, and whether the almost monthly warnings of the *gallows* have lessened the number of malefactors ?   Morality, which alone depends upon civil laws and fear of punishment, has always a very shallow foundation.   It acquires only strength and life, when it is grounded upon the moral feeling applied to conscience, which has its root in the breast of every man, and is nourished and strengthened by true religion.   To know that death is marked upon the removal of a silver spoon by a house theft, may deter many a domestic, but if the command, " Thou shalt not steal," thunders continually in the heart, and that the intention is known to the Highest Judge, who sees what is hidden, something more is gained for the cause of honesty and rectitude.

Thereto may be added, that at least much of what we hear treated of in the courts of justice, or read in the papers, is not at all adapted to encourage a moral feeling.   It may be, however, for example, that the public mention which is made of the names of all who are accused and convicted of adultery, prevents much repetition of the offence. For when conjugal infidelity becomes manifest in a woman, the better part of her acquaintance and friends desert her even more than would be the case in Germany; consequently, in comparison with the population, the trials of divorce are rarely considerable. But they are never wholly wanting; and is not many a corrupted mind made acquainted, upon the removal of the veil, as soon as the advocate demands it from the witnesses, with all descriptions of human errors, and frequently even with the most secret history of vice, of which, had it not been for this, it would have scarcely entertained a suspicion? Does not publicity in such processes particularly tend to destroy the delicate feelings of shame? Since the vexatious particularities, which there appear in language, become an object of the papers, which every one reads, do they not furnish perfect matter for ridicule and laughter at licentiousness? Follies may be chastised by the exposing to ridicule, and will sometimes improve the fool. If, however, wit and laughter are exercised upon sin and shame, we are no longer disgusted with the latter. The painters and judges of manners, like Tacitus, Persius, and Juvenal, did not contend against the vices of their times with wit and mockery, but with that noble anger which was enabled, not only to scratch and lightly wound the monster, but destroy him at once by strokes of the club. Finally, it is no proof of morality that the spectators, as often as these matters are treated of, are most numerous, and press forward to obtain places with the greatest eagerness.

After this, it appears to me doubtful whether the advantage is to be given so unconditionally to the decisions of the jury, or to those of a college of sentence (spruch collegiums) which, like the Royal Prussian Court of Justice, has ever enjoyed the reputation of honest impartiality. Von Vincke, too, who in other respects speaks of the English constitution with the greatest respect, is of this opinion :—" I acknowledge," says he, " according to the view which I have taken in England of the proceedings of the jury in civil and criminal matters, that I would much rather subject my life and property to the decision of a Prussian court of justice than to a British judge with twelve assistants ; that the form appears to me ill adapted to the present condition of culture in the state, where scientific preparation, ability, and incorruptible honesty are demanded from the judges, and secured by a correspondent income, trial, and education ; and where a regular protection is afforded against the errors they may commit."

Indeed, we do not at all comprehend why more love of truth, impartiality and uprightness, are to be supposed to animate the court of jury than any other which, at least, in proper comprehension of the cases lying before them, in maturity of judgment, in calm consideration and reflection, may very easily surpass any jury, even when the latter consists of the most upright individuals. In our courts too, it is not *one* voice that decides, and every judge has to dread the most severe observers of his conduct in the remaining members. Abuses, precipitation, humanity, respect of person, will not here be wanting. But is this not the case also in England? Does not the number of very striking examples which formerly Archenholy, Beschworner lately have collected, teach us this? How great a contrast do these bear to the assertion of Madame von Stael, " that we have no example for 100 years of the innocence of a person being acknowledged too late, as, (she adds in a declamatory manner) the citizens of a free state had attained so high a degree of sound understanding and so much controul of conscience, that with *these torches they never went astray!* Does not the personal appearance in the literal sense, which is peculiar to the public cultivation of justice, produce an influence, although an unconscious influence, upon the inclination, either to severity or mildness in the decision? It has indeed been said, " the decision of the jury is not founded upon a cold judgment, upon conclusion, comparison, or combination; it is at once the extorted *cry of the people.*" There is, however, far more truth in nature, than what must first pass through ideas, which mistake may too easily confuse. When, however, we know how easily this imaginary instinct of truth leads astray, it is impossible that the matter could be worse defended, since the ability of perceiving objects of experience, of coming to a probability or certainty upon facts and events, if not entirely, lies at least chiefly in the *understanding.* It has been said, " that not only the declarations of the witnesses, but the tone, deportment, confusion, the whole air of the accused has an effect upon the jury. But even if all this determine their *conviction,* is it *bail* also for the *absolute accuracy of this conviction ?*

The upright and collected man, who is to decide as member of a college of sentence, or a court of justice upon criminal acts, which have been carefully investigated, considers only *the action and the circumstances* under which that action has been committed. The *persons* are to him quite foreign. He is bribed by no deceitful voice of innocence, no eye darting around and piercing him for pity, no expression of inward calm or uneasiness. For the guilt which has been proved, no personal beauty of the guilty addresses his feelings ; and the want of outward charms never makes him indifferent to the *innocent.* At the court of the Old Bailey, more than once rejected plaintiffs have been besmeared with mud, not because they had demanded what was wrong, but because they had brought beautiful female thieves before justice, who might soften the heart of the judges, and in which females the sensuality of the spectators took an interest. It is very much to be questioned, whether so many voices would have raised themselves in favour of Sarah Price, who was lately executed for forgery, had not her exterior excited so great an interest ? Let every one ask his own bosom, whether, upon a refusal or an acceptance, upon an acquittal or condemnation, the personal appearance of the individual does not influence him ?

Moreover, has not the judge in his power to decide upon opinions ? If the representation of facts, upon which the jury has to decide, be short, and the mitigating or aggravating circumstances brought forward by him, either with a true or an artificial eloquence, the jury will not easily depart therefrom in their decision. If the delivery be long, which, as the result probably of monthly enquiries it often necessarily must be, how soon is the attention wearied ; and whoever of the twelve individuals shews himself the best informed and most capable of handling the business, finally prevails over the votes of the others.

I still have a very lively remembrance of having experienced a similar occurrence, which I myself had occasion to meet with, when my fellow-citizens, in the year 1800, reposed their confidence in me, and entrusted me with the direction of the business of the poor of the town, which then stood in need of a radical reform, and for which I had collected some information upon my earlier travels, by a nearer inspection of the excellent institutions for the poor in Hamburgh and Kiel. No small number of patriotic individuals of all classes were animated with a noble enthusiasm for the cause. Every one was ready to offer his council and to act. In earlier times the enquiry into the state of the needy, or those seeking assistance, had been made only very superficially. Premature compassion and partial recommendations decided, and the modest poor man was only too frequently overlooked. It was now agreed upon that the town should be divided into quarters and districts, in each of which a number of overseers of the poor should be appointed ; that these, however, were in common to enquire into want. The business gained visibly. The course became more steady and secure. But how clear was it here too, that the fewest persons, even with the best will, were fitted to enter into a thorough examination. Frequently, when certainly contradiction would have been the consequence, time pressed. They yielded, in order to come to a conclusion. Even the most excellent members were at times moved by inclination, by prejudice, by regards, or by passion. He who could speak with warmth for the poor of his district; be who possessed the talent to place their situation in a lively moving picture before the eyes of the assembly, found ready attention; while the man who frequently was more fundamentally informed, because he had examined the matter more dispassionately, was either talked down by the more eloquent, or overpowered by cries, and thus withdrawing himself from notice; it proved fortunate in the end that the voices were not counted, but that the opinions of the collective whole were guided by a few, who interfered between the contending parties. Similar experience has also been made in the few years, in which the trials by jury were imposed upon us by a foreign law. They did not even shorten always, as they expected, the processes, and this, too, is just as little the case in England, as that the expense of these processes is less. For, the preparations necessary to be made before it comes to the decision of the jury, often demand the greatest expenditure of time and money.

THE ENGLISH UNIVERSITIES.

The high schools of Great Britain have one common end in view with the German, that is, a high scientific education of the students, particularly those which are not catholic; but in their constitution, in other respects, they are wholly different.

Whoever has read the well known, and indeed frequently quoted writings of Wendeborn, Kuttner, Goéde and Meiner, upon the subject, and has them at hand, to him I shall have little new to impart.

I have often, however, perceived that this difference only appears to the learned in the more general and common points, without the peculiarities which mark the British universities having been explained to them. As I could only make myself acquainted with Oxford and Cambridge, I shall properly only have to speak of the English. For Dublin, in Ireland, as well as Edinburgh, Glasgow, and Aberdeen, in Scotland, are again quite differently constituted, and the latter have a far greater similarity with the German.

I hope that as brief a representation as possible will not be welcome merely to academicians, as universities are institutions on which all the learned citizens of a state, fathers and even mothers take the liveliest and most rational interest. Moreover, they are become, in our changeable times, very frequently the matter of discourse and contention; the public opinion has pronounced upon them, not altogether uniformly indeed, but louder than ever, that all the faults of German universities would be removed, as soon as we could change them *into English.* The more it will be expected from an old academician, that he should have devoted his attention entirely to these institutions. Far removed from either admiring or blaming what is *native,* unconditionally, I have given myself the trouble to compare them impartially. In imparting the results too, temperance and moderation have been my guides, which I think I have missed in many writers.

The strict attachment to antique forms and legal statutes, and the reciprocal jealousy of the respective institutions, which greatly contributes to prevent departures therefrom, that they may be without reproach, has indisputably had influence also upon the maintenance of a certain severe discipline; but this has also an effect upon the *tone* and *the manners.* It is certain, however, that the most severe discipline for the most part may prevent public demonstrations of vulgarity, and of the passions, but it is no reason why it should either improve the character or make the manners pure and innocent; and it would betray the greatest unacquaintance with human nature, and particularly with that of youth, were we to consider the English universities as the seats of virtue, and as places of preservation from all the errors to which students would be exposed, from our so called academic liberty. All unprejudiced observers allow, and many upright men, whose personal acquaintance I made there, did not deny, that there was no want of irregularities, and even excesses of every kind, which are probably only practised with greater foresight and more secretly than in Germany; that within these cloistered walls a disposition to laziness, luxury, dissipation, and inebriety, prevailed; that the long vacations and the frequent residence in the metropolis, were only too favourable thereto; and although personal enmity and bitterness may have been mixed with Knox's severe judgment, although he was formerly member himself of John's college, it was still not at all unfounded upon many considerations. The regular members, taking into view the princely salaries they enjoy, and enviable literary leisure, afford comparatively far too little for the sciences. Impartial people look for the foundation thereof in their particularly comfortable and agreeable situation, which, as formerly was the case in rich cloisters, gives too much food to idleness and sensuality, for a spiritual life to flourish amongst the majority. This cannot appear to us at all strange, since, in

Germany also, many of our clergy, particularly as soon as they have obtained a comfortable existence, free from care by considerable endowments and benefices, suffer their inclination for sciences to die away, and too frequently make an exchange of their books for gambling and cards, while others, who are animated by an inward and warm interest for learning, not only study for their bread, but remain faithfully devoted to their labours, amidst the oppression and the cares of life, and, by their literary diligence, prove themselves worthy of the sciences.

Probably too, the lively interest many members of the universities take in *public events*, is the cause of the little literary activity they display; since, wherever political ideas become prevalent, rarely do the scientific attract and improve in equal degree. Each university has two representatives in Parliament; and as they choose them themselves, and without the influence of bribery or other unworthy means, which are so often employed in parliament elections, every *fellow*, nay, every *magister*, may arrive at this honour; and, as he may become a bishop, may one day calculate upon a seat and voice in the Upper house. It is on this account that the universities have ever maintained a certain political character, and sometimes embraced the party of the *whigs*, at others, of the *tories*. Since they form a true free state, and, so long as they remain faithful to their statutes, depend neither upon the orders of the king nor of an archbishop, nor of a consistory, their voice upon certain occasions is very independent, and has not been without its influence. As, moreover, the English constitution finds the greatest support in the members of the evangelical church, the universities are already important to her, because they only belong to this church.

Both the towns of Oxford and Cambridge, with their large colleges and halls, particularly strike the traveller with wonder, who, probably for the first time, enters them quite unprepared. He would rather believe he was arrived in the residence of a prince or superior dignitaries of an empire, than at an university. For it is only necessary to go a few steps to have seen a number of buildings, many of which, in their circumference, in their antique as well as modern architecture, and whole appointment, resemble rather castles and large abbeys, amongst which some are so roomy and magnificent, that the ancient kings of England and Scotland hardly resided so sumptuously, and even at this day the royal and princely residences in London are far overshadowed by them.

As almost every one of the English colleges possesses its own antiquities and remarkable objects, the historian, the antiquarian, and the literary man, consequently finds in its monuments, inscriptions, collections, and archives, the choicest food for his intellect. The visitant at Cambridge likes to be told, in Christ's college, that he reposes under the shade of that mulberry tree which the greatest epic poet of England, Milton, planted ; willingly attends the conductor into the shadowy path which bears Addison's name ; or along the old walls, now transformed into a barn, belonging to the so called school of Pythagoras, on the Cam, where Luther's contemporary, Erasmus, taught Greek.

The lover of the arts finds also food for his wonder in these colleges. Many of them are ennobled by an excellent architecture, partly Gothic, partly Italian. They have been built partly by earlier monarchs, particularly the Henries, the Jameses, and the Charleses, or by high dignitaries of the state, such as cardinal Wolsey, with a royal magnificence ; and have been extended by rich patrons of the sciences, archbishops and former heads, who devoted to them their whole fortune. Time, war, and fire, have not been able to destroy any one of them entirely. At all times the preserving spirit of the nation, which suffers no possession to be lost, has either taken care that nothing should fall into decay, or that what has been somewhat decayed should rise again more magnificent out of the ashes, and they are continually rebuilding, beautifying, and improving. Portraits and pictures of the best schools adorn the interior, the general assembly rooms, the dining halls, the book rooms, and the chapels ; also busts and statues of great masters, such as Roubillac and Flaxman, whose chisel has lately completed the marble monument of the orientalist, W. Jones, celebrated as the editor of the *Asiatic Researches*, upon which a Brahmin explains to him the holy books of the Hindoos. Generally speaking, whatever member distinguishes himself in church or state by merit, or has attained to the higher dignitaries therein, may calculate upon being once accepted in the list of those who convert the great vaulted rooms into an historical room of pictures, and to look down with an exhorting and encouraging smile upon the youth who daily meet here, frequently by hundreds, either for completing propositions or problems for a premium.

England has ever set a great worth upon *painting in glass*. Hardly any chapel or hall is entirely without it. It answers the style of the old Gothic architecture, by the solemn chiarascuro which it diffuses in the churches. In modern times too, there has been no want of artists in this branch of the art, which certainly has become very rare in Germany. By their works they have often replaced what time, the warlike spirit of destruction, or religious fanaticism have destroyed

in a more beautiful form and design. As the great eastern·
window of Jervais, in Windsor, according to West's drawing,
is held for a master-piece, the magnificent glass painting,
which this master set up in the year 1777, in the new college
at Oxford, is not less so. In the splendour of the colours, the
size of the figures, and the beauty of the drawing, after the
originals by Joshua Reynolds, it was, to my mind at least, the
greatest and the most beautiful of this description which I had
ever seen in my travels. The western window of the chapel,
30 feet high, ten feet broad, is divided into two halves. The
lower partition represents, according to the old practice, customary in scholastic morality, the *four cardinal virtues,—Temperance, Confidence, Justice, and Prudence ;* and the *three
Christian,—Belief, Love, and Hope,*—in figures as large as life,
together with their chosen attributes : the upper division represents the birth of the Redeemer after the manner of Cor-
reggio.

The chapel of this college, generally speaking, is one, if not
of the largest, at least of the finest. White and black marble
squares adorn the ground, the sides of the marble altars,
bass-reliefs from the history of the bible; the steps of the same
are covered with costly carpets. A shrine in the vicinity contains, since the fourteenth century, the costly bishop's staff of
the founder, W. Wykeham, and represents him above in the
act of bending, kneeling, and praying. The organ separates,
as in many English churches, the high choir from the remaining part. As the pillars of the same are so placed that the
space left in the middle has the form exactly of the western
window, the large glass picture gives a finish to the view in
the most magnificent manner when you stand at the altar.

Stay in Oxford.

I should have remained in the above town wholly unknown,
even by name, where I knew nobody, for little do they know
in England of *German* professors or *German* authors, had I
not been furnished with the best letters of recommendation.
I was particularly indebted for them to the lady of the learned
Dr. Marsh, who had been just then nominated bishop of Peter-
borough, and was present at the parliament session in London.
This lady, by birth a native of Leipsig, assisted the German
stranger with the most friendly advice and zeal for his welfare.
The bishop being also professor of theology in Cambridge,
was himself and family well acquainted with the principal men
of both universities. I received letters to many heads of those
colleges. Moreover, I found in a young excellent orientalist,
whom duty of study had a long time connected in literary

pursuits with our Gesenius, Mr. Nichol, so agreeable a guide, not unacquainted with our language, that I found myself, almost upon the first entrance, by no means a stranger.

On the 10th of July the holidays begin. On that account most of the members of the colleges, as well as the students, were absent, but many an examination was still going on. Opportunity was not wanting, even during the vacations, of getting acquainted with the interior of the institutions and the life led in them.

I divided my time between the visit to the principal colleges, the public buildings, and some learned who were present. A beginning was made with botany the very day of my arrival. This branch of study interested the Baron de Geer, who had attended me to Oxford as a connoisseur, and had claimed my attention from very early youth as an amateur. The academical garden is not very large, but, under the care of professor Williams, is in excellent condition, and, as it appeared to me, very interesting for study. One of the buildings of the garden contained the library and very rich herb repositories, amongst which particularly a high value was set upon that of Dillens.

Professor Williams, as upper librarian, conducted us then into the Radcliff library. Dr. Radcliff, who gained a very large fortune in London as physician, was the founder of it, in the year 1749, and had devoted the sum of 240,000 rix dollars to its building and maintenance. It is one of the newest, and appears by its free situation one also of the most magnificent buildings. As you approach the town, the cupola of the rotunda, 70 feet high, raises itself majestically. We ascended the open gallery which surrounds it. At once the most beautiful panorama of Oxford lay before us. With one view we overlooked all the colleges, temples, and halls, works which cost the labour of six or seven centuries. Under their lofty roofs and towers all the remainder of the town, as it were, disappears. The library is particularly devoted to the history of nature and medicine. The elegant bookcases of mahogany are placed on the side of the great circle in the middle story and the upper gallery. The broad space in the middle of that circle, covered with a marble floor, afforded a superb local situation to the university, in the year 1814, to give a public entertainment to the conquering monarchs.

The far-famed Bodleian library is very inferior in situation, but much richer in literary treasures. With this library, Mr. Nichol, who is librarian, was enabled to make me best acquainted. The rich Sir Thomas Bodley found, indeed, the ground-work already laid by Humphrey, Duke of Gloucester, for an older collection which was much neglected, but took the

resolution, towards the end of the sixteenth century, of raising
it by what he possessed himself, as well as by rich legacies, to
the first rank.   His example has subsequently induced other
possessors of large collections to make a legacy of them to the
collection, and by his own fortune, which has fallen to him by
accident, he has been enabled to obtain an incalculable treasure
of printed and unprinted works, of which last the catalogue
alone of the oriental fills two folio volumes.   The learned
Nichol was now employed with the continuation and completion of the same.   Many highly important collections of very
old bible and classic manuscripts, as well as library rarieties, are
here to be found, and treasures which the libraries of the
archbishop Laud, Selden, and Pocock have furnished.   The
critical comparison of the manuscripts has already afforded a
rich food, and is too well known to the learned to make it
necessary to repeat it here.   For other readers, the mere
narration of many curiosities, for example, of the Latin writing
book of queen Elizabeth, of the mass book of Henry VIII., of
the coran of Tippoo Saib, would have just as little interest.
They can only awaken an interest by self-inspection.
    The same is the case with the picture gallery connected with
the library, represented in three rooms, wherein a little of the
excellent is lost amidst much of the mediocre, and the Thorn-
hill copies of the celebrated cartoons of Raphael in the Vatican,
chain the attention longest.   The Pomfret collection of antiques
is placed in a lower story of this same building.   It may possess a few valuable works of art.   To those who have seen the
British Museum or Dresden, it affords little entertainment.
    The collection of old inscriptions must not be left unseen,
in order at least to gain a perfect impression of the remains of
antiquity which defied thousands of years, and which, after
that the greatest number of centuries had passed them over
unheeded, have at once given employment to the diligence
of Seldene, Maittaire, and other learned men.   I speak
particularly of the marbles which the Earl of Arundel
bought up in the east, and which his son made a present
of to the university ; of the celebrated Parian inscription,
which is of such high importance to chronology and paleogra-
phy, since it begins its designs with Cecrops (1582 b. c.) and
the fragment which is still legible comes down to 354 years b. c.
    A portico of doric pillars leads into the Clarendon printing
office, not far from the theatre ; the nine Muses adorn the
front.   The history of the civil wars, which Hyde, earl of
Clarendon, left behind in manuscript, and which his heirs
made a present of to the university, brought so great a profit,
that they were enabled to raise this sumptuous building, and

devote it to a printing office. It bears, with justice, the name of the writer, to whom it is indebted for its existence. In Germany too, there is many a bookselling concern and printing office, which should more properly bear the name of the writers, who, probably suffering want themselves, have brought them to riches and honours.

There are some presses entirely in the service of the university, particularly for the older classes, as well as such works which otherwise would find a publisher with difficulty. I received from the superintendent, Mr. Collingwood, a couple of wet sheets of a new literal impression of the Greek lexicon of Scapula, which stood in need of so many improvements. But they choose rather to adhere to what is established. How little even does the expensive undertaking of the new impression of the Stephanian treasure of language content us, and how differently *German* diligence, which passes over no increase of knowledge, would have delivered it! Thus, at least, I have heard even English literati judge of it.

. Six presses are in uninterrupted work for English bibles, and for the common prayer. The university possesses the monopoly to the great regret of English booksellers. It was pleasing to me, once more to meet with something in England, which follows what we possess in our own vicinity. For in no respect can the Clarendon Bible Press bear a comparison with our Cansteinian, which, as has been already said, is now provided with twelve presses, and can furnish weekly the number of 70 or 80,000 sheets. This printing office of Canstein has never endeavoured to obtain a monopoly, and still less entertained the foolish intention of destroying, by their presses, all the printing offices in Germany, as the count Beugnot, when Westphalian minister in Cassel, earnestly assured me in the year 1807.

. After this, peep into the principal *buildings*, which belong to the whole university. I say nothing further of the single colleges, many of which I have visited. As the institutions upon the whole are tolerably alike, we see the same thing pretty generally every where. Much, as is usually the case, may still remain unknown to many persons who live even in Oxford, since we are frequently prone to neglect seeing, even once, what we have an opportunity of *seeing daily*.

Our attention is rivetted most by Christ church, which is the greatest of all institutions, from its size, its riches, the grandeur of its appropriations; the dwellings of the eight canons, who are always appointed by the king; the considerable collections of pictures and works of art; the large and very tastely decorated library, at the entrance of which we

willingly stop a moment to contemplate the statue of Locke, by
Roubiliac. There is hardly any college which can be compared
with this in cleanliness, elegance, and grandeur. The recency
of many alterations and decorations is visible in many places.
A lively remembrance is here excited of the first founders,
preservers, and benefactors of the institution, particularly of
cardinal Wolsey, who, before the plan was sufficiently
digested to be carried into execution, was hurled from
his pinnacle of greatness, and obliged to leave the completion
of it to king Henry the eighth, " whom," according to his own
words, "he had served more faithfully than his God."

I wish I had found the respectable head of Christ church,
dean Jackson, alive, who, according to the testimony of
all his contemporaries, has done infinite good, quite according
to the spirit of an early ornament of this college, bishop Fell,
who rejoiced when foreign merit obscured his own. Dean
Jackson enjoyed above all the highest respect. But the poorest scholar, as well as the most illustrious son of a peer, felt
himself attracted to him. On that account it was frequent to
hear the opinion pronounced, "This man is not like any body
else."

The more we become acquainted with the life led by the
heads and higher members of the colleges, the more we are
convinced that, for single men, there can be scarce one more
desirable or free from care, although, indeed, certain evils,
which are inseparable from that general life in cloistered foundations, are not entirely wanting here, and the colleges too,
amongst themselves, are not always connected in the closest
bonds of friendship. But, although apparently shackled, a
fellow is still a very free and independent man. It depends
upon himself, how much or how little expenditure he chooses
to make; to what employment he will devote himself; whether
he will live in solitude or in society; whether he will spend
his time more at home or abroad; whether he will wait for
his old age in this quiet situation, or accept one of the many
places which his college has to give away; and thus constantly
get higher and higher in the church. He may be every day in
the metropolis and take advantage of all its recreations and
pleasures, and every day visit the sister university; which,
however, appears to be seldom the case. The booksellers
deliver over to him every new literary production; the libraries, all the treasures of ancient literature in every branch.
This life is an uninterrupted *otium cum dignitate*, if he himself
only knows how to preserve its dignity. Still, contempt would
very soon follow the contrary. The superintendent of such a
college governs, as soon as he keeps a good understanding

with the fellows, his little state very happily, and is frequently as splendid and independent as a rich abbot. If he distinguish himself, he has still more certain prospects of a bishoprick, and may raise himself up to become archbishop of Canterbury, the dignity of primate of the empire.

Stay in Cambridge.

Not long before my arrival, at the period of the commencement, as the great promotion days are there called, the personal appearance of the chancellor of the university, the duke of Gloucester, had occasioned great festivities. Academic honours had been given away, prizes had been divided, solemn speeches were held, and balls, concerts, assemblies, and dinners had been given. I found the town by far more quiet upon my late arrival. We met with few academicians. Almost all the directors and members of the colleges, were taking recreation in the country. I was enabled to view more at my leisure the unmoveable curiosities, and thereby make some very agreeable acquaintances.

I had been particularly recommended to doctor Wood, theologian, master of the great John's college. It was impossible to meet with more benevolence and zeal. In spite of the almost continued rain which poured down, he chose to be my indefatigable attendant. May that excellent gentleman pass as many days and evenings as happily as he afforded them to me.

The university library, in the hall of which I took a passing view of the antiques which Clarke brought with him from his travels to Greece, is very considerable. The number of the volumes is reckoned, probably too high, at 100,000. There is a large treasure in manuscripts; amongst them the important Codex Cantabrigiensis, so well known to the critic, which Theodore Beza possessed, and made a present of.

The university church, an old Gothic building, bears a contrast to the modern senate house lying on its right. It has, however, gained a pleasing appearance in the interior by modern decorations. The high pulpit is at the same time the chair for the lectures, which bishop Marsh used to read.

The senate house is a very noble building, not yet one hundred years old. It consists properly only of a single large hall with a gallery, which may contain about 1000 persons. This is appropriated to all solemn promotions and other festivities. It is adorned with a variety of statues of kings and dukes. The finest represents Chatham's great son, William Pitt. Cambridge has the right of being proud of reckoning him amongst her former citizens.

Amongst the colleges, although many of them are indeed only built of brick, others may, without doubt, be placed by the side of those at Oxford, and probably surpass them in many respects. Trinity college bears, I think, at least in its magnificent exterior, a comparison with Christ church. The open portico is quite singular in its kind, which goes round three sides, each above 100 feet long, in the inner court, and the doric pillars of which support the upper story, in which is the library. What a walk this forms for hundreds in wet weather, and what an excellent locality, to entertain at times the whole university, as had just happened. We were straitened for time, and prevented from seeing the particular curiosities contained in the library. The most perfect collection of all the editions of Shakespeare, many hundred volumes of contemporary plays, designs of poems by Milton, a number of manuscripts of men important to history and literature, are certainly, as well as many other things, rarities of high value.

I passed some time with pleasure in the neighbouring college of Clare hall, which enjoys so pleasing a situation, commanding a fine view over the river and the smiling meadows, the more so as I had been received so hospitably by Mr. Leason, one of the members, who made me acquainted with the interior. I had accidentally made acquaintance with this gentleman in a bookseller's shop, in London. Amongst other things, we view with reverence the likeness of the excellent archbishop Tillotson, who here passed his youth.

Much as *King's college,* which is altogether modern, distinguishes itself by its grandeur and regularity, the large chapel, however, lays a claim to our greatest attention. This, as well as the institution itself, is indebted to Henry the sixth for its foundation, about the year 1441. At the view at once of this church, which looks like a cathedral, still more, however, at the entrance into the same by the western portal, we are struck at the magnificence of a building which many travellers declare to be the first in all Europe of the Gothic. We are enabled to comprehend, in some degree, the reason even of the architect of St. Paul's, Sir Christopher Wren, making an annual journey to Cambridge, in order to admire the boldness of the architecture, particularly the roof, 80 feet high, and which, as well as the chapel itself, 150 feet long, is not supported by any pillar.

Cambridge confirms us in the opinion too, that England is the country where we are not to reckon such large institutions amongst the distinguishing features, which appertain only to old times, and the sense for which is now departed. Thus, for example, in the year 1815, the rich earl Fitzwilliam made a present to the university of his library, which is so rich in fine works and many historical and political writings, of a sumptuous copper-plate cabinet, and a select collection of paintings, and devoted large sums to the building, and for its maintenance. How tastily is the hall decorated—how beautiful an appearance the new golden frames around every picture, (amongst which, one by Titian was shewn me, 3000 guineas in value,) make upon the crimson tapestry on the sides! Chests, furniture, every thing is after the finest forms. Happy university, thought I to myself, where such legacies are considered almost as secondary matters!

Cambridge, according to the opinion of many. who are nearer acquainted with the life of both places, is probably even before Oxford in cheerful sociability, and many other respects. I saw almost all its curiosities under the guidance of the worthy Dr. Wood. He made me acquainted with whatever was still interesting to me at a confidential dinner, I may say, which he gave me in the official residence of his college. We were quite alone. This was the more favourable for a free interchange of ideas. He united, with a warm interest, particularly for the service of religion, a mildness and reasonableness in his judgment, which is not the virtue of all episcopals. He was already in the possession of many works of German theologians, of Semler, of Rösselt and Michael, some of them even in our language, which is foreign to him, and listened only the more attentively to whatever had been produced since that time in the different provinces.

He spoke of the interior regulation of the colleges with the freedom of a man who every where sees clearly, and who will not justify what is faulty. Much still remained to be considered, when the evening came on. The time, however, for my return was pressing, and we heartily squeezed each other by the hand.

Departure from the Universities, and the Result of my Observations thereon.

I left both of those high schools with that mixed sensation of joy and sorrow which the goodness I had enjoyed, and the certainty of being for ever separated from them, leaves behind in the soul. How many instructive and agreeable hours would they not still have afforded me, could I have been enabled to await the return of the many learned and religious men who are here assembled!

Were I questioned upon the result, which was now become possible for me to draw upon the comparison of the English and German manner of conducting an university, I must allow, that the longer I think upon it, the more difficult it appears to me to form a thorough comprehensive judgment upon the subject.

The country, the national character, the future destination and plan of life of those who pursue their studies in them, all this is so closely connected with their constitution, and is in many respects so different, that both in universities and in schools, an unconditional transplantation of the one or the other into a foreign ground, would not be advisable. There is also in England no insignificant number of very genteel men of all ranks, who abound in knowledge, and who have never studied at an university.

Whoever, however, (as there are many amongst us who do) attaches himself not blindly to the antiquity of the German institution, or, as probably, still many more confounds not the merry life passed in his own university with that which is appropriate to study, and casts a liberal eye upon Oxford and Cambridge, will be able just as little to deny the good of certain peculiarities of those colleges, as to suppress the wish, that not indeed *wholly the same*, but much *similar* might be introduced into Germany. Only a few brief observations can be given here.

First of all, it is certainly an advantage for the greatest number of those who are just, and frequently very young, returned from the schools, that the further direction of their studies, by the aid of experienced men, is not at once retarded, and the school acquirements are not, by a sudden transition to the higher, become almost entirely supplanted. Not the third part of our young academicians, I know well what I assert, and I assert probably still too little, not the third part of them ever think of continuing the study of the classics, which is precisely the most excellent method of forming and exercising the mind; nay, many consider it hardly worth the trouble to remain, at least, in possession of their classic authors, as is well proved by the shops of the antiquary. Most of them follow the general stream, which carries them into lectures, even the name of which they frequently do not comprehend, and thus the most unmatured and weakest heads listen to that which scarcely the most excellent are in a condition to understand. We may, indeed, subject the ignorant to severe trials, adapted only to matured learning, by removing from them the supports upon which they leaned, but still not exclude them from the privilege of treading the academic career.

The education, in the English colleges of the university, is immediately connected with that which is imparted in schools, and the youth remains, although placed upon an higher class, following entirely the course of his former studies. He comes to maturity alike in the same soil in which his knowledge struck the first roots, instead of being placed in a hot-house, and shooting up, indeed, apparently quick, but receiving only an empty knowledge like vain blossoms. Whoever had an opportunity of becoming as closely acquainted with thousands who flock to the universities, as the many years connexion with great schools, and the duty of academic institutions have enabled me to be, would only lament to see so many of them participate in lectures, of which they are altogether unsusceptible. For few only follow the advice of dedicating the first year to the studies of humanity, or the easier preparatory parts of philosophy; and if even they wished it, how few are enabled to do so in the little time they enjoy, and from the still greater want of *property.*

This reminds me of the second advantage of the *English high schools.* With all the inequality of property which is to be found therein, the fewest number of all, probably only those who are received as servants in the colleges, are deprived, to a degree, of all means, as is the case in Germany with a great number. The man who is entirely destitute can hardly think of venturing upon an academic career, or if he once tread it, he finds so much support in the rich institutions, that he scarcely knows any thing of the deplorable poverty, which bears down to the ground so many of our young academicians, and makes it impossible for them even to provide themselves with the most indispensable of all means of assistance. If even these obstacles and difficulties to a free formation of the mind are overcome by an irresistible love of learning, activity, and employment of every little advantage, still single distinguished literati, who have worked themselves out of the deepest poverty, are always exceptions only to the general rule. On the other hand, the poverty of spirit of so many, who wish and are destined to study, the illiberality of their way of thinking, the vulgarity of their manners, the mere striving after employment and bread, without any love and taste for the sciences, are a natural consequence of the first education in the poorest ranks, who are not easily induced in England to bring up a son to the learned professions. There are, however, some institutions, as Christ's hospital, in London, and Christ church, in Oxford, wherein, even poorer boys who greatly distinguish themselves, are reserved for the study of the sciences. But these are so well taken care of by ample endowments, that they cease to be poor as soon as they are received in the institutions, and have, moreover,' a certain prospect of obtaining a chaplain's or a curate's appointment.

A third advantage, which the course of study affords in the first three or four years, I found to consist in the regulation, according to which, far more time is appropriated to individual labour than is the case in Germany. The English student is obliged to read much for himself, to write, translate, and make memorandums of many things; and when he is more mature in years, is made acquainted with the whole contents and spirit of the old capital works, which are only read and explained in schools much by piecemeal. He must himself dive into the compendium of history, of mathematics, and philosophy, more in a practical than a speculative manner. Many premiums for the best treatments of the subject, speeches, serve as an encouragement to zeal. He must render an account of what he has performed. How rarely is this the case, constituted as our universities are! Who troubles himself about the private industry of our scholars? And where is the professor who is in a condition to do so from his situation? Those whom we call the most diligent, often mis-spend five or six hours with hearing, and frequently with a perfectly mechanical, thoughtless, and insipid copying of what has been heard. Thus the most foreign subjects intrude, in the next hours, upon the impressions made by the first. Select talents only, among the many who are invited, reflect upon what has been heard, making attempts at writing, inventing, composing, delivery, whereby the youth developes himself, and learns to participate without prejudice. Thus the best head is overpowered by superabundance of matter. Like one plant destroys another which is too near it, while the single plant can neither take deep root nor flourish.

A certain important character distinguishes the academic discipline, with which the irresolute waverings and fluctuations introduced into many of our German universities form the highest contrast. In Germany, at times, an unseasonable severity, at others a prejudicial mildness, are resorted to; whilst impropriety in the application of the laws, or in the treatment of youthful minds, a tedious and ceremonial course of justice, where a prompt application would spare precious time, and prevent greater evils, predominate. With the yearly change of regulations, a change also of views and maxims is introduced; an effeminate adoption is made of prejudices, which have nothing to recommend them but their antiquity, which condemns the law, and takes opinion under its protection. There is not unfrequently, too, a courting of applause and favour by weak indulgence; and, generally speaking, a want of public spirit. All these are evils which have always been lamented, sometimes even exaggerated, and still more frequently have been considered too trifling, and, in which, at the same time, many scenes which are at once vexatious and unworthy the seat of the sciences, have their principal foundation. The last cannot thrive at all in a constitution which has such fixed forms and rules as the English. It becomes a matter of interest with the English university and its governors, that where every thing has a tendency to a spiritual education, and whereever we look, temples of religion and sciences advise us of the destination of the place of residence, a perfect outward appearance, at least, of tranquillity and order, should prevail. But they have the means, too, of doing much, which we must partly do without. Vulgar excesses are therefore very rare.

The age, which has been wonderfully enlightened during the last *forty* years, has brought ideas into circulation, which, rightly comprehended, and carefully applied, may bear glorious fruits, and have already, indeed, counteracted much of what was bad. The years of youth are, however, rather years of power than of reflection, and power, without measure and rule, may become a very dangerous element. On that account the wisdom of governments hence considered many measures necessary, which in England are not at all so. The youth, who is not wholly corrupted, will, upon the whole, follow nothing but what is good. From some errors, diligence is the best thing to secure him; from others, the school of life warns him. He may go astray, as daily history has taught us, but those who lead him astray and blind him, are the most culpable.

EXCURSIONS OUT OF LONDON.

Woodstock, Blenheim, Greenwich.

Notwithstanding all the economy I employed with my time, I found it still too short to visit many of the charming country seats and cottages, in which the wealthy pass the finest months of the year, or, if they are situated in the neighbourhood of towns, at least their Sundays. Woodstock is scarce two hours drive from Oxford, and is indebted to its vicinity to Blenheim for the frequent visits paid to it.

In this same Woodstock lived the greatest female ruler of England, four centuries ago. It was the melancholy place to which she was banished. Hated by her sister Mary, whose weak feelings were sorely wounded by the painful recollections that the powerful princess Elizabeth would be her successor, she had almost fallen as a participator in the rebellion of Wyatt, as well as lady Jane Grey, who was a sacrifice to suspicion. She had been already a prisoner in the tower. The undaunted defence she made liberated her from that suspicion, and she was indebted for the mild treatment she received from her superintendent, to Mary considering it more advisable to place her in the rural, but closely-guarded castle of Woodstock. Here she lived in solitude, devoted to the sciences, and, far from the noise of courts, attained that refinement of education, which made her afterwards, when queen, the wonder of her age. Probably the shadow of the great Alfred, who is said to have translated, in Woodstock, the books of Boetius *de Consolatione* into his native language, floated before her eyes. This Alfred still lives in the memory of the nation. The day before my departure I received, by the post, a very kind invitation to visit a certain Alfred club, which invitation I could not accept of, and could learn nothing further of the ends for which the club was established.

The great estate of the duke of Marlborough and his posterity, the mansion upon which was built in the reign of queen Anne, at the public expense, and for which parliament granted three millions of dollars, in the year 1705, bears the name of Blenheim, from a Bavarian village in the district of Höchstadt, where that great English warrior gave battle to the French and Bavarians, and returned to England crowned with victory. Few travellers omit paying a visit to the magnificent castle, so singular a monument is it of the national gratitude. It is surrounded by one of the most beautiful parks, adorned with the finest gardens. But almost all who have written of Blenheim, at times complain of the heavy style of the architecture, at others of the many fees which they have to pay to six or seven guides or attendants who wait upon them, as well as of the ennui which the lesson the latter have learnt by heart occasioned them during the long journey they had to make through the rooms, at the weariness of the passage through them, accompanied by many parties who diminished their enjoyment. I have, indeed, experienced a little of this myself, and I am afraid that the reader will not feel much pleasure were I to endeavour to entertain him with a long description of the place, which can alone be interesting to him, if it be a repetition of what he has himself seen. Where shall I begin? From the entrance of the great portal, which forms a triumphal arch, and which, according to the inscription thereon, was built by Sarah the wife of the hero, the proudest woman of her age, it is necessary to make a tour through all the innumerable windings of the park. Many hours are also necessary to view, with some attention, all the magnificent points of view which the castle offers, the sumptuous rooms, the picture galleries, and above all, the library, which is 200 feet long, the roof of which is adorned with sculpture and painting, and supported by two rows of expensive marble pillars cut out of one block.—For, in fact, every thing which can be separately met with in the castles of the great, constituting riches, elegance, convenience, and art, is here brought together upon one spot.

The great obelisk, situate upon the highest point of the park, gave me the least satisfaction. The statue of the Duke, placed upon it, appears paltry. The inscription is like a little treaty. It contains the whole act of parliament, which gives an enumeration of the deeds of the duke, and the donation which the nation has made to him.

We went down the river to the grand hospital of Greenwich, on one of the most cheerful mornings. Here quite another view of the incomparable panorama of the metropolis is offered to our eyes. What a continual change of prospect on both sides! What a contrast of riches and of misery, of the great exertions of commerce, as well as the little painful occupations which employ the inhabitants! On the one side, palaces; on the other, miserable fishermen's huts.; upon the right, the narrow close streets of Southwark; upon the left, the domineering tower, at the foot of the ramparts of which are the landing places, where formerly the sacrifices to death were so frequently brought by night time: further to the east is the view of the Surrey and London docks. Upon the river itself, what a continual throng of boats, which meet and get out of the way of each other with astonishing dexterity, gondolas and small boats with various coloured flags waving in the air; well dressed rowers and joyful bands of music.

At a distance we get the first sight of Greenwich. In the royal palace, which is now no longer inhabited, Henry the eighth's three children were born, viz.:—Edward the sixth, Mary, and Elizabeth, who were equally remarkable in history. The pleasing and animated little town is lost sight of by the contemplation of, as many travellers have assured us, the most magnificent and cheerful hospital, which is any where to be seen. It consists of two separated palaces, connected together by rows of pillars of the Corinthian and Doric order. To the north, it is bounded by the Thames, which is here so deep, as to bear fleets of merchantmen and men of war; to the south, by the park with its lofty groups of old oak and chesnut trees.

Upon the height lies the observatory, after the meridian of which all astronomical calculations are reckoned in England. The hospital, which is built in the most magnificent style, is better adapted to be the habitation of a monarch of Great Britain, than a charitable institution. It is devoted to the reception of sailors, who have become incapacitated by age, wounds, or other infirmities, as well as the widows and children of those who have lost their life in the service of their native country. The royal palace was begun to be built since, the beginning of the foregoing century, by Charles the second, and dedicated to the purpose which all succeeding monarchs, and particularly George the second, have promoted by the richest donations. About three thousand old seamen live here together, and cast a tranquil look, with probably sometimes a feeling of anxiety, upon the flood, and listen, as in a secure haven, to the storms and whirlwinds with which they once contended. This strong contrast, indeed, may not be adapted to make them contented, especially when brought into comparison with what they were so long accustomed to. But old age has still its place of security; the table is daily well covered, the lame and weak repose better upon their convenient beds, one of which is prepared for each invalid in large spacious rooms, than upon the unstable deck, or in the close quarters of a vessel.

If the seaman, according to an observation which has been frequently made, did not generally become as tacit at last as if he had never learnt to speak, what an inexhaustible entertainment must an intercourse with people afford, many of whom have landed upon all the shores of the world—are at home in all zones, who have tasted all means of subsistence, to whom no custom is strange; who have daily moved in danger of death, and have saved themselves, as it were, by a wonder, while thousands of their brethren have found their graves by the side of them in the waters. Every ship which sails up or down the Thames, passes before Greenwich, and acquaintances and persons unknown to each other, may shake hands upon the broad stairs which leads from the hospital to the Thames, with the veteran, either upon their departure or arrival. Every thing is grand, even in the decoration of the buildings. Over one of the colonnades, Nelson's death is celebrated. The four horses of the triumphant chariot are guided by bewailing Britannia. The hero lies lifeless in her bosom. Every where the pictures and bass-reliefs, particularly in the chapel, which is built in the most noble style, have reference to sea-faring matters, and call to the recollection the great scenes which have taken place upon that powerful element. Every old seaman may daily contemplate the mournful car which bore the body of Nelson, (of the Nelson who formerly probably led him to victory), to the burial place in St. Paul's cathedral.

The old men were cleanly dressed. Some kept guard. A chair still stands at the sentry box for those who are weary. Others were sitting upon their beds. Some were sauntering

about alone.   Many gave a cheerful answer to what I asked
them.   The children, for whose instruction a large school is
appointed, played and frisked around old age.   It happened to
be Sunday, and many parents and relations were paying them
a visit; groups were formed every where.   The sleeping rooms
were particularly cleanly ; the beds were hammocks, in which
the active boys swung themselves with astonishing dexterity.
Brought up early to the sea service, the reflection early steels
their courage, that should they become incapacitated, even
after a six years' service, they will still find an asylum here,
which, as it has done to their hoary fathers, will secure to them
an old age free from care.

Another part of these veterans live out of the hospital with
their friends, and receive a pension.   I doubt whether they live
not far happier in their little hut, than thronged together in the
sumptuous halls, which appear to me far too brilliant for their
destination.   With this impression, Mr. Symonds, the Gallo
American, left the hospital of Greenwich, and I participated in
his feelings.   The poor man, in my opinion, lives best in his
own house.

The invalid hospital at Chelsea, which lies in the neighbourhood of London, is a similar institution to this.   Here the
nation supports five hundred warriors, who are worn out by
service, but gives a pension to ten thousand.   There is a school
also here for the education of orphans of meritorious officers
and soldiers.

OF THE STATE OF THE THEATRICAL PROFESSION IN ENGLAND.

Whoever visits England as a traveller should not omit attending the theatre, because it furnishes him with an opportunity, partly of hearing a perfect pronunciation of the English,
for which the public, like the Greeks formerly, possess a fine
feeling, and partly because it may make him acquainted with
all the formalities of verbal delivery, such as discourse and
dialogue, from the deepest pathos to the most easy tone of
conversation.   I must confess, too, that the verbal delivery of
any poetical or dramatical composition, in which all the power
and magnificence of an elegant language, as well as the wonderful capability of voice and eloquence, appropriate to human
nature, are displayed, appears to me to appertain to the finest
enjoyments and recreations which a person of education can
indulge in.   I have attended many a representation, which
would have interested me but little on account of the subject,
entirely upon this consideration, and frequently read it afterwards line by line.   In this manner I have convinced myself
of the great difficulty which exists in comprehending the pro-

per tone and accent, whilst it appeared to me that the performers were frequently not equal to themselves, as is proved by the final syllables which were so strikingly dissimilar in rhymed poetry. In other pieces, however, the performance and subject interested me in like degree. It happened very lucky for me, that, during my residence in London, the six principal pieces of Shakspeare—Hamlet, Othello, Romeo and Juliet, and attractive Richard III., Henry VI., and VIII., were given. Some of the representations, particularly that of Richard III., appeared to me highly deserving of the applause which was bestowed upon them. Kean's acting displayed the dreadful truth of the tyranny of Richard; and I can hardly conceive any thing which touched the heart more, than the leave taken by the queen of her children, which announced the deepest feeling. I could not have supposed that the anguish of heart, breaking out into sighs and sobs, could have been given so nobly, and that an actress could succeed therein so well as Mrs. Glover did, who appeared to forget altogether the performer while she was representing the mother. Falstaff appears to be only at home upon the English stage. Miss O'Neil, the goddess of the public, and highly esteemed for her personal merits, gained all hearts in her representation of Juliet, as well as the younger Kemble did in Romeo. Yates, who filled five different parts in the *Coxenage,* the comic actor Munden, Mathews, who is so well acquainted with the manner of representing the peculiarities of his fellow performers, developed talents which certainly would be called rare any where.

Still, however, I could not participate in that unconditional admiration of the English theatre, with which I found many a German, who was not unacquainted with the merits of our performers, penetrated. The plain dialogue or, monologue often approached a lesson learnt by heart, and appeared recited in measured time. In expression of passion, they at least far exceeded the limits which we consider the extreme points to which an actor can go; and the conclusion was frequently made with those favourite *shrieks* or piercing cries, which were always rewarded with a clamorous applause. Even the prejudicial sarcasms of Richard III. often excited, particularly upon Kean's withdrawing himself, after the fashionable manner, rather laughter than disgust.

In making these passing observations, I am far from willing to appropriate to myself any particular privilege to give a decisive opinion of the present condition of this criterion of the national civilization. More perfect connoisseurs than I am are requisite for this purpose. They should be persons who have had longer time for observation, and I fear that I have already gone far beyond the sphere allotted to me. My views, however, of the subject are almost without exception in coincidence with those which our countryman, Goede, has given in a particular section of his celebrated work upon England. In England itself, too, people are pretty generally of an uniform opinion, that the taste for any thing noble is partly corrupted by the equestrian exercises and such like, which are exhibited indeed with wonderful dexterity in the theatres of Astley and Sadlers' Wells, and partly that the theatre is no longer that which it was at the zenith of its fame. This fame which it enjoyed, it is particularly indebted for to the two rare geniuses in their art, Shakspeare in the sixteenth, and Garrick in the last, century. The former was a man who was acquainted with, and depicted, mankind better than any who had gone before him, who was possessed of a mind inexhaustible in ideas, and a fancy rich in the greatest, as well as the most endearing, pictures, with a language which took possession of the human heart, both from the lofty tones in which it was written, the tenderest feelings it displayed, and was a man who was at once an endless fountain, from which, as the Greeks formerly did from Homer, innumerable British and German poets have drank.

Garrick, who, according to the general opinion, gave the most perfect idea of the rare spirit which animated Shakspeare, is still frequently mentioned. He has always served as a guide to the most respectable of his successors, such as Kemble, Cooke, and Mrs. Siddons, who once both heard and saw him. I know not how greatly the latter may be indebted to her pattern for the talent she has ever displayed; I only know that the reading of some of her principal parts, such as Lady Macbeth, Queen Catherine, of Arragon, readings which I attended in Cambridge, appeared to me to surpass every thing I had heard from other actors. This far-famed actress, (who was born in the year 1749) whose stately figure and dignity of features are little injured by time, preserved also, when off the stage, (from which she has some time since receded, as well as her brother Kemble, into domestic life) that power whereby she commands all the various cadences of tone, and is so perfect a mistress of the manner of preserving the fundamental principles of the character in which she speaks, that she adapts every expression to it with the most perfect harmony. She was not only loudly applauded by the whole company, but by the most impressive tranquillity, and that silent irresistible proof of a deeply felt admiration ensued, which Iffland used to say he valued far more than the repeated thoughtless tokens of approbation, evinced by the clapping of thousands of hands.

RETURN FROM LONDON TO HAMBURGH.

Fragments from my Journal.

" Farewell, Britannia, where the queen of arts
Inspiring vigour, liberty abroad
Walks through the land of heroes unconfined,
And scatters plenty with unsparing hand."

Harwich, 27th July, 1819.—The tumult of the metropolis
is silenced. We have been borne, as it were, upon wings,
fifteen German miles in a rather dark night. I am now
once more upon the coast of that country which, a short time
ago, lay before me enveloped in a mist, and which now floats
before my eyes like a magnificent and brilliant picture. For
a long time to come, I shall have no occasion to sigh for fresh
impressions, and may the more tranquilly reflect upon all that
I have seen and heard. If we should be enabled, upon our
landing upon the shores of another world, after our last journey
in this, to carry with us as lively recollections of all that the
earth has afforded us, we shall there too scarce stand in need
of new matter to occupy our minds ; and when our curiosity
has been satisfied, gratitude and admiration will continue to
warm our hearts, and to strengthen our memory.

The prospect of a good voyage is very unfavourable. The
winds refuse us our departure. An unwelcome leisure is,
therefore, afforded me to call anew to my recollection the last
hours I passed in London.

The inconveniences attendant upon getting ready my luggage,
the settlement of my debts in the house where I lived, and
other necessary matters, were over. Before I took leave of
my room, I cast another glance upon the noble Thames, and
the incessant bustle which prevails upon it. My amiable
hostess appeared unwilling to let me leave her. Her daughter
entreated me to play another German air upon her piano, the
execution of which appeared to afford her great pleasure.
With a heavy heart I took leave of my companion, the Baron
de Geer, who had gained my sincere esteem. I parted no less
reluctantly from the amiable families of Messieurs Bohte and
Ackermann.

On board of the Henry Freeling, the 29th July.

We went yesterday evening on board the packet. By singular coincidence it was the same which had brought me to
England. I greeted the narrow abode which was so well
known to me ; nor was I become a stranger to captain Hart
and the crew. The sky was cloudless, but there was not the

least wind. We were enabled to remain on the deck till a very late hour.

I wish the night had not only afforded us sleep and rest, but brought us further on our voyage. But we are still too near the English coast. The good company we have on board affords us some recompense.

July 30. Almost every body is sea-sick. No one feels a desire of entering into conversation. The hours, which lately passed as minutes, we wish we could accelerate with wings. They creep on so slowly, that we are frightened when we look at the watch, and hold it to our ears, in doubt whether it may not have stopped. Sleep appears to be the only friend of those that are well ; it deserts the sick like a false friend.

July 31. We have now lost sight of England. The Dutch coast stretches itself out before us, but we are obliged, from contrary wind, to be continually on the tack, to gain a little way. Thus the 300 English miles of sea may be made 900. At a distance we get a sight of the Texel, where the East India ships used to *rendezvous.*

The company on board are getting better. We begin to laugh at our own impatience, and to rebuke ourselves for wishing to change what is unalterable. I myself become more accustomed to the sea, and am already somewhat envied by my sick companions. I have begun to read the Mazeppa of Lord Byron with the English gentleman who is on board. He is very attentive to the errors I make, and, although he is unacquainted with the German language, he endeavours to explain in writing all the words I do not understand.

Aug. 1. We have passed a very solemn and quiet Sunday. The sea resembled a plain, over which green corn was waving. The sun shone down upon us with all its brilliant splendour from the beautiful azure sky. The ships bound to a contrary direction slid slowly by us in this perfect calm. All kinds of animated little forms were playing in the bosom of the ocean. The crew were dressed in their best clothes, and appeared well pleased at the returning tranquillity of the Sabbath. The sailors were laying upon the deck, either reading or in conversation. I saw the *Common Prayer Book* in the hands of many of them.

Aug. 2. We are beginning a fresh week. We thought we should have passed it upon our native soil. The captain does not appear in the best humour. The clouds, which are contracting together, bring us some hope. A storm arises ; lightning flashes around ; the motion becomes greater ; the labours of the crew are redoubled, and the lead is never still. We avail ourselves of some quiet hours for fishing, which costs several fine turbot and mackarel their lives.

Aug. 3. This morning brings us better tidings.   We are opposite Heligoland, before the mouth of the Elbe, and near enough, without assisting our eye-sight, to get a clear view of the whole island, which suddenly grew so rich, during the war between England and France, as the Depot of Colonial produce.

At breakfast a pleasing emotion arises in my breast, when I recollect that this day, nine and forty years ago, gave birth to one of the most respectable of monarchs.   There is no person around me who can participate in my feelings.   To make them generally known appears to me throwing them away. But different, however, as might be the political interests and sentiments of individuals, none refused to fill his glass, and all paid homage to the bravery, constancy, and domestic virtues which distinguish our prince and father of his people.   *God save the King.*

Aug. 4. The inviting Holstein village of *Brunsbüttel*, lays before us ; but as the wherry can not approach it, and we can hail no boat, we are prevented landing.   A violent storm comes on, with torrents of rain, which drives us all into the close cabin. It clears up, and we repeat our hailing of a boat ; fishermen draw near us, and bring us over the river, which is still sufficiently rough.

The ease, cleanliness, and comfort, which, in my former travels, I had found in all the villages of Holstein, are here confirmed.   Houses, rooms and furniture, are all superior to what we are accustomed to see in our part of the country.

Hamburgh in the Stadt London, 5th August.—About three o'clock in the afternoon we came before *Blankenese*.   Who is there who is not acquainted with this favourite resort of the inhabitants of Hamburgh and Altona ?

The travellers were now all of one accord to dismiss our boatmen, and to finish the remainder of our way upon a couple of Holstein carriages, which are always standing in readiness.

Every thing on this road bears marks both of opulence and increasing cultivation.   The elegant and tasty country seats and gardens continue in an uninterrupted line to Altona.   I hardly knew again the short road from thence to Hamburgh, so greatly was every thing changed, since I had first seen it in the year 1776.   We stopped at *Ottensen*, where Charles of Brunswick took refuge after the unfortunate affair of *Auerstadt*, and finished his days, and where Klopstock reposes ; we took a view of the tomb and monument of the sacred songster.

FINIS.

TRAVELS

IN

HUNGARY,

IN

1818.

BY F. S. BEUDANT,
MEMBER OF MANY LEARNED SOCIETIES.

Translated from the French.

LONDON:

PRINTED FOR SIR RICHARD PHILLIPS AND Co.
BRIDE-COURT, BRIDGE-STREET.

1823.

ADVERTISEMENT.

————◆————

HUNGARY is a country, of which our knowledge, from the very little intercourse maintained with it, is exceedingly imperfect. The duties of a recent traveller, M. Beudant, led him to explore and survey that remote unvisited region, with the design of collecting, ascertaining, and adopting, on a systematic principle, all such new, but scattered information, as was to be found in a large sphere of remark and enquiry, upon the subject of geology.

But while paying due attention to the principal and avowed object, he deemed it of importance to accomplish another by it, that of observing and describing what the means given, and the opportunities afforded, would enable him to learn, during his short stay, respecting the customs and manners, the taste, habits, and character, of the inhabitants, the chief part of which has been carefully preserved in the following translation.

G. SIDNEY, Printer,
Northumberland Street, Strand.

INTRODUCTION.

In respect of the diversities of its people, no country whatever can be compared with Hungary. They form an heterogeneous assemblage of nations, some of which descend from the primitive inhabitants, others from the different hordes that invaded them, including migrations from neighbouring countries, colonies invited thither, and individual families attracted by the fertility of the soil, or the hopes of commercial gain.

The following are the names under which the several nations may be arranged : Slowacks, Croats, Russniaks, Servians, Illyrians, Carniolians, Magyares, Kumans, Jaszons, Szeklers, Wallacbians, Bulgarians, Saxons, Suabians, Bavarians, Franconians, Austrians, Greeks, Armenians, Albanians, Italians, French, Jews, and Zingares.

Though attached for ages to the same country, united by a common interest, governed, in several respects, by the same laws, and living, for the most part, in good intelligence with each other, the diversities here enumerated remain distinct. Each retains, with a sort of pride, the remembrance of its origin, and the alliances they contract are within the limits of its pale.—Thus they preserve their dialect, manners, customs, and very often a peculiar physiognomy.

The Slowacks, called also Bohemian Slavi, designated, in French, by the generic term, Sclavonian, mostly inhabit the mountainous part in the north of Hungary. They nearly compose the entire population of the Comitats of Presburg, Niyitra, Trentsen, Thurotz, Arva, Liptot, Zolyom, Bacs, Gomor, Nograd, and Gran. These Sclavonians are probably the remains of the extensive Moravian kingdom, and, of course, the natural inhabitants of the country. They are more active and more industrious than the Hungarians, and have spread their colonies, in our times, into different parts of the flat country that were uninhabited before. One fact is remarkable, that wherever the Sclavonians form fresh establishments, the Germans and Hungarians either become blended with them, or soon disappear. Several even of the Town Mines, which are now become Sclavonian, as M. Schwartner observes, retain a decisive mark of their denationalization, in their names, as also those of many families, being of German origin.

The Slowacks are in general pretty well made, and they dress rather neatly, and at times elegantly, on their holidays. Their summer dress consists of cloth pantaloons, of buskins, of a cloth waistcoat without sleeves, garnished with very large silver buttons, in the form of little bells, and chased on the surface. The waistcoat open, lets the shirt appear, which is embroidered on the breast and sometimes on the sleeves. A leather girdle serves to fasten the clothes about the body; it incloses also the steel, the tinder-box, the pipe, and the tobacco-pouch. In winter a large pelisse of cloth, or of sheep skin, suffices to protect them from the rigours of the season. As to head-dress, it varies in different places; frequently the head appears bare, the hair oiled and pretty well combed. In some parts they wear a large round hat, in others a sort of high hood, a foot and a half in length, and without a brim; it is a coif or cap of felt. The women appear in buskins with copper heels, adorned with little bells; they have cloth petticoats and corsets without sleeves, mostly of a dark colour. Their chemise is commonly embroidered about the sleeves, which are sometimes edged also with a coarse lace. Young girls have their hair tied behind in a queue, trimmed with ribbands of all colours, that float on the back. The women adjust their head dress with a long cloth band, which, from the middle of the head, falls crossways on the chin; the two ends turned behind about the neck, are again brought forward so as to fall elegantly on the breast. This *coiffure* so completely overspreads the face, that scarcely is even the nose visible. Its singularity may be accounted for from the piercing winds to which they are exposed at morning, night, or occasionally in the day-time, and which prove very troublesome, if the neck is not well covered. To the same cause I assign the men letting their hair float on their shoulders. Though habituated to brave all the vicissitudes of the weather, I have often been obliged, at night and morning, to wear a kind of shawl about my neck and head, like many of the inhabitants in the hot countries.

The Russniaks, or Ruthenians, (properly Russians, and sometimes wrongly named Greeks, from the religion they profess) are originally from Red Russia, i. e. Eastern Galicia and

Lodomeria. When oppressed by the Russians and Polanders, they took refuge in Hungary, about the twelfth century. Here their local seat is in the comitats of Saros, Beregh, Ugots, Ungh, Zemplen, and a part of the Marmaros. Placed also on the limits of their natal soil, they unite with their countrymen that still remain in Galicia, in the circles of Stanislawow, of Stry and Sambor. Some also have settled in the Buckowine, and others have passed into Transylvania, where they are blended with the Wallachians. They appear to be of a dull and heavy temperament, and in general live wretchedly. Their number is not considerable, and they live on good terms with the other nations. Their language is a dialect of the Sclavonian, but they do not intermix with the Sclavonians, which is attributed to their religion. Some follow the orthodox, and others the schismatic Greek Ritual.

The Servians, called also Raatzes or Rascians, but among themselves named Serbi, come originally from Bosnia and Servia. Their country was incorporated with the kingdom of Hungary, in the beginning of the thirteenth century ; and from that time they began to pass the Save and the Danube, and to settle on the military frontiers which they now occupy. But when Bosnia and Servia fell under the dominion of the Turks, a number of others arrived. The kings of Hungary then became their protectors, and granted them considerable privileges, with the free exercise of the orthodox Greek religion, which they profess ; their bishops have also obtained the right of sitting in the diet. The Servians are pretty numerous, and in general in good repute with the other nations. They chiefly inhabit the military frontiers, and speak a particular dialect of the Sclavonian. We find them also in a considerable number in the southern part of the Great Plain, in the comitats of Temes, Torontal, Bacs, &c. also in Sclavonia and Croatia, besides a great number of them in Transylvania.

The Croats or Horvates form a remnant of the ancient Sclavonians, who, about the beginning of the seventh century, emancipating themselves from the dominion of the Avari, extended their conquests into the present Albania, Servia, Bosnia, Croatia, and Dalmatia. Besides Croatia, properly so called, this nation still occupies a part of the comitats of Sthulweissenburg, Eisenburg, Sumegh, Wieselburg, Œdenburg, and Szala, in Western Hungary. They constitute also a part of the population of Sclavonia, and are found mingled with Illyrians, Carniolians, Germans, and Hungarians, that were invited into their country, on the termination of those bloody wars, of which it had been the theatre, and during which the Turks had destroyed the major part of the inhabitants.

As a people, the Croats retain an air of rudeness in their manners and physiognomy, notwithstanding which, frankness and loyalty form the basis of their character, and the conduct of such as I met with was irreproachable. They appear tolerably neat in their dwellings, but their apparel is often coarse, and sometimes old enough. The women especially hunt for a medley of motley colours; I have seen them sometimes with petticoats of strong blue or brown cloth, streaked and speckled with ribbands of every colour; also with red stockings and yellow shoes, or with stockings striped transversely, red, yellow, brown, &c. But I may seem here criticising too freely, for I recollect, at Paris, not more than twenty years ago, our elegantes being caparisoned, about the legs and feet, in the same way. The women attire their heads pretty much like the Slowacks; their figure is, in like manner, half concealed; but in some cantons they wear besides, on the crown, a napkin folded square, and a muslin neck cloth or handkerchief, or else a piece of linen fastened to it, but so as to fall and spread over the back. Generally speaking, the costume varies materially in the different parts of the country which these people inhabit; the only predominant taste is for mottled stuffs, or clothing of different colours.

The Magyares form a considerable part of the population of the Hungarian provinces, but their number is inferior to that of the Sclavonians taken collectively. It is wonderful that they have not long ago been extinguished or confounded with the other natives, having had particularly so many wars and disasters to encounter and surmount. The Magyares, with their own maternal language, still exist as a separate nation, occupying all the flat country in the centre of Hungary. This people spread from the plains of Munkacs, where they first arrived, through all the fertile part of the country, driving the Sclavonians into the mountainous regions, and employing themselves in agriculture, or leading a pastoral life. Becoming Hungarians, they have also settled in Transylvania, where they occupy the comitats of Kruszna, Torda, Alba Inferior, Alba Superior, Dobaka, Hunyad, Klausenburg, Kukullo, Szolnok Interior, Szolnok Middle, Zarand, and the districts of Fagaras and Kovar.

The Magyares retain a distinct character, uniformly discernible. They are of the middling size, but of a robust make. Many authors describe the Hungarians generally as tall, but this rather belongs to the Sclavonians, who are commonly slender, and not so stout as the Hungarians. The Magyares are broad shouldered, with muscular limbs, have a well set figure, and a very masculine physiognomy, breathing an air of independence, that appears to most advantage when united with the qualities of the heart. They possess a degree of vivacity even to impetuosity; their frankness many would construe into rudeness, but it is accompanied with an accommodating temper, and they are ever ready to do services. A sprightly manner, blended with their vivacity, and mixed with a certain head-strong inconstancy, makes their character, to speak freely, resemble that of the French. Having been admitted into a number of companies where French was universally spoken, and remarking the gaiety of some, the impassioned manner of others, the lively turns of the discussion, the desultory interruption of conversation, combined with the affability of all, I have forgot for a time that I was in a foreign country. This description is not, however, more applicable to the Magyares than to the Sclavonians, and must be understood as restricted to the higher classes.

The dress of the Magyare peasant resembles that of the Slowacks, but it is of a ruder kind. Large pantaloons of linen cloth, which fall into the stockings or over the boots, and a shirt which only comes down to the loins; these constitute the summer wear. A large pelisse of sheep skin, often embroidered with other colours, thrown over the shoulders, or a rough great coat, with very long hairs, to resemble the fleece of a sheep, makes up the winter apparel. But if the dress of the peasants be generally coarse, throughout Hungary, that of the gentlemen is very elegant; it is modeled on the equipment of our light cavalry, originally copied from the Hungarian cavalry, which has ever been in great reputation. Our hussars have borrowed their name, their helmets are similar, and some of their accoutrements, as Sako, Sabrack, &c. are terms of Hungarian derivation. According to report, the word Hussar originates from an edict of king Mathias Corvin, ordaining that every twenty labourers should provide a horseman; he was called, in Hungarian, Huzzas, whence hussar has been formed.

The Kumans, called by the Hungarians, Kun, appear to be of Magyare origin; their name, perhaps, comes from the river Kuma, which, from the Caucasean region, falls into the Black Sea. We find, in history, a branch of the Magyare people extending to Caucasus, and on the banks of the Kuma, are the ruins of a town called Madschar, or Madjar, which may indicate their pristine residence. Their history becomes more apparent about the end of the eleventh century, and the beginning of the twelfth, when king Stephen, to recompence their valour, in wars against the Greek emperor, assigned them a district on the banks of the Theysse, now known by the name of Great Kumania or Great Kunia; in Hungarian, Nagy Kunsag.

In a later time, under the reign of Bela IV., a tribe of Kumans, from the northern plains about the Black Sea, came to claim Hungarian protection, and received a portion of territory, now called Little Kumania, or Little Kunia, in Hungarian, Kis Kunsag. Their language is a dialect of the Hungarian. The people are almost wholly occupied in rearing cattle, their situation and soil being favourable for pasturage.

The Jaszons appear to be also a tribe of Kumans. The name of Jasz, which the Hungarians sometimes give to the Kumans, generally, is thought to be derived from their skill in jaculating arrows, and from their being employed in the corps of lancers. In ancient acts, they are mentioned under the names of Balistarii and Balistei, and, by corruption, Philistei, words which refer to a similar import. The Jaszons inhabit a particular district in the comitat of Pest, designated by Hungarian geographers, by the name of Jaszsag, and which was granted to them by king Ladislas I. Their language is the same as that of the Kumans.

The Szeklers must be of the same origin as the Magyares, as they speak the same language and exhibit the same traits of character. They are of a middling size and robust make; their complexion is brown, their hair black, their physiognomy ardent and animated. The people are considered as the remains of the Kuns, and have been settled for ages in Transylvania, where history exhibits them in all the wars and troubles that have ravaged that country. They occupy the eastern part in the local seats of Haromeszek, Udvarhely, Csik, and Aranyos, all conquered by force of arms and secured by treaties, which have likewise guaranteed to them a number of particular privileges. They form one of the three nations of Transylvania; the two others are the Hungarians, properly so called, and the Saxons.

The Wallachians, called by themselves Romans, (Rumaene) seem to be actually a remnant of the ancient Dacians and Roman colonists intermixed. During the incursions of the barbarous hordes, they sought refuge about Mount Haemus, and afterwards found means to re-enter their own country. Their language is a mixture of corrupt Latin, or bad Italian and Sclavonian; and thus, with the exception of some words, a Frenchman, habituated to the dialect in the southern provinces of France, finds it easy to understand and converse with them. In writing they make use of Greek characters, disfigured more or less. These they have borrowed from the Sclavonians, among whom this alphabet was introduced by the two brothers, Cyril and Methodus, sent from Constantinople, about the end of the ninth century, to preach the gospel and translate the scriptures into their language. These missionaries added several particular signs to the common Greek alphabet, to express all the sounds of the new language they were to adopt. As to the word Valaque or Wallach, German, it seems to come from the Sclavonian word Wlach, pronounced nearly Valaque, and which signifies an Italian : just as the words Walen and Wallon, in the middle ages, designated a people whose language had affinity to that of the Romans.

The Wallachians are, in general, little and robust ; of an aspect rather lively, but of a brutal and perverse character. Their hair is black and clotted together, and of all the tribes in Hungary, they are the most remote from civilization. The men are naturally slothful, and if they can find means to satisfy the most urgent wants, are with difficulty excited to labour. Hence, they ever appear filthy and ill clothed, and they must drag out a miserable existence. From this indolence and wretched condition, De Sacy derives their name. He conceives that the Greeks, who first made mention of them, designated them by the name of *Blax,* which denotes idle, contemptible. The women, on the contrary, are very active ; we never see them unemployed, and if we meet them in the highways, it is always with the distaff or knitting in their hands. It is they who manufacture all the clothing for the family ; they assist, and often become substitutes for their husbands in the labours of the field. In their cabins they manage the household business, while the men are smoking their pipes, or reposing sluggishly in some corner of the tenement or garden, or waiting till their meal is brought them. This activity gives to the Wallachian women an advantage of an exterior more engaging than that of the men, attended at times with a certain elegance, and their costume in general has nothing in it disagreeable. They wear no petticoats, but their chemise, often embroidered with different colours, is always very long, and they spread over it two aprons set off with fringes, one before and the other behind. Their head-dress consists in a sort of little bonnet tucked out and rumpled, or in a handkerchief folded somewhat like a turban ; the young women have their hair plaited, and sometimes pretty neatly combed.

Maize forms the chief article of sustenance with the Wallachians ; of this they make a soup called memelige, and a sort of bad bread ; they have scarcely any thing else but milk and its produce, with leguminous plants and roots. The men are immoderately addicted to drinking brandy. Their national character is that of crafty, vindictive, pilfering, and superstitious, with no fixed principles of morality or religion. To which, when we add that they are destitute of arts and civilization, their condition must evidently be abject, and we need not wonder if the Hungarians, as well as other nations, treat them like slaves. They dwell chiefly in Transylvania and on the frontiers of Wallachia, but they are tolerated merely, and are not considered as forming a part of the nations that possess the country. Several, indeed, from some signal merits, have become members of these nations, and there are distinguished families among them, of Wallachian origin. The famous John Corvin Hunniades was of their race; history records his great actions in warring with the Turks, and his son, Mathias Corvin, was elevated to the throne of Hungary.

Exclusive of Transylvania, we find a great number of Wallachians in the Banat, where they are the most ancient inhabitants; we meet with them also along the frontiers of Transylvania, in the comitats of Arad, Bihar, Szathmar, and Marmaros. In general, the number of Wallachians is very considerable, and but little inferior, perhaps, to that of the Hungarians or Slowacks. In 1790 they rated their number, in Transylvania alone, at one million; at that time they were soliciting a participation in the privileges of the other nations. In Hungary, properly so called, they occupy 1024 villages along the frontiers of Wallachia and Transylvania. Their fecundity is very great, and in places where they inhabit, in common with the Servians, they supplant the latter, just as the Sclavonians do the Germans and Magyares. There are now among them, families of Russniacs, of Servians, and Bulgarians, which have lost every trace of their primitive language.

Next to the Sclavonians, the Germans undoubtedly form the most ancient nation of Hungary. In fact, many tribes of Germans settled in the western parts of the country, prior to the invasion of the Magyares, and especially after the destruction of the Awares. At the arrival of the Magyares, all the western part of the country, included between the Danube and the Save, had been subjected to the emperor Arnulph, and although that part was quickly wrested from him, a great number of the inhabitants would doubtless remain. But subsequently to the establishment of the Magyares, the number of Germans increased considerably. King, or Sainted Stephen, the primitive legislator of Hungary, feeling the necessity of augmenting the population, granted privileges to invite German colonists, which were carefully preserved by his successors. And thus, from the eleventh century, the Germans possessed settlements in different parts of Hungary. But it was more especially in the twelfth century, under king Geysa II., that they arrived in numerous bodies, so as to fill entire comitats and provinces. They mostly fixed their residence in the northern provinces and in Transylvania, so that from Presburg to the frontiers of Wallachia, they formed a sort of military cordon. They came from all countries, from Flanders, the Netherlands, Alsace, and the southern parts of Germany; they are designated, however, by the general name of Saxons.

These ancient Germans have proved a valuable acquisition to the country, compensating amply for the privileges granted to them. The civil professions of the state of burgesses originate from them; and to them may be attributed the opening and labours of the mines. By the Germans, industry was introduced into the towns, and a commercial intercourse with the north created. They early adopted the manners and costume of the country, though partly mixed with their own; but in some cantons they have a particular mode, which appears odd, of wearing a white chemise over a dark-coloured *culotte*. The ancient colonists look with an evil eye on the fresh comers from the Palatinate, Franconia, Suabia, and Bavaria, that arrived in Hungary at the beginning of the eighteenth century, after the expulsion of the Turks. These last go by the name of Suabians (Schwaben) which is become a term of reproach, " he is a Suabian, es ist ein Schwabe."

The number of those whose vernacular tongue is German, is comparatively small; a circumstance which is owing to the influence of the Slowacks. In many places originally founded by the Germans, we at present only find Sclavonians. The vestiges are few of that great girdle that reached from the foot of the Carpathians into Transylvania. It is in the comitat of Lips, in the centre of the Carpathians, that they mostly abound, their number exceeding 60,000. There is another numerous assemblage of them in Transylvania; there the Germans, under the name of Saxons, occupy the local seats of Hermanstadt, Nagysink, Medgyes, Reps, Segesvar, Szaszsches, Szaszvaros, Szerdahely, and Uj Egyhaz, together with the districts of Bistricz and Kronstadt. Here they form one of the three nations, and possess particular privileges which rank them above the state of burgesses. There are also many Germans in the Banat, colonists of the eighteenth century. We trace them again in great numbers towards the frontiers of Austria, in the comitats of Œdenburg, Eisenburg, and Wieselburg, besides which, there are many Germans scattered through all parts of Hungary. Several are to be found in all the mining towns, and whatever depends on industry or trading concerns, in the free towns, is chiefly in the hands of the Germans.

In the Population of Hungary, other nations require to be mentioned, though their number be, comparatively, inconsiderable, some employed in husbandry and others in trade. Of the former, is a little colony of French, that, in the time of Maria Theresa, settled in the plains of Hungary, between the Maros and the Bega, in a marshy, but very fertile territory. We find them congregated in the little town of Hatzfield, in the villages of Charleville and St. Hubert, and in those of Nagyjetsa and Csadat, in the comitat of Torontal. There are others at Breztovaez, in the comitat of Bacs; this last little colony has, hitherto, retained its language.

Some few Italians yet remain in Hungary; it is these that have introduced the culture of rice and the rearing of silk worms. Their number was, formerly, much more considerable, when the Hungarians had kings and queens of Italian families, and when there was a trade with Venice. They are now nearly limited to the village of Charlottenburg, in the Banat.

Commercial pursuits have attracted into Hungary a number of modern Greeks, Armenians, and Jews. The modern Greeks, or Macedonians, are mostly engaged in commercia speculations, and much of the specie or cash passes through their hands. Some reside at Pest, and there is a pretty great number of them at Hermanstadt and Kronstadt, in Transylvania. Many have no fixed residence, but traverse the interior parts of the country, especially in the great plain. Among themselves they have trading companies that extend from Vienna throughout the Levant. Their stay in Hungary is but temporary, their place being filled up by others of their countrymen. They frequently acquire a considerable fortune in Hungary, commencing with a very small capital. These Greeks have a particular costume which appears distinct from all other habiliments. Large pantaloons descending into the boots, these last of different colours, a silk camisole or under waistcoat, a woollen or cachemire belt or girdle, a short riding coat or frock open before, and a red cap or coif.

The Armenians who came to settle in Transylvania, about the year 1672, and thence spread into the plains of Hungary, are also engaged in trade, and particularly that of cattle; they are in possession of a considerable part of the grazing lands. The individuals of this nation are, in general, isolated in the middle of the plains of Hungary, where they lead a sort of Nomade or pastoral life. They have only one small parish, at Neusatz, opposite Peterwaradin. In Transylvania their number is pretty considerable, and especially in the towns of Szamos Ujvar, and Ebesfalva; elsewhere, they are scattered through the province, and here and there we meet with very rich families of them. Certain individuals, as also of the Macedonians, have been admitted into the corps of Transylvanian Noblesse.

The Jews form a very numerous body in Hungary, where their number amounted, in 1805, to 128,000; they must be considered as a particular people, as they marry only among themselves, and are not denizens in the eye of the law. In the middle ages, all the financial operations of the state passed through their hands; they only understood the art of coining, the rates of exchange, and the business of trade in general. The sovereigns, when their treasury was low, had no other resource than the speculations of Jewish capitalists; from these they obtained ready money, but it was by means ruinous to the state, though profitable to the speculators. M. Schwartner reports, that during the expedition of Andrew II., in Palestine, the finest domains or estates were alienated, and the royal rights, as to coinage and the salt duties, were transferred to the Jews, and that the dilapidation of the revenue made it necessary to declare the goods of the crown unalienable. The Jews were then excluded from the management of the finances; and later, under Lewis the great, their residence in Hungary was prohibited: but Sigismund, who was always in debt, re-established them in the kingdom, and in some measure legalised loans at usurious interest. The like disorders occurred under Lewis II., and in 1524, we find a Jew, named Isaac, at the head of the mint of Kaschau.

At present the situation of the Jews is very different. They are subjected to a *surveillance* rather rigid, which includes a particular tax, called the Toleration. They are prohibited by law from residing on the frontiers, as also from entering the mine towns. This extends also to several other places, so that, for the most part, they are held in little consideration.

The cantons wherein I observed the greatest number of Jews, are the frontiers of Galicia, and the banks of the Bodrog, in the eastern part of Hungary, and the comitat of Stuhlweissenburg, in the western part, and many remain at Karlsburg, in Transylvania; elsewhere they are scattered along the roads and in the villages, where they live in huts or keep little pot-houses. Many tramp about as pedlars, carrying on a small trade in wares of every kind. Their apparel has something in it odd, forbidding, and apt to excite distrust. It consists of a long robe of woollen or black silk, fastened about the body by a black-coloured girdle, a large broad-brimmed hat or high bonnet, of hair or black sheep skin, to which, add a long beard and an air of slovenliness in general.

In the last rank of human beings that inhabit the soil of Hungary, are the Zingares, by the Germans named Zigeuner, and that pass in France under the name of Bohemians. These are very numerous in Hungary, but no certain accounts have been given of their origin. Grellinian's Researches make it appear probable that they are descendants of a cast of Indians, the Parias, that were driven from their country about the year 1408, during the conquest of India, by Tamerlane. Some authors consider them as Egyptians, and from this notion the name of Pharaoni, or Egyptians, has been assigned to them. It is certain that they speak a particular language, that their features are not European, and that their first appearance in Europe was at the beginning of the fifteenth century; about 1417, we find them first noticed in the history of Hungary. They have ever lived a wandering life, and the means employed to bring them within the pale of civilization have only reclaimed a small number that have settled, as husbandmen, on the frontiers of Transylvania. The rest ramble about, encamping in the middle of woods, or near villages, in huts which they speedily raise, and that are truly wretched and filthy. They are indolent and vicious, and only work to procure what is indispensably necessary. Some are blacksmiths, and forge nails, knives, and hatchets, which the women go and sell in the villages; others tramp from town to town, playing slight of hand tricks, or on some instrument to which the peasants dance. They go all covered with rags, and the women especially are very disgusting.

The number of these vagabonds has been very considerable; from a census ordained by the emperor Joseph, in 1783, it appears that they amounted to more than 40,000; but they are now much diminished, either from being dispersed in the neighbouring countries, or from gradually mingling with the peasants and settling in different places.

Such are the varying tribes of people confounded under the name of Hungarians. The mass of population, of which this assemblage consists, amounts to more than ten millions. According to M. Schwartner, the enumeration of them, in 1809, might be rated as under:—For Hungary, Sclavonia, and Croatia, not including the noblesse, the clergy, regiments of the line, or the military frontiers, 7,555,920; for the corps of noblesse, 325,894; for the clergy of all religions, 15,600; for the regiments of the line, 64,000; for the military districts of Hungary, 777,406; for the military frontiers of Transylvania, 137,041; and for the provincial of Transylvania, 1,501,106.— Total, 10,376,967.

This population, uniformly spread over the entire superficies, as it existed previous to the treaty of Vienna, in 1809, gives a mean number of 633 inhabitants to the square league, or 1790 per square mile. The extent of the kingdom is about 16,390 square leagues, of 25 to a degree, or 5900 square miles, of 15 to a degree. If this number should seem small in respect to France, which contains at least 1000 inhabitants per square league, it will be considerable, compared with the population of Sweden, Norway, Russia, &c. But the population of Hungary is not distributed uniformly, as supposed above; there is an immense surface, consisting merely of mountains covered with thick forests, besides arid plains and vast marshes that are no better than deserts. The population is, of course, much more condensed in the habitable places, where it varies, however, according to circumstances. In 1809, M. Schwartner calculated 990 inhabitants per square league, in the comitat of Œdenburg; 924, in that of Presburg; 858, in that of Zips; 743, in that of Zemplen, &c. He computed the population of Transylvania at about 800 individuals per square league, which number may be augmented, in different cantons, if the uninhabited parts be subtracted.

On the whole, the population of Hungary is evidently increasing, as appears from the census of 1787, compared with that of 1805; the latter gives a surplus of 439,131 individuals. Instances are afforded in the comitat of Bekés, which a century ago was an immense pasture ground, with a few wretched hovels, and now contains flourishing towns and villages, with more than 90,000 inhabitants. The Banat of Temes, which, setting aside the military districts, contained, in 1799, about 318,000 inhabitants, in 1785, had 550,000, and in 1805, 636,000. This rapid augmentation is partly owing to fresh colonies, and partly to the improvements of rural economy. These would produce advantages much more considerable, were encouragement given to the clearing of uncultivated lands, the draining of marshes, and the propagating of a taste for the arts and sciences; of this a great number of Hungarian lords begin now to be sensible.

Hungary is a country which contains landscapes and productions remarkable for originality, and its history has scenes of great interest. It is situated in the most temperate part of our hemisphere, and watered by one of the greatest rivers of Europe, with a number of tributary streams. The soil, in general, in the lowlands, possesses an uncommon degree of fertility, and the mountains, where, from their height, they are deprived of cultivation, are not without circumstances interesting to the traveller, and uncommon to the naturalist; these consist in the superlative abundance of their mineral riches.

As to the people, the best picture that could be drawn of

them, would be formed by an exposition of their actions. To get a just notion of the genius of the nation, we should consider them as exhibited at different periods. For eighteen successive centuries, they had to resist the united attacks of foreign or neighbouring nations; their resolution and firmness appear in numberless wars, and they uniformly preserved the same spirit. Their military occupation, during perpetual wars, gave birth to an anomalous character, which their history, in its various stages and incidents, best describes.

The conclusion of their wars with the adjacent nations, the establishment of peace, and their reconciliation with Austria, gave another turn to the pursuits of the nation and the spirit of its government. We then take a political survey of them, as emerging from barbarism and a degraded state of humanity, as framing laws and assuming some diversities of character, when the general face of their country had become serene, delivered from the storms and convulsions which had agitated or destroyed it. The forms of their government are monarchical, and their institutions feudal; they are, however, no longer in a state of slavery or comparative misery, but enjoy such blessings as the country affords. In the general economy and order of their domestic polity, their privileges are many and great.

In surveying modern times and more recent objects, the immense variety of natural productions offers reflections, descriptive of the country, and conduces to set it in its true light. Their gold mines, the only such in Europe; their iron mines, resembling those of Sweden; their copper mines, opals, and certain lands that apparently exhibit, in their composition, phenomena, the peculiar produce of this country: these, with their beautiful plains and fruitful valleys, with their rich soils, woods, and forests, yielding plenty and variety of fruits and game, give importance and value to the subject, and render it interesting to the naturalist, the philosopher, and to readers in general.

Hungary, notwithstanding, in its various relations, is one of those countries with which we have the least acquaintance. Its situation, at one extremity of Europe, in part surrounded by nations not the most civilized, communicating but little with such as are, it seems to have been so shut up, that the curiosity of travellers has been seldom attracted to it. More than a century has elapsed since its interior has enjoyed perfect tranquillity, and a free communication with the rest of Europe; yet the Hungarians have made few observations to surprise, enrich, or invigorate science or art, though they have the requisite materials within their power.

It will be easily conceived, that something necessary to direct the public judgment in these matters, might have been expected from the Austrians, but though the disasters of wars and revolutions are soon repaired, in a natural way, their moral effects are not easily effaced. The people of Hungary have long lived in an insulated state, indifferent to the progress of useful studies or knowledge, devoted to ancient customs, and subjected to prejudices which have hitherto been held sacred. To describe them has been deemed a difficult enterprise, from the diversity of their language, which a stranger must acquire, more or less, before he can decide—exalt narration to truth, or reject it as fiction.

Other circumstances contribute to prevent, or to retard the progress of a foreign traveller. Hungary lies out of the way of all frequented roads, and has none of those facilities of communication which other countries contain. From the privations to be expected, the most experienced tourist would feel a degree of diffidence in exploring such untrodden ground. The climate, too, has been represented as prejudicial to health, the people as cut off from the rest of mankind, half barbarous, and tinged with an antipathy to the visitors of all other nations.

These reports are exaggerated ; much, indeed, must be left to time, habit, education, before society here can be freed from its incidental blemishes, can rise to that superior civilization, elegance, and embellishment, which are scattered over the face of some other countries.

To compensate for such defects, Hungary teems with materials and stores of curiosities which, duly methodised, would furnish a subject interesting to science and to men of letters. Among these it may be said, that as to the virtues of civil life, the people hold a distinguished rank. They retain, in their highest degree, a patriarchal hospitality, a noble frankness and simplicity of manners, such as an instructed mind would naturally turn to study. From every gentleman, or rather from every Hungarian, a stranger would meet with assistance, protection, and friendship, where, indeed, he would be least looking for it.

There have not been wanting Works, however, treating of Hungary ; some describing the different branches of its political economy, others investigating its antiquities, geography, numismatics, rural economy, natural history, and mineralogy. On this last head, Hungary is deserving of particular notice, being the only country on the continent of Europe that has mines of gold and silver. These have been worked for ages, and it has been found, by M. de Humboldt, and other scientific characters that have visited the mines in America, that the metallic earths of Hungary strongly resemble those of Mexico and Peru, and that all the geological circumstances are in accordance. This observation is too remarkable not to excite the curiosity, or occasionally the suspicion, of the penetrating naturalist.

The reflections here suggested had been duly appreciated by M. the Count de Bournon, director of the king's cabinet of geology, and he speedily procured his Majesty's consent and protection, that I should visit other countries, to collect facts, useful, interesting, or new, on which a system of geological science might be planned. Hungary was the last country that I explored; my labours in it were ended towards the close of the year 1817, but previous to my quitting it, I made it my business to collect materials of miscellaneous information. This I frequently obtained, by visiting a number of antique castles, seated in the midst of surrounding forests, and which had stood numerous assaults during the wars of eighteen centuries. The following contains a concise compilation of what is desirable in former authors, or the result of my own diligent investigation.

GEOGRAPHICAL NOTICES RELATIVE TO HUNGARY.

The kingdom of Hungary once included, in the conquests of its different kings, Bulgaria, Wallachia, Transylvania, Moldavia, Galicia, Hungary properly so called, Sclavonia, Servia, Bosnia, Croatia, and Dalmatia, with some parts of Austria and Moravia. But in the course of events, Bulgaria, Wallachia, Moldavia, Servia, Bosnia, and Turkish Croatia, have been subjected to the Ottoman empire, the archduchy of Austria* has resumed its detached part, Moravia is dependent on Bohemia, Galicia, which the kings of Poland had conquered, is re-united to Austria, and Transylvania, raised into a principality, has been ceded also to Austria, retaining its particular rights.

What constitutes the present kingdom of Hungary, is Hungary properly so called, and Sclavonia, with parts of Croatia and Dalmatia. Prior to the year 1809, Hungary extended to the Adriatic, and took in a part of the islands that lie along the eastern coast of that gulf. But by the treaty of Vienna, in 1809, Hungarian Dalmatia, the greatest part of Croatia and the Banat frontiers were ceded to France, and, together with Carniola and a part of Carinthia, were consolidated under the name of the Illyrian provinces. The kingdom of Hungary

---

* The name of Austria is a corruption of the German word Œstreich, denoting kingdom of the east, which was given, in the tenth century, to the eastern part of the German states.

then terminated at the Save, near the town of Agram* (Zagrabia) and this forms the present limit; for, although Austria has recovered all that it lost, from the Save to the Adriatic, these provinces have not been reinstated in the kingdom of Hungary.

The provinces, collectively, comprehend a surface of 5597 German geographical square miles, on which are found 90 cities, 706 towns, and 14,134 villages and hamlets.

Hungarian Croatia, (Horvat-Orszag, Hung. Kroazien, Germ.) and Sclavonia, (Tot-Orszag, Hung.) the extent of which last is very diminutive, are both included between the Drave, the Save, and a part of the Danube that passes between the mouths of these two rivers, from Eszek to Belgrade; Croatia forms the western part, and Sclavonia the eastern.

The principality of Transylvania† (Erdely-Orszag, Hung.) is bounded, on the north, by the comitats or counties of Marmaros and Szathmar; on the east, by Moldavia; on the south, by Wallachia; and on the west, by the Banat and the Hungarian comitats of Arad and Bihar; or rather, it is encompassed with groupes of mountains stretching in those directions.

Hungary alone occupies a space nearly three times as large as the above provinces, taken together. It reaches from the Danube and the Drave, to the lofty mountains that form the limits of Austria, Moravia, the two Galicias, and the Buckawine.

With respect to the configuration of the surface, here are mountains, whose summits are buried in everlasting snows, and vast plains, but little above the level of the sea. The mountains form a girdle round the country, as if to separate it from all others; it is open only on the south side, opposite the Ottoman empire.

There are two considerable ranges of mountains distinguished from all others by their elevation, the mountains of Transylvania to the S. E., and the groupes that form the boundaries of Moravia and western Galicia. These two grand masses, in relation to Hungary, appear like two citadels at the entrance of an immense gulf. This part of the girdle has been called the Carpathian Chain, though, strictly speaking, the name should be limited to the most elevated parts of the north west.

---

* The comitat of Zagrabia, which anciently covered 300 square leagues of country, lost, at that time, 213 of them. More also have been taken away by the Croat regiments, and the kingdom of Hungary has had a total loss or deprivation of 844 square leagues.

† This name was given to the principality, from its situation beyond countries covered with wood, that lay at the eastern extremity of Hungary, properly so called, and from itself consisting chiefly of forests. The Hungarian epithet, Erdely, comes from Erdo, a forest; Erderly-Orssag signifies a country or kingdom of forests.

The limits of eastern Galicia are formed of mountains of sand, with here and there some points of solid rocks interspersed. They constitute, apparently, a sort of talus, pretty uniform, from one extremity to the other.

Though the mountains cover an immense extent of the surface, there are also vast plains that become the centre of the country. Some of these serve as granaries for such cantons as, from their elevation, have not the benefits of culture.

The principal rivers which either pass through the Hungarian States, or compose its boundaries, are the Danube, the Theysse, the Save, and the Drave; into these a number of others, more or less considerable, disembogue, but all ultimately fall into the Danube.

The Danube, (Duna, Hung. Donau, Germ.) next to the Wolga, is the largest river in Europe. It rises in the Black Forest, and after traversing Suabia, Bavaria, and Austria, passes on one side of Hungary, at the point where it receives, on its left, the river Morave, or March. Below Presburg, it contains a great number of islands, and in its entrance and passage through the plains of Hungary, its waters spread over a large tract. At Neu-Orsova, it quits the Hungarian States, and proceeding through the vast plains of Wallachia and Moldavia, empties itself into the Black Sea.

The course of this river is very tranquil through Hungary, the country being flat, and the descent of the waters inconsiderable. The banks are frequently overspread with immense marshes that fatigue the traveller's patience with a disagreeable monotony. But between the mountains of the Banat and Servia, where the river is much straitened, it makes its way with a tremendous rapidity, which, with the shoals scattered here and there, renders the navigation extremely dangerous.

The Theysse, (Tisza, Hung. Tibiscus, Lat.) next to the Danube, is the most considerable of the Hungarian rivers. Its source is at the extreme limits of the Marmora, and the Buckawine, and after crossing the vast marshes of the comitats of Szathmar and Szaboles, at length enters the plains of Hungary, across which it proceeds to the Danube, and joins it between Semlin and Peterwaradin. In its course it receives all the waters of Transylvania, and the greatest part of those of the northern mountains of Hungary. The rivers of Transylvania are the Syamos, the Koros,* and the Maros, which last

---

* The whole territory traversed by the three branches of the Koros, (called the Rapid, the Black, and the White Koros) is extremely marshy. The baron de Vay calculated the lands covered by the Rapid Koros alone, at 55,000 acres, and the moist lands occasionally inundated, at 70,000.

quits Transylvania below Dobra, and passing through the plains of Hungary, falls into the Theysse, opposite Szegedin. Among other rivers that issue from the northern mountains of Hungary, are the Bodrog and the Hernat, with smaller streams, such as the Erlau, the Zagyva, &c. The Theysse, after its junction with the Maros, is not inferior to the Seine, at Paris. This river, with the Maros, the Koros, the Szamos, and the Bodrog, are navigable in detached parts of their course, but not throughout. Many attempts have been made to render some of them serviceable to navigation, by canals of communication, but hitherto they have proved fruitless.

The Save (Szava, Sclav. Sau, Germ.) which forms the southern limit of the Hungarian States, rises in the mountains of Carniola, crosses Styria, and enters into Croatia, to the Hungarian part of which it serves as a boundary. It frequently overflows, covering all the low tracts about it, and leaving water that turns stagnant a great part of the year. It is navigable nearly throughout, and is the channel by which grains, tobacco, &c. are exported to Dalmatia and Italy.

The Drave (Drava, Sclav. Drau, Germ.) rises on the frontiers of Tyrol, crosses Carinthia and Styria, enters the Hungarian States, and proceeds in a S. E. direction for the Danube, into which it falls below Eszek. This river forms the natural boundary between Hungary and the provinces of Croatia and Sclavonia.

There are two lakes in Hungary of considerable magnitude, the lake Balaton, and the lake Neusiedel. The former is about sixteen leagues from S. W. to N. E.; its greatest width is nearly three leagues. Its situation is between the comitats of Szala and Sumegh. The lake of Neusiedel, from N. to S., is about eight leagues, its greatest width two and a half. Its situation is between the comitats of Œdenburg and Wieselburg. There are many other collections of water, of a smaller description, in the mountainous regions.

Marshes are uncommonly numerous in Hungary, and particularly in the middle of the Great Plain, on the banks of the Theysse and the Danube, as also in the large vallies, through which run the Drave and the Save. Baron Lichtenstern estimates the surface of the lands overflowed, at 300 square leagues, or 108 geographical German square miles. Several lords have successfully attempted the draining of certain marshes; their example duly imitated, would restore an immense number of acres to cultivation, and secure the inhabitants from putrid miasmata, to which they are now liable. This malign influence, however, is confined within a compass of about 300 square leagues, and in more than 15,000 square leagues the climate is as wholesome as in France or Germany.

It is wrongfully that Hungary has been called the grave of foreigners; the climate, in general, is salubrious, and the natives retain their health and energy as long as in other countries. Precautions are requisite here, but not more than in other warm climates. The days are often extremely hot, and the nights cool; this unequal temperature makes plenty of warm clothing necessary. The quality of their wines, though excellent, is very spirituous; excess in the use of them would give rise to inflammations, or other serious complaints. I can vouch from experience, notwithstanding all the fatigues and privations I have undergone, during my residence in the country, that I never felt the effects of insalubrity, as represented in books, and of which I had heard a thousand absurd tales, at Vienna.

Hungary, properly so called, was divided, by former geographers, into upper and lower, or, which comes to the same, and is less liable to error, into eastern and western. The line of demarcation was the Theysse, which appears nearly in the centre of the country, and which, from Szolnok, turns from north to south. Hence, an ideal line is traced across the mountains to the centre of the Carpathians. The parts east of this line had the name, improperly, of Upper Hungary, and those to the west, of Lower Hungary, no less inapplicable. This division is now abandoned.

The territorial divisions of the Hungarian States are civil and military. These last, on the frontiers of the Ottoman empire, form a cordon against invasion; the inhabitants are both soldiers and husbandmen. They are designated by the name of Regiments, and are twelve in number. In Croatia, the regiments of Koros, and of St. George. In Sclavonia, do. of Gradiska, Brodi, and Peterwardin; in Hungary, do. of Tsaikists, German Banatic, and Wallachian Illyrian. In Transylvania, the first Wallachian regiment on the frontiers of Wallachia; second do., on the frontiers of the Buckawine; third Szekler regiment on the frontiers of Moldavia, and the second Szekler regiment on the frontiers of Moldavia and Wallachia. One of these, the battalion of Tsaikists, derives its name from Tsaikes, barks to defend the passage of the river Danube; this battalion consists of the boatmen that are to guard it.

The civil territorial divisions take the name of comitat, from the Latin comitatus, or otherwise, that of district. Of these, Proper Hungary comprises forty-six. The names are, Abauj,

Arad, Arva, Bacs, Barany, Bars, Bekes, Beregh, Bihar, Borsod, Csanad, Csongrad, Eisenburg, Gomor, Gran, Heves, Hont, Komorn, Krasso, Lipto, Marmaros, Nograd, Nyitra, Œdenburg, Pest, Presburg, Raab, Saros, Stuhlweissenburg, Sumegh, Szaboles, Szala, Szathmar, Temes, Thurotz, Tolna, Torna, Torontal, Trentsen, Ugots, Ungh, Veszprim, Wieselburg, Zemplen, Zips, and Zolyom.

There are, besides, certain detached lands, insulated within the comitats, and governed by particular laws. Some depend immediately on the king, others on the Palatine. Among the former, are the free towns of Zips, scattered in the comitat, but composing an assemblage or district. The Haidonical towns, in the country of Debreczin, that furnish a particular foot militia, are under the royal authority. The districts that depend on the palatine, are Little and Great Kumania, and the Jaszons, all three in the Great Plain, and insulated within the comitats of Pest and Heves. Sclavonia and Croatia have each three comitats, Posega, Syrmia, and Verocze, for the former, and Koros, Varasdin, and Zagrabia, for the latter.

Transylvania is divided into three nations, the Hungarians, the Szeklers, and the Saxons, and contains twenty-nine civil divisions. For the Hungarian nation, eleven comitats, Lower Alba, Higher Alba, Doboka, Hunyad, Klausenburg, Kraszna, Kukullo, Szolnok Interior, Middle Szolnok, Torda, and Zarand, with the two districts of Fagaras, and Kovar.

The Szekler nation has five local seats, Aranyos, Csik, Haroinzek, Maros, and Udvarhely.

The Saxons have nine seats or local portions, some of which are extremely impoverished, from the long wars, which have left marks of their desolations. The names are, Hermanstadt, Nagysink, Medgyes, Reps, Segesvar, Szaszebes, Szaszvaros, Szerdabely, and Ujegyhaz. There are, besides, two districts, Bisztricz and Kronstadt.

OF THE PRINCIPAL LANGUAGES AND RELIGIONS.

It will be readily conceived, from the diversified classes that inhabit Hungary, that there must be a confusion of tongues ; in fact, such has been the difficulty of a mutual understanding, that, for ages, the Latin has been in use for matters of common concern, both with the government and individuals. Notwithstanding which, there are really in Hungary but four constituent languages, the Sclavonian, the Hungarian or Magyare the German, and the Wallachian.

The Sclavonian is one of the most ancient languages o Europe, and the most extensively spread, in its different dia lects. Those of the northern people that had been civilizec by the Romans, and passed under their name; such of the Europeans as were ever at war one with another, such as rose up after the invasion of the Huns and Avari, these all spoke the Sclavonian language. One of its dialects, the Bohemian, had its golden age in the fourteenth century, and in the beginning of the fifteenth, when, agreeably to the statutes of the Golden Bull of Charles IV., 1359, emperor of Germany and king of Bohemia, every elector of the empire was to learn the Sclavonian Bohemian language. At the time of the council of Constance, in 1414, Bohemian literature was in a flourishing state, while in Germany and France the morning of letters had scarcely begun to dawn. With the Sclavonian tongue, a traveller might pass through Illyria, Dalmatia, Croatia, Bosnia, Servia, Hungary, Bohemia, Moravia, Silesia, Poland, and Russia, as the languages in all of these are but dialects of it. Most of the Hungarians that have devoted any time to literature, are acquainted, at least, with the three radical languages, the Sclavonic, German, and Latin; and among the noblesse, I have met with such as speak six or eight different languages.

The Hungarian or Magyare language, is *sui generis*, and has no more affinity with the German or Latin than these have with one another. There are a number of words introduced from other languages, such as Tatar, Turk, Persan, Arab, with others of Finland extraction, also Sclavonian and German words, more or less modified; but it has a particular and Asiatic character in its suffixes and affixes, at the end of substantives or verbs, in lieu of pronouns. The language has numerous vowels, and there are few words that a Frenchman would not easily pronounce, though a German could not without difficulty.

The Wallachian language is a mixture of Sclavonian and Latin, but strangely mutilated. In more than half of its expressions, it bears a striking analogy to the *patois*, in the south of France and Italy; with due attention it is easily acquired.

In the Hungarian provinces, we meet with little less diversity of religious creeds, than of its population. Each nation, each colony, has its particular mode of worship. The inhabitants, in general, profess the Christian religion, but are divided into a number of different sects. Here are Roman Catholics, Orthodox Greeks, Schismatic Greeks, Lutherans, Calvinists, Socinians, and Anabaptists; these, with the Jewish religion, comprehend the totality of creeds.

The Roman Catholic religion is that of the state, and of the great body of the people. Its establishment may be traced to the tenth and eleventh centuries, when the Magyares, who had overthrown its first altars, began to grow civilized.

The Greek Orthodox church, which was raised about the same time, has its adherents in most of the Russniacs, Wallachians, and Servians. They are subject to two bishops, one of whom resides at Unghvar, and the other at Grosswardien, both suffragans to the archbishop of Gran. This church has its members also in Transylvania, with a few in Croatia and Sclavonia.

The Schismatic Greeks comprise almost the whole of Sclavonia, and the major part of the Wallachians, of Transylvania and the Banat, besides others in some of the Hungarian comitats. Their patriarch, similar to an archbishop in the Roman church, resides at Carlowitz, near Peterwaradin; he has seven bishops under him.

Lutheranism has a number of partisans, that persecution only augmented and made bolder. Tranquillity was completely restored, by the toleration edict of Joseph II., and Lutherans are now to be found in every part of Hungary, especially in the northern parts where the Germans have settled.

Calvinists are more numerous than Lutherans, and abound chiefly in the plains of Hungary, and on the frontiers of Transylvania.

The number of Socinians is very small; they are chiefly found in Transylvania. That of the Anabaptists is still less; a few are found in the comitats of Presburg and Nyitra.

The Jews are tolerated, and have synagogues, but are divided, as in other countries, into two sects, the Karaites, whose Scripture is confined to the books of the Old Testament, and the Rabbinists, who give almost equal authority to the Talmud.

These religious denominations are sometimes more especially congregated in certain cantons; here we meet with a Roman Catholic village or an Orthodox Greek, there a Schismatic Greek, or one of the reformed religion; sometimes we find in the same village, three or four churches of different communions, though it may not contain fifty houses. But, in general, the Catholics exceed, and we may rate them, at least, at one half of the population, or at five millions, including the Orthodox Greeks, whose number amounts to six or seven hundred thousand. The Schismatic Greeks may amount to a million and a half, and the reformed religion may take in two millions and a half, whereof the Calvinists form two thirds.

OF THE FORM OF GOVERNMENT.

Hungary has been governed, for some centuries, by the House of Austria, yet it remains a distinct kingdom, with particular laws, magistrates, and privileges. By special treaties, the crown is declared hereditary in that family, and Hungary forms a part of the Austrian states, while the family remains on the throne; in the event of its extinction, the Hungarians would recover their right of election. At his accession, the hereditary prince is installed and crowned king of Hungary, independently of other states subject to his dominion. The coronation has its particular ceremonies, in accordance with the privileges of the nation, and is performed in presence of the states, consisting of the clergy, the noblesse, and the burgesses of the free cities.

Excepting the palatine of the kingdom, who is elected by the states conjointly, the king may dispose of the principal places and offices, but the person nominated must be noble and an Hungarian. He can also grant titles and letters of nobility, and the right of denizenship to noble foreigners. He disposes of all the ecclesiastical benefices, nominates to the abbeys, chapters, bishopricks, and, in the vacancy of any see, has the profits till the next installation. In all matters connected with public instruction, his power seems to be unrestricted. He can declare peace or war, dispose of the military force, and order a levy, in mass, by the nobles (called here an *insurrection*). In other respects, he retains only the executive power, which he is to exercise according to certain forms, with the right of proposing measures adapted to various exigencies. None of the existing laws can be modified, nor can any new law be established, without the consent of the nation. No extraordinary contributions, no levy of troops—in a word, nothing can be done without an assembly of the states, or diet, wherein the clergy, the noblesse, the great officers of state, the chapters, and the free royal cities have the right of sitting, or of being represented.

This numerous assembly, which the king can convoke, prorogue, or dissolve at pleasure, but which must be convened, at least, once in three years, is divided into two chambers. The former, or upper chamber, consists of *magnats*, that is, of the archbishops and bishops, the princes, counts and barons, and the governors of counties. The second comprises the abbots, and others of the higher clergy, with the deputies of the counties, of the chapters, and of the free royal cities, and the representatives of the magnats who cannot attend in person. These two chambers form, in reality, but one body, which has no other interest but that of the nation at large.

In this assembly, all the wants of the state are discussed and provided for. The king is there either in person or by commissioners. His propositions are considered, the levy of troops is fixed upon; the noblesse tax themselves with such charges as war or other circumstances may require. But the king has the right of a negative on the decisions of the diet, nor can any be in force till they obtain his sanction, when they are published in his name throughout the kingdom.

In his exercise of the executive power, the king's organ is a particular council, altogether independent of those which regulate the other parts of the empire. This is called the chancelry of Hungary, is resident at Vienna, and constitutes the first authority of the kingdom. The lieutenancy of the kingdom, or council of state, at Buda, over which the palatine, or viceroy, presides, has the direction of affairs relating to the interior. To this board the chancelry transmits the king's orders, the legality of which it has a right to investigate, and to forward them afterwards to the public functionaries. Every comitat or county has a governor, who corresponds, directly, with this central administration, which, moreover, has under it all that concerns the police, justice, the execution of government orders, and of those of the county.

The administration of the military frontiers depends immediately on the Aulic council of war at Vienna ; every regiment has a commandant, who has under him a number of officers. All business is transacted in a military way, the people being soldiers, though attached to and cultivating the soil.

The legislative code consists of laws enacted under different sovereigns, and accepted, generally, by the states, but various nations or divisions have their particular laws, and certain privileges granted to them separately, but assured to them, subsequently to their union, as a nation. Some among them are entirely governed by the Germanic code. Each of the states of the kingdom, each division of people, and, indeed, every city that has special laws, has its particular magistrates and judges, acting only among themselves : there lies an appeal, however, to the supreme courts, for cases not especially provided for.

With respect to the public revenue, it depends on the produce of the mines, and on the taxes which are levied on individuals, on cattle, on land, and articles of trade. There are no monopolies on the productions of the soil, but the annual contributions fall exclusively on the burgesses of the free towns, and on the peasantry ; the noblesse are exempted, having the right of taxing themselves. The gentlemen, however, contribute towards the temporary taxes fixed by the diet, for extraordinary occasions, as also to the charges of a war, when within the kingdom, and they arm a quota of men proportioned to their estates. Indeed, they are to rise in mass, when called upon by the sovereign, in defence of the state. This obligation was truly burthensome, in the disastrous times, when the Turks were making continual inroads, Hungary being the barrier of Europe against those infidels.

The noblesse enjoy very great privileges; besides holding all the places of public functionaries, being exempt from all the permanent contributions, sitting in the diet, and having a considerable number of votes there, they only are entitled to have lands in possession. The burgesses can only possess landed property within the territories of the free cities, and the peasantry have little other property than their moveables. The Hungarian gentleman is not, however, absolute proprietor of his possessions; in some respects, he has only the usufruct, for on the extinction of male issue, the property reverts to the state, which may dispose of it in favour of another family. Seigniorial lands cannot be sold; they may be mortgaged, and the original proprietor, or his children, may reclaim, on reimbursing the sums advanced. This is attended with an advantage to decayed families, and there are many examples to attest it.

So many privileges exclusively attached to the noblesse, are at variance with the notions now prevalent in most other parts, but the peasant here is not exposed to such inconveniences as might be imagined. There was a time when the Hungarian peasant was really attached to the globe; at present, he is free, and contentment appears in the cottage no less than in the palace. Such is the empire of the laws and of custom, that the peasant's lot in Hungary is often superior to that of the same class in countries that have more freedom. The noblesse have possession of the soil, and the lord is obliged to divide the land into farms of a certain proportion, and these he lets out to peasant cultivators. According to an *urbarium*, published under Maria Theresa, wherein all the customs of long standing were combined into a law, a complete farm was to consist of a mansion, with courts, barns, a garden, a certain number of acres of arable land, (forty-four Parisian) and a smaller for meadows, in the proportion of six to forty-four. The peasant takes a real interest in the soil, but for his location, he pays in daily labour and other services. One who has a complete farm owes to the lord, as services, fifty-four days' labour in a year, with a cart and a double train of horses or oxen. The farmer is also to deliver in annually, the ninth part of the products of the land, (for the first crop only, for if there be a second he pays nothing) the ninth part of his lambs, kids, honey, &c. He has to support other charges fixed and proportioned to different rights which he may acquire. But, if, with permission, he clears a portion of waste land, he pos—

cesses it without services or obligation, and the lord can only resume it by granting a suitable indemnification.

Thus, the Hungarian peasant, in some measure, enjoys the fruits of his labour. He may dispose of eight-ninths of the product of his crops, and he becomes proprietor of moveable goods, flocks, and herds, &c. which pass to his children. In addition to which, if from accident his crops should be lost, or his cattle destroyed, the lord must furnish him with sustenance, and even pay his debts and discharge other engagements, which he may have contracted with the seignior's approbation.

The peasant who has no lands to cultivate, suffers no disparagement on that account. If he dwells in a cottage, the seignior erects it, and supplies materials for its repairs; the service due is eighteen days' labour in a year. If he has a portion of land besides, he contributes the ninth part, either in stock or money, and his service of days' labour is only due when the ground is, at least, one-eighth of what would constitute a complete farm.

On the whole, the condition of the peasant is not inferior to that of many farmers in France.* The impossibility of acquiring land is matter of regret, but the peasant, with some formalities, may become a proprietor in the territory of the free cities.

The seignior is responsible for all that passes on his domain; complaints against the peasants are lodged with him, and he may be sued in the county court, or in the supreme court, for redress. He maintains a sort of police, and some have the right of criminal justice, but nothing is done in an arbitrary

* In the south west parts, the farmer has no landed property, but owes services to the proprietor, from whom he receives annual wages, the rate being invariable, in abundance or scarcity. The farmer receives 200 francs in money, 13 hectolitres (about 1300 English quarts, more or less) of wheat, 16 hectolitres of maize, and 13 of rye; 2 barrels of wine from the press, 1 hectolitre of salt, 20 pounds weight of oil for eating, 20 do. of oil for burning, 6 cart loads of fire wood, and 1 tenement for his family. The whole, taken at a medium, may be valued at from 8 to 900 francs.—These disbursements are indispensable on the part of the proprietor.

These advantages are on the side of the farmer, who seems hereby assured of the means of subsistence, but he has no chances of better fortune derivable from his industry, and is merely a tenant at will. Here the Hungarian peasant has an advantage, for the lord cannot dismiss him from the ground he occupies, except for bad management or conduct. An Hungarian farm, comprising an extent conformable to the urbarium, may be valued at from 15 to 1700 francs. The fifty-four days' labour, and the product of the ninth part, cannot equalize this sum, and in those parts of France where labour is dearest, would not rise to above 500 francs. The clear ninth produce at the highest, would only be from 2 to 500 francs; there would, consequently, be a benefit of from 6 to 700 francs, to be added to the eight-ninths remaining of clear produce, that will belong to the peasant.

manner. In respect to police, every village has a kind of judge, elected in a meeting of the inhabitants, out of three individuals presented by the seignior, and often from among themselves. To enforce execution, unless for causes or offences of minor import, the seignior convenes a court of justice, which pronounces legally on the case, or refers it to the county court.

From the forms of government, and the civil constitution of the kingdom, the principles of which are analogous to those of the most flourishing states, we might expect a high degree of civilization, and are astonished to find the tardy progress of letters, sciences, arts, industry, and commerce. To these, enlightened men of all nations are now directing their attention, and as the Hungarians are no longer in dread of revolutions, their melioration may be looked for. During the last thirty or forty years, the lords have begun to apply themselves to study, endeavouring also to diffuse the means of useful knowledge, and laying out their money to excite a spirit of industry. In this respect much has been done, but much more remains to do, and especially in matters wherein a government may proceed more effectually than individuals. Public instruction is much neglected, and excepting a few establishments which are very inferior to those of other countries, the youth here find it impossible to acquire learning, or even the elements of it, in a correct manner.

In the produce of general industry, the condition of this country is deplorable. With the exception of articles of the first necessity, manufactured in the towns where most of the workmen are Germans, others of almost every kind are imported from Austria. The few manufactures in Hungary are of inferior execution, and altogether inadequate to the consumption. There is reason, however, to hope that a change will take place for the better. There are now some manufactures of cloth, the most considerable of which are at Kaschau and Gacs, in the comitats of Abauj and Nograd. There is one at Œdenburg, on the lake of Neusiedel, where the finest cloths are made, and some, but inferior, at Modern, Tyrnau, and Skalitz; all others are of the coarsest description, and the men employed very few. The comitat of Zips has many manufactures of linen cloth, and this business is carried on also, in the most northerly mountainous parts, and at Kesmarck. There are bleaching grounds at Rosenau, and within a few years some cotton works have been raised, as at Sassin, in the comitat of Nyitra, and at Œdenburg; they have a pretty extensive sale. Fifty or sixty years ago, certain silk works were introduced with much zeal, but the fabrics, and the culture of worms and mulberry trees, are dwindled to an inconsiderable number. A few paper mills are scattered about the country, but the paper is very bad, and the quantity small. At Œdenburg are some brandy distilleries and a sugar house; also works for linseed and turnsol oil, and for snuff and tobacco, which last are in great reputation, and have a sale proportionate. The tanneries are pretty numerous, and their leather, dressed pretty well, forms a considerable article of exportation. The potteries are also pretty numerous; delft ware is made at Buda, Kaschau, Papa, Dotis, and at Holics, on the frontiers of Moravia; this last is a very ancient establishment. At Debreczin are some houses for making common glass, and for making soap; and there are a few alum works, the most valuable of which are in the comitat of Beregh.

If the productions of industry in Hungary are of minor importance, if they are inadequate to the internal consumption, its natural productions more than compensate. These are in such abundance, that the annual exportation is considerable. The dealings, however, in them, are mostly in the hands of foreigners, who, after amassing fortunes, return into their own countries to enjoy them. It gave me pain to find such a number of foreign traders selling their goods as dear as possible, and contriving, by various expedients, to render themselves necessary. This being the case, when are we to see public attention directed to the making of roads, the construction of canals, and rendering the rivers navigable? Several attempts have been made, and projects, at different times, laid before government, so far as to enter on the execution, but from the want of public spirit, or the difficulty of exacting sacrifices from the mercantile class, which are for grasping temporary benefits in preference to future good, most of these improvements have sunk into oblivion, and if actually commenced are now abandoned.

NATURAL PRODUCTIONS.

In respect of these, no country in Europe is more favoured. The abundance is such, compared with the adjacent countries, that we no longer wonder at the old national adage, "Extra Hungariam, non est vita, si est vita, non est ita." "There is no living out of Hungary—or, no living can compare with that in Hungary." In the southern and eastern parts of the Great Plain, the fertility is prodigious; so also on the banks of the Theysse and the banks of the Koros, in the comitats of Temes, of Torontal, Csanad, Bekes, Bacs, Syrmia, &c. But besides these places, grain of every species is cultivated with great advantage in all the southern parts of Hungary, of Transyl-

vania, Sclavonia, and Croatia; and, indeed, wherever the
height of the mountains or encroachment of the forests does
not affect the temperature. In various parts, where corn does
not thrive, they grow barley, rye, oats, and sarrazin, or black
wheat (polygonum fagopyrum). In good years, they export
more than 6,000,000 bushels of wheat into the neighbouring
countries. What would the produce be, if agriculture, which
is here in its infancy, were on a level with that in other
countries ?

Besides the Cereal plants (corn, and maize, &c.) millet and
rice are cultivated in Hungary. Maize is grown on a large
scale, in the Banat, in Croatia, Sclavonia, &c., and in less quantities in almost all the flat country of southern Hungary. In
Transylvania it is the main article of sustenance to the Wallachians and Russniaks, who make a kind of gruel with it; also
crumpets baked in the ashes, and even bread, which would be
pretty good were it rightly prepared. The ears of maize mixed with water, are so dressed as to form a sort of national
meat; it is, in fact, very good eating, and a stranger may
readily use himself to it, although it does not appear at the
tables of the great lords. Millet is generally cultivated in the
same places as maize, but especially in the more southern
parts. As to rice, it is grown in the marshy districts of the
Banat; there are rice plantations also in various other parts.
The baron de Vai had it in contemplation to form rice beds in
the tracts bordering on the three branches of the Koros; a
measure which would add immensely to the culture.

The vineyards of Hungary are in high repute, and their
wines constitute one of the most important branches of their
commerce. The vine is cultivated in all parts of Hungary,
excepting the most northern provinces and the most elevated
situations. The quantity of different wines made and exported into all the adjacent countries is immense. The white
wine of the country of Tokai, about the borders of the Theysse
and the Bodrog, is well known; in point of excellence it ranks
high. But the red wine of Menes, in the comitat of Arad, of
a very different gust, is not at all inferior, and is preferred by
some epicures. Besides these, there are many that have a
well-merited reputation. Such as those of Œdenburg and
Rust, on the lake of Neusiedler, with others too numerous to
quote. In general, Hungary takes the lead even of France,
in the variety of its wines; it has many not unlike our best
Burgundy, from along the Rhone, &c.; also others like our
sweet and our heady wines, but there yet remain others that
have no similitude whatever to any wines, the growth of our
vineyards.

M. Schwartner calculates the value of the annual growth, at a hundred and ten millions of florins, (289,300,000 francs) but he justly observes, that the quantity aimed at for exportation is too considerable, and that where the wines are indifferent it would be better to attend to the culture of grain.

Tobacco is another production of no small importance; its consumption being general throughout the country, and its excellent qualities making it a desirable article of export. No restraints are laid on the cultivation, but to enter Austria, exorbitant duties are imposed. Hence, the peasant can only gain a very moderate profit from his produce. After providing for the internal consumption, he must compound for the surplus with the Austrian officers, who go about the country and often buy up the tobacco before it is ripe.

In Transylvania are large plantations of tobacco, which is in great repute, but whether it be preferable the consumer must decide. Of the different kinds of snuff, those of Transylvania and of Fuzes Gyarmath appear to be the best. Tobacco for smoking is not subject to any very particular process, but the leaves are merely dried and chopped, or reduced to powder. Hereby it escapes that strong scent which the same sort prepared in Austria emits, and it takes an agreeable odour somewhat like the perfume of incense. The snuffs are never black like those in Austria, but take a yellow or chesnut brown colour; they are extremely fine, very piquant, and perfectly free from that ammoniacal smell, incident to snuffs prepared in the other parts of Europe. They are much valued.

The interior consumption of tobacco is immense, for the men almost universally, and youths of fifteen or sixteen, use it to excess. If, at a moderate estimate, we suppose one-third of the population in the use of smoking it, or of taking snuff, and each individual to consume a pound a month, the total would amount to 207,000 metrical quintals, or about 415,000 quintals, fixing the quintals at the ancient pounds of Paris. The exportation is also very considerable, and according to M. Schwartner, amounted, in 1802, to 187,200 quintals (ancient pounds of Paris.)

The immense forests that cover the mountains in the west, north, and east of Hungary, would acquire additional importance and value, were forges erected among them, and roads and canals made for the carriage of their materials. The woods rot in the mountainous parts, while the price is high, and getting dearer every day, in the plains. Besides timber for building and fuel, there would be supplies for the marine, as in those eternal forests of pines, are many straight and very beautiful trees that would serve for masts. But from the improvident management in a number of places, no other advantage is obtained from the wood than burning it to get pot-ash from the cinders.   Thus the major part of the forests, in the higher regions, are lost to the state, and in the lower parts, for want of proper modes of cutting, frightful mutilations and havock take place.   This has been found out too late, and several establishments on the roads, or at the extremities of towns, are in danger of being broken up.

The vast forests of oaks on the tracts less elevated, are serviceable in building, and their acorns feed thousands of hogs, half wild.   Of these we meet with numerous herds, especially in the western parts of the country.   Considerable quantities of gall nuts are also obtained from them, that are mostly used in the tanneries.

From the excellent pasture grounds, especially in the marshy parts of the Great Plain, the rearing of cattle has been much attended to, so as to form an article of exportation.   M. Schwartner reports, that in 1802, 158,600 horned cattle, 536,340 sheep, rams, goats, &c., and 170,068 lambs and kids, were sent out of the country.   The breeding of sheep, among which are many Merinos, has been brought to some perfection. Large quantities of their wool is used in the manufactories, and much also is sent abroad.   According to M. Schwartner, the exportation, in 1802, amounted to 14,278,870 ancient pounds of Paris.   Wrought into cloth, and different woollen stuffs, it finds its way back into Hungary.

The oxen are generally of a large size, their hair grey and smooth, their horns large and well formed, their head square. When fattened, they are allowed to be fine animals.   The horses, however, are small and ill made, and not a little attention is paid to improving the breed.   Many of the lords have particular studs on their lands, but the principal one is that of Mezohegyes, in the comitat of Csanad, established by Joseph II., in 1785.   It is endowed with a territorial domain of 47,350 acres, (Parisian) and never has less than from 8 to 10,000 horses, including stallions of all descriptions.   The superintendent is a colonel, who has under him a major, twelve officers, fifty inferior officers, and two hundred soldiers, with a number of other individuals held in employment.   There is another imperial stud at Babolna, in the comitat of Komorn. These establishments have supplied the army and the opulent classes with good and elegant horses, but the race in general is not meliorated.   The traveller every where meets with horses of an inferior size, that appear to be stunt or not well broke, and such as he would be timorous of making use of. They support fatigue, however, much better than animals of superior make and appearance. They are allowed to drink largely of water when heated ; a practice contrary to what prevails in other European countries.

As to fruits of every kind, plants, useful in the arts and for sustenance, game, poultry, fresh-water fish, Hungary yields to no country in these respects. The mineral kingdom also teems with immense resources, and the lofty mountains that encircle it on all sides, contain in their bowels riches of various kinds.

The gold and silver mines of Hungary and Transylvania, are the only ones in Europe of fixed and stable importance, and till the discovery of Peru, Mexico, and Brazil, were held of prime consideration. The well-known mines of Schemnitz and Kremnitz, with those of Kapnick, Nagy Banya, Voros Patack, and others, are still worked to great advantage, but it is not easy to appreciate their positive annual value. Their products, in times past, have been immense, but whether it is from negligence or a gradual impoverishment, the gains are greatly reduced. Besides these, wherein the metals are found in masses and veins, gold dust is collected in Transylvania, in pretty large quantities. There are also golden sands gathered in the river of Aranyos, (the word denotes bearing gold) which empties its waters into the Maros. And authors mention the Szamos, the Lapos, in the north of Transylvania, together with the Nera, in the Banat.

But besides these precious metals, Hungary contains copper mines of great importance, and indeed the richest in Europe; those of Oravitza, Moldava, and others, in the Banat; those of Iglo, Dobschau, Smolnitz, Herrengrund, Libethen, &c. in Hungary. Iron mines abound, and the mineral, from its excellent nature and quality, may be compared with that of Sweden or Norway. But the mining works are not sufficiently numerous or considerable, and are far, indeed, from answering the internal consumption, large sums being sent out of the country for this article. Some few mines of quicksilver are to be found, particularly at Szlana, in the comitat of Gomor, but the quantity extracted is small.

Salt is one of the most important mineral productions of Hungary. It abounds very much in the eastern parts of the kingdom ; considerable masses of it are formed in the centre of Transylvania, in the comitats of Torda, Klausenburg, &c. An immense depot is also found on the northern frontiers of that province, in the comitat of Marmaros, but its situation is so remote that but little is supplied to the internal consumption. The salt mines of Poland interfere with the exportation northwards, and those of Salzburg and Salz Kammergut, from their proximity to Austria, must operate against it. The quantity of salt employed in trade annually, may be rated at 1,200,000 quintals, ancient weight of Paris. This mineral substance is every where a royal right ; no individual can go to work for it on his own account, and provision can only be made from the large depots established in different places by the government. But the price, a matter of general import, is always fixed in the assembly of the states, where nothing that can contribute to the public welfare escapes attention.

There are several other salt beds or pans in Hungary, of more or less value, where salt is found, in solution, in the waters of the marshes and lakes about the vast plains of the country. In the heat of summer, the salt effloresces on the surface of the soil, and large quantities are gathered of it. Nitre (natron) is also produced in a great number of places, and especially in the eastern parts of the Great Plain. In the comitat of Bihar alone, more than 5000 metrical quintals are collected annually, most of which is employed in the manufacture of soap, particularly in the town of Debretzin. Saltpetre is gathered, in considerable quantities, on the surface of the pasture grounds, in the comitats of Szabolcs, Bihar, &c. In 1802, 3500 metrical quintals were obtained, and the produce would be much more considerable, should the wants of the State require it. The sulphate of soda, and the sulphate of magnesia, are found in the same places, and very large quantities might be procured, were it demanded for internal consumption.

During the last thirty years, attention has been attracted to a particular production, till then altogether unknown, certain alum rocks, perfectly resembling those of Tolfa, in the Roman States. These, under the management of M. Derczeny, of Dercsen, have already yielded excellent produce, and in tolerable abundance, not only sufficient for the manufactures of the country, but for exportation to Austria. The principal places where this valuable mineral appears, are in the mountains of the comitat of Beregh. It is found also at Parad, in the comitat of Heves, but it is there so blended with Pyrites, that the produce is much diminished by it.

Mines of pit coal would form a very desirable acquisition, but the country seems rather destitute in this respect, whatever may be asserted to the contrary by a French author, Marcelle de Serres, in his travels into the empire of Austria, in 1814. The only coal pits accurately ascertained, and where men are at work, are in the comitat of Barany, near Funfkirchen on one side, and at Egregy and Siklos on the other. Those near Funfkirchen are the only pits where the works are followed up with a certain regularity and advantage. The produce is absorbed in the circumjacent parts, or is conveyed to Pest, where it is chiefly in use with whitesmiths and blacksmiths. All other depots of mineral coaly matter, passing under the name of steinkohle or earth coal, consist of lignite, a coaly substance which contains no bitumen like coal, never swells or puffs when heated, is often difficult to set fire to, and diffuses an unpleasing odour. It is a remnant of wood that has lain buried in the earth, in ancient revolutions of the globe, and the woody texture is occasionally very apparent. Many vestiges of this combustible have been discovered in different parts of Hungary, but there are few places where it has become an object of regular labours. At Wandorf, near Œdenburg, large quantities are produced, chiefly for transport to Vienna. It is, however, highly probable that this mineral combustible might be worked, in a great number of places hitherto unexplored, and with obvious advantage. The mines of Sari Sap, at a little distance from Gran and Pest, are deserving of notice, from their situation in a part of Hungary where wood is getting scarce and dear.

Among other minerals, opal, which for ages has been the peculiar produce of this country, should not be omitted. Of late years, indeed, equatorial America has furnished samples of it for commerce. Opal is particularly found in the groupe of mountains that stretch from Tokai to Eperies, and it is about half a day's journey N. W. of the town of Kaschau, near the village of Cservenitza, that mining works have been carried on for centuries. This substance is discovered in several other places, but it no where else presents that life and vivacity of colours that make it in request with the jeweller, and so highly enhance its value. Ancient authors have recorded, and more recent authors have repeated, that emeralds, beryls, topazes, rubies, hyacinths, and lapis lazuli, have been found in the Carpathian mountains, but neither in my excursions, nor in the collections that I visited, could I trace any vestiges of such. I am of opinion that opal is the only fine or precious stone that Hungary affords.

There are mineral waters, in various parts, that have acquired celebrity in a greater or less degree. Some are hot, others cold; some are purely acid like those of Seltz, others are both acid and ferrugineous, acid and sulphureous. Some are used for bathing in, others for drinking. Those most frequented, and in the highest vogue, are at Bartfeld, in the comitat of Saros, at Lublo, in that of Zips, at Trentsen, Eisenbach, Glasshutte, about Schemnitz, and at Fared, on the borders of the lake Balaton. These are the principal, but there are other waters that require only a more agreeable situation

dle of the mountains of Tryberg, I beheld with pleasure, the
first waters of the Danube at their source; the course of the
river I was afterwards to pursue, though at a great distance.
At Riedlingen, the hilly country ceases, and all appearances
announce our entering into plains.

The vast plains of Bavaria, the soil of which is covered with
sand and calcareous fragments, reminded me of the plains of
Switzerland, of which they form a continuation. They are
only separated by hills of no great height, which mark the
division of the waters between the Danube and the Rhine.
The Bavarian plains are bordered by the same calcareous matters, as form the two sides of the great valley of Switzerland.

After crossing these plains very rapidly, I proceeded towards
Salzburg, intending, by the way, to take a view of the salt
mines, which constitute the riches of that country. From
Munich to Peiss, along the route of Rosenheim, we travel
throughout in a plain that has no undulations, but the country
rises gently afterwards, and we pass over a long ridge of hills,
in general, richly clothed with vegetation, and presenting
aspects extremely diversified. The lake of Chiem, which is
not less than ten leagues in circumference, and which we coast
along, in passing from Rosenheim to Traunstein, has a fine
effect, as surveyed with the hills that surround it.

At Traunstein, the town on the top of a hill pretty lofty, and
the immense buildings of salt works at the foot of it, communicating with the town by covered escaliers, (staircases) erected
on the slope of the hill, exhibit a total not a little striking, and
which, from the heights that border the lake of Chiem, on the
east, are truly picturesque. The buildings for the works, and
the large toll-house on the Traun, by which wood is conveyed
into the timber yards, must necessarily arrest the attention of
every traveller who would investigate the nature of great commercial establishments. There is an admirable order in the
management; the salt water is brought from Reichenhall, and
from Berchtesgaden, ten leagues distant, over two chains of
very high mountains, by machines and pumps at regular distances. The water is finally brought into an immense reservoir in the centre of the buildings, for evaporating it by fire.
Round the reservoir are eight large coppers and immense warehouses over them. The furnaces are very well constructed,
and the combustible materials are husbanded with exact
economy.

From the toll-house is a little causeway, and a very agreeable path that leads towards Reichenall. Advancing towards
Itzel, the hills get higher, and beyond that village are moun-

tains much higher still. Towards Reichenhall, the country assumes an aspect altogether wild, and the valleys are intersected with rocky precipices perpendicularly steep.

Along the road across the mountains, between Itzel and Reichenhall, we meet with a number of aqueducts that convey the salt water to Traunstein, as also conveyances of fresh water passing in an opposite direction. The machines and pumps are numerous, and are worked with singular precision. A machine does not occupy a space of more than four feet square, but the movements are executed with such punctuality and facility, that you scarcely hear the noise of the piston and suckers of the pump within it, at the distance of a few feet ; a person outside can form no idea of the enormous effort that is exerted. The engineer that constructed these works is M. Reichenbach, of Munich, the author of many other ingenious inventions.

The object of my excursion to Berchtesgaden was to visit the salt mine. The director could not accompany me himself, but sent me his secretary as a guide. The entrance to the galleries is at a little distance from the town. I was rather surprised to see the miners bring me a white cassock, like a combing cloth, being accustomed, in all my previous visits to mines, to throw a black cloth over me ; a large bougie was next put into my hands, in lieu of a miner's lanthorn. Those who accompanied me had the same costume ; thus accoutred, each with a bougie in his hand, and his tunic on his back, we marched in procession into the mines. They led me to all the windings, remarking on every interesting particular, and attending, with infinite complaisance, to all my goings and comings, so that I had every opportunity of studying the nature and variations of this depot that I could desire.

My first views encountered an argilous matter, replete with fissures, filled occasionally with veins or nests of salt. I came next to a mass of salt, very potent and nearly in a pure state ; we pursued the track of this down to the deepest part of the labours, it growing purer and purer as we proceeded. This mass is reduced to powder, and detached portions are conveyed into reservoirs, where, by solution, the salt is cleared of its earthy particles. The water is then made to pass to Reichenhall and Traunstein, for evaporation.

The interior of the saline regions of Berchtesgaden, cannot but prove interesting to any that would study the nature and structure of those depots of ancient seas, but I experienced also, the satisfaction of a general traveller, in surveying the most beautiful scenery imaginable.

After passing through a long gallery, we came to one of those

vast cavities from which large quantities of salt had already
been extracted.   It was a sort of subterraneous gulf, but
then it was illuminated by the miners through its whole outline, and even in the sinuosities of its deepest recesses.   A
glimmering light was every where visible, but not clear enough
to distinguish objects ; this cast a mysterious air over the
whole, so as to form a scene truly magical.   The effect was
still more imposing, from being blended with terror, when I
catched a glimpse of the steep walls of the surrounding precipices, with the ladders and machines for drawing up the salt.
The view was tremendous and enchanting, and produced a
sensation, of which no description can convey an adequate
idea.

. Quitting Berchtesgaden, I proceeded next for Hallein.   The
entrance of the galleries was at Durnberg, where I arrived in a
direct course, though I was obliged to pass to Hallein, to get
leave of the directors to visit them.   Hallein lies in the bottom
of a valley, the descent to which is very rapid, by a way cut
out of the abrupt declivities of the mountain ; to a stranger it
has a very picturesque effect.   The district no longer forms a
part of Bavaria, having been lately ceded to Austria.   At
Durnberg, the master miner had, by appointment, agreed to
accompany me.

This entrance is by an horizontal gallery, lined with solid
walls, in all the first advances ; afterwards we come to a timber
wainscoting, and then appear masses of saliferous argile, solid
enough not to require supports or props.   In the midst of
these argilous walls, we see pretty large portions of pure salt,
grey or reddish.

I had not at Hallein the view of an illumination as rich as
at Berchtesgaden, but by the light of their little lamps, the eye
could trace a number of large lakes, on which are conveyed the
saline substances, dug up by the workmen.   These lakes were
thirty-two in number ; I launched into the middle of one of
them, on the same *radeau* as had served the emperor Francis.
At the time of that monarch's visit ; the whole area was lighted
up with great magnificence, and to judge from the space which
the lamps occupied, the scenery so enlightened, and shining
with so great a lustre, must have been very imposing.

One particularity attached to the works of Hallein, is the
inclined planes on which we glide to pass from the higher to
the lower galleries.   The number of these is considerable, and
much of the time is spent in the exercise.   It may seem strange
that we thus glide, pretty rapidly, in an obscure path, over declivities of from eighty to one hundred feet in length, holding
a bougie in one hand, and the rope which serves for a guide in

the other. The old miner that conducted me was in a transport of joy to see me move along as nimbly as himself. These miners, in general, expect to receive money from visiters, but when a stranger takes an interest in their labours, converses freely with them, and shuns no difficulties, betrays no fears in following them, they redouble their efforts to satisfy and inform.

After sliding thus a long time, from top to bottom, we arrive at a large gallery, whence there is a way to get out. There we find miners with little wheel-barrows, that bring us up to day light in a quarter of an hour, though to pass on foot would require thirty-five minutes.

This long gallery, partly dug or hollowed in the saliferous mass, and partly in the calcareous, exhibited a phenomenon rather unusual. We should naturally look for moisture as an attendant on the saline substances, and if dryness could be supposed any where, should expect to find it in marbles or calcareous masses, but here the effects are directly the reverse. In the interior parts it is quite dry, where the congeries of salt appears, but the calcareous masses are found to be every where dropping. Two causes may be assigned for this; one, that the argilous mass, which in some measure incloses the salt, is not easy to be penetrated by water, which slides over it till it finds a vent or issue; another, that what little of moisture penetrates, is firmly retained by the argile as well as by the salt, and cannot leak or run out. But a calcareous mass, even the most compact, will easily let water filter through it; and, besides, it is sure to contain a great number of fissures.

While I was at Hallein, I made an excursion to the valley of Salza, surveying the adjoining mountains with the eye of a geologist; on my return, I took the straight road for Vienna. I passed through Salzburg some days after a calamitous event which was every where the subject of conversation. A dreadful conflagration had destroyed eighty-eight houses in the city, together with the superb Chateau Mirabella, which had been ever recommended as an object of curiosity to strangers; also four churches, and the little village of Frosheim. While the inhabitants of this latter were affording their assistance in the city, their own dwellings had become a prey to the flames. The prospect from the mountain of Monchsberg, in the neighbourhood, is magnificent, exhibiting the whole country like a map to the eye of an observer. The landscape was beautiful in itself, but to me was clouded by the smoking ruins that tinged it with a sombrous hue.

After passing through Molk, St. Polten, and Burkersdorf, we enter the plains of Vienna. Here are many pleasant villages that announce our approach to a great city. We leave the imperial palace of Schonbrunn, which contributed not a little to improve the prospect on our right. The day of my arrival was a holiday, and the road was thronged with caravans going and coming with great rapidity, sometimes containing not less than twenty passengers; they raised terrible clouds of dust, which intercepted the sight at a few paces distance. I reached the barriers at length, and proceeding through the suburbs, which took up half an hour, I entered the city. Upwards of an hour was spent in the search of an apartment with furnished lodgings; the hotels and auberges were full, or otherwise not to my taste, and I at last accepted the recommendation of my postillion, who removed me to Leopoldstadt, one of the suburbs, in an island of the Danube. Here I found suitable accommodations, and regretted that I had not followed his advice sooner.

The city of Vienna, (Wien, Germ. Vindobona, and Vienna, Lat. Bets, Hung.) stands on the right bank of the Danube, in a pleasant situation, lat. 48°, 12′, 40″, N. long. 17°, 32′, 30″, E. of London, and about 413 feet above the level of the sea. Some authors trace its origin to a village of the Windes or Wendes, in the same place, the name of which must have been Windewohn, a dwelling of the Wendes, whence the Romans made Vindobona. Others assert that it took the name of Fabiana, or Faviana, from a Roman governor named Fabius, or from a king of the Rugians named Fava, the word being afterwards corrupted to Viana, and then to Vienna.

At Vienna we must make a distinction between the city and the suburbs. The city occupies but a very small space, and is surrounded with fosses and fortifications. As it includes the ordinary residence of the court, and is the centre of all the public offices, and the seat of commercial transactions, it naturally becomes the most populous. The streets are extremely narrow, the houses very high, and the whole population is exceedingly straitened. Though the number of palaces, hotels, and superb buildings is more considerable, in proportion, than in any other great city, the aspect of the whole seems dark and melancholy, breathing an air of austerity beyond the common standard of German gravity.*

The suburbs are much more extensive, and infinitely more agreeable; the houses are more spacious, less crowded together, the streets wider, and the gardens are in great numbers, diffusing a gay appearance over the whole. The suburbs

---

* According to an average observation of the barometer, of 17 years, at the mean temperature of 12°, 5′, 8″, for the mercury, and 10° for the air, it will be at 0m, 7478. The hall of the observatory, wherein the barometer is fixed, is at 55″ above the confluence of the Vienne and the Danube.

form a sort of rural district to the city, and there, at the return of fine weather, the great lords, who have erected magnificent palaces with delightful gardens, spend a part of the summer. There is also a considerable number of handsome public buildings, such as the school of surgery, the polytechnic school, with numerous churches, among which is that of St. Charles, considered as the finest in Vienna. There are several very pleasing promenades, in the midst of parterres, wherein the vegetation is rich and abundant, the city affording nothing of the kind.

But notwithstanding these advantages, there are also inconveniences, which no doubt will be removed hereafter, but at present are disagreeable. In the suburbs, the principal streets only are paved, and the rest, in winter or rainy weather, are covered with mud. The boulevard, which we pass over to enter into the city, is also filled with it ; add to which, that in summer, in the dry weather, we are scorched by the sun, and stifled with dust.

The suburbs have all been raised since 1684; those prior to that period were destroyed, in 1683, at the approach of the Turkish army, during the revolt of count Tekeley, in Hungary.

They have not always made a part of the city ; several formed distinct villages, till Joseph II. incorporated them with Vienna. They have been since increasing rapidly, and an extensive line drawn round the city would take in about 6000 houses and 180,000 souls ; the city alone may have 1400 houses, and 46,000 inhabitants. The suburbs are thirty-three in number ; the principal and most beautiful are Leopoldstadt, Wachringergasse, Alvergasse, Josephstadt, Maria Hulf, Wieden, and Landstrasse. The Prater, the finest promenade in Vienna, and perhaps in Europe, is in Leopaldstadt. It is a sort of magnificent forest at the gates of the city, in a large island of the Danube ; it is more than a league in length, and half a league wide, and contains oaks, beech, lime, and chesnut trees, all of a superior description. Superb avenues, with flowery meadows on each side, have been cut through it, interrupting the monotony which the thickness of the foliage would occasion, and giving animation to the scene. A multitude of booths and little *auberges* are scattered in various directions, forming detached hamlets, exhibiting spectacles, games, horsemanship, &c. The Prater is, in summer, the rendezvous of the whole town, and when enlivened by a crowd of splendid equipages, by the gay assemblage of the population, diversified with Turks, Greeks, Armenians, Jews, &c. all in their national costume, the traveller of sensibility will feel himself highly gratified.

If Vienna, in its interior, presents few attractions, this must be attributed to the height of the houses and the narrowness of the streets, for there are few cities, and especially fortified cities, that contain, in proportion, so great a number of palaces, hotels, and genteel buildings. These are mostly of pretty recent construction; few, or none, however, display any thing remarkable in their architecture. The imperial palace is an immense structure, but having been enlarged at different periods, there is little of symmetry in the exterior, and its general appearance falls below the idea that one would form for the mansion of a great Sovereign. Certain parts of it look beautiful, and others have an air of imposing grandeur, but here, as throughout Vienna, every thing is crowded; the palace is concealed on one side, by the houses of the town, and by the rampart on the other; nor is there any other entrance or egress than by arcades that are necessarily public, and of course generally encumbered with carriages and foot passengers. Among the churches, that of St. Stephen is well deserving of attention; its architecture is a beautiful Gothic. The spire, which is not so high as that of Strasburg, but bolder and higher than any in Paris, is 414 feet above the level of the pavement.

Within the city, the number of places or public squares is pretty considerable, but they are, for the most part, irregular, and thronged with little stalls of hucksters. In their centre appear fountains and monuments, but often overcharged with ornaments, and generally in a bad taste. The place Joseph may be considered as one of the courts of the Chateau; it has an air of dignity which would be greatly enhanced were it more spacious. The statue of Joseph II., which occupies the centre, is frigid, and not without its imperfections; it adds, however, to the embellishments of the place.

The houses of Vienna are mostly of bricks or timber; buildings of any consequence are of stone. Some are of a particular free-stone, greyish or yellowish, of which I observed a series of mountains, previous to my reaching Vienna. Others are of calcareous, coquiliferous stones, from the borders of the lake of Neusiedel, in Hungary, and resembling those most in use at Paris. The streets are pretty well paved; on each side are causeways for foot passengers, consisting of large flags of grey granite, from Saiblingstein, on the banks of the Danube. The middle of the street is of grey-coloured free-stone, partly brought from Burkersdorf, where I had occasion to notice some quarries, and partly from other points of the same mountains.

In treating of Vienna, I must not omit mentioning their mode of paving under coach gateways. In lieu of stones, they nee cubes of wood, placed one beside another as in ordinary pavements, so that the edges of the wood lie vertical. In this way, a carriage passing under the gate makes no shaking or harsh noise, as when the paving consists of stones. Fir is the timber employed, and this sort of pavements will last for a long time.

The number of hotels with furnished lodgings, is not considerable at Vienna, which seems rather unaccountable, considering the vast influx of strangers. In the very heart of the city the accommodations are not the most inviting, and a stranger feels little inclination to stop there. But in the auberges of the suburbs it is otherwise, and the terms reasonable; in this respect, Leopoldstadt may be recommended for a traveller who means to make only a short stay. The air is salubrious, and the Prater is nigh at hand, where, every day the promenade is respectable, and on Sundays it is thronged with all the various classes of society. In most of the auberges you may have your meals, either in your own apartment or at a common table. But these meals are regularly from twelve to two, and from eight to ten; nothing can be had in the intervals, unless previously ordered. The auberges where liquor only is to be had, are distinguished by a bundle of shavings, moulded into the form of a bell; those, where eating is provided, are noted by a bunch of fir. Some of the *traiteurs* are in very great vogue, and there are many coffee-houses; some are pretty well furnished, and here all the voluminous gazettes of the German States may be read. One particular, incommoding to a stranger, is, that the hackney coaches, which are pretty numerous and ready at hand, either for town or country, are subject to no fixed prices, so that you must agree with them beforehand, or you may expect disagreeable altercations.

Such is the general outline that I sketched of Vienna, during the short time of my residence, going through and returning. As to the various institutions, such as the university, the academy of surgery, the gymnasia, the polytechnic school, the academy of commerce, that of the fine arts, the normal school, the academy of oriental languages, the general seminary, the institution for deaf and dumb, the hospitals, the establishments of a benevolent description, of which there are many that do great honour to the inhabitants, and some to the care of government, I had no time to examine or treat of in detail, inspecting some very rapidly, and others not at all. In general, I may remark, that, as to the primary bases of instruction, it appears less forward here than in other parts of Germany. The polytechnic school has no resemblance to ours; it is limited to providing a certain number of young persons with instruction merely elementary in the arts and commerce, so far as to construct plans, and in the practical parts of stone cutting; these extend also to chemistry, physics, natural history, as connected with the arts and commerce, also to history, geography, and the languages. The plan of this establishment is more assimilated to that of our schools of arts and trades, but is more comprehensive.

Vienna, in its aggregate, contains very numerous collections of every description. The imperial library adjoining the Chateau, passes for the most considerable in Europe; report assigns to it more than 300,000 volumes, (the royal library in Paris has more than 500,000) also a great number of MSS., and of samples in the art of printing, from 1435 to 1500. The apartments wherein these valuable assemblages are deposited, are very suberb, and if there is any thing objectionable, it is the superfluity of gildings, marbles, paintings, and other articles of luxury. The cabinet of antiques and medals is also in the imperial palace, together with the museum of natural history, the present director general of which is M. Schreibers. This establishment is very rich in minerals, many from Hungary, also in shells, marine polypi, &c.

The gallery of paintings at the Belvidere, on the Rennweg, has an immense collection of works of all the different schools; it was first formed by Joseph II., and has been gradually increasing since. There are very capital paintings in the different churches; these have also their mausolea, the most remarkable of which is that erected by duke Albert de Saxe Teschen, in 1805, to the memory of his wife, the archduchess Maria Christina. This monument is in the church of the Augustins, adjoining the palace; it was executed by Canova; the whole has an air of dejection and grief so natural, that the sympathising spectator cannot but follow the figures, slowly moving, as it were, to the tomb.

At a little distance from the Belvidere, in the Rennweg, is the botanic garden, belonging to the university. It is under the management of the baron Jacquin, son of the botanist to whom we are indebted for the Flora of Schonbrunn. The number of rare plants is not very great, but the establishment is very well adapted for the instruction of the students.

Besides the collections of a public character, there are a great number that belong to individuals. Indeed, there are few cities wherein a taste for the arts is more generally diffused among the opulent classes. There are collections of paintings, of statues, of antiquities, but a great deficiency of those in natural history. M. Vondernull has a collection of mineralogy, of which M. Mohs has published a descriptive catalogue ; another also of precious stones, cut and polished. This last has been since sold to count Archinto.

The environs of Vienna are, in general, agreeable. We find scattered around, elegant villas, chateaux, palaces, surrounded with the richest vegetation, in situations the most picturesque, and abounding with natural curiosities. For further descriptions of Vienna and its environs, I must refer the reader to the work of M. Marcel de Serres, on the Austrian monarchy, who has handled this subject with very considerable detail, and to other authors.

Some notice may be taken, however, of the imperial palace of Schonbrusur, the park of which especially merits the attention of naturalists, from the immense number of plants distributed throughout its numerous inclosures. This is partly owing to the munificence and special care of the reigning emperor, who is not a little attached to the study of nature. Occasionally the traveller will see foreign birds fluttering about the plants of their natal soil, though generally confined in cages. The menagerie is not very rich in animals, though superior to that at Paris. At Schonbrunn are also the Alpine collections of the Archduke John. The archdukes, the archduchesses, and the emperor himself, are frequently occupied in the investigation of the objects of natural history.

The imperial chateau of Lachsenburg, excites an interest of another kind, in the variety of its objects of fancy. Here are temples and pavilions of curious foreign architecture, also buildings and their furniture, throughout, in the rustic style, with village fishing and farming. One building, called the House of Caprice, is singular in its architecture, and in its odd and grotesque contents, some of which are so contrived as to be rather mischievous. But the most striking object, at Lachsenburg, is the little Gothic castle, built by the present emperor, on the model of the castle of Ambras, in the Tyrol, which is as old as the fifteenth century. It forms a truly curious picture of a castle of the middle ages, giving a complete idea of chivalresque manners, monuments, furniture, &c.

The chateau of Dornbach has a very delightful park, and that of Schœnau, two posts from Vienna, contains the famous temple of night, the descriptions of which resemble those of the palaces of the fairies. About Vienna are not a few neat villages, with elegant houses and chateaux, more or less remarkable, where a stranger may entertain himself during the fair season, amidst a profusion of materials, accumulated by art and caprice.

In one of my excursions as a mineralogist, I came to Sifring to survey two quarries, from which vast quantities of stones had been taken, so as to lay open the composition of the interior soil. I remarked there, in prodigious quantities, the remains of plants and vegetables, that had changed their nature and become a carbonaceous substance.

One object of my staying a little longer at and about Vienna, was to make preparations for my journey into Hungary. I wished to procure such maps and descriptive notices as were not to be had in Paris. I expected to find in the learned bodies and their collections, new documents respecting the country I intended to visit. But herein I was greatly disappointed; at Vienna the information was as defective as at Paris, and, besides, strong prejudices existed against the people and country. Many were for prepossessing me with groundless apprehensions for my personal safety, but I had formed my resolution, and could account, from history, for a kind of national antipathy in the Austrians, the result of so many ages of incessant wars. To this I also attribute certain incivilities, on the part of the police, when I made known my intentions of proceeding into Hungary. Recent circumstances might have inspired some distrust of the French name, but all difficulties vanished on addressing myself to the higher officers, and I met with nothing but complaisance and facilities. M. le Comte de Caraman, French ambassador at Vienna, demanded himself the passports I should require, at the Hungarian chancelry, and procured also, from the chamber of mines, the necessary orders for my entering and inspecting the mines of the state.

CHAPTER II.

JOURNEY FROM VIENNA.

I quitted Vienna, May 26, 1818, but difficulties lay in my way in passing through the barriers. A clerk stopped the carriage, and asked a number of questions, and when, in reply, I assured him that I had come from Paris, and meant to travel through Hungary, he repeatedly exclaimed, striking his head in astonishment, " Von Paris, nach Ungarn ! From Paris to Hungary !" To the Austrians, Hungary is tantamount to Siberia. The clerk, after examining my ample papers, added, " How learned this gentleman must be !" and after asking if Dominus Magnificus, in the passport, was my Christian name, to which I gravely answered in the affirmative, I was allowed to proceed on my journey.

For a long time, we pass over a plain in pretty good cultivation; the islands of the Danube skirt the horizon on the north, and with the forests that cover them, serve to amuse the traveller in his passage. In front are the Laita Mountains, stretching from N. W. to S. E., and in some measure connecting the Carpathian mountains with those of Styria. In the neighbourhood of Peternel, in the middle of the fields, we perceive the remains of a triumphal arch, attributed to the Romans. I arrived at Presburg towards night.

The city of Presburg (Posonium Lat. Posony, Hung.) is one of the most considerable of Hungary. Though at the frontier extremity of the kingdom, it was long the seat of government, while the Turks were in possession of Buda, or in a condition to threaten its security. It is generally considered as having been founded prior to the time of the Romans, from whom, however, it derived the name of Pisonium, or Posonium. Presburg is pleasantly situated on the left bank of the Danube, which is here about 270 feet in width. It is tolerably well built; there are many good houses, and some large buildings, called palaces, among which the palace Batyani is undoubtedly the most magnificent, though unfortunately pent up among other buildings. The churches are in a plain style, but appear very neat in the interior. The streets are mostly narrow, and often turning; they are paved, but not well, in the town, and in the suburbs are only causeways on one side next the houses; the middle is a channel, very muddy in rainy weather, and in dry seasons nauseating and stifling from the dust.

The castle royal, destroyed, in part, by a conflagration, stands on a gentle eminence, on a bank of the Danube, and is commonly considered as the first promontory of the great chain of the Carpathians. Its height above the Danube is about 180 feet. The castle is large and well built, but has nothing remarkable in its architecture. There is a fine view from the mount on which the castle stands, but misty weather prevented me from entirely commanding it.

At Vienna, I had heard so much of the harsh treatment strangers experience in Hungary, that I was not without apprehensions, when one of the town servants brought me an order to appear before the police. These were dissipated when I presented myself before a magistrate, who, with the greatest civility, assured me that my reception, as a stranger, would be every where agreeable. In fact, I witnessed the noblest hospitality on the part of the gentlemen, and an interesting affability in all classes of the people.

I quitted Presburg by the road of Posing, having on the right a very large plain, well cultivated, and the primitive

mountains on the left.   Near Posing is a vein of quartz, producing gold ; at Malaszka is one of antimony, and near it another of gold and silver ; all of these have been worked.   Those
of silver or gold are similar to what is yielded by the primitive
earths at Botza, in the comitat of Lipté, but cannot be compared with those of the country of Schemnitz, which are in a
soil very different, marked with particular characters, only to
be found, elsewhere, in the mines of the New World.

The lower parts of these mountains, from Presburg to beyond Posing, are covered with vineyards that produce very
good wine, known by the name of St. George ; together with
the wines of Buda and Œdenburg, it passes at Vienna for one
of the best of ordinary wines.

Having reached Moderna, I quitted the road that leads to
Moravia, for that of Tyrnau.   Travelling in this direction was
unpleasant ; it was over a flat not very fertile, extending on
the west and south as far as the horizon, and bounded on the
north by very distant mountains.

Tyrnau is a small but pretty handsome town.   I was struck
with the air of neatness that pervaded all the houses, which
had been lately white-washed, and the window-blinds painted
green.   Though not really better than cottages, their appearance was sprightly and gay.   There are several churches ; at
some distance nothing appears but steeples, which gives an
air to the place of being much more populous, and hence, it
has been called Little Rome.   The streets are wide and kept
clean ; there is a good choice of inns, but I had been recommended to the best, the Black Eagle, in the Place, or Market,
fronting a large street, at the end of which we discover some
part of the buildings of the university.

Leaving Tyrnau, I had to cross plains where the road serpentines, so as frequently to appear diverting us from the
object intended.   Perhaps my guide had lost the road, but this
he would not acknowledge; I was six hours, however, in
reaching Freystadt, (Galgotz, Hung.) a distance of only four
leagues.   Here, after crossing the Vag, we find along the
water side a very agreeable promenade, on the declivity of a
hill which has a castle on its summit.   The situation was delightful, and formed a contrast with the dreary plain I had just
been traversing.

At Freystadt I noticed a considerable magazine of mill-
stones, conveyed from the quarries of Konigsberg.   Leaving
Freystadt, I had to travel up and down hill, with no shelter
from the sun, and afterwards through a wood, where the shade
was doubly refreshing.   I then reached a point of view where
the city of Nyitra lay in a sort of basin below.   It was pleasant

to see an end of this day's toil, for I had been partly on foot and was fatigued, yet had my doubts as to readily procuring lodgings in one of the great cities of Hungary.

In less than half an hour I had reached Nyitra. I came first to the suburb of the Jews, called the Judenstadt, but from old prejudices, was averse to stopping in a Jewish *auberge*, and passed on to look out for one in the town. I entered one of very decent appearance, the Golden Stag, but the master, after eyeing me from head to foot, assumed a theatrical air, exclaiming, that he neither could nor would provide me with a chamber. I then, in my turn, with a lofty demeanour, planted myself in the house, sending my servant out for the judge. In the interval, by shewing these people my port folio, and other parts of my paraphernalia, they found me a chamber, and brought into it a dry mattrass, and an enormous pillow that was to serve for a covering; no bed-clothes. When I asked for some, and a pullet for my supper, the house became a scene of uproar, which was only terminated by the arrival of the judge. This gentleman, on inspecting the large seals of my passport, and my relays of assignation, *(forchepan)* took his hat off, with many tokens of respect, and seriously reprimanding my landlord, departed. The latter then was all civility and complaisance.

In general, throughout Hungary, a person that arrives on foot is but little considered. The reason is, that the lords, the public functionaries, and all that are provided with relays of assignation, have a right, on payment of a small sum, to be conducted by the peasants, who are obliged to furnish a carriage and horses. Hence, it so happens, that one who can afford to eat a pullet is rarely a foot traveller. The peasants are accustomed to it, being inured to a hard life. In entering an auberge, they do not even ask for a chamber or a stable to sleep in ; if they do not find some corner on the ground floor, they throw themselves down in the middle of the court, wrapped up in their bunda. This is a large pelisse made of sheep skin, and their only clothing in summer and winter. In cold weather, they turn the woollen side inward, and the contrary in warm weather. They even prefer this covering to any other. A person travelling in a carriage is every where well received and entertained. This is the case with such as travel in hay-carts, which is very common in Hungary, even with the great lords.

The reception I had met with, insensibly gave me a dislike to the town ; it has, however, some fine houses, and it lies in a very pleasant situation on the side of a hill.

My next object was to make an excursion to the mountains

of Gimes.   When I came to the village, it was only with a
Jew that I could have a small chamber, and that not in the
neatest order.   Observing a capital house at some little distance, I recollected the advice given me by the magistrate of
Presburg, and was not long in introducing myself.   It was the
mansion of the count de Forgacs, lord of the district, who received me in the kindest manner, inviting me to stay with him
while I was exploring the parts adjacent.

Hungary is a country that its neighbours are ever misrepre-
senting, and we have, in France, notions not much in its favour.   The lords, however, are in general very well informed,
speaking several languages, and the French habitually, which,
indeed, is usually the language of good society.   But their
distinguishing characteristic is a noble politeness ; a stranger
is uncommonly well received, not only by those to whom he
is recommended, but by those to whom he is entirely unknown ;
a dignified simplicity will add grace to the reception.   To be
lodged in an ill-conditioned auberge, belonging to one of his
farmers, would be a sort of reflection on the lord, or the stranger would be deemed as holding himself inferior to polite
society.

The peasantry are very well behaved, and I had never the
slightest reason to complain of any.   When obliged to have
some with me, in my little expeditions, I always found them
remarkably attentive, and ever eager to accompany me somewhat further.   This proved to be the case universally, and I
am unable to account for the boisterous declamation of travellers, respecting the manners of the inhabitants.   Our reception
depends much on the mode of presenting ourselves ; if we
will not conform to the usages of the people, if we treat the
peasant with hauteur, or ridicule his appearance and behaviour,
no wonder that disagreeable consequences arise, and more I
should look for in Hungary than elsewhere.   Some of their
customs are uncommonly singular, but I submitted, unre-
servedly, to them ; and this little complaisance, which costs
nothing, contributed not a little to render my stay in the
country agreeable.

In fact, what could seem more odd to a Frenchman than to
see the dessert served up as soon as he is sat down to table ?
then comes chocolate, then an omelette cut into small bits,
and these arranged symmetrically on a plate of prunes, then a
piece of veal on baked pears, a plate of maize baked in a dish,
with water, &c.   A bottle of liquor and a glass are then
brought, at which every one helps himself in his turn.   After
the repast the men fall to smoking, the ladies being the first
to offer a pipe ; and this occurs every where.   The Hunga-

rians are so truly polite when we adopt their customs, that we cannot with a good grace refuse to be accommodating.

We should still more make it a point to conform to the manners of the peasant, who seldom or never reasons, and judges of others by himself. One of his greatest civilities is to offer you drink out of his bottle; he drinks first, and again after you; if you comply, you are instantly in his good graces, but otherwise if you slight his kindness. It is well, however, not to make one's self too familiar, avoiding, at the same time, all appearance of hauteur.

When I arrived at an old castle, the resident of the lord's game-keeper, a young girl came to open the gate, and instantly took my hand to kiss it. I was a little startled at this gallantry, witnessing it, for the first time, at the gate of an old forsaken castle, in the midst of a forest. My surprise disconcerted the girl, and being desirous to speak with her, I found she only understood the Sclavonian. She again took my hand to kiss, and I no longer declined it. I have since been frequently a witness to this usage, which is very common. A peasant never appears before a well-dressed man without practising a similar ceremony. Children and young persons learn and practise it not only with their relations, but with company of every description. Gentlemen kiss the hands of the ladies; and a lady paying a visit to another, superior to herself in age or quality, tenders this mark of respect; if the latter would give an instance of politeness in return, she conceals her hands and makes a prompt offer of her face.

From the top of the castle there is a very fine view of all the surrounding mountains, which are every where covered with trees. In one excursion, I found a handsome wood, wherein the count de Forgacs has cut a number of little avenues and paths that serpentine in every direction. In an adjacent warren is a variety of game, with fish ponds; these, with the situation entirely rural, render it a very pleasing promenade.

I could not stay long at Gimes, notwithstanding the pressing instances of the count de Fergacs; I was impatient to visit certain problematical rocks, that formed a principal object of my journey. I left my new friends, much pleased with their affability; the count supplied me with his carriage, and I took the road for Konigsberg.

I might observe here, that the most elevated point of the country is the mountain of the castle of Schlossberg, called here the Mountain Gimes. Its height is about 1536 feet above the level of the sea. Annexed are some barometrical observations, June 1, 1818.

Schlossberg, at noon	height of the barometer, temperature, fair weather.	719 mill. 19 gr.
The village, at 10 o'clock	height of the barometer, temperature, fair weather.	738 mill. 19 gr.
Observatory at Buda, at 2 o'clock	height of the barometer, temperature of the air, do. of the mercury, flying clouds.	742 mill. 19 gr. 3 15 gr.

The new observatory of Buda was the point of comparison which I assumed for all the barometrical observations I made in Hungary.

At the village of Aranios Marot, I found an auriferous lead mine, and along the road I was now travelling, met with large blocks of a porphyritic stone, to which M. Haüy has given the name of trachyte. These must have descended, washed away by some great flood, from the hills to the north-east. At the village of Szent Benedek, (St. Benedict) which is adjoining to those hills, I observed blocks of trachytes exactly similar to those in the walls of the castle of Gimes. On the summit of one is a monastery, which has been ceded to the chapter of Gran, and overlooks a pretty good landscape, though the features of the country are harsh and severe. At the foot of it runs the river of Gran. The whole district is a champaign, covered with sand and vegetable earth, and the few neighbouring hills are very low and round. Little is to be seen all the way to Konigsberg.

This little town, called by the Hungarians Uj Banya,* would scarcely deserve the name of a village in France. The only object worth noticing, is the town-house, built, in 1382, by queen Mary, for her own residence; in front of it is an inn, where a traveller may find tolerable accommodations. The houses of this royal free city are scattered up and down, without order or neatness, and the environs have a wild appearance, except an opening that commands a valley, which here produces an agreeable feeling from the effect of contrast. Lofty mountains, crowned with thick forests, the little scattered dwellings of the miners interspersed among the trees, the roofs of the engines and buildings for the machinery, a church on a little eminence, these look well at a little distance, but on approaching them, from the heaps of rubbish thrown out by the miners, the illusion vanishes.

---

* The name of Banya often occurs in Hungary; it signifies a mine. Uj is an adjective, meaning new; Uj Banya, the new mine.

At and about Konigsberg are rocks that are worked into for mill-stones; they bear the name of Muhlstein. They are found also at Hlinik, which is about four leagues to the N.N.W. on the banks of the Gran. The trade in these mill-stones is very considerable throughout all the S.W. parts of Hungary.

I visited the mines of Konigsberg, which are situated above the town, and found the metalliferous parts every where in the midst of earthy rocks. The minerals consist chiefly of auriferous sulphurated silver, found in masses or in small veins, and portions scattered over a soft substance easily diluted in water. Native gold also is found in fine parcels, mixed with earthy matter, and it is sometimes found in veins of quartz. Sulphurated antimoniated silver, fragile sulphurated silver, and sulphurated antimony, are also occasionally found. There is a very great quantity of sulphurated iron, in little crystals, spread through all parts of the rock.

The mines of Konigsberg are extremely ancient, and, in earlier periods, were abundantly productive. The payment of the miners consisted then of the gold-dust that would attach to their clothing. This prosperity gave such importance to the place, that queen Mary 1., in 1382, built a mint here, and a palace for her own residence. A considerable diminution has taken place, and in lieu of 300 workmen, at present there are only 80.

The labours of the workmen are not conducted according to the usual methods, but enormous transversal galleries have been formed, constantly pursuing the earthy rocks to indefinite lengths, and only terminating with the mineral, in deposits more or less considerable. This shews that the labours exerted in the masses met with here and there, have furnished, at times, an immense produce, at others, hardly covering the expenses. The parts abandoned, whatever the miners advance to the contrary, seem completely exhausted, and their operations are at random, without any fixed data as to the metalliferous depots.

I traversed the mountains on both the right and left side of the valley of Gran. In the latter, one general character presented itself, a number of cavities, which appeared like the remains of so many craters. They are covered with a thick vegetation, almost impassable, and contain no vestiges of scorified matter, to denote the quondam existence of an ignivomous aperture. There are, however, near the village of Magospan, in the declivities and lower parts of the earthy sides, basaltes, evidently significative of volcanos, posterior to the formation of the trachytic rocks. These basaltes are in mass, and but seldom divided into distinct prisms; their colour is commonly a dark grey. In some points, remarkably cellulous, the colour is a pretty deep black. On the surface of the soil are found considerable quantities of black scoriæ, twisted, and as evidently produced by the action of fire, as those of Nugere, Puy de la Vache, &c. in Auvergne, or as those of volcanos in full activity.

These, and other observations made in the vicinity of Konigsberg, could not lead to any decisive conclusion as to the origin of the rocks, whether igneous or neptunian. It is evident that the trachytic earth is mixed with substances really scoriaceous, and that the basalte contains scoriæ, turbinated or twisted, which would denote a probability in favour of an igneous origin. The existence of metallic depots, in the heart of substances produced by fire, is not peculiar to Konigsberg ; it is the case in the gold mines of Telkevanya, in Upper Hungary, in those of Viltalpand, in Mexico, and perhaps in the mines that Strabo makes mention of in the Isle of Yschia, on the coast of Naples. But this will not apply to the mines of Schemnitz, and a number of other places, where every thing, on the contrary, points to a neptunian or aqueous origin.

CHAPTER III.

COUNTRY OF SCHEMNITZ, &c.

On quitting Konigsberg, we pass along the right bank of the Gran, by mountains of molar porphyry, that stretch to beyond Scharnowitz. After crossing the river at the village of Rudno, we meet with trachyte rocks, extending to beyond the village of Unter Hamer, and to the mine works that lie before the village of Hodritz, where are various other rocks of different kinds.

The village of Hodritz, overlooked by wooded mountains, or the dark foliage of pines, contrasts agreeably with the bright green of other trees, and has a cheerful aspect. On a height, a little before it, is a spot covered with little habitations, neatly white-washed, and which have a fine effect, from the verdant scenery with which they are surrounded.

After this coasting along the left bank of the river, we meet here and there with detached houses. We then begin to ascend by a noble road, cut out regularly on the right declivity of the valley. When arrived at the highest point of the road, we discern on the N. W., the valley of Eisenbach, and on the east, after turning the Paradelsberg, or Mountain of Paradise, which, till then, obstructed the view, we overlook another open country, and approach the basin wherein we survey Schemnitz and Dulln. This country has acquired considerable celebrity, from the immense mineral riches that it contains. The traveller's attention is arrested, when he reflects that it has been the nurse of geologists, Jacquin, Delin, De Born, Scopoli, &c. The engines for extraction seem numberless, and may be every where distinguished by their conical roofs, exhibiting all the appearances of bustle and activity. All around are immense *haldes*, heaps of excavated matter now re-agglutinated from decomposition, and attesting the antique origin of the mines, by the prodigious mass of their materials drawn from the bowels of the earth.

The road descends rapidly on Schemnitz, and I arrived there early, to trace a rapid sketch of the environs, and form a general notion of the country. The little town of Schemnitz (Selmecz, Germ. Banya, Hung.) is situated at the northern extremity of the comitat of Hont, on the southern border of a little basin, encircled on all sides by groups of mountains. In the middle of the basin rises the mountain Calvarienberg, with a conical form, and completely isolated. A chapel on the summit, and certain stations constructed on the southern declivity, give it, from the plain, an inviting air. Its summit is about 2239 feet above the level of the sea, and 101 above Schemnitz. The view from it is very much narrowed by the surrounding mountains, but their sinuous elevations, with the forests that cover them, form a delicious panorama. The town of Schemnitz, which lies southerly, appears from it like an amphitheatre of houses, which, blended with verdure, in carpets of grass that partially cover the country, exhibits a landscape that never fails to be attractive.

Here I may remark, that the Germans have, pretty generally, given name to various places wherein they have settled; sometimes it is a corruption of the native name, and sometimes a word that has no relation to it. Most places have various names, and one or other is used as the discourse is directed to an Hungarian, a Sclavonian, or a German. There are even Latin names pretty common, modelled on one or other of these languages.

Schemnitz, according to report, was in being under the reign of St. Stephen, the first king of Hungary, about the year 1000 of the Christian æra. It was then partly built on a rocky point that lies to the N. W. near the town, and which was overthrown by an earthquake. There were gold mines then working at Dulln, when those of Schemnitz were first discovered. Tradition relates, that this was effected by a hog, which, grubbing up the earth, made bare the indications of a famous treasure of minerals, near the place where now stands the principal inn of the town.

The position is somewhat disagreeable, from its lying open to the north winds, and being excluded from the south by mountains; the weather is cold in all seasons. There is nothing in the interior to invite attention, no pleasant promenade to recreate the inhabitants during or after their labours. There is, universally, an arid appearance on which ever side we turn; mountains of rubbish covered with ochre, and exhaling a sulphureous scent. All around we must scale more elevated situations to come at a temperature more refreshing, trees, green grass, and the sweets of vegetation.

The valleys which descend to the S. W. are agreeable, though in their higher parts less pleasing; thick forests of pines cover the declivities as well as the tops of the mountains, and appear as if intended to conceal the depths of the adjacent precipices. The lower parts are more agreeable, the declivities more gentle, and various parts are covered with oaks, birch, and beach trees, whose lighter foliage contrasts with the darker tints of other trees.

The valleys of Eisenbach and Glasshutte contain baths of great celebrity, and much frequented in the fair season; they then become points of assemblage very entertaining. But we do not find in these establishments all the conveniences that might be wished. Throughout Hungary the traveller takes with him his bed, linen, and other articles of prime necessity. Woe to one that arrives without this immense luggage, for a wooden bed, often too short by a foot, straw, two or three bad chairs, and a coffer or chest of fir, constitute the whole furniture of a chamber, though always very neatly white-washed; and the baths here can offer him no better.

The school of mines established at Schemnitz, by the empress Maria Theresa, acquired, at its outset, a well-merited reputation. The encouragements given to the students, the talents of the professors, the curious improvements in the processes of extraction, &c. attracted from all parts a numerous concourse of pupils, as also of eminent scientific characters. At present, few traces remain of that transient splendour. They are now more intent on realising products than propagating useful knowledge. The chamber of mines is chiefly or wholly occupied in financial arrangements; all that regards science and the practical improvements of art, are subordinate objects hardly deserving notice. Here are no professors devoted to the study of different branches of mining as a science; some officers go through some courses, but it is like works of supererogation, sacrificing time snatched from other business. Here is no difference between the engineer and the miner; the same lessons serve for both, and are unsuitable either for one or the other. For a laboratory, there is a hall without any of the necessary implements, and for a collection, a confused heap of samples, ill selected, confusedly thrown together, and covered with dust. Such is the state of this once celebrated school. Among the officers of the mines are men of merit, but their efforts are paralysed by the lucrative spirit that pervades the superior management. The quantum of the products is, in some measure, prescribed beforehand, and the chamber refuses to advance the disbursements requisite even for improvements that would augment the profits.

A country as important as that of Schemnitz, from its mineral riches, which for ages has been the object of subterraneous labours the most extensive, might readily be considered as well known with respect to its mineral constitution. But the authors that treat of Hungary, notice Schemnitz but slightly, though its district forms a type of comparison for all others of the same kind.

As to the nature and position of the soil or earth, Becker and others consider the whole mineral mass as entirely formed by water; others consider it as the production of volcanic depots. There is a great contrariety among authors; M. de Buch, however, has demonstrated, that there have certainly been volcanic depots in Hungary. Admitting this, my own opinion is, that the mines of Schemnitz are not of igneous origin.

CHAPTER IV.

DIFFERENT EXCURSIONS IN THE COUNTRY OF SCHEMNITZ.

Within this range, there are several mining works of greater or less celebrity, as in the flanks of the mountain of Szalas, in the valley of Eisenbach, in the lower part of the valley of Hodritz, to within a little distance of Unter Hamer, some hours journey from Schemnitz. To the south also, the mountains that rise behind Schemnitz give vestiges of numberless excavations and subterraneous labours. But the mining country is surrounded with a number of sterile tracts.

Those mine works, in general, within the country of Schemnitz, appear included within a space nearly quadrangular. The valley of Eisenbach seems to be the most interesting in the whole district, from the numerous veins, argentiferous, and auriferous, that constitute its riches. The village of that name lies at the entrance of a vast basin, about which the mountains are not so lofty, their summits are more depressed, their declivities less rapid, and covered with a refreshing vegetation lighter than the dark tints of the firs; the temperature also is milder, and nature presents, as it were, a new face. The bathing house, the only place where a stranger can conveniently lodge, is at a little further distance. The house is a very good one, and most agreeably situated; in front is a little square, and in its centre a little Chinese parasol, in a bad taste, and somewhat degraded from the gypsies, in the season of the waters, playing airs there, to me very disagreeable, for whole days together. The house, for an *hotellerie* of Hungary, appears genteel in its interior; it is exclusively appropriated to the bathing visiters, but the season was just commencing, and they were willing to take me in, on condition of not stopping longer than three days. I was conducted into a vast corridor, with a number of chambers on each side, on each of which the price was fixed. Some, towards the back part of the house, were taxed at a florin per day; others, more to the front and in a better light, at a florin and a half. With difficulty I procured one on this side, under a promise of removing, should it be asked for by any one taking it for the season. These chambers are not elegant, but remarkably neat, and, being all newly white-washed, had a gay appearance. A *couchette*, at least half a foot too short, and some stuffed chairs, not in the best condition, made up the whole furniture. Going out soon after on a visit to the mountains, the servant wished me to leave the key, that they might make my bed, but when I returned in the evening, I found my room just as I had left it. They imagined that my bed and wardrobe would arrive after me, and they had made preparations for receiving them. There was no mattress in the house, and I was glad to content myself with a bottle of straw. The only covering I could get was a very dirty coverlid; the borders I wrapped as carefully as I could with the napkin that had served me for supper. The *bourgeois* (my landlord) did not approve of this, but it was my only resource, and would be so to any other visiter that should arrive on foot, and with no other luggage than a hammer in his hand.

Along the roads, in the valley of Eisenbach, intermixed with others yet in activity, I observed a number of mines that had belonged to individuals, but had been seized by the Austrian government, which now holds the major part of them. The proprietors were even compelled to melt, in the government forges, the minerals which they had prepared. It gave me pain to see buildings and establishments in ruins, the multiplicity of which attest the inherent riches of the soil. All the implements for pounding and stamping with belong to the state; their number is pretty considerable, and their clattering, in a sort of cadence, helps to break through the solitude of the valley wherein we seem to be secluded from the world. Everywhere I met with miners reduced to poverty, whose pale figure and particular dress, most commonly covered with mud, strongly attracted my sympathy. From their earliest years they have been habituated to the hardships of a miner's life, but these alone were comparatively overlooked.

At the extremity of the valley of Eisenbach, I met, for the first time in Hungary, with gypsies, known both in Hungary and Germany by the name of Zigeuners. It was at the village of Bzenicza; they were in a little hut made of branches and clay, and they were lying together, men, women, and children, on a little straw and dried herbs. In the vicinity of their cabin was a forge where they made hatchets, knives, &c. for sale. One of them was an aged person, had been in Germany and spoke the language; I entered into discourse with him, but could learn nothing as to the origin of his nation; all that he knew was, that he was born in Transylvania, and that his children and grand children were born in different places. When I asked why they did not fix in some village where they might live more comfortably, he made a sign with his head that it was not agreeable to their inclinations.

The Zigeuners, in general, retain a particular national character, and this has been observed for three centuries, as they never marry but among themselves. They are of low stature, mostly meagre but well made; their complexion is tanned, or rather copper coloured, their eyes black and vivid, teeth white; in fact, their physiognomy has something in it foreign to the European. The women, partly from the negligence of their attire, are disgusting, and reminded me of those old mummies that we find in cabinets of antiquities. It is wretched living that so disfigures them, for the girls are well made, and their figure is far from being disagreeable.

The general opinion is, that marriage does not take place among this class, but that the women and children are in common. The latter remain entirely naked to an advanced age, and I have sometimes seen girls of their full stature, and well formed, in a state of nudity; I remarked, however, that they always shunned the presence of strangers. A set of naked children, with their dark skin, ill combed hair, &c. seemed to

me, like little fiends, and I always surveyed them with painful sensations blended with pity.

The Zigeuner has ever been addicted to a rambling life,
neglecting advantageous offers on the part of the sovereigns.
Maria Theresa and Joseph II. endeavoured to fix them in
Transylvania and the Banat, but could prevail only on a small
number that applied themselves to agriculture. When they
remove, they take their all with them, that is, a few rags and
certain instruments to carry on their trade. They live much
in the woods, or near to the villages, where they sometimes
stop several years, and, at last, decamp suddenly without previous notice. We see nothing in their cabins but a few earthen
pots and a little straw, and, in winter, much of their time is spent
smoking together—men, women, and children. They appear
very fond of the caustic and oily soot, nauseous to the scent,
that lodges in the tube of their pipes. They ask, pressingly,
for this, when they see any one cleaning his pipe before them.

These gypsies are indolent and vicious, never working but
from the pressure of necessity. The most common trade
among them is that of blacksmith, and it is they who manufacture the little iron or copper hatchets with cane handles
every where met with. Not a few are musicians, and some
have risen to celebrity; they then roam about the villages
playing to the peasants on holidays. They have their slight
of hand tricks and posture masters, though less in Hungary
than elsewhere. They are subtle and active, and pilfer any
little articles that fall in their way ; but I never heard of gross
enormities among them. I have frequently met with them
in woods where they might have robbed me with impunity,
but they never spoke, unless I addressed them first, and then,
after answering, they would ask for some tobacco.

The Zigeuners have a peculiar language that has no analogy
with any other. They are not originally European, and were
not known in France till the beginning of the fifteenth century.
It is certain that they were in Hungary in 1417, and that then
great numbers of them were scattered throughout Wallachia,
Transylvania, Moldavia, the Buckawine, &c. In 1427, a band
of them came to Paris, representing themselves as inhabitants of
Lower Egypt, first converted to the Christian faith, relapsing into
Mahometanism, and admitted to penitence by Pope Martin V.
who, by way of penance, ordered them to travel about every
where for seven years, without sleeping in beds. The Parisians
would not receive them, and they were sent to la Chapelle, near
St. Denys, where people went in crowds to hear them tell fortunes. Their conduct, however, was complained of, and the
Bishop of Paris, to prevent greater disorders, excommunicated

all who pretended to tell fortunes. These vagabonds then left the country, but either they or others returned, for an ordonnance of the states of Orleans, in 1560, ordered all impostors, under the name of Bohemians or Egyptians, to quit the kingdom under pain of being sent to the galleys. It was, probably, in the fifteenth or sixteenth century that they arrived in England, where they are known by the name of gypsies.

Authors differ as to the origin of the Zigeuners. Some trace them to Cilicia and Assyria, others consider them as Persians, of the branch of the Usbecks; others derive them from Zingitania, in Barbary, turning the word Zingare into Zingari and Zigeuner, names given them in Italy and Germany. According to some, they are real Egyptians, having been called Pharaoni, while others bring them from Asia Minor, in 1403, after the defeat of Bajazet by Tamerlane. Grellman refers their descent to Hindoos of the cast of the Parias, who were driven out of their country, at the time of the conquest of India, by the same Tamerlane. It is generally agreed that they are not originally Europeans. As to the name of Bohemians, this is applied in France to vagabonds of every description; the first gypsies that arrived had probably passed through Bohemia; the appellation, however, is considered as injurious.

The Zingares have appeared, at times, in such numerous bodies as to excite uneasiness in the inhabitants of the countries through which they were passing. More than 60,000 have been counted in Hungary and Transylvania, and when the Buckawine was ceded to Austria in 1778, out of 7000 inhabitants, 1000 were Zingares. In the census, under the Emperor Joseph in 1783, the number for Hungary amounted to 40,000. There are many also in England, but in France, Spain, and Italy, where they must conform to somewhat of a civilized regimen, their number is very small. The children among them are much fewer, in proportion, than among the peasants of the countries where they reside.

EXCURSION IN THE VALLEY OF HODRITZ.

I made excursions through all parts of this valley; the mines are pretty numerous about Hodritz, but terminate there. Coming to a village called Kopanicza, inhabited by Germans, from Austria and the frontiers, I was preparing at the church to take the height of the barometer, when I found myself presently surrounded by all the women of the place. They were astonished at the novelty of the spectacle, and were disputing about the nature of the barometer, (that of Fortin) which sparkled in their eyes, and they deemed it a wonderful machine. One of them then became a Ciceroni, and explained to the others that it was an instrument to observe the firmament with. I could not perceive one man while I stopped in the village, which was more than an hour, or even in the neighbourhood. One woman offered to conduct me on a road that would take me to Viszoka, but I walked quicker than her, and she left me with a direction to go on straight forward, although there was no road.

Arriving at the heights near Viszoka, about four o'clock, I found myself very much fatigued, having, for two nights, slept in a manner in the open air. After leaving Hodritz, where I dined on a bacon salad, I could get nothing to eat but black bread and milk. In lieu of descending to Steinbach, where I might take post, I renewed my ramble, and was near being lost in the mountains of Szitna; my compasses became my guide in the woods, and night did not overtake me till I had reached the heights of Windchacht, where I recovered my knowledge of the road. About eleven I reached Schemnitz, so exhausted that I was unable to stir out the next day. This was one of my most fatiguing journeys, and brought on a pain in my eyes that was very troublesome and did not leave me while I remained in the country. I attributed this to the coolness of the nights, the more dangerous from the great heat of the day-time. Frequently after 20 or 25 degrees of heat during the day, I have known the thermometer fall down to 12 in the night. Such a difference, with the humidity that attends it, produced an effect on my organs only to be conceived by those that have had the like experience. I would earnestly recommend to foreigners, travelling in Hungary, to wear warm clothing sufficient to be a protection in case of passing the night abroad. The peasants, who often lie in the open air, have the precaution to carry about them pelisses of sheep's skin. For my own part, obliged to be frequently on foot, and having sometimes two or three men with me that would soon be loaded with stones, I was unable to make a due provision beforehand, and though my constitution was robust, my health was somewhat impaired. I would not advise any one to venture himself in Hungary as I have done, without previously consulting his physical and moral constitution. Much depends on the force of habit, on energy of character, and, above all, on the enthusiasm of a naturalist to brave the privations and fatigues incidental to such journeys.

EXCURSION IN THE VALLEY OF GLASSHUTTE.

There are two roads to pass from Schemnitz to Glasshutte, one a footway over the mountain of Szallas, the other a high road through the basin of Schemnitz, to the foot of the mountains that border it on the west. It would be requisite for a geological traveller to take both these roads, but, to avoid fatigue, he might go by the Szallas, where the greatest part of the way is on a descent, and return by the high road, which is the easiest.

In leaving Schemnitz, along the high road, we pass at the foot of a mountain, named Rothenbrun, that overlooks the town and stretches nearly from east to west. According to tradition, one part of the town of Schemnitz formerly stood on this mountain, and was overwhelmed by an earthquake. It might have been a partial fall of the mountain, as the rock, in its upper parts, appears cleft perpendicularly to a vast height.

About an hour's journey before we reach the village of Glasshutte, there is a gallery of mines, now neglected, as the profits did not answer the expenses. It contained veins of argentiferous lead. The village is in a pretty agreeable situation, though the walks about it are rather difficult. There are several bathing houses that are well frequented in the fine season. The mineral waters that supply the baths proceed from a mass of calcareous tuft that contains remains of plants and terrestrial shells; they form a hill on which stands the church of the village.

The waters are acidulous and ferrugineous; their temperature, at the springs, is 43 degrees (Reaumur), that of the air being 14'. But in other springs that I met with, at the foot of calcareous mountains, the temperature was only from 24 to 30 degrees. In an excursion from Glasshutte, I had to pass over some mountains bristled with wood, and where, at every step, are steep precipices or rapid descents, vast fragments of rocks, and a number of antique castles, raised on points scarcely accessible. Those which I have met with elsewhere, in the midst of the wildest forests, might seem to have been the haunts of robbers, or served perhaps as retreats to the victims of those disasters, the horrors of which are traced in every page of the Hungarian history.

JOURNEY FROM GLASSHUTTE TO SCHEMNITZ.

My return to Schemnitz was by the mountain of Szallas. I took a little foot-path that ascends towards the mountain, but lost myself a second time in the woods, though assured by a peasant, my conductor, that, having worked in the forests of the country, he was well acquainted with the way. I wandered about the whole day, depending on his pretended knowledge, but towards night was obliged to take my compasses for a guide. My conductor was perplexed and puzzled, roaming about in every direction, and I had some difficulty in persuading him that I could find a way out of those winding gorges and antique forests. Throughout Hungary, the peasants are afraid to trust themselves half a league from their village ; I have frequently met with some that would not pass the summit of the mountain that overlooked their valley. In general, I was advised not to venture too far, as robbers, they said, haunted the heights. Many dismal stories were told me on this head, but I have explored all parts, without apprehension of danger. These prejudices seem to have descended from ancient times, when it would have been imprudent to advance far into the woods, which now may be penetrated with safety.

The point of Szitna is the most elevated, not only of these parts but of the whole circumjacent country. Its height above the level of the sea is 1338 yards. June 9, 1818, the height of the barometer, on its summit at noon, was 686 mill. 8 gr. temperature 6, 5 : weather cloudy ; wind, a strong northerly.

In one of these excursions, I visited a gallery of mines where the workmen had found what they called large pieces of wood, with remains of vegetables, in the heart of coaly substances. The officers considered them as anthtracites, but I am inclined to adopt the opinion of the miners, that they are lignite, though I cannot pronounce positively, not having seen them. Near the village of Illia, the miners, in their labours, find bituminous pieces of wood, and also wood opalised.

Returning to the mountain of Snitza, which in my rambles I had lost sight of, I found its point or summit completely overlooking all surrounding objects to the distance of many leagues. A little square pavilion has been erected here, by Prince de Kohary, which is visible at a very great distance, and which, from the plains of Schemnitz, appears like a shepherd's hut. A balcony runs round it, whence, at our ease, we may survey a vast extent of country. In this magnificent view the observer traces, on the south, the plains of Hungary. His eye, glancing over the mountains of Dregely, reposes on an immense horizon. On the east, various groups of mountains stretch, successively, to a great distance, and to the north, we perceive the lofty granitic and calcareous crests in the comitats of Zips, Lipté, &c. and which join the central groupe of Tatra. The cimex, or highest point of this last, is the most elevated in the whole kingdom of Hungary. M. Waldenburg makes it 2666 yards above the level of the sea. The peak of the Calvarienburg appears, from Szitna, like a point in the middle of a plain ; Schemnitz and Duller look like heaps of hovels, and the villages and buildings for the mines can scarcely catch attention. The castle of Antal, belonging to the Prince of Kohary, is the only object to arrest the spectator's view. On the 10th of July,

1818, the height of the barometer, from Szitna, was 674 mill. 3. Temperature 15 gr. flying clouds, wind northerly.

At Tiszolez, I was informed that opalised wood was in such abundance about Uhorska, that the church of that or some neighbouring village was wholly constructed with it.

The environs of Palotja are somewhat remarkable from the depots of lignite, and relics of shells of various descriptions. They have evidently been deposited under waters, tossed about in every direction, and the waters must have covered them long enough to allow of their living and multiplying there. The quantities of the remains of the molluscæ kind are immense. At the southern foot of Szitna, an argilous matter is found which has long been in use for the manuufacture of porcelain at Vienna.

EXCURSIONS TOWARDS THE PLAINS OF HUNGARY.

By the road which leads directly from Schemnitz, we advance to a flat, where we see the mountains lowering successively, and the eye catches a glimpse of the vast plains of Læva. We then seem to breathe a new air. Nature seems becomingly to smile, decorated with forest flowers and richer apparel, and we quit, with pleasure, the cold and savage country wherein Schemnitz lies. As mineralogy was one principal object of my journey in Hungary, 1 may here insert some observations that I made generally.

The quantity of gold, silver, and lead, that the mines of Schemnitz supply annually, is not correctly known. It is certain that the products, at present, are much inferior to those at former periods. Often, from the pressure of different wars, the lateral veins have been neglected; these and the parts less rich were resumed in times of peace. M. Schwartner assumes for a term of comparison, the eight years of peace that elapsed from 1780 to 1788; he rates the products of the mines of Lower Hungary at 12 or 1300 marcs of gold, and from 58 to 59,000 marcs of silver. Adding to it the products of Upper Hungary, he makes out a total of from 15 to 1700 marcs of gold, and from 70 to 74,000 marcs of silver, per annum. But this does not appear to be an average term, as at periods, both before and since, the products have been much greater.

It is well known that at Kremnitz, from 1680 to 1693, more than 200,000 marcs were procured annually. In 1772, the mines of Lower Hungary remitted to the mint at Kremnitz, 53,860 marcs of silver, and 2291 marcs of gold. From 1740 to 1773, a hundred millions of florins were obtained from Schemnitz and Kremnitz, which would yield annually a sum of more than eight millions of francs.

M. Heron de Villefosse computes the products of all the mines of Hungary at 2600 marcs of gold, 80,000 marcs of silver, and 6000 quintals of lead. The gold and silver would then furnish an annual sum of 6,344,000 francs. But these numbers, which represent, pretty well, the mean annual products of times more remote, are much superior to the products of the present day.

Hungary (higher and lower) supplies about half the gold that the mines of Europe produce. Transylvania furnishes nearly the other half.

The total quantity of gold extracted from the mines of Europe may be calculated at 5300 marcs. How immense the difference compared with the produce of America, which rises to 70,647 marcs !

The quantity of silver drawn annually from the mines of Hungary, is somewhat more than one-third superior to what is yielded by the mines in the rest of Europe, the total of which may be estimated at 216,000 marcs.

In these products France can enter into no sort of comparison. The quantity of gold drawn from our rivers is inconsiderable, and our mines of argentiferous lead do not yield above 7500 marcs of silver.

Generally speaking, the mines are wrought at Schemnitz as in other countries, but on a larger scale. The pits and the galleries are very well executed, and quite compact; the reservoirs of waters are disposed with much art ; several fine arrangements evince the care and grandeur of conception manifested under the special protection of the sovereigns. If science and their improvement of the art were more attended to, Schemnitz would again become one of the finest establishments in Europe, and rival that of Freyberg, in Saxony.

CHAPTER V.

THE COUNTRY OF NEUSOHL.

The district of Newsohl formed one part of my scene of observation ; the road lies through the valley of Koselnick. Here the declivities are less abrupt ; vegetation has not lost its strength and beauty, but covers the face of nature ; the gloomy fir trees disappear. From Altsohl to Neusohl, the road winds along the banks of the Gran, in the bottom of a broad valley ; approaching the town, we arrive at the foundry to which the minerals of Schemnitz are conveyed.

The town of Neusohl owes its origin to a colony of Saxons invited thither by King Andrew II. for the purposes of mining, but the German race is now extinct, and the place is wholly inhabited by Sclavonians. Its situation on the banks of the Gran, at its confluence with the little river Bistricza, with the high wooded mountains that at a distance appear to advantage, exhibiting an amphitheatre of verdure, might characterise it as a very agreeable town; but, detached from the rural scenery, it has a sombrous aspect, and is, in general, ill built, except a few houses; among these we may distinguish the palace of the ancient bishop. At my first coming, it seemed as if it had been consumed by a conflagration, though I soon found it was owing to the construction of the houses, at least in the principal street. Most of these have but one story, surmounted with a very lofty roof, but to represent a second story, an isolated wall appears to conceal the roof, and which terminates in a cornice. In this wall are one or two openings in the form of windows, but without glasses or a sash, and we can see the dark tints of the roofing through them. But the first impression arising from this singular construction is, that the house is in ruins, that the roof and windows are decayed, and that the case only is left. The mistake is soon detected, and these false windows appear intended to pass through them a heavy piece of timber that serves for a gutter. In some houses somewhat more of luxury appears, and real window blinds, painted green, are annexed to the wall for a deception; however, these enormous gutters, conveying water through window blinds to the distance of ten or fifteen feet, in the middle of the street, must have an odd appearance.

At my first arrival I became acquainted with M. Zipser, one of the first mineralogists in Hungary, and also with M. Beniczki, notary or secretary to the comitat, who, to a variety of general information, adds a particular inclination for geology. Their collections contain interesting details relative to Hungary, and from their conversation I derived useful instructions for the rest of my journey. Among other civilities, I might notice their accompanying me in several of my excursions.

In one of these we visited Herrengrund, where copper mines have been worked from the thirteenth century. The kinds of copper are the pyritous, the grey copper, and the green and blue carbonated copper. The decomposition of the minerals produces a great quantity of sulphate of copper, which dissolves in the waters that filtrate from all parts of the works. These waters are carefully collected in cavities, where they have a process to decompose the salt, and so to extract copper by cementation.

In another excursion, M. Beniczki accompanied me to an old lead mine which had been abandoned, and where he had again set men at work. The old entrance lies at the foot of an immense wall of rocks, in a situation truly picturesque. There was always a natural cavern, which the mining labours have extended. Of the minerals, the principal masses are a brown earthy carbonated iron, and an earthy oxydated iron, in which are portions of sulphurated copper and galena, more or less considerable. There is also carbonated copper, green and blue, carbonated lead, phosphated lead in mass, sometimes, but rarely, crystallised, and of a greenish yellow; also calamine in little square masses.

We came afterwards to the little town of Libethen, elevated to the rank of a free and mining town, by king Lewis I., son and successor of Charles Robert. Though founded by the Saxons, invited thither by king Andrew II., it is now wholly inhabited by Sclavonians. The town suffered much from wars and revolutions. About the end of the fifteenth century, during the wars of Mathias Corvin with the Bohemians, it was attacked suddenly, when one part of the inhabitants were driven to quit the place, and the rest, who had fled to the mines, were miserably suffocated by the fire and smoke thrown into them. The town then remained desolate forty years, till the mines began again to be worked, at the beginning of the sixteenth century. The town is but indifferently built, and lies in rather a wild situation, at the bottom of a valley, with groupes of mountains on every side. It is not larger than one of our smallest villages about Paris. We came also to the village of Sajba, famous for the most beautiful opal jasper and opalised wood; hence come those samples of a yellowish white opalised wood, and others of a very brilliant grey, that have long been in our collections at Paris; they are found here in every shade of colour, lustre, and pellucidity.

Tradition reports that the country of Libethen anciently had gold mines, but it is certain that, for a long time, nothing but copper has been worked. The mines must have been very important to raise the town to the rank of free and royal, but now it is partly abandoned, and the number of workmen greatly diminished.

CHAPTER VI.

THE COUNTRY OF KREMNITZ.

We can go from Neusohl to Kremnitz by a foot way, to the W. S. W. of the town, by traversing the range of mountains that form the limits of the two comitats. The forms of these are often very grotesque, from having been rent into various shapes. A very narrow path rises very rapidly, and in the declivities of some of the mountains I observed a very thick vegetation, which, though unfavourable to the geologist, would offer an ample field of research to the botanical enquirer. Here were plants, to a great number of which I was a stranger; unfortunately, those I had collected during my travels were lost, among many other objects of natural history. I particularly regret a multitude of insects, collected in different countries and elevations of the mountains, which required classification in the various branches of entomology.

The town of Kremnitz (Kormecz Banya, Hung.) is one of the most ancient royal free towns of Hungary. It is said to have had mines worked in the time of the Romans, but in the middle ages, the Germans resumed the labours, and gave rise to the town. It is they, in fact, who have successively renewed it, after the various devastations it underwent, in common with other places. Many Germans yet remain in the country, who speak an unintelligible Gothic German, as harsh in pronunciation as the German Swiss. The town lies in the bottom of a narrow valley, overlooked on the right and left by high mountains; its position is far from being agreeable, and its interior has little to exhibit but the mint, to which all the gold and silver from the mines of the whole kingdom is conveyed to be inspected, and where all the preparatory operations, as that of acids, &c. are conducted on a great scale. Out of this establishment, which also stands in need of improvement, there is little worth seeing, and a stranger would find it difficult to get a decent lodging. I could not have procured a lodging in the only public house that was shewn me, if an individual, to whom I applied in the street, had not generously pleaded my cause with the hostess, who, yielding to his request, helped me to some bad soup, and to something of the same nature, called *kneps*. She assured me that there were no eggs in the town, and to get a wretched fowl at night, my servant was obliged to threaten the hens that were running about the house. It was a Friday, and the people here, scrupulously adhering to the laws of the church, observe meagre days, and cannot conceive how a traveller dare do otherwise. I have sometimes dined with the curates on these days, and meat then was provided for myself, while they contented themselves with a few vegetables.

One general observation I made respecting Kremnitz, that it is only in one species of earth or soil, trachyte, that the mines are found. In that, and the concomitant characters, there is a striking analogy between the local stratifications of Schemnitz and Kremnitz.

At the bottom of an immense cavity, formed by a perpendicular dislocation of the mountain, I observed a pool of ferrugineous water, with bulrushes, of the most beautiful green I ever beheld, growing in the middle. Some attribute the colour of the plants to the influence of the waters, and it is a fact, that, wherever I have noticed them, the green colour of the vegetation is much more intense than elsewhere. The cold at the foot of this immense excavation was insupportable, but I was astonished to find the thermometer not lower than 13°, that is, only 2° below the temperature at the top of the mountain. In places of this kind there is a humid vapour which penetrates the clothing, but which, from the warmth of the body, soon becomes a dry vapour; hence, we feel a cold much more piercing than what comports with the temperature of the circumambient air.

In one of my excursions from Kremnitz, I came to the village of Perk, where every thing reminded me of journeys that I had made in the south of France. The face of nature was gay, the sun's vital beams and heat were every where felt, bright and shining forests of firs on the left, penetrating, as it were, through the gloom that surrounded them, and perfuming the air with a resinous scent. Hid from the public walks of men, I thought I discerned some of nature's finest touches, though different parts of the soil were sandy and dry.

In my road to St. Kerest, I remarked siliceous, fissile substances of a black colour, but which grow white before a fire, and that retain all the appearances of vegetable impressions. De Born, in his description of the same tract, makes mention of petrifications, which he compares to vegetables, or to corals. Ferber has noticed these organic remains, and compares them to the roots of marine plants, and to the stalks of one that grows in marshes, the *thypha palustris*. M. Esmarck also alludes to them, under the designation of calcedonies and petrified reeds.

The town of St. Kerest is beautifully situated on hills that border the Gran; it was the residence of the ancient bishop of Newsohl. There is a very stately chateau, and a number of neat dwelling houses, with an excellent auberge, at the posthouse, where even pedestrian travellers are treated with great civility.

The village of Prochot is inhabited by ancient Germans, whose language my servant, though a German, found it very difficult to understand. A stout young man, about thirty years of age, made a tender of his services, as a guide to a mountain in the neighbourhood, but we had no small trouble to get his mother's permission. The good woman was alarmed and afraid of me. She was overjoyed at our return, and I received from her afterwards, every mark of civility. These simple people, not without reason, harbour a distrust of the inhabitants of the towns; to manage them requires a certain frankness without rudeness, and little occasional liberalities. When once gained, their attachment grows fervid, and no exertion will be spared to render themselves accommodating and agreeable. The good woman herself was an instance of this, offering me some crumpets she was baking in the oven, and wishing to detain me till I had explored every corner of the adjoining mountains. One of these, which I scaled, had an immense plateau on the crust, covered, not with resinous, but with hazel-nut and juniper trees.

At St. Kerest I again met my travelling companions, and we set out together for a fresh excursion into the country of Schemnitz. But the sum of my observations there, of a general kind, have been already noted. My stay in Hungary had been longer than what I had contemplated; I had almost exhausted my stock of ready money, and the dates of my letters of exchange, for different parts of Hungary, had expired. I found it necessary, therefore, to return to Pest, for the re-establishment of my pecuniary concerns.

CHAPTER VII.

VISIT TO CERTAIN MOUNTAINS IN THE COMITAT OF NOGRAD.

I shall introduce here a little adventure that occurred, while exploring the groupe of the mountains of Dregely. I intended fixing my head quarters at Nograd, which is marked in the maps as a market town, and where I had supposed the assizes for the county were held. But on my arrival I soon found my mistake; it is but a small village, and cannot be much frequented, as it does not lie on any road. I was conducted to an auberge where I might have had accommodations, but for the uncouth and avaricious humours of those who kept it. I ordered a supper, being hungry and fatigued with my day's journey, and reckoning upon it, I walked up to the castle and other parts of the village.

From the remains of the towers and walls, the castle must have been very strong and extensive, and a place of importance. A great part of it was destroyed in 1685, by the explo-

sion of a powder magazine; the Turks had a garrison there, but
they abandoned it.   Nograd, now a wretched village, had been
a considerable place in ancient times, but was desolated by
successive wars.   Returning to my host, I was equally surprised and mortified to find no culinary preparations.   The
mistress had been at a neighbour's in search of a pullet, and
made free to fetch one away in the absence of the family ;
this, however, was soon reclaimed, or its value fixed at a florin.
The *aubergiste* would not pay more than half, and the other, in
a foaming fury, snatched the fowl, then ready for eating, from
the spit, threw the latter in the face of my hostess, and ran
home.   I now promised to pay for the pullet, cost what it
might ; I even repaired to the house of this neighbour, but she
had retired elsewhere, probably to devour the fowl at the house
of another neighbour.   I was then forced to be content with
three eggs, which I had to share with my servant and the
peasant that had been my guide.

In my journeys I visited the mountain of Dregely, which is
a conspicuous object, and one of great notoriety in Hungary.
Its form is conical, and it stands altogether detached from the
mountains that surround it.   Its height above the level of the
sea is about 1260 feet.   There are some remains of its old
castle, consisting of dilapidated walls, cemented with a mortar
not very solid, of lime, siliceous sand, and pebbles of quartz
and granite.   In the eastern quarter are a door and a staircase,
both cut out of the solid rock.   From the top of the walls is a
commanding prospect over the whole country, which takes in
many extensive ranges of distant mountains.   On the 28th of
Sept. 1818, the height of the barometer from the castle of
Dregely, was 724 mill. ; temperature, 16 gr. ; weather, flying
clouds ; sun very hot.

In my journey to Vissegrad, the road winds along the
Danube, and sometimes approaches so near that we pass
through the water.   The castle of Vissegrad was formerly the
residence of several kings of Hungary, and its apartments and
gardens were decorated in such a style of magnificence, that a
pope's legate, in the reign of Mathias Corvin, gave it the name
of the Earthly Paradise.   When it was built is unknown ; it is
first noticed by Hungarian historians, in the reign of Lladislas I.
in the eleventh century, as the prison of king Salomon, after
the defeat of the Wallachians, whom he had incited to insurrection.   It was probably then of minor importance, till enlarged and beautified by succeeding kings.   Charles the First
preferred it to any of his other houses, and entertained in it,
with extraordinary pomp, the kings of Bohemia and Poland.
Mathias Corvin embellished the gardens with marble statues,

basins, jetteaux, &c. The royal habitation and the gardens were at the foot of the mountain, on the banks of the Danube, where they could not occupy a very considerable space, but the castle was on the isolated point of an eminence, about 650 feet above the Danube, which, in this part, may be about 400 feet above the sea. Vissegrad is a Sclavonian word, and derives its name from its position ; Vissi, most high, and Hrad or Grad, a castle.

It was in the castle of Vissegrad, then considered as the most secure in Hungary, that the crown sent by pope Sylvester II. to St. Stephen, as a gift from heaven, was preserved. This was agreeably to an ordinance of Lladislas II. ; it was placed in the most inaccessible part of the fortress, and confided to keepers, selected from among the Grandees, who were under an oath only to resign it to the nation assembled, and to lay down their lives in the defence of it. This consecrated crown, however, was often carried away during the troubles ; sometimes by the dethroned kings, who, by that means, prevented the coronation of their successors, and sometimes by those who pretended to the throne. It has frequently given rise to bloody wars, and thousands have fallen victims to preserve or to regain it. Such was the high importance attached to it, that the place of its custody was fixed by a decree of the nation assembled, nor was it to be removed but by a similar order. Joseph II. had it removed from Presburg (where it had been deposited by an order of the assembly of 1608) to Vienna, but this act of authority was considered as arbitrary, and derogating from the rights of the nation. It contributed not a little to retard the various reforms which that monarch had projected. Fears were entertained of a general insurrection, and Joseph, in rescinding many of his acts, addressed a manifesto to the nation, which shewed that his object was the general good, and that his intentions were grounded in purity, justice, and equity. The crown was lastly removed to Buda by another order of Joseph, Feb. 18, 1790, two days before his death, and this event was hailed with transports of joy throughout the whole kingdom.

The castle of Vissegrad, taken and retaken alternately by the Germans and Turks, is now a huge heap of ruins. Close to the Danube we yet find some old towers and a wall, with bastions, ascending thence to the summit of the mountain, to communicate with the principal fortress. The ruins of the latter are very considerable, in walls and round towers. We may plainly distinguish the double walls that formed the exterior inclosure, between which lay the pathway that led to the fortress. In the interior appear two successive fosses, one

above another, and in the centre stands the castle on an isolated rock, cut perpendicularly to the height of several yards.
In the remnant of the castle are certain chambers and apartments, with ogive gates and windows, ornamented with little
pilasters, round or square, strongly reflecting the taste of the
ancients. But, in general, we see nothing but walls thrown
confusedly one over another, and filling the fosses with rubbish. In the inner court is a cistern in the shape of a bell,
into which all the waters from the different roofs emptied
themselves. Opposite this, in the middle of the wall, we observe a sculptured stone, containing some coats of arms, with
a Latin inscription half defaced, and the date of 1493 in Roman
ciphers. From the top of the walls the eye traces the course
of the Danube; meandering to the west behind the mountains,
and then turning abruptly to the south, his stream rolls onward
through the champaign districts of Pest, and the vast central
plain. As a comprehensive and animated view of the productions of nature, I was enchanted with it.

As to the whole range of walls, they are composed of the
rocks whereof the mountain consists, but the gates and windows, and all parts that require to be cut in regular forms, are
of very solid calcareous tuf, that contains in it a vast number
of vegetable impressions. These tufs have been brought
from the neighbourhood of Old Buda.

In the environs of Vissegrad I first noticed (though I found
them, afterwards, in other parts along the Danube) two species
of fluviatile, or river shells, that are not common in Europe.
One belongs to the menalopside genus, and the other to the
Paludine; the latter has obtained the name of Naticoide,
in a work now publishing by M. de Ferrusac. I was very
desirous to see their molluscæ, or living animals, in order
to study their characters, but could not succeed : the shells of
both are defended with corneated opercules.

Here I may observe that immense collections of fossil shells,
such as are only to be found in the sea, have been excavated
in the hills of freestone that run from north to south, between the rivers of Gran and Ypoli. I have remarked also
numberless beds of different shells, with strata of lignites, in
carbonaceous substances, in my rambles through Hungary.

On the flanks of the freestone hills, and on the banks of the
rivers that intersect them, are still found the remains of large
animals, as teeth, heads, thighs of the elephant and mammoth ;
several of these are deposited in the cabinet of Pest. There
are specimens of the elephants of Asia and the elephants of
Africa. Those bony fragments have been found in various

other parts, as also in the plains of Hungary, but, more commonly, in the soil of alluvion than in masses of freestone.

To other observations made in and about the mountains of Dregely may be added some notice of Acsa. It is chiefly remarkable for the castle and park of Baron de Pronay. From the terrace there is a fine view over the surrounding mountains. The little town of Watz is deserving of notice, being one of the most agreeable in Hungary. According to history, it was built in the reign of Geysa I. who, on gaining a decisive victory over Salomon, caused a church to be erected in the midst of the forest that covered this country. The name of Watz was that of a solitaire or recluse who lived in the forest. It became afterwards a considerable place, and the see of a bishop ; and later, the cradle of letters and philosophy. The town suffered much in the invasion of the Mongols, notwithstanding the vigorous resistance of the inhabitants. It was exposed to similar disasters in the reign of John de Zapola, in his wars with Ferdinand of Austria. It was taken also and retaken several times by the Turks ; their incursions, whether as enemies or allies, contributed to retard the progress of civilization. The entrance of the town is distinguished by a beautiful triumphal arch at the extremity of a fine avenue of trees ; this is on the side of the Danube. There are several very good houses, and some public buildings, for affording the means of instruction. Among others is an institution for the deaf and dumb, founded by the Emperor Francis, in 1802. And what is not the least recommendation to a traveller, here are several good inns.

CHAPTER VIII.

THE MOUNTAINS OF MATRA, AND THE ENVIRONS OF ERLAU.

I arrived at Pest, July 17th, towards evening, and on the 20th, in the morning, I was on the road for Aszod, where an announcement to the Baron Charles Podmaniczky had already preceded me. The two intermediate days had been devoted to the arrangement of my pecuniary concerns, to visiting the museum of natural history and that of the observatory, as also to an acquaintance I had formed with Dr. Haberle, Director of the Botanic Garden. I obtained here some valuable information relative to certain parts of Hungary, and for which I have also to thank M. Schuster, Professor of Chemistry in the University.

In renewing my pedestrian excursions as usual, I passed by Godolo, where there is a fine chateau belonging to Prince Grassalkoritzs; it stands on the right hand of the road, but very near to it, and the grounds contain a number of plantations and inclosures. The next object to attract notice was a gibbet, the first I had met with in Hungary, bearing the carcase of a criminal who had suffered six months before. The spectacle seemed too shocking for the feelings of women and children, and the sensibilities of humanity are outraged and nauseated by it.

These impressions I retained till my arrival at the castle of Aszod, where my gracious reception and entertainment soon effaced the disgusting sensation. The neighbourhood was not favourable to the leading object of my journeys, and I departed, the Baron accompanying me to Gyongyos, where he introduced me to several officers of the Palatine regiment.

Lieut. Col. Baron de Edelsbacher and Count Teleky gave me letters for the Baron D'Orcy, at Parad, in the northern part of the mountains of Matra. I set out with the horses and servants, supplied by these gentlemen, and attended by an hussar, whose presence might inspire the greater security. This amiable and preventing kind of hospitality I witnessed throughout the country, and I cannot but speak highly of the generous attentions of the good Hungarians. At Parad my entertainment was no less agreeable, and the Baron D'Orcy accompanied me, in my rambles, with all the promptitude imaginable.

The village of Parad is but small, but there are ferrugineous waters that, in the fine season, attract company. The Baron D'Orcy's habitation is only intended for occasional residence in the summer. Every thing has an air of the greatest simplicity, and the whole appears rustic and rural. It forms an assemblage of small buildings with only the ground floor, and disposed, on each side, so as to make a broad street or place. Some serve for the accommodation of the Baron and his people, and others for the reception of visitors. In the middle is a chapel, and in summer, the whole looks more animated and gay than some more stately chateaux. The amiable affability of its possessors might tend to strengthen this feeling.

I intended to visit a certain crater, mentioned by Fichtel, but the baron was eager to conduct me thither, and we accordingly set out in a caravan, the baron, the colonel of the palatine regiment, a neighbouring curate, and myself, with seven domestics or guides. In our way we went to visit some of the baron's alum works, long established, and I was instantly struck with the resemblance of the rocks to some of Mont Dor, in Auvergne. The experiments that I made, after my return to Paris, on some specimens that I brought away, confirmed the analogy in the materials of the two places. With some precautions, alum might be procured at Parad, nearly as pure as that of Munkacs or Musaj, and, of course, like the fine sort known in France by the name of Roman alum.

After this we renewed our excursion to the mountain. For two hours we passed through very thick woods of oaks and beeches, and at different points I observed the *rosa spinosissima* in prodigious quantities, which, with the *crategus aria*, produced a very agreeable diversity. In all this tract I saw none of those eternal firs that appear every where, on equal heights, in the mountains of Schemnitz and Kremnitz.

Arriving at the crater, I found its depth about 180 feet. The whole cavity was filled with very large beech trees, also with crab apple and hazel-nut trees, and brambles, which it was often difficult to get clear of. The sides or walls are perpendicular in some points, and at others have a pretty rapid descent. I could not trace, either on the sides or in the parts adjacent, any vestiges of scorification, such as one would expect to find, had there been an ancient ignivomous aperture, similar to what exist in the extinguished volcanos of Auvergne. I examined every part, the sides, top, bottom, and am convinced that it never was volcanic; it has not even the ordinary form of a crater, an inverted cone, nor is it in the usual position, at the summit of a mountain.

Having acquired a certainty that M. Fichtel and others have been mistaken on this point, we again set out on our return to Parad. In about an hour, descending towards the village, we found the steward and a party of the baron's people, who had prepared a very good dinner, under a tent of branches and foliage. They had brought with them also a relay of horses.

In another excursion which I made to Erlau, I arrived at the town of Sirok, in a valley, through which runs the river Torna. Its ancient castle was built on the point of a white rock, nearly isolated, the flanks of which are torn by deep ravines, and not a tree to be seen about it; it is now in a ruinous state. The higher parts of the rock are almost every where perpendicular. Several chambers of the castle were dug or hollowed out of it. On these great walls we see fragments, and blocks of all sizes and colours, white, yellow, grey, &c., and in one of the caves, others of a black colour. In short, the walls, the courts, and fosses, exhibit, in a numerous collection, all the varieties of massive rock. This castle was taken by assault, in 1596, by the Turks, and the crescent waved on its walls for a long time; at present, it is so encumbered with ruins that it is impossible to form a correct opinion of its strength and construction; from the space which it occupied it must have been very large.

The town of Erlau (Eger, or Jager, Hung. Agria, Lat.) is situated nearly on the confines of the Great Plain that forms, in some measure, the centre of Hungary. It was built by king Stephen, who made it the see of a bishop, since raised to that of an archbishop. It is one of the richest benefices in Hungary; the revenues were so considerable, that the ancient kings ordered the see to be reserved for their fourth son. The town is pretty well built; there are several very good houses, but, in general, it looks dull, which is common to all the small towns in Hungary. The most remarkable buildings are those of the university, constructed at the charge of more than two millions of florins, by the bishop, count Charles Esterhazy. Convenience, neatness, and beauty, are alike consulted; the professors are well lodged and accommodated; the classes, the apartments, are handsome and correctly arranged; the chapel, the library, the hall of conferences, are extremely elegant, and furnished with paintings of uncommon beauty. The buildings are surmounted with a very lofty tower, intended for an observatory, but, unfortunately, it was ill provided with instruments. The cathedral, and several other churches, the episcopal palace, and the house of the comitat, are structures which would not disparage other towns more populous, and from the heights, they give to this an aspect truly imposing.

Behind the town we discern the site of the ancient castle, now scarcely distinguishable by some remains of rubbish. Count Esterhazy, the bishop, was allowed to demolish it, and the materials were made use of in the construction of the University and other buildings. The battlements no longer exist to attest the valour of its ancient inhabitants, but the pages of history retain the remembrance. The town was completely destroyed, in the reign of Bela IV. by the invasion of the Mongols, who carried fire and sword into the heart of Hungary, and turned the most populous countries into vast deserts. But raised again from its ashes, defended by some fortifications, and yet more by Hungarian intrepidity, it sustained, with incredible energy, the most dreadful assaults and sieges. We cannot survey, without admiration, the sanguinary details commemorating the vigorous resistance of its inhabitants against the Austrians and against the Turks.

I shall quote here a passage from a French writer, concurring, with other testimonies, in favour of that patriot zeal which transforms the feeblest into heroes. Erlau was besieged in 1555, by Mehemet Pacha. On the approach of the enemy's army, the whole town resounded with acclamations, men, women, soldiers, all vowed adherence to the following conditions : " the word capitulation is proscribed; death shall be the punishment of him that mentions it. Should the enemy invite to proposals of peace, the answer to be by discharges of artillery. In the case of provisions failing, we will devour one another, and the lot shall determine the victims. The women shall be employed in repairing the walls; they may follow their husbands to the breach, or at the sorties. To prevent any plottings to surrender, no assemblages of above three or four to be allowed within the town."

These desperate conditions were strictly observed; in vain Mehemet sends a trumpet with offers of peace; no answer is returned, and while he is haranguing at the foot of the walls, the inhabitants, in gloomy silence, place four pikes on the rampart, and on them a coffin covered with black, to indicate that the town should be their grave. The trumpeter reported to his general this terrible but eloquent reply; salvos of artillery soon dismantled the castle and unroofed the houses, but the first attack was repulsed, and 8000 Turks perished at the foot of the ramparts. Mehemet orders four assaults at the same instant; the women run to the breach, some rush among the enemy, others roll huge stones, or pour scalding oil on the assailants. The wife, seizing the arms of her husband, pierced by her side, the mother, those of her son, and all, forgetting their weakness and danger, think only of defending their country and religion, and avenging the death of their friends. These examples of female heroism gave a fresh stimulus to the energies of the besieged, who soon became the aggressors, and compelled the Turks to retreat, after the loss of more than 30,000 men.

The hills about Erlau are, in general, covered with vines, that produce a wine much esteemed, but very heady. It strongly resembles some wines from the banks of the Rhone, in Languedoc. Among these hills are some rocks of a grey, compact, calcareous substance, from which issue the hot springs that feed the baths of Erlau. My stay here was short but agreeable. The Baron D'Orcy had obligingly made his house in the town my home, though not present himself, and had my stay been prolonged, I should have met with more friends. The Abbé Titel, a young astronomer, who had spent some time in Paris, entertained me with perfect cordiality, and the Archbishop, Baron Fisher, testified his regret at my hasty departure. I had intended to return to Erlau, after visiting the comitat of Gomor, but proceeded so far, in another direction, that the time would not have sufficed.

In general, I may observe, as a geologist, that an entire analogy exists between the mountains of Matra, the scene of these last excursions, as to the nature and disposition of the rocks that compose them, and those that I had more studiously explored in the country of Schemnitz. Among other points of resemblance, I found, as a naturalist, about Erlau, trunks and branches of opalised wood, as also various kinds of shells, fragments of obsidian, &c. As to the pretended crater, it is simply the upper end of a little valley, partly stopped up with a number of blocks that have fallen from the heights, and thrown in heaps one above another.

CHAPTER IX.

BASALTIC BUTTS OF SALGO, &c.

Quitting the mountains of Matra for a northerly direction, the most prominent object is the point of Salgo at a distance, the conical mass of which rises, in an isolated situation, above all the surrounding heights. On this mountain, according to Busching, the earth, charged with sulphureous vapours, kindled and burnt for two months together; this was in the summer of 1767. I shall not dispute the fact, though I could find no tradition or report concerning it; but if it took place, it could not have been occasioned by sulphureous vapours, the nature of the mountain not warranting the presence of such a combustible, though it was probably of igneous origin.

In exploring the mountain of Samos Ko, I came to an old castle on the summit, which must have been very spacious. Several stories are yet remaining; the walls are composed of basaltic prisms, laid one upon another, and cemented by a very rough mortar, of little solidity in its present state.

The mountain of Salgo, at about three quarters of an hour's journey from the village of that name, is a basaltic mass, rising up among woods and forests scarcely penetrable, and every where exhibiting marks of volcanic productions. They bring to mind the masses of scoriaceous substances about volcanoes, whether alive or extinguished, such as frequently are seen in the Vivarais, under or between layers of basalts. The summit of Salgo is a very narrow point; the castle which bounded it could never have been very extensive. Nothing is to be seen, at present, but some remains of walls, which more resemble a tower for observation than habitations to reside in. Its mean height is about 1920 feet above the level of the sea. Barometrical observations, July 27, 1818. Summit of Salgo at eight in the morning. Height 710 mill. temperature 17 gr. Flying clouds, wind easterly. At the foot of the basaltic mass, half past seven, height 728 mill. temperature 17 gr.

About half an hour's walk from Salgo, is a mountain called Medve, similar in its formation. In piercing through the woods to arrive at it, scoriaceous matter appears scattered over the soil, though often concealed by a vegetable earth that has all the marks and colours of having been emitted from a volcano. At the mountain itself, the characters are so strongly marked that the most hardy neptunist could not call in question their igneous origin. I proceeded in search of a crater in these parts, but the top of the mountain exhibits only a *plateau,* or a level surface, pretty extensive and covered with trees. Scoriæ, however, of every description, abound, inclosed in a red earth, that seems to have proceeded from their decomposition.

In the midst of the plains of Fulek, is another mountainous crest of basaltic formation. It is on it that the remains appear of a strong castle, which, in the fifteenth and sixteenth centuries, was taken, alternately, by the Turks, Germans, and Factions of different parties. But here are no masses of scoriæ, but basaltic tufs of the colour of yellow ochre.

CHAPTER X.

THE ENVIRONS OF TISZOLEZ AND CERTAIN MOUNTAINS IN THE COMITAT OF GOMOR.

Renewing my excursions, I arrived one night, about ten o'clock, at Tiszolez, a little town inhabited by Sclavonians, and situated in the middle of a valley, through which runs the little river Rima. There was no inn, and to procure a lodging I made application to the judge, who had me conducted to a wretched *cabaret,* where was nothing but straw to sleep on. Unluckily, six Jews had arrived before me, whose filthy beards and squalid appearance obliged me to retreat elsewhere. I was taken to a small chamber filled with onions, butter, and cheese, and where a young man, the son, was snoring tremendously. Here I and my domestic passed a part of the night, and the guides, I believe, slept in the street.

In such circumstances I was not long detained in the arms of Morpheus; before day I was in the middle of the village, imbibing the fresh air, and by six o'clock, had advanced a good way towards some mountains I was in quest of. On my return, I inquired for the evangelical minister, soliciting permission to introduce myself to him. Here fortune became propitious, M. Schulek received me with the most engaging kindness, and both he and his lady lodged and entertained me with cordial hospitality.

At Szlana are quicksilver mines, which I entered and explored. The works have been very extensive, but at present the quantities of mercury extracted are not considerable. I next entered the valley of Sajo, on my road to Bethler. The mountains, on both sides, are uncommonly rich in metallic substances, and especially in copper and iron; here are mines which have been, and yet are worked, in a great number of places. At Bethler are iron mines, establishments for forges, foundries, &c. of great importance; they are the property of Count Androssy. These minerals bear a strong resemblance to those of Sweden and Norway, where are whole mountains consisting of them; the analogy prevails also in the rocks that contain them.

In some mountains of these parts are caverns, of no small celebrity in Hungary, partly from their extent, and partly from ice being preserved in them during a great part of the summer. In caverns like these, it is generally thought that they are much colder in summer than winter, nature appearing here in contradiction to itself. I conceive this to be a mistake, from not accurately analysing the circumstances. These caverns are always in the temperature of melting ice, that is, at zero, in summer; and the sensation of cold is more intense as the external heat is greater. On the contrary, in winter, they are never below the external temperature, and no difference of sensation is perceived in entering them. In the first frosts the caverns retain the temperature of zero, on a supposition of ice yet remaining, whilst the cold without has reached several degrees; a sensation of warmth is then felt on entering them. It may be observed, further, that no ice, or very little, is found in these caverns at the beginning of winter, and the contrary occurs in the beginning of summer. In the first case, it is evident that the ice had not melted during the preceding summer, and that the frost had not lasted long enough to acquire fresh forms. In the second place, all the ice appears that had accumulated during the winter, and which had not yet had time to melt.

As false notions prevail on the above subject, I may add, that at the cavern Chaux, in the department of Doubs, it is evident that the ice is formed during the winter. The temperature within the cavern is always as low, in that season, as the external temperature. The water then drops from the vault, in greater or less quantities, and congeals into stalactites and stalagmites, that continue increasing through the winter, the quantity of ice being greater in proportion to the length and the rigour of the frost. It increases even when the frost without is gone, as the air of the cavern is a long time in acquiring an equilibrium of temperature, and the maximum of the quantity of ice obtains only in the spring. Then it begins and continues melting through the summer, so that it is entirely melted, or considerably diminished by the return of winter, when similar phenomena recur. Both the caverns of Szclitze, where I then was, and that of Chaux, and many others in the mountains of Jura, have their apertures turned to the north, which must facilitate the lowering of the temperature during the winter, and keep it, at the same time, from rising rapidly during the summer.

The town of Dobschau* (Dobsina, Sclav.) is one of the most ancient mining towns of Hungary, and situated in the most mountainous part. It was founded by some Germans, in the beginning of the fourteenth century, for the sake of working its mines. Its mountains contain immense mineral riches; here are mines of copper, iron, and cobalt, the productions from which were very considerable, when strict attention was paid to this branch of revenue. According to the miners, all these minerals are in couches or beds, more or less condensed, and very few in veins.

CHAPTER XI.

PLAINS OF IGLO.—MOUNTAIN OF TATRA.—SALT-MINES OF VILLICZKA, &c.

After quitting the comitat of Gomor, my next excursion was to the frontiers of Galicia. Passing through the plains of Iglo, I came to the town of that name, which is but a small place,

---

* This word is often pronounced and written Topfschan, and hence, it has been derived by many from Topfschaven, to look into a pot. The arms of the town represent the circumstance of a miner looking into a pot. This refers to a tradition, that the original miners having assembled to give a name to the town, agreed to take for it the word that the first miner, coming out of the mines, should utter. One of their comrades soon appearing, drew near the fire, exclaiming, " Er muszle zu seinem topfschauen,—I must look into my pot." Others, however, derive it from the situation of the town, appearing, from the very high mountains that surround it, as lying in the bottom of a pot.

though the principal of the sixteen free towns of Zips, and the centre of the royal administration.

It was about half a day's journey from Iglo to Mount Tatra, which I meant to visit. On the way, I called at Gross Lomnitz, on M. Berzeviczy, for whom I had letters of recommendation; he received me in a manner most agreeable to my feelings, and I had no little satisfaction in his society and conversation. In countries so remote, and generally deemed, though erroneously, only half civilized, in comparison of the rest of Europe, to meet with a man so well informed, scientific, and learned, was a source of high gratification. Before supper we walked to the heights behind the castle, and had a magnificent view of the Tatra. Its most acute cone, known by the name of the Peak of Lomnitz, rises majestically, like a nine-pin, above every object around it, and is about 5700 feet above the plain that lies at its foot. It stands completely isolated, and its flanks are marked by deep ravines, produced, in 1813, by a water spout that fell on the summit, unrooting trees, dragging along enormous portions of rock, and hollowing the soil to a great depth. The mountain of Tatra has been described by geographers, as connected with others that branch into Transylvania, but I had many proofs of the contrary. Though I did not scale the summit, I had opportunities of surveying it on every side.

We set out from Lomnitz with very good horses, proceeding in a straight line for the farm of the same name, and reached it in about two hours. The lower parts of the rocks, as we advanced, were partly cultivated with an indifferent kind of oats, further on were meadow grounds, and at the farm appear juniper and fir trees. Here we breakfasted, and leaving our horses, set out on foot, with attendants that carried provisions for a dinner. M. Fabritzi, the fiscal or steward of M. Berzeviczy, would accompany me in this excursion, and this rendered it doubly agreeable. We entered a valley called White Waters, from the usual colour of its white muddy streams that empty themselves into the White Lake. After two hours march among rocks, we discover the elevated peaks, contiguous to that of Lomnitz, which form the natural limits between Hungary and Galicia. Here are varieties in the vegetation; those declivities of the mountains that are not too steep, exhibited thick forests of different pines, with the *sorbus aucuparia*, and the *vaccinium uliginosum* was in great abundance. Approaching the White Lake, the vegetation grows more scanty; the other species disappear, and we find only the *pinus pumilio*, the spreading branches of which form tufts that are sometimes twenty feet in diameter.

After three or four hours' further march, (for the naturalist cannot always reckon distances rigorously) we came to the Green Lake, (Grüne See) so named, as, from the hills that surround it, green spots are seen here and there on the black surface that covers the rest of its waters. Approaching near, I remarked these spots, as arising in places whence issue the little springs that feed the waters, and where the bottom is a white sand, composed of little portions of mica. This lake is at the northern foot of the Peak of Lomnitz; from this point that acute cimex appears quite as high as from the plain. It exhibits a pyramid rising to a peak, and at length, almost vertically above us. It stands in a spacious basin, surrounded with rocks perpendicularly steep, at the foot of which lie, n heaps, the blocks and fragments that are constantly falling from the heights. We heard several *avalanches,* or downfalls, while we were traversing this part. Very near the Green Lake, at the foot of a rock almost perpendicular, in the shape of a needle, is another lake very deep, but much smaller, called the Black Lake, from its waters reflecting a blackish hue. Snow, I am told, never rests on the summits of Tatra, but it is found in the valleys, where, sheltered from the winds, it does not entirely melt throughout the summer. I should have observed, that the White Lake is so named from the waters that roll from the surrounding mountains, being often impregnated with a white calcareous matter.

We were descending very quietly, without any signs of bad weather, but, in this region, naturalists must, it seems, endure the shock of the elements. M. Wahlenburg complains of it, and prefers the climate of Lapland to that of Hungary. M. Townson was unlucky here, also; and just when I was felicitating myself on my better fortune, a clap of thunder, in the mountain, was harbinger to an assemblage of clouds, and the rain fell in torrents. It did not last above half an hour, and our clothes, though well soaked, had time to get dry, so that we returned safe to Lomnitz. I was inured to these sinister adventures, and concerned to find M. Fabritzi, who had accompanied me from complaisance, not a little incommoded.

There are several mines in the mountainous groupe of, or about, Tatra, and especially mines of copper. There is an auriferous vein, inclosed within quartz, towards the summit of the Krivan, but the mines of Botza are in the greatest repute; these are of argentiferous and auriferous copper, and have been worked a very long time. The surrounding mountains give numerous indications of similar materials.

Parallel to the groupe of Tatra, is another mountainous range, rich also in mines. In the valley of Lipto, which is in these parts, are the numerous caverns noticed in maps of Hungary, especially that of Demanova, and described by some authors as containing ossified remains of animals. The valley itself, from its magnificent vegetation, has acquired the surname of Hungarian Switzerland. There are, however, other caverns in the comitats of Arva, Thurotz, &c.

Finding, at Lomnitz, that I was but three days' journey from Villiczka, I felt an inclination to visit its famous salt-mines. I made preparations accordingly, taking care to have my collections sent directly forward to Pest. My baggage I had removed to Eperies, and I took with me only what was necessary for my little excursion into Poland. I set out with horses hired at Gross Lomnitz.

The Polish auberges are many degrees inferior to those of Hungary; this I had soon an opportunity of witnessing. Being obliged to stop at Relyo, in a wretched *cabaret* kept by a Jew, for my bed I had nothing but a bottle of straw spread in the middle of what served me for both chamber and kitchen, wherein I had scarcely room to stir, and which, moreover, was very near the stable. My Jew was very apprehensive of defiling the dirty porrengers that served for his own use, and would have conversed with me, seated on a chair, had I been in a humour to listen to him. My supper was an omelette of fried eggs badly cooked. To enhance my misfortunes, several peasants came in at ten at night, to drink potatoe brandy; the place was nauseating with it, and they would have remained till next morning, had I not assumed the character of a great lord, and dislodged them.

When day appeared, I quitted my laire without waiting for breakfast, though it was my custom to take refreshment before setting out. At the town of Altendorf, I had to undergo an examination by the officers of the customs; this, however, was soon dispatched, as I had only brought a shirt with me, but my passports were only for Hungary, as, from information I had received, there would be no difficulty in passing the frontiers. The clerks, however, thought otherwise, alleging that I should have had letters for quitting Hungary, and that, besides, an order of the Hungarian chancelry could not be valid in an Austrian *douane*, as if every Hungarian must repair to Vienna in quest of a passport for Galicia. The director whom I called upon gave an order for instantly signing my passports, but his wretched scribes stood haggling with me, and seeing me take snuff, pretended to confiscate nearly an ounce that I had in my snuff box. I then threw the whole about the place, and as it was fine and dry like all the snuffs prepared in Hungary, they presently decamped, not caring to come in contact with it.

The whole country of Poland seems very poor; we see nothing but oats and potatoes in cultivation, and an air of wretchedness pervades the peasants. Their clothing consists of a surtout of coarse brown wool, fastened about the body with a leathern girdle; under this few of them wear a shirt; and they have nothing else but linen pantaloons, commonly without stockings or shoes, or in lieu thereof, sandals bound with thongs that pass under the feet. On their heads they wear a round hat, or a woollen bonnet; their hair, filthy and greasy, hangs down behind. The villages contain cabins or hovels of earth or clay, and in the town of Myslinicé, excepting the inn, which is a neat building, and the Town-House, which has nothing in it remarkable, the other dwellings are of a similar description.

After two or three days' travelling, wherein one part of the road lay between two hills very near each other, and on the tops of which we could see the remains of old castles, that defended the passage, and were celebrated in the last wars between Poland and Hungary, I arrived on the heights of Villiczka. Here we survey a vast horizon with not an elevation that deserves the name of a mountain. At a little distance, in the west, the city of Cracow (*Krakau*) appears to great advantage, and even Villiczka exhibited an object on which the eye might repose. Hence, in less than a quarter of an hour, I arrived at the town, the entrance to which is by a kind of suburbs. This part was inhabited by Jews, who, with their large black robes, long beards, and huge hair bonnets, reminded me of Robinson Crusoe in his island. In the town I was shewn to a wretched auberge, the only one in it, where my chamber, perfumed with onions, was a sort of warehouse to the kitchen adjoining; indeed, the passage lay through it. The windows and doors were opened to let in the fresh air, but this had not been done of some years, and they made me a bed as well as they could. About three in the morning I heard the crowing of fowls; I thought, at first, they were under my window, but one of them mounting on the bed, I found there were half a dozen others perched on a pole. As I wished to get rid of them, I had some exercise in driving them out at the window, and this thoroughly awoke me. I was for getting out also, but the doors being secured, I followed the fowls and jumped out of the window.

The little town of Villiczka is situated on the verge of the plains of Poland, and at the northern foot of the mountains that separate it from Hungary. Tradition reports that the mines, which constitute its wealth, were discovered by a shepherd, named Villiczk, and that Queen Cunegonde had them opened about the beginning of the fifteenth century. Its salt mines exceed all others in Europe in their extensive produce, and in the execution of the works and labours. On the day of my arrival I had solicited permission to visit the mines, and the next day the director sent an engineer to accompany me, so that I had an opportunity of examining every thing in detail.

The usual entrance into the mines is by the great well of extraction, as the descent is more speedy than by escaliers, and such precautions are adopted that there is no danger to apprehend. This well or pit is about ten feet in diameter at the mouth, but widens considerably lower down. It is about 200 feet in depth to the first gallery, beyond which we every where descend by superb escaliers. The upper part of the pit is lined with timber, as it passes through a quicksand; the lower parts, which have been cut through the mass of salt, or in the saliferous argile, require no support. The mode of an expeditious descent has nothing frightful in it to a miner; nor am I surprised that all the persons employed would ascend and descend, in a manner instantaneous as it were, rather than traverse four hundred and seventy-six steps by the escalier. In the mines that I had visited heretofore, I descended either upright or seated on the edge of the basket that brings up the minerals, holding the rope in one hand, and a lamp in the other; but, at Villiczka the descent is by a singular process, whereby several, seated in a sort of rope arm-chairs, in divisions, or rows, one above another, are let fall, in a few seconds, in a ythat seems frightful to persons not accustomed to it. Every one here carries a bougie in his hand, so that it appears like a set of chandeliers one above another: the movement is effected by horses.

The saliferous depot of Villiczka has long been the subject of notices published at different times. The stupendous labours in the execution have often excited the enthusiasm of travellers, and have given rise to pompous descriptions, wherein not a little of the marvellous has been mingled. I shall confine myself to a slight sketch of what relates to the works, and what is most remarkable in the mine.

The works at Villiczka are on a grand scale, conducted with perfect regularity, and even with a sort of luxury. Beautiful galleries, large and elevated, form easy communications between all the works of each story; superb escaliers, cut in the saline mass, or constructed of solid timber-work, in the heart of the different excavations, produce a general circulation, and points of junction between the upper surface at the aperture, and the labours throughout, even where they are the deepest.

Exclusive of these magnificent works, which are essential to the mining, and which contrast, in a striking manner, with mining labours in general, particular decorations have been added on certain points. Here is a spacious hall, agreeably ornamented, in the middle of one of the cavities, produced by the clearing away of the salt; there appears a chapel, with columns, statues, &c. cut in the salt itself; in other parts are terraces on the brink of the excavations, also gates representing the entrance of a strong castle, an obelisk commemorating the visit of the Emperor Francis, all regularly fabricated of rock salt. We find also, in different points, inscriptions noticing the presence of the sovereigns; decorated radeaux, on which they pass over the collections of waters and lakes; consecrated paintings, dedicated, by the veneration of the workmen, to the patrons of the labours. Nor is this all; at every step we find traces of magnificent illuminations which have been made, at different periods, in the heart of these depths. Such are the real facts, which have been embellished by a thousand fictions. Some of these may be quoted here; springs and streams of fresh water, a windmill, houses with several stories, as in a town. It has been further reported, that the workmen, when once entered, never quit the place, but this is only true as applied to the horses. Among other fabulous reveries, children were born here that had never seen the day.

In general, this depot may be considered as an immense mass of argile, called by the workmen, halda, disposed, not in strata, but in vast bodies unusually voluminous, to which, names have been given according to their respective positions, and the degree of purity in the salt. The works are divided into stories; the first, or uppermost, is a coarser sort, called *gransalz*, or green salt. The second story exhibits a purer salt, named spiza, immense quantities of which are exported to foreign countries. The third and last story, named szibik, is lamellated, that is, divided into a number of thin plates.

These different collections of salt, as also the saliferous argile that contains them, are of great solidity. Each of them, when worked, is nearly cleared throughout, and then appear immense excavations, the walls of which are well able to support themselves. In the lower parts, the works are only advanced into such bodies of salt as, by their position with respect to the upper galleries, cannot, by fresh cavities, impair the solidity of the rest. From the solidity of these masses, combined with the facility with which they are penetrated, those beautiful escaliers, with the spacious galleries and architectural decora-

tions, by which this mine is distinguished, have been, with less
difficulty, executed.

Several of these cavities contain considerable collections of
water, and even large lakes, into which, as they are cleared
and emptied, portions of the saliferous argile are thrown.
Boats and radeaux are in use on several of them.

The dryness generally remarked in this mine, has not escaped the attention of naturalists, but the same phenomenon
occurs in all salt-mines.   It often contrasts, in a striking manner, with the excessive humidity that pervades works that pass
through earths of another description, previous to arriving at
the salt.

Organic remains have been occasionally discovered in this
mine.   Remnants of cray fish, and the shells called *chamites,*
have been found in the heart of the saliferous argile.   It is not
unusual to meet with ammonites, and other marine shells,
even in the salt itself, and in the argile, petrifications, and pit-
coal.   M. Townson noticed little bivalve shells in the argile
that incloses the spiza salt.   Some have mentioned elephants'
teeth, and the ossifications of quadrupeds, but these have
rather been found in the lands, increased by river slime of the
adjacent plain, than in the saliferous depot.

It may be further observed, that this mine lies at the foot of
a great chain of mountains, consisting of free-stone and argile,
that reach to the Buckawine, and the mountains of Marmaros,
and that all the depots of salt, and all the salt springs of Galicia
and Hungary, are exactly in a similar position.

The greatest depth of the labours in the mine of Villiczka is
about 960 feet below the surface.   The descent into the mine
is about 150 feet below the level of the sea.

As to the organic remains peculiar to these mines, they consist of lignites, or fossile carbonised wood, scattered through
the salt, and marine shells inclosed in the saliferous argile.
The fossile wood is so abundant in the spiza salt, that it is
hardly possible to break off a piece wherein some will not
appear.   Some have nearly passed into a state of jet by trans-
formation, others are altogether bituminous, and retain their
figure.   There are very large trunks and fragments, as well as
very thin branches of trees.   I have been informed that leaves,
in the form of cords, have sometimes been found.   I observed,
in the director's collection, a fruit of a round form, of the size
of a nut, in tolerable preservation.

This fossile appeared to be of a ligneous description, something like the shells of nuts; but I could not distinguish to
what genus of plants it belonged; it had passed into the bituminous state.

What struck me the most in these bituminous lignites, was the very strong and nauseating smell which they emitted, not a little resembling truffle at the height. This becomes insupportable in a chamber where fresh samples are stored; in the mine it is qualified by circumstances, perhaps by the muriatic acid. Indeed, it is not easy to discern it there; the smell that is perceptible, resembles what we find in places confined and not frequently cleaned.

Another more remarkable singularity is, that this smell is exactly like what some species of the medusa, molluscæ, and marine animals, thrown up by the waves on the shore, exhale. The alcohol, in which these animals are preserved, takes the same smell very strong, especially when the decanters are not well stopped up. This is the more noticeable, as I have never observed any vegetable putrefaction with the like property. One instance may form an exception, certain fossile madrepores of Italy, that have been extracted from depots as modern as those of Villiczka.

The shells are found in the saliferous argile, but never in the salt itself. The largest that I have seen are bivalves, from four to five lines in diameter (a line is the twelfth part of an inch). Such as I collected were, apparently, of the genus *tellines,* but they would not bear handling, dissolving instantly into dust. Besides the bivalves, the argilous mass contained an infinite number of fluted, microscopic univalves, very much resembling those found in immense quantities in the fine sands of our seas, and in certain marine depots that have not been very long discovered, in the environs of Paris.

Though I could find no remains of animals in the pure salt, there appears in the king's private cabinet of mineralogy, at Paris, a very distinct fragment of madrepore, in a portion of salt that looks like the green salt of Villiczka.

The circumstances above noted, of lignites, or bituminous wood, found in large quantities in the mines of Villiczka, with the fluted shells, &c. are the more remarkable, as we know of nothing similar in other saliferous depots.

Here, also, I might observe, that in certain mountains to the north, on the banks of the Vistula, in the middle regions of which are lead mines, are calcareous substances, exactly similar to such as appear in the mountain Lime, as it is called, of Derbyshire. To which may be added, that all the depots of salt, at Villiczka and Bochnia, with all those in Gallicia and the Buckawine, as well as in Hungary, are found uniformly in one position, i. e. at the foot of a chain of mountains. Also, that the saliferous depots of Poland are always on the borders of plains, and only at the height of about 760 feet above the level of the sea, while in the depots of the Alps, that are, apparently, of more ancient formation, they are found at the height of 4850 feet above the same level.

The salt-mine of Bochnia is not above four leagues from that of Villiczka; it exhibits similar characters, and is probably a continuation of it. The whole substance of the soil, between the two towns, is homogeneous. But at Bochnia we find, about the town, and on the very surface of the soil, an argilous matter that prognosticates the vicinity of the saliferous argile.

In some of the neighbouring forests, which are covered with vast numbers of *sapinettes*, a very elegant species of fir, and here and there with the thayd, I remarked ant-hills of extraordinary magnitude; some were not less than ten feet in diameter at the base, and in height exceeded my stature. They formed hills of small bits of wood, accumulated into a congeries. There were many others smaller, but more considerable than any that we meet with in the woods of France. These forests are extremely solitary and of unknown antiquity.

While in these parts of Poland, I was proceeding one day, on a Sunday, to Altsandec, where all the inhabitants, peasants, were promenading the village in their best apparel. This might be reckoned pretty good, but I never could reconcile myself to that singular mode, though almost universal, of having the shirt hanging down over a blue *culotte,* and adjusted to the waist by a dark-coloured flannel waistcoat.

Approaching the frontiers, I found the roads extremely dangerous, from passing along declivities where are no traces of a visible path, and where carriages frightfully incline to a descent. The inclination sometimes appeared so considerable, that I was eager to take the measure of it, but how was I astonished to find it, where the descent was most rapid, at not more than from twenty to twenty-five degrees. The fact is, that our senses misled us frequently in these approximate computations; however, no carriage could travel here with security, were the friction less considerable. In France, the high roads, where the descent is most rapid, are, by law, restricted to five degrees inclination. Occasionally, roads of this description are met with in Hungary, but mostly in the mountainous parts; where they are descending, the drivers pass without hesitation, though sometimes at the risque of getting stuck fast at the bottom. Indeed, throughout Hungary, the roads are in general execrable. Horses and carriages drive over such points as no one in France would ever think of passing.

Proceeding towards Lublo, to enter again into Hungary, over some hills of moderate height, I found an old castle, (an occurrence pretty frequent) and soon after, at the bottom of a valley, had to go through the ruins of a village, destroyed by an inundation; to prevent similar accidents, it was rebuilt on the hill. Lublo is a pretty considerable town, and has baths in its neighbourhood, of some repute. Unfortunately, I arrived on the eve of a great market-day, and the inn, and both public and private houses, were full of guests, so that there was no possibility of getting a lodging. No doubt my equipage would appear singular; I was taken for a comedian. The inn-keeper would gladly have entertained me, when I promised him much diversion, but I was obliged to retire and re-pass the river Poprad, in quest of a cabaret, where the peasants were dancing, and they usually continue the sport through the night. I then had the bed removed to the coach-house, where I slept quietly; my domestic lay in the pantry, and my coachman on some straw in the stable.

The little town of Bartfeld, where I arrived next, is tolerably well built; its situation is pleasant, and it would be an agreeable place, were it not encumbered with the ruins of its ramparts, which bear an impression of desolation. It has ranked among the royal free towns since 1376, and has a pretty considerable trade in wines, wool, and corn, forming an entrepot between Hungary and Poland. About half a league north of the town are baths of great celebrity, and deservedly so from the excellent quality of their acidulous waters. They have nothing of that hepatic smell, commonly emitted by similar springs in Hungary, nor of that iron taste which is often disagreeable, though the waters may be very wholesome. They are in a situation extremely picturesque, and are the most esteemed of any in Hungary, being exported to considerable distances, as were formerly the waters of Seltz, till artificial means of producing them were discovered.

On leaving Bartfeld, I descended the valley of Topla, and there my coachman contrived to overset the carriage, in as good a road as any in Hungary. To enhance my misfortune, we plunged into a brook, and my barometer was broke in the fall. All the samples that I had been collecting, since my departure from Kesmark, were immersed in the water, and the sack which contained them rolled also into the stream. I had not paper enough to wrap them in a second time, and, to remedy these disasters, I was under the necessity of repairing to Eperies. But misfortunes seldom come alone, and in crossing certain hills, over roads which I shall call diabolical, the carriage rolled over a second time, and the coachman, who had not learned caution from the first accident, here broke his shoulder bone.

One general remark may be made here, that the salt-springs and saliferous depots are constantly found conterminal with (i. e. more less bordering on) sands, whether of a deep solid mass or otherwise, mixed with argilous couches. This remark will apply to Eastern Galicia and the Buckawine, taking in the depots of Dobroniel, Drohobicz, Lisovice, Delatyn, Kossow, Solka, &c. stretching from NW. to SE. and passing on to Bochnia and Villiczka. A similar remark may be made, as applicable, in some measure, to the numerous iron mines and works at Smolna, Orow, Skole, Myzun, Weldzicz, Rotzniatow, &c. as also in the Buckawine, and on the frontiers of Moldavia, these are found between the couches of argilous sand and the free-stone with calcareous cement. To which may be added, that it is especially in the districts occupied by this free-stone and argile, that all the salt-springs and saliferous depots, at the northern foot of the Carpathians, from Villiczka and Brochnia to Portestye in the Buckawine, are found. And further, these saliferous depots differ materially from those in all other countries, as containing a considerable quantity of organic remains. These may be here recapitulated, as consisting generally of bivalve shells, that appear to belong to the telline genus, of small microscopical, multilocular shells, of the renalite, rotalite, or discorbite genera; and lastly, of lignites, in larger or smaller pieces, wherein are lodged trunks and branches of trees, intermingled with fruits and leaves.

———

CHAPTER XII.

MOUNTAINS BETWEEN EPERIES AND TOKAI, OPALS, &c.

My arrival at Eperies could not repair my disasters, as I had no tubes for the barometer in the baggage I had forwarded thither, and unluckily, though I ranged about the town, I could not find one *barometmacher* in it. The bad weather, too, prevented my geological perambulations in the mountains, and M. Sennovitz, the only naturalist I wished to see, being absent, I spent my time in promenading the town with my umbrella. Judging of it, under such circumstances, Eperies appeared to me very large, well built, and, what is not common in Hungary, the streets are decently paved, and have rather a neat appearance. The inhabitants may be rated at from 7 to 8000, consisting of Germans, Sclavonians, and Hungarians. The first are by far the most numerous, and the Hungarians are but few in number. This town was raised to the rank of a royal free town towards the end of the fourteenth century, and it is now the most considerable of any in the comitat. The other free royal towns are Zeben and Bartfeld; the former (Sabino, Sclav.) takes its name from Sabina, sister to king Bela III. Eperies is surrounded with walls that are in pretty good condition, but it was often taken by the Polanders, by Ragotzky, and others, and suffered much in different wars. It is now one of the chief towns of Hungary. Here is a tribunal and a garrison; the trade is pretty considerable, and there are several manufactures. The Lutherans have a college here of some reputation, and they are very numerous. There is one very good inn, but they charged me very high for my entertainment.

The weather clearing up in the afternoon, I walked out of the town towards the hill Calvarienberg, on the sides of which are several little chapels painted white and red, and a church at the top. These different buildings, intermingled with trees, present a varied and magnificent scene.

Among some freestone hills, a little east of the town, are the salt-mines of Savar, that have been worked for several centuries, but were more considerable formerly than at present. The salt-springs issue immediately from the freestone, and are covered here, as in the plains of Poland, by arenaceous or sandy beds, not solid or consistent. It is probable that deeper researches would lead to very considerable depots of salt, as the geological relations are analogous to those of Villiczka and Bochnia.

I returned to Eperies with an intention of proceeding to Kaschau, and having ordered horses at the post-house, I set out in rainy weather. Arriving at Habsany, the first post station, meaning to visit a depot of opals, and somewhat in ill humour with the weather, fortune befriended me. As chance would have it, the office clerk went to consult his master about promising me the horses, but he soon returned with an invitation to enter the chateau; here I found, in lieu of an ordinary post-master, a gentleman of singular affability, M. Edward Bujanovics; he would have me stay dinner to judge of the weather, and promised me the company of the tutor to his children, as far as to Cservenitza. The accident of my barometer was also repaired; he tendered me one constructed on the plan of Reichenbach, that he had purchased at Vienna. I took knowledge of the quantity of mercury that it contained, should an opportunity offer of comparing it with another, the better to ascertain the correctness of my observations.

In my route from Habsany to Cservenitza, I first crossed

the plains of Hernat and Tarza, consisting of depots of alluvion or of cultivated lands. I then passed over some hills also under cultivation, and at length arrived at the opal mines, which are at some distance beyond the village of Cservenitza.

These mines, which constitute the riches and reputation of the country, have been worked for ages; the labours are very considerable. Fichtel reports, from papers in the archives of Kaschau, that in the year 1400, three hundred workmen were employed in the county of Cservenitza, either in the search of opal or in the quicksilver works. It is not very likely that these were in regular employment; they might be peasants of the neighbourhood, who anciently enjoyed the privilege of seeking for opal wherever they could find it. It was only at a more modern period that the labours in quest of this precious stone became individual property. The Austrian government had possession of it for a certain time, and then abandoned it. The Baron de Brudern has lately obtained some right herein, on condition of employing workmen regularly; till then the works had been carried on without any general plan. At the passage where I descended thirty men were at work, at the rate of 40 kreutzer per day, (about 14 Sous of French money.) Two comptrollers were here to superintend the men and conduct the works, also to see that no labours were carried on in the adjacent parts. When at Vienna the Baron de Brudern had promised me a letter, but not having seen him since, I should have had no little trouble in getting permission to visit the works, had I not been accompanied by the governor of the children of M. Bujanovics. The comptrollers, however, conducted me every where with a degree of complaisance, but watching my every movement. My object was to examine the rock, and to ascertain the variety of opal, the most important in respect of science, though of little value in common estimation.

I visited successively the principal mines, commencing with the mountain of Dubnick. Here the opal is found in a rough long conglomerat, in veins more or less extensive, the opaline matter filtrating into fissures which it fills up in whole or in part. The most common sorts are the opaque opal, of a yellowish or reddish white, and the milky opal, more or less pellucid; there is also the *fruar* opal, or opal of fire, in pretty good abundance.

At a little distance is the Pred Branya, south of Dubnick, and near that another mine, at the mountain named Libanka. It is here that the works have been prosecuted with the greatest activity, sometimes in open air, and sometimes by subterranean excavations. I found much to reprehend in the plan and disposition of these labours.

In the above long conglomerats, which are always more or less ferrugineous, are veins of a very fine matter, wherein the oxyde of iron, or rather the hydrate of iron, is very abundant. Sometimes these veins are conjoined with veins of a siliceous opaline matter, and the two substances get mixed. From them results a true opal jasper, more or less ferrugineous, also opals mingled with iron. The finest stones, such as we have in our collections, mostly come from a variety of trachytic conglomerat in this mine, as also the opal prisms. In this part the labours have been most considerable. Some years ago an opal of the finest sort was found, of the size of a small crown piece; it was disposed of, according to report, for 30,000 florins, or about 79,000 francs. In the conglomerat the opal, for use in commerce, is found near the surface, as well as at remote depths.

The environs of Cservernitza are not the only places of these mountains where the opal is found; there are mines, it seems, at Bunita, at Erdoske, and near Sovar, as also towards the south, at Herlany, at Kenieneze, &c. In these points, last mentioned, large quantities of common opal and of opal jasper are excavated, erroneously designated by the name of pechstein. In former times there were also opal mines at Zamuto, which were rather prohibited than abandoned, and at present very fine stones are, occasionally, discovered there. In general, opals are extremely abundant in all this trachytic groupe of hills, and indices of them unexplored I thought I could discern in various points, but none are so beautiful or in such abundance as in the environs of Cservenitza—and what is rather remarkable, a particular character attaches to the conglomerat that contains it.

After this excursion I returned to Habsany, intending to proceed afterwards to Kaschau. M. Bujanovicz had obligingly provided me a lodging in his house, though he was absent from home. The day after my arrival at Kaschau I found myself detained by rainy weather, though I had little occasion to prolong my stay. The Abbé Este, professor of physics in the university, for whom I had letters of recommendation, was going to spend his vacation in little journeys among his friends. I had recommendations to several of them, and the Abbé offering me a seat in his carriage, we so adjusted matters that for fifteen days, consecutive, we were frequently together; the society of this old gentleman being every way agreeable, and his attentions to me unbounded.

Kaschau (Kassa, Hung. Kossiec, Sclav. Cassovia, Lat.) is the principal town of Upper Hungary; it was founded by certain Saxon families that came to settle there in the reign of Geysa II

Here they raised two villages, one of which, the present town, was raised to the rank of a free town, by Bela IV. It was then surrounded with walls, and became one of the strongest places in Hungary. The inhabitants are from 6 to 7000; here is an administrative chamber, as also a garrison and a commandant. The town is pretty well built, and there are several very neat houses, but the way of living is in general simple, and without luxury. In the winter, the neighbouring gentry come to reside in it. To these belong certain great houses that might pass for hotels in Paris. There are several spacious caseans and churches, both catholic and reformed. The principal church, built in the fourteenth century, is a very handsome structure, of an agreeable Gothic architecture; it forms the most prominent object to shew to strangers. The university was founded about the middle of the seventeenth century, by the bishop of Erlau, benedict Kisdy; the reformed have also erected a college. In short, Kaschau is one of the first towns of Hungary, and has every thing to render it agreeable to a stranger; next to Pest, Buda, and Presburg, I would give it the preference for a constant residence.

The hills about the town are mostly covered with vineyards; further on are the mountains of Dargo, all covered with thick forests, consisting entirely of oaks. Pursuing this excursion to reach Talkebanya, I crossed the plains of Ondava, covered with little eminences of a sandy formation, and with few marks of cultivation. Further on, from the summit of some hills above Galzecs, the prospect is most beautiful and extensive, and the weather being favourable I drew a sketch of it; the forepart exhibits a level country under cultivation; the first hills have, here and there, groves or patches of wood, but all the loftier region behind is entirely covered with it.

Telkebanya is a village at the foot of the mountains that formerly had mines of gold of some celebrity. I found an auberge in it, kept by a jew, who provided me with a very neat little chamber, after warranting an assurance that I meant to pay him. After that, I had no reason to complain; I was well entertained at a moderate expense, and the next day he took care that I should not be overcharged by the guides that I was obliged to hire. I must here observe, with regret, that the Jewish publicans, against whom I had entertained prejudices, were in general far more reasonable, in my dealings with them, than others of the catholic faith, who frequently extorted from me in a most unchristianlike manner.

In the evening I had provided a guide to the mines, and next morning early we were on our journey. The country was partly covered with vegetation, and partly under cultivation. I observed also large quantities of jasper, and pebbles of molar porphyry, more or less siliceous. After three quarters of an hour's walk, we arrived at the mines, where, my visit being short, and the labours having been ill conducted, I could only collect, in general, that the auriferous depot is found in the trachytic mass, or more particularly in rocks that strongly resemble molar porphyry.

There were but three or four men at work, employed occasionally, but from bad management they seemed to be losing their time and labour. I may observe here, that the map which Fichtel gives of this district, and of the whole tract between Eperies and Tokai, is not to be depended upon ; I detected a number of false positions. I may further remark, that the opal of this district (Telkebanya) is in nothing more remarkable, than in an exact likeness to that discovered by M. Humboldt, at Zimepan, in Mexico ; the geological circumstances are in strict analogy, and the samples from the New World, now at Berlin, could not be distinguished from those at Telkebanya, if the labels attached to them were lost.

Passing through a valley covered with a forest of beech and oak trees, and afterwards over mountains in horrible roads where we were up to the ancles in mud, we arrived at Tolcsva, wet to the skin from a heavy rain, and bespattered with dirt up to our ears. We had, indeed, the look of banditti rather than of persons used to good company. M. de Szirmay, for whom I had letters, was not at home, and the only individual in the house was a girl, to whom my appearance was but an indifferent recommendation. She received me after some hesitation, when I had explained the particulars, conducted me into a chamber and made preparations for supper, which was as necessary as a lodging. Next morning M. de Szirmay arrived, and expressed not a little concern that I had intruded myself, as it were, into his house. M. de S. was only occasionally at Tolcsva, but he made me promise to meet him at Uj Hely, to proceed afterwards to his house near Hommona, at the foot of the mountains of Vihorlet, which I wanted to explore.

The town is pretty considerable, and may contain three or four thousand souls. The Jews are so numerous, that at first they seemed to be the only inhabitants. Out of the town are numerous plantations of vineyards, as also caves hollowed out in the pouncy conglomerat, with stone doors to them ; and about a quarter of an hour's walk from the town are extensive quarries of mollions, a coarse rough stone used for ordinary buildings.

I then proceeded across the mountains, which are entirely

their mutual pressure runs a syrup, very thick, extremely sweet and aromatic, which is collected with great care. The quantity may be augmented a little by pressing the grapes lightly, but so as not to bring away any of the pulpous matter, as that would tinge the taste of the juice. This juice sometimes takes the name of essence, it is mixed, in a certain proportion, with the juice of the common grape as it comes from the hogshead, before the gross matter is submitted to the press. This mixture, after fermentation, produces the real ausbruch, a term which corresponds to what is called in French *mere goutte*. The maslas is made by mixing the residue of the half-dried grapes, after squeezing them harder, to crush the pulp, with the common wine, both that which is obtained from treading and that which comes from the press.

The wines that pass under the name of Tokay are very dissimilar, and very often the resemblance is merely nominal. I have tasted all the different sorts, and among them have found some that may be called very bad. Some are of a straw colour, with a slight greenish tinge; in general I consider these as the best; others are of a brownish yellow, more or less strongly marked. Some are clear, others thick and turbid, but these last are often very excellent; they had, probably, been bottled before the sediment had settled. In fact, the wine, as exported in little barrels, contains a large quantity of mucilaginous matter that settles very slowly, so that when it arrives at its destination some time must elapse before it will be fit to put into bottles. On the *mare* or gross substance of the grapes, it is common to pour a fresh quantity of good wine, which, when well shaken, takes a sweet and very agreeable flavour; to this new mixture they also give the name of maslas.

Wines of the best quality are soon disposed of, with a reserve of some for the domestic consumption of the owners. A very large quantity goes into Poland, and there they are found to be the best, from the custom of keeping them a length of time. The prices vary according to their age; in the district of Tokay Proper, good wines of some years standing are at a ducat (twelve francs) a bottle, but in Poland they are at two, three, or five ducats, as kept longer or shorter.

A notion generally prevails, at least in France, that the real Tokay is only made in places where the imperial family have possessions, and that it is only from their cellars that it can be had in perfection. The Hungarians deny this, and allege that many land owners have vines of the very best quality. They assign the pre-eminence to the environs of Tarezal, and the second rank to the canton of Erdo-Benye, where the exposure to the sun is peculiarly favourable. This distinction I have

derived from other parts of Hungary, as there was no safe re-
lying on the pretensions of the two rival cantons.

The genuine wines of Tokay are supereminently excellent,
having a particular flavour which I cannot well define, and not
to be found even in such as come nearest to them. But the
superiority will not make amends for the price they are at in
France, compared with the wines of Frontiniac and Lunel,
which very strongly resemble them. I have no doubt but that
equal care in the culture, as to the maturity and desiccation,
with the precaution of throwing out spoiled grapes, &c. would
produce wines in Languedoc that might match with those of
Tokay. The wines that are fabricated with grapes dried artifi-
cially, are somewhat like the Tokay, and are not seldom sold
under that name.

In various other parts of Hungary luscious wines are made
according to the methods in use at Tokay. Some are white,
others red, but in general they are of an inferior quality. Indeed the wines of Memes, on the frontiers of Transylvania,
may enter into rivalship; it is red, sweet, and very spiritous,
with the finest and most agreeable flavour imaginable. Several
prefer it to the wine of Tokay, and I am one of the number—
yet I think it still more unlike Tokay than our best Lunel.
But whatever its good qualities may be, its reputation falls far
short of what it deserves—the name of Tokay is uppermost in
the market.

I shall now resume the course of my mineralogical journeys. In quitting Tokay I returned to Toclsva, to pack up
my collections, and send them on to Pest. Then, setting out
from Toclsva for a series of mountains that form the frontiers
of the Marmoros and the Buckawine, the first part of the
road lay in a plain, with nothing particularly observable till I
came to the banks of the Bodrog, which are very agreeable,
along which we coasted to near Saros Patak, where we turned
out of the road to visit a mountain, at some distance, famous
for its mill-stone quarries. On our arrival, I observed a
striking similitude, in all the varieties and accidents of geological circumstances, between these quarries and those of Konigsberg and Hlinik.

I then returned to Saros Patak, where I had left my carriage,
and proceeded in the direction for Uj Heby; on my arrival I
found M. de Szirmay waiting for me. I alighted at the house
of the comitat, where was an assemblage of persons occasioned
by a squabble, like what occurs sometimes on the frontiers of
France and Spain. For a long time, the inhabitants of a tract
bordering on that of Erdo-Benye, had complained of their
neighbours for pasturing their cattle on a mountain which be-

longed to them, as they alleged. For this violation of their rights, one fine day in the year 1818, they proceeded to bring away the whole herd to their own village. Then the inhabitants of Benye, with the judge at their head, came, *vi et armis*, to reclaim possession. A bloody contest ensued, wherein several individuals were killed, and a number of women and children wounded. The people took back their cattle in triumph, but eventually it will prove a serious matter to them and to the judge. Here M. de Szirmay presented me to the baron Malony, who politely invited me to dinner.

CHAPTER XIII.

MOUNTAINS OF VIHERLET.

On quitting Uj Hely I proceeded next for the Udva, near Komona, where M. de Szirmay resided occasionally. At Lazony I stopped a little at the house of M. Paul Szirmay, where the Abbé Este met me by appointment. My reception here was most agreeable, and I took leave with regret, the next day the Abbé Este accompanied me to Udva, and afterwards to Munkacs. On the summit of a mountain we passed by the old castle of Barks, and found the town of Homona, lying in a sort of basin, surrounded with hills of freestone. These connect with the mountains that form the boundaries of Hungary and Galicia. The village of Udva is at a little distance among the hills.

I left Udva early the next morning, on a visit to the mountains of Vihorlet; at Dluha I took up M. Alex. Szirmay, who would accompany me in this excursion. Leaving Dluha we came to a forge, where men were at work on different minerals, the most valuable of which was carbonated iron, from Ostrosznicsa; its colour was a light grey, with a tinge of yellow. Here were also minerals from Varano, much mixed with earth, and in the middle of them concreted parts of hydrated iron. I surveyed the whole establishment, and took notes of the different minerals that were lying in heaps about it.

Our course was then directed for the rock of Szinna, which may be discerned at a very great distance. Our guides insisted that it would require four hours to reach the summit, but being inured to the ascent of mountains I judged otherwise; in fact, we arrived there in a hour and a half. All these mountains are covered with thick forests, through which now and then we discerned some slight traces of road. The rock of Szinna is an abrupt high and steep precipice, but the ascent is pretty easy from a number of steps, though of an irregular description. The summit is a little plain, pretty level, commanding a view of the whole country. We descended then in quest of a lake at the bottom, on the banks of which, near a wood, our attendants lighted a great fire, prepared provisions, and we encamped for the night. Awaking at intervals, I promenaded the little valley adjacent to the lake. In this solitary scene my sensations were of a truly singular kind. The profound obscurity that pervaded the forests, the expansive sheet of still water, the stars reflecting a twinkling light on its surface, produced a beautiful and affecting scene, gratifying not only to a man of taste, but to a philosopher, and such as no poetical similes could do justice to.

The lake is every where surrounded with mountains of some height, and it receives all their waters. These have a passage through a winding and very narrow valley, with a forge and a flood-gate at the end, to regulate the volume of water. The sides of the mountains are very steep hereabouts, and it proves very fatiguing to scale their summits. They are interrupted by a great number of little valleys, through which it is often difficult to find the road.

After this excursion we returned to Dluha, and thence to Udva. Next day we set out (the Abbé Este was with me) for another excursion on the mountains of Vihorlet. We had intended dining at Vinna, but entering the chateau of Ormezo, we were so importuned to stop, that we could not resist the invitation. Here we found a numerous company, several being of the most considerable families in Hungary, and I had the pleasure of being introduced to their acquaintance. The society was excellent, and the dinner party very lively and gay; we took leave, however, proceeding for Nagy Mihaly. The maps which I had of this part of Hungary presented a number of hills, but our road lay wholly over a plain.

At Nagy Mihaly, we alighted at the chateau of Count Albert Staray, the exterior of which is in the modern style, with every regard to convenience and symmetry. The architect has skilfully availed himself of two ancient towers that had a gloomy appearance, and uniting them by a portico, with a terrace over it, every semblance of antique fortification has disappeared. The interior is also decorated with a display of taste and elegance that forms a striking contrast to the simplicity that reigns, in general, throughout the dwellings in Hungary.

From Nagy Mihaly I made an excursion to Vinna, where I had the honour of visiting the Countess Wallenstein. The village lies at the foot of a mountain, and her old castle is situated on an isolated point adjacent. It is the fate of travellers, and especially of the naturalist, to break off an acquaintance abruptly, which it would be his highest pleasure to cultivate. Setting out early from Vinna, it was evening before we reached the residence of Count Barkoczi, at Palocz. The country was level, but a marsh intercepted our direct route, and we had frequently to wind about it. Next morning we set out early for Ünghvar, but rainy weather coming on, the rest of my journey became toilsome. Several excursions that I had projected I was obliged to abandon, and to content myself with such information as I could collect from different quarters. In some of the mountains, in the parts adjacent, consisting of trachytic conglomerats, are found the minerals of iron, or rather, of silico-ferrugineous matter, in use at Domonya, and partly to aid the fusion of other minerals.

At Munkacs, we alighted at the house of M. Derceeny, distinguished by his various scientific researches, and more especially by his discovery, in Hungary, of aluniferous or alum rocks, exactly resembling those of Tolfa, in the Roman states. These, which are in the comitat of Beregh, furnish a new and very important branch of industry to the district.

The country of Munkacs was the cradle of the Magyars, where they settled towards the end of the ninth century, under their chief, Alom. It is one of the finest and richest countries of the kingdom. The town of Munkacs has a melancholy aspect; it was formerly surrounded with walls. The fortress, which has been notified in history by the wars of Tekely and Ragolski, was built in 1360, by Theodore Keriatovics, duke of Munkacs, and enlarged afterwards at different times, by the princes of Transylvania, in whose possession it long remained. It stands on the summit of an isolated butt, in the middle of the plain, and is in very good preservation. For some time it has served as a place of custody for state prisoners, but had none at the time of my visit. In the interior, every thing was extremely neat, but the different partitions intended for the prisoners, were such as to excite horror. The windows are so contrived as to intercept every view of the country; the walls are remarkably thick, and pierced obliquely, so that the day-light can only enter from above. The aperture, however, is large enough, thoroughly to lighten a little chamber, so that the prisoner may have the benefit of reading, or of employing himself in some labour. In one of the apartments of the castle, we find portraits of the Ragolski family. I know not how far they exhibit a resemblance, but they have an ill-looking aspect, and the last chief of the insurgents, with somewhat of a military air, appears also ungracious and forbidding, so that I felt no inclination to regret his memory. The mantle of this last is preserved in the church among the sacerdotal ornaments.

The aluniferous rocks that formed a principal object of my visit to this part of Hungary, are not at Munkacs, but in the country of Bereghz Sasz, where they are found in abundance. There is only one quarry of alum works at Munkacs, where M. Dereseny has introduced the process in use at Tolfa. The minerals are so intermingled, that an average product is obtained in the rate of about twelve for a hundred. They first go through an operation by fire, and then are removed to a sort of threshing floor, where they are constantly watered to reduce them to a paste, and after another operation by hot water, and evaporation, they are deposited in tubs to let the alum crystallise.

The weather continued unfavourable, but I was under the necessity of quitting Munkacs. The Abbé Este then returned to Unghvar, and I took the direction for Bereghzasz. In the afternoon I reached Bereghzasz, and presented my letters to the baron Pereny. Among the adjacent hills I observed a great number of vineyards that produced a pretty good wine, the exposure or situation being favourable.

The baron Pereny had sent for the director of the alum works at Deda, to accompany me to Musaj, and we set out next morning. At the village we found some alum works, and M. Wobry, the director, ordered a young man to attend me in my visit. Quarries of mill stones were formerly worked here, and are still occasionally, though considered as inferior to those of Saros Patak, and Hlinik, but the aluniferous rocks, discovered by M. Derceny, have greatly enhanced the importance of this whole tract.

Petrified wood is found here, in the midst of the aluniferous rock. Fragments are found partly in a siliceous state, and partly in the state of compact alunite. M. Derceseny shewed me some beautiful specimens, and presented me with some, the characters of which are strongly marked.

A question here arises, whether the facts observed at Musaj are analogous, in their circumstances, to those at aluniferous depots in other parts of the globe? Probabilities may be founded on the apparent identity of the products, and we may adopt one general remark, that when there is an exact conformity between rocks, in a pretty considerable number of their samples, it is rare that the same does not exist also in the geological relations. But if we compare the products of the mountains of Musaj, with those collected at Tolfa, at

Piombino, in the islands of the Archipelago, as Milo, Nipo-
ligo, &c., the resemblance would be so perfect, even in minute
particulars, that if the samples of the different collections were
confounded, it would be impossible to point out their local
origin.

As to the alunite, or the substance that, from its intermix-
ture, furnishes alum by calcination, the samples that I collected
at Musaj make it appear that it is a very distinct species, to
be determined by its chymical and crystallographical characters.

CHAPTER XIV.

BRIEF NOTICES RELATIVE TO TRANSYLVANIA AND THE BANAT.

Towards the central part of the principality, in a westerly
direction, on the groupe of mountains that rise above Carls-
burg, are a number of mines of salt, and of salt springs.   In
several places the labours are very considerable, the works
being conducted in large galleries.   Such are those of Thorda,
of Dées, Kollos, and Szek, also of Viz Akna to the south, in
the vicinity of Hermanstadt.

Near to Sibo, on the banks of the Szamos, gypsum is found
in large quantities, either white or more or less coloured; ornamental articles, of various kinds, are made of it.

In one part of Transylvania, the country of Kapnik, the
mountains in the north, are pronounced, by Fichtel, to be volcanic formations; but this opinion is inadmissible.   The rocks
which he calls Lavas, are, in reality, porphyric grunsteins.   I
had positive proofs of this, in the collections of M. Schuster,
at Pest.   Near to Fekeleto are mining works, from which are
produced the red mottled calcairs, known by the name of
marble of Grosswardein.   There are also variously coloured
marble mines about Belenyes and Vasko, and at Funacza is a
cavern of considerable magnitude, wherein the ossified remains
of quadrupeds have been found.   In general, the mines that
form the riches of Transylvania are found in the porphyric
grunstein.   The mines, in that part called the Banat, are uncommonly rich, and particularly in copper, with an intermix-
ture at times with silver and gold.   The superb specimens of
blue carbonated copper, of Moldava, Oraircza, Dognazka, &c.,
are well known, and are only inferior to those discovered of
late years, at St. Bel, near Lyons.   In these mines also are
found those beautiful green granets, of which some mineralogists are for forming a particular species.

Such are the general facts that I could collect respecting Transylvania; it is, however, a country abounding in objects interesting for a naturalist to visit.

CHAPTER XV.

DEBRETZIN, NATRON LAKES, &C.—THE AUTHOR'S RETURN TO VIENNA.

The continuance of rainy weather for eight days together, and the very bad roads, rendered my future progress discouraging. My papers had been frequently wetted, and I was unable to preserve what I was collecting, or to make regular connected observations. I had intended to cross the mountains of the Marmaros, but then I should have been under the necessity of sleeping in the open air, which then was impracticable. I determined for Debretzin, and quitting Ardo, began to cross the plains of Szaboes. I had been told of the difficulties of travelling through districts overspread with marshes, but could have formed no idea of the horses being up to the belly in mud, and the carriage in danger of sticking fast in it, and even of being overturned. To aggravate my misfortunes, I could only procure oxen to the first station, and to reach the second; besides oxen, I was obliged to have two Wallachians for my guides. This was the first and only time I had to complain of the Hungarian peasants; these were ill-looking figures, whose dress and appearance prejudiced me against them from first setting out. From a negligence which disgusted me, they proceeded to ill-humour, and at length grew insolent. I was seriously exasperated, frequently threatening them with my cane, and with the bastinado on reaching the next station. My cool and determined air had its effect, and though we were at night-fall in the midst of the marshes, we arrived safe at Nagy Kallo. Here the fellows asked my pardon, dreading lest I should put my threat in execution.

At this place I was in danger of starving, as all the provisions in the auberge had been consumed, and I had to content myself with a small loaf and a glass of bad wine. Nagy Kallo was marked on my map as a post establishment, but for six years no demand had been made on the post-master, and I was obliged to have recourse to the worspan or judge. I had to wait some time, as he could only find oxen, and would hardly propose my taking horses extraordinary, that is, paying the double station. Assuring him that I would readily do this, and treat him besides with wine, my generosity was not thrown away, for, instead of oxen and Wallachians, I had four good horses and a well-behaved guide, with whom I advanced rapidly to Teglas.

At Teglas I had a letter for M. De Bek, who happened to be absent. I was kindly entertained, however, by madame de Bec, with whom I found two French, or rather Belgian young ladies, her relations, that agreeably brought my own country to recollection. Before dinner I promenaded the gardens, and had only one fault to find, their being in a plain perfectly level.

Previous to my entering Debretzin, the aspect appeared barren and cheerless, and at the return of day, my judgment of it was still more unfavourable, as most of the houses have but one story, and if two or three, here and there have two stories, the buildings, in forming a comparative estimate, would be little valued in any other scene. The streets are not paved, and already, though the season was not far advanced, and the rains had only lasted a few days, it was hardly possible to pass from the middle of the street to the houses without considerable deviations, to find some fragments of a causeway.

Natron is found in abundance in the environs of Debretzin, in a state of solution, among the marshes and lakes that spread on all sides of the plain. It is found, more or less, from the plains of Szathmar, to those in the comitats of Bacs and Pest, also in those of Stuhlweissenburg and Œdenburg, but more particularly between Debretzin and Nagy Varad, where it has been obtained a long time, from several lakes that get dry in summer, the salt then appears on the ground. This saline efflorescence, in the middle of summer, looking like heaps of snow, has procured them the name of white lakes in Hungary. The salt, when taken away, is reproduced every three or four hours, and this lasts through the fine season. Magazines are formed of it at Debretzin, both for exportation, and the manufacture of soap. The annual produce is more than 10,000 quintals, and there is no doubt of its being made much more considerable, were attention paid to some very rich lakes that are at a greater distance.

The existence of nitron in the middle of plains, in the waters of the lakes and marshes that cover them, is one of the most interesting facts in geology, but the least known. It is a phenomenon not exhibited only in Hungary; it occurs in the immense deserts that overspread different parts of our globe. From what we know of this mineral production, as discovered in Egypt, in Arabia, Persia, the Indies, Thibet, China, Siberia, the plains about the Caspian and Black Seas, in Asia Minor and Mexico, it is found every where in analogous relations and circumstances. Such are sands mixed with marle and argile; it is accompanied with several other salts, whereof the common sort is the most plentiful. There was a succession of rainy weather which prevented my researches into other particulars, though my curiosity had been ardently excited.

I spent one entire day in peregrinating the borders of these lakes, but the earth was every where a flat surface, and there was no ravine, to explore its composition in detail. Thoroughly to investigate the phenomenon, it would be requisite to make excavations, and examine such as have been made occasionally in certain pits or wells. Ruckert, who for a long time was employed in extracting the natron, and had leisure to explore the soil, states that the sands are not more than four or five feet in thickness, and that they rest on a layer of blue argile, and sometimes contain particles of iron in grain. He observed waters always lodging in the deeper parts, and therein is contained a great quantity of carbonate of soda, from 50 to 60 for the hundred, and which crystallises in the cold nights of autumn.

Not being able to remark on the saline efflorescence of the soil or surface, where every thing was in a state of re-dissolution, I examined the natron that had been previously collected. It was mixed with a pretty large quantity of grey argilous matter, and contained much muriate of soda, with a certain quantity of sulphate. I had afterwards an opportunity of seeing some among the peasants in Great Cumania, collected in the marshes that border the Theysse, and I noticed the same salts, though in a less quantity. The same observation occurred in the natron gathered in the plains about the lake of Nieusiedel. I conclude that the carbonate of soda is never pure, but that in Hungary, as elsewhere, wherever found, it is ever mixed with muriate of soda, more or less.

As to the origin of the natron, we have not data in a sufficient number to pronounce on it with certainty. We are reduced to speculations which, as being founded on facts, independent of any hypothesis, merit a degree of attention. With respect to sub-carbonate of soda, to which Ruckert attributes it, by a certain process of nature, this opinion rests on no positive observations, as no excavations have been made, purposely, for the sake of such. Nor is it in analogy with the depots of rock-salt, ancient or modern, and the waters of our seas, which deposit salt on the shores, contain no trace of it. In this last case, there does appear, however, to be a formation of natron, but in very small quantities, which effloresces on the surface of the soil, and must be attributed to the decomposition of muriate of soda. This takes place in different ways, varying only in the promptitude with which the operation is performed. Advantage has been taken of it, for the fabrication of the sub-carbonate of artificial soda, and applicable successively, to a number of processes, more or less profitable.

So also it is, in the decomposition of muriate of soda, that we are to look for the origin of natron. M. Berthollet accounts for the daily formation of this salt, in the valley of natron lakes in Egypt, in a probable manner. He imputes it to the reciprocal action of muriate of soda, and carbonate of calx, aided by the efflorescence, which determines the successive separation of the carbonate of soda, and thus allows a continual and indefinite decomposition to take place. Ocular inspection will show that the lakes contain a great quantity of muriate of soda, lodged in a calcareous soil, the rock of which pierces here and there the sands which cover it. We meet, likewise, with strata of gypsum, which probably accompany the depots of rock-salt, which the waters perforate before they enter the lakes. This explication very well agrees with the natron lakes of Hungary, for the richest are found in the eastern part of the great plain, at a little distance from the calcareous mountains that form the advanced posts of the high mountains of Transylvania. In the middle of those, or behind them, are considerable masses of salt; more to the west the plain is filled with rough calcareous depots, like those in the environs of Paris. The carbonate of calx seems very abundant through the whole plain, and forms daily deposits of strata, more or less dense, at the bottom of the marshes.

Every thing indicates that there is much muriate of soda in all the plains of Hungary. Most of the saliferous argiles, that I have had occasion to observe, as well as the argilous masses on the borders of the natron lakes, contain a quantity of carbonate of calx, and all are, more or less, sandy. These mixtures naturally prepare the decomposition of muriate of soda; one, by directly furnishing the substance that is to produce it, and the other, by rendering the mass more porous, and thereby facilitating the efflorescence of the natron. If the decomposition does not operate in the mines, it is from a scantier supply of heat and of moisture, and especially of fresh air. It is evident, that in tracing the course of these plains, where muriate of soda is constantly found in the waters, they lead, in an unvarying continuation, to the masses of salt that form the object of considerable mineral works.

Another salt is also found in the plains of Hungary, more difficult still, perhaps, to explain, salt-petre, which is found in very large quantities in the plains of Hungary. It effloresces, also, on the surface of the earth, in the comitats of Szathmar, Bihar, and others. The labours for collecting it are pretty considerable, sufficient to answer the demands of Hungary and Austria. Near 7000 quintals were taken on the account of Government in 1802, but the produce might have been much augmented.

My next route was from Debretzin to Pest, a journey of four days, across the great plain, which constitutes in some measure, the centre of the whole country. The superficial extent, from the Danube to the mountainous parts, is not less than 40,000 square leagues. In all this range, the traveller, especially in the latter part of the season, might fancy himself in the heart of a desert, with no apparent road, and whatever dwellings might be traced, would lie scattered, in various directions in the chief towns, at vast distances one from another. And what are a great number of these habitations ? wretched hovels, built of earth and straw, or a sort of rough bricks dried in the sun. Not a tree, not a hill, for the eye to repose upon ; and the flat surface, from the effect of refraction, seems every where to rise and fall in gentle slopes. At the extremity of the visual horizon one might, in some measure, take the height of the stars, as at the horizon of the sea. Sensibility seems to recoil at the idea of such an immense expanse, bounds to which the eye in vain looks for. A profound silence reigning throughout the day, it is not without satisfaction, therefore, that the traveller, fatigued with so monotonous a *tableau*, hails the approach of night, that will relieve the stretch of vision and fancy, by fixing it within the range of his narrower optical sphere. The silence is then interrupted by the cries of water-fowl, and soon the numerous fires, kindled by the herdsmen, the peasants, and by the drivers of carriages, &c. that lodge in the plain, afford an aspect more gay and cheerful. Then, indeed, the traveller does not appear alone, in a desert. But the fires are often, in reality, at very great distances, though to an observer, little used to survey objects over so vast and level a superficies, they may seem very near. It has been my lot, more than once, to spend two hours in a voiture with four horses, to reach one of those fires, that I had thought of coming at in ten minutes. This made me speculate on the angular distances of the fires, which seemed disposed in circles about me, and so near to each other, that the parties might easily form an intercourse. Those distances were not less than two or three leagues.

This plain becomes the receptacle of all the waters of the east and north ; in general it is extremely humid, and as it every where keeps its level, the rivers that traverse it, not being confined within their banks, render the lands miry, or form impracticable marshes. The eastern part especially, that is to say, all the plain to the left of the Theysse, exhibits a sort of extensive marsh, from a number of little streams descending from the mountains of Transylvania, that serpentine, in a thousand directions, and leave stagnant waters on their banks. In this part, however, the lands that are under cultivation have been successively gained from the marshes; and the soil, consisting partly of vegetable and animal remains, is remarkably fertile, so as to become, in some measure, a granary for the rest of the country. The land is black, and very dense; and the cereal plants, (grain generally,) yield 20 and 30 for 1. This is not the case to the right of the Theysse; in the part of the plain between that river and the Danube, most of the lands that are not inundated, produce only heath and brambles, and have an aspect of extreme aridity. The plains of Kekskemet are covered with white and moveable sands, which the winds raise and transport like clouds, to great distances. It is certain, however, that a vast extent of meadow and arable land, by draining the marshes, on a soil filled with fine mud and organic remains, might be reclaimed with infinite advantage.

Besides the arable lands, which produce in excessive abundance corn, maize, millet, &c.; besides the marshy lands in use for the culture of rice; there are vast pastures in these plains, comprehending about 90,000 French acres, where numberless herds of horned cattle and horses are fed. Winter and summer they remain in the plains, abandoned as it were to chance, but entrusted to the care of a few herdsmen, each of whom may have from 12 to 1500 under his care. In summer the cattle are exposed to the violent heats that dry up all the plain, and when the winter approaches, they have no shelter against rain, cold, and tempests; hence, from accidental circumstances, a great number of them sometimes perish. Sad examples are quoted, wherein the loss has amounted to 50, 60, and 80,000 head of cattle in a single night.

The herdsman, assimilated to the animals that he superintends, is in a very little better situation. With no other shelter than his bunda, or mantle of sheep-skin, he must also, night and day, summer and winter, brave all weathers, not having the resource of the mountain shepherds, of digging holes in the sides of the hills for shelter, in a rainy season. But these guardians, as rude and savage as the animals among which they dwell, seem to make little account of circumstances that would be intolerable to others. Their tanned complexion, mustachios, ill-combed beard, hair hanging down, and rustic accoutrements, with a hatchet constantly in their hands, altogether form figures not very agreeable to the eye, and hardly to be surveyed without apprehension. A frightful air of filth must be taken into the account, and often a nauseating smell of fat, from a custom they have of greasing their bodies, and plastering their shirts with grease, to keep them, they may, from vermin, which would otherwise breed, as they some-times do not change their linen till it falls into rags.

It is, no doubt, owing to the extreme humidity of many parts in the plains of Hungary, that the inhabitants rear such a number of buffaloes; we meet with them, sometimes, in considerable herds. This animal seems intended for marshy tracts, and proves of great use to the peasants, in labours that require draught. Two buffaloes will draw a heavy load better than four stout horses, and they are easily kept and fed on very indifferent provender. Thus, they thrive wonderfully in moist places, where the ox and horse could not long be preserved in safety. The buffalo is smaller than the ox, and much lower, his hair is of an uncommonly black colour. His horns, striated transversely, curved in a semicircle, and flattened, are thrown behind, so that the animal has little use of them, either for attack or defence. There is something hard, rough, and coarse, in his aspect and manner; no care is taken to keep him clean, as the creature takes a pleasure in miry and marshy waters. He is easily tamed, and does not appear of a mischievous character, but is soon irritated, and throws himself from one side to the other, if in harness, or escapes into the marshes, if at liberty. The milk of the female is full of cream, much better tasted than cow's milk, but is yielded in less abundance. The butter is very good and white, but like grease, and not pleasant to the eye. It is usual, in many places, at milking, to keep the young buffalo before the mother; but I have often seen them stand very quiet, without such precaution, and believe they might be trained to it, like cows. It is curious to mark them, when again entering the farms and places where they have been used to eating and drinking, every movement indicates an extravagance of joy, which they express, also, by a low grunting, not unlike that of hogs. The buffalo is useful for labour, but his flesh is not well tasted, unless very young, and then there is something disagreeable. The skin is valuable for different uses, and particularly in the works for extracting salt, throughout Hungary and Transylvania. The horns are massive, and in great request for many purposes, having the preference to those of oxen, for durability and beauty.

In passing over these plains, the eye of the geological traveller is wearied with the barren and uninteresting prospect. In a space of 100 leagues, he has not seen a pebble larger than a pea, and the soil, a perfect level, shews him nothing but siliceous sands, more or less micaceous, mixed with argilous and vegetable matter. Nor can he have recourse to a ravine, to explore the nature and succession of those modern alluvions which have equalized the soil, as all the rivers have very low banks, and are almost every where surrounded with impracticable marshes.

Having had occasion to mention the notary, I should observe that the word is not to be taken in the sense we use it in France. In the Hungarian villages, they are a sort of mayors, employed to execute orders transmitted by the lords, or directly, by the comitat; all ought to know Latin, which is the language of office and business throughout Hungary. Their appointment is by the lord to whom the village belongs, but the inhabitants of the place may depose him and demand another, if his conduct should not give satisfaction. Every village has also its judge, but he is subordinate to the notary, and, in a variety of cases, must act by and with his advice and consent.

The marshy plains of Hungary, in a zoological point of view, must be highly interesting. The number of aquatic and river birds is immense, among which there exists species it would be difficult to find in the plains of Europe, and especially in France. Such, for instance, are the Glareola Austriaca, or ordinary Sea Partridge, the Charadrius Asiaticus, or Solitary Plover, found on the banks of the salt lakes in Southern Tartary, the Tringa Gregaria, or Social Lapwing, in the plains of the Volga, and a multitude of other species well deserving of attention, mingled with other birds more common. Birds of prey, of every kind, are here in immense numbers, some of them weighing from twenty to twenty-five pounds. Mammiferous animals, of diminutive size, which often occasion much damage, are numerous in the plains, and would be interesting as objects of study. And, lastly, in these vast marshes I have found testaceous aquatic molluscæ of every species, genus, and particular variety; to the study of which I could have devoted myself with pleasure had time permitted. I had collected several varieties that were afterwards lost, and can only recommend the assemblage to the notice of future travellers.

Pest and Buda may be said to form but one city, the two parts of which are separated by the Danube. Pest is on the left side of the river, at the end of the Great Plain, and Buda, on the right, at the summit and on the point of some hills of no great height. A bridge of boats maintains a free communication between the two towns, during a great part of the year; but the rapidity of the river, from heavy floods at times, interrupts the intercourse. Old Buda, which forms a particular precinct, is not properly separated from New Buda, and one might pass from one to the other without perceiving a difference, were it not for a sort of barrier such as we meet with between a town and its suburbs. The result of this union is a very long street along the Danube, between it and the hills that border it; it requires an hour and a half for a pedestrian to proceed from one extremity to the other.

The present importance of these towns is such that they may well be considered as the capital of Hungary. Their height above the sea, (according to the mean level of ten years' observations, barometrical) at the observatory of Buda, is about 330 feet, the barometer being about 250 feet above the river. The population of these towns, including old Buda, may amount to 50 or 55,000, nearly two-thirds of which are at Pest. It has augmented considerably during the last fifty years, and every thing announces a much greater increase.

The town of Pest, therefore, is now the most considerable and handsomest of Hungary; being pretty near the centre of the kingdom, and from its position on the Danube, it has an easy communication with Austria and Turkey, and becomes a principal entrepôt of commerce. This has attracted a number of Germans, from all the different states, and every day new sources of industry are arising that will ere long rank Pest with the greatest towns in Europe. New buildings, new works of every description, appear in all directions, and the improvements are planned on a symmetrical scale. A commission of embellishment has been established, which obliges the proprietors to build in a manner more agreeable to the eye; the results produced excite the fairest hopes as to the future, and the town already exhibits a great number of elegant and beautiful houses. Their construction is simple but in a good taste, and they run in a right line. The entrance to the town, on the banks of the Danube, has an imposing effect. As to grand structures there are but few; the only one that can be called magnificent is the hospital for invalids, built by Charles VI. and which now serves for a casern. The churches are very ancient and have a poor appearance, recalling the bad taste of the times. There is one hotel for the exhibition of spectacles, very large and handsome; another is building to form an national theatre, for Hungarian pieces only, but the subscribers are very scanty, as there are but few Hungarians in the town. Doubts are entertained whether it will ever be finished. There are no public promenades in Pest that can properly be called such. Some trees, indeed, have been planted along the Danube, and on one of the avenues to the town; this last will probably become a sort of *Boulevard*, but considerable improvements will be requisite to form it into an agreeable retreat. We must go half a league out of town ere we arrive at any shade, in a sort of promenade, called the Stadwald; but it is of little notoriety, either for extent or respectability.

In quitting Pest for Buda, we have, on the bridge, a view of scenery altogether of the finest order. Water constitutes one of its principal features; the majestic Danube is seen to full advantage, and the eye enjoys the replication of its course to a considerable extent. In this part the river is nearly four times the breadth of the Seine, at the Garden of Plants in Paris. Its islands are covered with verdure, and the mountains in the back-ground, with their craggy precipices and retired glens, shaded, at intervals, by stately foliage, produce an effect truly picturesque. To complete the attractions of the spot, Buda presents an amphitheatre of houses that contrast with the rusticity of the other scenery, and the palace of the Viceroy, on the summit of the hill, fills up a space of ground, insulated from the other buildings.

In Pest we have the bustle and activity of a commercial town; compared with it Budha has a sequestered character, and with some might appear to superabound with solitude. It has no other trade than what its daily consumption requires, and throughout the fine season the noblesse retire to their estates, when their absence leaves a chasm which the other enjoyments of life seem unable to supply. In winter the scene changes, cheerfulness and vivacity return; it becomes the festive season of the year, and families repair in whole groupes to Buda, where the townsmen may welcome them as an annual boon. We then no longer view the place through a gloomy medium; we enjoy the first society, and from the diffusion of that wealth which the opulent possess, others are enabled to support more comfortable establishments. The town is not so extensive as Pest; its situation on a hill proves an insurmountable obstacle to this. It is pretty much in the same situation it was in fifty years ago, but as it was long the residence of the kings, and is now of the viceroy or palatine, it becomes of course the rendezvous of a part of the noblesse. Indeed, the town is very well built, and in a manner far superior to Pest. There are many superb hotels, or mansions, that have an air of grandeur more easy to conceive than to express, and not be found in a mere trading town. Their interior also is very nobly fitted up. The palace of the Viceroy, in some measure rebuilt by Maria Theresa, is of an immense extent, and being very agreeably situated, it is but justice to say that it forms a splendid, and even princely residence.

In Hungary, horses are not harnessed in pairs, but one to draw behind another. Three horses will answer the purpose best, so that one may be less fatigued than the others. It would even be advisable to have one horse running loose along side, each to have this indulgence in rotation.

My first object, after leaving Buda, was to visit certain hills on the road to Marton Vasar, which, from their collections of calcareous shell-work, more strikingly resemble the quarries about Paris, than even those at Pest. The cellars and caves in and about the villages, and at Promontorium, have been worked in these depôts.

Among other depôts of shells, I visited one on the sides of a height, between Biske and Ober Galla, where the quantity is immense. They consist of various genera, but it was not possible to characterise them distinctly, as the portions of test which remained, had passed into the state of spathic calcaire. I remarked, in general, however, that these organic remains had no sort of analogy to what I may style the Parisian Calcuires of Pest, Promontorium, &c., and that they much more resemble the calcareous formations of the Jura.

Throughout this part of the journey, I saw only little low hills, though, on the maps, were marked mountains of considerable elevation. These hills appeared to me to consist entirely of free-stone with lignites; they were covered with forests of oaks, which yielded sustenance to thousands of half-wild hogs, from their produce of mast. These animals, throughout Hungary, are very small; they have much more vivacity than those that are brought up tame in France, and have even something ferocious in their manner. Their hair is black, most commonly frizzled on the body, and bristled about the sides. It is not very safe being among them with dogs, for when they discover one, they assemble to a peculiar grunt, and pursue him with the keenest antipathy; if he cannot escape, they will tear him in pieces.

I next took the road for Veszprim, calling up the people of the auberge early, according to my custom, and leaving Palota, which lies in a plain, I passed by some mountains which I was not looking for, my map having marked the spot with marshy plains. The town of Veszprim, which my map places in a plain, stands on a calcareous plateau of some height, though a number of houses, which form a sort of suburbs, stretch along the edge of a valley. The descent is considerable, along very bad streets, wretchedly paved, and I had no small trouble to advance with my carriage, it being market-day, and the whole town thronged with people, carts, cattle, &c. But this crowd gave me an opportunity of marking the varieties of Hungarians, Croats, Slowacks, &c. diverting to one of my taste, and presenting, in a lively contrast, various new objects to engage my ideas in contemplation. The dress of the women threw around them an air of singularity in a mixture of genuine rusticity, and studied embellishments, that seemed to bear the semblance of a romantic wildness. Red stockings and yellow shoes, petticoats of strong blue cloth, red corsets without sleeves, or with sleeves of varying colours, a number of ribands, also, of different colours, with a very clumsy head-dress—these, in correspondence, displayed a scene of oddities truly imposing, and such as could not fail to interest and amuse. The head-dress appeared to me to consist of two neck-handkerchiefs, more or less fine, but sometimes coarse enough, one of which, folded like a napkin lengthways, rests on the fore-part of the head, one end falling on the nose, the other, loose and unfolded, is put behind, and covers the shoulders. The former is then tucked up and thrown behind, or otherwise wrapped about the head, as we wrap a napkin about eggs. The men have mostly round hats, or else, feltcoifs or caps ; many had ill-looking hoods of coarse white cloth, and large linen pantaloons ; some, rather more elegant, had a *culotte* of strong blue cloth, over which the shirt hung down, with a cloth waistcoat of a bluish grey colour. All these accoutrements met me in every direction, and my promenade was frequently winding into new paths, to enjoy the variegated prospects before me—the whole, however, accompanied with horrible *tintamarre.*

I arrived at Keszthely, at night-fall, and repairing immediately to the chateau of Count Festctits, was received with all that benevolent philanthropy and tender respect, which form admirable traits in the character of an Hungarian gentleman. The count sent for the whole of my baggage, which he would not suffer to remain at the inn.

In lieu of making mineralogical excursions about Keszthely, I intended visiting the different establishments of rural economy which count Festctits had created on his estate. These required a particular attention both from the manner in which they are conducted, and from their being an inlet for the introduction of agriculture into Hungary. This was the first object I was eager to explore next morning, and the count and his son accompanied me, to detail the particulars. Among these, I was most struck with the Georgicon, or school of agriculture, designed to qualify young persons for the superintendance and management of estates. In Hungary such are called officers of economy. It is intended, also, to provide the peasants with such instruction as may make them expert in gardening and farming. This establishment is maintained entirely by the count, who has endowed it, for the purpose, with a considerable farm ; there being different professors for different courses of study. These, for such as are to become officers of economy, include what is necessary in geometry, mechanics, the art of drawing, and, more especially, architecture, with the designing and construction of plans, &c. In the latter part of their time the pupils are practically employed in various concerns about the establishment, as keeping accounts, and, alternately, through a round of other duties. Some part of their time is devoted to botany, and to the acquiring of some knowledge in physics and chemistry. On finishing their studies, the young persons either return home with certificates of their proficiency, good behaviour, &c. or are disposed of by the count, on his own domains, or transferred to other lords that may stand in need of their services.

The young peasants intended for gardening and farming, are taught reading, writing, and accounts ; nor is instruction in religious duties neglected. They attend to all such improvements in cultivation, generally, as may be suggested in the modes of rearing cattle, in models of the different implements for plowing, of which there is a complete assortment on the establishment. Every department of the school appeared to be well adapted and conducted; what is essential to be known is taught, and nothing further. In the gardens are collections of various kinds of kitchen vegetables, cereal plants, fruit and timber trees; utility being the object to which every thing is directed. There is also a small botanical garden.

The lake Balaton (Platten See. Germ.) is the largest in Hungary. Its greatest length, from S.W. to N.E., is about 16 leagues; its greatest breadth, which is at its eastern extremity, is about three leagues. It grows wider and narrower at various points successively, and, at the point of Tihany, is not above half a league in breadth. In many parts it is bordered with very extensive marshes: the total surface, including the latter, is estimated at 66 square leagues. The lake is fed by a number of small streams, that descend from the mountains, and especially by the river Szala, which rises in the most western part of Hungary. The quantity of water supplied by the streams is but small, compared with the surface of the lake, and there does not appear to be an outlet, unless the little river of Sio be such, which we find in the middle of the southern bank. The lake abounds in fishes; the most remarkable, or that which is most in request, is the Fogas, a kind of perch, the best eating fresh-water fish that I ever tasted. It is highly valued in Hungary and Germany, and occasionally exported to considerable distances; according to report, it is found only in the lake of Balaton. On the banks which I traversed, I observed swans, ducks, drakes, and molluscæ, such as we have in our ponds. The adjacent marshes swarm with water-fowl. The bottom of these marshes is commonly covered with turf, of which use would doubtless be made, were wood less common. It is in use, however, in several places, and especially for various manufactures. It appears that iron, mixed with slime, is often found in the marshes. In the country of Balaton, generally, there is an ample field for researches to the naturalist, it being a most interesting part of Hungary.

I made but two mineralogical excursions from Œdenburg, but I could not refrain from taking a survey of the famous chateau of Eszterhazi, which had been much spoken of, as a princely and magnificent structure, and which has cost immense sums. It is, doubtless, the grandest and most spacious in Hungary; it stands about four leagues east of Œdenburg, on the borders of the lake Neusiedel, but the locality, in a flat and marshy tract, is not well chosen. The palace itself may be held up as displaying much stateliness; I have seen few to exceed it. It is exceedingly well built; the architecture is noble, and the various offices are of an elegant and embellished description. In these respects it far surpasses the actual residence of the prince at Eisentadt. It is also more extensive, containing 200 chambers completely fitted up; I counted 148 window-casements in the principal front, and 200 in the garden front, without including a number of pavilions on the ground floor.

We enter the court-yard through an ornamented iron gate, not unhandsome, but too small, in comparison with the rest of the building. The court yard forms an ellipsis, in one of the foci of which, we find a basin of no great magnitude. The anterior part is occupied by low buildings, with only a ground floor, and which serve for offices and apartments to the steward, housekeeper, &c. At the lower end is the chateau or mansion; the middle part forms an elevated structure, with a terrace on the top and on the two sides, buildings like wings two stories high, arranged in portions of a circle. An exterior escalier, of a congruous and interesting appearance, leads to the first story of the middle building. Here is the great saloon for receiving company; though in an antique taste, it is scarcely to be equalled for the ideas of magnificence and beauty which it affords. The ceiling is as high as the building itself; the paintings are but indifferent; the flooring is of inlaid work, in white and brown colours. We find some very superb chandeliers, and over the mantel-piece a time-keeper, small and but ill suited to its costly accompaniments; I observed others also in the corners of the casements, of a similar description. The bed-chambers and smaller apartments on the right and left of this vast mansion, contain nothing extraordinary, and from the contrast, sink in importance and respectability. On the ground floor are shewn the minor apartments of the prince; the most remarkable is a little saloon, the wainscoting of which is a varnish of gilt china, which must have cost immense sums, as every piece must have been ordered for the purpose; but the features which characterise it altogether, are far from proving gratifying to the eye. The interior of the chateau, speaking generally, by no means corresponds with the exterior, though the grand saloon may form an exception. It is deserted by the family, which may account for its being stripped of its best furniture, and for the wainscotings and parquets (floorings) going to decay. A quantity of other china is also shewn to strangers, and I saw a number of large dishes, plates, vases, &c., but inferior to the porcelain of Sevres. There are some dishes, shut up in coffers, that appear-

ed to be of European manufacture, but the drawings on them,
except two little designs of a field of battle, were not comparable to those fabricated at Sevres, Berlin, and Vienna.
The same magazine contained also a large quantity of grotesque
china ware, in glaphic talc.

The gardens and woods behind the chateau have nothing very
agreeable, as the soil is not well adapted for vegetation. The
plantations have not been judiciously planned; they are modelled
on the antique French taste, but the proportions are ill observed,
and we have, on the whole, a very ordinary garden, crossed by
straight alleys. The statues, that formerly were its ornament,
have been removed to Eisenstadt.

The chateau of this last is a square building, on which the
eye reposes with an exhilarating effect, though it does not exhibit that richness of grandeur which Eszterhazi possesses. It
was built, in 1683, but fitted up, with a number of additional
embellishments, especially on the side of the garden, by the
present prince. The front towards the villas, is ornamented with
busts of all the ancient kings of Hungary. I noticed these with
a passing glimpse, but there was nothing in them to draw my
particular attention. The entrance is through a gate that seems
too small for the building; then, passing through a vestibule that
has nothing remarkable, we arrive at a square court, surrounded
with buildings of some height. The effect of these is rather
sombrous; at the opposite extremity we find a little low arched-
way, which leads to the garden. There the prince has erected,
in front of the building, a very beautiful perystile, with a gentle
semicircular descent on each side, for the convenience of carriages arriving at the first story. This is an elegant structure,
but not in accordance with the rest of the chateau. The gardens
are in the English style, and there being sheets of water interspersed, and the ground undulated, I felt the glow of satisfaction
at the artificial creation, and must acknowledge the sublime
effect which the scenery produced on my mind. Opposite the
castle, they were building a kisque, which was to be called the
Temple of Night; it is raised over a piece of water, encircled
with artificial rocks, cut with too much uniformity, and ill suited
to the taste of a geologian, accustomed to expend time in exploring the vast recesses of primitive nature.

In one part of the garden, on the slope of a hill, are the
plantations which the prince has constructed, in imitation of
those of Schronbrunn; they contain an immense collection of
plants of all countries. I was most struck with the beautiful series imported from New Holland. The collections from China
are not less remarkable; and, altogether, the botanical establish

ment may rival that of Schonbrunn, and appears to me to be o.
the first consideration.

As to the interior of the chateau, the apartments that I saw
were very small, dark, and ill fitted up with decorations.   In
general, though it is doubtless a noble structure, in a situation
very agreeable, with gardens like a paradise, it does not rank so
high, in the character of a splendid and august edifice, as that
of Eszterhazi.   The principal defect of the latter, is its disad-
vantageous situation.   The chateau of Eisenstadt, from the embellishments introduced, reminded me of the English country-
houses, where the manner of building and living was, at once,
convenient and comfortable, but not well befitting the character
of magnificent.   Many chateaux that I have seen in Germany
and France, are not so handsome or elegant as this ; which,
however, is an object by no means so well calculated to fill the
eye with its grandeur, or to inspire emotions of admiration.

I entered Vienna again about the middle of November, exceedingly fatigued with my excursions, after leaving Kesztely, and
standing greatly in need of repose.   After spending a few days
at Vienna, I prepared for my departure, but winter had already
set in, and though it was fair weather, the thermometer was ten
degrees below zero.

G. SIDNEY, Printer,
Northumberland Street, Strand.

TOUR

OVER THE ALPS

AND IN

ITALY.

BY ALBERT MONTÈMONT.

Translated from the French.

LONDON:

PRINTED FOR SIR RICHARD PHILLIPS AND Co.
BRIDE-COURT, BRIDGE-STREET.

1823.

ADVERTISEMENT.

The following work contains much correct information; the occasional observations of a man of taste and learning, addressed to a congenial spirit upon the various materials which, with an easy elegance, in a clear and animated manner, he briefly analyses and examines. In addition to the acquisitions previously communicated by other meritorious writers, he has brought together many facts, characteristic and highly descriptive of the countries and their inhabitants, in the little scenes and incidents which awaited him—the little pleasing pictures which he happily sketches, scattered here and there through the letters.

In an area so crowded with magnificence, intercourse with its novel and curious circumstances, however frequent, varied, and habitual, will never produce satiety—will never lose its hold upon the mind.

The spirit of patriotism and good sense, the impress of generous feelings, which pervade the author's elegant and gentle mind, cannot be more advantageously exhibited than it is throughout the volume. But to enjoy the full force of many particular topics, which give an insinuating interest to the narrative, the inquisitive Reader must apply to the Book itself.

G. Sidney, Printer,
Northumberland Street, Strand.

TOUR

OVER THE ALPS,

AND

IN ITALY,

IN LETTERS TO A FRIEND.

LETTER I.

EXCURSION FROM PARIS TO GENEVA, THROUGH DIJON, DOLE, POLIGNY, AND THE MOUNTAINS OF THE JURA.

On the 9th of August, 1820, our varied peregrination commenced ; my companions through the progress of it were two of my pupils, committed to my care by their relations. The first incident that took place was forming an acquaintance with two Scotch gentlemen, whose humour led them to set down minutely, from memoranda on the spot, such observations as would occupy immediate attention, as they successively arose. They wished to accompany us in our route ; their remarks on the principal cities, people, and places, that we visited, being such as would interest the general traveller rather than the philosopher. Our curiosity to explore fresh continental scenery, the majestic ruins of Nature, buried in the bosom of Solitude, or the new paths that industry is gradually opening, through the great discoveries and noblest works of art, was no less ardent. Added to which, we meant also to note regularly, to relate and describe unaffectedly, whatever might appear to deserve notice in the various stages of our journey. With such a similarity of tastes, we formed, altogether, one of the completest companionships for such an undertaking that chance could bring together.

These Scotch gentlemen were strangers to the French language, but they brought with them *la bourse bien garnie des guinees*—a necessary interpreter, that will find provisions of due kind and quantity, that will foster an intercourse among different nations, be they ever so dissevered by land and ocean, ever so discordant in manners and religion. But this interpreter is sometimes at a loss, and cannot entirely determine about every thing.   The two Caledonians could only converse in the idiom of Shakspeare, and they necessarily became our correspondents, in most things acquiescing in our judgment.

Their tour became subordinate to ours, but it was at their own request.   We cordially embraced them as descendants from the Bravoes of Morven, as wanderers, roaming far from the woody hills of their land, from their shining streams that warble ceaseless inspiration.   All new and original as they were, we had pleasure in the thoughts of being any ways serviceable to them.

We crossed the plains of Burgundy, where the waving harvests were bending beneath the breeze with extreme rapidity. In two days and two nights we reached Dijon, famed for its groves and arbours of vine-trees—for its wines of choicest store.   Here we approached the Saone, in the Stygian gloom of whose lazy current many a son of old Silenus has voluntarily ingulfed himself, anticipating death's domain, to which he must soon have yielded.

We were now landed in a country that must raise respect and admiration, that must command our praise, from the worthies of other years and times—it was the country of Buffon, Cribellon le Noir, Bossuet, and the caustic Piron.   After an excellent supper, the fleeting moments passed swiftly—the hoary head, with his wrinkled brow, would have felt his cares most sweetly soothed by the high-flavoured wine of Vougeout. Next morning, ere Sol's sacred lustre had gently brightened into day, we were sweeping over the beautiful landscape, and the opulent city of Dijon, its beauties veiled in the shade, and growing dim to the eye, was disappearing.   Speedily we scud across the plains, along the banks of the Saone, the scenery embellished with forms of varied and graceful hue, and the feathered choir enchanting the eye with their beauteous plumage. While contemplating and comfortably enjoying the shifting scenery of the traveller's life, we had entered Auxonne, saluted by some salvos of artillery, and were set down at Dole, on the banks of the Doubs.

Here we had time to rest and refresh ourselves; after breakfast, changing our voiture, we began to ascend and traverse the very wide expanse of the Jura mountains, and had the satisfaction of arriving, in a few hours, at Poligny, built on a lofty, commanding site.   From its elevated ground may be seen an extensive tract of country, to great advantage, the eye following the course of it as far as to La Franche Comté.

In the evening we arrived at Champagnole, where the

charms of a siren singer detained us some hours, in festive glee, till the instant of our departure. Our Scotch companions, social in their dispositions, yet detesting dissipation, seemed to be warmed with no common-place feelings of pleasure. Astonished at the harmonious powers which the French language possesses, as varied in the sweetness and melody of her voice, they availed themselves of the opportunity to enjoy her company, and it was evident they were doing no violence to their inclinations. They complimented her with much vivacity, and were happy to do any thing that could be agreeable to the lovely creature.

At half-past eleven at night, we set out from Champagnole, and pursued our rambling; but though all the splendour of the day had fled, it was not a sad lifeless evening shade, set in mists and darkness; the moon's sacred lustre hallowed the dun gloom with its beams, and by the dawn we had reached certain elevated points of the Jura. Wildness is the distinguishing feature of the valley of Lavatay, and in this respect its districts possess and present all that the solitary mind could desire to contemplate. We descend in it as into an abyss. Innumerable blocks of stone, mouldering fragments, and huge ruins of rocks, lie scattered through the valley, but chiefly near the bases of the mountains from which they have fallen. The picturesque effect of this extensive area occupied our imagination for some seconds, and in five or six hours more we reached the heights of Gex, from which we discover in front the lake of Geneva, and the great Chain of the Alps.

Here all was enchanted ground. Had I faith, like the ancients, in the existence of genii locorum, I should believe or imagine that the presiding spirit, the genius Loci alone could depict the new charms every where diffused on the scenery, could alone impart the solemnity, strength, and elevation, of nature's stately ornaments. But here the grave and lofty subjects, whereon her powers are so peculiarly and expressively displayed, are blended with that liveliness, that great diversity of style and manner which appear, in numberless instances, as marked by the hand of art. Here is no continued, quiescent, irksome monotony; the eye is pleased, *ad infinitum*, with the regularity, copiousness, sweetness, arising from the variations of the latter, inspiring sentiments and emotions of a more delicate texture, while ideas of an order exceedingly different are raised in our minds, while the majestic qualities and characteristic properties, of which nature is susceptible, and herein is fertile, in so eminent a degree, render this spot superior to all others; it is not excelled by any of which we have knowledge, and is, perhaps, the happiest for itinerant contemplation

of any in the known world.   The panorama, in its circle of
expression, its powers of accommodation suited to different
tastes, displays such an evident abundance as I am unable to
pourtray at full length.

A near hand view of the country presents the increasing
growth of cultivation in spacious plains, fields, and vineyards,
of great luxuriance and beauty—innumerable towns, villages,
and orchards, which lie all around—dusky groves, and pine
forests, that stretch themselves on the sides of the green hills
—castles erected on elevated ground, the cantons of Berne,
Zurich, Lucerne, &c. inhabited by an active, hardy, industrious
people, with different parts of the Valais, and the city of Sion,
the capital of its episcopal government.   Here Zephyr breathes
upon the azure waves of a peaceful ocean, here the heart glows
with a softer scene; there, at a distance, under a lowering
sky, the savage beauties of the Alps, simple, but grand objects,
surprise us with awe.   I observe the cloudy heads of those
stately piles, those towering rocks, those stony ridges, with the
sylvan gloom of the deep valleys extended at their feet; I see
the haughty crest of that huge Mount Blanc, scowling to the
vast arch of heaven, and involved in endless sleet.   His wide
stretching arms clasp the boundaries of my view, and a pale
zone of unmelting snow closes the fair landscape scenery.

At the foot of the Northern Alps runs a ridge of mountainous wrecks and fragments, more than 5000 feet in height;
these are a sort of calcareous tombs, of innumerable generations of marine animals of every description.

And thus, while I felt the influence of grace, beauty, order,
on the banks of the lake of Geneva, my wondering eye, filled
and charmed with the bright blooming colours of art, the bold
air and wild hydra forms of the Alps, overwhelmed my breast
with a kind of gloomy night and Gothic horrors.

Descending from the heights of Gex, we arrived at Geneva
about sun-set, whence the silvered head of Mount Blanc, irradiated by the sun's departing beams, had all the appearance of
a brilliant illumination.   But this gave way to other feelings
when we found ourselves among a people always distinguished
by an ardent love of liberty, in a country where, in the language of the patriarch of Ferney,

> On ne méprise point les travaux nécessaires,
> Les états sont égaux, et les hommes sont frères,

where contempt awaits not those whose hours are devoted to
labour, where no invidious barrier arises between rank and
talents, where, with a jealousy of individual power, the happiness of the community is the hereditary feeling!

I bid you adieu for the present. Let the simple annals of private life recorded in this short epistle, pass for my introduction.

LETTER II.

GENEVA, FERNEY, THE LAKE OF GENEVA, LAUSANNE, VEVEY.

WHAT must a lover of Rousseau tell you, respecting his country, that has not been repeated from one to another by privilege of common-place and monotonous succession? Let me, however, give my opinion on the subject, as, if I do not differ widely from others, I shall aim at being more clear and distinct.

The city of Geneva is situated at the southern extremity of the lake of that name. The Rhone, whose source is hid in the mountains of St. Gothard, after watering all the plain of the Valais, empties itself by several mouths into the same lake at its northern extremity, and issuing from it at Geneva to continue its course, divides the city into two unequal parts. The least considerable, which forms a sort of suburbs, is on the side bordering France. In this part, the house is yet shewn wherein the author of the Social Contract was born. At the entrance of the threshold appears this modest inscription : " Ici est né J. J. Rousseau—Here J. J. Rousseau was born." The street wherein the humble dwelling is situated, has acquired the name of Rue Rousseau. The house is at present tenanted by a watch maker, the profession of Rousseau's father.

The other part of Geneva contains the public establishments, and the finest buildings. The surface of the ground is not every where level, and to promenade the interior parts of the city will be attended with some fatigue. Cæsar mentions Geneva as an ancient city of the Allobroges ; he made it a place of arms, and Charlemagne passed through it in 773, when marching with an army into Italy. Clement Marot, when persecuted in his own coubtry, fled hither as a refugee, in 1543, eight years after Calvin's reformation.

Omitting historical details, it is sufficiently obvious that Geneva is one of those places that abound most in instances of literary fecundity. .This mental industry, producing the happiest effects, has been fully displayed, not without its due celebrity, in our days. In the admired performances of Saussure, the correct productions of Bonnet, the indefatigable powers of Pictet, with the extensive merits of Bourrit, and a multitude of other eminent literati, extraordinary efforts of genius have been exhibited. As to Rousseau, he is what he appears, all originality, invention, and fertile imagination; his first thoughts, formed with great facility, have reversed the usual notions and ideas of mankind on points of political economy, and, notwithstanding some extravagancies, the improvisatorial talents with which he was gifted, enforced by vigour of conception, and brilliancy of diction, render the character which he has obtained of the most durable kind. The delirium of love is carried to its highest pitch, in the letters of Julia and St. Preux.

In this metropolis of Calvinism, there is a public library, a museum, and a cathedral, which may be justly recommended to attention; the character and genius of their objects appear to be well consulted. The library contains 50,000 printed volumes, and 200 MSS. Here are 80 volumes of Calvin's sermons, also certain homilies of St. Augustine, written in the sixth century, on papyrus, and a fragment of the book of expenses of Phillipe le Bel, of the year 1314.

The judicious arrangements of the museum make it a pleasing and improving exercise for observation and study. It comprehends five grand divisions—minerals, shells, birds, antiques, and medals and paintings. On the second story are apartments for a literary society, similar to the Royal Atheneum of Paris. This forms a depository for all the various journals, French, German, Italian, and English, with any compositions, literary articles, &c. of real merit and celebrity, as they appear; the library is select and very numerous. The liberal and enlightened members constantly favour the admission of foreigners among them. I was introduced by M. de Chenevière, professor of theology, and a minister of the reformed church. The virtues, amiable manners, and established reputation of this gentleman, as a scholar, entitle him to an honourable testimony.

The cathedral is a large Gothic structure, containing a number of antique monuments. The steeple appears as a prominent object; from its elevation, the eye can survey the town at large, with the whole immense sheet of the Leman Lake and its crystal-like waters. On the east is seen the village of Carouge; to the south arise the Chain of the Alps, and Mount Blanc, which last seems to lord it paramount over its allied hills, like the Grand Signior over his mistresses and innumerable vassals. In the north we discover Ferney-Voltaire, and the mountains of the Jura; and at about a quarter of a league from Geneva, the junction of the Rhone, and the Arve, which last is a muddy minor stream, and descends from Mount Blanc.

Those who visit Geneva will derive satisfaction from forming an acquaintance with some of the higher classes, among whom he will find eminent men of various descriptions, though in manners they are very plain. But nothing can exceed, in its proportion, the great mass of information residing in the middle ranks, nor are the lowest sunk into a state of ignorant apathy. Their ancestors valued themselves on the advantages of liberal discussion and extensive inquiry, and the present generation are by no means disposed to resign them.

The citizens have never been backward in patronizing all such inventions, for manufacturing purposes, as may seem to be improvements in mechanics. The horological business, or making of clocks and watches, continues to be a leading object with them, and the Genevese spare no pains to merit this kind of distinction. Connected with the arts is the hydraulic machine, which feeds and supplies the waters of the town. The plans in relievo of the Alps, by M. Gaudin, cannot be contemplated without a degree of wonder—a testimony of approbation. Strangers who visit the botanic garden and the new palace which adjoins it, as also the hall of spectacles, from motives of curiosity, will reap utility as conjoined with it. In a municipal point of view, their *grande rue,* or principal street, is deserving of particular mention ; its timber arcades rise, like a Gothic frontispiece, to the very roofs of the houses.

In the town itself is nothing very remarkable ; the grand and permanent source of its opulence and prosperity, is the activity and industry of its ingenious mechanics. The intelligent traveller will enlarge his general plan of survey, by extending it to the environs ; here he may pursue a vein of prospective discovery in a great variety of situations and points of view. He will find charming promenades along the right bank of the Leman Lake, and on the side of St. Jean. Near the junction of the Rhone and the Arve, is the beautiful country house of M. Constant, a relation of our celebrated publicist, and at no great distance is the rural seat, Les Delices, that was occupied for some time by Voltaire, before he removed to Lausanne, and finally fixed at Ferney.

To enjoy the magnificent optical illusion of Mount Blanc and its Glaciers, illumined by the setting sun, no spot can be more favourable than a height between the village of Ferney and that of Le Grand Sacouney. In the evening of August 15, my companions and I had a fuller and more curious view of that most interesting object than we had before anticipated. We could not contemplate the scene without emotions that excited a sort of soul-transporting enthusiasm. This fine day had passed rapidly away in excursions to satisfy our curiosity, and we set out on our return to enjoy the convenience of rest and refreshments after our fatigues. While night was over-

shadowing us, we often heard the nightingale pouring forth exquisite notes of her delicate, tender, animated composition.

Next day we went to visit Ferney, two little leagues from
Geneva. When Voltaire took possession of the property in
1759, here were only eight cottages; at his death nearly a
hundred houses, built at his expense, covered the domain, occupied by more than twelve hundred inhabitants. He raised
also a manufactory of clocks and watches, and another of
eartheuware, and procured an exemption from the visits of
the officers of the *Douane*.

Here Voltaire afforded an asylum to Delille Desalles, pro-
scribed for his *Philosophie de la Nature :* here he protected
Marmontel, a writer of great celebrity, but persecuted likewise
for that respectable publication, his Belisarius, in which he
alluded obliquely to the degenerate and profligate character of
some modern governments ; here was the retreat of the count
Morangies, robbed of his patrimony by usurers. Here also
Voltaire revived the memory of Calas, of Sirven, of Martin, of
Montbailly, and saved the wife of this last from the scaffold.
Here he supported his character, producing a bold and striking
apology for the unfortunate Lally, as also for Labarre, and for
12,000 Serfs depending on the canons of St. Claude, in Mount
Jura ; here he portioned the grand niece of the great Corneille,
with a fortune of 90,000 francs, also the daughter of Madame
Dupuits with 100,000, and *Belle et Bonne*, when he married
her to the marquis de Villette, with 150,000. His old friend
Thiriot, after spending a year with him at Ferney, on his return
to Paris, found a purse of 50 Louis at the bottom of his trunk,
slipped in by Voltaire, and one day when the latter had been
to visit Madame Dupuits, then lying-in, he contrived to leave
in her buffet a superb silver vase, wherein was a receipt for
12,000 francs that M. Dupuits owed him. A labouring man
of Ferney was in prison for 7500 francs ; Voltaire had him released by paying the amount ; and when informed that this
man had a numerous family, and that it would be like throwing money away, he made answer, " Money given in alms is
not thrown away, and here I am restoring a father to his family, and a citizen to society." Another labouring man, who
was not of Ferney, having lost a law suit in the parliamentary
court of Besançon, in his despair had recourse to Voltaire, who
examined his papers, and finding his cause good, " Here,"
said he, bringing three bags of a thousand francs each out of
his closet, " with these repair the injuries of justice ; go to law
no more, and if you are willing to settle on my lands, I shall
make it my business to find you employment." The Jesuits
of Ornex wished to round their territory, by purchasing land

of some miners that was mortgaged for fifteen thousand francs. The speculation would have been ruinous to the mining concern, but Voltaire laid down the money for them to the bailliage of Gex, and thus rescued their patrimony from the rapacity of the Jesuits.

The anniversary of St. Bartholomew was ever a day of mourning with Voltaire, and on that day, as some will have it, he was more or less subject to a fever.

We approached to the house of this great man with a sort of homage, not unlike the pilgrims of Mecca before the tomb of Mahomet. In due time we arrived at the chateau, and were introduced into the apartments of the monarch of French literature. The bed-chamber and the saloon for receiving company, are just in the state wherein he left them, setting out for Paris, where he died. We found, in his bed-chamber, portraits of the following personages:—Frederick the Great, his early friend ; Catherine II., empress of Russia, embroidered in needle work by herself; Voltaire, at the age of thirty-four; the marchioness de Chatelet, or the sublime Emilia ; Le Kain, the Talma of his day : more than one amateur had . cut away pieces of the canvass to lay by as a relic; Washington, with this inscription in the hand of Voltaire—Ne quid detrimenti capiat respublica; Milton, Racine, J. Delille, with this verse of Horace, inscribed by Voltaire—Nulli flebilior quam mihi, Virgili ; Isaac Newton, who died in 1727, at the age of eighty-five, a bachelor ever retaining his virginity ; Benjamin Franklin, born at Boston in 1706; Corneille, Marmontel, La Fayette, the veteran votary of liberty in two hemispheres; Pope Clement XIV, in 1769; Antoine Thomas, Helvetius, Mairan, D'Alembert, le Duc de Choiseul, and Leibnitz. At the bottom of this last, Voltaire has placed this stanza :—

> Il fut-dans l'univers, connu par ses ouvrages,
> Et dans son Pays meme, il se fit respecter ;
> Il instruisit les Rois, il eclaira les Sages,
> Plus sage qu'eux, il sut douter.

His elaborate compositions were of first-rate merit, and the world did honour to his genius and science. In his own country he was distinguished, and succeeded in a respectable degree. Kings were instructed by his extraordinary learning, and sages by his well-grounded notions in philosophy; and more especially in his valuable performances, he *doubts* of many things that had received the stamp of authority, herein wiser than those who, wedded to an opinion, will never resign upon knowledge or good reason.

Over a canopy appears " Mes manes sont consolés, puisque

mon Cœur est au milieu de vous," and over a sort of urn, " Son esprit est partout, et son Cœur est ici." It is the same image or sentiment, differently appropriated, denoting that his heart is here ; but this is no longer the case, as the marchioness de Villette has it in her possession.

The portraits here specified shew the diversified manner wherein Voltaire indulged his taste. This indulgence forms one of the most elegant of literary recreations. Of his well-informed mind, the verses which he addressed, in 1736, to M. de la Roque, editor of the Mercure de France, give good evidence.

> Vers enchanteurs, exacte prose,
> Je ne me borne point à vous,
> N'avoir qu'un goût, c'est peude de chose,
> Beaux arts, je vous invoque tous :
> Musique, danse, architecture,
> Art de graver, docte peinture,
> Que vous m'inspirez de desirs !
> Beaux arts ! vous etes des plaisirs,
> Il n'en est point qu'on doive exclure.
>
> *(Temple du Gout.)*

Herein Voltaire displays the riches of his imagination ; his genius embraces not merely the individual interests of poetry ; his soul is elevated to comprehend the entire mass of the fine arts, music, sculpture, &c., and the philosopher who possesses sensibility will see how his expansive mind knew how to embellish topics suitable to his taste and character.

From the terrace of the garden, we have a prominent view of Mount Blanc. In the garden there runs an alley, a quarter of a league in length, edged with poplars; Voltaire promenaded in it occasionally, but was most partial to an avenue, hedged with a particular sort of elm-trees. There was a little cottage, wherein he spent much of his time, but it is replaced by a plantation of trees.

Voltaire's gardener is still living. He has by him a collection of seals from the letters of his master's correspondents ; underneath, for amusement, he would put the names of those correspondents. Under some, in lieu of the names, he put the word " fous, childish, silly." When a letter came, he compared the seal with that on his register ; if there was an evident identity, and the fatal epithet appeared, he sent back the letter to the post office without opening it.

This old gardener has also in his possession, Voltaire's bonnet, set with a gold border by Madame Denis. The marchioness de Villette, with strict propriety named *la Belle et*

Bonne, has the night gown, and the great armed chair wherein he used to read and write.

In front of his chateau is a church, which he was at the charge of erecting. On the façade we read the following inscription :—Deo erexit Voltaire. On the outside, annexed to one of the walls of the temple, is the tomb which he had prepared for himself.

Every object that we saw reminded us of the useful principles which that celebrated man displayed in action, and which the following lines discover, having appeared in some of his writings :—

> J'ai fait un peu de bien ; c'est mon meilleur ouvrage,
> Mon sejour est charmant, mais il etoit sauvage ;
> Depuis le grand edit, inculte, inhabité,
> Ignoré des humains, dans sa triste beauté,
> La nature y mouroit, Je lui portai la vie
> J'osai ranimer tout. Ma penible industrie
> Rassembla des colons, par la misere epars,
> J'appellai les metiers qui precedent les arts ;
> Et pour mieux cimenter mon utile entreprise,
> J'unis le protestant avec ma sainte Eglise.

Here the author, with the frankness of a philosopher, developes certain truths. A person endowed with such a mind, finding no satisfaction in countries where princes are unceasingly occupied in politics, hostile to the interests of their subjects, irritated at the stupor in which the latter are too often plunged, this remarkable man, whose head is replete with energy and sensibility, withdraws himself from a sphere unsuitable to a thinking being, and retires to a simple and happy solitude, to discharge the functions of his self-appointed office, that of doing good.

Voltaire did every thing in his power to decorate his new semibarbarous situation, with all the philanthropic succours of which it stood in need. Facts mark his temper and genius more distinctly than a laboured character. Touched by the art of genius, a new creation appeared around him, exhibited in all the beautiful variety of which the scene was capable. In lieu of a waste and lonely gloom, emerging groves robed in green, and habitations, the asylum of calm domestic life—feeding flocks, flowers, living waters, and waving blades of corn, sprang up like an enchanting vision. His was the nobler part of generous friendship, to soothe the anguish of sorrow, to beam cheering smiles round the bed of affliction, to pour consolation where sickness and grief vented their moanings. It was his, too, blessing and blessed, to rear the pile, the altar around which a Christian throng might bend in holy prayer—

be taught to renew the purer heaven-atoning rites of justic
peace, immortal mercy, and all the angel train of charities.

I have since seen at Paris, preserved by the marchioness de
Villette, the bed gown, and the gold-laced waistcoat, long worn by
Voltaire, as also the crown of laurel adjudged to him at the *Theatre Francois*, in 1778, and the great chair with a writing table and
moveable desk attached to it, wherein he often sat.

At length we quitted Ferney and returned to Geneva, to make a
tour of the lake in a boat, and survey its beauties nearer.   It is 18
leagues in length, but would only be 14, were it in a straight line.
Its greatest breadth is about 3 leagues ; near Vevey, in the environs
of Meillerie, it is 950 feet in depth.   The lake never freezes.   Its
eastern part, or that where the town of Lausanne is situated, is
the most interesting.   It is fifteen leagues from Vevey to
Geneva, but boats, with a favourable wind, will make the passage
in four hours.   The air is remarkably pure on the banks of the
Leman; it has a sort of flux and reflux depending on the variation
of the atmosphere, and its pressure.

Lausanne, capital of the Canton de Vaud, buttressed, as it were,
to three hills on the banks of this lake, enjoys a very fine climate,
and presents a landscape, wherein the eye may, for ever, trace
some new found undiscovered charm.   Here are a library, an
academy, colleges, two gazettes, &c.   Tissot, a celebrated physician, lived here from 1770 to 1776; Voltaire, from 1757 to 1759,
and Haller at the same time.   M. Ebel assures us, that the
great Haller would not visit the author of the Henriade.   To be
in want of the sanction derived from the good opinion of others is
an evil, but I presume that many, like myself, will dispute the
justness of that sentiment, which prompted the great Haller to
such conduct; I have ever hitherto considered it, as an act illiberal and injudicious.

The same M. Ebel supplies us with another anecdote, which it
may be useful to detail, remarking, at the same time, that the
agents in it have a much better right to censure and disgrace.
In 1479, the Bishop of Lausanne and his Chapter cited with due
formality, before their tribunal, the May bugs, that were then very
troublesome, and as they did not obey the order, they were adjudged contumacious, excommunicated, and banished from the
diocese of Lausanne.   According to report, the original act of
this sentence is preserved with the greatest care.

The ancient parliament of Paris brought themselves into no less
disrepute, when, by an arret of February 7, 1314, they confirmed
the decision of the Judges of the county de Valois, who, on the
deposition of witnesses, had condemned a bull to be hanged for
goring a young man to death with his horns.

It is with regret we observe the tendency of such superstition, but I recollect another circumstance which will represent it in the most disgusting light. In Greece, when inundating rivers, at times, carry away the harvest, the inhabitants present a formal request to the Judge, that he would lay an injunction on the insolent stream to withdraw within its channel. A sentence is presently pronounced, in favour of the petitioners, but if the waters still keep rising, the Cadi, accompanied by the complainants, repairs to the scene of desolation and throws a copy of the juridical Act at the rebel current. The people then hurl invectives at the water, shoot at it with vollies of stones, pay the fees of the court, and entertain no doubt on the subject of the effect to be produced, thus betraying the decision of idiots.

The little town of Vevey is placed in a situation more agreeable than even that of Lausanne. Here nature displays a new plan and larger map of the Lake, with the rocks of Meillerie, noticed by Rousseau, the mountains of the Valais, and the glaciers of St. Bernard, including other points of view, characterised by sweetness and novelty.

Let us now return to Geneva, which is the Paris of Switzerland. It is not doing more than justice to the inhabitants to affirm, that they discover much of that spirit of freedom which distinguishes the present race of Frenchmen. In private life, the general cast of their manners is smooth, easy, and interesting. Striking specimens of science, taste, and genius; of diversified ingenuity well judged, and excellently managed, with some strong marks and symptoms of a pleasing experienced affability, every where offer themselves to observation. Here are no poor to be seen, every one is employed, and there is employment for every one. If I were to point out the least excellent part of their character, they are too closely bent on the *utcunque Rem.* To get rich, better his fortune, and promote his family interest, is the motto of the Genevese—" Let those be Spartans, he says, that will."

Here I am constrained to leave them, and to stop my career— you will find more ample details respecting Geneva, in the letters of a recent traveller, M. Raoul-Rochette, who has studied their society, under all the various aspects which arise from the different degrees of its civilization, and from the influence of their Government.

LETTER III.

FROM GENEVA TO CHAMOUNY BY BONNEVILLE.—CLUZE, THE
VALLEY OF MAGLAN.—A VAUCLUSIAN SPRING.—THE BATHS.
AND CASCADE OF ST. GERVAIS.—THE LAKES, &c. OF CHEDE.
THE GLACIER OF *Les Bossons,* AND THE VALLEY AND VILLAGE
OF CHAMOUNY.

A DILIGENCE conducted us from Geneva to Sallenche, that is,
about two-thirds of the way to Chamouny; we pass by Bonneville and Cluze. Bonneville is a little town of Savoy, situated
on the Arve, about five leagues from Geneva, at the southern
foot of the mountain called *le Môle.* The village of Cluze is
about three leagues further on, at the foot of woods and rocks
extremely picturesque. Here the face and forms of nature exhibit a curious contrast; in one part peaceful groves, and all those
charms of softness which please and captivate the eye, in another
dire ruins of majestic sternness, monstrous uncouth shapes of
rent and fallen rocks, which fill the traveller with a pensive
melancholy as he espies them; the scene here glowing with
bright colours, there consigned to blank confusion, and terrific to
behold. Could a kindred genius, his taste classical and congenial to the landscape, trace it with his pencil, it would exhibit
beauties to discover and study, blended with objects, in the same
proportion, the most austere and hideous.

We next enter the valley of Maglan, bordered with steep rocks,
often well wooded and sometimes naked and bare. Every now
and then appear patches cultivated, and sprinkled with dairy
houses, holding provisions for the winter, and so contrived as to
contain the cattle during the fair season. Such haunts as these,
remote from noise and strife, mad ambition would never be tempted to roam in—the tranquil heart only will seek the spot, and call
it his home.

Is there any happiness in solitude? Milton says,

—Who can enjoy alone,
Or all enjoying, what contentment find?

Had he visited this spot he would perhaps have tarried and
loved to rest here.

Numberless are the sinuosities in the valley of Maglan, through
which, with its rocks descending to their base, their tops seeming
to reach the clouds, from the novelty of the imagery and local
scenery, the traveller advances, apprehensive that he shall find no
outlet.

The Arve, a stream which waters this valley, at times inundates the whole plain, foaming, dashing, and raging against the road, with his oozy billows ; and at other times withdraws his wide waters.

Near the village of Maglan, above the hamlet of La Balme, we perceive the entrance of a grotto, that penetrates to the depth of 620 feet into the bowels of the mountain.   We find also, just before arriving at the village, close to the road side, a spring of water remarkably limpid and no less cooling.   It issues in such abundance as to form a little river, which falls into the Arve a little lower down.   It forms a miniature of the fountain of Vaucluse, with this difference, that the latter is hid, but this is uncovered and open.

In the same place is an echo, startling the traveller from a hundred giant voices, that seem to grow out of it, repeating the same sound.   The rocks resound as with the report of a pistol, while the strolling reverberation trails its slow length along.

Further on, to the left, is a magnificent cascade, the waters of which fall from a height of 800 feet.   Its detached features correspond with the general character of the valley, and enhance the effect of the leading circumstances.   As an accompaniment, may be added, that its murmurs were audible all the way to Sallenche. This is a little town on the left bank of the Arve ; here we changed our voitures to take caravans, or mules, for the village of Chamouny.   Sallenche lies in a vast bason, whence we have a very distinct view of the silvered crest of Mount Blanc.   Both the poetical and the common traveller would be surprised at the sublimity with which its highest part soars to the heavens, as if it could not descend an inch below the sun, moon, and stars.

About a league beyond Sallenche we arrive at the baths of St. Gervais, sequestered in the bottom of a valley, agreeably overshaded with larch trees.   Close to the buildings, the Bonhomme, a turbid boisterous torrent, pours a flood of whitish-coloured waters, and behind them is a fall of the stream, forming a grand cascade, the most interesting, perhaps, in all the Alps.   Approaching to near the fall, we feel a sudden change of temperature ;   a gentle warmth arising from thermal waters in the vicinity alternating with the cold effluvia of the falling spray. The descent is about 300 feet, rushing down with such violence that the leaves of the trees round about are shaken.

For about half a league the darksome torrent rolls through a hollow channel, sunk two hundred feet deep among rocks ; each side is fringed with a wood of larch trees.   At the summit of the cascade appears, on the right, a well-turfed parterre, surrounded, as in a plantation, with forest trees.

Both I and my companions were eager to multiply our comparisons, and seeing that nature was lavishing her stores in this climate, we could not miss the opportunity of visiting the beautiful cascade of Chede, on the left of the Chamouny road. Its limpid waters, in the reflection of the sun's rays, will exhibit, to those who brush the morning dew, a very beautiful rainbow.

Half a league farther on is the charming little lake of Chede, in the pleasing scene of whose surface the azure sky again gaily smiles, while the gloomy shades of the neighbouring mountains yield a prospect of sterner magnificence.

Next appears an agreeable troop of children, with smiling complaisance and songs, offering us cooling draughts out of their cups. Innocence was in their looks, the boys presenting the pure crystal liquid, the girls milk and cream, with such a grace that we found it hard to resist them. Such offers as these we had for four or five leagues, as far as to the village of Chamouny. One of my companions yielded to their solicitations more than twenty times. We repaid their complaisance, which was not wholly disinterested, with several little pieces of money.

A little beyond the lake last mentioned, the traveller should visit the bridge of goats, thrown over the foaming waves of the Arve. Four rams, I think, might pass in front, but if two men should meet on it and neither would retire, they must both fall into the water and make food for fishes. At a little distance from this bridge, as antiquarians report, there was a flourishing town in the time of the Romans, but the traces of it are as hard to ascertain as those of Nineveh and Babylon.

A lengthened ledge of cascades, formed by the Arve, beyond this bridge, in a wild savage retreat, almost as free as nature first made it, gives a picturesque effect very well deserving attention. Near it still appear the ruins of a mountain, the whole of which fell down in 1751, and overwhelmed the valley to the distance of five leagues. As a spectacle of destruction, a great part of it was of a melancholy air, but after happily clearing a dangerous piece of water, called the Black Torrent (very properly so denominated) we came, in time to breakfast, at Sorvez, where are gold and silver mines.

In the subterranean of one of these mines, on the side next Arve, a noise of water is heard, which might be cited as a comprehensive instance of all that is dreadful in the catalogue of sounds. Thunder, or the perpetual confusion of a raging tempest tearing from the mountain's height a ponderous mass of rocks, would produce an effect infinitely inferior. Had Dante been a witness of all the horrors that decorate the scene, he would, doubtless, have placed it at the entrance of his infernal regions. Our guide would by no means let us descend far into the vast labyrinth, his courage seemed to fail him. Amongst other highly unpleasant circumstances which he detailed, as conjoined with the frightful tumult, din, and uproar, was the frequent falling of stones from the vaulted roof, which might have accelerated our end, as in the case of the king of Epirus.   We followed his advice, however, like simple mortals, who value their own lives more than that of any king in the world.

It is time now to tell you of our arrival at Chamouny, but I must stop a little to bring into notice another of the disasters to which human life is exposed.   Young Eschen, a Saxon poet, who as such had undoubted claims to superior honour, in the year 1800 fell a victim to his courage, in a crevice of the Glaciers of Buet, obstinately disregarding the advice of his guide.   At the moment when the latter was exclaiming, for the last time, " Arretez, stop," the unfortunate youth disappeared, plunging into a dark gulf, which a recent fall of snow had masqued from his view.

From Sorvez to the valley of Chamouny the distance is a small league.   Nearly the whole of it is an ascent, with the Arve in view rolling its waves under the long, high, steep brows and ridges of those rude irregular eminences that overhang its banks. We could see through the firs and green swarth with which their dark flanks are garnished.   I can but notice what came immediately under our observation ; a drawing of the scene would most fully describe the principal subjects of our attention and wonder.

On quitting a little wood and entering some meadows, we found ourselves in the valley of Chamouny.   From these meadows it reaches about six leagues, nearly in a right line, to the Col de Balme, on the frontiers of the Valais.   It includes several villages, the chief of which has the name of Priory of Chamouny, from a convent of Benedictines, established in 1099, one hundred and odd years after the foundation of the Hospitium of Great St. Bernard.   We pass through the villages of Les Onches and Bossons, above which last appears the beautiful Glacier of the same name, at the foot of Mount Blanc.   The ardent votary of nature should pay it a transient visit, as its superb and beautiful pyramids of ice, fantastically coloured by the sun's rays, and viewed through the firs, look like a sea of glass with its smiling gay reflections, and are admirably calculated to claim attention. Fancy, in its wildest strains, could not aspire to ornaments more delightful and cheerful, than what an extensive view of the situation commands.

We arrive next, in about half an hour, at the priory ; that is, at the village of Chamouny, situated on the Arve, between Mount Blanc and Mount Breven, in the centre of the valley.   This last is diversified with woods, meadows, cultivated fields and glaciers. Chamouny is the usual place of departure and return, when travellers make excursions to Mount Blanc or the surrounding mountains.   The village contains about 300 houses.   We saw here two cabinets of minerals and birds, including several chamois, with some living young wild goats.

Chamouny is 3174 feet above the level of the sea. The winter lasts here nine months ; in the height of summer they are often obliged to kindle fires, the air and its keen blasts are so piercing. Excellent honey is produced here, and the mountains afford pasture for chamois and wild goats. The lower parts of the valley are well turfed with grass, and feed a great number of cattle. Nature, as if to indemnify the inhabitants for the length and sharpness of their winter, confers on their fields and meadows greater powers of vegetation than in our plains. What they sow in June they reap the product of in August. What takes five or six months to ripen throughout Burgundy, is effected in three, in the valley of Chamouny. As the snow falls in large quantities in winter, the inhabitants, to melt it the sooner, cover it with a black earth, this colour being a better conductor of caloric, and absorbing more heat than white. In the fine season, such of the men as are able to work, repair to the lower countries in quest of employment ; the women and old men guard the cattle, and labour on the lands. They make their bread to last a year or eighteen months, according to the quantum of their harvests. In winter, the stables serve both for dining and sleeping rooms. A partition is allotted for the cattle, and the rest is occupied by those of the household. The windows are mostly of paper well soaked in oil. On All Saints Day, the people generally kill a cow and a pig, and keep the flesh in salt for Sundays and occasional festivals, living on other days on milk and potatoes. A singular custom prevails here in the mode of their courtship, having the appearance of eccentricity. Ten or a dozen years are lost amidst the wildering mazes of platonic affection ; during the nine months of winter, the professed lovers play at cards and other amusements, that with variety may give a little power over the passions. Sometimes instances occur of early marriages, but they are very rare. A girl that should fail herein would be sure to have a nickname fastened on her, that would leave an indelible stain on her character. It is very difficult to account for these peculiarities. Parisians dames, I would, on many accounts, particularly recommend to you not to let that subject of delight, your personal attractions, grow dulled by age, as at Chamouny. Here, however, I must stop for a few days, having other excursions in view.

LETTER IV.

MOUNT BLANC, ITS GLACIERS AND AVALANCHES.

THERE are objects that impose on the visual organs, such as those La Fontaine refers to, De loin c'est quelque chose, et de près, ce n'est rien ; that is, giants at a distance but dwarfs near hand. Just as in common life affectation or pedantry may be mistaken for erroneous dignity, or classic lore, but, with a little familiarity, they soon degenerate into tinsel pertness and clumsiness. But nature, in producing Mount Blanc, has furnished a sample of the true and great sublime, so comprehensive and expressive as to afford a type of majesty in all its qualities and possible shades, exhibited in the scale of still increasing gradation. It is not without a degree of terror, mingled with surprise and admiration, just as when the mind is full of any great event, that the eye measures the aerial throne of this Alpine sovereign resting on mountains of ice, as old as Time.

Mount Blanc rises to the height of 14,700 feet above the level of the sea. The Chimboraço, in America, rises to 19,302 feet, but no mortal has ever yet reached its summit, unless, perhaps, we except M. de Humboldt. Mount Blanc has, several times, been felicitously scaled ; its elevation above Chamouny is 300 feet more than that of Chimboraço above its dependant valley of Tapis.

The summit of Mount Blanc has acquired the name of the Dromedary's Back, from a sort of lengthened bunch or ridge running from east to west in a direction nearly horizontal, and very narrow at its highest part. It gets wider as it descends easterly, and forms, in the west, a kind of front roof.

On the side of Italy Mount Blanc is inaccessible ; the descent is so steep that snow and ice cannot lodge in it. On the side of Savoy the mountain has gentle declivities, and discovers his flanks covered with eternal glaciers that descend down to the valley of Chamouny.

Although it would be scarcely two leagues in a bird's flight from the village of Chamouny to the summit, it requires, at least, ten hours' march to reach it ; dangerous passages are to be avoided by winding circuits, and there are 11,520 feet to ascend. The journey will take up three or four days, and sometimes more, if overtaken by bad weather. A number of unsuccessful trials had been made before the exploit was achieved by an intrepid peasant of the village, named Jacques Balmat, and by a physician of the same village, named Paccard. It was in 1786 that they scaled the prodigious ascent, and thus could assume the merit of being the first mortals that had ever succeeded in the enterprize.

M. de Saussure, a celebrated naturalist, was equally fortunate the year following; he was the first that made scientific experiments on the cimex of that immense aggregate of rocks and ice.

To engage in the hazardous undertaking, one should be inured to a mountainous region, and be able to contemplate the most frightful abysses with sang froid. Provisions for 4 or 5 days will be requisite, as tempestuous weather may occasion delays in the passage. There should be also a ladder to scale the crevices of the glaciers, and ropes that, when tied together, may form a line of communication. Without this precaution, it would be running a tremendous risque of stumbling into precipices concealed by the snow, and formed by the chinks of the glaciers. At making the least false step, the traveller would lose his presence of mind, and perhaps slide from one depth to another, to the base of the mountain, or disappear in one of the gulfs that might be near where he fell. Black crape is also necessary to cover the face with, while the sun is darting his rays on the ice, or we might incur the risk of losing our sight, and having the face well nigh excoriated, from the force of the solar beams. Nor is this all; there must be shoes with large and very sharp-pointed nails, as also a hatchet to make holes in the ice, for the feet to catch in, where the descent is rapid, and large staves pointed with iron, to bear ourselves up in the ascent, and still more in the descent. Also a tent to lodge in on the ice, for at the distance of three leagues from Chamouny, in a gradual scaling of the colossus, we have a series of glaciers to the cimex.

After the first journey we sleep on the ice, at the foot of rocks that are called "The Great Mules." This is after clearing a dangerous glacier, abounding with crevices. It is not above a quarter of a league to the highest part of this glacier, and yet it will take up, sometimes, three tedious hours to accomplish the feat in.

Next day we proceed to one of the shoulders of Mount Blanc, called *le Dome du Gouté.* Near it M. de Saussure fixed his tent in the snow, at the height of 5790 feet above the level of the sea, and 540 feet higher than the Peak of Teneriffe.

On the third day we begin to scramble up to the last plateau. Here great caution is called for, as there are a number of rapid descents, with crevices in the glaciers, hid by recent falls of snow.

The nearer we approach the highest point, the air becomes more rarefied, or, in other terms, the more the azote gas predominates, the more the oxygenated diminishes, or grows subtile. We cannot advance ten paces together, without stopping to take breath; but when the summit is gained, the fertile and active mind, unchecked in its career, contemplates the dimensions of space, expanded in a high degree, and from the situation and characteristic circumstances, becomes susceptible of the strongest sensations, and most lasting impressions. The horizon is immense, the eye being lost in its endless range.

When the air is clear, we can see to the distance of 68 leagues. From Lyons and Langres, about 65 leagues distant, in a right line, the cimex may be distinctly marked ; and M. de Saussure thinks he has had a glimpse of it from the heights of an eminence near Toulon.   M. Bourrit is confident, that from the top of Mount Blanc he has recognised some parts of the Mediterranean.

The wind here is uncommonly sharp, and the cold insupportable, but descending a little to the south, the temperature is not disagreeable.   As M. de Saussure observes, if shelter can be obtained from the direct impetus of the wind, it will not be felt. This is reversed in the plain, for though sheltered from its direct action, you feel its reflection ; dense air has the effect of re-percussion on the wind, which air rarefied has not.   As we approach the top the air gets dryer, and we are teazed with a sort of unquenchable thirst.   Melted snow will only add to it, and the only resource is melted ice, the water of which will be very potable.

On this elevation the appetite loses its relish, and prepared provisions fall into a congealed state.   We respire with difficulty, and the pulse beats as quick again as in the plain.   The train of epicures, with Vitellius at their head, would here feel an unaccountable aversion to wine and strong liquors.   The sky, here, is of a darker blue than in the plain.   This circumstance gave rise to a sudden fright in the guides of M. de Saussure ; when drawing near the top, the heavens appeared dusky, seen through a sort of embrasure, on a height which they had reached.   They started back, taking it for a vast gulf yawning before them.

From the great purity and transparency of the air, the stars may be seen by day-light, if the head be well covered and shaded. But, as if uncongenial with the human frame, we feel uneasiness, a general lassitude prevails, with a want of sleep, an ardent fever, and sometimes fainting fits.

There are many who cannot ascend to above 9000 feet.   Mules, at the height of 10,000 feet, on the mountains, feel so stifled, that they utter plaintive moanings.   Animals do not force nature, voluntarily, but man forces his, to make experiments and discoveries, or to gratify his vanity.   We travellers might have some in our sack, but we felt not its weight, for vanity is light.

At the height of 15,000 feet, under the equator, as M. Ebel reports, any violent exercise will produce fainting : and those who rise to upwards of 17,400 feet, will bleed at the eyes, lips, and gums.

On the cimex of Mount Blanc, we find no traces of any animals.

M. Saussure, who stopped here four hours and a half, saw only a couple of butterflies passing by him.

Sound is very much impaired, the rarity of the air diminishing its elasticity, and the force of its vibrations. An echo is scarcely perceptible; the explosion of a well-loaded pistol would give a report not louder than that of a pop-gun in an apartment.

In these mountains it is the descending winds that bring fair weather; the ascending prelude to rain and tempests.

You may well imagine that glaciers enter, as a capital ingredient, into an account of Mount Blanc, and have obtained a part of its renown. Those of Mount Blanc, like all others of the Alps, are formed by vast masses of snow, that have imbibed water, which becomes congealed in the winter. The figure of these enormous masses depends on the surface whereon they rest. If the soil is a rough declivity, the clefts are numerous, and the glacier will be like the waves of the sea. If it is a valley, pretty level and even, with a gentle declination, the crevices will be few.

In winter, a profound silence reigns among the glaciers; but in spring and summer frightful noises are sometimes heard, attended with vast concussions, that shake the mountain. Every fresh crevice is formed with a noise accompanying it like that of thunder. It is the frequent renovation of these clefts that renders the glaciers so dangerous to the traveller.

From the crevices issue frequent currents of a very cold air, that carry along with them small particles of ice, and scatter them at a distance, just like flakes of snow.

Every where among the glaciers, the murmuring of dashing waters is heard, working passages through the walls of ice. Sometimes we light on wells of a circular form, wrought out vertically, and filled with water to the brim.

The forms of the glaciers get renewed every month, and if any stone or other substance falls into their crevices, it is soon disgorged, and thrown back to the edge of the glacier.

There are many, however, whose surface is impure and blackish, in this respect varying from the rest; it proceeds from the ruins of rocks that the avalanches drag along with them; in decomposition they turn to a slimy or muddy earth. In the course of time the stones are often thrown out of the glacier, or finally form a sort of hills, arising, sometimes, to a hundred feet in height. And very often the astonishing force of the glaciers reduces these very heaps of stones to a sort of sand and gravel, from the compression which they undergo between the ice and the rocks of the mountains. The ice is not compact, like that of rivers and lakes; it consists of pieces and grains, several inches in length and thickness. Their forms are tortuous and odd, and they so dovetail into one another, that there is no detaching them from the mass but by breaking several. Hence they acquire a sort of movement, as in the articulations of a limb or member. It is an undulating movement, wherein the lower part comes uppermost, and vice versa.

At the bottom of the glaciers there appear a sort of vaulted archways, which serve as a passage to carry off the waters. They get formed in the winter, but are cleared away when the snow melts. The water is of a whitish blue, and retains its colour for several leagues, if other streams do not mingle with it.

From Mount Blanc to the Tyrol 400 glaciers have been counted, which might, says M. Ebel, form a sea of ice, of more than a hundred square leagues.

The avalanches, so common where there are glaciers, constitute, likewise, one of the most imposing curiosities of the Alps. These add an interest, though of a melancholy tendency, because the chilling impartiality of their history records catastrophes occasioned by them, the superior impression of which is still left. The falls of snow, known by this name, exhibit a phenomenon no less terrible than extraordinary; they take place in winter, spring, and summer.

The winter avalanches are formed of flakes of fresh snow, which, detached by the winds, and falling along the rocks, increase to a frightful volume, and then roll to the bottom of the valleys, dragging along trees and rocks, and changing the course of waters. The winter avalanche, formed of fresh snow, and not hard, is not so dangerous as that of the spring.

This latter is composed of masses of compact snow, that get loose from the rocks, in a thaw. From their weight, or from the impetuous rage of winds, they tumble, with extreme violence, into the lower parts, sometimes overwhelming whole forests, and covering an entire valley with their ruins. The ringing of a bell, or the sound of a voice, the least noise would give them an impulse, and precipitate their fall. In the places where they appear, the traveller must walk quick, and with the greatest silence, setting out early, before the sun has softened the snows. There is no describing the force of the spring and winter avalanches; the air, in their fall, receives so violent a percussion, that sometimes cottages are overset, and men thrown down and stifled, at considerable distances.

The summer avalanches only take place on the highest parts of the mountains. In their fall they might be taken for a river of crystal, pouring down abruptly, with a cloud of fine snow surrounding it. At every descent the mass augments, and a report is heard like thunder. The echoes prolong it, in their extensive route, with many a still lingering note, along those sequestered haunts. This last kind of avalanche is most to be dreaded in approaching the cimex, and in descending from it. They sometimes fall in the presence of the traveller, and block up his passage, as if indignant at his audacity.

Having mentioned Jacques Balmat as the first who scaled the summit, let me add, that his daughter would accompany him, and actually reached the brow of the colossus. If the attempt was creditable to her courage, it was unhappily contrasted by the event, as she returned almost blind, and was subjected to a weakness that lasted several years.

Enough of Mont Blanc, its glaciers and avalanches : in my next I must report other interesting particulars connected with the valley of Chamouny, for nature, here, is inexhaustible in the general merits of her phenomena, her metamorphoses, and the different objects of her composition.

LETTER V.

THE ARVERON, OR FOUNTAIN-HEAD OF THE ARVE.—MONT ENVERS.—THE SEA OF ICE.—CROIX DE FLEGERE.—MONT BREVEN.

THE Valley of Chaumont forms an article which I cannot discuss, as a tourist, without bestowing upon it a considerable portion of praise. To the eye of fancy it presents a grand spectacle of powerful and improving effect, from the variety and well combined structure of its parts; as such, I recommend it to the sedulous attention of tourists. Throughout the whole valley variety is never once lost sight of. Here is greatness of dimension, inspiring ideas of infinity, with terror, stillness, darkness,—rocks of every eccentric form and character, lakes and rivers, deep and majestic water-falls, trees, roughness and irregularity.—These are the obvious and avowed works of simple nature. But combined with this scenery, though subordinate to, and depending, as it is were, on it, art has employed, and, in some degree, displayed effects illustrative and ornamental, in decorations, that by a transition not too sudden seem necessary to please the eye and the mind. Throughout the valley, buildings and the architecture of country towns, &c. improve the landscape in many essential points which enter into the composition of the picturesque. Here are all the metamorphoses of Proteus, blended with a thousand attractions of Vertumnus.

It was in this district, so highly distinguished by the originality of its objects and character, that the author of La nouvelle Heloise forgot the fluctuations of his fortune, and supported his character of independence with spirit and consistency. To me it conveyed pleasing incitements to wisdom and the love of virtue, every thing seemed calculated to improve, entertain, and fortify the mind.

Travellers whose moral or physical constitution will not admit of their ascending Mount Blanc, should not fail to visit an important object, the sources of the Arveron. This is a rapid, boisterous stream, that, within a quarter of a league of its spring head, loses its name in uniting with the Arve. The Arveron descends from a vast glacier, named Les Bois, which communicates with the Sea of Ice. This torrent dashes down from the lower part of the glacier along a great arch of ice, more than a hundred feet high by nearly as many in breadth. It is dangerous approaching too near this superb vault and cavern, as oval arches and blocks of ice are continually tumbling from the heights. The waters of the torrent which carry along with them spangles of gold sand, rush with a foaming and tumultuous rage from the vault, often rolling enormous fragments of ice. The vast mouth of the Arveron is surmounted with lofty pyramids of ice, and encircled, as in a frame, with the beautiful forest trees of mount Envers and Le Bouchard. Here the traveller must be careful not to discharge fire arms, or to make the least noise in the vicinity. A Genevese family disappeared, and was lost among the falling blocks, from accidentally firing a pistol, which shook the vault and unloosed its component parts.

At no great distance is the village of Les Bois, inhabited by Albinos, a race of men that excite compassion rather than envy, from the imbecility of their physical constitution. They seem scarcely able to bear the day-light, and what little work they do is in their houses, to provide subsistence and satisfy their wants, which, happily, are but few.

Mount Envers lies at the foot of another called the Needle of Charmoz, which is contiguous to Mount Blanc, and 5724 feet above the level of the Sea. It is the largest of the glaciers of the Alps, and has acquired the appellation of the sea of Ice. The imagination is dazzled with the naked masses clustering all around this ocean of ice. It is a sort of pompous desert, where an eloquent silence reigns, penetrating the soul with profound and durable emotions. The panorama, from the distinct and exclusive character which it possesses, might seem to belong to a new world.

About half way up, we come to a fountain that yields a very scanty flow of water, but delicious and refreshing. Here there is a sudden and unexpected variation in the view. Every object appears soft and beautiful, light and playful, but it is within a narrow confined circle, as, all around, every thing indicates and represents a wild and desolate scene. Near this fountain we find the amiante, a singular mineral, consisting of delicate threads of an argentine ash-colour, of which the ancients made a cloth like linen, but incombustible.

Advancing a little higher, the road becomes very dangerous, from the frequent fall of avalanches and pieces of rocks that get loose from the sides of the mountains. All along we have the valley of Chamouny in view.

Having once gained the height, in lieu of beauty or any other qualities which are the foundation of a scene *riante*, we discover a large and extensive valley, entirely of ice, environed with gigantesque mountains, whose crests seem lost in the Heavens. Their bald and arid appearance, blended with their lofty fronts and steep flanks, infused a terror which it was impossible to surmount. If there is a man in whom the sensations and impressions of dread would not be excited by the view, he must have a heart thrice bound with adamant.

On the top of the green swarth which overlooks Mount Envers, is a neat pavilion, erected by M. Felix Desportes, then ambassador from France to Geneva. This little temple, dedicated to Nature, (so the inscription on the front purports) will afford shelter to travellers that may pass the night there.

The Valley of Ice, whose surface resembles that of a sea suddenly frozen, in a moment of calm, is an immense icy plain, of a magnificent green colour, that extends from the glaciers of Les Bois to the Col du Geant, near Cormayeur, in Piedmont, through a space of about ten leagues.

When from the grassy summit of Mount Envers we begin to descend, it is by a very rapid path, among Rhododendrons and Larches, to the brink of the glacier, where enormous accumulations of stone and sand rise to view. We next advance, but with extreme caution, to acquire a just notion of its extent. A piece of the ice gives immediate relief to the head-ache, by preventing the ascension of the blood. The inhabitants of the district make use of it for the purpose. At the southern extremity of the Sea of Ice, an arm of this sea, which has the name of the Glacier of Talefre, becomes exposed to view. The naturalist will there discover useful materials to form an acquisition to his knowledge, and the philosopher, who possesses sensibility, will contemplate the expansive scene with pleasure.

The traveller, here, will make a little turn to the left, passing by pyramids of ice, that threaten to crush any who approach them, and scale a rock called *Le Couvercle*, and after that, ascend a plateau, a sort of oasis or island in the midst of the glacier. This, in the month of August, becomes a parterre of very fine turf, embellished with beautiful alpine flowers. It has obtained the name of the Garden, and has all the appearance of one, being bordered with stones and sand, thrown out of the glaciers, and making a sort of inclosure about it. This flowery garden rises 8484 feet above the level of the sea, and 936 higher than the Hospitium of great St. Bernard. It lies in the midst of snow and ice, in situations the most arid, and on the highest mountains of the ancient continent.

A curious proof was here exhibited of the fact that glaciers will not retain foreign substances. During the time that French troops held the valley of Chamouny in military occupation, a post of observation was established on Mount Envers, to apprehend deserters, then very numerous. Here, upon information that a party had crossed the Sea of Ice, and that an individual had sought refuge on the Garden, it was resolved to surprise him there. While traversing an ocean of ice, one of them slid into a crevice, hid under recent snow; his comrades make a cord of their handkerchiefs, great coats, &c. and draw him out, but without his fire arms. Sometime after, another party found his fusee on the surface of the glacier.

A tradition is prevalent that the space now covered by the Sea of Ice was once a valley well cultivated and inhabited, and that it formed a passage to go from Chamouny to Piedmont, through Cormayeur.

La Croix de Flegere is one of the finest mountains about the valley of Chamouny. Ladies might ascend it without difficulty, and a great part of it lies through a forest. Having passed all the trees, we soon arrive at a cross, where a view opens that will take in the whole valley, and all the sea of glass, which last appears here in two grand divisions, with lofty precipices every where overhanging them. On the right and left, on the other side of the valley, we can clearly distinguish all the glaciers, the Col de Balme, all the different needles, and Mount Blanc, a bold, unbroken, broad mass, of a magnitude, shape, and features to constitute an order of superior eminence. At an humble, inferior distance, are seen, as permanent parts of the landscape, in this farewell view, rocks and mountains, hanging forests, and sudden precipices, rivers, dingles, cascades and headlong torrents, so mingled with diversities as if nature had studied and consulted this object; and, as before observed, the wildness of nature is, in many parts of the valley, subjugated by art.

Mount Breven is at a little distance from the Cross of Flegere, and rises 7836 feet above the level of the sea. It retains most of the solid features of the last-mentioned landscape, and will command the admiration of every judicious beholder.

My Scotch companions had a spirit of enterprize which these adventures were admirably calculated to excite; their ingenuity and industry were often shewn in them to advantage. Both had cultivated religious sentiments; one of them, from the solemnity of his demeanour, was the Nestor of the troop.   The character of the other, bold, prominent, and decisive, marked him out as our Achilles, and, like Homer's Hero, swift footed.   From his agility we called him the Chamois,—but woe to any of those animals that fell within his ken, death or captivity was sure to be their lot.

The eldest of my pupils rivalled our Achilles in vivacity.   In bounding over torrents and precipices, he, at times, out stripped the Caledonian, having learned of our famous dancer, Deshayes, to trip it, in all the whirling movements of Vestris and Duport. With constitutions such as to defy all common rules of conduct, incident to the grave manner usual with grave characters, these two might exclaim, with one of Tasso's warriors, ' Fatigues, dangers, I like best to take counsel of you.'

The Caledonian Nestor and my second pupil had a conformity of character, but from the diminished irritability of their nerves, it was in making their advances with calmness.   This caution, as any one may think, would be of importance in their case, securing them from little accidents, of which their rivals often incurred the risk and felt the inconvenience, but without material injury.

LETTER VI.

FROM CHAMOUNY TO MARTIGNY---THE VALORSINE---TETE NOIR. ---TRIENT---COL DE FORCLAY---A VIEW OF THE RHONE, IN THE VALAIS---ALPINE ANIMALS.

BIDDING adieu to Chamouny, its valley and glaciers, with the earliest tints of dawn we had left the central village, aiming next for the Valorsine and the Col de la Tete Noir, in our way to Martigny en Valais.   We came in good time to the hamlet of Trelafin, whence we may discern that of Tour, at the foot of the Col de Balme, where, every winter, snow falls to the depth of 12 or 15 feet.   The inhabitants are then obliged every morning to sweep away the snow before their houses.   During one very rigorous winter, they remained eight months buried under the snow, deprived of all communication, and not able to pass from one house to another.

To this hamlet of Trelafin we may apply a passage of Voltaire, when, in his Journey to Berlin, he treats of certain countries in Westphalia.

" In some large hovels that I have seen here, called houses, we find animals, called men, that live in the greatest cordiality, and pell-mell with other domestic animals.   A certain hard, black, and glutinous substance, made, according to report, of a species of rye, forms the principal sustenance of the inmates."

In my third letter, I noticed a hard kind of bread, made to last for a year or eighteen months,—this is similar to what Voltaire mentions. It is cut with a large knife, like that which wooden shoe-makers use in polishing their shoes. Pieces of it are then thrown into hot water, and when sufficiently steeped, they eat it with cheese and potatoes.

About half a league above Trelafin, we have gained another ascent, and we then enter into the Valorsine, a valley of a much wilder aspect than that of Chamouny, and for this plain reason, because it is more elevated. It stretches from west to east, towards the Valais, and is watered by a torrent that issues from the glaciers of Buet. However wild, it is not without some beauties, skirting the sinuous valley, on either side. Here are diversities of tint, of light as well as shade, so modified as to feast the eye and fill the imagination : pastures, orchard plots, cultivated fields, with the foliage of the larch in its blooming groves, clothe naked nature to the best advantage, at least, as far as the inhabitants know how. Winter continues long, and it is only in the month of June that the snows disappear.

The valley may contain about 600 inhabitants, scattered along the extent of the elevation, in several hamlets depending on the village of Valorsine. During the three months of their fine weather, the men go abroad to seek employment in the Valais and the Tarentaise. The church of the Valorsine is protected by a high mountain that serves it for a rampart against the avalanches, by which, in different situations, it had been more than once overset. There is only one auberge at Valorsine ; here a *gastronome* (epicure) would be ill at ease, as he could get nothing but milk, cheese, eggs, and bad wine, with bread a year old. This auberge had no sign, and we gave it a name, calling it the hotel *des vrais amis,* of true friends.

At Valorsine we met with a young person of uncommon personal beauty, that, far enough from being wild, was, however, to a certain degree, timid. Her hair floated in waving ringlets on her shoulders, as blown on by bland zephyrs. Her eyes, under her sunk eye-lids, unmasked the sweet passion of love in all its sensibilities. Her complexion was the incarnation of the rose blended with ivory. Said I to myself, " Where will this beauty nestle and find a mate?" and I paid her several compliments : among others, " Madam," said I, " you ought, at least, to bear the name of one of the Graces." " Sir," replied she, the carnation glowing on her cheeks, " my name is Cecilia."

She appeared so young that I could not feel it unpolite to ask her age. She said she was sixteen, and was born in the village of Valorsine. The backwardness of the climate prevented her fair alabaster skin from developing the plenitude of its polish.

Her breasts, though rounded by the hands of the Graces, were as yet only budding. They were partly, but not entirely, concealed. No ornaments distinguished her apparel; but the *simplex munditiis* only made her the more. attractive. She was the very Galatea, or Estelle, that figures in our romances and idylls, in short, the Shepherdess of the Alps, in the whole range of ideal perfection that the title may seem to import.

One of our Scotch gentlemen asked her if she would accompany us, adding many flattering promises; but the smile that she gave him in return, made it appear that she knew already what it was to love and to be beloved. And, in fact, he saw a very handsome young fellow soon after come and plant himself by her, take her hand and kiss it,---nor would he afterwards leave her. The young Scot, with ardent eyes, coursed over the charming hands, the vermilion lips of this Alpine nymph, whose eyes darted traits of a curious sensibility that were irresistible.

But we must tear ourselves from this dazzling vision, our horses were waiting, and our guide was hastening our departure, fearful of being benighted : so we bid farewell to the fair Cecilia. Her *new* lover clasped her hand, exhaling a sigh that was not re-echoed, and which flew away on the wings of the light winds.

Quitting Valorsine, we enter next the mountains of the Valais, advancing into the heart of a forest of larches, to visit La Tete Noire. We proceed along a rugged path to a rock shaped as a cavern, where an English lord with his lady passed a disagreeable night, waiting for the parts of his carriage, which had been taken to pieces and carried on the backs of mules, that he might have it said, that a carriage had passed over these frightful solitudes. It was a whim which cost him seven or eight hundred francs.

As we approach Le Col de la Tete Noire, the aspect of the country grows wilder; the road serpentines all along among trees; but it is edged with precipices eight or nine hundred feet in depth, with a deep torrent at the bottom, of a whitish water, foaming and brawling with a deafening roar, over ragged projecting rocks.

On the left we see, on the opposite side of the valley, the village and church of Finio, which look as if suspended in the air. It is difficult to conceive how vegetation and the dwellings of men can be maintained in such an elevation.

At length we arrived at a place called Malpas, or Mapas, with dangerous steps, rudely cut out of the rocks. We were struck with terror, catching a glympse of the abysses close to the road on the left, and of the rocks on the right, threatening to overwhelm us. This place is called La Tete Noire, (the Black

Head,) it being, in fact, a height every where of that colour from the dark rocks and firs that cover the flank of the mountain.

We come next to a descent, or rough declivity, which leads to the valley of Trient, where we observed peculiar situations, in all the varieties of a most romantic form. As a lover of the picturesque, I remarked also a bridge over the torrent, near a hamlet, and surrounded with trees, green plots, and the majestic perspective of mountain towering above mountain. These little diversities, though of secondary consideration, created attraction. From the valley of Trient we ascend to the Col de Forclay, from the height of which we clearly discover the sinuosities of the Rhone, in the Valais, together with the plain along which it pours, in its serpentine meanders, and the city of Sion, in the centre. The scene is interesting, commanding at one view, the romantic course of the river and a most extensive reach.

The bleak rocks of the Col de Forclay cast their long shadows over an area of more than equal sterility to that of La Tete Noire. Here we find vegetation at a stand, and natural productions shrinking from the stern blasts of winter.

It may afford satisfaction to those curious in natural history to be informed respecting the different animals that inhabit these mountains. I forgot to treat of them when at Chamouny.

Besides most of the quadrupeds and birds common in France and Germany, we find in the Alps, the lynx, the white hare, the black squirrel, the wild goat, the chamois, the black and fallow bear, the marmot, or mountain rat, the great eagle, and the white wood-hen.

Of the lynx, the ancients reported, that his piercing sight could make its way through opaque bodies; this was a fiction. Our lynx cannot see through stone-walls; but his eyes are unusually brilliant: he utters a cry somewhat like that of the wolf. He is not so large, nor does he stand so high on his legs. In general, he is about the size of a fox, but walks and leaps like a cat. He lives by the chase, and pursues his game even to the tops of trees, strangling his victims when seized, and sucking their blood. After opening their heads to devour the brains, he will often abandon them in quest of other prey.

The white hare in his manners resembles the rest of his species; but is wilder.

The black squirrel lodges constantly on the highest trees, and is still more afraid of water than of the ground. He is very sprightly, and remarkably clean. In summer he makes a provision of nuts, and lives on them in winter.

The marmot and the bear pass the winter in abstinence and fasting. When the bad season commences they are very fat; but at the return of spring as lean as cuckows. The marmot is so torpid in his winter sleep, that when surprised in the earth he may be tossed about, and even torn to pieces, without emerging from his lethargy. When the warm weather returns, he re-assumes his ordinary functions.

The bear is not so lethargic as the marmot; his fat helps him to support hunger, and he seldom quits his lair but when very much pressed by hunger. This animal is capricious and irritable, and dislikes fillips on the nose or muzzle, though not averse to the caresses of women.

A company of French grenadiers patroling Mount Cenis, one day surprised a bear in the forest dragging a young girl to his laire. He had perched on his two hind legs, and with one of his front-paws seemed to be giving her the arm. They surround him and make him let go his prey, presently killing him. The poor girl, half dead with fright, coming to herself, declared that the bear had attempted to do violence to her person. She died eight days after. The Captain of the detachment, M. Turquois, an eye witness, vouched to me for this fact.

Another incident, not less extraordinary, took place in the mountain of Chaillot. A shepherd's daughter, tending her flock, was seized by a bear, and carried away in his paws. Her cries and groans were heard by the shepherds and huntsmen; but they arrived too late. The animal had gratified his brutal passion; but in his rage to be interrupted, he tore the girl to pieces. Another bear came up to the spot, and would dispute the other's claim to the female; but both were cut to pieces by the hunters.

In another mountain of the High Alps, the wife of a shepherd going into the forest was carried away by a bear, and lived for some time in his den. After some months the huntsmen, hearing a bear making dreadful howlings, pursued and killed him. The smell of a corpse exhaling from his cavern, they enter it, and find that of a woman; she was known by the guide of the huntsmen to be the person they had been so long in quest of.

The great eagle of the Alps is four feet four inches in length, and nine feet four inches between the extremities of his wings. He disdains the smaller animals, and contemns their insults. *Aquila non capit muscas.* If he punishes the insolence of the crow and the magpie with death, it is not till they have long teazed him with their importunate chatterings. He looks for an enemy worthy of his resentment, and has been known to attack oxen, and, as fame reports, to precipitate them from the top of the rocks.

Descending now from the Col de Forclay, we come to Martigny, a little town in the Lower Valais, famous in the time of Cæsar, who took possession of it to secure the passage of the Great St. Bernard.

Martigny stretches along a mountain very near the Rhone. The suburbs border the torrent of the Drance, which descends from St. Bernard and empties itself into the great river. Martigny will be our rallying point in certain excursions in the vicinity.

LETTER VII.

EXCURSION TO GREAT ST. BERNARD.—VALLEY OF ENTREMONT, &c.—ST. PIERRE.—VAL DE PROU.—HOUSE OF REFUGE.—COL DE ST. BERNARD, &c.

THE passage of Mount St. Bernard was not rendered practicable till the time of Cæsar. That great captain, in spite of the elements, made a road over it, but it was to enslave the free people of the valley of the Rhone and the Allobroges, Geneva being one of their principal cities. The French armies renewed this passage, under the standard and direction of Napoleon Bonaparte.

The torrent of the Drance takes its rise, pouring from a mountain near the Hospitium of Great St. Bernard; it then passes through the valley of Entremont, one of the most interesting among these mountains, and after frequently swelling to a dreadful flood, spreads itself over the surrounding level, till it mingles its whitish waters with the muddy current of the Rhone. It is often destructive in its career.

From Martigny, we proceed to St. Branchier, a village on the banks of the Drance, where the valley of Entremont begins, but reaches four leagues further to the little town of St. Pierre, the last village on the road to the Hospitium of St. Bernard.

Before we enter St. Branchier, we pass under a vaulted roof cut in the live rock, on the right bank of the Drance, in 1818, after that torrent, in its infuriated course, had entirely swept away the road. This was at the time when the ice broke up in the unfortunate valley of Bagne.

Next to St. Branchier we come to the village of Orcieres, and so keep advancing through the valley of Entremont, enlivened with the luxuriance and mellow tints of green meadows, in the middle of which the Drance no longer rages with impetuous eddies, but rolls its silver streams with serenity through a country adorned with golden harvests on the sides of its hills.

After a journey of about an hour and a half we arrive at Liddes, a large village half way between Martigny and the Hospitium, agreeably situated in the midst of meadows. The church steeple bears the date of 1008.

Leaving this village the valley grows wilder. It was here that our artillery was dragged up to the height of St. Bernard by the soldiers and peasants, in an ascent of four leagues across snow and ice. M. Tuillard thus describes this operation. A hundred and twenty men harnessed to a long rope, drew along the cannon and their carriage. Besides their arms, ammunition, and provisions for five days, each soldier of the division Watrin carried also the provisions of the division Loison. The weight of this double load was estimated at more than seventy pounds, but the ardour of our men was inconceivable. When benumbed with cold and harassed with fatigue, the volunteers found their courage and strength sinking,—they called out for the drums to beat a charge, and, inspired by their drums and martial songs, they succeeded in reaching at length the summit of St. Bernard. In passing the southern side of the mountain the men slided over the snow to the bottom of the declivity, Bonaparte and all the officers imitating them.

From the hamlet of Alleve, about which Napoleon had placed his cavalry in the month of May, 1800, we ascend to a village called St. Pierre, 5000 feet above the level of the sea. The entrance of this village, on the side next the Hospitium, is defended by a wall, gates, and a bridge of one arch, thrown over a torrent whose deep channel, a quarter of a league higher up, falling from a rock, forms a very fine cascade of 200 feet in its fall.

Having once gained the height of St. Pierre, we have a view of Mount Velan and the Glacier of Menoue, and soon enter into the valley of Great St. Bernard, at the distance of three leagues from the convent.

In tracing a little descent, along which the road goes toward the Drance, we pass the edge of a precipice where the first consul was in danger of perishing, by sliding from his mule into the snow. A peasant caught him by the coat, and received a thousand francs in recompence.

The further we advance the more vegetation degenerates. At Martigny we were gratified with the bloom and foliage of the oak and chesnut trees, and in proceeding to St. Branchier, with groves of beeches and yoke elms. The valley of Entremont had its characteristic charms, its lands being uniformly covered with verdure; but this rich decoration, which has so excellent an external appearance, diminishes in proportion as we ascend. Afterwards, scattered here and there, we see maples, alders, lote trees, and firs. In our next situation we had larches and willows, at the height of 5400 feet above the level of the sea, and after that trees disappeared, and we saw nothing but wild rose plants and rhododendrons. Advancing to an elevation of 8000 feet, we should find nothing but moss and certain Alpine plants, but these, on reaching a higher story, disappear, and at the height of 10,600 feet would be nothing but lichens overspreading the surface of the rocks, and at another height all vegetation whatever is at a stand.

In proceeding through the valley of St. Bernard we keep alongside of the Drance, among some pasture grounds and dairy houses that belong to the Hospitium, till we come to a plateau named le Prou, whereon we find seven little barns about a hundred paces distant from the great dairy of St. Bernard, wherein cows are kept and cheese is prepared.

On the left, in front, we discover the mountain of the Drome, where three companies of grenadiers passed over snow and ice, 10,800 feet above the sea, to surprise an enemy's post on the southern declivity. At the word of the first consul they darted over the dangerous height, and fortune crowned their enterprize with success.

To approach the Hospitium we keep along the Drance, here only a large brook, 6000 feet above the level of the sea. Soon after vegetation disappears, and a picture of desolation and sterility presents itself hardly to be imagined. We now walk over stones and moss, and in about half an hour come to two little buildings, one of which serves as a house of refuge for travellers, and the other is to preserve, for a time, the bodies of such individuals as perish in the snow.

This place has the name of the hospital, and hither provisions are brought by the dogs of St. Bernard, accompanied by their masters, and, especially in great storms, care being also taken to make out a path for the traveller.

This region is exposed to what is here called a *tourmente*, a hurricane attended with vast shoals of snow, that suddenly in a few seconds, rise to the highest part of the gorges and deep cavities, covering and overwhelming wherever it finds them. A traveller surprised in these openings, is in the greatest danger, for he cannot keep his eyes open so as to explore his way, or if in the plain road, it is soon obstructed, and he is in danger of falling into some abyss. In such cases the intelligent dogs and the worthy religious of St. Bernard, often constitute a resource superior and permanent.

We soon had the satisfaction of accosting those venerable ecclesiastics, so devoted to the kind offices of mercy ; every glance, every line and feature of which has its animation and character, eloquent of sympathy, and forming the perfection, the sublime of human nature. Entering their hospitium, it is but justice to remark, that from the active zeal and public spirit which pervade that benevolent institution, we were welcomed like children long absent from their loving parents.

The Hospitium of Great St. Bernard stands on the highest part of a mountain, in a very narrow gorge, between steep and desert rocks, 7560 feet above the level of the sea. Its situation is at a point where the north and south winds meet, with all the varieties of sound, from the faintest murmuring to the sullen roar, and, at times, combating with a boisterous rage and awful impetuosity, not to be conceived by those unacquainted with the scene. We saw no signs of vegetation, excepting some wretched garden plants which the good fathers were trying to raise; and as to their provisions, they fetch them from a distance of four or five leagues. St. Bernard stands on the very point most convenient as a refuge for travellers in a tempest.

This habitation, the most elevated of the old Continent, was founded by St. Bernard, in 962, and he presided, as its warden, for the space of 40 years. It consists of three ranges of buildings, the charms of which depend not upon the accidents of decoration, for the most perfect symmetry, and all its corresponding ornaments, would here be graces of inferior magnitude, and the beauty itself of art, would make but the smaller part of loveliness. The whole beams with expression, abounds with character, descriptive of some kind or elevated passion, with superior charms, that never cloy nor fade.

The *Corps de Logis*, or principal mansion, stands at the end of a very deep lake, frozen over in winter; it is capable of receiving nearly 200 persons at a time. In the right, are offices for the domestics; they are so constructed as to intercept, at one of the angles, any avalanches that from an adjacent mountain might overspread the Hospitium. On the left, and more to the north, is the chapel wherein individuals are deposited that are found dead in the snow. They are ranged one beside another, as in a camp mortuary, the bodies, from the dryness, vivacity, and free circulation of the air, corrupting very slowly. The traits of the countenance remain unaltered for years, and the bodies, when dried, take the semblance of mummies. I noticed some dead three years and more, that still retained their hair, and the skin appeared in good preservation. What seemed the most striking was the body of a mother, with that of her child, both of whom had perished under an avalanche. The mother was clasping the child in her arms, death could not part them.

On the col of St. Bernard, advancing a little towards Italy, they shew a place where, in the time of the Romans, there stood a temple and an Hospitium, dedicated to Jupiter Hospitalis. The mountain was then called *Mons Jovis*, of which was made *Mont Joux*, which it retained till the tenth century. In the ruins have been found Ex Votos, or Votive tables, in great numbers, engraved on plates of bronze; they shew that from the earliest times the passage of St. Bernard was considered dangerous. The Almoner of the convent introduces amateurs to a cabinet that he has formed of the antiquities found in the ruined temple. · We noticed a collection of medals of Roman Emperors, many small figures in bronze, two of Hercules and a Mars, a very curious hand, a sepulchral lamp, gilded ears of corn, and a little Jupiter holding the thunder. These different objects are distinguished by the variety and perfection of their mechanical improvement, such as give honour and importance to the arts, and also for their excellent conservation.

The church of the Hospitium is a handsome structure. The arched vaulting is of a noble fresco, which has not called for any reparation since 1686, when it was raised. The altar is supported, by four large pillars of black marble, all of a piece.

When entered, we see on the right in the wall, a monument in white marble, representing General Desaix, rendering his last sighs at the battle of Marengo. The work is a master-piece of the sculptor Lemoine. The hero appears in the attitude of uttering the last words which escaped him : ' Go and tell the first consul that I die with regret, not having done enough to immortalize my name with posterity.'

In the chapel we also find several paintings of the great masters, and a beautiful organ, surmounted with an angel.

The dogs of St. Bernard are of a superior description, and very ready to caress strangers. These faithful friends of man, clear the way, in a time of snow, from the Hospitium to the Hospital, and sometimes further, bearing on their necks a flaggon of brandy to offer to the travellers, whose arrival they instinctively can prognosticate at considerable distances. These interesting and intelligent animals never mistake the right road, though overlaid with snow.

At the end of Autumn, in 1820, a domestic of the establishment, going his rounds, observed the dog that he had with him stop suddenly, and barking with all his might, run away in another direction. At the same time, he hears a rumbling noise, and takes a resolution to follow the dog; he thereby avoided an enormous avalanche, wherein he must have been engulfed, had he slighted the foreseeing instinct of his faithful companion.

One of the dogs patroling the vicinity one day in bad weather, found a child that had taken refuge under a vaulted roof of snow. The mother had just before disappeared under an avalanche, and the child was in danger of perishing. The dog was importunate in his caresses, and the child mounting his back, was brought to the Hospitium, by his sagacious liberator.

These animals do not lose their beneficent instinct by a change of climate. At Lisow Castle, near Liverpool, are two of the St. Bernard dogs, conveyed thither by a Swiss merchant, and consigned to an aunt of my pupils. One day, some children were hunting for shells on the sea shore, when one of them was caught by the reflux of the tide. This being observed by the others, their piercing cries brought up one of the dogs then in the neighbourhood, which plunging into the water, caught the child by his clothes and brought him safe to land.

All the fathers of St. Bernard go on a mendicant tour, making gatherings to support the expenses of their convent. Their tour does not reach beyond the frontiers of Switzerland, and if other mendicant brothers itinerate further, they are not of this establishment.

As the air is unusually keen on this elevated situation, none of the religious remain here above six years. We find no aged persons, but young men in their full vigour. When age or infirmity approaches, the religious are appointed to serve cures in the villages about the valley of Entremont as far as to Martigny, where the Prior of the convent generally resides.

A hundred cows are maintained on the establishment, that supply it with cheese, also fifty horses or mules that go in quest of provisions into Piedmont and Switzerland. Their wood comes from a distance of four leagues, in the valley of Aoste. They have nothing but what is brought from a considerable distance.

We were not a little astonished at our entertainment at supper, which was equal to that of the best auberge in Geneva. After two services, we had the dessert and wine extra, which last was not inferior to Madeira. The religious did the honours of the table with a politeness and kindness not to be expressed. The servants all alert, at the least sign, executed their functions with correct precision. After the dessert coffee was offered us. The gaiety of the place was well adapted to our feelings and to the occasion, with nothing in it to call impropriety; it helped to season our relish, though indeed the appetite never fails here. After the repast, one of the fathers performed on the piano-forte some pleasing melodies, for they all have a taste for music, and listen to it with a cultivated ear. A very agreeable marchioness, that was at supper with us, sung some favourite lively airs of the French music, and I cannot but speak of her efforts in the language of praise; for a moment we fancied ourselves at Paris, in the Theatre Favart.

At length we took leave of this disinterested and patriotic society, wherein good sense, agreeable conversation, and suitable conduct so pleasingly preside, and set out on our return to Martigny, intending to proceed to Simplon.

Previous to our re-visiting the village of Liddes, we noticed, on the side of the road, a large quantity of little black balls rolled up in heaps. Our company then consisted of from 15 to 20 persons, all of whom had been entertained at the convent. One of the party, 47 years of age, took these little balls for natural productions of the country, and beginning to chew one, presently threw it away, with a sputtering noise, as bitter, or not very pleasant. This traveller might be reckoned not over fastidious; what he thought good fruit, his eye dwelling on it with pleasure, proved to be sheep's dung. This hoggish misadventure not a little entertained the groupe of our fellow travellers, among whom, a young Parisian Marchioness, handsome and amiable, said she should never forget it ;—it helped to beguile the time all the way to Martigny.

There we took leave of the fair Parisian, who, with her husband and father, took a different road. . One of our Scotchmen, both of whom were distinguished by a cheerful, good-humoured, and obliging disposition, paid his attentions to her, with all the courtesy and urbanity of a well-educated cavalier.

As a postscript to this letter, I add the following observations, from a memoir I have just perused, by M. Parot, Professor of Physics at Dorpat, and Russian Counsellor of State.

The cold and moisture at St. Bernard make it a sort of tomb—this may be attributed to various causes. The buildings are buried in snow, during eight months of the year. The whole region is so wrapped up in mist, that scarcely fifteen days in a year are quite serene. The walls of the convent require an interior lining of bricks and double windows; at present, they are dangerous conductors of both heat and humidity. Other materials for fuel might be had as substitutes for wood, or it might be economised by stoves. At present, the consumption of fuel is considerable, and it takes near five hours and a half to dress victuals, from the diminution of the pressure of the atmosphere.

The religious of this establishment seldom live above five and thirty years, and more die between twenty and thirty, from the effect of cold and the humidity of their habitation. This mortality would be far less rapid, were precautionary measures more extensively contemplated.

LETTER VIII.

THE VALAIS, ITS EXTENT, AND SITUATION—THE TOWNS OF ST. MAURICE, MARTIGNY, SION, AND BRIEG—MANNERS OF THE VALAISANS, &c.

THE Valais has been treated of in different publications, and among others in the famous letter of J. J. Rousseau, one of the finest in his New Heloisa. He does not enter into the design of St. Preux, which was, to entertain Julia with all the curiosities of the country. " We must, (he says,) reserve our correspondence for matters the most interesting to ourselves, personally." He merely depicts certain aspects of the country, that present themselves on every side, and communicates some liberal opinions respecting the manners of the people in the Upper Valais. He forbears dwelling on the majestic course of the Rhone, the towns, the natural productions, the resources, the extent, and customs peculiar to the country in general. On these points I shall furnish some details, without omitting those of the great writer last mentioned.

The Valais is the longest and most considerable of all the valleys of Switzerland. The Rhone traverses this Canton through its whole extent, which is 35 leagues, by 1 in breadth. It is surrounded with the highest mountains of the Alps, from St. Maurice, which is at the entrance, to the foot of Le Simplon, at the other extremity.

In this lengthened dale, excavated by nature, between the mountains, appear, at successive distances of from 6 to 8 leagues, four little towns, St. Maurice, Martigny, Sion, and Brieg.

St. Maurice lies in a passage so straitened by parallel mountains, that, with the bridge over the Rhone, it might, as a key, lock up all entrance into the valley. Near this town we find the beautiful cascade of Pissevache, where the water tumbles perpendicularly from a rocky height of 300 feet. The transparent stream, in its headlong fall, takes the appearance of a brilliant gauze, veiling the rock.

Martigny, of which some notice has already been taken, is a little town near the junction of the Drance and the Rhone, at the foot of the valley which leads to Great St. Bernard. It still retains some tourelles, or turretted battlements, which remind us of the feudal prerogatives in old times.

Sion is the capital of the Valais, seated in its central part, between Brieg and Martigny. It is surrounded with ramparts and old towers; these are the ruins of strong castles, constructed by the Romans and their successors. The town lies on the widest part of the valley of the Rhone, buttressed against hills enriched with vineyards.

Brieg, the last town of the Valais, is situated at the foot of Le Simplon, at the entrance of the valley which leads to St. Gothard, and very near the Rhone. Its towers, garnished with enormous globes of tin, give it, at some distance, an air of riches and grandeur; but this idea must be discarded on entering the place.

The Valais is divided into Upper and Lower. In the Lower Valais the French language is universal; in the Upper, German, and a little French, are spoken.

The valley is mostly shaped as a plain, from one end to the other; and the Rhone, which waters it all along, at times, when swollen and enraged to a high degree, urges, bears down, by its daring torrent, and whirls away every thing in its course, shattering whole plantations, and causing a general wreck. If the inhabitants, however, would combine their efforts, they would succeed in securing the valley from such universal deluges.

It possesses one peculiarity, that is unusually interesting, that of combining the temperature of every climate, from the polar ocean to the torrid equatorial regions. Here is a rapid transition from scenes of terrible and tumultuous grandeur, to mingled impressions of beauty, from viewing, studying, and consulting nature, in her other rich diversities.

This eternally varied line of tints, of light and shade, so modified, was deeply impressed on the imagination of the philosopher of Geneva.

" I was eager," said he, " to ruminate, but was ever interrupted in my reveries by some unlooked for spectacle. Sometimes, the wild forms of immense rocks and hanging mountains threatened sudden ruin over my head ; sometimes, lofty and precipitous cascades, foaming and roaring over ragged strata, besprinkled me with their mingled misty spray. Sometimes, a dashing torrent poured upon us from on high, and laid bare to my view the steep slopes of some dangerous chasm, at the prospect of which the eye sickens, and we dare not look down upon its depth. Sometimes, I lost myself in the long recesses, (gloomy as the darkness of cheerless night,) in the solemn silence of some tufted wood. Sometimes, emerging from a deep hollow, my eye was suddenly feasted with the minuter beauties which constitute the attraction of meadows. The astonishing mixture of wild and cultivated nature : haunts, where one would think man could never penetrate, combined with accidents of less majestic, but beautiful scenery, produce and impress on the solid features of the landscape, independent charms, which nothing can exterminate and destroy.

" Close to the wide expanse of some cavern, we see dwelling-houses, vineyards, where we should look only for brambles, excellent fruits on the slippery summit of rude cliffs, and cultivated fields among high precipices and profound gulfs, whence the shrinking eye recedes.

" It is not the hand of man only that has rendered this singular tract so oddly contrasted. Nature seems to have taken pleasure in appearing in opposition to herself, under different aspects, in one and the same place. Towards the east, the gaiety of spring, or the luxuriance of summer, and mellow fruits of autumn ; in a northerly direction, mountains covered with a veil of snow, the atmosphere thick with vapours, the earth locked in icy fetters, the leafless grove, the dismantled plantation, nature unclothed and with a repelling nakedness, if I may so express myself. In such a country, summer glowing with its yellow harvests, and winter with its howling tempests, have many varieties, and their phenomena are always more or less beautiful and sublime."

Such is the Valais, in which we find nature in her bolder, broader style, happily contrasted, relieved with a vivacious, penetrating effect, by many engaging and animating, sweet and striking touches of art.

With respect to the inhabitants, they leave an interesting impression on the mind, but it is not so gaily conceived. Most of them, men and women, boys and girls, have enormous goitres, that form a great drawback on the general merits of their physical composition. Where these complaints are found incurable, we may see the subjects standing before their doors in summer, in a state of entire listlessness, shewing those disgusting protuberances, with their olive-coloured complexion, and unsightly features. Some of them can apply to certain light labours, but in general they are incapable of any application. When any discourse is addressed to these last, all the answer you can obtain consists in certain inflections of the voice, like the cries of animals, accompanied with a frightful smile.

Their disorder, (called by the author, cretinism,) is attributed partly to heat, partly to the stagnated air, and partly to the quality of the water. It is ascribed also to the want of cleanliness in the inhabitants, they being generally considered as indolent and heavy, and without a proper share of industry. They appear strangers to cheerfulness and gaiety; when at labour they have a melancholy air, and they have not spirits sufficient to enforce, in a due degree, that style of singing airs and songs, which, when persons are at work, is found to produce agreeable and serviceable effects.

During the calamities that befel their native country, in the course of the French Revolution, their apathy seems to have been denounced and banished. In several instances they spurned, with a becoming indignity, at the insolence of oppression, acting with a spirit of manly and laudable independence. They had it not in their power to controul the occupation of their country by France, but, indeed, during that period, many abuses of their civil establishments were reformed, and many useful institutions adopted, which they still retain. Odious distinctions, that had existed for ages in the Upper and Lower Valais, and all along the magnificent route of Le Simplon, were extinguished for ever. A new æra has been established by that revolution, in some respects.

Three leagues from Sion, on the side of Brieg, appears the handsome little town of Sierre, inhabited by the noblesse and opulent families. It is the first place where we hear the German spoken. The water here is insalubrious, and when drunk cold renders the voice hoarse.

From Sierre there is a ready communication to the baths of Leuk, which are much frequented in the fair season, from the superior efficacy of their waters. The town of Leuk is situated on a height on the right bank of the Rhone, about five leagues from Sierre.

Leaving Sierre we soon enter a forest of larches along the Rhone. At the village of Tourtemagne, there is a very good inn, and a cascade which may vie with that of Pisse Vache near St. Maurice.

As we advance forward the valley grows narrower, and we pass through Viège, a little town that has two Gothic churches, decorated with very odd figures; and lastly appears the town of Brieg, at the foot of Le Simplon, on the left bank of the Rhone.

With the exception of salt, their country supplies the Valaisans with all the necessaries of life. Meadows and their cattle form the principal source of their riches. Generally speaking, they are kind and hospitable, and an equal mediocrity, remote both from misery and luxury, illustrates the character of their domestic economy.

Of the Valaisans, it may be said as of the Athenians, in all things they are too superstitious. A traveller, M. Echasseriaux, as quoted by M. Mallet, takes notice of their hermitages, their ossuaries, or depositaries of relics, their chapels cut in the rock, or scattered about its base, or on the sides and summits of mountains; " these," says he, " contain abundant sketches of the religious humour which pervades the character of the people in the different parts of their country. Here stands a cross in front of the enormous ruins of a mountain overset, there another has been planted before a torrent that menaces devastation;" to which, it is added, that while the house of the citizen is poor, the church of the hamlet is always richly ornamented.

At these chapels, as M. Mallet remarks in one of his interesting letters on the route of Le Simplon, the labourer comes to implore rain for his field, and the shepherd to pray for divine aid against the disease that attacks his flock. The chapel, from which numberless vows are addressed, stands beside a field, dried up with heat in the midst of a pasture ground wherein the flocks are languishing, and not far from the avalanche which had occasioned destruction to one on a contiguous site.

From Martigny to Brieg, we have kept along the valley in the course of the Rhone, sometimes on the right, sometimes on the left, and crossing it over neat wooden bridges. We have been hemmed in with mountains, as in a longitudinal cavity, respiring

an air hot and gross from the concentrated localities. Among
the Valaisans there are but few handsome persons, unless, perhaps, in the higher mountains, where the *cretin* does not exist.
Julia's lover makes mention of some charming figures there.

We shall now quit the Rhone, which, on our left, descends
from Mount Gothard, and proceed to ascend Le Simplon by the
new route bearing its name, and forming one of the wonders of
our age.

LETTER IX.

OF THE MOUNTAIN LE SIMPLON, AND THE GRAND ROUTE OR ROAD BEARING ITS NAME.

THE new route of Le Simplon is one of the boldest undertakings
which the genius of modern times has conceived and executed.
To clear a mountain fourteen leagues in extent, to fill up frightful
chasms, to pierce through a valley of rocks, striking out a passage
therein, to correct or to combat mountainous declivities subject
to avalanches, to make a number of turnings in different passages,
to mitigate the inclination of the road, to fix bridges over depths
which the eye is almost afraid to measure, all these difficulties
our engineers surmounted, by the labours and perseverance of
somewhat less than five years.

Le Simplon is a mountain situated between Great St. Bernard
and St. Gothard. It is rightly considered as one of the most interesting passages of the Chain of the Alps; it is also one of the
richest in vegetables. Formerly it was only passable on foot or by
mules, and was not a little dangerous in riding along the precipices, and from the risk of avalanches. This passage is now
the easiest and most agreeable of any, without even excepting
Mount Cenis, the route of which is infinitely inferior in objects
that attach the eye and satisfy the mind.

On the side of Switzerland it is entirely covered with larches,
even to its crest. On the side of Italy it is much wilder; here
the labour of man appears most prominent, here are those immense rocks, through the interior of which the new way has been
made to pass.

The route of Le Simplon, ordered by Napoleon in 1801, was
completed in 1805. General Thureau, and the engineer in chief,
Ceard, traced the plan of the works. The execution was consign-
ed, under the direction of this last, to Messrs. Lescot, Houdard,
Cordier, and Poulonceau, for the side of Switzerland, and to
Messrs. Duchêne, Cournon, Maillard, Gianella, and Bossi, for the
Italian part. These are imperial arts, and worthy kings.

The inclination of the road is so gentle, that there is no occasion to trig the wheels; the width is every where about 30 feet. We find pallisades of larchwood, or flat stones guarding the edge of the precipices, and broad ditches on the sides of the mountain to carry off the waters. From one half league to another, both on the northern and southern quarters, are houses of refuge, occupied by cantineers, a sort of publicans, where a traveller may purchase wine, brandy, and provisions, and also procure a lodging. On the highest part of the mountain is an hospitium, and a little lower down, on the side of Italy, is a village with a good inn, and where a traveller may pass the night. Post relays are established along the whole route, where the service is punctually attended to. At certain distances, large poles are planted to point out the road, when the track is buried under snow.

From Brieg it takes us six hours to arrive at le Col du Simplon by the new route. We may set down three hours to pass from the Barrier, near the new hospitium, to the village of Le Simplon, and between five and six from this village to Domo d'Ossola, the first town on our entering Italy. This lies at the foot of the mountain, on the Italian side, as Brieg does on the side of Switzerland. In the passage intervening, we have to clear twenty-two bridges, and seven galleries, or arched vaults, pierced through the interior of the rocks.

The first of these works that appears remarkable, we find on our quitting Glisse, a village near the town of Brieg; here is a superb bridge over the torrent of La Saltine, which descends from Le Simplon, and falls into the Rhone. It is one of the largest along the whole route, but consists of only one arch. It is built of larch wood, as more durable than fir, and is the only bridge under cover; the timber work of the arch is also sheltered from the rains.

Passing this, we ascend insensibly the windings of the route, with a number of little oratories on the right and left, where the inhabitants go on pilgrimage. All along, from the circuitous turnings, the inclination is very gentle, and at times the level is so observed, that we seem travelling on a plain. The first ascent is in the midst of meadows, and afterwards we proceed under the shade of larches till near the summit.

Here, if from the midst of forests we turn our looks backwards, a scene appears which may be viewed with delight and rapture. In tracing the landscape, villages and meadows, with an endless number of streams that pour into the Rhone, combine to adorn, in bright glowing colours, the immense panorama. The Rhone, a king of floods, rolls his expansive and whitish waters, his rapid, high-surging waves, murmuring across the plain. His banks are enriched with a variety of vegetation. On the flanks of the mountains, we discover smiling cottages surrounded with meadows, and occasionally several handsome houses, and not inelegant edifices, among cultivated fields and rising grounds, that give a cheerful look to the country; churches add also to its beauty. Above these fields are groves of larch trees; and lastly, we contemplate romantic rocks, naked or covered, with eternal snows bordering the distant perspective.

Nearly about half way, the route passes along the bottom of a valley, wherein the beautiful bridge of Ganter is established over the junction of two torrents, in a place exposed to frequent avalanches; it rises 80 feet in height. The art employed in its construction secures it from those irruptions of snow, and enables it to brave the floods; its elegant architecture is a pleasing novelty after passing through so many surrounding woods.

Works of this description alter the face and appearance of the country, and evidently for the better. Travellers only come here as visiters, when it has burst from the icy chains of winter, and partly assumed the vivid hues of spring—nipping frosts, and the bleak, keen north-east wind, speedily resume their subsequent empire.

In the vicinity, and about the middle of the valley, we still discern the huts that general Bethencourt erected for his men, in the year 1800, when passing Le Simplon, at the same time as the first consul was clearing the passage of Great St. Bernard.

A rough bridge, thrown over an abyss of 60 feet in breadth, had been carried away by an avalanche. Here a grenadier undertakes an hazardous exploit; he fixes his feet in the holes wherein the posts of the bridge had been inserted, and passing from one hole to another, happily arrives at the other end of the precipice. The general passes the second, and all the men imitate him, suspended to a rope between the open air and the cavity, loaded with their knapsacks and arms. Five dogs remained behind, which threw themselves headlong into the chasm; two only emerged from it, and joined their masters besmeared with blood. The names of the officers were engraved on an adjacent rock.

At a little distance from the bridge of Ganter, appears the handsome *chalet*, or cottage of Berenzaal, in a situation very agreeable during the summer. At the end of autumn the shepherds quit their cottages and regain the plains, but the family of Berenzaal remain on the mountain through the winter. A flambeau of resinous larch is kept constantly burning through the long nights. The custom of lighting with wood in lieu of tallow, wax, or oil, is of high antiquity, and noticed by Virgil in that passage, where the lighted cedar beguiles the passing time of Circe, daughter of the Sun, while her industrious and most expert hand is busied in the labours of the loom :—

—— tectisque superbis,
Urit odoratam nocturna in lumina **Cedrum,**
Arguto tenues percurrens pectine telas.

Like Circé, the Berenzaal family are weavers, but not under
tectis superbis, though the house is solidly built, with capacious
barns and out-offices. In the time of the *tourmentes,* and very
chilling cold, the traveller here will find a refuge, and bless Providence for affording him a secure shelter and a generous hospitality, in the substantial goodness of its inmates.

On quitting the larches we pass through the first gallery, and
the second half à league further on, close to some superb glaciers,
the water of which, in its descent, forms cascades of the most
imposing effect, to awake the traveller's attention.

From the second glacier we arrive at the barrier, where we pay
a toll of six francs per horse, for keeping the route in repairs.
This barrier, or gate, is between two ranges of buildings, one of
which forms an inn, and the other coach-houses, stabling, &c.
On the wall of the latter we read the following inscription :—
"Hic Bonaparte viam proprio patefecit olympo—Here Bonaparte opened to himself a road to immortality."

Advancing some paces further, we reach the plateau of the
mountain. It is covered with a green parterre, with rhododendrons and Alpine plants, and rises 1168 feet above the level of
the sea.

On the left of the road, as we proceed towards Italy, we see the
walls of the new Hospitium, which is to be 60 metres in length,
and 20 in breadth. The services are to be performed, (or this was
the original intention,) by fifteen ecclesiastics of Great St. Bernard, on whose jurisdiction it depends. The emperor Napoleon
had endowed it with a revenue of 20,000 francs. The ancient
building is seen a little further on, in a hollow recess, to the right
of the road. It is built in the form of a tower, and contains six
stories ; the duties are discharged by two fathers of St. Bernard,
who admit poor travellers, and entertain them, gratis, with food
and lodging.

The plateau of Le Simplon is contracted in its view, on the
side of Italy, by the mountains that rise in front ; but towards
Switzerland every thing, as before observed, is either grand or
romantic, either highly interesting or picturesque, from a more
studied culture, as towns approach, and increasing population is
more discernible.

The extent of the plateau is pretty considerable. We descend,
by a slight declivity, to arrive at the village of Le Simplon, which
stands on a height, in a wild place, near a forest of larches, and
on the banks of a little torrent, among meadows wherein vegetation languishes. About some of the houses we see little gardens,

with a few kitchen plants and pot-herbs. From the vivacity of the air the inhabitants are obliged to keep up fires all the year round. They have stone stoves, in the shape of pillars. In the three months of the fine season, they tend their flocks, trim their meadows, and some fields which they have, and go in quest of provisions to lay up for winter. In winter they work on the roads blocked up by the snow, and become carriers of goods, merchandise, &c. Potatoes cannot come to maturity in a climate so rigorous. But notwithstanding these disadvantages, in the months of July and August the eye will dwell, with a degree of pleasure, on such few varieties of fertility and vegetation as the environs may appear enriched with.

As already observed, it is generally three hours' travelling from the Barrier to the village of Simplon. Our voiturier, (driver,) a merry fellow, and everlasting votary of Bacchus, traversed this distance in less than an hour, to reach the inn before other carriages on the road, and to secure the best beds. Our entertainment was excellent, but dear enough, according to custom. He had taken a glass extra, to sleep the better, but had left in the stable a lamp, which set fire to some straw. Luckily, the master of the house, going his usual rounds, discovered it time enough to give the alarm of fire! His cries, with a voice like thunder, roused every one from sleep. Our voiturier comes down, in his shirt, bringing with him the servant maid Louisa, from an upper garret. The landlord falls upon and beats him, rolling him in the straw that had caught fire, and water arriving from all quarters, the poor culprit was so inundated, that he thought the heavens were opening for another deluge ; as yet he had scarcely come to himself. The landlady falls on the servant, with heavy blows, that fearfully resounded. We get the flames under, while the two lovers are thus doing penance, and as we had further occasion for one of them, we petitioned for pardon for both, which was granted, with some reluctance. The whole furnished a comic scene, that reminded us of the droll interchange of pugilistic blows between the Hero of La Mancha, the Muleteer, and Sancho, in an inn, where a female servant gave occasion to the adventure.

Leaving the village of Simplon, as we proceeded towards Italy we wind about a long circuit of road, to soften the descent. It leads to the entrance of a wild gorge into which the torrents of La Dovina fall, the road inclining to it, as towards an abyss.

Here we immediately enter into the first gallery on the side of Italy; passing it we come to a Cantine or house of refuge, which serves also for an asylum to passengers, when exposed to the *tourmentes* and the inclemencies of bad weather.

Here we contemplate a scene of great and infinite terror; the imagination takes flight, soaring on the wings of wonder, at the vast climax, the continued chain of horrors. The Gorge is extremely narrow, the whole breadth of it being occupied by the channel of the torrent; not the slightest trace of vegetation; immense rocks rise on each side, that seem to touch the skies; they resemble two parallel walls, between which we advance, as through a prison. Sterility pervades the entire solitude, and the sun-beams never penetrate.

The road continues along the Live Rock, sometimes on the left, sometimes on the right of the torrent, passing over some neat stone bridges, till we arrive at the Second Cantine, and then at the Grand Gallery. It extends 200 metres in length, is 30 feet high, and 30 feet broad, with two vast apertures over the abyss, to let in day-light. The rock, through the interior of which it penetrates, loses its head in the clouds, while its base reposes at the bottom of an abyss, the depth of which the eye dares not measure. In the execution of this enterprise, war was, as it were, declared, not only against the torrent, but against the terrific masses of the rock itself. Security has been thereby afforded, against avalanches, and the danger of floods.

The resounding of the horses' feet, and the wheels of carriages, under this superb vault, ring a change on the ear, the combined effect of which is so powerful as to render it attractive and pleasing. At its exit, or lower entrance, we discover a very fine bridge over a torrent that forms a lengthened cascade, and plunges into La Doveria, at the bottom of the abyss.

On the vault of the gallery we read this simple inscription: " Ære Italo, 1805 ;" that is, the expenses of this construction defrayed from the Italian revenue. In this the name of Bonaparte appears prominent, and may be adverted to with the alluring contemplation of a tutelary genius, a wise and benevolent benefactor.

Going out of the great gallery, we continue descending along the torrent, between bare, perpendicular rocks, of a sombrous colour; these are called the Solitudes of Gondo. Vegetation and life, are here unknown, but after three hours' journey the traveller arrives at Gondo, a wretched village, the buildings of which are oddly constructed, and the inn, with its eight stories, and little iron grated windows, looks like a prison. Under the village, some scattered sun-beams glance, as by stealth, from the tops of the rocks, to animate some little gardens, the leguminous plants of which seldom arrive at maturity.

A quarter of a league lower, we pass by a chapel built on the borders between Italy and the Valais.

In the contours of the road, should a number of carriages be successively moving forward, at due distances, they would, in the range of the eye, appear to be one above another.

Half a league beyond the last-mentioned chapel is the village of Issel, where Piedmontese Douaniers politely search your effects, but are often troublesome enough. Here it is satisfactory to behold nature somewhat improving, and the hand of man somewhat more successful, in fertilizing all around him. But every where about the torrent it is still the contemplation of nature; we perceive birch-trees, smiling grass-plats, and, higher up, some woods and copses of larch, with an endless number of cascades and running waters, sportively bounding, in every possible direction.

Soon after, we survey the delightful valley of Frontano, and the village of that name situated in a bason enriched with vegetation in a country profusely covered with farm-houses, cottages, arable-lands, trees of all kinds, orchards, and a never-ceasing variety of an increased population, and consequently cultured and fertile spots. There is an alteration for elegance in the appearance of handsome houses and spacious edifices; architecture appears to predominate as one of the characteristic traits of fair Italy.

To this consoling view succeeds another ordinary, meagre, hard-featured, and coarse, which I shall call the last scene of horror; it adjoins the last gallery, which has a large window over the torrent.

On clearing this gallery, the rocks, hitherto contiguous, widen gradually and open to us a view of the magnificent bridge of Crevola, extending from one mountain to the other, and closing up the valley. It constitutes the last of the labours of Le Simplon.

From the bridge of Crevola we discover, at the end of a long line of road, the town of Domo D'Ossola, small but very commercial, and, as already observed, the first that can be called a town of Italy, to those advancing along the new road.

I should have mentioned certain auxiliaries or appendages to the route of Le Simplon, wherein the labours have been very considerable and costly. As in the lower Valais, blowing up the rocks of Meillerie, and raising a causeway, 1500 feet in depth, along rocks, on the banks of the Leman Lake. I can but barely allude to the enormous expenditure in erecting a causeway from Domo D'Ossola to Sesto Calende, above lake Major; the road rises along it, 15 feet above the water, and it is protected with a wall against the overflowing of the lake. In short, the works of Le Simplon, and improvements of the route, speaking generally, from Geneva to Milan, have cost upwards of twenty millions of francs.

The route from Paris to Geneva is 103 leagues, and from Geneva to Milan 74.

From Domo D'Ossola to Bavena, a town on the northern bank of lake Major, is a distance of six leagues, through a fine open champaign country.

THE BOROMEO ISLANDS.

MONT-BLANC.

LETTER X.

LAKE MAJOR—THE BOROMEO ISLES—STATUE OF ST. CHARLES
BOROMEO—THE LAKE OF COMO.

ARRIVING, at length, on the banks of Lake Como, where both
the towns and country assume a more cheerful look, where the
site of every place renders it pleasanter and more healthful, I
find my spirits cheered, and my toils repaid. Here, while taking
delightful walks on its shore, the sky unclouded, while commanding a fine view of the water, and its fertile banks, I seem to have
burst, as it were, by enchantment, into a fairy-land. This azure expanse stretches over an extent of from fifteen to sixteen leagues.
All around it appear towns and villages, hamlets, and country-
houses, with hillocks rich in the blessings of Ceres, Bacchus,
and all the rural gods. To these hillocks succeed, in the
back-ground, high mountains of the chain of the Alps, which, at
the east and south, lower by degrees down to the plains of Lombardy; towards the north they extend, with an augmenting elevation, as far as to the silvered cimex of Mount Rose, almost as
high as Mount Blanc.

This ocean is not quite so tranquil as that of the Leman Lake.
It is subject to storms, as is the Lake of Como. It is, however,
more abundant in fish, particularly excellent trouts, and eels of
unsual magnitude. Its greatest breadth is two leagues and a half,
a league less than that of the Lake of Geneva.

Lake Major receives a number of rivers, that appear to be engulfed in its depths. These are waters that issue from the vast
contour of mountains, stretching from Mount Rose to St. Gothard to Le Simplon, to Le Bernardin, and Le Jorisberg. The
Tesin (Ticinus) issues from a lake to the S.E. near Sesto Calende,
and expanding into a wide channel, falls into the Po, a little
below Pavia.

Lake Major branches itself out into two parts. In the centre
of the northern branch, looking towards Le Simplon, appear the
delightful Boromeo Islands: they seemingly owe every thing to
nature, but in reality owe much to the curious works, &c. which
art has constructed in imitation.

The Boromeo Isles are three in number—Isola Bella, the beautiful island Isola Madre, Mother Island, and Isola dei Pesca-
tori, Fisherman's Island. They were naked barren rocks, when,
in 1671, Prince Vitalien Boromeo, of Milan, had them covered
with earth, and decorated with ornaments, profusely flowing,
that form a living picture, that charm us with their cheering

smiles, their flowery wreathes, the lovely dyes of rising spring and summer.

Isola Bella is within musket shot of the Road; when first discovered, it might seem an enchanted island, so much does exulting genius glory in the graces, order, beauty of its ductile earth, of its forms and shapes, in which art successfully moulds and polishes fair nature, invoking the poets' song, and the plaudits of the critic. Palaces, magnificent gardens, odoriferous trees, among which the winds whisper gently, crystalline fountains, statues, groves, flowers and flowering shrubs exceedingly beautiful—every thing here has felt the influence of man, freely and frequently indulging in such novelties, variations, and inventions, as the most fertile imagination can abound in. The variety of sights, and the mixture of trees and vaulted terraces, rising one above another, gradually lessening and forming a sort of pyramid, on the southern side, fully display views on which the eye may gaze with rapture.

Approaching the Isola Bella we breathe an air embalmed with the gales of Eden, the sweet perfumes of plants, our surprise at which is so great, that the observation may be regarded, at first, as among the most predominant of this place. The whole island about the palace is covered with groves and enrobed in springing green plantations of orange and citron-trees, cedar, laurel, cypress, rose bushes, myrrh, jasmine, and a thousand other sweet-scented shrubs, of different colours, and young flowers that seem always new. Oranges and citrons thrive here as well as in Sicily, notwithstanding the difference of climate. The Acanthus, Valerian, and Caper-tree grow naturally on the walls and gardens. The vine also appears on the walls of the houses.

The art which created these beauties has taken no fleeting stand here, but dwells, as in a safe retreat—art concealing art.

The interior of the palace breathes an air of luxury and Asiatic magnificence. The apartments, in whose storied walls the polished fancy may for ever trace, clothing some new charm, the brilliant execution and highly-finished drawings of the great masters, are not too highly elaborate for the general cast of the buildings, but flow into each other with much ease,—great skill and contrivance appear in their construction. The grand saloon, newly embellished, offers striking specimens of the architect's science and taste. But the most remarkable part of the palace is a subterranean apartment, the columns, walls, and cieling of which are lined with mosaics. On the floor, are statues of white marble; one of them represents a dolphin ejecting a fountain. The whole palace and the ten terraces, the highest of which rises a hundred and twenty feet above the surface of the lake, are supported by arched vaults that here take the name of carcase of the island.

From these terraces we discover, on the south, Lavenc, on the east, the hills of Varese and the beginning of the plains of Lombardy on the west, the Fisherman's Island, and on the north, the icy summits of Mount Rose, Le Simplon, and certain points of St. Gothard.

Near the palace of the Isola Bella, which the Boromeo family repair to, in the fine season, is a little village consisting of Fishermen's houses; among them we find a pretty good inn.

In the vicinity, but nearer to Baveno, is the Fisherman's Island, which, from the uncommonly simple style of its buildings, agreeably and happily contrasts with the spirited excellence and uniform magnificence which in general characterise the Isola Bella. The inhabitants live on the produce of their nets, but the fish of Lake Major are not so docile to the hook, as some noticed by Ariosto were to the voice of the fairy Alcina, though she had neither net nor bait.

The houses of the Fisherman's Isle so press on rocks, that there would hardly be the means of raising a vine arbour before them. They are overlooked by a steeple, which forms the prominent object, and in the progression of curiosity, though it possesses nothing very new, seems pleasingly conceived to close the scene. The manners of the inhabitants are strongly interesting, and discover much of that original simplicity which so pleasingly accords with the subject of their labours.

Very few that visit the Boromeo Isles, deign to notice the Fisherman's—but had I a statue to erect to Happiness, I would consign it with contentment, a certain quantity of which I have calculated, to the worthy inhabitants of this island. Relief is afforded to their few wants, and hence a relative union is introduced between a satisfaction far above mediocrity, and the whole of the temper that distinguishes and accompanies them,

> " Latius regnes, avidum domando
> " Spiritum, quam si Libyam remotis
> " Gadibus jungas, et uterque Pœnus
> " Serviat uni."

Command your desires, says Horace, and you will possess an empire more spacious than if you had Libya added to the distant Cadiz, and both African and Spanish Carthage formed a part of your dominion.

The third of the Boromeo Islands, Isola Madre, distant about half a league from Isola Bella, towards the N.E. contains seven terraces on which a palace has been raised. The climate is still milder than that of Isola Bella, as under better shelter from boisterous winds, so that there is no need for covering the orange groves in winter. It is thickly planted with groves of orange and laurel trees; we find also the superb cypress and rosemary trees of a considerable size. Pheasants and pinkadoes are pretty numerous. The rural simplicity, rather familiar, of the island is of a most popular cast, though without that importance and dignity which result from the majestic march of grandeur, in the great labours of the stately piles of Isola Bella.

J. J. Rousseau was for making the Boromeo Islands the residence of his Julia, but, from finding too much of the art of man in them, he gave preference to the Isle Bienna. So Voltaire preferred the lake of Geneva, for a better reason, that a sage liberty fertilizes its contiguous districts. In lake Major you see poverty on one hand and excessive opulence on the other; the privileges of the highest classes, and the people subject to humiliating distinctions which degrade the condition of man. Equality of fortunes is an idea that I scout, but equality before the law, the right of being subject to it alone, that of expressing and writing our opinions, of chusing our vocation and disposing of our property, of going and coming without having to ask permission of a priest, the right of assembling with other individuals to deliberate about our common interests, and lastly, the right of every man to share in civil functions, as well as another, be his rank or birth what it may, these are no longer chimeras, but what we have reason to expect, and may confidently look for, though from the ferocious and treacherous character of despots, such an event may be retarded. The French Revolution has left on the mind and heart, exalted, fervent, characteristic impressions, grave and slow in ripening, but greatly superior to the light, transient, and volatile effects flowing from the political manœuvres of certain privileged families.

Night is coming on, and we must pay a visit to the statue of St. Charles Boromeo, which I espy on an eminence close to the road. This colossal statue, representing a Cardinal Archbishop of Milan, whose memory is held in great veneration throughout the north of Italy, was erected about the year 1697. It is 66 feet in height, and the pedestal on which it rests has 46 additional. The head, feet, and hands are of bronze, the rest of the body is copper; withinside is a mass of weighty stones to give stability to the figure. It contains also an escalier to lead to the head. The hollow of one of the little fingers is almost wide enough to include a man.

Hence we returned to the Route of Le Simplon, intending for Sesto Calende, a little town of Lombardy, eight leagues from Milan, at the southern extremity of Lake Major, seated on the left bank of the Tesin, which we pass over by a boat for want of a bridge.

It will be long ere I forget the delicious spectacle, the gay changing scene we had, the same evening, from a window of our inn at Sesto. By moon light we could distinctly recognize, to an immense extent, the fair expanse of Heaven's blue vault, the bright tints of that clear mirror of Lake Major, with fishing vessels gliding through the smiling vale o'er the soft breast of the Tesin, their crews chanting evening songs, bold and unrestrained, as they paced along its silver winding stream. To us, there dwelt a charm in the free musings of their sweet voices.

The Lake of Como is but three or four leagues from Lake Major; it is 9 or 10 in length, and as many in breadth. It is surrounded with mountains, and a number of rivers, the principal of which, the Adda, the Lira, and the Mera, flow into it. The scenery of nature is grand, and all around the champain forms an enchanting scene, when we survey the cultured gardens, the verdant lawns, the soil which art has known how to chuse, as its fairest, favourite residence for nobler man. Navigation on the lake is dangerous, from the squalls and pelting storms of wind that, at times, ride over it.

Caroline, Queen of England, here courted the silent, calm retreats of contemplation. She has been charged with levities and little immoralities, but these were surely gross and wilful misrepresentations, which we may attribute to certain designs, unjust and insidious, fomented by those who had not the power to resist corruption. Such a set of witnesses, in whom it was impossible to place implicit confidence, nor could any one be convinced, or determined, by their testimony—unsanctioned, too, by the names of any one person of character. As a matter of enquiry, the case was not fully investigated, in behalf of the defendant. And what could be expected by such as were anxious to know the truth and had no other object in view, but a quashing of the prosecution? The dry non-solicited answer of Non mi Recordo, when the arguments evidently applied to the circumstances and situations, will not easily be forgotten :—none of us may live to witness the like again.

LETTER XI.

MILAN, ITS SITUATION, CLIMATE, INDUSTRY, PUBLIC ESTABLISH-
MENTS, CHURCHES, PALACES, &c. PAVIA.

In approaching Milan, the triumphal arches at the gates announce, in an imposing manner, the *grandiose* of the interior. It is situated in the midst of a vast plain, watered by the Adda, the Tesin, and a prodigious number of artificial canals. The city was originally built by the Gauls, who, under Bellovasus, fixed themselves in Italy, about the year of Rome, 170. After the third Punic war, it was reduced, by the Romans, and was long considered as their second city. Milan became, afterwards, that theatre of bloody wars, being several times taken and destroyed, but ever rising again from its ashes. As Hannibal, in Horace, says of Rome, ' Merses profundo, pulchrior evenit.' The city was destroyed, by Attila, king of the Huns, afterwards taken by the Goths, who massacred most of its inhabitants, was raised again by Narses, taken by Belisarius, from the Ostrogoths, and recovered by the latter in 539, who, by the sword and famine, cut off 300,000 inhabitants.

After the reign of Charlemagne, the city flourished some time in prosperity. In 1162, it was besieged, by the Emperor Frederick the First, surnamed Barbarossa, who razed it to the foundations, on which he plowed and sowed salt. Under the protection of Pope Alexandria, in 1171, it appeared again, as in triumph over Barbarossa, and adopted a Republican Government. In toto, the city sustained 42 sieges, and was taken 24 times.

In 1796, the French established a republic here, under the name of Cisalpine; in 1805, it was transformed into a monarchy, and in 1814, Lombardy again passed under the Austrian dominion.

The territory of Milan resembles a delightful garden. The soil is fertile, the air salubrious, though moist at times from the rivers and canals that water it; but these give it the appearance of spring even in winter. Vegetables of all climates will readily thrive there.

In respect of trade and manufactures, Milan is still one of the first cities of Italy. Here are fabrics of steel, alabasters, leather, ivory, silk, cotton, bronze, gilding and for goldsmith's work, also for making chocolate, hats, wax, corals, cutlery, cylinders, woollen cloths, Cologne water, aqua-fortis, delft ware, paper, glass, &c. Mathematical and astronomical instruments are brought here to great perfection. Carving, engraving and sculpture, as also the bookselling and printing businesses, are in a flourishing condition.

The palaces, churches. and public establishments, are very numerous. The Cathedral, Palace of Arts, and the Theatre of La Scala, are master-pieces of architecture. Here are public and private libraries, cabinets of physics, observatories, lyceums, and schools of every description.

The new monuments may contest the palm of splendour with the ancient, and it is difficult to conceive how, in less than twelve years, labour so considerable have been erected.

There are a number of hospitals for the sick and indigent, and we see no shocking extremes of opulence and misery, Milan being rather a city of industry than of luxury.

The Milanese is gentle, gay, sensible, and free, but without rudeness. He has a taste and aptitude for the sciences and arts. He receives strangers with politeness, is not averse to good cheer, and enjoys public spectacles. Towards evening, in the promenade, 500 coaches, of superior elegance, may be seen at a time. The women are, in general, small but handsome. In summer they hide half of their face with a veil to prevent being sun-burnt, and to keep off insects. Their complexion is not so fair as that of our Parisian belles.

The city is about 30,000 feet in circumference, and 9240 in length. Its boulevards serves for promenades. The streets have flagging for foot passengers, and the middle is so contrived that carriages make no rattling noise.

The population is about 140,000. The hotels for lodging and eating, in public or in private, are of all sizes and descriptions. In a thousand other respects Milan may be hailed as the Paris of Italy, the manners and fashions of Paris being also very prevalent.

The windows of the apartments which we occupied in the hotel de l'Europe, in the centre of Milan, looked down on the boudoir of a young Italian lady, that had but just reached her fifteenth year. One of our fellow tourists was not the last to remark this circumstance, and taking counsel only of that little urchin cupid, he contrived to insinuate himself into her company, and, as it should seem, to touch her sensibilites. He frequently visited her, and as an obsequious cavalier, escorted her to the promenades and spectacles. She spoke English, French, and Italian fluently, which enhanced the satisfaction of her admirer. Every morning early he might be seen, in a dishabille, under her window, with his guitar, serenading the idol of his heart.

Something may be added in respect of the edifices. In the palace of the Viceroy the interior is most magnificent. The paintings, in fresco and other similar embellishments, were executed under the government of Prince Eugene, whose memory is held dear throughout Italy. The palace of sciences and arts is the most beautiful and interesting in Milan. A portico of the Doric order, and the grand staircase, are of a very superior architecture. The library contains about a hundred thousand volumes, and many valuable MSS. Next to the library is the school of engravings; it has a collection of very interesting designs. The palace of arts was distinguished by nothing remarkable till the arrival of the French in Italy; it owes its present consequence to Napoleon and Prince Eugene. The cathedral looks like an immense quarry of marble, worked into shape; it is in the Gothic style, the architecture appearing rather odd than elegant. The foundation was laid in 1386, but it is not yet finished. The immensity of the labours lavished on it by Napoleon is indescribable. The dome, or cupola, overlooks 5000 pyramids, with a multitude of statues and other embellishments drawn from the sacred history.

Of seventy churches in Milan, next to the cathedral, the most remarkable is that of St. Alexander. The façade has marble steps to it, and the principal altar is sprinkled with oriental agates, jasper, and other precious stones. The Ambrosian library is one of the most ancient of Italy. Besides a number of MSS. here is a volume of the history of Josephus, on Egyptian papyrus, a Virgil with notes, in the hand of Petrarch, the code of Leonard de Vinci, some MSS. of Pindar, Sophocles, Eschylus, and Euripides, the original Cartoon of the school of Athens, by Raphael. Some paintings of Michael Angelo, &c. The library contains about 100,000 volumes.

The Great Theatre is one of the first in Europe, for extent, richness of decorations, spectacles, dances, ballets, and the skilful selection of the orchestra. There are six rows of boxes, large, convenient, and superb in their ornaments. One might lose one's self in the parterre (pit), and I was struck with astonishment on entering it.

In the Champ de Mars, where 80,000 men might manœuvre, is a noble amphitheatre, one side of which commands a view of the troops, and the other that of the horse races and gymnastic exercises. It may hold 30,000 spectators, on ten rows of seats, and was built by order of Napoleon.

In the environs of Milan, distant about half a league, is an echo of a truly singular description. It proceeds from an old charter house now abandoned, and when any sound is emitted from the window of a second story (for anywhere else it is mute) the repetitions are so rapid and frequent that, sometimes, it is hard to count them. The voice will be heard again, at least, ten times, and the report of a musket thirty-six.

Beyond the echo, at the distance of another half league, is the country house of the Litta family. It would require a volume to describe the riches of art and nature displayed in the palace and adjacent grounds. The grottoes reminded me of those depicted by Fenelon, as occupied by Calypso and her nymphs.

At Somma we are shewn an enormous cyprus tree, the trunk of which measures thirteen feet in circumference. Near it, according to the report of tradition, 230 years prior to the christian æra, Hannibal, with his elephants and a numerous cavalry, passed the Ticinus, wounded one of the Scipios, and drove his army out of the field.

The city of Pavia is about ten little leagues from Milan. We proceed to it along a very noble road well shaded. All around appear canals of irrigation, which diffuse coolness and fertility throughout the country. About three leagues from Binasco, on the left of the road, is the Charter House of Pavia, an immense structure, commenced in 1396, and not finished till some ages after, but now deserted. It was one of the finest residences in

Lombardy. Two leagues further on is the city of Pavia, situated in a vast plain on the banks of the Tesin. The Tower is yet to be seen, wherein the unfortunate Boethius was confined. The ferocious Theodorick, of odious memory, after putting to death the father of the poet, was seized with remorse, and, according to common fame, thought he saw the head of his victim in that of a pike served up at his table next day.

Pavia has some fine buildings, the streets are broad and straight. The University contains a rich library, a museum, a cabinet of physics, and a garden of plants. The territory is so fertile that it is commonly called the garden of the Milanese.

Why, alas! in these fine countries, should the public spirit be corrupted, the only sources of moral and political instruction be diverted from their purposes, so as to deteriorate the general character of the inhabitants, merely to cloke the faults of inefficient and unprincipled governments?

LETTER XII.

FROM MILAN TO TURIN—GENERAL OBSERVATIONS—NOVARE. VERCEIL—TURIN, AND ITS ENVIRONS—MILITARY RECOLLECTIONS IN PIEDMONT.

Quitting the capital of Lombardy, our next route will be that of Piedmont. From Milan to Turin commonly passes for one day's post travelling. Nothing remarkable appears on the road, and the sooner we traverse it the better. Beggars innumerable assail you, of every description, at and in the inns, at the ferries, with postillions and their masters, &c. &c. To come here without money a traveller would hardly escape dying of famine. What a fine climate but what an expenditure of money, what an exhaustion of chagrin to pass through it; Montesquieu says, " see Italy in a transient visit, think and meditate in England, travel in Germany, but live in France." " Voyez l'Italie, pensez en Angleterre, voyagez en Allemagne, et vivez en France."

The author of the Spirit of Laws had a purse open for the wretched, but was not fond of plenary indulgences that were to be paid for. Before he left Rome he went to take leave of Pope Benedict XIV., who felt an esteem for his personal and intellectual merits. Said the Pontiff, " my dear president, before we part, accept some pledge of my friendship. I authorize you, *de faire gras*, to be excused from meagre days for the rest of your life. Montesquieu thanked the pope, and bade him adieu. The chamberlain bishop then conducted him to the

Datary's Office, where the bull of dispensation was expedited for him, accompanied with a rather chargeable note of expenses for this singular privilege. Montesquieu alarmed at the amount returns the brevet to the secretary, with these words; "I thank his holiness for his benevolence, but the Pope is of a truly honourable character—I refer to his word, and my conscience will sanction me herein."

Madame de Frenoy, in one of her novels, considers Italy as a place of exile to a Frenchman. She was delighted with the country of Lombardy, and thought it another Eden—but every where, even at Milan, with the music celestial of its opera, with all the magnificence of its entertainments, the monotonous ceremonial of the people wearied her. The most exquisite wine could not elicit from them a sprightly sally or repartee, and she regretted the dinners of Paris. The Milanese ladies, she says, have more beauty than grace; they excite admiration but do not please. In the theatres the actors were always actors, and never the characters they would represent.

What would she have said had she been exposed as we were to the rapacity of Cisalpine and Piedmontese vultures?

The first town on the road from Milan to Turin is Novare, or Novara. It is far, indeed, from being handsome, but contains streets of considerable length. Whether arising from taxes, or other circumstances, the inhabitants bear the impress of such as find themselves in no pleasant situation, with but a scanty stock of individual enjoyments.

We breakfasted at Vercell, the head place of the ancient department of La Sesia. It is a pretty large town, but dirty enough and ill built. We paid dear at the Auberge, being taken for English, who are always charged dearer than others.

We arrived at Turin on the same day, and alighted at the hotel *de l'Univers*. Here the entertainment corresponded with exterior appearances. Splendid apartments, rich furniture, exquisite perfumes to regale the sense, highly flavoured meats, for epicures, with the wines of Asti and Casal, and the delicious liqueurs of Turin.

This metropolis is regularly built, very handsome, and perhaps, the most elegant of all the cities of Italy. The situation is in a charming plain, at the confluence of the Doira and the Po; running water is distributed from a sluice, and the streets are kept constantly clean. They are uniformly straight, and the principal ones lead up to the grand place *de la Cour*, wherein our inn was situated. In the centre of this is a palace, which would be better elsewhere than here. About it, embanked against two of its walls, are barracks, rather offensive from misery being so nearly contrasted with opulence.

The street of the Po has arcades very convenient, and well set out with shops ; it leads to the new bridge over the river, constructed in the time of the French. It is a magnificent work, entirely in the Roman style. A report prevails, that the king of Sardinia, in 1814, returning from the island of that name, would not pass over it because it was a monument of the usurper. If this anecdote be stated right, it was not in the natural order of things, and does not savour much of magnanimity.

The street of La Doira is very long, and has neat flagging for foot passengers ; with its reverberating lamps, especially on the night of an illumination, joined to other accidental ornaments, an effect is produced that may be counted truly elegant.

The promenades may rival those of Milan in beauty, both on the side of Rivoli, and along the banks of the ancient Eridanus, which rolls majestically, scattering plenty through the plains of Piedmont. The great theatre is not so spacious as that of Milan, and is but seldom opened. Taste and coolness reign in the interior. The little theatre of Carignan is open every night. The architecture of the palaces and houses is every where excellent, and the environs of the town prove a rich collection of new kinds of objects to characterise and illustrate the survey. The palace of Stupinis, three little leagues from the city, is uncommonly handsome, and becomes the residence of the court in summer. The chateau of La Superga, on an eminence on the other side of the river, is well deserving of attention : it is the burying place of the sovereigns of Piedmont.

In the city is a public library, and an academy, which has been dignified by the learned and scientific labours of many eminent characters. Medicine is cultivated here very successfully, and the arsenal and printing offices will repay the trouble of inspection. But what a disproportion between the industry of this city and that of Milan. Comparatively speaking, the streets of the former seem deserted, while the latter are every where thronged with the busy hum of men. In point of extent, Milan occupies more than twice as much ground as Turin ; Milan is all business and life, Turin a beautiful statue, but cold and inanimate. Its scientific establishments are also few in number. If we rate Milan as the Paris of Italy, Turin may be its Nancy or Manheim.

The women at Turin are generally handsome and amiable, nor are they deficient in wit, but their Piedmontese jargon and disagreeable accent, repel the magic charm of their impressive tongues, and forbid the high-prized beauty to point the dart, to thrill the bosom, to ensnare and wound the breast of taste. A secret also may be found in the vivacity of the

Milanese ladies; with a due leaning, however, to the liberal side, the characters of the Piedmontese belles are not entirely devoid of it.

Turin was formerly encircled with ramparts. The French demolished or converted them into promenades. Nothing of its fortifications remains, but the citadel raised on a little rising ground near the city.

LETTER XIII.

GENOA AND ITS ENVIRONS—GULF OF SPEZZIO—ALEXANDRIA AND MARENGO.

Our original intention was to return from Turin directly into France, but recollecting the little distance to Genoa, and that we had felt regret for not visiting Venice, we changed our preconcerted resolution.

A striking analogy pervaded the character of the two cities; both had upheld a distinguished figure in modern history, their forms of government were similar, both had been pursuing the career of commercial and naval grandeur, both had magnificent ports and buildings in accordance with their pristine opulence, and both had acquired foreign dominion in the east and in the Mediterranean. Both cities had at times changed masters, and both had now passed under a foreign yoke.

Genoa is raised on the shores of the Mediterranean, at the extremity of a gulf, to which it gives its name. It is embanked against a mountain of the Apennines, and appears like an amphitheatre, placed between two torrents, or rivers, one called Bisagno, and the other Polcevera. The eastern coast extends to the gulf of Spezzia, and the western to the principality of Monaco. From whatever quarter we arrive at the capital of Liguria, either by water or land, the perspective is admirable. This effect is produced by the number of palaces and houses of pleasure, or country houses, that look down from the eminences, and seem to form a part of the city. Round about the port it is semicircular, and the unevenness of the surface gives to the whole the look of an amphitheatre. Its tide-washed shore, decked with towers, art screening and shadowing naked nature with many a touch of her hand, so as to disclose a general metamorphosis, will appear to the greatest advantage at the distance of about a mile at sea. Surveyed hence, it would be unjust to refuse it the title of *superb*, which it enjoyed in the days of its independence and prosperity.

Genoa, besides some fortifications, has two walls. The outer one, begun in 1626, takes in a compass of twelve miles on the elevations of the mountain. The interior one is of about six miles. Between the two walls are different forts, known by the names of Richlieu, Les Eperons, Les Rats, &c. In 1800, the city sustained a siege under Massena, nor would he capitulate to the Austrians and lord Keith, till reduced to the last extremity by disease and hunger.

The streets are remarkably narrow, and it is but in a few of them that carriages can pass. The houses rise to the height of six stories; hence the sun-beams never irradiate the ground or level of the streets. In this respect it is the Grand Cairo of Italy, for there the streets are also very narrow, and the houses very high. Formerly all the houses were decorated in front, with paintings in fresco, but of these nothing is now seen but a few fragments. On the tops of the houses is a terrace in lieu of roofing. In the evenings they take the fresh air there, and have little beds of orange and citron trees, with flowers that, at Genoa, thrive in all seasons. There are three streets remarkable for their extent and beauty, and may, in fact, be said to constitute one, from the Gate St. Thomas to that of L'Acqua Sola. These three become promenades, and have a sort of causeways, but not raised. The first is called Strada Balbi, the second Strada Novissima, and the third Strada Nuova. It is this last that Dupaty, in his letters on Italy, considers as the finest on the surface of our globe. These, and the others, are in general paved with broad flag stones, as in the galleries of the Palais Royal at Paris. Fame reports that these formerly were of the lavas of Mount Vesuvius. The streets are always clean, from a number of gutters and common sewers that have their outlets in the sea.

The air here is very pure, and the water is excellent; this last is conveyed by a superb aqueduct, about four leagues in length. A number of monumental fountains recall some subject of mythology; besides which, there are, as at London, conduits, or works, which sometimes furnish a sufficient quantum to every house.

The port is very capacious, and the largest ships of war might find anchorage in it. On the top of a high tower, mounted on a rock, appears a pharos, or light-house, for vessels that arrive in the night; near it is the lazaretto, which exhibits nothing remarkable.

In the eastern part of the harbour is the " Free Port," where the merchants have their magazines. It is encompassed with walls, and may be considered as isolated. It forms the entrepôt of all foreign merchandise that comes to Genoa, and is hence transported to Switzerland and Germany.   The porters here are very troublesome, elbowing and pushing, loaded or not, and turning out of the way for none.

The arsenal still retains the arms and cuirasses of certain Genoese dames that had taken the cross, in 1301, on a military pilgrimage to the Holy Land.   The pope advised them to contribute, by their purses ; he was thinking of money, their enthusiasm was aspiring to deeds of heroism.   Here is the rostrum of a vessel of antiquity, and a sample of leather, of the most original invention.

The churches are thirty-nine or forty in number; all are handsome, but those of St. Lawrence and Carignan are the most distinguished.   The former is as old as the year 260 of the Christian æra ; it is faced with black and white marble within and without, and paved with the same.   In the sacristy they pretend to shew the emerald vase that formed a part of the presents offered by the queen of Sheba to Solomon.   Marvellous cures and conversions were ascribed to it.   The Carignan is one of the masterpieces of Perugino, and stands on a height which overlooks the sea and the whole amphitheatre of Genoa.   Its architecture and ornaments are noble and solid ; the form is that of a Greek cross.   Before the principal entrance appears a bridge of several arches, connecting the hill of Carignan with that of Sarzano.   It was raised at the charge of a descendant of the founders of the church.   Its height is so considerable, that all the houses underneath, which are six or seven stories high, do not reach to the twentieth part of it. In the church of the Annunciad, I observed the tomb of the Duc de Boufflers, who died at Genoa, in 1747, commanding a body of French troops sent to succour the republic.

There are several charitable foundations at Genoa; the principal is the albergo dei poveri, or asylum for the poor.   The profusion of marble columns, staircases, statues, &c. is wonderful.   They are ascribed to the ostentation of certain Patrician families, that would successively commemorate individual benefactors.   The albergo is an immense building, and serves both for a house of charity and one of correction.   Some parts are appropriated to licentious females.

As to palaces, forty or fifty are reckoned within the city. The palace Negro is all of marble; that of the mint has some valuable antiquities, that of the Jesuits is no less beautiful than spacious ; the inner court is embellished with marble columns, escaliers, and galleries of the greatest magnificence.   The front of the palace Durazzo seems immense, and looks like the residence of a sovereign prince rather than of a private person. The palace Carega carries also a royal splendour with it, and the same may be said of the palace Doria; the situation of the last is one of the finest in the world. The theatres do not correspond with the elegance of the other buildings; they are alike incommodious for the spectator and the spectacle.

Commerce and industry are the deities of the Genoese; they excel in working silk, velvet, and hosiery; their artificial flowers are in high vogue throughout the continent. Oils, oranges, and citrons, form a considerable branch of commerce. Cedrats, an ever-green, ever loaded with flowers and fruit, and of an odoriferous scent, constitute the chief ornaments of their gardens.

The inhabitants are devotees in appearance, but sceptics in reality, and ardent votaries of Plutus. In former times, stillettoes were instruments of many illegal acts, and *sicaires*, professional assassins, here, as in some other countries of Italy, were ready to execute any order of a noble, inscribed in the golden book. The nobles had also satellites, called Sbirri, who, though a part of the police and guard, would ever second the hostile animosities of their masters. The wives and daughters of these Sbirri were subservient to the debauches of the noble class, and popular prejudices existed in favour of those Genoese houries. The Sbirri formed an isolated cast, but such distinctions have now disappeared; thanks to the French Revolution, and to the light which it has diffused.

The Genoese ladies copy the Parisian modes; their dress, in general, is truly neat and elegant. There is no want of diamonds and jewels, but the parade dress is black. They are remarkable for a veil called mezzaro, which forms a substitute for the hat of the French ladies. They are addicted to still, rather than bustling pleasures; their eyes and complexion enhance their other embellishments.

The man of their confidence is here called their sigisbeo, or patito; he ministers to their pleasures, and becomes a major domo. But they have credit for entertaining correspondence with others, unknown to their confidant. After about a year's marriage, the wives seldom stay with their husbands, who, moreover, are sure to set the example of parting.

The priests maintain a considerable influence over the common people. They reckon at Genoa 21 confreries, that every 3rd of May march in grand procession about a large machine, called the *cassa*, that is surmounted with statues, and with its accompaniments, makes a weight that 30 men can scarcely carry.

In the time of the Republic, the Doge possessed great authority, but his responsibility was no less. His election was only for three years. In the hour wherein his functions expired, at the sounding of a great bell, he threw off his robes of dignity, and, clad as a simple citizen, appeared at the bar of the Senate, in the presence of the assembled people. There he was bound to reply to any accusations that might be urged, and if convicted of injustice, be the complainant who he might, he must make reparation on the spot.

The environs of Genoa are extremely picturesque. The valley of Bisagno and that of Polcevera are overspread with palaces and country houses, many of which are from designs, by Michael Angelo, especially that called Paradise.

Not far from Genoa is the Gulf of Spezzia, completely a work of nature, and every where deep enough for the reception of vessels of the largest dimensions; according to some histories it was the port of the ancient city of Luni, a flourishing Etrurian colony, till swallowed up by the sea.

Now, again, we resume the route of Turin, leaving some towns on the right and left, but tarrying for a moment at Alexandria. It is situated on the Tanaro, and passes for one of the strongest places in Europe. For this it is indebted to the French, but nothing else appears remarkable, except the hotel de Ville, or Town Hall, which is a decent structure. Near Alexandria was fought the battle of Marengo, which decided the fate of Italy, and compelled Austria and Naples to sue for peace.

LETTER XIV.

RETURNING TO FRANCE BY MOUNT GENEVRE, PIGNEROL, PEROUSA, &C.—FENESTRELLE, &C.—MOUNT GENEVRE—THE HOSPITIUM—SOURCE OF THE DURANCE AND THE DOIRE—EMBRUN—GAP—FROM GAP TO GRENOBLE.

To return hence into France, there are two roads : one passes from Mount Cenis, through Savoy, the other from Mount Genèvre, through the department of the Upper Alps. The former is the finest and most frequented, the other exhibits more of nature's various and original models. Of these, from the liveliness of our imaginations, we had become passionately enamoured, and led on by our love for the wonderful, we gave preference to the latter. Mount Cenis is but a miniature of Le Simplon, and besides, curiosity pressingly solicited us to undertake another and different excursion, to Briançon and Grenoble, as containing materials more interesting to the general tourist than Chamberry.

We then hired a voiture, that through the valley of Pignerol conveyed us in two days from Turin to Briançon, a fortified place in the northern flank of Mount Genèvre, the distance about 20 leagues.

On the first day we breakfasted at Pignerol, a town of Piedmont, agreeably situated in a fertile valley of the same name. It is rather small, but very commercial, and the inhabitants feel the full effect of their activity in the valuable benefits which it produces, comfortably enjoying the fruits of their industry.

Proceeding from Pignerol to Fenestrelle, we observed, with singular pleasure, the views improving, into the spirit of which we could well enter.

Half way from Pignerol to Fenestrelle, we come to the village of Perousa, Mount Viso terminating one extremity of its valley. This gigantesque mountain, whose inaccessible peak is constantly covered with snow, may be seen at very great distances in the interior of Italy. At the foot of this peak are the sources of the Po, issuing from a rock; its waters at first, distinguished by their easy flow, descend into the Valley of Salluce, increasing into a large brook, then a river, and soon, by tributary torrents, that pour from every quarter into it, become a King of Floods, bounding through the plains of Piedmont till finally absorbed in the Adriatic.

The Col of Mount Viso, close to the peak, is also covered with snow throughout the year. This proving an inconvenience to travellers, the Princes of Salluce, about the year 1100 caused a vaulted way to be cut through the mountain, about half a league from its cimex, that is where the snow begins, so as not to be obliged to clear it. This subterraneous route, which is now abandoned, is 8 feet high by as many broad; in length, it extends nearly a quarter of a league.

It was in the valley of Perousa and Pignerot, that a number of French Protestants took refuge, when persecuted, after the Revocation of the Edict of Nantes.

From Perousa it is but two or three hours' journey to Fenestrelle, a large village at the foot of the mountain of Sestriere. It is a strong place, and guards the entrance of Piedmont, being also a receptacle for state prisoners. Luckily we only stopped a night in it, lodging in a wretched auberge, pell mell, with soldiers, peasants, and drunken fellows. The mistress helped us to a supper and some wine, called by the name of the country, but both alike detestable.

At Fenestrelle nature appears almost as savage as the jailer of the prison and the inhabitants; but leaving the village and ascending the Col of Sestriere, we find a more pleasing vein and agreeable turns of her fancy, smooth, placid, and easy, if not particularly engaging, in sequestered groves of larches, meadows, fields and attractive verdure.

From Fenestrelle to Briançon, we have to pass two Cols, that of Sestriere, and that of Mount Genèvre. Here we have to ascend, descend, re-ascend and re-descend.

It is three hours' journey from Fenestrelle to the top of the Col de Sestriere; it takes nearly the same time in the descent, when we find ourselves at Sezanne, a Piedmontese village at the foot of Mount Genevre. It has acquired notoriety from the rigour of the *Douane* officers, in their official visits, and its terrible swarms of lice. At breakfast, our whole company was placed in a state of siege! lice were running about and getting under the petticoats of some ladies that were with us. In all haste, we took leave of this fatal village.

Ascending through woods of larches, in about two hours, we arrive at the top of the Col de Genèvre. Here we find two villages, one on the side of Italy, and the other on the French part. We halted at this last to undergo examination by the Gallican Douaniers, who were not quite so rough as their neighbours.

Near the village of Mount Genèvre stands an obelisk, commemorating the opening of the new road by Napoleon, that passes over the mountain. Opposite, and concealed in a grove of larches, is the source of the Durance and the Doira; both issue hence, the former proceeding towards France, and the latter towards Piedmont.

In this village is an hospitium, where, as at St. Bernard, Le Simplon, and Mount Cenis, travellers that call are entertained with cordial hospitality.

While the Douaniers were inspecting our carriage, a man, who called himself a soldier and an ex-courier, accosted us, telling us we must make haste, if intending for Briançon that night, for, added he, the gates will be shut very early. I was no stranger to the distance, and well knowing that there was no auberge about Briançon, except one or two little pot-houses in a village called St. Margaret, and both I and my companions being surfeited with the fare of some wretched hotelleries, we accepted the offer of the ex-courier, who proposed to lead us. He sets off like lightning, we follow him at a distance, along numerous turnings made by the road, which descends the northern flank of Mount Genèvre. In less than an hour our man arrives at the end of his course, and waiting on the king's lieutenant in a vein of ill-timed pleasantry, would have him believe that we were personages of superior consequence, and desiring that the gates might be kept open some time longer.

The fellow persuades almost as readily as Nestor would of old. The good-natured commandant, willing to oblige, dispatches his adjutant with orders to shut the gate of Italy half an hour later.

The lieutenant was preparing to compliment our highnesses, while, in the mean time, we had arrived at the foot of the ramparts, with a very indifferent dismantled voiture, and two sorry jades of horses.

It was the hour of the Angelus; the bells were ringing their double chimes, the drums were beating the retreat, and the soldiers of the post were under arms. We make our entrance, the courier being a little at the head of our carriage. No sooner was the gate opened, than we were beset like strange wild beasts, but with respect, the military being anxious to learn where we wished to lodge. We refer to an hotel that I well knew, and they attend us thither, people of all ranks going and coming, with a sort of distracted attention. We knew not what to make of this bustle, but coming to within a few steps of the hotel, we were forced to alight, from the cragged nature of the streets of Briançon. The hotel was thronged, and we had to force our passage through. The master comes to salute us, hat in hand, with profound reverences. He instantly knows me, and introduces us. "Ah, Sir," he exclaimed, "you are become a prince!" "How! explain yourself," I rejoined. "Your courier has announced you as relations of the royal family."

We laughed heartily at this *mauvaise plaisanterie*, but immediately sent forward our passports to the commandant, then attired in his grand uniform, and preparing to harangue our highnesses. On reading the passports, and learning the real particulars from our maitre d'hotel, he fell into a violent fit of laughter, but the author of the joke had to pass a night in prison for his pains, our intercession for the culprit proving fruitless.

Briançon is a very strong place, having on its ramparts and in its forts, three hundred pieces of cannon. The principal forts are on the flank of a mountain, the crest of which is 7800 feet above the level of the sea; it has a fort on it. A superb bridge of a single arch, over the Durance, forms a communication between the town and the forts. The town is built on rocks, so steep that carriages cannot descend them; they stop near the church, in the higher part of the town.

The inhabitants are very industrious, and with much information have no less address. They breathe a pure air in these mountains, and are strangers to provincial vices. A love of liberty pervades their character.

In the fair season the men go abroad for employment, in countries more favoured by nature; the old men and wives cultivate the lands. The women, with a cart and an ass, do the heaviest work nearly as well as the men.

In the Upper Briançonnois bread is made for a year. In winter the inhabitants have their kitchens and beds close to the cattle and stables. Their bed clothes are mostly woollen cloths, washed only every six months; owing to the rigour of the season, which keeps the waters frozen, and will not allow the bleaching of linen.

Towards Le Lotaré wood is so scarce that they make a sort of cakes of cow-dung for winter fuel.

It would be difficult to express the satisfaction with which the natives return to their rocks and cabins after a temporary absence. In the long evenings they rehearse what they have seen and heard, and thus beguile the tardy hours.

Departing from Briançon to proceed for Embrun, we took no small delight in contemplating, above the village of Labecey, some traces that were shewn us of the route that Hannibal had taken.

From La Roche, a little village famous for its trout, where we breakfasted, we passed on to Fort Mount Dauphin, a work of the famous Vauban, as are those of Briançon. It defends the plain on the side of the Durance, as it does also the valley of Queyras, one of the wildest but most interesting of the Upper Alps. The rocks approach so close, in the passage from Guillestre, to Fort Queyras, that they threaten a downfall on the traveller's head. In winter this passage is very dangerous from the very frequent fall of avalanches. This valley brings to mind the solitudes of Gondo, in Le Simplon.

From Mount Dauphin we descend to Embrun, a town containing about 3000 inhabitants; it is built on the back of a vast rock, washed by the Durance. Here was formerly an archbishop, who, at one time, bore the title of Primate of the Gauls. At present it seems only a remnant of its ancient splendour.

Proceeding through the large village of Ghorge, about three leagues below Embrun, and reported to have been a considerable place in the time of the Romans, the first town we come to is Gap, head place of the department of the Upper Alps. It is ill built but has fine walks about it. In the chapel of the church is a superb marble monument to the memory of the Constable de Lesdiguieres, who was born in the environs.

It was through the town of Gap, lying on the high road from Marseilles to Grenoble, that Napoleon passed, in 1815, when returning from the Isle of Elba.

The passage from Gap to Grenoble is altogether mountainous, over a very fine road but bordered with tremendous precipices. Here are points where fifty men with cannon might repel a whole army. My companions were not backward in remarking this, and wondered that he was not arrested in his march. I was at that time employed in the Alps, and can vouch for the following fact.

A battalion of 600 men of royal guards, was stationed at this Gallic Thermopylæ. General Cambrone, their commander, retreated, having orders not to oppose force to force. Bonaparte advances, *solus*, to the 600 men. " Qui vive ?" they cry " Napoleon," said he. While the commandant was recalling the men to their duty, the ex-emperor opens his breast, and crossing his hands over his head, "if you do not recollect," said he, " your general, who has so often led you to victory, he is here, fire." At these words the battalion disbands and speedily appears under the colours of the usurper.

LETTER XV.

GRENOBLE, ITS ENVIRONS, AND THE GREAT CHARTREUSE.

NEXT day after our arrival we set out to survey the town of Grenoble at our ease. It is fertile enough in sources of amusement, though there might not be sufficient to gratify a Sybarite. It is in one of the most agreeable situations to the amateurs of embellished nature, and the mountains that surround it on all sides, are cultivated to their very tops. The bason of Grenoble makes a part of that valley, wherein the river of Isere meanders, in a thousand turns, to join the Drac, a wild and muddy torrent.

The capital of Dauphine is surrounded with ramparts. The Isere divides it into two parts ; one, consisting of suburbs, is hemmed in between the mountain and the river ; and the other, which composes the town, lies in the plain between the Drac and the Isere.

There are some very good buildings, such as the Prefecture, the Cathedral, the Bishop's Palace, the School of Law, and the Court of Justice.

Here are a great number of manufactories and workshops. Works in metal of all kinds, with gloves and ratifiat, are in high reputation. The wines and liqueurs are excellent ; plantations of vineyards appear in every direction.

Grenoble has produced a number of men celebrated in the sciences and arts, or for their military genius; Bayard, the pink of French chivalry, the profound Condillac, Vauccanson the mechanist, Mably the historian, and others.

The Library here is capacious and well constructed; the Museum contains valuable drawings; the cabinet of medals is very rich, and there are several literary cabinets, with capital printing offices, and private libraries. There is an old proverb, " *Dauphinois, fin, fourbe et courtois.*" " The Dauphinese are courteous, but sly and roguish." I shall give them credit, however, for a great deal of courtesy, urbanity, and wit.

The ladies possess vivacity and grace; in general they are of a frolicsome or waggish humour, and very volatile. Among them are fine shapes, clumsy shapes, Hebes, Venuses, and cruel Dianas. Some of these last, the missionaries have converted, and by teaching them to love God, have taught them also to love their neighbour.

Society here is divided between the noblesse and the bourgeoisie. The ancient dowagers are said to be too nice in their selection of visitors; but I am persuaded that Fame herein outshoots the mark; for education may often compensate for the absence of fortune; and, after all, as Juvenal says,—" *Nobilitas sola atque unica virtus,*"—True nobility consists in virtue alone.

The Grotto Notre Dame, and the bridge of Cleye, about a league from Grenoble, are well worth seeing. The latter consists of a single arch, very bold and very large. It rises over the torrent of the Drac, at the end of a delightful plain, which serves for a public promenade.

These two last are included within the seven wonders, assigned by common fame to Grenoble. The other five are beneath notice, but there is one truly great wonder, in the environs,—the Chartreuse, founded by St. Bruno, and on which were dependent all the Chartreuses of Germany, France, and Italy.

This ancient monastery stands about five leagues from the town, in the midst of a desert, shut up on all sides by inaccessible rocks. Two roads lead to it. I had contemplated, among the Alps, scenes as solemn, romantic, and stupendous as I could conceive possible; but in the solitudes of the great Chartreuse, I found expressions of nature no less forcible, and the combined effect of her productions, her highly elaborate compositions, no less powerful.

Going from Grenoble to the Great Chartreuse, and scaling the first ascent, we see under our feet the town of Grenoble, the valley of Isere, wherein that river, like the Firth of Forth, in Scotland, has a thousand sinuosities and replications, with the whole bason of Grenoble. Continuing to ascend, at the end of an hour and a half we come to the village of Sapey, among meadows scattered about it.

We then descend into a thick forest, for about an hour, and leaving the woods, we advance, as in a plain, to the entrance of the convent.

This entrance is by two perpendicular rocks, of a tremendous height, and so close to each other, that a couple of wicket gates, fixed on each side, completely block up the passage, with the help of a bridge thrown over the torrent that rolls at the bottom.—When these gates are closed, there can be no entering, and the eye is lost among perpendicular rocks, that seem to touch the skies. Prior to the Revolution women were not allowed to pass this entrance, but now they may advance to the gate of the convent, but are not to enter.

From these gates to the monastery is about an hour's walk. We leave the torrent on the left, and move along a rugged road, through a thick forest of beeches and firs. Every thing here appears so gloomy, that at mid-day, we might think it was midnight.

Quitting this, we arrive at an immense meadow, and there discover the first building of the monastery, that is, a vast range of cow-houses, for keeping cattle and preparing milk. On one side, below the road, is the cemetery of the servants and domestics.

Keeping along the meadow, we discover, at last, at the other extremity, the convent itself, and its roofs surmounted with a multitude of turrets and steeples. It stands exactly at the entrance of another forest, overlooked by frowning desert rocks, whose prodigious height is not a little alarming. All around we see nothing but these, excepting that some of them are wooded. In the middle of the meadow, we seem as if landed in the infernal regions of Danté, or in some prison, whose walls are joined to the skies. It might seem to be an immense fortress, built by Nature, and needing no other guardians than its two entrances. The woods, the meadows, the rocks, the dwellings, and the inhabitants, every thing here has a sombrous aspect. No pleasing productions of art are introduced, which might contrast agreeably with the other objects, except a few shady bowers, with some pellucid streams, and beds of flowers, on which the star of day is not niggardly of his beams. The only cultivated grounds are the gardens, which are inclosed within the area of the convent. Every where else, we have meadows, forests, or rocks, composing a savage spectacle, and supplying only grave materials for thinking.

At our entrance a grave porter gravely opens the door; I thought he had the look of a magician. We cross an adjoining court, when a corridor expands to view that we might have taken for a part of the Chinese wall. Our guide moves for-

ward, and the principal friar on duty slowly paces towards
us, from the lower end of the immense corridor.   Apartments
are then opened, but in a profound silence; and lastly, a little
fire is made for us in a large chamber, with five closets attached, and a bed in each.   At a large table, a little supper is
served up for us, but without flesh meat, which the chartreux,
and all belonging to the establishment, abstain from, and visitors must submit to this restriction.   Our supper consisted
of an omelette, of fish, fried potatoes, cheese, fruits, bread,
and wine.   Supper ended, every one repairs to his cabinet to
repose on beds not quite so soft as one might have wished.

As soon as rosy-fingered Aurora had opened the gates of the
morning, and the porter those of the monastery, we walked
out to visit the chapel and haunts of St. Bruno, sequestered
further up in the forest.   There the solitaire, at the foot of a
naked rock, lived on vegetables, with a streamlet of spring
water that ran by him, serving him for beverage.

He might then say, with the vicar of Wakefield,

> No flocks that range the valley free,
>   To slaughter I condemn,
> Taught by that power that pities me,
>   I learn to pity them.
> But from the mountain's grassy side,
>   A guiltless feast I bring,
> A scrip with herbs and fruit supplied,
>   And water from the spring.

On a nearer view of this rock, where St. Bruno spent most
of his days, both when the season was fair and otherwise, our
eager fancy was alive to depict, in a pensive mood and with silent
thought, the mournful doom of one who could lonely seek such
a state of torpid existence. . Voltaire says—"C'est n'etre bon
à rien de n'etre bon qu'à soi—To be of use only to one's self, is
to trifle the hours of life away in dullness and insipidity."

What a difference between the sweet sympathies with which
mercy gilds the seat of St. Bernard, among those who know
how to live in the tempest, and come as mild companions to
the sufferer, often wandering over the trackless waste, and the
unfeeling gaze of the useless inmates of the Chartreuse; their
looks cheerless and dark as winter, unblest with companionship, one charm of life, as they seem scarcely to know one
another.   No voices to touch the ear, no soul-inspiring accents
of benevolence and tenderness, but as if shrinking from visiters
that wander thither with intrusive feet, making them pay dear
for the hospitalities conferred.

On returning from the chapel to the monastery, a domestic
shewed us the principal apartments.   The fathers were walk-

ing up and down in long corridors, wrapped up in woollen gowns, and with hoods on their heads. Instantly on seeing us, they disappeared, each one retiring to his cell.

The church, which stands in the middle of the other buildings, is very handsome. We visited, successively, the apartments of the superior, while he was at prayers with the other chartreux; the library, which is already pretty well filled, considering the little time that it has been re-established, that is, since 1814, and the great hall of audience, wherein all the generals of the order assemble once a year. It is very extensive, and is not unlike the hall of the marshals of France in the Tuilleries. As the portraits of the French captains are placed one beside another, so the generals of the order are painted, one after another, on the walls of the great saloon.

As to the extent of the principal range of buildings, they make up nearly a league in circumference. They form an oblong square of one quarter of a league, in a right line, and two principal corridors reach from one extremity to the other.

The gardens are cultivated exclusively by the chartreux; each has his particular portion on the terraces of the convent.

This vast structure was rebuilt eight or nine years before the revolution, at the charge of upwards of a million, but the riches of the chartreux were then immense, as they had in possession eighty leagues of forests. The buildings have suffered nothing from the revolution, being remote from all communication. The architecture is simple, noble, and solid.

The fathers can only converse together on Sundays and holidays. It is on such days only that they eat together, at other times they eat in their own cells. Flesh meat is never seen among them, being prohibited by their regulations, but fish, vegetables, eggs, cheese, wine, &c. are not wanting.

In lieu of shirts, the chartreux wear woollen robes; for beds, they have mattresses of bulrushes. They rise every night at eleven, and attend prayers till one in the morning. This interruption of sleep must be inconvenient, but custom diminishes the effect of it.

We quitted this solitude with pleasure, and took the road of St. Laurent and Voreppe. At every step we pass along frightful precipices, and after an hour's walk arrive at the principal entrance of the monastery. Here are large gates and a porter's lodge; all the circumstances and situations are wild and savage as a desert. At a bridge which passes over the torrent, the view is appalling. All the entrances lie through narrow passages of high parallel rocks, with bridges and gates in conformity with the situations, and the roads at times cut out of the rock itself.

Emerging from the possessions of the monastery, we first notice the hamlet of Les Charbonniers, where a number of saw-pits are at work.

Let me take here a retrospective view of the particulars, as there is scarcely a parallel for the grand Chartreuse, to be found in the world. . We descended through thick forests, under perpendicular rocks, between two parallel heights, but then every where wooded. We had next to cross a dangerous torrent, which receives all the waters of the desert, and carries them to the valley of St. Laurent. In this part many grand cascades water the road, and we proceed among precipices 5 or 600 feet in depth. This passage is very dangerous in rainy weather, or at the melting of the snow. Stones and avalanches fall frequently, at such times, and block up the road. The cascades then are so impetuous, that an effort is required to resist them. The summer season is the only time to visit the great Chartreuse.

From the first entrance of the monastery, which is only a little distance from the greater one, we go in about an hour to the village of St. Laurent, where the generals of the order leave their voitures. From this village to the convent we must pass on foot or on horseback, a distance of three leagues.

From St. Laurent to Voreppe, there are five or six dangerous torrents to cross: the distance is three leagues. Two of these we pass on a plain, the third is over a pretty rapid descent. We then enter again the high road to Voreppe, and can procure Diligences for Grenoble, which is also about three leagues distant.

LETTER XVI.

LYONS—THE BANKS OF THE SAONE—CHALONS SUR SAONE, &c.

RETURNING at length from the great Chartreuse to Grenoble, and thence resuming the route of the capital, we again took our departure in the Lyons Diligence.

Between Grenoble and Lyons the only town is Burgoin. It is a small place, but the people, as throughout the fertile plains of Dauphiné, are of an industrious character and seem to live comfortably.

Our diligence broke down on the road, but it was in the night; our entrance into Lyons was thereby retarded, as we should otherwise have arrived at break of day. But arriving some hours later, we had a far better opportunity of reconnoitring the environs of the city.

The plains of Dauphiné and La Bresse lay like a map before us, stretching out to an immense horizon. Behind us the Alps were plainly in view, the considerable distance intervening only adding to their majesty. At length we reach a plateau, whence we have a noble view of the second city of France. It is seated at the confluence of the Soane and the Rhone, and at the foot of the hillocks of Le Beaujelet. The distance is about two leagues from Lyons, but there is no point where the varied magnificence, the noble grandeur of the spectacle, can be better assumed.

We descended, however, from the plateau and arrived at Lyons, through the suburb de la Guillotière, separated from the town by the Rhone. It was Sunday; immense crowds, in elegant apparel, were promenading, with a sort of busy throng and bustle, along the gentle Saone and the Rhone; the scene illumined by the frank and amiable graces of the young and fair, and gay, thrilled harmony, joy, and ecstacy through our faculties. My companions bore an honourable testimony to these attractive and pleasing circumstances, having before adopted erroneous and illiberal prejudices concerning Lyons and its people.

The next day after our arrival we visited the principal curiosities. The hotel de Ville is a superb building, in the place *des Terreaux*; the ascent to it is by a large escalier. In the vestibule we observe a magnificent antique Tourobole, or Sacrifice of Bulls, with a table of bronze, on which is engraved a speech of the Emperor Claudius to the Roman senate, in behalf of the inhabitants of Lugdunum.

The Great Theatre, behind the hotel de Ville, is very elegant, but has no seats in the parterre or pit. It is open every night, as is also the little theatre *des Celestins*.

On the place *des Terreaux* is the Museum of Arts and Commerce. It contains some valuable antiquities, large paintings, a mosaic, hardly to be matched, found in the environs of the city, and a cabinet of birds.

The City Library is well situated on the banks of the Rhone, and may well be distinguished by the choice and number of works that it contains, about one hundred thousand volumes.

The Cathedral also is well worth seeing; we noticed an ancient clock in it, of a very ingenious construction.

The Grand Hospital, as a building, may vie with the hotel de Ville; the inside is much more respectable, in point of grandeur, ornament, and beauty, and its distributions are more judiciously planned. A number of sisters (a religious coterie) wait on the patients, in their tedious and painful indispositions, as friends, benefactors, preservers. Every candid and judicious traveller must be sensible of the irreproachable character and amiable demeanour of those kind females, in general, as united in the bonds of peace, and stretching out their friendly arms to the distressed.

To the amateurs of expanded views I would recommend to ascend the dome of this structure. I should have mentioned that a crocodile was once taken in the Rhone, under the bridge *de la Guillotière*, which is now suspended to the vault of the dome of the hospital.

We proceeded next to visit *la Salle Gallier*, the most spacious and beautiful coffee-house in Europe, next the juncture of the Rhone and the Saone, then the elegant bridges thrown over this last river, as also the place Bellecour and Fourviéres, where the prospect is still more comprehensive than from the dome of the hospital.

We did not fail to pay our respects to the manufactories and workshops, which I should not only praise but hasten and delight to praise. It may be justly remarked, that in this distinct view the city possesses a peculiar and durable fame. Here are very considerable fabrics of stuffs in gold, silver, and silk, also of lace, hosiery, ribands, hats, &c.

Having heard of the banks of the Saone, as characterized by much sweetness and novelty, from Lyons to Chalon, we entered a great barge, which conveys passengers from one place to the other. Here we passed by a grotto wherein the philosopher of Geneva passed a night with six splendid shillings in his pocket. It is included within a garden, and a very limpid spring of water issues from it.

At Chalous sur Saone we quitted the high road for Paris, to spend a few days in the country of the Abbé Geoffroy and Madame de Genlis, near Marcigny, where the amiable author of *la Gastronomie* resides. Here also we parted with our Scotch fellow tourists, of whom it may be said, that they judiciously knew how to realize and practise those rules to which travellers should not be inattentive. As men they were sensible and affable, of a mild and polite demeanour, of a communicative turn and liberal opinions, and never assuming supercilious airs.

√

NARRATIVE

OF A

Journey from Egypt to the Western Coast of Africa, by Mahomed Misrah.

By an Officer serving in Sierra Leone.

Fort Thornton, Sierra Leone, April 8, 1821.

At the request of several of my friends, I am induced to send you an account of a journey performed by a Mahommedan priest, over land from Egypt to the Western shores of Africa; the details of which I have collected at several recent interviews.

Mahomed Misrah, a Moslem, was born in Alexandria about forty-five years ago. When a young man, he remembers an army of white people taking possession of his country, who, about three years afterwards, were driven from it, having been beaten in a battle with other white people, who spoke a different language. Mahomed was within hearing of the guns, but did not see the engagement, he, and a great many more of his countrymen having retired from the scene of action through fear. A few years after this period, feeling himself conscientiously impelled to propagate his belief, he set out on a journey westward along the shores of the Mediterranean, and travelled as far as Fez, where, finding an insurmountable barrier in the great desert of Sahara, to his advance to the southward amongst the Kafir nations, he turned his face towards the rising sun, retraced his steps to Alexandria, and (to use his own expressions) sat down there for some time, uncertain as to his future intentions; at length, without any fixed or determinate plan, he departed from Alexandria, and following a southerly course, arrived in nine days at Ariff, four at Dongola, and in ten arrived at Sennaar, a low sandy country, abounding with camels, horses, and cattle; the Nile, which he describes as running from the S. W. or country of the Kafirs, where it bears the name of Baher el Abeed, is about a mile in breadth here, and is slow and majestic in its progress; the natives of Sennaar are Mahomedans, and the king is named Khamadoo.

Turning his back upon Sennaar, the Kolunjumi (Red Sea) and Mecca, he arrived in one day at the eastern frontiers of the kingdom of Kordofan, which is only habitable on the borders, the centre being a desert of ten days' journey across, and not to be traversed during the dry season : here Mahomed was under the necessity of awaiting the departure of a caravan which took some time in collecting, and did not eventually set out till the wet season had been pretty well advanced. In this part of his journey, the priest suffered much from the scarcity of water, that which they carried in skins having evaporated, and there being no oasis or well in the desert, at which they could procure any ; in this dilemma,

they spread their garments at night on the sand to catch the rain or
dew, and in the morning, a scanty supply was procured by squeezing
them; which (says the priest) is the practice always resorted to in such
cases, and it is for the sake of this advantage, that the journey is always
performed during the rains. The king of Kordofan is named Musa
Báh, and his subjects are rigid Mahomedans.

After having traversed this desert, which occupied eleven days, and
having skirted the northern boundaries of Dar For, he found himself at
Noomdroo, the most eastern town of Wadda, or Dar Bergoo; in fifteen
days more, pursuing a direction to the N. W. he arrived at Warra, the
capital of that country. This is a very powerful kingdom, and of much
greater extent from east to west than is generally represented in the
maps; the sovereignty is held by Saboo, a prince of unlimited authority,
who occasionally sends large armies into the field, but seldom accompanies them himself; his troops are not furnished with fire-arms, but
they maintain desperate conflicts with the spear, an instrument which
they direct with much precision, and handle with great dexterity. Many
of the natives of Wadda are great travellers, and trade to countries far
distant; their beasts of burthen, like as in most of the sandy districts
of Africa, is the camel. From Warra proceeding to the northward of west,
in two days he fell in with Fitrée al Fitrée, or Belála, situated on the large
lake of that name; this lake receives the contents of a large river (perhaps the Gir of Ptolemy, the Baher el Miselad of Browne) which rising
among some small mountains or hills on the confines of Kordofan, flows
to the westward through Dar For, and afterwards in a north-westerly
direction till it reaches its termination where its breadth is about four
hundred yards. Mahomed has made the circuit of lake Fitu, and positively declares, that it has no outlet; this stubborn fact, may (with the
sequel of his route, which is perfectly consistent, and shews that he
crossed no river of any magnitude between Fitri and Nufi,) prove a serious objection to the continuation of the Gir, which has been lately supposed to flow from Lake Fitri, and after traversing an immense extent
of country, to unite with the Niger, and thus account for the quantity
of rain-water, which finds its way to the Bight of Benin through the
broad channels of its numerous rivers. The soil around Lake Fitri
during the dry season is soft and slimy, owing to the retiring of the
water, and at this time, myriads of musquitoes are engendered, which
cause a visit to its banks to be very disagreeable. The natives of the
country are Mahomedans, carry on a great trade with the Arabs, but
are subject to the kingdom of Wadda, to which they pay an annual tribute.

A journey of one day north-west, brought the priest to Baghermi.
The prevailing religion of the inhabitants is Mahomedanism; they trade
with the Arabs, and pay tribute to Bornou: he reached Katucko in one
day more, and rested the day following at Mandara, where he found
himself only one day to the eastward of Bornou Brinée, the principal
town of the extensive kingdom of that name; Katucko and Mandara
are both dependent upon Bornou; the chief or headman of the latter is
known by the name of Abdul-Labi. Bornou Brinée is a large and populous town, and is much resorted to from all parts of northern Africa;

the merchandise, however, is entirely conveyed to it upon camels and horses, and Mahomed Misrah declares there is no river of consequence within ten days' march of it : being questioned as to its distance from the Niger, he pointed towards the south, saying, "Three days will carry you to Mooskoo, and seven days to the country of the Kafirs ; the Joliba runs through that country, but is known there by a different name." That part of the kingdom of Bornou through which he passed, (with the exception of Brinée, which is surrounded with sand,) is more fertile than any he met with during the whole of his journey ; abundance of vegetable provision and plenty of fine corn are produced, and extensive pasturages crowded with cattle, are seen in all directions. The natives are Moslems, and their king, Ahamdoo, receives tribute from most of the circumjacent nations.

Departing westward from Bornou Brinée, he arrived in three days at Angaroo ; one day S. W. by W. brought him to Tassina, three days west to Awoyak, and three days W. by S. to Kano, generally written Cano, Ghano, and Gaub ; all these countries are flat, clear of brushwood and bush, and like Bornou produce plenty of corn. Kano is a kingdom which ranks high among the nations of northern central Africa, and every thing said of it by the priest corroborates the statements already given by others ; the natives are amazingly adventurous and persevering ; they trade to Nufi, Timbuctoo, and various other remote countries situated along the north bank of the Niger, the inhabitants of which are known by the appellation of Muley Ismahel's people, a great Arab chief, whose empire extends along the southern skirts of the great desert. He performed the journey from Kano to Kashana, generally written Keshna and Kassina, in five days, travelling W. by S. through districts sometimes verdant, occasionally sandy ; the natives are Mahomedans, of a very deep black complexion, of commercial habits, and not disposed to quarrel, or make war ; the country of Zanfara lies to the southward of Kashana, according to information received there by the priest.

Proceeding in a direction considerably to the southward of west, he arrived after a tedious journey of twenty days at the town of Nufi, situated on the Niger, which is here called Kuorra, is only about four hundred yards broad, and pursues a course a little to the southward of east with great rapidity, into the nations of the Kafirs. On his route from Kashana, he passed many inconsiderable rivers running from north to south, traversed a country tolerably clear and fertile, though occasionally interspersed with extensive deposits of sand ; and as he approached Nufi, met with many villages, at all of which he received cordial welcome, being inhabited by tribes of the purest Mahomedan faith. Nufi is but an insignificant town, and is full of pagans, a circumstance which appeared to have given Mahomed great concern ; it is situated on the left bank of the Niger, and further from its source than Boussa, where many coinciding reports agree, that our unfortunate countryman, Mungo Park, lost his life by shipwreck.

In one day's march S. W. from Nufi, Misrah reached Yarraba, where he states that a singular trade is carried on, between the natives and a tribe of white people, said to be Christians, who come down a river which flows into the Niger from the southward, and exchange commodities without personal intercourse.

In five days after leaving Yarraba, he reached Azzogo, situated in a country flat, sandy, and barren ; he then proceeded W. by S. to Goingia, a journey of ten days, through a barren country, to the southward of which lies Dahomy, a very bad country, where he understands people eat one another ; four days west, through beautiful and well cultivated regions, abounding with every description of provisions, brought him to Degumba, to the left of which are to be descried lofty mountains, extending along the horizon as far as the eye can reach ; these are of course the mountains of Kong, which were formerly supposed to stretch across the whole breadth of Africa ; along the road to Degumba, numbers of women are to be met with inhabiting booths, in which the traveller may repose, and be regaled with milk, fruit, and other refreshments, in exchange for kolas and kowries ; the former, a fruit so much prized by all Africans, grows abundantly here, and is the means of attracting the surrounding nations, who flock in great bodies to Degumba for the purpose of procuring it in exchange for European and African produce. Gourma is the next place at which our priest arrived, having travelled in a direction a little to the southward of east, passing through many small towns and villages, and a country rather fertile than otherwise ; three days more, pursuing the same course, brought him to Mousi, a country which produces almost every article of food required by the Africans, excepting kolas, to get which they are obliged to trade to Degumba ; and although the distance is so trifling, yet such is the estimation in which that article is held, that six or seven are said to be a handsome price for a fine Mousi horse : this noble animal is very plentiful in this part of Africa, and arrives at great perfection. growing larger and stronger than at any other place which the priest has visited. The principal vegetable productions of Mousi, as well as of those countries which he passed through after crossing the Niger at Nufi, are yams, rice, and corn, the latter of which grows luxuriantly in most of the interior regions : the natives of those districts are not a mixture of converts and pagans, but Mahomed regrets that while the proportion is materially in favour of paganism, the Mahomedans are very firm in their faith. From Mousi, turning towards the north-west, and passing through various small towns and villages, about a day's journey from one another, he arrived at Jenne, or Janne, in fifteen days, but did not fall in with any river running to the northward.

In seven days from Janné pursuing a south-westerly course, Mahomed Misrah reached Sego, the capital of the kingdom Bambarrana, at which town I shall leave him to prosecute the remainder of his journey by himself, as this part of the country is already well known to us through the medium of European travellers, and as it is to be presumed that, before this time, an account, more circumstantial than any that has hitherto appeared, may have issued from the pen of staff-surgeon Dochard, who passed several years in the interior, and a considerable length of time on the banks of the Niger ; I nevertheless think it necessary to observe that I have in my possession the route of the priest, as well as of many other natives, from Sego to the coast, and that although

I am perfectly satisfied, from the agreement of the statements with other accounts, that the whole of Mahomed's information, as far as regards his own personal observation, may be relied on, yet I do not perceive any thing of sufficient consequence in the remainder to interest those who have already perused the travels of Mungo Park, Mollien, and others.

The priest supposes his day's journey might average about twenty miles, the whole giving a distance of 2720 miles, from Misrah to Sego, and as we know that Sego is about 700 miles distant from the colony of Sierra Leone, the whole extent of his journey may aggregate about 3620 miles, from which, if we deduct 400 miles completed for the deviaton of the courses which he has himself given from the straight course between Misrah and Sego, 3020 miles will be left for the journey, had it been possible to perform it in a direct line ; this at once exhibits a very extraordinary and satisfactory coincidence, for it will be found to differ but little from the straight measurement on the map, which is about 2925 miles. The attention is here naturally arrested to admire the accuracy and astonishing capacity of this priest, for had he travelled with an intention of marking his route, and been furnished with suitable instruments for the purpose, at the same time having a knowledge of the use of them, he could hardly have accounted for his ground more correctly, which is a very desirable fact to be certain of, as it enables us, in conjunction with other circumstances already detailed, to attach a considerable share of importance to his information respecting the Niger. He appears to be quite positive that the Nile is a continuation of the Niger, and that Bahar el Abeed is the link of connexion ; for he has met people who have told him that they travelled along its banks, from Nufi to Sennaar ; that it is very broad, and frequently overflows its banks, inundating the country to an immense extent. But while I attach little or no credit to what he has heard (being well aware that the native travellers too often consider themselves privileged to deal in the marvellous), yet I think, presuming the height which would be required for the source of the Niger not to be an objection, the only other is its great breadth at an early stage of its course, and the consequent magnitude which it would necessarily attain from tributary assistance, previous to falling in with the range of the Nile. But although a little very simple reasoning might in a measure cancel the latter objection, yet were there does exist one, let it be ever so trifling, the hypothesis cannot be allowed to be valid.

The intercourse between the nations in the interior and the colony of Sierra Leone has of late years become very great, and, to a common observer residing in the colony, it must appear evident that the intercourse is daily increasing ; indeed, to such an extent is good faith now established, that little excursions, in the shape of parties of pleasure, are frequently made by the inhabitants among the neighbouring tribes.

ACCOUNT

OF THE CAPTIVITY OF ALEXANDER SCOTT,

Among the wandering Arabs of the Great African Desert, for a Period of nearly Six Years.

ALEXANDER SCOTT, a native of Liverpool, at the age of sixteen years, sailed as an apprentice in the ship Montezuma, commanded by Captain Knubley, and belonging to Messrs. J. T. Koster and company, of that port. The vessel sailed on the 26th October, 1810, for Brazil, but was wrecked on 23d November, at three o'clock in the morning, on the African coast, somewhere between Capes Noon and Bojador. In the course of the first day, the crew, who had reached the shore, were visited by two persons (one of whom was a negro,) belonging to the Arab tribe of Tobórlet. They had with them a camel. Scott, the cook, and a Portuguese boy, named Antonio, were desired by Captain Knubley to accompany those men to their habitations. The natives finding that Antonio had a knife and some copper-coin, took his knife, and cut away the pocket containing the money; in consequence of which, the Portuguese refused to go farther, and returned to the coast. Scott and the cook proceeded chiefly on foot, but occasionally riding on the camel (after their fears at its appearance had subsided,) for eight or nine hours, when they arrived at a valley called Zérrohah, on the sides of which about 100 small tents were scattered. These tents were low, and formed of a coarse mat-like stuff, manufactured by the Arabs of the hair of goats and camels, intermixed with wool. There might be about six or seven persons inhabiting each hut; their complexions were very brown; both men and women were bony and slender. Scott and his companion were consigned by their guides to the care of some women.

Next day the captain and the rest of the crew arrived; but on the following day Scott was carried by the same two men who had been his guides, to other tents about two miles off. He remained altogether about three weeks at those two places; during which period all the people were scattered about, but Scott and Antonio remained together. They had skins to sleep on, and a thick porridge of barley-meal for food. Scott had remarked, that two pigs, saved from the wreck, had been killed by the Arabs; but their flesh was either left on the beach or thrown into the sea.

The Arabs now began to break up their tents, and sold Scott to an old man, named Sidi El Hartoni, who had with him three camels. He carried Scott away, and they fell in, on the evening of the same day, with another Arab, who had purchased the remainder of the crew, with the exception of the captain, a passenger, and two seamen.

On the following morning, the old man carried Scott to the spot where the vessel had been wrecked, and there they remained for three days. From thence they departed for the south, and after two days, during which Scott occasionally rode on a camel, he fell in with the Portuguese boy in possession of another Arab tribe, also moving southward. Here the two boys attempted to escape from their masters, but were pursued, caught, and beaten. They were immediately finally separated; Antonio and his master set off in a S.E. direction, and Scott was carried, as near as he could judge, due south, travelling all the way not far from the sea, sometimes within sight of it, and occasionally along the beach. Their route was continued for fifteen days more, and the rate of travelling he estimates at fifteen miles a day; every night they rested at the tents of some tribe, and were always hospitably received.

The country they traversed principally consisted of a soft sand. A part of the road lay through a valley, watered by a salt river, and containing a deep thicket or wood, in which Scott observed trees resembling firs, and some from which whitish gum exuded. This last had sharp spines, the stem thicker than a man's body, not very high, growing, as Scott expresses it, "all of a rook."* This valley is named Wad Seyghi, (Wad, in the language of the country, signifying a valley, in which there is running water).† Here Scott saw an animal, which he describes as "a large beast almost like a cow, covered with hair of a grey colour, with large horns, thick at the root, and spreading outward, a very short tail, and feet like those of sheep. This animal is eaten by the Arabs, who call it Row-y-and."‡ After the seventeen days' travelling, they came to an encampment of thirty-three tents, in a part of a district which Scott says is named El Ghiblah, and is bounded on the west by the sea. Here they remained several months. The place of their abode was the highest part of that country; its soil is principally rocky; its distance Scott computes at upwards of 200 miles southward of the place where he was sold to Sidi Hartoni, and he supposes it to be about twenty miles from the ocean, the roar of which he occasionally heard when the wind blew from the west. He also remarked a circumstance which inclined him to think the coast not far distant.

---

* Rook is a Lancashire term for a heap or close bundle. This tree is perhaps an Acacia.

† It is thought by competent judges, that Wad signifies a valley, with or without water, and is certainly employed to denote a valley without running water.

‡ The Buffalo apparently.

The water of the wells at the beach was much fresher than that of the place of encampment, and the Arabs, who were often sent to fetch it from the coast, usually left home in the morning, and returned on the evening of the following day.

In this district Scott saw "plenty of wild fowl, occasionally foxes, wolves, deer, or animals like deer, with a red back, white belly, tapering black horns, with prominent rings, and tips bent forward, eyes black and large. Some of these animals have straight horns :—it is called El Mochae."*

Scott remained at El Ghiblah for some months, but about the month of June (as he supposes, from his recollection of the length of the day and the heat of the weather,) he was told that " the tribe would go a long journey to Hez el Hezsh, and that he must go with them, and there change his religion or die."

The old man, his master, his three sons and three daughters, with many others of the tribe, composed a caravan of twenty families.

The party mustered between 500 and 600 camels, of which fifty-seven were the property of Sidi El Hartoni. Each family was provided with a tent, which, with provisions, water, and all their effects, were carried by the male camels, while the young camels, and those that gave milk, had no load whatever. The number of sheep belonging to the caravan was above 1000, and their goats were nearly as many. They had only five horses, which during the journey were chiefly employed in chasing ostriches, the feathers of which were carefully preserved, and the flesh eaten. They carried with them two jack-asses, and many dogs, chiefly of the greyhound and bloodhound breed, with which the people killed hares, foxes, and wolves ; and on the flesh of all these this tribe occasionally fed. When travelling, the sheep and goats of each family were kept in separate droves. The animals go close together, except where they meet with some vegetation, when they spread, but are easily brought together by the whistling of their driver, or by the sound of his horn. The latter is the most usual method, and soon collects the flocks around the driver, an effect supposed to arise from their apprehension of wild beasts, which drives them to the protection of their keeper. It is said, that they can distinguish by the smell the approach of a wolf at the distance of half a mile.

---

* On shewing Scott the plates in Shaw's Zoology, he immediately pointed to the following animals as those which he had met with in the African Desert and its confines, while he described the peculiarities of each with considerable accuracy : Antilope oryx, or Egyptian antelope ; A. gazella, A. cervicapra, or common antelope ; A. euchore, or spring antelope.

The tents were pitched every night, and the camels and flocks belonging to the family were disposed in front of the family tent, near which fires were kindled for cooking.   Should there be any apprehension of an attack during the night, all the tents are pitched in a circular encampment called Douar, within which all the cattle are driven, and the men lie among the camels, which immediately rise up on the first alarm.

The sheep and goats are very different from those of England, being much larger, with longer legs, and are much accustomed to travelling.   When they have sufficient food, they will keep up with the camels on a journey, and they can occasionally run as fast as a greyhound.

The camels can go long without food or drink; they browse on the scanty herbage of the desert, where they find it, and drink as much at once as will serve them a long time.   Scott never saw or heard that this animal ever swallowed charcoal, and thinks, that had this substance ever been its food, he must have observed it, as he has often seen the camels reduced to great extremity for want of herbage.

For the first four or five days, the route of the caravan lay over hard clayey ground, very barren, producing only wild bushes, but not a blade of grass.   They then came to a sandy district called El-e-Buscharah, consisting of hills and valleys of sand, having water only at a deep well about ten miles southwards of the place where they entered on it.   From this well the camels were loaded with water.   The Arabs told Scott that this well had been made by Christians, who once possessed this country, until expelled by the Moors or the Arabs.

In this sandy district they saw no beasts, except a few deer in the valleys.   Scott describes these deer as of a nankeen colour, with black stripes along their sides, near the belly; the nose, eyes, and tongue black; the male had small straight horns without branches, the females none; their legs were long and slender; they were so fleet that the greyhound could not catch them; their size was inferior to that of an English sheep.*

The only vegetation of this country was small bushes, and a low tree, called by the Arabs El Myrreh.   The tallest of them is about three yards high, it has a red broad branch like a palm, and running roots like liquorice, about as thick as the finger, and sweet as sugar; the roots are called Ferrada by the people, and eaten both by them and the cattle.   The cattle were fond of this root as food, and it was reckoned good for them.

---

* This is evidently an antelope, and probably a new species. It has some affinity to the antilope oryx.

There were here some birds, and the eggs of various wild fowl were found in the sand, among which Scott particularly mentions one by the name of Wild Peacock.*

For eleven days their route lay through this sandy district, and then they entered upon a more firm sort of soil, which sometimes presented a hilly surface, and occasionally extensive plains of hard clay, sprinkled over with some bushes, but without any other vegetation. The hills sometimes shewed rocky sides, on which "dry mosses"† grew. This sort of country continued for about two months, during which they went through several valleys containing small streams of water, so brackish that it could not be drank ; and they passed by some mines of salt, and brimstone. The former appeared like white rocks in some valleys, and the latter looked like white and yellow rocks. Scott knew the salt by its taste ; and having broken off a piece of the brimstone, he found it to be very bitter, and on throwing it on the fire at night, it burnt with a blue flame, and almost suffocated the people, who beat him heartily for causing this annoyance.‡

The tracts left by camels in the clay soil, in wet weather, (which is not very frequent in that country,) guided the caravan through this desert region. They often met other Arab tribes travelling like themselves, but they never pitched their tents near each other. This arose partly from fear, and partly from the scarcity of water and food for their cattle.

After passing through a wood, which they traversed for two days, they again came to a sandy soil. This wood was the boundary between the clayey and sandy districts. During their passage through the forest, they saw several lions, which did not attempt to come near them.

Scott remarked, that beasts of prey seldom attacked a party unless they were first molested ; but their flocks were attacked in this wood by a tiger.§ The camels can smell this animal at a considerable distance, and its approach is known by their refusing to advance. This occurred in the wood, the men prepared their arms, the tiger approached with little noise, and fell upon the sheep; the people endeavoured to drive him away, and fired at him, on which he suddenly turned on them, killed three, two of whom he struck down at once, and wounded five others. He then seized a sheep, which he carried off with great ease, in his mouth.

In this wood they met with a party who had a tame elephant.

---

* Perhaps a bustard.   † Lichens.
‡ The bitter taste perhaps arose from a mixture of sulphate of magnesia, which occasionally occurs with sulphur ; or it might be owing to sulphate of ammonia.
§ From Scott's description of this animal, it would appear to be the panther.

These people were of a darker complexion than the tribes of
El Ghiblah. They belonged to the tribe of Or Ghêbet, and
came from El Sharrag, and said they were going to some town
(the name of which Scott did not hear) to fetch corn. They
cautioned the Arabs with whom Scott was, to beware of a
people called Baurbarras, black savages, who lived in the wood,
and had done them much damage. In the wood were date-
trees, cocoa-trees, and wild oranges.

On leaving the wood, the caravan entered on the sandy district already noticed. It was varied by valleys and small sandy
hills, and was watered by many running streams a little brackish; although the weather had been long hot, and very little
rain had fallen. In about a month they got through this sandy
district; and, without having had any distant view of it, arrived
on the shores of a vast lake or sea. The day was extremely
clear, and two mountain tops on its opposite shore were just
visible, almost like clouds on the sky.

The point at which they arrived was not that which they had
intended to reach; for it was an uninhabited country. They
proceeded, therefore, northward, along the banks of the lake,
and in the evening arrived at a number of fixed huts, built of
canes and bamboos, called El Sharrag, and belonging to the
Or Ghêbets. The surrounding country was of a soft sandy
soil, not much wooded. There were many low bushes; and
near the beach high trees, with tall stems, and bunches of
leaves at the top, something like a cocoa-tree, but taller.

From the time of their leaving El Ghiblah, until their arrival
at the lake, the route of the caravan was pretty uniformly in
one direction, except when the intervention of hills or rivers
caused occasional deviations; but as soon as these obstacles
were passed, they resumed the original direction.

Scott was unprovided with any means of determining the
true line of their march, but, judging from the position of the
sun at his rising, it appears, that at setting out, the line of
route lay a little to the southward of east, and gradually inclined more to the south as they advanced.[*]

They travelled more or less every day, except when they
tarried three days in the wood, to bury those who had been
killed by the tiger. The first day was, in consequence of this
occurrence, a day of rest; the second was employed in burying
the dead; and the third was occupied in placing stones over
the graves, to secure them from wild beasts. Some days,

---

[*] Unfortunately there are no more precise data from which this important point
can be ascertained; and this mode of estimating by the eye, especially in the
observations of an ill educated lad, sixteen years of age, cannot be considered as
any thing more than a rough approximation to the true line of route.

when very hot, they stopped at 2 or 3 o'clock for the day.
Scott was of opinion, that the distance travelled was generally
twenty miles, and seldom less than fifteen miles a day.

In all this journey, they did not pass through, nor did they
see any thing that could be called a town, nor any permanent
habitations of any kind, until they reached the lake. They did
not pass near, nor did they cross any high mountains. They
did not meet with any large river or stream which was not
fordable. They frequently met other parties like themselves,
who all spoke Arabic, which Scott now began to understand
tolerably well; but many of them spoke also another language.

During the journey those who chose rode on the camels; the
women and children often did: Scott was permitted to do so
sometimes. Scott's occupation was chiefly to attend to his
master's sheep and goats, in which he was assisted by one of his
master's daughters; and at night he was employed in grinding
or bruising barley between two flat stones. The Arabs fared
very scantily, and Scott still worse. His feet and legs were
blistered by the burning sand: he was cruelly beaten for trifling
faults, and if he slept too long in the morning, he was beaten
with a cudgel. The whole party were often short of water;
and at one time, when travelling over the hard ground near
the salt and brimstone mines, they were in great distress,
having been six days without any water. Their resource then
was the milk of their goats and camels; and they frequently
collected the urine of the latter, as a drink in this extremity, or
preserved what water was found in the stomach of those that
died. The urine of the camel is occasionally taken as a pur-
gative medicine. It is usually given for three successive mornings, and operates much on the bowels. The Arabs did not
take breakfast; they generally had only one meal a day, and
that after sunset. It consisted usually of goat's milk and a
thick porridge of barley flour; but if they had no corn, they
drank the milk of their goats and camels, and ate the flesh of
the camel, whether the animal died a natural death, or was
killed accidentally, or on purpose. They even occasionally devoured the hide of the camel, which is tough and thick. It is
first beaten quite thin between two stones, and then it is roasted. A large fire of wood is kindled on the ground, the glowing
embers are mixed with the sand, and the hide, or other animal
food, is covered over with the mixture, when it is soon roasted,
and devoured by the Arabs, without any nice attention to the
particles of sand which may be adhering to it. They also occasionally eat locusts, which are roasted in a similar manner.

At El Sharrag, all the camels, sheep, and goats, belonging to
the party, with two persons of each family, were left, and a

large boat was hired to convey them across the lake. This boat was very long,—was built of a red wood, something like mahogany,—appeared to have no iron about her,—and even her rudder was fastened by ropes of straw or grass. Between seventy and eighty of their party embarked in this boat, amongst whom was Scott. The boat was commanded by an Arab of a darker complexion than those with whom Scott had travelled, and manned by six blacks, whom Scott considered to be slaves, from the treatment they experienced from their master; for he observed, that they, as well as other negroes, who are numerous at El Sharrag, were often beaten by the Arabs. The boat started at sunrise, and was rowed with six oars, until a little before sunset, at a rate (as Scott imagined) of about two miles an hour. The oars were very short and clumsy; the blacks sat two on the same seat, with their faces to the stem, rowing with quick and short strokes, and raising the body at each stroke, not sitting steady, and making a long pull, as English sailors do. They rested half a dozen times through the day, for about ten minutes or a quarter of an hour at a time. A little before sunset, a large stone, which served as an anchor, was let down with about twenty fathoms of cable, and the boat remained stationary all night. They weighed anchor again at sunrise, proceeded as before, till sunset, and then again cast anchor. Soon after day-break on the third day, they again got under weigh, and proceeded until about two o'clock in the afternoon, when they arrived at the opposite shore. Their course was straight for the two mountains already noticed, and they landed at their foot, in a country called El Hezsh.

The lake is named Bahâr Tieb.* Judging by the position of the rising sun, Scott thinks that the greatest extent of this Bahar is from N. E. to S. W. When on it, he could not perceive any boundary in those directions; and he was given to understand that it extended very far in both. Its breadth he could not state, except as far as an inference may be drawn from the time they took to cross it, at this, which seemed its narrowest part.† The water during their passage was smooth,

---

* According to Scott, " Bahar signifies a water on which boats can go," and " Tieb or Tee-eb, fresh." The name is therefore the " Fresh Water Lake or Sea."

† Suppose their course the first day　　　12 hours,
　　　　　　　　　　　　the second day　　　12
　　　　　　　　　　　　the third day　　　　8
　　　　　　　　　　　　　　　　　　　　　　———

we have for the whole　　　　　　　　　32 hours;
but we must deduct for the resting of the rowers,　3 hours,
　　　　　　　　　　　　　　　　　　　　　　———
which leaves for the whole sum　　...　　...　29 hours;
and this, at the rate of two miles per hour, would indicate fifty-eight miles as the breadth of the Bahar at this point. We may perhaps say, in round numbers, sixty miles.

with a great deal of weeds floating on its surface.   Some had broad green leaves, but none of them looked like sea-weeds. All resembled fresh water weeds, and abundance of rushes grew near the shore.   The water under the weeds was clear, and fresher than that of the country, which was all brackish. When further questioned, Scott stated, that though the water of the Bahar was comparatively fresh, yet it would not be reckoned fresh in this country.   The Bahar had no perceptible current; had any such existed, he could not have failed to observe it.   Both nights when the boat was brought to anchor, the bow was as nearly as he can recollect towards the moon, when rising about ten o'clock;[*] and he remarked that its position did not appear to be changed during the night. The sky was cloudless, the winds were calm, and a very heavy dew fell.   The moon was full, two or three days before they crossed the Bahar.   The Bahar contained turtles, something like those brought to England from the West Indies, but much smaller; of these Scott killed some, but did not eat them. Fish of different kinds abounded in the water, and were caught with great ease by nets let down from fishing vessels, or hauled on the beach.   He saw some like mackerel, others shaped like eels, but thicker and much larger.   Some had no scales; but he did not see any with long feelers at their mouths.

There were many fishing-vessels on the Bahâr, but no boats larger than that which conveyed them across the lake, which was capable of carrying about 200 people.   Its ends were both alike, rising up like those of a canoe, very sharp, decked for about three yards at each end, with several thwarts or seats for the rowers across it, on each of which two men sat when they rowed, each with a separate oar.   The boat was very flat-bottomed, was ceiled in the bottom and up the sides, had no mast, but there was a step for one in the keel, and a hole in the seat over it.   The cable was formed of a rushy grass, which he was told is taken when green, is flattened by beating it when wet, and then twisted into ropes, which become afterwards yellow.   The boat in the language of the Arabs is called zourgos, but by the natives of El Sharrag and El Hezsh, flook.

With the master of the vessel Scott had no opportunity of speaking.   This man wore a white cotton shirt, with a red girdle, and was armed with a musket and cutlass.   The dress of the boatmen had some resemblance to an English carter's frock, but was made of woollen.[†]   They all wore yellow slip-

---

* Rather about 8ʰ or 8¼ʰ by the moon's age.
† This is a pretty accurate description of the dress of the poorer class of Moors on the northern coast of Barbary

pers, lined with red, and of the same width from the toe to the heel.* These people spoke the Arab language, and also another called Schlech. In the former Scott conversed with them, and found that they were apprehensive of being attacked while on the water, by people who come from the upper or northern part of the Bahâr in boats, and who inhabit the eastern side of that part; are small in size, and are a different race from the Arabs. Scott thinks they told him, that this race (whom they named Zachah) do not believe in Mahommed.

The boatmen also told him, pointing to the southward, that in that direction lay a great salt-water sea; that the one they then were on run into it; that there was no end of it; that there were plenty of Saffina el Kabeer, or large ships on it; and that they called it Bahâr el Kabeer.† They stated, that to the southward was a harbour called Bambarry,‡ where a great number of ships came. They further stated, that a long way to the southward (pointing in that direction), and before they were born, there had been great battles, both on the Bahâr el Kabeer and on land, between the French and English;§ that where the battle had been fought on the land, the bones of those killed were yet lying.

At the place where the party landed were a number of huts built of logs of wood, placed perpendicularly, lined with canes on both sides, with bushes in the intervals, and covered with rushes taken from the banks of the Bahâr. The name of this place is El Tah Sidna Mahommed, signifying " The place of a chief called Mahommed;" and the name of the tribe is El Tahsi del Hezsh. On landing, the Arabs all kissed the ground three times, and washed their hands and faces with sand, as they did at all times when they prayed. Scott refused to do so, and the men beat him with a stick; but the women begged he might not be further punished. They remained all night at these huts, but the next morning at sun-rise, they left the village, taking Scott along with them, and telling him they were going to Hez el Hezsh, to Sidna Mahommed; that he must go there, change his religion, and be circumcised; and that if he did not become of their religion, Mahommed would rise up and kill him.

---

* This is the exact counterpart of the Barbary Slipper.

† Great Sea or Water.

‡ There is a district not far to the south of the Congo River called Bamba, where the Portuguese have been in the habit of slaving. But the bones, the fighting, and the river, must all belong to different stories. Scott was young in Arabic; and the Arabic was not the vernacular tongue of his informant.

§ When questioned on this head, Scott affirmed, that he is certain they said Frencese and Inglese." These negroes were probably slaves brought from a distance.

The country bordering on the sea was sandy, but a little way back it was a mixture of sand and clay, with many large rocks which were quite "full of chinney weed," called in Arabic Tomkīlet.* They then traversed a mountainous country, by a winding path (which tended southward,) until about three o'clock in the afternoon ; when they arrived at a valley between two high mountains, the sides of which produced large oil trees. The branches of this tree resemble an oak, and produce " green plums," with a hard shell and a kernel in each, which, when boiled, affords oil. The process for obtaining this oil is as follows : The nuts are broken, the kernels dried in the sun, then ground, and boiled with water in clay-pots ; the oil is skimmed off as it rises.

The valley is about three quarters of a mile across ; there was no grass in it, but small bushes grew in a clayey soil, mixed with a black slaty stone.

Here stood a solitary building, " about the size and shape of an English barn, or haystack." The lower part was formed of rough red rockstones, bedded in clay ; the upper of canes and boughs of trees : the whole was covered with rushes. It appeared as if it had been long built, being quite black with moss on the outside. One end of this building was to the north, and the other to the south. In the south end was a square-headed door, which was not opened while Scott was there. There was no window, nor any thing like a chimney, or other projection, except a long pole forked at the end, rising out of the rushes, on the east side of the roof, and sloping upwards. It was so long that the forked ends were beyond the line of the wall, and each extremity was covered by an ostrich egg. Immediately below these was a large wooden bowl capable of holding five or six gallons, and placed on three large stones, which supported it about two feet from the ground. This building they told him was the grave of Sidna Mahommed. This, he says, does not mean the grave of the prophet, whose title among them is Uhrr-soël,† but of some great man con-

---

* Chimney is the vulgar name for archil,—a substance prepared chiefly from Lichen Rocella.

† Before receiving this account of the grave, he had been told that it was the burial place of the prophet Mahommed, (as he supposes, with the intention of more readily inducing him to change his religion,) but having read when at home, in some book respecting the East Indies, that Mahommed's burial place was Mecca, which is a large town, and that his coffin was hung up in a large church, he therefore knew that this story could not be true. After his return to El Ghiblah, he was told that another great man, called Sidna Ali, was buried in the building above described ; that this person was born where the prophet was, and married his daughter Fatma-Min t'Uhrrsoel, who is also interred there. Scott's master likewise read to him from a book, the names of many who were buried

nected with, or a relation of Mahommed the prophet. The personage here buried was laid (as he was told) on his side with his head to the north, his feet to the south, and his face to the east,* the usual mode of interment in that country. In the ground adjoining the building, were the graves of many pilgrims who had died in El Hezsh. These were marked by small hollows, with a stone upon each, with other stones placed on edge along the sides, and one at each end.

The party was accompanied by five pilgrims, who were dressed in a kind of white cotton shirt, with a red belt round the waist, and each carried a brass box containing books and papers. When they had arrived on the ground, all, in a standing position, cried aloud ; "Allah ackibar shekou il lahi el allah.—Shedowna Mahommed de rassoul allah."† They bowed their heads thrice to the ground, then got up, and walked to the front of the building, to the door of which the pilgrims first approached. On one side of the door was a brownish stone, set in the ground two feet high, which the pilgrims kissed, and their example was followed by all the party, Scott excepted. The stone was quite smooth and rounded at the top, seemingly hard and clean, but the sides were rather mossy.

The people here threatened to kill Scott, if he did not turn Mahommedan, shewing him a knife with which they said they would destroy him. He told them " they might kill him, for he would not turn ;" and they gave him until next morning to think of it ; but after this time they did not trouble him any more about changing his religion.

Tents and provisions had been provided by the pilgrims, and the party staid all night in the valley. Next day some of them walked five or six miles into the neighbouring country, and saw three or four ruins of large buildings, one of which had walls standing, that were pierced by two or three square windows. The walls were of " rough rock-stone," with clay for mortar. These ruins covered a great deal of ground, and had evidently been once inhabited, but the people with whom Scott was, did not seem to know any thing about their former use. At night they remained in the tents, and next day returned to the sea-

in the above described building, some of which he recollects, as Sidna Braheim, Sidna Mouss, Sidna Bak-har, Sidna Hammed, Sidna Bo-hcida, Sidna Solleh.

The errors in Scott's description of the tomb of Mahommed, and of the place of his burial, are not uncommon in such popular works as he probably consulted.

* That is towards Mecca.

† These words are put down as nearly as possible, according to his manner of pronouncing them, as are the proper names which occur in the narrative. Compare this sentence with Ali Bey's Account of the Religion of the Western Arabs, vol. 1, p. 89 and 90,—and the ceremony of kissing the stone of the Kaba, vol. 2, p. 52.

side. Before setting off, and also at day-break on the preceding day, the Arabs said their prayers at the building.   During their stay on that side of the Bahâr, Scott was never again taken to the grave, though he believes that the party went to it almost every day,* with camels and mules.   He was confined in the hut where he was lodged, and was never allowed to go farther than the door, in consequence of his refusal to become a Mahommedan.†

While he remained there, many people, some of whom wore red caps on their heads, came on mules and camels, as pilgrims from the southern side of the lake, to offer (as it was said) sheep and goats at the grave; and there were also frequent arrivals of parties like their own, who came in boats from the northern side of the water.

The people of El Hèzsh eat in the middle of the day as well as at night.   Their food, as also that of the people of El Shanag, consists chiefly of corn-bread and dates, as they make much less use of goats' and camels' milk, and camels' flesh, than the other Arab tribes do when stationary.   They make, however, kouskusû.‡

Their dress differs from that of the pilgrims already mentioned.   It consists of a dark-blue linen shirt, a pair of short trowsers, which reach to the knees, a red girdle, a knife at their side, and a musket.   Their legs are bare, and on their feet are slippers of yellow leather lined with red, or sandals.

The women have red slippers, bare legs, and a white haïck, with a broad plate of silver hanging in front of each shoulder, and a belt of yellow and green worsted plaited together.   "The women of the head-men have a dark-blue millicha," which is worn like the haïck of the inferior orders, but has its corners and edges fringed with the same colour, and they wear also a belt, which is sometimes all red, at other times white, or a mixture of yellow and green.   The children wear a sort of woollen frock with short sleeves, which, with the breast of the frock, are worked with red worsted.

There are many black slaves at El Hèzsh.   There are no houses better than the huts already described; but the latter

---

* It is customary with Mahommedans to pray at the tombs of their holy men; and this pilgrimage might be substituted for that to Mecca, the distance to which being too great for the wandering tribes to undertake.

† The firmness of Scott in this particular is highly praiseworthy.   It had been reported before his return that he had renounced Christianity, and embraced the faith of Mecca; but the writer of this note has decisive proof, that he never had conformed to the ceremonies of that religion.

‡ An excellent African dish, much used in Morocco, made by seething a fowl in a pipkin filled with granulated flour; its juices are absorbed by the farinaceous matter, which is thus rendered very palatable.   It is a pilau.

are very numerous. Tents are also used, when a part of a family is obliged to go in quest of food for the cattle.

About a month after their arrival on the Bahâr, the party to which Scott belonged, having taken leave of some of the pilgrims by shaking hands, and kissing the top of the head, left El Tah Sidna Mahommed El Hêzsh, embarking in the same boat which brought them thither, and which had been, in the interval, employed in carrying over passengers as they arrived.

Scott remarked, that the opposite shore of the lake was not visible, even in the clearest weather, from El Hêlsh, on account of the lowness of the land. There being more wind than when they came, and it being fair, they placed two oars across each other by way of a mast, and spread on them a long narrow blanket, such as they wrap round their bodies, as a sail. They left the shore of El Hêzsh, a little after mid-day, and arrived on the opposite side at day-break the next morning, (as he supposes, about six o'clock.) In this voyage they had the advantage of sail and oars, and continued under weigh all night.

Scott had no conversation with the boatmen during this recrossing of the Bahâr. On account of his refusal to change his religion, he was not permitted to speak to them, and was refused every indulgence.

On landing, they found that several of the camels had died, owing, as Scott supposes, to their having swallowed stones and gravel while feeding on the low bushes, which are so close to the ground that the animals could scarcely feed without taking up gravel with them; and considerable quantities of it were found in their stomachs after they were opened. As soon as the hire of the boat was settled, (which amounted to three camels for every family taken over and brought back,) the party set out on its return, by the same route which they had followed in coming to the Bahâr. They travelled for a month without any particular occurrence, until they came to the wood before described. While going through it, they saw some of the black people called Bambarras, who were armed with bows and arrows, and quite naked. The Arabs attacked the negroes, and a short contest took place, when several of the Arabs were wounded, but at last the blacks were beaten, and eight of them made prisoners. These were brought to the tents, bound hand and foot, and the next morning carried away by the Arabs, who pursued their journey. The negroes were *tattooed* or marked by three diagonal cuts on each cheek, and a horizontal one across the forehead.

After this the caravan travelled for about a month and a half over hard ground, with small hills, covered with low wild bushes, but without trees of any size; but there were trees of considerable magnitude in the low ground through which they occasionally passed. About this time they came to a large valley, where there had been much rain, and a considerable quantity of fresh water was in it. The trees and shrubs were quite green; there grew no grass, but a herb like the green-sauce of England, a flower like the dog-daisy, and a yellow flower about eight or nine inches high, of which the camels, sheep, and goats ate. The " green-sauce" and goat's milk were here the principal food of the party. They remained about six moons in this valley, during which time the men frequently went out to fight, and brought back camels, corn, &c. which they had plundered. When this valley could no longer afford food to their cattle, they sent a party to look out for another place of encampment; and when they had discovered a suitable spot, the whole party set out for it, taking three days to reach this new district. Here they remained two or three months without any thing remarkable occurring, until the trees began to lose their leaves, all the vegetables withered, and the ground dried up, when the whole caravan set out direct for El Ghiblah.

For a week or two they went over hard ground, and then came to sandy valleys, quite barren, and without any vegetable on them, except the palm-like tree El Myrreh before noticed. In little more than a week they got over this sandy district, and in about another week again arrived at El Ghiblah, but not in the exact spot from which they had taken their departure.

They pitched their tents, however, by some wells, and seemed to consider themselves at home. They always avoided going too far to the northward, for fear of being taken by the " Moors" or subjects of the emperor of Morocco, between whom and the wandering Arabs, or Moors of the desert, there is a deadly hatred and perpetual war. The tribe with whom Scott lived was often at war also with Arabs to the southward.* At El Ghiblah, the black prisoners taken in their contest with the Bambarras, were sold to some people from Wadnoon, who gave eighty dollars for each.

The tribe was now held in much greater estimation by their neighbours than before their journey into the interior, and the men were called Sidi El Hèzsh Hezsh. To Scott, however,

---

* During these long journeys Scott saw various animals, not noticed in the preceding pages, as monkeys, squirrels, porcupines, wolves, foxes, leopards, which are cowardly animals, hares, deer, with and without horns, various kinds of wild cattle, and an animal like a bear. Birds were seen of the eagle species, —a large one of this kind Scott has seen to carry off young kids. There were different kinds of hawks and crows. He saw a bird like an eagle, but larger, which preys only on hares. There were many ostriches, peacocks, cranes, red-legged partridges, parrots, " green and red birds with long tails," a large green bird, with the under part of the bill like a spoon.

this journey was a source of trouble; for since his refusal to
turn Mahommedan, they treated him much more cruelly, beating him almost daily with sticks.   This he acknowledges,
however, sometimes arose from his sleeping too long in the
morning, when they thought that he should be attending to
their cattle.

Scott states, that the district in possession of the Arabs commences some distance from Wadnoon, and is divided into four
parts.   The northern Till lies about 100 miles south of Wadnoon, and has a small river called Ourerab, and a ward or
valley running through it.   The western part is named Sachal,
is divided from Till by the large wad called Zerrohah, the one
being from the other ten or twelve days' journey.*   This wad
is only a part of a much larger district called also Zerrohah,
which lies to the eastward of Till and Sachal.   It is a high,
but not mountainous land, and sends down a large wad, as
above mentioned, which reaches to the sea.

The fourth division El Ghiblah lies to the south, and is divided from Sachal by the wad Seyghe.†   The tribes are in
general terms distinguished by the name of the district they
usually occupy, as the Tille-eêns, the Sachal-eens, the Ghiblah-
eens.   In each of those divisions, however, there are particular
tribes scattered, the special names of some of which he recollects, viz. the Mujatts, and Zurghiêm tribes, which dwell in
Till, are always at war with the Ulled D'Leims.   The El
Arosiem and Ulled Missebah, which belong to Zerrohah.
Those of Toborlet (into whose hands Scott fell when cast
away,) of Lemmiheir, Fyeketts, Ulled Tiderary, Ulled Emouk-
sor, and Ulled Emiâra, are all of Sachal, or as it is sometimes
called Sachara, are now considered a very peaceable people.
In El Ghiblah are the tribes of Ulled D'Leim, Ulled Edono-
chalab, Ulled Teggadow, Ulled Emouss.   Scott mentions also
the Arab tribes of Orghebets and the Scarnas, who belong to
El Sharrag, near the Bahâr El Tieb.   These distant tribes he
has seen, the former often, the latter sometimes, in El Ghiblah
and in Sachal, having come there on fighting expeditions, or
for corn.   This appeared to him less extraordinary, because
his own master was once absent for more than twelve months
on an expedition of some kind; and the people of El Ghiblah
sometimes go far to the southward, to a place called Llumgaufra,‡ the chief man of which is called Wildibacaab, and

---

* In this account there is some indistinctness, as ⬛ have not been able to ascertain from what point in Till to what point in Sac⬛ this computation extends.
† It was on the coast of Sachal that the Mon⬛na was wrecked.
‡ In spelling this name, the Welsh doubl⬛ ⬛ been adopted to give an idea
of the sound.

whence the Arabs obtain black slaves in exchange for horses, in the proportion of three or four slaves for each horse. These slaves are again sold at Wadnoon. Scott was also told, that at Llumgaufra there is a very large river, which runs a long way through the country; and that on the other side of this river the people are not Mahommedans.* He could not obtain any name for this river, but the general one of Bahar El Tieb; which is not, however, applied to small rivers. The name for them is Illimon Sacharah, or running waters.

Scott found that hostilities are also commenced by the Arabs; for the blacks never come in a hostile manner amongst the former.

The Arabs generally remain in the place where they pitch their tents, as long as the herbage affords sufficient food for their cattle. When this is exhausted, or dried up, the tribe removes, and some of the sheep and goats are killed and eaten. The skins of these are taken off with particular care. The head is first removed, and while the body is yet warm, the hand is introduced beneath the skin of the neck, and worked round until the two forefeet are drawn out. The skin is then stripped off, so as to be without any cut on it, and thus forms a sort of bag, which is used to carry water or other liquid.†

The dress of the Arab men is nothing more than a blanket or shawl which is folded around them. The thick strong ones are called Lixsa, the thin ones Haïck. The turban is worn by those called Sidi, who are generally elderly people;‡ and also by the chief men of the tribe, either old or young.

The women wear the same kind of blanket, the corners being fixed over the shoulders by silver clasps, and secured by a belt round the middle. They have generally blue linen on the head. The women of the wandering tribes do not use veils. Their persons are slender, and the old ones are much wrinkled.

The Arab marriage among these wandering tribes is not attended with any particular forms. A man inclined to take the daughter of his neighbour to wife, applies to her father, and generally gives him a number of camels. The number of these may amount perhaps to ten. This concludes the match, and the girl lives with her husband. Scott thinks that the parties may separate at the pleasure of either; and a man may have

---

* Is this river the Niger?
† This practice appears to be extremely ancient. The present Spaniards adopt it, probably from their Moorish conquerors, and in such bags wine is carried from one place to another through the whole peninsula.
‡ Are they not the descendants of the family of Mahommed?

as many wives as he chuses to maintain. Both boys and girls are much fairer than when the skin has been exposed to the weather in advanced life. The sexes come quickly to maturity, and girls are sometimes married at ten and twelve years of age.

The funeral of these Arabs is not attended with any particular ceremony. The body is washed, and placed in the ground, on the same day that the person dies, and bushes and stones are placed over the grave, to preserve it from wild beasts.

Children are taught to write with black ink, formed of charcoal and milk, and applied to a smooth board, with a split cane or reed, by way of a pen.*

In ten or twelve days after the arrival of the tribe in El Ghiblah they went on a plundering expedition, taking Scott along with them. Their arms were muskets, and a weapon of

---

* Scott was so taught; but from specimens of his skill which he has exhibited, he does not appear to have derived much advantage from his instructors. His proficiency does not now reach to the formation of all the characters of the Arabian alphabet. He can, however, write several of the letters, and repeat the names of the rest; but his attempts at writing show him to be by no means an expert penman. He, however, probably speaks the dialect of El Ghiblah, which is said to be a corrupt Arabic, with fluency. The following list of a few names of things is noted down, as nearly as the ear can collect the sounds from his mode of pronouncing the words. There, as in the other proper names introduced into this narrative, *ch* is strongly guttural, the simple vowels have the sound of the Italian vowe's, the final *e* is pronounced, and the accents are introduced to convey an idea of Scott's pronunciation.

Sun,	Simse.	Oil-Tree,	She-dàfer-grèen.
Moon,	Gammátr.	Oil,	Zàt.
Stars,	Injour.	Fig-Tree.	Kara-móos.
North,	Till.	Prickly-pear,	Teckanáret.
East,	Sharrag.	Chinny or Archil,	Tomkilet.
South,	Ghiblah.	Dog,	Kelb.
West,	Sáchal.	Fox,	Vil or Thib.
Valley which has		Wolf,	Zubàh or Athhá-
a stream or river			bàh.
in it,	Wad.	Tiger,	Gurrzahe˜e.
Gum-Tree,	Tolch.	Lion,	Sebáh.
Male Camel,	Ishmaël.	He-Goat,	Artroos.
Female Camel,	Annâg.	She-Goat,	Liang.
Young Camel,	Achwâr.	Ram,	Kabsh.
Goat,	Màz.	House,	Dàr.
Sheep,	Nàzshe.	Water,	Illimah.
Deer,	Rosèlléd.	Elephant,	El Hàzsh.
Fish,	Seheut.	Moving Sand form-	
Christian or Infidel,	Kaffre.	ing hills,	Loggrhàd.
Christian,	Nazerenne.	Rocky Mountains,	Kuddeah.
Christian Boy,	Inferanne.	Tree,	Sadrhu.
Ship,	Saffina.	Date-Tree,	Unghól.
Boat,	Zourgos.	Date,	Attomór.
A Man,	Ærak aròzshel.	Gold,	Edhéb.
A Woman,	Ærak heilemaráh.	Moorish Soldiers,	Umhal ta Sultàn.
Cow,	Bagg˜ve or libgher.	Ostriches,	Nàm.

the sabre shape, not so long, but as broad as a sword, which had a sheath and handle of brass. The chief of the tribe had a brace of pistols, and a sword, which had belonged to the Montezuma. In three days they reached the tents they wished to plunder, and meant to attack them in the night; but the dogs gave the alarm and prevented the surprise, and the two tribes fought in the morning. Scott's companions beat the other party, killed several of them, took their camels, and burnt their tents; but in five days afterwards they were attacked and beaten by their adversaries, obliged to fly, leaving all their property behind them, and took refuge in the Wad Seyghi, close to the sea-shore. There they remained two months, and were at one time almost starved for want of food; at which time, Scott says he was of essential service to them; for the Arabs have so great a dislike to salt-water that they will not wet their feet with it if they can avoid it; and, should this happen through necessity, they take the earliest opportunity of washing their feet with fresh water; but fish being now their only resource, Scott was lowered down from high rocks to the beach, where he collected muscles and fishes for them.

At length they departed from Wad Seyghi, got a fresh supply of arms, and went in search of their old enemies, whom they found and attacked in fourteen days, but were resisted. In this action Scott was placed near his master, who threatened to kill him if he did not fire his piece, (having on a former occasion omitted to do so.) The head man of the enemy came towards Scott's master, who drew a pistol and shot him. Another, in the mean time, advanced on Scott, who was ordered by his master to fire, which he did, and the man fell from his horse. The rest of the party were soon beaten and dispersed. It was on this occasion given out that Scott had killed the chief of the enemy, which was not true; however, he was considered worthy of a particular name, as having slain an enemy in battle; and, instead of calling him Christian or Alewk, (their mode of pronouncing the abbreviation of his name, which he had told them,) he was afterwards styled "Mahommed the Christian."

On another occasion, three Arabs were sent with Scott on a plundering expedition. On arriving at the enemy's tents, they waited till about day-break, meaning to steal what they wanted; but on approaching, a dog barked, and they fled, but were pursued and taken prisoners by some of that tribe, who carried them to their tents, deprived them of their arms, and detained them three days, threatening to murder Scott. In the middle of the third night, one of Scott's companions looked out of the tent where they were confined, and perceived the guards asleep.

Accordingly, they endeavoured to make their escape; and leaving the tent, saw five men with guns, all fast asleep : they took the arms and slew the men ; seized twenty-seven camels, and made off, but were pursued and overtaken, when one of Scott's companions was killed, another wounded, and he with the other escaped with difficulty. After wandering five days without any provision but what herbs they could find, on the sixth they reached their own tents.

Soon after this last adventure, Scott having, while watering his sheep at the wells by the sea-shore, seen a brig at sea, conceived the idea of making his escape, and ran away : he took shelter for the night in a cove among the rocks, which, from some foot marks at the entrance, he supposed might be the den of some wild beast.* He was, however, traced by the prints of his footsteps, and retaken by the Arabs, who severely bastinadoed him on the soles of the feet, which they struck with a hot iron rod, so that it was two or three months before he recovered from the effects of this punishment.†

From this period until his final escape, he was kept with the tribe, wandering from place to place, to procure food for their cattle; often attacking the neighbouring tribes, and being frequently attacked by them, sometimes beaten and plundered, at other times victorious, and robbing their enemies. In the latter end of July, or beginning of August, 1816, the tribe encamped in a place called Lah Thinn, a little to the southward of the wad called Ourerah, in the district of Till ; Scott was, as usual, tending the sheep and goats, accompanied by his master's daughter. It happened that they both fell asleep. In the mean time a "wolf" came, killed three sheep, and dispersed the rest of the flock, so that when Scott and his companion awoke, the dead sheep were those only in sight.

Fear of the punishment which this negligence would certainly draw down on him, seconded his resolution to attempt an escape. He desired the girl to go and look for the sheep in one direction, while he searched for them in another. He instantly fled towards the sea-shore, along which he travelled for four days and nights in a northerly direction.

During this time his only sustenance was a little fresh water.

---

* It is probable that the dread of being overtaken by the Arabs overcame every other fear ; but Scott attributes his resolution, in part at least, to a belief that some gunpowder which he had about him was a sufficient protection, even against a lion, which is said to have the greatest antipathy to the smell of it.

† Scott has been repeatedly asked whether, on this or any occasion he observed any thing peculiar in the appearance of his wounds, especially whether those on his shins (which were not uncommon,) shewed the bone white; but he says that his wounds were all red, though many of those on his shins were severe : all healed easily.

Early on the fifth day, he saw to the eastward a great smoke and some high mountains: he made the best of his way towards the smoke, and when in a hollow, near some houses built of stone, whence the smoke proceeded, he was met by a Moor, who pointed his gun at Scott, and desired him to throw away his knife, and take off his clothes. "On his refusal the man threatened to shoot him, when Scott said he might fire if he chose." Hearing himself addressed in the Arab tongue, the man put aside his musket, and asked Scott who he was. His question was briefly answered, when the Moor advancing, took Scott by the hand, told him he was safe, led him to his house, and gave him food.

He afterwards desired Scott to write to the English consul at Mogador; and Scott did so. This man, leaving Scott under the care of his brother and his son, set off with the letter; and after an absence of eight days, returned with a letter from William Willshire, Esq. the English consul at Mogador,* who sent a horse for Scott to ride upon, and 27 dollars to buy provisions.

After recruiting himself for three days longer, Scott, accompanied by the Moor, set off, and arrived safe at Mogador in five days, during which they travelled at the rate of at least thirty miles per day.

As the place where Scott encountered the Moor is not above a mile and a half from Wadnoon, that place may be considered as about 150 miles from Mogador. Near the Moor's house was a river as large as canals usually are in England. This river flows through the town of Wadnoon, and is fresh until it meets the tide from the sea.

From the neighbourhood of Wadnoon, Scott saw to the eastward mountains whose tops were covered with snow, which he was told remained on them all the year round.†

At Mogador and at Wadnoon, the language spoken is called (by Scott) Schlech. He received every kind attention from Mr. Willshire, during his stay at Mogador, who paid his ransom to the Moor, on account of the Ironmongers' Company of London. Scott reached Mogador on the 31st August, left it on the 11th of November, in the brig Isabella of Aberdeen, captain James Cummings, and got to London on the 9th of December, 1816.

---

* The humane attention of this amiable gentleman is gratefully acknowledged by Scott, Riley, and other unfortunates; and the willingness with which the Moor entered into Scott's restoration to freedom, is the best proof of the fidelity with which the important office of redeeming Christians from slavery, is executed by the representative of Britain at Mogador.

† The ridge of Atlas.

APPENDIX.

I.—*Observations on the Geography of Mr.* Scott's *Routes in North Africa.* By Major Rennell, F. R. S. &c. &c.

The geographical notices contained in this narrative are scanty, but appear to contain internal evidence of their truth. The most important part of them relate to the nature of the Sahara, in the place where the traveller crossed it; that is in its widest part; and which no other European, that I know of, has hitherto given an account of. We have been accustomed to regard the Sahara as having a continuous surface of loose sand, of forty to fifty caravan journeys across; but here it appears that nearly two-thirds of it have a much firmer surface than sand: and valleys occur in which large trees are growing. However, no grass, nor any drinkable water, is found there (on the surface at least), the soil being highly impregnated with salt, which is, indeed, the common character of the northern belt of Africa.

The place where the *Montezuma* was wrecked can only be approximated, and that by an inquiry which may appear tedious to ordinary readers. But it happens that the place of the wreck is the only point of departure that can be referred to in the arrangement of the position, from whence the route across the Great Desert or Sahara sets out. Scott himself only says generally, that the ship was wrecked between the Capes of Nun (or Noon) and Bojador, and within the province or district of Sachal. This is one of four contiguous provinces in this quarter, whose positions are described in the narrative: it is included between Till on the north, and El Ghiblah on the south; all the three extending along the coast of Africa to the southward of Morocco, and having a small portion or tongue belonging to the fourth province named Zerrohah (which lies inland), intervening so as to form a common boundary between Till and Sachal. This narrow portion of Zerrohah consists of a wad or valley, which has a streamlet of water in it, and serves as a communication between the body of the province itself and the sea-coast. It is named from the province to which it belongs, the wad or valley of Zerrohah.

The shipwreck took place at eight or nine hours' camel travelling (or about twenty English miles) from this valley; and to the southward of it, of course, because the shipwreck happened on the coast of Sachal, of which the valley itself has been described to be the northern boundary.

The province of Till is known to extend northward to the neighbourhood of Nun (a cape and town well known in African geography); and southward it includes the valley of Ourerah, often mentioned in the course of the narrative, and from whence Scott finally escaped to Nun, after four days and nights' travelling, and a part of the fifth day; and probably as fast as he could go. Allowing, then, that he went in direct distance 100 to 110 geographical miles in a direct line, this will place Ourerah at that distance to the south-west of Nun, and directly opposite to Fortaventura, the nearest of the Canary Islands to the mainland of Africa, and a little to the northward of Cape Juby.* How far the province of Till may extend to the south of Ourerah is not known, but probably not far, as so large a part of it lies beyond Ourerah to the north-east; as also from the circumstance of the general trending of the coast in that quarter, as it bore on the supposed cause of the shipwreck. For this was doubtless the operation of a south-easterly current on the ship, which had carried her gradually, though imperceptibly, towards the land, all the way from the parallel of Cape Finisterre.† As her course would naturally be south-westward, that part of the coast which trends to the westward, was more likely to have arrested the ship's progress than that which has a southerly direction; and this change of position takes place not far from Cape Juby. It seems probable, therefore, that the ship was stranded thereabouts (and, indeed, most of the shipwrecks happen in this quarter). Had the ship been farther to the south, its course would have carried it parallel to the coast, and within sight of land, during the preceding day; whereas it was probably to the north of Cape Juby, during that day, where the land retires far back to the eastward, and out of sight.

Thus, we are induced to look for the place of shipwreck, and in consequence for the valley of Zerrohah, in the quarter of Cape Juby; and which opinion receives strength from the circumstance of Ourerah being in the vicinity of Cape Juby.

By the narrative it would appear, that seventeen days were employed between the place of the wreck and El Ghiblah, an encampment not far from the sea-coast, in the province of the same name, and stated to be the southmost of the four provinces occupied by the wandering Arabs, with whom our traveller had communication. If this journey of seventeen days is calculated on the ordinary rate of caravan travelling, 250 or 260 geographical miles in a straight line may be allowed; and these will reach to the river Del Ouro of the Portuguese. If fifteen instead of seventeen days, be the true reading (as it appears doubtful in the MS.), thirty miles should be deducted, and the camp of El Ghiblah placed so much farther to the northward. But this will scarcely affect the general line of the route across the Great Desert. Caravan rate is here taken, because the party was so small; it consisting only of one family, attended by three camels; whereas the journey across the Desert was performed by a large party, with 2500 animals of different kinds, and, moreover, was continued more than six times as long. The time employed in this journey is roundly given in months, with the exception of three intervals of eleven, five, and two days; of course no accuracy is attainable. Most probably the new moons regulated his time; but, after all, the memory was to be trusted, and it would be unreasonable to expect a more consistent result than the one about to be reported. The total number of days may be taken at 106, unless the three

---

* It may be that the *Arca* of M. Delisle is meant for *Ourerah*.
† See the remarks on this current in the following Article.

days' halt in the wood, are to be included in the gross number of days given for the march.*

Considering that the party was composed of 115 to 120 persons, men, women, and children (Patriarch fashion), and that the latter classes did not always ride; moreover, that there were about a thousand goats (besides as many sheep, and 500 or 600 camels), which goats could only keep up with the camels when they had sufficient food; that camels travel only at the rate of $2\frac{1}{2}$ English miles per hour ; it is probable that 2 or $2\frac{1}{4}$ might be the rate of march, since the slowest goers must of necessity regulate it.† It must also be taken into the account that nearly two-thirds of the way was not sandy, and therefore not so well suited to the feet of the camels, a great number of whom were loaded. No halts are spoken of (except the three in the wood, on an extraordinary occasion) ; and it appears probable that their daily marches were so short, as to enable them to persevere, without incurring such a degree of fatigue as would induce the necessity of frequent halts.

Perhaps, then, their rate was below that of great armies, which has been calculated at a mean, on marches of long continuance, at about $14\frac{1}{2}$ British miles on ordinary roads ; and when reduced to direct distance and geographic miles, at about $10\frac{1}{2}$ each day. Perhaps, in this case, 10 may be amply sufficient.

This report of the general direction of the line of the route, cannot be expected to be more accurate than that of the distance, perhaps less so. The sun, however, would furnish him with a good mark. mornings and evenings, if he made allowance for its great declination at that season ; for it was about the month of June when they set out. At their outset, it is said that their route was a little to the southward of east, and gradually inclined more to the south as they advanced, which is as clear as could be expected. If, then, we suppose a curve of this kind, it will terminate in the direction of the Lake Dibbie of Mr. Park, and will not even err very widely in point of distance, considering that the geographical construction on both sides is made up of calculations on very extended lines of distance ; for the place of the Dibbie Lake rests on its proportion of the distance, reported to Mr. Park, between his lowest stations on the Niger and Tombuctoo ; whilst this latter is placed by the meeting of lines of distance from Morocco, Tunis, and Tripoli ; but which did not differ much in point of parallel from that given by bearings pointed out to him during his route eastward.

On the map,‡ then, about 1000 geographical miles may be measured on the curvilinear route across the Desert, between the encampment in El Ghiblah and the Lake Dibbie, whilst the 106 days at ten, give 1060, or sixty more than the map. It would be useless to reason on the ground of such data ; for there seems, from the names and general positions of the Lakes respectively described by Mr. Park and Mr. Scott, no reason

---

* The time given for their journey back, does not materially differ from the other ; it being, as well as the loose manner in which it is given (and probably could only be given) only *a few days short of it*. This tends to shorten the surplus distance arising on the calculation which follows.

† The sheep, it appears, travel faster than the goats in that quarter.

‡ See the general map of Africa in Mr. Park's Travels.

to doubt that they are one and the same. The D is often changed to T, and Tieb, or Tec-eb, differs little in root from Dib-bie. The 1000 miles give only nine, and somewhat less than a half, instead of ten, for each day.

The Lake, as described to Mr. Park, is much smaller than the one seen by Scott : but no one will regard the two accounts as of equal authority. Mr. Park says (p. 213), "Concerning the extent of the Lake Dibbie (or the Dark Lake,) all the information I could obtain was, that in crossing it from west to east, the canoes lose sight of land one whole day." On the other hand, Scott reckons the passage across twenty-nine hours, at two miles per hour. However, it is difficult to conceive how a vessel, capable of conveying 200 persons across so wide an expanse of water, could be rowed or paddled by the same six persons, at the rate of two miles per hour ! Probably, instead of 58 miles, 43 may be a sufficient number. It may be concluded that they crossed it from the N.W. to S.E., as Mr. Park's informant told him, that in going towards Tombuctoo, they navigated it from west to east (in effect, in the direction of the general course of the Niger), and consequently in the line of its greatest length ; for river lakes occupying a portion of the valleys or hollows through which the courses of the rivers lie, have their greatest length in those directions. Scott, therefore, may be supposed to have crossed it in the line of its breadth ; and it must consequently be a large lake.

He observed no current in the lake, whilst the vessel lay twice at anchor, but her prow pointed to the eastward, although during calm weather. In a lake of that extent, the current of the river would be dispersed, and, therefore, it is difficult to account for the constant position of the vessel. Possibly there might be a light air of wind, but it escaped his notice. There could be no counter current in the middle of so wide a lake. With respect to the report of the boatmen on the lake, if they could have been supposed to possess any proper knowledge of the future course of the Niger, it would have been worth the attending to. But having the Shilah for their vernacular language, they doubtless came from the northern quarter of Africa, and were not likely to have any knowledge of the subject but from report. The opinion of the North Africans has, in all ages, been in favour of its communication with the Egyptian Nile, which probably arises from an idea that it must necessarily reach the sea somewhere. At the same time it may be remarked, that in the inland parts of Barbary, there are not less than five considerable streams between Morocco and Tunis, which run inland towards the Sahara, and, forming small lakes on its border, are either evaporated or swallowed up by the sands.

In respect of the quality of the soil in the central part of the Sahara, in the line of the before-mentioned route, it may be observed that in the maps there are two tracts of land in the nature of islands or oases, or, at least, marked as being different from the sandy tract. They are named Gualata and Taudeny It may well be, that these parts of the tract described by Scott as being free from sand, and although described to be in a position wide of the route, northward, yet either they may be farther to the south, or the direction of Mr. Scott's route may have been more northerly. As he set out in June, when the sun's northern declination was very great, he may not have allowed for it sufficiently in his estimation of the eastern and western points of the heavens. The watered valley in which they sojourned so long, falls very near the western part of Gualata.

It appears that they returned nearly in the line on which they advanced, until they came near this valley, which was about three-fourths of the whole way. But then they evidently deviated, because they traversed the sandy tract in seven days, which took them eleven in their way out, and also came to a different encampment from the one they had quitted in El Ghiblah.

Remarks on the Currents between the Parallels of Cape Finisterre and the Canary Islands, which may be supposed to have carried the Montezuma out of her course. By Major RENNELL, F.R.S., &c. &c.

I SHOULD consider myself highly culpable if I neglected to state, by way of caution to navigators, the result of my inquiries respecting the current which appear to have caused the shipwreck of the Montezuma, and of a great number of other ships of our own and other nations, on the western coast of Barbary ; having examined a multitude of journals of ships that have sailed in that track, with time-keepers on board, and which have also, when opportunities presented themselves, had their rate checked by celestial observations.

The general result is, that navigators who depart from the parallel of the southern part of the Bay of Biscay (or say 45°), and sail in the usual track southward, will be assailed first by a S.E. current, and then by an easterly one, until they have passed the parallel of Cape Finisterre ; when the current will again turn to the south of east, and gradually become a S.E. current, till having passed Cape St. Vincent, it becomes easterly again ; owing, no doubt, to the indraught of the Strait of Gibraltar ; and this easterly current is pretty general across the mouth of the bay between Cape St. Vincent and Cape Cantin.

Beyond this bay (which may be deemed the funnel, of which the Strait itself is the spout), the current again becomes SE., or rather more southerly, (as it is more easterly towards Cape Finisterre,) and continues as far as the parallel of 25°, and is moreover felt beyond Madeira westward ; that is, at least 130 leagues from the coast of Africa, (beyond which a SW. current takes place, owing doubtless to the operation of the north-east trade-wind.)

The rate of motion of this current varies very considerably at different times, that is, from twelve to twenty or more miles in twenty-four hours. I consider sixteen as rather below the mean rate. I have one example of 140 miles in eight days, in one of his Majesty's ships, equal to 17½ miles per day ; and in another of only twelve. And in a very well kept East India ship's journal, 170 in nine days to Madeira, or nineteen per day. The direction of the stream likewise varies, but commonly more towards the south than the east, after passing the mouth of the Strait.

Near the coasts of Spain and Portugal, commonly called the Wall, the current is always very much southerly, owing perhaps to the falling obliquely on the shore, of the great mass of water brought by the SE. current; which can only run off towards the south, and round Cape St. Vincent towards the Strait's mouth. And amongst the Canary Islands, and between them and the coast of Barbary, the currents are less regular. I have endeavoured to describe this in the sketch.

It may be taken for granted, that the whole surface of that part of the Atlantic Ocean, from the parallel of 30° to 45° at least, and to 100 or 130 leagues off shore, is in motion towards the mouth of the Strait of Gibraltar.

According to what has been said in the course of the above remarks, it must be expected that a ship sailing in the usual track to Madeira or the Canaries, will be carried to the south-eastward at the rate of sixteen miles per day; that is, even if she has a fair wind, she will be carried by the current 150 or 160 miles to the south-eastward, in the course of her voyage to Madeira or the Canaries; and, consequently, on a SE. by S. course will be carried eighty or ninety to the eastward of her intended port. If we suppose a SE. course, the error in easting will be no less than 109; which distance, if they were bound to Teneriff, would carry them to Allegranza or Fortaventura, and if intending to make Allegranza, would place them on shore on the coast of Barbary. The French and Spaniards report, that their ships have often made Allegranza when they supposed themselves on the line towards Teneriff. It must be added, that if a ship had a long passage, the error would be greater in proportion, and might possibly amount to 200 miles of easting.

It would seem advisable, therefore, that every ship going to the Canaries, or intended to sail between those islands and the mainland of Africa, and being without time-keepers, as that class of merchant ships commonly are, should, to every day's reckoning, add ten miles to easting. This would, in the first instance, prevent them from deceiving themselves as they went forward; in like manner, as it is better to set a clock forward at once, than to charge one's memory constantly with its being too slow. Ten miles does not seem too much as a cautionary measure, as a ship has very lately been carried ninety-nine miles to the east in eight days in that track. What would not have been the error, had she had even a moderately long passage?

It is this current which has furnished the roving Arabs of the desert with their victims from every nation, and the good Mr. Willshire with objects of benevolence.

J. RENNELL.

LONDON,
27th February, 1819.

G. SIDNEY, Printer,
Northumberland-street, Strand.

NARRATIVE

OF A

VOYAGE TO INDIA;

OF A

SHIPWRECK

ON BOARD THE LADY CASTLEREAGH;

AND A

DESCRIPTION OF NEW SOUTH WALES.

BY W. B. CRAMP.

LONDON:

PRINTED FOR SIR RICHARD PHILLIPS AND Co.

BRIDE-COURT, BRIDGE-STREET.

1823.

G. SIDNEY, Printer,
Northumberland Street, Strand.

NARRATIVE

OF A

VOYAGE TO INDIA,

&c. &c. &c.

SECTION I.

THE AUTHOR'S DEPARTURE FROM ENGLAND—DESCRIPTION OF THE CEREMONY ON CROSSING THE EQUINOCTIAL LINE, AND HIS ARRIVAL AT MADRAS.

On the 8th or 9th of January, 1815, we proceeded, in the Princess Charlotte, Indiaman, to North-fleet Hope, and received on board our cargo. On February 28th, we sailed to Gravesend, in company with the Company's ships Ceres, Lady Melville, Rose, and Medcalfe, and arrived at the Downs on the 3d of March. Our dispatches not being expected for some time, we moored ship. Our time passed on very pleasantly till the 27th inst., when the weather became rather boisterous, and accompanied by a heavy swell. On the evening of the 28th, as the Hon. Company's ship Tarva, from Bengal, was rounding the Foreland, she struck on the Goodwin Sands, and was forced to cut away her masts to lighten her, and get her clear off. The Ceres drifted almost on board us; we slipped our cables, and with difficulty escaped the Goodwin Sands.

On the 1st of April the pursers joined their respective ships, and on the 3d we made sail with a fair breeze, and soon cleared the English channel. Nothing was now heard but confusion; the pilot having just left the ship, the hoarse voice of the captain resounded through a speaking trumpet, while the seamen were busy in making sail. We had a fine steady breeze till we made the Bay of Biscay, when we had a strong gale for three days.

After the hurry and bustle of the gale was over, we had a fine steady breeze; I then began to feel an inward pleasure, and to rejoice in the predilection I had imbibed from my earliest years.

We arrived on the equinoctial about eight o'clock in the evening of the 19th of April, when one of the oldest seamen is deputed Neptune; when he went into the head and hailed the ship in the usual form, Ship, hoa! ship, hoa! what ship is that? The chief officer replied, The Hon. Company's ship Princess Charlotte of Wales, and that he would be glad of his company on the morrow. Gladly would I have dispensed with it. On his quitting the vessel, as is supposed, a pitch cask was thrown overboard on fire, which had the appearance of a boat till lost to view.

The next morning, about nine A. M., Neptune hailed the ship again, when he was invited on board (from the head). On the fore-part of the gangway and after-part of the long-boat, a boom was placed across, and a tarpauling was hung in form of a curtain, so that when they were in readiness they took it down, and the procession moved on towards the cuddy, twelve of the officers walking in the front, two by two with staves (broomsticks); next followed Neptune's car, (a grating with a chair covered with sheep skins) with Neptune, and his wife and child, (a recruit's child, as we had 250 on board, of his majesty's 46th regiment) Neptune bearing in his hand the granes with forks uppermost, and the representation of a dolphin on the middle prong, and Neptune's footman riding behind (barber) his carriage, dragged by the constables. The captain and officers came out to meet him, and presented him with a glass of gin, which was on this occasion termed wine. After the captain's health was drank, he desired them to proceed to business, and to make as much haste as possible; they then proceeded to the starboard gangway, and Neptune placed himself upon his throne (on the boom, close to the long-boat and wash-deck tub) the slush tub being filled with balls, and lather made of slush, and the barber standing ready to begin his work with a razor made of a long piece of iron hoop well notched; the engine was brought on the quarter deck, and began to play, to force those below that had not crossed the line. I had not been long below before an officer from Neptune came to me, and demanded me, in his name to appear before him at the starboard gang-way, whose summons must not be disobeyed. On my arrival at the gang-way, the usual questions were asked me, whether I had been that way before?" Without waiting for an answer they placed me on the wash-deck tub, and the barber rubbed me with the back of his razor and then let me go, upon my previously having given an order upon my bottle.

I had hardly got upon the poop, when one of the men was brought upon deck who was neither beloved by the men nor officers; they then placed him upon the tub, and asked him several questions, and while he was in the act of answering them, they thrust some black balls into his mouth, and then rubbed his face and neck over with lather, and scraped it in an unmerciful manner till the blood run in several places; they next pushed him into the tub of water and kept him under for the space of a minute, which tended to smart and inflame the wounds. It was at least a fortnight before he could wash himself perfectly clean; but now several more shared the same fate. The sun was setting fast before the amusements of the day were finished. The clouds presented the most beautiful appearance, and the rippling of the sea, together with the flying fish, scudding along the surface of the water, afforded the mariner a great field of thought. At so grand a display of the great and wonderful works of God, what mortal can be unmoved, or deny the existence of a BEING which nature herself proclaims!

The evening was very fine and beautifully star-light, and the moon shone with resplendent brightness. After the company had withdrawn to their evening refreshments, I amused myself with walking on the solitary poop. The sea appeared to be an immense plain, and presented a watery mirror to the skies. The infinite height above the firmament stretched its azure expanse, bespangled with unnumbered stars, and adorned with the moon '*walking in brightness;*' while the transparent surface both received and returned her silver image. Here, instead of being covered with sackcloth,* she shone with resplendent lustre; or rather with a lustre multiplied in proportion to the number of beholders.

Such I think is the effect of exemplary behaviour in persons of exalted rank; their course as it is nobly distinguished, so it will be happily influential; others will catch the diffusive rays, and be ambitious to resemble a pattern so commanding. Their amiable qualities will not terminate in themselves, but we shall see them reflected in their families.

---

* I must be excused for the ideal extravagance of "clothing" this nocturnal luminary in "SACKCLOTH," on adverting to that unlimited flight of poetic imagination, which speaks of "*Heaven peeping through the blanket of the deep. Vide Shakspeare's Macbeth.*

My readers, I trust, will not wonder at my meditations on these sublunary objects, when they consider that they are the seaman's guide, and from them the greatest sources of nautical information are derived.

In the midst of these pleasing reveries, I was aroused by the ship being taken a-back, the watch being completely intoxicated, and it was only with difficulty that they could do their duty. Nothing material happened till our arrival at the Cape, when we experienced a severe gale for three days. The sea being heavy, she pitched her portals under water. We were running at the rate of ten knots per hour, under bare poles; and we soon after made the trade winds.

On the 23d of June we arrived in Madras roads; from the deck the view of the land has a magnificent appearance; the different offices have, to the beholder, the appearance of stone, and they are formed along the beach in a beautiful manner; they are built with piazzas and verandahs, and they extend about one mile along a sandy beach, while the natives parading along the shore, and the surf spraying upon the beach, gave the scene a very picturesque appearance. The surf beats here with so much violence that it is impossible for any ship's boats to land without being dashed to pieces.

On our making land we espied a small craft, called a katta-maran, making towards us; it was manned with two of the natives naked, except a handkerchief round their waist, and a straw round cap (turban) made with a partition in it to keep letters dry. This bark is made of three long hulls of trees, about ten or twelve feet in length, tied together with a rope so as to make in the centre a little hollow; they sit upon their knees in the centre, and have a long flat piece of wood, about five feet in length and five inches in width, which they hold in the centre, and keep continually in motion, first on one side and then on the other, and in that manner they force the katta-maran swiftly through the water.

It is very remarkable that these poor creatures risk themselves through the surf for a mere trifle, to carry letters for the different commanders to their respective vessels, at a time when the surf is at a dreadful height. When these poor fellows lay themselves flat on the kattamaran, and then trust themselves to the mercy of the surf, they are often driven back with great force, and they as often venture again, till they effect their purpose. They generally get their living by fishing, which is done by hook and line, and they offer them alongside the different ships for sale.

For two days the surf being so violent no boats could come off; but early on the third morning there were several came off

with debashees (merchants) on board.   They brought such
things as might be wanted by the ship's company and officers.
Their boats are made to carry passengers and cargo.   There is
not a vestige of a nail to be seen in them, their seams, instead
of being nailed, are sewed together with coir rope ; and they
are generally manned with six or eight men.

SECTION II.

THE AUTHOR'S DEPARTURE FROM MADRAS AND ARRIVAL AT
    BENGAL----DEPARTURE THEREFROM----HIS VESSEL RUNS
    ASHORE ON THE PULICAT SHOALS, AND GETS SAFE AFLOAT
    AGAIN, AFTER BEATING SIX HOURS AND FORTY MINUTES---
    HIS SAFE ARRIVAL AT MADRAS, AND DESCRIPTION OF THE
    DIVERS---ARRIVAL AT BOMBAY---THE SHIP BEING DOCKED,
    THE AUTHOR IS SENT TO BUTCHER'S ISLAND WITH THE SHIP'S
    COMPANY---A DESCRIPTION OF THE ISLAND OF ELEPHANTA·--
    HIS JOINING THE SHIP AFTER HER LEAVING THE DOCK---HIS
    WORDS WITH HIS COMMANDER, AND BEING TURNED BEFORE
    THE MAST IN CONSEQUENCE---HIS DEPARTURE FROM BOM-
    BAY, AND AFTER A SHORT PERIOD HE IS REPLACED IN HIS
    FORMER SITUATION---AND ARRIVES AT MADRAS.

WE sailed from Madras, August 23d, and arrived at Bengal on the 30th.   The scenery on the entrance up the river
was indeed sublime, and inspired us with a sensation of gratitude to the Giver of all good.   I went up to Calcutta with a
craft of cargo ; but having been sent down immediately, I
could form no idea of the place.
    On the 20th December we sailed from Bengal bound to
Madras, in company with the Honourable Company's ship
Marquis of Wellington.   We kept a-head of her on the morning of the 25th, till she was almost mast down, and expected
to bring-to about twelve o'clock in the Madras roads; but
our expectations were greatly damped by the following circumstances :---At 8 A. M. the ship struck on the Pulicat rocks
with such great violence, as to knock almost every man off
his legs ; the lead was immediately called, which, to the disgrace of some one, was not on deck ; in the course of two
minutes she struck again with as much violence as before;
sail was immediately taken in, and after sounding, we found
we drew about three and a half feet water.   We then made
signal of distress, by hoisting the ensign union downwards,

and firing a gun. The Marquis of Wellington by this time hove in sight; all was confusion and consternation, the ship having beat several times with great violence. The Wellington hove to, and sent their cutter with four men and a second mate to our assistance, and then made sail and passed us, without rendering us any other assistance. The pinnace and long-boats, booms and spars, were immediately sent over the side, and the kedge-anchor was placed in the long-boat; but she leaked so very fast, that with all the united efforts of the seamen they could not keep her above water.

The weather was now very cloudy and black, and threatened a severe gale; so that our present situation became very disagreeable, as no assistance could be rendered us off shore, should necessity require it. But owing to the exertions of the officers and men, we effectually swung her head to the wind, which was blowing strong from the shore, and by 7 P. M. we anchored safe in the roads.

On the following morning we were busily employed in discharging our cargo and sending it on board its destined ships, (Honourable Company's ships Stratham and Rose.) After our clearance, the divers were expected from off shore, to examine the damage the ship's bottom had received; but, owing to the inclemency of the weather, it was impossible for them to get off from shore.

A seaman on board, by birth a West Indian, engaged to dive under the ship's bottom, and to acquaint us with the state of it, which was gladly accepted. In his youth he had been a fisherman on the coast of the island of Jamaica; the weather being rough, it was thought unsafe for him to venture; but on the following morning, it being quite calm, he prepared himself for his expedition: after he had jumped overboard, he walked, or rather trod water, round the ship; he informed us the copper was much battered above water, and in many places whole sheets of it were broken off; and after he had made us perfectly acquainted with the damages we had received above, he dived under her counter, and abreast of the after, main, and fore hatchways;—when he came on board, he informed us, that about twelve feet of our false-keel was knocked off, and about six feet of our copper abreast of the main-hatchway, besides a quantity of copper in different places, all of which we found to be true after we were docked.

We received considerable damage on board; the bolts were started from her side about three inches, and the main-beams sprung. Three days after he had dived, the captain came on board with two native divers, and several officers of the different vessels lying in the roads, to survey the ship

When they went under they brought up the same account as our man had first given. After about an hour's consultation, our ship was ordered to Bombay to be docked, it being the most convenient one for a ship of our burden. In a few days after we proceeded on our passage, and arrived in safety, keeping the pumps in continual motion during our passage.

The Island of Bombay is situated on the west coast of the ocean, and one of the three Presidencies belonging to the Honourable East India Company, and is in Lat. 18° 55′ N. and Lon. 72° 54′ E. of Greenwich. As soon as we had discharged all our cargo, and the ship was docked, the ship's company and officers were sent to Butcher's Island.

Butcher's Island is a small island situated about four miles and a half to the westward of Bombay, and is in circumference about one mile and a half, and has been a very formidable garrison. In the centre is a small fort and two barracks, the latter we took possession of for the ship's company. Soon after our landing on the island, a party of us went over to the Island of Elephanta.

The Island of *Elephanta* is about one mile and a half to the west of Butcher's Island, and is inhabited by 100 poor Indian families. It contains one of the most stupendous antiquities in the world : the figure of an elephant of the natural size, cut coarsely in black stone, appears in an open plain, near the landing place, from which an easy slope leads to an immense subterraneous cavern, hewn out of the solid rock, eighty or ninety feet long and forty broad, the roof of which is cut flat, and supported by regular rows of pillars, about ten feet high, with capitals resembling round cushions, and at the farther end of it are three gigantic figures, mutilated by the bigoted zeal of the Portuguese, when this island was in their possession. After spending the day very pleasantly we returned.

The serjeant (an old invalid) who had charge of the fort, had a beautiful little garden; thither in the morning I frequently resorted, to enjoy one of the most charming pieces of morning scenery that I had ever witnessed.

> " Awake ! the morning shines, and the fresh fields
> " Call you ; ye lose the prime to mark how spring
> " The tender plants ; how blows the citron grove ;
> " What drops the myrrh, and what the balmy reed ;
> " How nature paints her colours ; how the bee
> " Sits on the bloom, extracting liquid sweets."
> MILTON'S PARADISE LOST.

How delightful this fragrance. It is distributed in the nicest proportion; neither so strong as to depress the organs, nor so faint as to elude them.   We are soon cloyed at a sumptuous banquet, but this pleasure never loses its poignancy, never palls the appetite; here luxury itself is innocent; or rather, in this case, indulgence is not capable of excess.   Our amusements for the forenoon were our nautical studies, and in the afternoon officers and men joined in cricket. In the evening, after my duty of the day was dispatched, and the sultry heats were abated, I enjoyed the recreation of a walk in one of the finest recesses of the Island, and in one of the pleasantest evenings which the season produced.

The trees uniting their branches over my head, formed a verdant canopy, and cast a most refreshing shade; under my feet lay a carpet of Nature's velvet; grass intermingled with moss, and embroidered with the evening dew; jessamines, united with woodbines, twined around the trees, displaying their artless beauties to the eye, and diffusing their delicious sweets through the air. On either side, the boughs rounding into a set of regular arches, opened a view into the distant seas, and presented a prospect of the convex heavens.   The little birds all joyous and grateful for the favours of the light, were paying their acknowledgments in a tribute of harmony, and soothing themselves to rest with songs.   All these beauties of Nature were for a while withdrawn.   The stars served to alleviate the frown of night, rather than to recover the objects from their obscurity.   A faint ray scarcely reflected, and only gave the straining eye a very imperfect glimpse.

The day following that the ship came out of dock we joined her.   Our labours were now unremitted, to get her in readiness for sea.   Amidst all our exertions it was impossible to give any satisfaction; our chief mate was very arbitrary, and vented his spleen upon the defenceless midshipmen, besides making the backs of the poor seamen sore with *starting*. Starting is a term used for rope's-ending a man, or otherwise laying a *Point* severely across their shoulders till they have not the strength to wield it any longer; a point is a flat platted rope, made for the purpose of taking in reefs, or otherwise to fasten the sail upon the yards.

At length my life became so truly miserable, that I was determined in my own mind not to endure it, if there was any possibility of avoiding it. For that purpose I wrote on board his Majesty's frigate, Revolutionnaire, for a situation, when Captain Wolcombe generously offered me one, provided I could get permission of Captain Craig to leave my present ship.   I was at length forced to leave Bombay, through this and other circumstances.

On our arrival at Madras every preparation was made for receiving our cargo on board, which was speedily done, and in a short time was ready for sea.

SECTION III.

THE AUTHOR'S DEPARTURE FROM MADRAS, DESCRIPTION OF A WATER-SPOUT—HIS ARRIVAL AT ST. HELENA AND DEPARTURE THEREFROM, ARRIVAL IN ENGLAND—JOINS HIS MAJESTY'S TRANSPORT SHIP, TOTTENHAM, BOUND FOR NEW SOUTH WALES—HER RUNNING ON SHORE IN THE RIVER AND PUTTING BACK TO DOCK—HE AFTERWARDS JOINS HIS MAJESTY'S TRANSPORT SHIP, LADY CASTLEREAGH. HIS DEPARTURE FROM DEPTFORD AND ARRIVAL AT PORTSMOUTH—HIS DEPARTURE THEREFROM AND ARRIVAL AT NEW SOUTH WALES.

As soon as our dispatches were in readiness, we proceeded on our passage for England; the morning was beautiful, and as the men were heaving up the anchor, my heart felt an inward sensation of joy and gratitude to our Creator, that he had been pleased to bring us so far safe on our voyage; we made sail with a steady breeze, and soon lost sight of land. After we had been at sea about two days, close on our weather-bow we observed a water-spout; when we first saw it, it was whole and entire, and was in shape like a speaking trumpet, the small end downwards, and reaching to the sea, and the large end terminating in a black thick cloud: the spout itself was very black, and the more so the higher up; it seemed to be exactly perpendicular to the horizon, and its sides perfectly smooth, without the least ruggedness where it fell. The spray of the sea rose to a considerable height, which had somewhat the appearance of smoke; from the first time we saw it, it continued whole about a minute, and till it was quite dissipated three minutes; it began to waste from below, and gradually up, while the upper part remained entire, without any visible alteration, till at last it ended in black clouds, upon which a heavy rain fell in the neighbourhood. There was but little wind, and the sky was otherwise serene.

On our rounding the Cape we experienced a very heavy gale, which continued for the space of ten days. We arrived at St. Helena in about ten days after clearing the Cape of Good Hope.

The approach to this Island is tremendous, it being an immense large rock in the midst of the sea, on which there is not the least appearance of verdure, houses, or indeed any sign of inhabitants, till you arrive at the anchorage, which is to leeward of the Island; and in turning round the corner of the rock is a fort, close to the water's edge, from whence they make all ship's heave to, till they have sent a boat on board from the Admiral; and in case no attention is paid to their signal, they fire a shot. After proceeding a little way, the town is discovered in the midst of a valley, and has a very picturesque appearance.

The produce of the Island is potatoes and yams. The yams are used in time of great scarcity of wheat, for bread; the inhabitants are under the necessity of boiling them 12 hours and baking them, before they can eat them; and in fact, many of the Islanders prefer them to bread. The coast produces an amazing quantity of fish, particularly mackarel, which are in great abundance, and run in shoals about six fathom under water. At this time Napoleon resided at Longwood.

After staying here 12 days, we proceeded on our passage to England, and arrived there in six weeks and two days.— The distressed state of England, and scarcity of employment determined me again to try my fortune abroad, and for that purpose I made several applications to the different owners, but for some time was very unsuccessful. At length I was engaged by Messrs. Robinson, to join his Majesty's Ship Tottenham, bound to New South Wales with 200 convicts. On June the 8th I joined her. After receiving all the ship's and government stores on board, we proceeded to Woolwich, and received on board 50 of our number, and in the afternoon of the same day we made sail, and on a sudden struck on a reef at low water; we were lying high and dry; every means was used to get her off, but without success, till we sent our convicts up to the hulks, and discharged our stores into the different crafts sent for that purpose, and by that means lightened her so, that at the flood she drifted; she was so materially damaged, it was deemed necessary she should return back to Deptford to Dock.

I had not waited long in London, before another vacancy occurred on board His Majesty's Transport Ship Lady Castlereagh, lying at Deptford, bound to the same Port. Shortly after I had joined her, we sailed to Woolwich, and received on board our guard, which was composed of a detachment of his Majesty's 46th regiment of foot, and after receiving a portion of our convicts, we proceeded on our passage to Portsmouth : we received another portion from Sheerness, and in two days arrived at Portsmouth. The remainder of our prisoners not being in readiness, we were forced to bring up and moor ship a cable each way.

Spithead is a spacious road for shipping, between Portsmouth and the Isle of Wight, and where they in general lie after they are in readiness for sea. I went on shore to see the town of Portsmouth. It is situated inland of Portsea ; the streets are generally narrow, and rather dirty, owing to their not being properly paved.

The Dock-yards, as there are several, resemble distinct towns, and are under a government separate from the garrison. Here is a commodious arsenal for laying up cannon, and the fortress may be justly considered as the most regular one in Great Britain. The number of men employed in the different rope-yards generally is considered to be between eight or nine hundred, and the garrison is very large. The town of Portsmouth contains about 40,000 inhabitants, and the harbour is reckoned one of the finest in the world, as there is water sufficient for the largest ships, and is so very capacious that the whole of the British navy may ride in safety. The principal branch run up to Fareham, a second to Pouchester and a third to Portsea Bridge ; besides these channels there are several rithes, or channels, where the small men of war lie at their moorings. Opposite the town is the spacious road of Spithead. On the 20th of December we received our convicts, and the following day we made sail and passed through the Needles, which are two sharp-pointed rocks at the N. W. end of the Isle of Wight, so called from their sharp extremities.

The prisoners, during their voyage, behaved themselves with great propriety, considering the variety of characters which we had on board. We arrived at New South Wales on the 26th of April, 1818, after a pleasant passage.

SECTION IV.

DESCRIPTION OF NEW SOUTH WALES—DEPARTURE THEREFROM
—ARRIVAL AT VAN DIEMAN'S LAND.

WE now made for the eastern coast of New Holland, southward of Port Jackson; the coast has a most beautiful appearance, being constantly green during the year. From the south
cape, about five leagues to the northward, is a most spacious
bay with good anchorage, and sheltered from all winds. The
natives are very ferocious; few vessels put in without partially
suffering by their depredations, particularly seamen who,
having ventured from their parties, have been by them cut off,
robbed, and murdered. This place is called Two-fold Bay;
ten leagues farther north is Bateman's Bay. Here is good
anchorage and plenty of fresh water, but it lies open to the
E. N. E. winds, and when they prevail they are accompanied
by a heavy swell, so that it is impossible for vessels to lie secure. Seventeen leagues farther north is Jervis's Bay, and an
excellent harbour and good shelter from all winds, with a fine
sandy bottom. Round two small islands, at the mouth of the
bay, there are two very large kinds of fish, which are caught in
abundance with hook and line, called king fish and snap-
pers.

The next harbour to the northward is Botany Bay, which is a
capacious bay, with excellent anchorage for shipping; but
the entrance is very dangerous to those commanders who are
strangers to the coast. At the head of the bay is George's River,
which extends about sixty miles up the country, and is navigable for small vessels of about 40 tons burden; on the banks of
this river there are several settlements, which I shall hereafter' describe. Nine miles farther north are the heads of
Port Jackson; on approaching the heads from sea, the entrance
is so narrow, and the rocks so perpendicular, that the opening
is not perceivable at a distance.

On the south head is a look-out house, and a flag staff, on
which a yellow flag is hoisted on the approach of any vessels
from sea, which is answered by another signal staff on a battery at the north end of the town, alled Davis's Point Battery,

which is to be seen from all parts of the town, so that a vessel is known to be approaching before she enters the port. After entering the heads, the river runs due south for six miles, it then turns short round a point of land on the north shore, called Bradley's Head, which runs due west for twenty-four miles. After rounding Bradley's Head, the town of Sydney is perceivable, about three miles distant on the south shore. The anchorage is a small cove, as still as a mill-pond, land-locked around on all sides ; the principal buildings in view are the stores and dwelling of Mr. Campbell, a Bengal merchant ; they are built of white stone and have a noble appearance : the next is the government stores, a large stone building, at the end of which is the hospital, wharf, and stairs, the only public-landing place in the cove ; here are two centinels continually parading the quay. From the landing place is a fine wide street, called George Street, with several fine stone and brick buildings, extending a mile and a half long, and joining the race ground. The public buildings in this line are the governor's secretary's office, an orphan school for female children, and the military barracks, with many fine private buildings, shops, &c. On the S. E. side of the cove is the government house, a low but very extensive building, surrounded with verandahs, and built in the eastern style, with an extensive park and garden surrounded with a high stone wall. About a quarter of a mile south of the government house is the general hospital, a large and extensive building, erected without any expense to government, the whole having been completed and paid for by three private gentlemen of the colony, for the grant of certain privileges. One mile further S. E. is Wallamolla, a fine brick and stone mansion, the property and dwelling house of John Palmer, Esq., formerly Commandant-general of the colony.

Between the general hospital and Wallamolla is the race ground, a fine level course three miles long, planned and laid out after the model of Doncaster race course, by order of his excellency Lochlin Macquarie. The races commence on the 12th of August, and last three days, during which time the convicts are exempt from all government duties. Convicts that are placed in the town of Sidney are in many respects happier than those farther inland ; those who are employed in the service of government are under the inspection of the superintendent of the public works ; they assemble at the ringing of a bell, in the goverument-yard, soon after day-light, and are mustered by their respective overseers and conducted to their work by them, having received their orders from the superintendent on the preceding evening. The overseers are themselves convicts of good character, and perfect masters of their different trades. They labour from day-light until nine o'clock, and they have then one hour allowed them to break-fast, then they return and work till three in the afternoon, and from that time they are at liberty to work for whom they think proper.

On leaving Sydney, the next settlement is Rose Hill, or, called by the natives, Paramatta, and it is situated due west up the river. Between Sydney and Paramatta there is but one settlement, about half way, which is called Kissing Point, and close on its banks is a large farm, kept by Mr. Squires, who likewise carries on an extensive brewery. The principal edifice at Paramatta is the government stores, a large stone building; close to the landing-place, and leading into the town, is a street about a mile long. They are generally small cottages, and are mostly inhabited by the convicts; and to each is attached a small garden, which they are compelled to keep in good order.

There is also a large manufactory of flax, the produce of the country, of which they make coarse cloth of different descriptions. This town is under the direction of the bishop of New South Wales (Samuel Marsden) and is the place where the noted George Barrington resided many years as chief constable, and died in the year 1806, highly respected by the principal men of the colony. At eight miles distance, in a westerly direction, is the village of Galba, which is a very fertile soil, the farms being in high cultivation, the ground clear of timber, and numbers of sheep and oxen seen grazing in its fields. Two miles south of Galba is the village of Castle Hills, in appearance resembling Galba; and a number of farm houses scattered about as far as the eye can reach. About fourteen miles, in a S. E. direction, is the town of Liverpool, on the banks of George's River; here cultivation is making rapid progress; and on each side of the river are numerous farms, till the traveller arrives at its termination. From George's River a branch runs in a N. W. direction, is about twenty miles in length, and is called the Nepean River. Here the eye of the agriculturist would be highly delighted at the verdure that constantly appears in view; the farms are but thinly dispersed, as the Nepean is not navigable.

At the extremity of the Nepean is the most extensive tract of land that has yet been discovered. This tract is laid out in pastures, which are literally covered with wild cattle, the produce of six cows and a bull which escaped from the colony about forty years ago. They were discovered by a runaway convict, who returned to the settlement and reported his discovery, for which they pardoned him his crime of desertion. After leaving the cow pastures, due north is the town of Windsor, the most productive place in the colony for grain of every description, which is brought to be shipped on the River Hawksborough, in small crafts for that purpose. Windsor is sixty miles from Sydney, and the river is navigable all the way from the sea; its entrance is called Broken Bay, and is fourteen miles north of Port Jackson, and thirty miles north of Broken Bay.

The town of Newcastle is situated about seven miles up the river, called the Coal River, in consequence of coals being found there in great abundance, of very good quality. This town is a place where all are sent to that prove refractory, or commit any crimes or misdemeanors in the colony, and is much dreaded by the convicts as a place of punishment.

Newcastle is the last settlement to the northward of Sydney; the natives are black, and appear to be a most miserable race of people: they live entirely naked, both men, women, and children, and they possess not the least shame. They carry fish and game to the different towns and villages inhabited by the English, which they barter for bread, tobacco, or spirits; they are, in general, of a light make, straight limbed, with curly black hair, and their face, arms, legs, and backs are usually besmeared with white chalk and red ochre. The cartilage of their nose is perforated, and a piece of reed, from eight to ten inches long, thrust through it, which seamen whimsically term their spritsail-yard. They seem to have no kind of religion; they bury their dead under ground, and they live in distinct clans, by the terms Gull, Taury Gull, or Uroga Gull, &c. They are very expert with their implements of war, which are spears made of reed, pointed with crystal or fish bone; they have a short club made of iron wood, called a waday, and a scimeter made of the same wood. Those inhabiting the coast have canoes; but the largest I ever saw would not hold more than two men with safety.

Their marriage ceremony is truly romantic; all the youth of a clan assemble, and are each armed with wadays; they then surround the young woman, and one seizes her by the arm, he is immediately attacked by another, and so on till he finds no combatant on the field, and then the conquering hero takes her to his arms.

The different kinds of game which the colony produces, are several kinds of kangaroos, of the same species, but differing in size and colour. Beasts of prey have never been seen in the colony. The birds are, parrots, cockatoos, and a large one called *emus*, which have very long legs and scarcely any wings; they in general live upon fern, and weigh from seventy to eighty pounds; there are likewise a number of black swans. The woods abound with a number of dangerous reptiles, such as centipedes and scorpions.

Government not being disposed to receive all our convicts, we were taken up to proceed to Van Diemen's Land, with a crew of two hundred convicts, besides a detachment of one hundred and sixty rank and file of his Majesty's 46th regiment of foot. We sailed from hence, and arrived at Van Diemen's Land after a pleasant passage of six days.

Van Diemen's Land is situated south of the Cape of New Holland, and is a dependency under the controul of the Governor-General. Here is a Deputy-Governor, who resides at the principal town, called Hobart's Town, situated about thirty miles up the Derwent; it is a town at present consisting of small cottages, or huts, built of wood, and with but few free inhabitants. The soil of the country is good; but there is a very inconsiderable trade. The Derwent runs ninety miles due west up the country. North of the Derwent, about twenty miles, is Frederick Henry's Bay, an immense deep bay, with good anchorage and shelter for shipping; and north-west of Henry's Bay is another fine river, called Port Dalrymple; it runs south-west ninety miles inland; at the head of it is a town, called Launceston; the inhabitants are principally convicts, and are employed in clearing the land for government. The native inhabitants of Van Diemen's Land are nearly the same as those of New Holland; and they at present hold no intercourse with the European inhabitants. After our prisoners were received on shore, they sent us another detachment of 150 rank and file of his Majesty's 46th regiment for Madras, and we began to prepare for sea.

SECTION V.

DEPARTURE FROM VAN DIEMEN'S LAND AND ARRIVAL AT MADRAS—AN ACCOUNT OF A SEVERE GALE, AND THE GREAT DANGER OF SHIPWRECK, TOGETHER WITH HER WONDERFUL ESCAPE FROM IT, AND HER SAFE ARRIVAL IN CUDDALORE.

THE morning was beautiful, and the noise of the crew weighing the anchor, created much life and bustle; and as we proceeded out of the harbour Nature seemed to smile, and bid us welcome to the watery element we had been so long traversing. A few days after, we entered the Endeavour Straits, which are about ten leagues long and five broad. We had several canoes off from the shore of New Guinea. It is a long narrow island of the South Pacific Ocean, and north of New Holland, from which it is separated by this strait, except on the north-east entrance, where it is counteracted by a group of islands, called the Prince of Wales's Islands. The land is generally low, and covered with an astonishing luxuriance of wood and herbage. The inhabitants resemble those of New Holland, omitting the quantity of grease and red-ochre with which the New Hollanders besmear their skins.

Their canoes are neatly carved, and are about twelve feet in length; they have outriggers to keep them firm on the water, and they are formed out of the hulls of trees; they carry about five or six men. They brought on board a quantity of shells, bows, arrows, and clubs, besides other trifling articles, and they would exchange with us for bits of old iron-hoops, or in fact any old thing, however trifling. The breeze freshening, we soon lost sight of the native merchants.

We arrived at Madras on the 12th of September, 1818, after a tedious passage. Owing to General Munro's intended departure for England, our cargo was immediately got ready, and as expeditiously received by us, and we were ready for sea on the 20th of October; but our dispatches not being in readiness, we were forced to remain at our anchorage, and on the morning of the 24th the clouds looked very black, and threatened a severe storm; but no preparations were made on board, and at 4 P.M. signal was made from the shore for all ships to leave the roads, which unfortunately was not noticed by many of the officers of the different vessels. At 5 P.M. the gale commenced; but through neglect the royal and top-gallant yards were not sent down, nor could the officer commanding be persuaded that any danger would arise from remaining at our anchorage; the ship's company now came aft and expostulated; but the officer in command called them all cowards, and said he would not start her anchor if it blew the masts out of her.

About 2 A. M. on the 25th, the gale commenced with the utmost fury, and she rode her scuttles under water, but as they were not secure, the sea came inboard and made very fast upon us. At 6 A. M. the water was three feet on the lee-side of our gun-deck, and from the continual working of the ship the chests broke from their fastenings.

After seeing a vessel go down at her anchors close on our starboard bow, the officer then gave orders for our cable to be slipped, which was immediately put into execution. John Gardener, a seaman, wishing to go aloft, and not taking proper hold, was blown from the rigging, and never seen again. We set the fore-sail, which immediately split; the mainsail, met with the same fate; the gaskets of the topsails gave way, and the sails split. At half past eight we found we had sprung a leak, owing to the ship's labouring so much; in the course of ten minutes we sounded, and found three feet water in the hold. The pumps were choaked; by 9 A. M. they were cleared, and by this time we had eight feet water in the well, and three on the gun-deck; the ship rolled very much, and the chests, guns, and water-casks, being all cast adrift, were dashing from larboard to starboard with the greatest fury. At 10 A. M. the ship labouring so much, and her being eight streaks of her main-deck under water, abreast of her main-hatchway, so that we had very little prospect of her living two minutes above water, it was thought necessary to send her mizen-mast by the board, in order to righten her; but while going, the mizen-mast heeled to windward and caught her royal-yards in the top-sail tye, and stayed her so, that we were compelled to cut away the main-mast, which carried the fore-top-mast and jib-boom; and, while in the act of going by the board, it knocked an invalid down and killed him on the spot. The ship rightened a little; but the sea was very boisterous, and we appeared to be in a valley in the midst of a number of tremendous high mountains, which to all appearance seemed ready to fall and crush us The carpenter came forward, and informed us, that we had sprung another leak, and that we had ten feet water in the well; the men, as by one accord, dropped the pumps, and appeared to despair; we might all have well exclaimed with the poet,

     " Heaven have mercy here upon us !
     " For only that can save us now."

" The atmosphere was hurled into the most tremendous confusion, the aerial torment burst itself over mountains, seas, and continents. All things felt the dreadful shock; all things trembled under her scourge, her sturdy sons were strained to the very nerves, and almost swept her headlong to the deep."

It would be in vain to attempt to give a description of our feelings at this critical moment, tortured as we were with anguish and despair. Every man seemed now as if all was given over for lost, when the carpenter came forward and informed us the leak was found out, and that with a little exertion it might be stopped; the men then rose with great vigour, flew to the pumps with renovated strength, and gave three cheers. The cabins were all washed down, and a party of men were busily employed throwing every thing overboard,—self was not considered,—the very last rag was committed to the furious elements without a sigh. At 11 A. M. the sea struck her starboard quarter-gallery and forced it from its birth, and as we were busily employed, a cry was heard, the starboard fore-mast port was carried away, and the sea forced itself with great rapidity along the deck; but the seamen flew to meet this new misfortune with the vigour of tigers, not considering the dangers they had to encounter, and thus effectually succeeded in stopping the leak.

While the seamen were busily employed, the troops were desired to pump, which they firmly refused, and said they would sooner sink, except a poor blind man, who could not keep from them; his reply was truly noble, and, I am sure, my readers will excuse my repeating it. " I am unworthy of the life I have if I do not exert myself in this hour of distress; if it has pleased God to deprive me of the blessing of sight, he has not of the feelings of a Christian." At half past eleven the gale greatly abated, and by this time the carpenter had stopped the leak, by using all the gunny bags and blankets that could be found; the damage was occasioned by the masts beating under her counter. By 12 A. M. it was a perfect calm; the men were now busily employed clearing the gun-deck, and securing every port-hole and scuttle in which they effectually succeeded by 1 P. M.

" For a moment the turbulent and outrageous sky seemed to be assuaged; but it intermitted its wrath only to increase its strength; soon the sounding squadrons of the air returned to their attack, and renewed their ravages with redoubled fury; and the stately dome rocked amidst the wheeling clouds. The impregnable clouds tottered on its basis, and threatened to overwhelm those whom it was intended to protect, the vessel was almost rent in pieces, and scarcely secure; where then was a place of safety? Sleep affrighted flew, diversion was turned into horror; all was uproar in the elements; all was consternation among us, and nothing was seen but one wide picture of rueful devastation.

" The ocean swelled with tremendous commotions; the pondrous waves were heaved from their capacious beds, and almost lay bare the unfathomed deep; flung into the most rapid agitation, they swept over us, and tossed themselves into the clouds. We were rent from our anchors, and with all our enormous load were whirled swift as an arrow along the vast abyss. Now we climb the rolling mountains, we plough the frightful ridge, and seem to skim the skies; anon we plunge into the opening gulf, we reel to and fro, and stagger in the jarring decks, or climb the cordage, whilst bursting seas foam over the decks. Despair is in every face, and death sits threatening in every surge." The whistling of the wind and roaring of the sea, together with the voice of despairing seamen, and the dreadful shrieks of the women, made us truly miserable; but we were forced to exert ourselves with assumed courage and vigour, which could only be imagined but by those placed in a similar situation,—our exertions were for life or death, knowing that if they once failed, that nothing was to be expected but to perish in a watery grave.

We kept the water under to about three feet during the time of this dreadful gale; about 4 P. M. it abated, and about 5 P. M. it blew a steady breeze from the south-west; and at 6 P. M. we went round her to examine the damage we had sustained; when, dreadful to relate, we found that a man and child had been washed out of their hammocks and perished; on proceeding along the waste we found two invalids had been jammed to death between two water-casks and the ship's sides, making a total of six lives lost during the storm.

The hatches were opened about 8 P. M.; but the provisions being so salt and sodden with the sea-water, they could not be eaten, on account of the scarcity of fresh water. After the watch was set we laid ourselves down upon the upper-deck with no other covering than the starry heavens.

On the following day we commenced clearing the wreck, and rigging up jurymasts, which we happily effected before sun-set; and on the 28th we arrived at Sadras, which lay south by west of Madras, distant fifteen miles. We lay here till the 30th without any tidings of the captain.

The men from fatigue and pain, from sleeping on the wet decks, and continual pumping, came aft, and said the clouds threatened another storm, and that the monsoons were growing very strong, and in case the weather should alter for the worse, they had not strength left to work the ship in another gale, from want of nourishment; and that provided the officers did not think proper to remove to a place of safety, they were determined to take charge of her and proceed to Trincomalee, and deliver the vessel into the hands of the underwriters. All our remonstrances to them were in vain, until the chief mate pledged his word and honour, that if the captain did not join her the next morning, he would, ill as he was, take charge of her and proceed there himself.

On the following morning the captain joined her, with the hon. L. G. K. Murray, secretary to the board of trade at Madras, when they brought on board a quantity of provisions, which we stood very much in need of, and immediately made sail and arrived the same day at Pondicherry. The governor sent us on board a new anchor, as our own was sprung. Pondicherry is a town of Hindostan, under the French government, and situated on the coast of Coromandel, seventy-five miles S. S. W of Madras.

On the following day we run into Cuddalore, a little above the first bar. Cuddalore is a town of Hindostan, one hundred miles S. S. W. of Madras. Thirty of the ship's company being sick, they, with me, were compelled to leave the ship, and forced to proceed on shore to the hospital. I was about this time seized with a violent fit of the cholera morbus. It is supposed to originate from the cold damp airs which are very prevalent at this time of the season. A gentleman's bungalore was humanely given up as a hospital, or friendly receptacle, for our incapacitated seamen, during our sojourn at Cuddalore.

The possibility of visiting the native town was precluded by the peculiar strictness of the regulations imposed upon us.

SECTION VI.

THE AUTHOR'S DEPARTURE FROM CUDDALORE AND ARRIVAL AT PONDICHERRY—DEPARTURE THEREFROM, AND ARRIVAL AT MADRAS, WITH A DESCRIPTION OF THE SAME—ACCOUNT OF THE RELIGION, CUSTOMS, AND MANNERS OF THE NATIVES—DEPARTURE FROM MADRAS, ON HIS ROUTE TO NAGPORE,—ARRIVAL AT PONAMALEE, AND DESCRIPTION OF THE SAME—HIS DEPARTURE AND ARRIVAL AT CUDDAPAH.

AFTER I had thoroughly recovered, through the interest of a young German widow, I obtained my acquittal from the ship, and then proceeded to New Town for my passport. New Town lies about two miles and a half E. N. E. of Cuddalore, and is the residence of the Europeans in that neighbourhood; the houses of the Europeans are generally built of brick and those of the natives of wood. The day after I had obtained my passport I proceeded on my route and arrived at Pondicherry the same evening.

Pondicherry is about four leagues in extent; the houses are built with brick, but the Indians use only wood, in the manner which we call lath and plaster. In a few days after I arrived in Madras, and took up my residence with a friend in Pursevaulkum.

A few days after my arrival I proceeded with my friend to town. Madras, or Fort St. George, is a fort and town of the peninsula, on the coast of Coromandel. It is the principal settlement of the English on the east side of the peninsula, and is a fortress of great extent, including within it a regular well-built city. It is close to the sea shore, from which it has a rich and beautiful appearance, the houses being covered with a stucco, called *chunam*, which, in itself, is as compact as the finest marble, bears as high a polish, and is equally as splendid as that elegant material. There is a second city, called Black Town, nearly four miles in circumference, separated from Madras by the breadth of a proper esplanade. Madras, in common with all the European settlements on this coast, has no port for shipping, the coast forming nearly a straight line, and being incommoded with a high and dangerous surf. The citadel is situated in the middle of the White, or English Town, and is one of the best fortresses in the British possessions. The town is also encompassed with a strong wall of the same stone as that with which the citadel is built, and is defended by bastions, batteries, halfmoons, flankers, and mortars. Opposite the west gate of the citadel are barracks and a convenient hospital for the company's soldiers, and at the other end is a mint where the company coin gold and silver.

I was shortly after engaged as an overseer in the Madras Advertiser printing office, and as an assistant to the Madras Nautical Academy; but not agreeing with my employer I left it, and obtained permission to stop in the country as a free merchant.

Mr. M. R***, with whom I resided, used all his interest to obtain for me some permanent situation under government, but it could not be effected. At length, being tired of an indolent life, I opened a school, which succeeded very well, when

I was forced to relinquish it, owing to my ill state of health the confinement and severity of the weather brought on a languishing complaint, which would have terminated in my death had I persisted in continuing in my present employment.

My friend being obliged to quit Madras, left me and his brother in charge of his house. My friends, during his absence, greatly contributed to my amusement, and, in short, spared no expense. One morning, passing through Vessory Bazar, I was greatly shocked at seeing the nabob's elephant take up a little child in his trunk and dash its brains out against the ground; the only reason that could be observed was, that the child had thrown some pebble stones at it; and the only redress the poor disconsolate mother could obtain was a gift of fifty pagodas from the nabob, which is about equal to twenty pounds sterling.

During my friend's absence his mother and brother were carried off with the cholera morbus. The general estimate of deaths through the settlement is at least three hundred and fifty in one day; the natives have been known to sacrifice in one day and at one pagoda, fifty cocks and fifty kids, to appease their angry gods, and, in fact, some of the poor deluded creatures will go with a sword run through their cheeks in the fleshy part, and kept hanging in that position for some days, continually dance backwards and forwards through the different bazars; others have the palms of their hands pierced with a sword; others have their breasts burnt, and others again have an instrument run through their tongue in order to calm the wrath of their offended deities; nor can they, in their opinions, put themselves to sufficient torture.

Shortly after my friend returned, I went to reside with a friend at Royaporum, south of Black Town, and soon afterwards I was engaged as an examiner in the accountant-general's office. After I had been a short time in this employ, I received an order to prepare for my departure for Nagpore, in the service of his highness the Rajah. On my return from the Fort St. George, I was greatly surprised at seeing an old man standing with his bare feet upon two pieces of wood in the form of a pair of pattens, with pointed pegs uppermost; he stood in that position for several days, with the blood running in torrents, and several of those who passed by gave him what their circumstances could well afford. A few days after I was invited to witness an Hindoo ceremony. We took our station at the top of a rich Persian's house, opposite a spacious esplanade and contiguous to a large pagoda; in the centre of the esplanade was fixed a capstern, with a pole about sixty feet long, which was fixed so as to be occasionally raised or lowered. Shortly after our arrival, a native, decorated with flowers, proceeded slowly towards the pagoda with tom-toms, and all kinds of Asiatic music ; after he had prostrated himself in the pagoda, the Brahmin, a kind of priest, struck his side with a leather thong till it swelled to a considerable size, and then forced a butcher's hook through his side ; he then composedly walked to the machine, and suffered himself to be fastened to a rope and suspended in the air with no other support than the butcher's hook ; he went at least three times round a circle of about one hundred feet, and he kept his arms continually in motion during the whole time, fencing and throwing flowers among the bye standers, which were immediately picked up by them and kept as a religious relic. This ceremony is performed yearly for the purpose of those who have lost their cast, and may regain it by voluntarily undergoing this treatment. Eleven of them went through this torturing ceremony.

I now began to put myself in readiness for my departure. On the morning of the 8th I dispatched my baggage and tents, together with a guard of eight peons (native police), which my friends had obtained for me, through their interest with the superintendent of the police. By the time I had taken leave of all my friends, and thanked them for their disinterested protection to a distressed seaman, I proceeded on my route (after receiving several more marks of their favours, Mr. C**** having presented me with an Arab horse, four baggage bullocks, and five hundred rupees, besides several letters of introduction) at eight o'clock in the evening. I travelled about five miles down the Ponamalee Road, and stopped at a village a little below the main guard, a small place with scarcely any fodder for the cattle. On the following morning, at a very early hour, we proceeded on our march, and arrived at Ponamalee about eight o'clock, where I found several of my friends waiting to take leave, as they expected that Ponamalee would have been the first stage.

After having taken farewell of each other they returned back to Madras, and I hired for the day a small bungalow (or garden house) opposite the fort, where I determined to stay. Ponamalee is about fourteen miles W. S. W. of Madras. This small and beautiful town is situated upon a rising ground, which commands an extensive view of the adjacent country. The number of Europeans residing here is but few, as it is entirely out of the road for traffic. There is a fort which is situated upon a rising ground, and gives the village a romantic appearance. It forms a complete square, and on each angle is a small place erected in form of the body of a wind-mill, which was used formerly for the purpose of solitary confinement when the troops were quartered here, but is now occupied as lumber rooms ; the fort is garrisoned by pensioners. The grand entrance is on the south side, and a small wicket is usually on the west. The fort is surrounded by a large moat about thirty feet in depth, the water is very clear and good, and is drank by the natives. The inner part is far from being roomy, owing to the extreme width of the ramparts. There are two or three small buildings for the use of the commanding officers, but now the residence of a school-master and two serjeants; in the centre is a small building with a dome on the top, which was used formerly for a chapel, but is now converted into a school for the instruction of the poor soldiers' children, and the two barracks are occupied by pensioners.

On the following morning, about two o'clock, we prepared for our journey, and in a few days arrived at Naggery, a distance of about two hundred miles W. N. W. of Madras. The natives here are Hindoos, and the village is remarkably clean. The pagoda, or place of worship, is a fine large building, built in an oblong form, and beautifully gilt and carved all round with monkeys and apes. The Hindoos, in their manner of diet, are very abstemious, refraining from flesh; in fact, they will not eat any animal food; they are very regular in their morning ablutions, which they do by washing and marking themselves with chunam in the centre of their foreheads, according to the mark of their different casts. If any one neglects it he is immediately turned out of the cast, and his relations disown him, nor will they permit him once to enter their house. Such is their strictness, that the father has refused to see his son and the mother her daughter; and if they happen to perceive him at any distance they fly from him as they would from a serpent, thinking that his touch would pollute them.

The roads here are very bad, being principally jungle; their principal cultivation is paddy (a kind of oats). On my arrival at Nundihall I was determined to rest for a couple of days, as two of my servants were in a very ill state of health. Nundihall is a beautiful town, the houses are built of brick, and are generally from three to four stories high; the streets were very dirty, owing to the number of paddy fields that surround the city, as the growth of it requires that the earth should be completely covered with water. The natives are generally Hindoos and Moors. The town is surrounded by a high brick wall.

After leaving the town of Nundihall the roads were very bad, owing to the quantity of stones, and hills which were very steep and difficult to ascend. On the roads I had several disputes with the natives passing through Wuntimuttall, owing to my servants and the peons stealing the toddy from the trees. Toddy is a liquor which is extracted from the top veins of the cocoa-nut trees, which runs continually into a pot placed for that purpose. The liquor is very pleasant, and is reckoned very wholesome when drank early in the morning in a small quantity; if drunk in the heat of the day it causes acidity in the bowels, and often is the cause of the death of many Europeans. The natives drink it continually, and often get quite intoxicated with it.

We arrived at Cuddapah on the 21st instant; it is a large and commodious town, and is inhabited by Mussulmen. Cuddapah is situated N. W. of Madras, one hundred and fifty-one miles distant, and the general estimate of inhabitants is at about two hundred thousand. The principal houses are built of brick and the inferior ones of mud.

The Mahometans divide their religion into two general parts, faith and practice, of which the first is divided into six distinct branches—belief in God, in his angels, in his scriptures, in his prophets, in the resurrection and final judgment, and lastly, in God's absolute decrees. The points relating to practice, are prayer with washings, &c., alms, fasting, pilgrimages, and circumcision.

The Mahometans pray five times in twenty-four hours, viz.: in the morning before sun-rise, when noon is past and the sun begins to decline from the meridian, in the afternoon before sun-set, in the evening after sun-set and before day is closed, and again in the evening and before the watch of the night. They fast with great strictness during the whole month of Ramadan, from the time the new moon first appears, during which period they must abstain from eating, drinking, and all other indulgences, from day-break till night or sun-set.

The Europeans reside about two miles to the west of the native town, and have commodious houses, with fine spacious gardens; they are built of brick and much after the form of a gentleman's seat in England, but on a larger scale. I proceeded to the house of the collector, and on my road, my horse taking fright, I was thrown, and lost my purse containing all my money. My distress was now indescribable. Being left pennyless in the midst of a people totally destitute of Christian feeling, and without the probable means of obtaining the common necessaries of life, I arrived, in this miserable state of mind, bordering on despair, at the collector's, Mr. Hanbury, and after making him acquainted with my circumstances, he generously rendered me his assistance, paid my servants' wages that were in arrear, and kindly advanced what I thought sufficient to defray my expenses, having previously sent my peons back to Madras, and supplied me with fresh ones to proceed with me to Hydrabad.

On the following day the rain came down in torrents, accompanied with thunder and lightning, which kept me within my tent and caused me to exclaim with Dr. Henry, "O, ye lightnings, that brood and lie couchant in the sulphureous vapours, that glance with forked fury from the angry gloom, swifter and fiercer than the lion rushes from his den, or open with vast expansive sheets of flame, sublimely waved over the prostrate world, and fearfully lingering in the affrighted skies!" " Ye thunders, that awfully grumble in the distant clouds, seem to meditate indignation, and from the first essays of a far more frightful peal; or suddenly bursting over your heads, rend the vault above and shake the ground below with a hideous and horrid crack!" In the evening the weather began to clear up, which induced me to walk out, when taking two peons as a guard, I proceeded south of the town, on a beautiful plain: the pleasantness of the weather, and the stillness of the evening, tempted me to prolong my walk, and inspired my mind to contemplate on the wonderful works of Providence, who had so lately showered down his blessings upon me, in preserving me from want in the midst of a heathen world. The sun had almost finished his daily course, and sunk lower and lower till he seemed to hover on the verge of the sky!

The globe is now half immured beneath the dusky earth; or, as the ancient poet speaks, " is shooting into the ocean, and sinks into the western sea." The whole face of the ground was overspread with shades, and what the painters of nature call "dun obscurity." Only a few superior eminences, tipt with streaming silver, the tops of groves and lofty towers that catch the last smiles of day, were still irradiated by the departing beams. But, O how transient is the destination—how momentary the gift! like all the blessings which mortals enjoy below, it is gone almost as soon as granted. How languishingly it trembled on the leafy spire, and glimmered with dying faintness on the mountain's sable brow! till it expired and resigned the world to the gradual approaches of night.

SECTION VII.

THE AUTHOR'S DEPARTURE FROM CUDDAPAH—DESCRIPTION
OF THE DIFFERENT VILLAGES, AND ARRIVAL AT HYDRABAD
—DESCRIPTION OF HYDRABAD, AND DEPARTURE THERE-
FROM—ARRIVAL AT NERMUL.

ON the morning of the 27th, I proceeded on my route over
the chain hills, with which the town of Cuddapah is surrounded;
the roads are very good, but the steepness of the hills made it
very fatiguing: in six hours I arrived at Batoor, a distance of
twelve miles. Batoor is a large village, the houses are built of
mud and bamboo, and form a motley groupe; the only protection
they have from the number of robbers which infest that part, is a
small fort, about two hundred square feet; the ramparts are about
fourteen feet in thickness, and at each angle a small gun is
mounted upon a pivot, about three feet from its walls; the fort
in general is very much out of repair; the inhabitants are Hindoos, and are very indolent; the land is quite barren and free
from cultivation. The cruelty with which Europeans in general
act towards these poor captives is really disgraceful, and cannot
but be censured by all who cherish the least trait of humanity
with their breast.

When an European passes through any of the villages, and is in
want of any coolies, or porters, to carry his baggage, he orders
his guards to press every man he can meet with, and compel him
to carry whatever his barbarous protector chooses he should labour
under, and if there is not sufficient men, to press the women,
without considering whether they have any family to provide for.
It has been frequently known, that the mother has been forced to
leave her infant babe from her breast upon the bare earth to provide for itself, to carry the baggage of a merciless enemy, whose
only payment, after going fifteen or sixteen Indian miles, is, if
she complains, a *bambooing*, (that is a caning,) and, perhaps,
after she gets home, which cannot be till the next day, she finds
her poor infant dead for want.

We passed through Parmunsa, and arrived at Moorkandah,
which is a small village, and in a very ruinous condition, as it is at
the foot of the Ghaut; the inhabitants are but few in number, and
are principally brahmins, consequently provisions are very scarce;
on my requesting the cutwall, or headman of the village, to bring

some fowls, he refused, and said there were none in the place, although I repeatedly heard the crowing of a cock. The impudent manner in which the man answered me, made me doubt the truth of what he said; in order to ascertain it, I took two peons and my gun and went round the village, and found a full grown cock; I caught it, and ordered it to be carried to my tent and killed; the natives by this time were in arms, and before any of us were aware of it, they had secured the peons and surrounded me, demanding the cock: when they were informed of its death, they all began to weep and raised a most lamentable cry, and said it was devoted to their god, and that the heaviest curses would follow me. I expected their denunciations would have paid for it; but in that I was greatly mistaken, for they demanded payment for it; and to avoid any injury to my peons, I offered them one rupee, considering that it would be equal to the price of eighteen cocks; but they disdainfully refused it, and said that they must offer gifts to their god to appease his anger, and to pay their sadura to intercede in their behalf. I remonstrated with them; but to no avail, as they would not take less than ten rupees. I tried all in my power to make my escape from them; but when they perceived my intentions, they drew their scimeters, and held them to my breast, and said, provided I did not accede to their offer, they would not spare the lives of my peons nor myself, as they could not get it replaced for forty times that sum, which was presented to them by their rajah. The price I considered to be extortionate, (but I paid it,) as fowls are sold in the different villages round that neighbourhood for one penny each, sheep for ten-pence, and every other article in proportion.

On the following morning, at a very early hour, I crossed the Ghaut; in the centre there is a very great declivity on each side the road, about two hundred feet in depth, and the Ghaut is very steep, and covered with flint-stone, which made it very difficult for the horse and cattle to pass: it is about twelve miles in length, and at the foot of it is the village of Badnapore. The inhabitants are very peaceable, and the village is close on the borders of Khristnah river. We made all possible haste to cross, which was effected by means of a large round basket, which is continually whirling round in the river. The river is about a quarter of a mile in width, but the heavy current carried us nearly two miles down; and owing to the exertions of the cattle, we encamped close on its banks. On the following day we passed Pungall-hill fort, which is situate on the summit of a very steep mount, and is built of mud, and large enough to contain ten thousand troops; it is only accessible on the north-east angle, which is easily blockaded in case of necessity. In five days we arrived at Hydrabad.

Hydrabad lies about 350 miles north-west of Madras; the houses are built of brick, and generally run four and five stories high. The inhabitants are principally Mahometans interspersed with Hindoos.

The Mahometans will not suffer a Christian to touch their cooking utensils or fuel by any means, and if such should be done, they consider them as polluted, and they will instantly break and destroy them; and while they are in the act of eating, if touched by any one of another sect, they will not swallow what is even in their mouth, but will throw it out, and go through a regular puri-cation by washing and prayer.

After I had been at Hydrabad a few days, I joined a small party to view the interior : while we were taking breakfast, a cavalcade of elephants came up to the door with a number of peons. After we had mounted them we proceeded through the south gate into the city; the streets were particularly dirty, owing to there being no drains. The town is supplied with water by a well about two hundred feet in circumference.

On our entrance into the minister's house we were surprised at seeing a battalion of female sepoys (soldiers) presenting arms to us. We stood to see them go through their military manœuvres, which they did with dexterity; we then proceeded towards the house, which is built entirely of cedar-wood, but in a very ordinary manner, owing to the number of apartments: every room is carved in a beautiful and masterly style, from the cieling to the floor. This ornament is very common among the lower classes, who have the devices of their gods carved on the doors of their houses. The apartments form a complete square, and in the centre is a stone tank. We next proceeded to a gallery of looking-glasses; the only one worthy of notice is about eighteen feet long and sixteen wide; there is likewise a whole length paint-ing of Earl Moira, Governor-General of India. We afterwards proceeded to the palace of the Rajah: on our entrance into the inner court, we were agreeably surprised at seeing a quantity of tea-cups, saucers, &c. of various colours, placed against the wall in form of elephants, tigers, serpents, &c. in the most superb manner; in the centre is a large tank, containing a great quan-tity of salmon-trout. I had the honour of being introduced to the Rajah's sons, but his Highness was not present.

After having obtained a guard of twelve sepoys and two naigues, I proceeded on my route, and in a few days arrived at Nermul.

Nermul is a large and beautiful city, surrounded by a fort, and is about three miles in circumference, and is on a rising ground, 205 miles north-north-east of Hydrabad, and in the heart of the jungle, it is under the command of Major Woodhouse. The inhabitants are principally Moors.

I pitched my tent in the middle of a burying-ground, by the side of a running stream, and owing to the fatigue I had experienced, I now resolved to sojourn for two days. This place suited my present state of mind.

My attention was soon attracted by a magnificent tomb, and upon examining the inscription, it proved to be a rajah's. The gardens were ingeniously planned, and a thousand elegant decorations designed ; but, alas! their intended possessor is gone down " to the place of sculls !"

While I am recollecting, many, I question not, are experiencing the same tragical vicissitude. The eyes of the Sublime Being, who sits upon the circle of the earth, and views all its inhabitants with one incomprehensive glance, even now behold as many tents in affliction as overwhelmed the Egyptians in that fatal night when the destroying angel sheathed his arrows in all the pride of their strength; some sinking to the floor from their easy chair, and deaf even amidst the piercing shrieks of their distracted relations ; some giving up the ghost as they retired, or lay reclined under the shady harbour to taste the sweets of the flowery scene; some as they sail with a party of pleasure along the silver stream and through the laughing meads ! nor is the grim intruder terrified though wine and music flow around.

" Those who received vast revenues, and called whole lordships their own, are reduced to half a dozen feet of earth, or confined in a few sheets of lead ! Rooms of state and sumptuous furniture are resigned for no other ornament than the *shroud,* for no other apartment than the darksome *niche!* Where is the star that blazed upon the breast, or the glittered sceptre? The only remains of departed dignity are the weather-beaten hatchment. I see no splendid retinue surrounding this solitary dwelling. The princely equipage hovers no longer about their lifeless master, he has no other attendant than a dusty *statue;* which, while the regardless world is as gay as ever, the sculptor's hand has taught to weep."

SECTION VIII.

AFTER remaining two days, I proceeded on my route; and on the
following day arrived at Wadoor, a distance of fourteen miles,
across a long succession of hills, the roads over which are very
rugged and covered with stones; Wadoor lies in a valley, at the
foot of a large mountain, and is hardly perceivable from the top.

On the 20th December, we travelled along a beautiful and finely
cultivated country, the produce of which is cholum and paddy,
which grows in great quantities; the inhabitants are very civil,
and principally Moor men. On the 25th December, 1821, I
arrived at Nagpore, and on the same evening was seized with the
Nagpore fever, which is always accompanied by fits of the ague.
The fever is supposed to originate from the excessive heats of the
day, and the extreme cold of the night.

I endeavoured as much as possible that my ill state of health
should not keep me from my employment, but attended to it
very assiduously; which I persevered in till the 27th of March,
when the doctor informed me, that I had better leave the Presi-
dency or I should endanger my life, as the hot winds generally
set in in the middle of April, which frequently prove very dangerous to European invalids.

On the 2nd of April, after having previously obtained my passport and a guard of twelve Seapoys, I proceeded on my route,
and towards evening arrived at Tukea, where, owing to my ill state
of health, I was compelled to stop two days.

On the 12th I arrived at Ouronty, which is S. W. by W. of
Nagpore, about 100 miles. The town is very large, and is surrounded by a brick wall; the houses are built of brick, and are generally three stories high. The inhabitants are Mussulmen. In
the afternoon I went to the palace of the Rajah, (Rajah ram.)
His palace outside is very dirty, owing to his guard making fires
against the walls for cooking. On my desiring to see the Rajah, I
was conducted through a long dreary passage, with the walls, to

all appearance, covered with grease and filth, at the end of which is a large court-yard, which has a very different appearance, the Rajah's apartments being all round; at the end were six Peons waiting to conduct me to his highness, with silver staves, about eleven feet long, with a device of Mahomet on the top; on my introduction to the Rajah's apartment, he was sitting cross-legged with his hooker; at my entrance he arose and made three salams in token of respect to the British nation. After questioning me where I was going to, and my reasons for so doing, he presented me with two camel-hair shawls, by placing them across my shoulder; then taking his leave.

On the following day, I proceeded on my route, and on the 20th arrived at Luckenwarry; where there is good encampment and water, and the natives are principally Hindoos. Early on the following morning we began to cross the Luckenwarry Ghaut; the roads were steep and not above ten feet wide, and [on each side a vacuity of about 250 feet deep. The light in the lanthorn being extinguished, and the moon being obscured, my horse, had it not been for the horse-keeper, would have precipitated me to the bottom; I instantly dismounted, and the horse-keeper led him till he was clear of the Ghaut. On the centre is a large gate, which stands about forty feet high, and which, during the war, had withstood a three months' siege.

Passing through the jungle between the villages of Curróne and Chickly, we were greatly surprised at seeing a large party on camels; we hailed them and enquired who they were, but we could not by any means obtain an answer; when finding they persisted in their obstinacy, the Naigues suspected them of belonging to the party of Sheik Dullah, a noted robber who had already committed many depredations in that neighbourhood, and on our desiring them to move to the left of us if they were friends, they made a sudden halt; the sepoys then drew up in a line, and the followers began to guard their baggage, but when they saw our number, they went off to the left of us, grumbling.

On the 24th, we arrived at Jaulnah. It bears W. by S., of Nagpore, distant 180 miles. On the following day, after I had taken sufficient rest, I presented my passport to the Adjutant-General, and delivered up the guard, having previously obtained another. Jaulnah is a large town, surrounded by a brick wall, about twenty feet in height; the houses are generally of brick, and from three to four stories; the inhabitants are principally Hindoos, interspersed with Persians and Musselmen. The cantonment is the head quarters of the British army on this side the Deccan.—Jaulnah has a civil and military government.

After staying two days, I proceeded on my route, and on the 19th of May I arrived at Poonah. It bears S. S. E. of Bombay, and is in the territories of the Peishwa : it is about forty miles distant from Bombay. I took up my residence with a friend, commander of the Sebundaries : during my route, I passed through Armigabad, Amednagur, and Seroor; which is the residence of Europeans, and has detachments of different regiments quartered at each town : their houses are in general of brick and stone, their religion is Hindoo.

The Hindoos are divided into four tribes, first the Brahmin ; second, the Khatry ; third, the Bhyse; fourth, the Sooders ; all these have their distinct sects, and cannot intermingle with each other ; but for some offences they are expelled their sects, which is the highest punishment they can suffer. In this manner a kind of fifth sect, called Pariah, is formed of the dregs of the people, who are employed only in the meanest capacity. There is a kind of division which pervades the four sects indiscriminately; which is taken from the worship of their gods VISHNOU and SHEEVAH ; the worshippers of the former being named Vishnou bukht, and of the latter, Sheevah bukht.

Of these four sects the Brahmins have the superiority, and all the laws show such a partiality towards them, as cannot but induce us to suppose that they have had the principal hand in framing them. They are not allowed the privilege of sovereignty ; but are solely kept for the instruction of the people. They are alone allowed to read the Veda or Sacred Books. The Khatries or sect next in dignity, being only allowed to hear them read, while the other two read the Satras, or commentaries upon them ; but the poor Chaudalas are not allowed to enter their temple, or to be present at any religious ceremony.

In point of precedence, the Brahmins claim a superiority even to princes, the latter being chosen of Khatary or second sect. In fact the Brahmin claims every privilege, and the inferior sects give place to him ; the Hindoos are allowed to eat no flesh nor to shed blood. Their food is rice and dholl, and other vegetables, dressed with ghee (dholl is a kind of split pea, ghee, a kind of butter, melted and refined to make it capable of being kept a long time) and seasoned with ginger and other spices. The food which they most esteem is milk, as coming from the cow ; an animal for which they have the most extravagant veneration, insomuch that it is enacted in the code of Gentoo laws, that any one who exacts labour from a bullock that is hungry or thirsty, or shall oblige him to labour when fatigued, is liable to be fined by the magistrates.

The Hindoos are remarkable for their ingenuity in all kinds of handicraft ; but their utensils are simple to and in many respects inconvenient, so that incredible labour and patience are necessary, for the accomplishment of any work ; and for this the Hindoos are remarkable. The religion of the Hindoos is contained in certain books, called Vedas; and, though now involved in superstition, seems to have been originally pure, inculcating the belief of an Eternal Being, possessed of every divine perfection. Their subordinate deities, Brahma, Vishnou, and Sheevah, are only representatives of the wisdom, goodness, and power of the supreme god Brahma; whom they call the principles of Truth, the spirit of Wisdom, and the Supreme Being; so that it is probable that all their idols were at first only designed to represent these attributes: they believe in ten Avators, or incarnation of the Deity, nine of which have taken place for the punishment of tyrants, or removing some great natural calamity; and the tenth is to take place at the dissolution of the universe. Several of the Avators inculcate the transmigration of souls, and the ninth of them, which forbids the sacrifices of animals, gave rise to the religion of Gauda Boodma, or Fo.

Their deities are extremely numerous, and are generally supposed to have first originated in Italy and Greece.

After stopping six days, I proceeded to Bombay, and on the 30th of May I arrived there. After delivering my passport, I made application for a ship for England, and was some time before I could get one; and the great expense I incurred in living at a tavern, made me entirely pennyless, so that I was forced to dispose of the shawls which I had presented me by the Rajah of Omrouty, and for which I received three hundred rupees each. But before I was finally settled, I had not above ten rupees left.

Bombay is an island of Hindostan, on the west coast of the Deccan, seven miles in length, and about twenty-one miles in circumference; the ground is barren, and good water scarce; it was formerly considered very unhealthy, but by draining the swamps and bogs the air is much improved; the inhabitants are of several nations and very numerous, but are principally Persians.

The religion of the Persians is, generally, Paganism, directed principally by the priests of magi, men of strict austere life, forbidding the use of either ornament or gold; making the ground their bed, and herbs their food. Their whole time is spent in offering to the gods the prayers and sacrifices of the people, as they only might be heard.

The people are *Gentiles*; as to their religion, they worship the sun and moon, and various heavenly bodies, from whom they suppose they derive every blessing of light and warmth; and every morning they gather themselves round the beech and present their morning oblations, by pouring into the sea quantities of milk and odoriferous flowers, and prostrating themselves with their faces to the earth, as a mark of adoration to their rising deity (the sun.) Besides other gods which the Gentiles worship, they are great idolaters of fire, which they offer sacrifices to in time of peace, and carry it with them, as their tutelar deity in time of war. Their adoration is so great, that the first candle they see lighted, let it be in whose place it will, they immediately stop and repeat a prayer. In their habitation they never put it out after it is once lighted.

Besides the town of Bombay, which is about a mile in length, with mean houses (a few only excepted), there is a capacious harbour or bay, reckoned the finest haven in the east, where all ships may find security from the inclemency of the different seasons. After remaining here for the space of three months, I was engaged as captain's clerk on board the Hon. Company's Ship Marquis of Huntly. We sailed from hence July 25, 1820, and arrived at the new anchorage in nineteen days' sail; soon after I went up to Calcutta on duty for the ship.

Calcutta, or *Fort William*, the emporium of Bengal, and principal seat of India, is situated on the western side of the Hoogely river, at about ninety-six miles from its mouth, which is navigable up to the town for large ships. This extensive and beautiful town is supposed to contain between four and five hundred thousand inhabitants. The houses are variously built, some of brick, others of mud and cow-dung, and a great number with bamboos (a large kind of reed or cane) and mats. The bamboos are placed as stakes in the ground, and crossed with others in different ways, so as to enable them to make the matting fast, when for the roofing they lay them one upon the other, when a large family lie in that small compass of about six feet square, which makes a very motley appearance. The mixture of European and Asiatic manners observed in Calcutta is wonderful; coaches, phaetons, hackeries, two-wheeled carriages drawn by bullocks, palanquins carried by the natives, and the passing ceremonies of Hindoos, and the different appearance of the faquirs, form a diversified and curious appearance. The European houses have, many of them, the appearance of palaces or temples, and the inhabitants are very hospitable.

After the cargo was sent on board I returned to the ship, but on our passage down the river we were compelled to lie out in the river, owing to the great boar, as it is called; it is a quick overflowing of the water, which rises in a great body and with such violence that it breaks down all before it. It arises from the narrowness of the river, and the force which it makes from the sea; in the course of two minutes it rises to the height of four or five feet.

Lying in one of the creeks till the tide was turned, I was really alarmed by the men getting into the boat in great disorder and telling me that it was a crocodile which I had for a long time observed, and mistaken for the hull of a tree. A crocodile is an amphibious voracious animal, in shape resembling a lizard. It is covered with very hard scales, which cannot but with difficulty be pierced, except under the belly, where the skin is tender. It has a wide throat, with several rows of teeth, sharp and separated, which enter one another.

On my arrival on board every thing was in confusion, as we expected to sail in a few days.

SECTION IX.

THE AUTHOR'S DEPARTURE FROM CALCUTTA, AND ARRIVAL AT CHINA—AN ACCOUNT OF THEIR RELIGION, CUSTOMS, AND MANNERS, AND OF HIS BEING ROBBED ON DANES' ISLAND—THE AUTHOR'S DEPARTURE FROM CHINA AND ARRIVAL AT ANJURE POINT—THE CUSTOMS AND MANNERS OF THE MALAYS—DEPARTURE THEREFROM, AND ARRIVAL AT ST. HELENA—DESCRIPTION OF THE EMPEROR NAPOLEON'S TOMB AND HOUSES—DEPARTURE FROM ST. HELENA, AND ARRIVAL IN ENGLAND.

WE sailed from Bengal in company with the Hon. Company's Ship Dunira, October 19th, 1820, with a fine breeze, and arrived at Pulo Penang, or Prince of Wales's Island, on the 6th of November. The houses have a noble appearance, and are built after the form of those in Calcutta. The inhabitants are principally Malays ; of them I shall speak more hereafter. After having received on board a quantity of rattan, as private trade for the captain, we made sail and arrived at Macao, on January 26th, 1821, after a long and tedious voyage.

Macao, a town of China, in the province of Canton, is seated in an inland at the entrance of the river Tae. The Portuguese have been in possession of the town and harbour since the early part of the seventeenth century. The houses are low and built after the European manner ; the Portuguese are properly a mixed breed, having been married to Asiatic women. Here is a Portuguese Governor as well as a Chinese Manadarin. The former nation pays a great tribute to choose their own magistrates. The city is defended by three forts, built upon eminences ; and the works are good and well planted with artillery.

On the 29th we anchored off the second bar, and found lying here the Hon. Company's Ship Canning, and two or three other Company's ships; on the 30th weighed and made sail, but there not being water enough, removed back to our old station. On the following day we crossed Whampo. After the cargo was discharged I went up to Canton.

Canton is a large and populous city, situated in one of the first rivers in the empire. It is the capital of the province of Quantong, and the centre of the European trade in that country. The streets are long and straight, paved with flag stones, and adorned with lofty arches. The houses are remarkably neat, but consist only of one story, and they have no windows to the streets. The covered market place is full of shops. The inhabitants are estimated at about 1,000,000; many of whom reside in barks, which touch one another, form a kind of floating city, and are so arranged as to form streets. Each bark lodges a family and their grand children, who have no other dwelling. At break of day all the people who inhabit them depart to fish or to cultivate their rice.

The frugal and laborious manner in which the great live, the little attention which is paid to the vain and ridiculous prejudice of marrying below rank; the ancient policy of giving distinction to men and not to families, by attaching nobility only to employments and talents, without suffering it to be hereditary; and the decorum observed in public, are admirable traits in the Chinese character.

There is little distinction in the dress of men and women; rank and dignity are only distinguished by the ornaments they wear, and they dare not presume to wear any thing without proper authority, without being severely chastised for it. Their dress in general consists of a long vest, which reaches to the ground, one part of it, on the left side, folds over the other, and is fastened to the right by four or five small gold or silver buttons placed at a little distance from one another. The sleeves are wide towards the shoulder, and grow narrow towards the wrist—they terminate in the form of a horse-shoe—round their middle they wear a large girdle of silk, the ends of which hang down to their knees; from this girdle is suspended a sheath, containing a knife, and over all they wear a loose jacket down to the middle, with loose short sleeves, generally lined with fur, and under all they wear a kind of net to prevent it from chafing. The general colour of these dresses is black or blue.

Their religion is idolatry, their principal idol is *Fong Chon*, and they are very superstitious, believing in magic and invocation of spirits, and the art of foretelling events by divination.

While receiving our cargo on board, a Chinaman belonging to one of the craft, stole a box of tea, but, by the exertion of our officers, the culprit was taken and immediately sent on shore to

Dane's Island to the mandarine. He was found guilty of the crime, and his punishment three dozen blows with the bastinado. The instrument of correction, called pan-tsee, is a bamboo a little flattened, broad at the bottom, and polished at the upper extremity, in order to manage it more easily with the hand.

The culprit, after the mandarin has given the signal for punishment, is seized and stretched out with his belly flat on the ground, his breeches are pulled down to his heels, and on the mandarine throwing down a stick, of which he has a number by him, one of the officers in attendance uses the pan-tsee, and gives him five severe blows, which are succeeded by several others till the number is complete. When it is over, the criminal must throw himself on his knees, incline his body three times to the earth, and thank his judge for the trouble he has taken in his correction.

The mandarines are of two classes, viz. ; those of letters, and the inferior sort are styled mandarines of arms. The latter class do not enjoy the same consideration as the former.

The Chinese in general are much addicted to commit depredations on the pockets, or, in fact, on any unguarded property. After all our cargo was received on board, I went in company with two midshipmen, Mr. C******* and Mr. R*********, on Dane's Island. After we landed some Chinese came and decoyed us to their village, which was at the back of a number of hills and out of sight of the shipping, under a promise that they would let us have some of their country fruit, such as they sent us on board. The length of time that some of them were absent, and the sun going down fast, made us rather doubt the sincerity of their intentions; those that were with us begged that we would stop till the sun was down, but we began to be afraid of our lives. When the men saw that we were determined to wait no longer, they gave a dreadful whoop, which was answered by others stationed on the hills; they immediately seized hold of us and rifled our pockets.

On March 25th we sailed down to Macao, and on the following day we took our departure, and on the 24th of April arrived at Anjier point, and is a settlement belonging to the Dutch ; it lies to the east of Batavia. The houses are generally built of bamboo ; the inhabitants are of various casts, Pagans, Mahometans, and Chinese. The barbarism of the Batta Tribes is horrible, for they kill and eat their criminals or prisoners of war, or even sacrifice their own relations when aged and infirm, not so much with a view to gratify their appetites, as to perform a pious ceremony. Thus, when a man becomes infirm and weary of the world, he is said to invite his own children to eat him when salt and limes are cheapest. He then ascends a tree, round which his friends and offspring assemble, and as they shake the tree they join in a funeral dirge, the import of which is, the season is come, the fruit is ripe, and it must descend. The victim descends, and those that are nearest deprive him of life, and devour his remains in a solemn banquet.

In a few days we made sail. We arrived at St. Helena, on the 19th of July, 1821. This island is situated in the South Atlantic Ocean, its circumference is about twenty miles, and at a distance it has the appearance of a large rock rising out of the sea. On rounding the island it has a very romantic appearance; the town lying in a valley presents to the eye a beautiful chain of scenery. It has some very high mountains, particularly one called Diana's Peak, which is covered with wood to the very summit. There are other hills also, which bear a volcanic appearance, and some have huge rocks of lava, and a kind of half-vitrified flags. James Town is erected in a valley at the bottom of a bay, between two steep dreary mountains, and has from the shipping a noble appearance.

Accommodations are tolerably good, and the inhabitants, generally speaking, are very hospitable. Their villas are pleasantly situated, and have a fine view of the sea; the whole face of the country is really romantic; the hills are immensely high, and the valleys very narrow; and in many of them there are a few houses, which give the whole island a very picturesque appearance.

After obtaining a passport from the Adjutant-General, I went over a long succession of hills to see the habitations of the late Emperor Napoleon Bonaparte. The roads were very difficult to ascend, and particularly rugged. The remains of this great and illustrious personage are buried in a deep valley, about three miles from James town, and about two miles from his late residence at Longwood, under the peaceful shade of three weeping willows, and which also, (as in respect to his dust,) lend a solemn air of reverential darkness to the memorable *well*, from which, during his pilgrimages, he was wont to receive his refreshing draughts.

No stately monument marks the spot; no polished alabaster, or the mimicry of sculptured marble marks his grave: the real excellency of the patriot is written on the minds of his countrymen; it will be remembered with applause as long as the nation subsists, without this artificial expedient to perpetuate it.

Let the poor pass by his grave, and thankfully acknowledge, there lies the man who gloriously fought for his country and his subjects, to free them from the galling yoke of tyranny and oppression: no tablets are written to mark his actions, but those which are written in the heart of his subjects.

The depth of his tomb is about twenty feet, and his coffin rests upon two pedestals, ten feet high., His body is enclosed in four coffins, first lead, second deal, third mahogany, and fourth marble. What is very remarkable is, that part of his tomb is made of the flag-stones of his new house, taken out of one of the kitchens. After viewing the tomb of the man who was the most brilliant meteor in the political world, I proceeded up to Longwood, to take a view of the habitation in which he died.

After presenting my passport I had permission to inspect the premises : the officer took great pains in shewing me the very spot on which he quitted his troubles and persecutions, when he kindly left me to make what sort of reflections I thought proper. The darkness of the room gave it a very solemn appearance, and suited the mind to contemplate upon this late extraordinary character;—but a short period past he was the terror of the world, and now, alas ! what is he ? He is laid low in the tomb, unregretted and unpitied by his merciless enemies. A gleam of light through the casements reflected a dead glimmer through the gloomy mansion. The *most illustrious* have claimed the *tomb* for their last retreat ; rooms of state are resigned ! the sceptre has ceased to wield, and sumptuous banquets are neglected for no other ornament than the winding sheet ! "Where is the star that blazed upon his breast, or the coronet that glittered round his temples ?" Alas ! they are resigned and given over, through the power of the tyrant hand of death.

I have often walked between the impending promontory's craggy cliff; I have sometimes trod the vast spaces of the lonely desert, and penetrated the inmost recesses of the dreary cavern ; but never beheld Nature lowering with so dreadful a form ; never felt impressions of such awe striking cold on my heart, as under this roof ; every thing seemed to participate in grief for their deceased lord. The rooms were very dirty and much neglected. The plants in his late garden seemed to droop their heads in sorrow for the loss of the hand that reared them.

I next proceeded to the palace which had been sent from England, and really it would have reflected honour on the British nation, and no sovereign in the world need wish for a more magnificent one, had it been placed in a more healthy part of the island.

We sailed for England on the 29th, and arrived on the 13th of September, 1821, after a speedy and pleasant passage.

THE END.

RECOLLECTIONS

OF

SICILY,

BY COUNT DE FORBIN.

I EMBARKED at Toulon on the 10th of February, 1820, for the purpose of visiting Sicily. We intended to go direct to Palermo; but contrary winds having detained us at sea for a week, during very severe weather, we were happy to take shelter in Porto Longone, in the island of Elba. Expectation has become the habitual state of all the inhabitants of this island. Still impressed with the marvellous circumstances of the fall, the exile, and the departure of Napoleon, the inhabitants of Elba seemed not to believe that this great drama was concluded. If a few vessels were seen approaching their coast, they all ran out to look at them, persuaded that some new court was approaching to re-animate their melancholy and deserted shores.

I was viewing the house which Napoleon had inhabited, when our consul acquainted us with the new crime which plunged France in mourning. Struck with consternation at this crime, I saw nothing more, and hastened to quit the solitary streets of Porto Ferrago. We set sail shortly afterwards, but a violent west wind obliged us to put into Civita Vecchia, where, being quite tired of the sea, I resolved to proceed to Naples by land. It was night when I arrived at Civita Vecchia, and I was impatient for the return of day.

I have never seen Italy without a hasty emotion. The sun rose, and showed me this country which I love in its languor. I was then in Italy! I again trod those shores with a heart full of affectionate feelings! It was also like a native country to me, adorned with all the reminiscences of my younger years. The charm of Italy cannot be painted or expressed; without endeavouring to teach them to those whose observation it escapes, I shall content myself with relating them. The sight of the happy country produces in the soul a sensation which can only be compared to the effect of distant music, heard in the ceremony after a day of sorrow. So long as age shall not have chilled my blood, I shall always return to seek the promontories of Italy, its azure sea, and its mild light.   What is more noble than her passed existence? what is greater than her history?   Let us respect even her slumber; it is that which follows immense labours.

A few days at Rome, in the spring, would suffice to reconcile the most wretched man to life.   The deliciousness of that season is beyond expression; a crowd of soothing and pleasing ideas occupy the imagination and the heart.   Disinherited of the sovereign purple, humbled, she seems to exert herself to conceal, beneath a robe of flowers, the mutilation of the monuments of her past glory.

The fever, however, was desolating these beautiful countries; it is only by that, in a manner, that the Romans are sensible of life.   At Montcrone, between Civita Vecchia and Rome, the Tertian ague regulated the order of departure of the postillions; this fatal calender assisted them in counting their melancholy days.   Thus we were drawn through this charming country by persons who were in a dying state.   The horizon was of a dazzling brightness, the bushes were covered with birds, and we frequently drove over the ancient way, which travellers leave with regret, for the papal road is only a quagmire.   Nobody has a better right than the Pope to say, in the words of Scripture, "My kingdom is not of this world."   Every step you make in the states of his holiness, you meet only misery and suffering.   I have seen no action, no agitation, no activity here, but in the pulpit.   The preachers gesticulate violently; with the sweat of their brow they fertilize the vineyard of the Lord, while the farmer sleeps in profound idleness.

Within sight of the dome of St. Peter's, and near to Rome, we found every where traces of the fever; we met with it as an advanced guard before the gates, marking at random the houses which it attacks.*   This destructive scourge seems to besiege the sacred city; every year it makes itself master of a street, of an immortal hill.   Vast habitations, gardens, colonnades, strike the sight; you approach, and find them deserted : the porticoes are falling down, the fountains are dry, the arbours overturned; the roof has given way, leaving exposed to the storm, walls covered with paintings, and whatever announced the luxury of the ancient proprietors of those forsaken palaces.

The silence of the suburbs of Transtevere and of la Longara, is interrupted only by the noise of the carriages of some strangers, looking for the house of Scipio, or going to admire Raphael at *La Farnesina*.   The triumphal car of the victor is succeeded

---

* It frequently happens that one house is infested and that adjoining perfectly healthy.

by the chariot of a cardinal ; an enormous umbrella, the symbol of the dignity of the princes of the church, figures on the top of this Gothic carriage, and replaces the Roman ensigns.

I have again visited the Forum Romanum, the vast sepulchre of columns and temples : it has become the field of battle of all the antiquaries in Rome, particularly of Messrs. Fea and Nibby. In their train their disciples dispute, and after them all those who understand, or pretend to understand, any thing of the matter. A brick forms the subject of a consultation, the most insignificant vault is baptized ; and in short, all the decisions consecrated by time are overthrown. How discouraging is this to travellers, who, when they revisit Rome find themselves every where at a loss, and after having spent so much money to learn names they are obliged to spend as much more to unlearn them.

Two foreigners, the duchess of Devonshire, and the duke de Blacas, were at that time causing researches to be made in the Roman Forum. The constant and enlightened efforts of the latter threw a great light in the plan of that most interesting part of ancient Rome. He had just ordered a space of 500 feet long and 600 feet broad to be cleared, in which stood the temple of Venus and Rome. Adrian, while superintending himself the construction of this edifice, the plan of which is said to have originated with him, intended it to have surpassed in magnificence the Forum Trajanum, the master-piece of Apollodorus. The emperor is reported to have been too jealous of the architect, who lived a victim to this singular rivalship.

This temple of Venus and Rome, amphiprostilus and pseudo-dipteros, appears to have had two *cella* leaning one against the other. Ten white marble pillars, of the Corinthian order, decorated each principal front ; it seems to have had only nineteen on the sides. This edifice was surrounded by a portico formed of columns of granite, one side of which adorned the sacred way. Pope Honorus I., in the seventh century, obtained permission of Heraclius to remove the brass roof from this building, to cover with it the basilica of St. Peter. The *Summa Via* passed opposite the temple of Venus and Rome. The same labours have just made us acquainted with the whole of the Via Sacra, and what depended on the edifice known by the name of the Temple of Peace. This basilica was erected by Maxentius ; in fact, the construction and the details evidently belong to the epoch of the creation of the arch of Constantine. According to Aurelius Victor, the entrance of this monument, consecrated by this same prince, was then placed towards the Coliseum.

The duchess of Devonshire employs her mornings in encouraging letters and visiting the ateliers of the artists; and in the evening she does the honours of Rome. It is to the taste for antiquity that we owe the completion of the excavations of the column of Phocas, an insulated monument, which was conjectured to have belonged to a temple or a portico.

Every thing has been said on the effect produced by the church of St. Peter; but, in my opinion, the agreeableness of its internal temperature has not been sufficiently commended. When the sacred music adds its charms to the splendour of this sumptuous monument, the Roman people easily persuade themselves that they enjoy a foretaste of Paradise. All, even to the perfumes, heightens the illusion, and it is only at the gates of this noble temple that they return to their miseries.

The majesty of the Deity is too often disregarded at St. Peter's; gallantry sometimes chooses this church for a rendezvous. We were witnesses of the unhappy termination of an adventure of this kind. A beautiful Roman woman had remarked a foreigner at one of the ceremonies of the holy week. The timidity of the young man was overcome, and a rendezvous agreed upon in a *villa*. As well to avoid the heat as to enjoy secrecy, the two lovers penetrated into the vaults of these catacombs; stopping near a fountain they enjoyed the treacherous coolness—but their lips had pronounced words of tenderness for the last time! Their blood was chilled—death destroyed them both at one blow! Their double funeral terrified the Roman youth who followed them into these same caverns, the depository of innumerable bones.

On leaving St. Peter's, where I had just heard a vehement sermon against nudities and indecency, I entered the Musio Peo-Clementino, where I saw two hundred statues, Venuses, Ledas, &c. restored by the care of the popes. Under each is written in large characters, *Ex dono et munificentia. Pii Sexti,* or *Pii Septimi;* I may therefore admire with a safe conscience.

At that time the people at Rome were mourning for a celebrated lawyer, Bartolucci, whose funeral I met. He had just finished, by order of the pope, the incorporation of the ancient pontifical code, with the French laws, and said a few days before his death, "*Morró contento; sono infine riuscito di vestire da abbate il codice Napoleone.*

I often walked in the ruins of the golden palace of Nero, the theatre of so much magnificence, and of so many crimes. I, too, enjoyed a fête in it, but it was one that nature gave. The sun sinking into the sea illumined the Campagna of Rome, rich in those lines of ruins—rich, too, in its desolation, and beautiful in its mourning. The reflections of a golden light marked all the outlines from the Circus Maximus to the shores of Ostia.

The ivy, the myrtle, the flowers, hanging in garlands from one arcade to another, floated above my head. The eagle still darts from the summits of this monument; but he no longer guides victorious legions; he terrifies only the thousands of birds that hover among the arches, and are now the only inhabitants of the vast palaces of the masters of the world.

I found great changes in the society of Rome; I missed something in the persons whom I had formerly known as the most distinguished for vivacity and wit. I do not speak of beautiful countenances that were faded, but of all the friends of my youth who had rapidly advanced into the vale of misery. How can mature age avoid being melancholy? It has had time to see, what it believed destined to immortality, forgotten —to hear that which it fancied so admirable, condemned, to view the destruction of all the idols of its happier days.

Far from participating in the prejudices usually entertained against Italian society, I think, on the contrary, that we may find in it much intellect, frankness, and sincere affections. It is necessary to have it known in one's youth to be pleased with its tranquil monotony. The Italians habitually follow the beaten track in the thorny path of life; in them there are no illusions, no reveries, none of that melancholy which is the mother of talent, and sometimes as powerful as genius; never any of that sadness to which even happiness pays a voluntary tribute. The Italian women do not ask of life more lively joys than it can give. In vain should we seek among them those fleeting shades, that happy mixture of weakness and of dignity which renders the society of the women of the north so pleasing and so attractive. Truth in their sentiments, good faith in their passions, but little taste for wit and friendship; these seem to me, in general, to characterise the Italian women. I allow, however, all the exceptions, and have myself met with several. Let us not, like some travellers, judge of the Italians by the laquais de place, at Rome, nor of their monks by certain lay brethren who go about begging in the inns.

The sceptre of the arts falls from the hands of Italy. The death of Canova re-established them in a republic; nobody well knew the power or the inclination to assume the influence, which he exercised in a manner so noble, and so just to the artists of all countries. No one ever made a better use of a considerable fortune and well-merited credit, than that illustrious statuary, who was a special benefactor to his native town. This eulogium cannot be suspected from a Frenchman, who regrets the time lost to the arts, and so ill-employed by that able sculptor during his last stay at Paris.

The Italian writers who wish to have their share in the immortality of Canova, because they have so long proclaimed it, are about to enjoy their prerogative, and create or destroy the reputation of the schools. It is according to their decision that an artist will henceforth be either *poverello* or *celebrissimo*. At that time they extolled a young Roman, who patiently makes copies after Raphael and Andrea del Sarto. The custom of copying great masters, and veneration for their works, is fatal to originality in the Italian artists. The statuaries ape the antique instead of being inspired by its master-pieces; the painters follow, with more or less success, the steps of Carlo Maratti. The Germans, who live at Rome, go back to the source of the art, and find no truth and elevation but in Giotto and Ciambué. They are fully persuaded that the Italian school was irretrievably led astray by the last manner of Raphael.

I set out for Naples as soon as possible, being eager to go to Sicily, though I did not wish to reach it before the great heat set in. After having greatly alarmed us with the report of banditti, some persons proposed to me to make an agreement with them. I could not place any kind of confidence in the man to whose hands I must have entrusted myself; a gloomy countenance, large diamonds on his fingers, and pistols in his pockets; all these, added to his unintelligible patois and profound bows, disgusted me with the negotiation. I had no reason to repent, for I met with no accident on my journey. Having left Rome in the night, I was in the morning at the commencement of the Pontine Marshes. A fine road crosses them; the vast canals carry off the water; the sea is kept within its natural limits. When we ask to whom the Roman states owe these great advantages, we read upon a plain stone the following inscription :—

OLIM PONTINA PALVS,
NVNC AGER PONTINVS.
OPVS PII VI.
ANNO MDCCXCIII.

I travelled rapidly to Terracina, the ancient Anxur. At Fondi, in the kingdom of Naples, I was struck with the great number of beggars, and the fine appearance of the troops; they are without doubt the same soldiers on whom Toachim founded such flattering hopes, because they manœuvred like the French ex-guard.

I stopped at Gaëta, where the mild warmth announces the South of Italy. The inn is near the sea side. The ruins of a temple, said to have been part of Cicero's villa, are concealed in

an orange grove, laden with fruit ; some cypresses rise above it,
and vary the line, and white doves hover fearlessly around.   The
costume of the women of Mola di Gaëta is picturesque ; it has,
probably, never varied since the time of Horace; the young
girls whom he admired wore their hair in tresses, and rolled on a
piece of stuff, fastened with a large silver bodkin.   The other
villages on the road are not so pretty as Mola.   Itri at a distance seems to be a charming place : it is divided by a valley,
which supplies it with an abundant spring: it is also crowned
with palm-trees, but in the interior all is ruin, misery, and
poverty, and the people are very ugly.

You would think on entering Naples, that the city was occupied by foreign troops ; they have so exactly copied the uniform
of other nations.   The naval officers wish, above all things, to be
taken for English ; the troops are stuffed in Russian or Austrian
habits, and yet the true national costume is the monk's frock, the
ecclesiastical habit of the Spanish fashion, the military uniform
of taffety, and the simple drawers for the Lazzaroni ; all the rest
is borrowed.

Strangers are always surprised at the great number of princes
and dukes at Naples.   If these titles were the awards of great
services, few countries have produced more heroes and useful
citizens than Naples.   But Italy has always swarmed with
people bearing titles.   Tassoni makes one of his heroes kill thirty
marquisses in a single battle.

Ancient Rome, or modern Europe, are indebted to Naples for
the first idea of Punchinello.   A painting found at Herculaneum,
and which is found also on several vases, represents this comic
character ; below was written *Civis atellanus.*   The attitude, the
physiognomy of the ancient Punchinello, are a complete bur-
lesque.   The jests, the gluttony, and above all, the poltroonery
of punchinello delight the Neapolitan, and amuse even foreigners,
though they cannot feel all the finesse of the double-entendres
of these buffoons, nor the aptness of their frequently very biting
satire.

Before I embarked for Sicily I resolved to revisit Pompeii. The
states of the king of Naples may be said to be double : he has
as many cities under ground, as inhabited, and almost as many
statues as subjects.   We returned from Pompeii by Vesuvius,
which was not so threatening as I had before seen it.   On reaching the summit of the crater, I looked down into the furnace,
whenever the wind drove off the sulphureous vapour and the
cloud of black and reddish smoke.   An immolated rock of a
pyramidal form was in the middle of the crater. Its base seemed
to be sulphur, its summit a pure red, and bands and efflorescences
of every colour formed to it a brilliant crown.   We ascended and

descended on scoriæ and dross of iron. A spring of hot water flowed at our feet, and further on a stream of fiery lava slowly descended towards Resina. The night was dark and stormy : and without perceiving the sea, we heard it at a distance break upon the shore. Here thought is only prayer. Every thing vanishes before Him who created the world, and whose Omnipotence shews a river of fire to the *Campania felice.*

I embarked at Naples on the 24th of April, 1820, at 4 P. M. on board the packet boat, *il Tartaro.* I was accompanied by M. Clérian, a young landscape-painter, and M. Van Cleemputte, an architect of the French school at Rome, and from the assistance of these two artists I derived great advantage.

The Tartaro was part of a convoy of seven vessels carrying troops to Palermo, under the protection of the Capri of seventy-four guns. The wind soon became contrary, and it was three days before we reached the Gulf of Olivieri, near Mazzara, on the coast of Sicily. On the eminence above the beach of Olivieri, a poor ruinous village, are the ruins of Tyndarus, a part of which, as well as the promontory, has long been covered by the sea.

We were eighty miles from Palermo and thirty from Messina.

Tyndarus, formerly rich and populous by its commerce, was situated on a very elevated platform, which projected into the sea, near a small convent, dedicated to the Virgin, (Madona di Tindara.) Vestiges of a citadel, of a theatre, and an amphitheatre, are still placed in a picturesque manner, half-way down, surrounded by wild vines and carob-trees ; and I was sorry that I could not stay here some days. There is a very fine view from the point of the promontory. The ruins of a temple, which might be that of Ceres, covered a neighbouring hill. Near it was that of Mercury, from which Verrès carried the statue of that deity, which Scipio had placed on the altar, after the taking of Carthage.

Large white stones piled on each other mark the circuit of the walls of Tyndarus and its principal gates ; the road still passes in the same place as the ancient way. I afterwards went to visit the church of the Virgin, which was founded in the fifteenth century. I ascended to the monastery with much labour, by a rough road, sometimes at the bottom of a ravine, sometimes over steps cut in the rock ; the fatigue gave an additional relish to the excellent malmsey.

While ascending to the monastery, wherein I turned to take breath, a cool north-west wind came from the sea, which broke below, and I perceived in the horizon all the Eolian islands. I had passed between these islands at sun-set, in a high gale ; the sea was then agitated, and the vapours condensed upon the mountains, looked like clouds of thick smoke violently emitted by volcanoes. In fact, from time to time, the fire of Stromboli broke and dispelled these clouds. We passed under this dark canopy, and in the back-ground, Mount Etna, covered with snow, and still dazzling with light, announced Sicily with inconceivable grandeur.

I had intended to travel along the coast as far as Palermo, passing by Pattè, Santa Agata, San. Stefano, Cefalu, and Termini; but I was disgusted by the cupidity and bad faith of the man who hired me three horses, and offered to accompany me. Every body assured me, that it was not safe to travel without the support of the Campieri, (game-keeper to the barons,) and without letters of recommendation to the captains and syndics. The recent introduction of the conscription had filled the woods with vagabonds, whom it would not have been agreeable to meet. All the inhabitants of the country whom I saw at the beginning of my journey, appeared to me poor, superstitious, and cunning. I must say, however, that experience has given me more confidence in the people of Sicily.

Our journey from Olivieri to Palermo was pretty expeditious. We passed opposite to the abandoned village of Joyosa Vecchia; its ruins are on the summit of a mountain, near Cape Orlando, formerly Agathyrnum. Below are the islands of Felicudi and Alicudi, which are part of the Eolian Archipelago. All this country appeared very wild, yet little hamlets are here and there concealed in the valley.

PALERMO.

The first emotion of surprise which a traveller feels on beholding the picturesque physiognomy of a people is always favourable to the purpose of catching it and painting it. Habit afterwards effaces this impression. On the contrary, it seems to me, that the character and manners of a nation are better studied in time, since every day brings new information.

What most struck me at the first sight of Palermo, was the singularity of the physiognomy of its inhabitants, and its marked character. Palermo has little resemblance with the cities of Italy: several palaces and churches put me in mind of Burgos and Valladolid. The whole of their habits and manners complete their resemblance with the Castalians. I landed on the quay at six o'clock in the evening: a balloon had just been launched; it was not to go very far; but it was a novelty to the Palermitans, who testified the highest satisfaction. I took refuge under the protection of a chaise, which advanced slowly, not to be crushed by a crowd of abbeés, military, lazzaroni, and women half-veiled.

The moon lightened this quay; but I had scarcely passed by a triumphal arch into the street, when I found nothing but profound obscurity; some lamps, nearly extinguished, before a Madonna, and gloomy palaces, resembling the abode of the Gusmans, the Sanchez, and the Olivares.

Nothing is so piquant when you land in Sicily for the first time, as the mobility of the features of the inhabitants. A bending of the eyebrow, a method of lengthening the chin, a contraction of the nostrils, compose an animated conversation; they are clear and positive questions and answers. Afterwards, when they begin to speak, their gestures are so eager, the fingers become such rapid auxiliaries, that the eye can scarcely follow them. The *Cassero*, the principal street of Palermo, presents a succession of comic and varied scenes. The streets are thronged with monks of all orders, every one desires a look of these good fathers, and approaches respectfully to kiss their hands.

Palermo is intersected by two principal streets, and the central point where they meet forms an octagon. The architecture of this place, which is of the year 1592, under the reign of Philip III. is in the Florentine style; it is magnificent, but it will not bear strict examination. One of these streets, which goes from the sea to the country, bears indiscriminately the name of *Cassero*, or Toledo. *Cassero* probably comes from the Arab *el cassar*, either because this street led to a castle, or because a castle was built on this spot. It is also the quarter for business, where every one desires to live. The equipages of the nobility of Palermo go every evening through the Cassero to the sea-shore, which is the fashionable promenade.

The popular custom of placing small marble fountains at the corners of the streets, dates from the time when the Saracens were masters of Sicily. Each of these fountains has its bason, its *jet d'eau*, and glass vessels of pure waters; oranges, citrons, lemonades, and ices, are sold there at extremely moderate prices.

Nearly all the houses of the street of Toledo have, in their upper stories, projecting balconies, and grated boxes; and I learnt that these galleries belonged to convents of nuns. Sometimes a monastery at a great distance, has paid a high price for the advantage of enjoying a sight of this fine promenade, the nuns belonging to them, come by subterranean passages, communicating between the gallery and the monastery. Young ladies of noble families inhabit these convents, which are generally very rich. They formerly received visits in the parlour, and gave breakfasts and little spiritual concerts. They were seen

on the balconies of the Casseros, at the hour of the promenade ; persons desirous of seeing them, take lodgings near
this place ; they conversed by signs, but all this is changed.
The present nuns of Palermo, pay the penalty of the gaiety
which animated their abode forty years ago, and of what in-
discreet travellers have related. The churches of these convents are highly decorated ; the dormer windows, grated with
silver, about two feet in diameter, are placed three feet from the
pavement, and serve for confessionals.

The people of Palermo complain of the heavy taxes ; on the
door of a toll-house at the entrance of the city, there is written *Dazio de ficri,* tax on flowers. Is it not too cruel to tax
flowers, while heaps of filth are tolerated in the streets ?

The *Bugaria,* situated about three miles from the city,
adorned with country seats, is celebrated in the annals of the
pleasures of Palermo. It might be thought that its name
comes from *baccaria,* a place consecrated to Bacchus ; in fact,
the reverse of the medals of Panormus has a bunch of grapes.
I saw at *la Bugaria* only enormous buildings erected on rocks,
not a tree or a meadow : the prospect is, however, varied by
the sea, which terminates it. No traveller omits to visit the
house of the Prince of Patagonia, who had the strange taste
to decorate his gardens with statues of monstrous deformity ;
several still remain, though his son has had many of them
broken. The servant who shewed the inside of the house,
speaking of the mania of his master, said : *Povero nomo non
amava ne donne, ne gioco, ne teatro ; ma si divertiva di quelle
bestialità.* We found two monks playing at billiards, waiting
for the dinner hour of the Prince. I recommend to the curious
the gallery of portraits of the family of the Princes of Patagonia.

Soon after my arrival, I went to see the ruins of Soluntum,
near la Bugaria, and Mount Catalfano. The origin of this town
is not known, which was long in the possession of the Carthaginians. A narrow road led to two temples, built upon a hill.
The little that can be discovered of these monuments, shew that
they were of moderate size, and that their foundations were hewn
in the rock ; and it is with much difficulty that some Doric capitals are found under the briers and bushes which conceal them.

We slept at Termini, near which are the ruins of the ancient
Himera. This town is at the foot of Mount Termini, one of the
Nebrodes. The principal church of Termini, is supposed to
have been erected on the ruins of an ancient edifice, said to
have been the palace of the pro-consul Athenius. We made a
drawing of a statue wearing a toga, which the inhabitants call
that of the Consul.

The interior of the chapel of St. Rosalia, on Mount Pellegrino, is very picturesque. When a beam of the sun penetrates through the ivy and the bushes into the church, which is hewn in the rock, its uncertain light throws a magical gloom over the gilded altar, and the image of the Patroness of Palermo.

Saint Rosalia had lived in her youth at the court of King Roger, of which she was the ornament. An unhappy passion induced her to abandon the world about 1220; and not finding the rules of any community austere enough, the fair penitent retired into a grotto of Monte Pellegrino, where she died soon after. Being buried by angels, the perfume of roses issuing from her tomb, betrayed the place of her sepulture.

The cathedral of Palermo, built in 1185, by Gautier, Archbishop of this city, was dedicated to Saint Rosalia, whose intercession saved Palermo from the plague. The outside of this monument, the architecture of which is Moorish and Greek of the Lower Empire, is very striking. The tombs of porphyry of the Emperors Frederick and Henry, are much admired; whose epitaphs were composed by the Canon Roger Paruta. I think that these enormous blocks of porphyry were brought from Syria. I have myself seen some of large dimensions in the port of Cesarea in Palestine, which seemed to have been prepared to be sent to Europe. This church is illuminated in the evening of the fête of Saint Rosalia, by five hundred lustres, with wax candles, the splendour of which is heightened by looking glasses skilfully arranged, so that the view of this immense cathedral at that time is extremely brilliant.

The fête of Saint Rosalia, which is celebrated at Palermo in the month of July with the greatest pomp, will in future awaken the recollections of the late troubles. The fire-works which preceded that solemnity, were the signal of the terrible conflagration. This was the death-blow to the prosperity of the Palermitans, and the brilliant spectacles which the people so highly enjoyed. Nothing can give a better idea of this fête than the engravings in the Travels of Saint Non, after the designs of Després.

Guided by father Francisco, we visited the catacombs of the convent of the Capuchins. The gardens are planted with large trees; alleys of myrtle crowned by orange-trees, bending under the weight of their fruit; while streamlets of limpid water murmurs at their feet and nourish them. A staircase faintly lighted leads into a subterranean crypt, through a long square gallery, the walls of which are as it were lined with skeletons, half covered with a tanned skin. Some of these bodies, dressed in Monks' garments, still retain something of their physiognomy. Their arms are sometimes stretched out, sometimes placed by the side of the body, and sometimes crossed over the breast.

Below, in chests covered with armorial bearings, are the women and young persons. I saw there the name of a young lady of Vintimilli, who died in 1819, aged seventeen. Even here there is a distinction of ranks; a citizen lies far from a Lord, who is not permitted to lie near a Prince. My guide, familiarised with the sight, replaced some corpses which had been moved. The property of this place to preserve from corruption the bodies deposited in it, is so surprising, that little children still seem to be playing together.

The art of painting is entirely neglected in Sicily. The works of Signor Velasquez, though highly praised by his countrymen, have no similarity with those of his celebrated namesake of the Spanish school. As for sculpture, nobody applies to it, the Sicilians have retained an exclusive admiration for Gaggino, a productive statuary of the 15th century.

Palermo has two theatres; in the first, the *Carolino*, they perform serious operas, in the other little Sicilian comedies, and low farces. A Sicilian performer, whose acting is full of nature, was highly applauded. The Opera of Iphigenia was then a very great favourite; Achilles was acted by a woman who sung wonderfully well, so that nobody was sensible of the ugliness of the hero, and the grotesque costume of the Greek army. The taste for music is as lively at Palermo as in Italy; their manner of expressing their satisfaction is equally passionate, they always say with Tassoni; *A chi l'armonia non piace, indemoniato o bestiale, e de dire che via.* I found here in the boxes, the same monotony of customs, visits, and gossipping as in all the theatres of Italy.

What sweet repose do we enjoy in the garden of the convent of Maria dé Giesù, about two miles from Palermo! This convent is on the side of a mountain, the declivity of which is gentle; the hill, which is covered with rich verdure, is planted with cypresses, pines, oranges, and large aloes; the terraces crowned with arbours, are made amidst this forest, and abundant springs fall in cascades, and form at each stage of these terraces, basons of delicious coolness :

> ——————Illic vivere vellim,
> Oblitusque meorum obliviscendus et illis,
> Neptunum porcul è terra spectare furentem.
> (Horat. Epist. lib. 1 ep. XI.)

The purity of the air, the sound of the convent bell, the lovely vegetation of this place, the view of the port and city of Palermo, the distant noise of a populous city, the silence of this retreat, and the contrast of all these various interests, excite a pleasing and profound reverie.

A magnificent road leads to the abbey of Monréale, four leagues from Palermo, across a beautiful and fertile plain, covered with palm, curob, and plantain trees ; an ascent excellently contrived leads to this church, built in a splendid style, by William II., the greatest part of which was consumed by fire in 1811. Gates of brass, vaults incrusted with gilded mosaic work, fifty columns of granite or porphyry, a high altar of massive silver, and innumerable monuments, were all devoured by the flames. I saw in the convent, which was saved, a fine picture by Pietro Novello, called *le Monréalese*, the friend and rival of Vandyke ; Novello died at his native town, Monréale. A broad pencil, vigorous and pleasing colouring, distinguished the works of this artist, who had first followed the manner of Spagnoletto : but he may be accused of weak and often incorrect drawing. The artist's daughter, the pupil and rival of her father, sometimes worked with him. The productions which proceeded from this union of talents, are remarkable for grace and harmony of colouring.

The fire in the church of Monreale spared the tomb of William the Good. The editor of the travels of Saint Non, supposes that this work is of the twelfth century, whereas it bears the date of 1575. It is the monument of William the Bad, which is of 1177. A square cloister, supported by two hundred and sixteen columns of white marble, beautiful gardens, fountains, a delightful situation, made me envy the fate of the rich and numerous Benedictines who compose the community of Monréale. The monks seldom visit their library, or their collection of medals. I then went to the monastery of St. Martin, built by Gregory the Great, and its magnificence made me forget even the sumptuous abbey of Monréale. We must not look in these monasteries for Calmets or Montfaucons ; we more commonly find there a calm oblivion of the affairs of this world, peaceful relations with mankind, and only some ambition to become prior or abbot. The monks of this country are generally inclined to tolerance, for which I have heard them reproached by austere persons, who are often as inexorable to others as to themselves.

The prince royal of Naples, the duke of Calabria, who then governed Sicily with the title of regent, often resides in a beautiful mansion (Bocca di Leone) near Monréale, where he indulged in his taste for agriculture. It is impossible to have more solid knowledge, and more ardently to study the welfare of his people, than this prince, whose manners are mild and unaffected. The duke of Calabria and his august consort are adored at Palermo.

Loaded with kindness by his royal highness, and furnished

with letters to the intendants and the superiors of the religious communiters in Sicily, I bade adieu to Palermo from the summit of Zizza. This moorish château, as curious as the alhambra, is the work of an Emir, who bestowed on this elegant monument the name of his daughter. To another castle near Monréale, he gave the name of his second daughter, Tuba. William II. caused to be translated into Latin, a Chaldean inscription, found near the Zizza, of which the following is the substance:

"While Isaac, the son of Abraham, reigned in the valley of Damascus, and when Esau, the son of Isaac, governed Iduméa, a great number of Hebrews, accompanied by several inhabitants of Damascus and Phenicia, landed in this triangular island, and chose their habitation in this beautiful spot, to which they gave the name of Panormus."

A second inscription, in the same language, is preserved over one of the gates of the city; the following is the sense:

"There is no God, but one only God; there is no power but this same God; there is no conqueror but the God whom we adore. The commander of this tower is Sépho, son of Eliphaz, son of Esau, brother of Jacob, son of Isaac, the son of Abraham. The name of this tower is Baych, and that of the neighbouring tower Pharat."

The nobility of Palermo do not have such frequent assemblies as in 1777, when the editor of St. Non speaks of the brilliant fêtes, and the spirit of gallantry which still animated Sicily. They hardly exist, except in the boxes of the theatre; and the house of the princess of Paterno, of the illustrious family of Moncade, was the only one which still afforded to strangers the relief of the most refined and attentive hospitality.

After having turned round a barren mountain, we perceived the little village of Carini, the ancient Hyccara. Alcamo, founded by the Saracens, is on the summit of a mountain thirty miles from Palermo, three from the sea, and nine from Ségeste; Alcamo contains a great many convents, both of monks and nuns. I recommend to lovers of painting a fine picture of Angelo de Fiesole, which adorns an altar in the church of the Zoccolanti.

We were very well lodged at Alcamo, at the palace of Pastore, thanks to the kindness of the princess of Paterno, but I quitted it without regret to visit the ruin of Ségeste. The country between them is extremely rude. This city is great and striking, and does not deserve to be ill spoken of, as it is in the travels of St. Non.

Sitting in the shade of the columns of the temple of Ceres

or of Venus, which has been so much admired and so often drawn, I did not trouble myself to know to which of these two goddesses it might have been dedicated. I enjoyed the charms of a delightful day, which thousands of birds celebrated with their rival songs. The sparrow hawks flew screaming from the summit of the ancient edifice, and lizards, of an emerald colour darted from the crevices of the columns, gilded by the sun. This monument remains the only testimony of the piety and the wealth of the ancient Ségeste. The rival of St. Selinuntium sleeps like her in the dust; and time has effaced even the inscriptions which attested the reciprocal hatred of these two great cities. The temple of Ségeste is of the same order, but not so pure as that of Pœstum. I do not know where the draftsmen, employed by the Abbé de Saint Non, could see trees near this Doric monument. After having made a drawing of this temple with great care, and without fanciful embellishments, we ascended the hill where are the ruins of the theatre. It is evident that this edifice, the walls of which are forty-feet high, and the vomitoria, still to be seen, was surrounded by habitations. Heaps of square stones are lying on all sides. Here, and no where else, we must seek for the ancient Ségeste. Castel-a-mare, on the sea coast, is the ancient emporium of Ségeste. This place is between Palermo and Trapani.

From Alcamo to Trapani we did not follow a regular road, but narrow paths, which traverse round uncultivated and desert hills. We left Calatafimi on our left; it was there that Des Porceleds commanded; a Provençal gentleman, whose virtues caused him to be excepted from the massacre of the Sicilian vespers. Philippe de Scalambre, a French gentleman, governor for Charles I. in the Val di Noto, was also spared in the massacre at Messina, some days after that of Palermo. The hills are covered with short and slippery grass; and in the valley are small streams half dried up. The rude flute of the shepherds, who tend numerous flocks, has none of the graceful modulations of that of Bion or of Theocritus. If you meet country people mounted on their mules, they first respectfully take off their cotton cap, commonly worn by the Sicilians, and the next thing the good people do, even when they are biting an enormous piece of bread, is to come up to you and say, " you see very well that I am dying with hunger."

Nothing can be more like Palestine than those abandoned fields. As you approach Trapani, you find little cultivation on the beginning of a high road. We passed Mount Saint Julien (Mont Eryx.) Some walls, on the summit of a square rock, are said to be the remains of the temple of Venus Erycina, so celebrated for the beauty of its priestesses. It is worthy of remark, that the women of the little town of Saint Julien, placed like a citadel on the summit of the mountain, are the most beautiful in Sicily. These successors of the priestesses of Venus, have retained only the features of their predecessors. Great austerity of morals prevails at Saint Julien ; doors hermetically closed, and grated windows, clearly denote the jealous and unsociable character of the inhabitants.

The heat of the day had been so intolerable that we were exhausted with fatigue when we reached Trapani, a town of 12,000 inhabitants, on the sea side, and tolerably fortified. The streets, like those of Palermo, are paved with large flags of a shiny stone. I saw some fine palaces, but their doors were not opened to us. The magistrates assigned me a lodging, from which the fleas and their auxiliaries expelled me, and I was obliged to sleep in the public square wrapped in my cloak, and my head resting against a fountain.

The island of Saint Pantaleon was, formerly, joined to the continent ; Motya, where the Carthaginians were besieged by Dionysius, the tyrant, was situated on this spot. These Africans made an island of it. From the summit of Mount Pantaleon, Cape Bon, in Africa, may be distinctly seen.

Trapani now complains of the decay of trade ; it formerly exported, with advantage, works in ivory, coral, shells, and alabaster ; it also traded in sumac, wine, oil, and soda. But this last branch of commerce is almost extinct. Trapani has retained nothing of its ancient lustre but the irresistible beauty of its women, who were reckoned the handsomest in Sicily. Though they are wrapped in black mantles, the elegance of their figure is very remarkable. Their eyes are large and mild, their features have the Grecian purity, and their expressive smile is a favour. We journeyed along the sea-coast to Marsalla, formerly Lillybæum, which was destroyed in the Punic wars, and the Saracens built upon its ruins the modern Marsalla, which, in Arabic, signifies the Port of God. It was afterwards enlarged and fortified by the Normans, and destroyed by Charles the Fifth ; some subterraneous vaults are the only remains of the baths and sumptuous abodes of the Greeks of Lillybæum. I could discover only a few vestiges of its walls ; on the sea-coast nothing remains of it but the quarries that furnished the stone for its monuments, which are now no more. I saw however in the Town Hall of Marsalla, a stone group, larger than life, which was formed under ground at Lillybæum. It represents two lions devouring a bull ; though very much decayed, it seemed to me to belong to the finest era of the arts in Greece. A Latin inscription, in the same palace, is of the time of the Roman dominion.

I was lodged with the monks of the Franciscan order. They are numerous and hospitable, but their convent is poor. When I heard their prayers before meals, when I again saw before me the pewter plates, the broken fork, and the tin drinking cup, I fancied myself again at Rama, or with my venerable hosts at Jerusalem. Though the good monks obligingly took us wherever they imagined there was any thing that could interest us, I found nothing worth drawing. Mr. Goodhouse, an Englishman, has established, at Marsalla, a manufactory of wine, as profitable to himself as advantageous to the inhabitants; his inexhaustible charities maintain them in years of distress, and his name is blessed by all the inhabitants of Marsalla. The wines in the cellar of Mr. Goodhouse rival the best Maderia. I would not advise any body to take the road by Trapani, when he may proceed from Alcamo to Castel Vetsano. The road which I took was burning hot, unwholesome, and uninteresting. The way from Marsalla to Mazzara is seldom more than two miles from the sea-coast. It is an uncultivated low plain, intersected with marshes, and extending further than the eye can reach; not a mole hill; not a tree to break the monotony of the scene. At last, after a journey of fourteen miles, some quarries indicate the vicinity of an inhabited country. Mazzara, containing about three or four thousand inhabitants, was the ancient Mazarum. Ancient marble sarcophagii, ornamented with bas-reliefs, are placed in the cathedral. Mazzara, though now so inconsiderable, was once the residence of Count Roger, whose statue is still standing over the door of the principal church. We proceeded from thence to Castel Vetrano, by roads begun with considerable magnificence but suddenly abandoned. Thus, what has been done is suffered to go to decay; and the means of communication are very dear and often impracticable. People and cattle have infinite trouble in extricating themselves from these marshes during rainy winters. Briars cover the vast quarries of Campo Bello, from whence the Selinuntines procured the large stones which they employed in building their temples. Vases of columns, capitals rough hewn, lie still in the quarry on the road. How did they move these masses of thirty feet in length? Would not this be an interesting subject of inquiry?

The landscape of Campo Bello was, at that time, worthy of the pencil of Claude: the sun was setting in the Lillybæum sea; goats having, on the summit of the quarry, placed themselves as a portion of a rock already hewn into a column, others climbed on a capital of gigantic size, half concealed by fig-trees and dwarf palms; the steeples of the village of Campo Bello enriched the back-ground, and elegantly varied the line of the horizon.   It was pretty late when we entered Castel Vetrano, which some affirm to be the ancient Entella. Castel Vetrano is the birth-place of Maggio, a famous musician of the seventeenth century, who was the Rossini of his time. On our arrival they were celebrating the festival of the patron saint of this little town, which was terminated by fire-works. Our arrival attracted some attention, and we soon became exclusive objects of the curiosity of the public.   The Syndic ceremoniously opened the letter recommending us to his care. After a long conference between this magistrate and his inferior officers, we were taken to very good apartments in the palace of the Duke of Monte Leone.   I was impatient for daybreak to visit the ruins of Selinuntium, commonly called *li Piglieri*, which are on the sea shore, seven miles from Castel Vetrano. To reach them we traversed a fertile plain, intersected by a wood which I shall never forget; it was a forest of wild olives, cork trees, and evergreen oaks, bushes of white thorns blossomed beneath them, and numerous nightingales saluted the rising sun.   But an hour later I felt an African heat while I was drawing among the temples.   The remains of an ancient way led us to the three temples, situated on an eminence, the foot of which is washed by the sea.   It may here be seen that a violent earthquake could alone humble the pride of man by so completely overturning his most majestic works, and which he must have thought the most durable.   All is fallen, and the temples are only mountains of ruins.   The rhododendron, the wild vine, usurp the sanctuary, and twine among the cornices, the bases, and the capitals.   We supported ourselves by the branches to endeavour to find the place, the measure, the destination of these innumerable fragments.   The temples of Selinuntium, which our guide assured us had been overthrown by an earthquake at the moment when Jesus Christ expired, are still perfumed : incense no longer burns upon the altar, but nature has been so prodigal of her sweets, that it is impossible to remain long. The space which separates the temples, and which was, doubtless, the forum of Selinuntium, is overgrown with enormous thistles.   This great and populous city was destroyed in a few hours by the brutal fury of the soldiers of Hannibal ; from one of its two ports an immense staircase led towards the city, a fine avenue to three other temples, which likewise covers, with their ruins, a tolerably high hill.   Storms often clear away the sands which have filled up the ports of Selinuntium, and shew, for a few moments, the quays, the columns, and other remains, melancholy vestiges, which the fury of waves again conceals under moveable sands.

A watch tower is at present the only inhabited dwelling.   The ladder, which is taken away at night for fear of the Corsairs, served me to climb into this gloomy abode, which thirst induced me to enter.   Two old men occupy three or four dark and decayed rooms ; one of them, who called himself an artillery man, was nearly blind.   His daughter could only give us some brackish water.   This young woman, who was suckling a child, was handsome, notwithstanding the wretched state of her picturesque dress.   When this only female inhabitant of Selinuntium came down, and seated herself on the fragment of a column, she seemed to me to personify this poor Greek city, the vestiges of which inspire so much pity and surprise.

We travelled, without stopping, the twenty-four miles between Castel Vetrano and Sciacca, a little ruinous town, which retains nothing of the charms of *Thermæ Selinuntiæ.* Some Gothic ruins, which command Sciacca, still remind its inhabitants of the long feuds of two rival houses, the Barons of Luni and Perollo ; these rich and powerful houses fortified their palaces. Under the reign of Martin and Maria a beautiful heiress was sought in marriage by two of the most accomplished young men in Sicily, Artale de Luni and Jacques Perollo.   The king favoured Luni, because he was of Spanish origin ; he was preferred ; and rage seized the heart of Perollo.   The two rivals bequeathed to their sons the hatred which they had inherited from their fathers, and which divided Sciacca and all Sicily.   Recourse was had to poison and assassination, and even the holy sacrament was witness to the most sanguinary combats. All this passed in the 15th and 16th centuries, under the kings of Arragon.   These two families, sullied by their crimes, were at length banished, when the government became sufficiently strong to check the feudal wars, by incorporating the estates of its great vassals with the domains of the crown.   The enormous dungeon of the castle of Luni commands a whole quarter of the town of Sciacca, which its inevitable fall, threatens with speedy ruin.   The materials, which form the basis of this monument of feudal barbarism, are imprudently suffered to be carried away by piecemeal.

Sciacca has been celebrated for the perfection of its pottery ; and, in fact, most of the beautiful vases of great Greece were manufactured here or at Gela.   At present they manufacture vases of a light and porous earth, which have the property of cooling the liquid which they contain, as much as the Egyptian *basdaques* of Kéné.

Eager to visit Agrigentum, we proceeded rapidly along the beach. Rice fields, and immense plains which are very unwholesome, are inundated by the rivers. Istrus and Camicus came down nearly to the sea-side. We perceived upland the ruins of Calata Balota, a Moorish castle, which was afterwards the fortress of the house of Luni. Cottages covered with thatch, placed all along the coast, at a distance of a mile from each other, are inhabited by officers of health. I endeavoured to find at least a stone of the ancient Heraclea, but the last ruins of that Greek city sunk into the sea a few years ago.

Continuing our route by the sea-side, we came to the port of Girgenti, situated about four miles from that city, which occupies the same site as the ancient citadel. This little port had an appearance of business, some feluccas, and a little trade. The ascent to Girgenti is rough, unpaved, and the horses are in constant danger of falling into the ravines. It is impossible to give an idea of the bad state of the roads, and still more of the streets, in the villages, and even in the towns of Sicily. I complained of it to an inhabitant, who answered, shrugging his shoulders, " I am here only for a few moments ; I should " have too much to do, to try to better myself : the father of " my father was as badly off as I am ; besides it is hot ; I am " going to seek for a cool place to sleep. I advise you to do " the same, and leave every thing else, as I do, to the Holy " Virgin." The eye turns aside from this modern village, to contemplate that wonderful line of temples, the second line of ramparts, which is far more elegant and magnificent than the military architecture of Vauban. There are the temples of Juno Lacinia and of Concord ; and, lastly, a whole plain is covered with the ruins of the temple of the giants. Farther on is the piscina, which is six thousand toises in circumference. These innumerable tombs are those of the besiegers ; those of the besieged are farther on, and the modern Girgenti itself seems to be only a sepulchre. The greatest austerities of the Christian religion and its most gloomy penitents, have succeeded to theatres crowned with flowers. Spectres, covered with haircloth, wander amidst the remains of temples and theatres, and the psalmody of the *Miserere* is alone heard among these mighty ruins.

The citadel of Agrigentum was upon an elevated spot. Below it are vestiges of the temple of Jupiter Polieus ; and that of Ceres and Proserpine ; now the chapel of Saint Blaise. The road which passes under the ruins of a gate of Agrigentum, leads to the temple of Juno Lacinia, which contained the picture of Zeuxis, for which the painter had five of the handsomest young women in Agrigentum for models.

About three hundred steps from the temple of Juno is that of Concord ; which is the best preserved that I have yet seen in Italy, Greece, or Sicily. It wants only a roof, a piece of the pediment, a portion of the cornice, all the rest is standing. This edifice is doric pseudodipteros and amphiprostylus. The columns are fluted without a basis; the temple rests on six steps; it is 143 feet 10 inches 9 lines in length, and 51 feet four inches broad. The period of its foundation is as uncertain as its dedication to Concord; this supposition having no other foundation than the following inscription, found in the modern city:

CONCORDIÆ, AGRIGENTINORVM SACRVM,
RESPVBLICA. LILYBETANORVM,
DEDICANTIBVS. M. ATTERIO, CANDIDO, PROCOS.
ET. L. CORNELIO, MARCELLO. Q. PR. PR.

Mr. Houel and M. Denon are mistaken; the openings made in the Temple of Concord date from the era of the introduction of the Christian worship, when this church was dedicated to San Gregorio delle Rupe, bishop of Girgenti. We are also accused of this act of barbarism (for all this is uncertain). Beato Mattei, bishop of Girgenti, also entirely overthrew the antique altar in 1620. It is therefore believed, that it was he who caused the six doors on the sides to be opened, the bad effect of which is ascribed, by almost all travellers, to the original architect of the temple. Still following the walls we come to the temple of Hercules; it was of immense size, of the Doric order, and the columns fluted without base. Near to this are the remains of the wonder of Agrigentum, the Temple of the Giants, dedicated to Olympian Jupiter, which was so worthy of the majesty of that god, such as is represented by Homer and Phidias. Excavations, ordered in 1802, shewed the place of this edifice. According to Diodorus, it was 340 Greek feet in length, and according to new measures and the reduction of the English to the Greek foot, it must have measured 356 feet, 8 inches, 4 lines; its breadth of 160 feet, according to Diodorus, would be 177 feet, 2 inches, 8 lines English; and, lastly, its height, according to him, 120 feet, would be but 110 feet, 11 inches, 9 lines.

The Punic war prevented the completion of this monument, and it may be imagined that it never had any roof. The exterior of the temple was composed of a wall with columns, let into the wall by half a diameter, or rather, projecting at least this half diameter; it is not certain whether Diodorus, in his measure, meant to comprehend or to include that of the columns. These columns, which were fluted, are stated to have been 40 feet in circumference; a man could easily conceal himself in one of the flutings, whence Diodorus says, (Book III., chap. 24) "Tanta Striarum, amplitudine ut corpus humanum inserere se aptè queat." Fazelli *De rebus Siculis*, is the first who speaks of these great ruins: he quotes some

Latin verses in rhyme, dated 1401, which were found in the Archieves of Girgenti. These verses commemorate the recent and fatal day (the 9th of December, 1401) in which three of the colossal statues fell, the neck and shoulders of which seemed to support this great mass. According to Fazelli, these three colossuses, or giants, which long remained standing upon three columns amidst the ruins of the temple, furnished the ground for the arms of the city of Girgenti, the motto of which still is, "Signat Agrigentum mirabilis aula gigantum."

Father Pancratio, who wrote on the subject during the last century, calls it "Palace of the Giants." It appears certain that the two fronts of the temple had also only columns let into the walls ; their number was 14 on the sides and 7 in front. These colossuses, measuring 25 or 26 feet, formed of several blocks of stone of the country, were necessarily covered with stucco, and placed with their backs to square pilasters. Their two arms bent over their heads, called to mind the attitude of the porters. In fine, the style of the sculptor is evidently Eginetic. The learned world are now looking with impatience for a dissertation upon this monument by Mr. Cockerell, an able English architect, who has applied to this labour with much zeal and perseverance ; his work will certainly throw great light upon this important point of ancient architecture.

It is very remarkable, that in the ruins of so rich a city, which, in the time of Empedocles, had 800,000 inhabitants, the traveller finds so few traces of marble monuments. The streets, the public squares, had to follow the variations of the ground, which is extremely irregular, and the spot where the city might be, was on the side of a mountain, exposed to the scorching rays of the sun. One is surprised at the narrowness of the public ways, among others, that which passed under the Porta Aurea, below the Temple of Hercules, and under that of Gela. There certainly was not in the ancient city of Agrigentum a single palace equal to the Louvre or the Vatican. I met with only a marble cornice belonging to an unknown monument, in the possession of Signor Panetieri, the Precentor in the cathedral,—and even this was of the age of Septimus Severus.

We lodged at Girgenti, with the Dominicans, who did not receive us very well; they would have thought themselves more certain of the price of their masses from the English. " *Le una gran bella natione,*" said the prior. " It is impossible," added he, " that God should not shew mercy to it, and give it credit in the other world for all the money which it spends in this." However, the affection of the Sicilians for the English nation is easily accounted for, by all the good which the latter has done them, by the advantages they derived from its alliance, and by the abode of the British troops in Sicily. On the other hand, I was loaded with civilities by Monsignor Panetieri; this learned ecclesiastic possesses a collection of Greek vases. He shewed me the torso of a statue of Pentelic marble, of the most admirable workmanship: it may be by the same master as our Venus of Milo; I brought home a cast of it, which M. Panetieri had the politeness to give me. It is impossible to be better treated than I was by the Marquis Palerma, civil governor of Girgenti, who executed with mildness the difficult task which had been assigned him, to diminish the immense influence of the clergy, to introduce regularity into the administration, and to accustom the people no longer to regret the arbitrary justice of the barons, and to bear the law of the conscription. The last article was not the most easy, and was a continual and general subject of complaint.

The revenue of the bishop, which amounted to eighty thousand piasters, had just been reduced to twelve thousand. All the clergy murmured still less at this, than at seeing two priests withdrawn from their jurisdiction, and from the ecclesiastical immunities, who were accused of having assassinated their superior at Palma. The new laws consigned these men, who were already imprisoned in the dungeons of Girgenti, to the criminal tribunals. The details of this affair, the refinements of cruelty exercised by these two men, excited general indignation. One of the accused had chaunted a requiem over the body for the soul of their victim. It was hoped that these wretches would soon receive the punishment due to their crime.

The seminary of Girgenti is so considerable that two hundred young men were going to receive priests' orders.

The modern Agrigentines speculate on the ashes of their ancestors. They ransack the sepulchres for the vases, which amateurs purchase at such high prices. I obtained several; but I was disgusted with negotiating with the peasants, who are greedy and deceitful. Whole days pass in conferences, messages, in lies on their side, and impatience on the part of purchasers; they generally come and wake you in the middle of the night, to accede to the bargain, which they refused the day before. If the ancient Agrigentines took too much care of their children, if they covered them with pearls, and robes embroidered with gold, the most considerable people of Girgenti leave theirs in a state of neglect, which is truly disgusting. The clothes of the infants are laced so tight as to make their heads swell, to distort their features; and these poor creatures, thus suffering and disfigured, are left for hours together on the threshold of a door. The consequence is, that you see children of five or six years old with the dropsy; the only remedy known here is to dedicate them to St. Francis.

The population, in consequence of this kind of education, has become frightfully ugly; and when the *contessine* and the ladies of quality attempt to make up for the defects of nature, by dressing in the extreme of the French fashion, it is not always easy to preserve your gravity.

I quitted the groves of olives and the beautiful palms of Agrigentum for the arid mountains of Aragona, Regalmuto and its mines of sulphur, Camarata, Castronovo and its quarries of marble, and lastly, Bivona, the country of Saint Rosalia. I found no trace of the ancient Hippone: my curiosity was more satisfied by what the Sicilians called *Casali de' Greci.* These are four villages, founded by some Albanians in 1480; these victims of the despotism of the Turks, sought an asylum in this country. Remaining faithful to their religion and their dress, their priests marry, their rich women wear the veil, wide sleeves, fringes, and a robe fastened by a silver girdle of pretty good workmanship. This Greek colony is composed of the villages of Contessa, Piana, Mezzo Juso, and Palazzo-Adriano. All those who now escape the Turkish scimitar will, doubtless, imitate this example. May these fugitives at length find repose in an hospitable land! May my country open her doors to them, place them under the safeguard of her paternal sceptre, and the egis of her generous laws! I was directed to the ruins of the ancient city of Entella, but unfortunately missed them. Near Calta Nisetta they shewed me, in the sulphur mines of Stretta, a fountain of sulphur which is intermitting. Calta Nisetta had, before the last revolution, sixteen thousand inhabitants: this town, which boasted of being the ancient Nisa, was burnt and entirely destroyed by the people of Palermo in July, 1820. The unfortunate inhabitants wander now among the ruins, plunged into the most terrible misery.

On the way from Agrigentum to Alicata you stop at Palma, a poor little village, with four churches. The country, however, is always the same, fertile in spite of the inhabitants. Then you come to extensive solitudes, heaths, and torrents, the course of which is marked by oleanders, which have a charming effect. We arrived early at Alicata, which pretends to be the ancient Gela Alicata, and is the point nearest to the coast of Africa: there is some appearance of activity in its port for the shipment of corn; but the town is dirty and wretched, and you are devoured by clouds of insects.

The numerous descents of the corsairs of Tunis and Algiers lately desolated all this open coast. They took advantage of the darkness of the night to land and approach the solitary habitations. These robbers then dispersed, fastening to their necks a little bell. The country people, imagining that their mules had escaped, or that their neighbour's oxen had broken into their fields, went out without suspicion, and did not go four steps before they were loaded with irons.

After the bad night that I had passed at Alicata, I rested under some orange-trees, in a garden half-way between that town and Calta Girone, where we were to pass the night. During this journey, which was thirty-eight miles, we saw labourers of a miserable appearance, leave fields of wheat a league in length, to come and ask us for alms. They have nothing of their own, they cultivate the inheritance of a master they never see ; lawyers, and intendants, always stand between the labourer who dies with hunger, and the great nobleman whom they ruin.

The heat appears to me to be more stifling in Sicily than in Africa. The sun scorches your head, and the earth burns your feet. Water is scarce and unwholesome ; so that when the journey is long, men and animals are dying with thirst before noon ; if they perceive a stream all are eager to reach it. The people complained, that abundant and regular streams had disappeared : in truth, we found fountains and reservoirs now useless. When the calcareous valleys of southern Sicily are heated to this degree, walking is a torment. A burning sky causes tempests to be regretted ; if a slight wind rises, it is inhaled with delight ; but it is from Africa that it comes ; soon the mouth is parched, the throat dry and hot, and all objects appear through a vapour waving like a flame. How delightful is it then to find in a village water cooled with ice, which, with the juice of a lemon, makes a delicious beverage

After leaving on one side Modica and Noto, we climb by terrible roads, much worse than that of Girgenti, up to Calta Girone, or rather Calata Hierone. Calta Girone, placed on the summit of a mountain, is a little town, the university of which has a revenue of eighty thousand piasters. The professors rise late, the students never come, consequently their studies are not very profound. Calta Girone consists only of churches, and is inhabited only by priests. They are great admirers of a statue of the Virgin, by Gaggini, in the church of the Recollets.

After the long descent from Calta Girone, we made drawings of aqueducts and substructions, which may have belonged to the ancient Eubéa, *(Licodia.)* The subterraneous way, hollowed in the rock, and which, probably, terminated at the ancient citadel, is a very curious monument of the art of the ancients, which would deserve to be carefully examined. Many other roads branch out from this principal one ; but they are all choaked up with rubbish, which might easily be cleared away. Vases, little idols, lacrymatories, medals, and mosaics, in tolerable preservation, are found every day in the environs of Licodia. There are also many sepulchral chambers, part of the gates of the city, and of its walls.

All these remains have a character of grandeur and solidity. An excavation made in 1808, produced very curious results. Three urns of lead were found near each other, in a state of perfect preservation ; several leaves of gold, evidently made to imitate laurel leaves, were placed in one of them.

I did not see Terra Nova, formerly Callipolis, which carries on a pretty brisk trade with Malta. Not far from it, are the ruins of Camarina, a flourishing Syracusan colony, now entirely destroyed. Ragusa, *Hybla Minor*, which has bituminous springs, and sepulchral grottos. Scicli, Casmene, Spaca-Forno, are uninteresting ; but the latter opens the valley of Ispica. This valley is near three leagues in length. Its rocks are every where hollowed into grottos, square chambers, stair-cases, and human habitations now deserted. The history of its inhabitants, who are supposed to have been Troglodytes, is enveloped in impenetrable obscurity. These caverns are often placed in almost inaccessible situations : some of them are spacious, and communicate with each other by stair-cases : the roofs are often supported by square pillars.

I proceeded by Stafenda, towards Pozello, Marza, and its Cyclopean walls, lastly cape Pachynum, one of the three points of Trinacria. Some walls of a temple of Apollo were pointed out to me. I had before me the islands of Marzameni and Vindicari. We left the ancient Elato, after crossing the river Helorus, and passing near the triumphal monument of Hippocrates. It is a column about forty feet high, and ten in diameter; and was erected in honour of the victory gained by the king of Gela, over the Syracusans in the year 461, before the Christian era.

After stopping under a tree at Patagonia, on the banks of the river Terias, I reached the *Leontinus ager*, so celebrated for its fertility, and went to sleep at Lentini, the ancient Leontium, where vases and medals are still found every day. At Lentini, which is fifteen miles from the foot of Ætna, one forms a better idea of this volcano, which covers a full quarter of Sicily.

We proceeded the next day to Syracuse, by difficult roads, but of the most diversified aspect ; I particularly recommend to painters, a valley more poetical than that of Tempe ; more smiling than any site of Arcadia or Thessaly. Large trees cover the banks of a cool and transparent river, which flows at the bottom of the valley. It sometimes insulates some of these trees, and the islands, sheltered by enormous masses of rock, seem to be the happy domain of the shepherds of Theocritus. The wild vine crosses the valley, and forms bridges adorned with scolopendria, bindweed, and convolvulus, of a rose colour, which descend in festoons, from a height of more than a hundred feet, down to the river. This whole country calls to mind at every step, the verses of the greatest painter of Nature.

" Hîc gelidi fontes, hîc mollia prata, Lycori ;
" Hîc nemus ; hîc ipso tecum consumerer ævo.
(Virg. Eclog. X. v. 42.)

We returned to the sea-shore pretty near the port of Augusta ; this little town has acquired a melancholy celebrity by the cruelty with which its inhabitants massacred the crew of a French frigate, at the time of the expedition to Egypt. A tempest had driven our unfortunate countrymen, on this inhospitable shore, and not one escaped.

I had scarcely set my foot on the territory of Syracuse, when my eyes saw a monument of the glory, or of the misfortunes of its inhabitants ; for it is not known whether this ruin, consisting of a round tapering column placed on a square base, was erected in memory of the success of Syracuse against Nicias, or of the triumph of Marcellus.

SYRACUSE.

A road hewn in a flat smooth rock, which follows the sea-coast, and where the marks of the wheels of the ancient cars are still visible, leads to modern Syracuse. Some quarries, and some tombs are upon a hill, from the summit of which you behold Syracuse, now confined to the island of Ortygia, which is pretty well fortified. What first strikes the eye is a confused mixture of bastions and steeples ; you afterwards see the great port where the power, the glory, and the good fortune of the Athenians expired ! Then the Epipolæ appears, lastly the ruins of Tyche, the Latomies of Dionysius, and a portion of the theatre. The soil is rocky, stony upon the summit, and wonderfully fertile below ; a brook is almost always surrounded with aloes, fig-trees, oranges, and a thick and verdant turf; this contrast with the nakedness and the greyish blue colour of the surrounding rock, is striking and picturesque.

You enter Syracuse through three or four gates furnished with draw-bridges. Causeways extend a great way into the sea, which fills the ditches of the fortress. The waves beat against walls built at the expense of the ancient fortifications, and of the most sumptuous monuments of old Syracuse. It is no longer a Greek soldier, who guards this gate ; it is a poor sallow meagre Neapolitan, muffled up in an Austrian uniform. I have always seen this guard asleep. We were lodged at the handsomest inn, the best apartment of which reminded me of that which I shared in Cairo with all the rats and weasels in the quarter of the Franks. The Cook of this inn has retained nothing of the skill of Heraclides and Mythecus. Some Gothic carriages slowly promenade in the evening on the quay of the fort. The horses are execrable, and the servants ill dressed.

The trace of the cars enables us to discover the direction of the streets, which must have been very inconvenient both for foot passengers, and for carriages. It is certain that the houses were small, built on the naked rock, without either foundations or substructions. Nothing remains of the stones of which they were built. It would be impossible to imagine that a populous city could have stood on this spot, but for the aqueducts, formed in the rock, at a considerable depth, which branch out in every direction, shew the streets and squares and communicate with wells dug in every house. There are as many as three stories of these aqueducts which still bring abundance of the purest water. The subterraneous murmur of these waters, is now the only noise heard in this place ; where, according to the expression of ancient authors, a crowd of people thronged and pressed against each other with the same agitation, as the waves of the sea in a narrow streit.

What generation can more justly conceive than ours these great disasters. Is it to prove to us the truth of the misfortunes of ancient nations, that Providence shews to the universe the fatal glare of the flames of the Greek cities, and terrifies us with the bloody scenes of Chios, Ayvaly, and Corinth ?

I fear I shall be accused of Vandalism for not indulging, as my predecessors have done, in the enthusiasm with which the theatre and amphitheatre, at Syracuse, inspired them. Though I find it impossible to fancy so easily as others the ancient splendour of these monuments, it is no less true that these ruins, viewed from a certain point, compose one of the grandest sites, and, perhaps, the most elegant lines, I ever saw in my life. A river falls in cascades over the seats of the amphitheatre, having forced its way from an aqueduct, which rests upon rocks covered with ivy.

Syracuse has still a senate, the sole employment of which is to guard the shrine of Saint Juliana. The silver statue of this saint is here held in greater veneration, if possible, than that of Saint Rosalia, at Palermo. The people of Syracuse are the more superstitious, as the neighbourhood of Etna easily persuades them that they are nearer to hell than others. This fear, increased by the smallest shock of an earthquake, gives rise to numerous practices, and to a taste for the marvellous. I have seen people kiss the hands of the monks with much more compunction when the thicker smoke of Etna gave reason to fear an eruption of the volcano; the sentiment of religion becomes stupid when it is excited by terror. This people cannot admire the sublime morality of Jesus Christ; it is not preached to them. The majesty of God is concealed from them by a multitude of saints, whose credit extends only five or six miles round. The Sicilian mingles in his respect the celestial hierarchy, the martyrs, and the recollections of paganism: we meet with the mountain of Saint Venus, people pray in the chapel of Saint Mercury, and I have seen the well of Saint Juno.

I am far however from pretending that many priests, and a great number of Sicilians, may not frequently have real and profound piety. A burning climate, complete indolence keeps the imagination in a state of indefinite and ardent sensibility. Hence lively joys and profound griefs, afflictions which religion alone can console, delusions against which the sanctuary is the only refuge. Whenever the passions are exalted, the worship of the divinity is more fervent, faults more frequent, and it is well known that repentance prays better than innocence. The fear of the devil has the same effect upon the minds of the Sicilians as stories of ghosts upon the imagination of children; they utter loud cries, are dying with terror, and yet wish the story never to come to an end. The poorest Sicilian gives to a begging friar rather than to an unfortunate cripple. He often does it only to satisfy his conscience for the fault which he contemplates, or that which he has just committed.

It appears certain that Saint Paul introduced christianity into Sicily. This apostle, who stopped only three days at Syracuse, left disciples in this country. Bachillus, Beryllus, and Marcian preached the faith to the Sicilians, and were the first bishops of Messina, Catania, and Palermo. The blood of the martyrs which flowed in abundance under Diocletian and Maximinian, cherished the seed of the gospel.

The Inquisition, introduced into Sicily in the thirteenth century, was not severe, except under Ferdinand the Catholic; but as soon as Sicily ceased to be under the direct sovereignty of the Spanish monarchy, the Sicilian people freely indulged in their aversion to this religious tribunal, and it was at last suppressed, in 1781. It must not be omitted that the Inquisitors were as tolerant and prudent in Sicily as they have long been at Rome. The population of Syracuse amounts to about fifteen thousand souls, and there are eighty convents of monks and nuns, a great number of religious conservatories, of churches and seminaries. The whole city is enrolled under two brotherhoods, that of Saint Philip and that of the Holy Ghost. In certain fetes the members of the first of these

associations endeavour to surpass those of the other in expense
for wax candles and gilt paper, and the greater number con-
demn themselves, for this expense, to a sort of daily abstinence ;
but then they place Saint Philip on a car, four feet higher than
that which their rivals consecrate to their patron ; and this
success indemnifies them for a languishing and sleepy existence of a whole year. I am far from criticising these customs
of the inhabitants of Syracuse, and proposing our example as
a model.   I do not advise them to renounce tranquil pleasures,
to adopt ours, to establish an opera, twenty other theatres,
gambling houses, in short every thing which excessive civilization has rendered indispensable to us.

Guided by a hermit, whose countenance was not calculated
to inspire confidence, I visited the Catacombs of Saint John ;
it is the labyrinth of death.   Passages of interminable length,
round saloons, square halls, hollowed in the tuff, are provided on
the right and left, with openings of different dimensions,
which contain the corpses of the dead of all ranks and ages.
Nothing that remains of ancient Syracuse can give so good an
idea as these catacombs of the immense population of the
city.   Near this labyrinth of sepulchres, which extends several
miles under ground, is the subterraneous church of Saint Marcian, which is supposed to be the oldest christian monument
in Sicily. It was here that the first words of consolation
sounded in the ears of the most unfortunate people on earth.
This inspiring word lightened their chains, dried their tears, and
hope then opened to servitude, weakness, and misfortune, the
gates of eternity.   We made a drawing of this crypt of the
first faithful, the effect of which is extremely picturesque, and
would be an admirable subject for Granet.

The Naumachia appears to me too small to receive a population of two millions.   Besides, we may be allowed to doubt whether
combats between little barks could give much pleasure to a people
who had before them the sea, and a port, the bustle of which is
said to have been prodigious.   We ascended the river Anapus,
the only navigable stream in Sicily, which rises under the walls of
Buscemi, thirty-six miles from Syracuse, and falls into the great
port, after its junction with the limpid waters of the fountain of
Cyane.   I remained for a long time leaning over the side of my
boat, and never was weary of admiring the perfect purity of this
cool water ; the eye perceives, at the depth of forty feet, gold-
coloured sand, little pebbles, which might be taken for emeralds
and topazes ; and a multitude of fish sport in this delicious
stream.

The cathedral of Syracuse is founded on the ruins of the temple of Minerva.   Fourteen Doric columns support the modern

building. There are scarcely any traces of the temples of Jupiter, of Æsculapius, of Apollo Temenites, and Fortune, and of many other monuments celebrated by ancient authors. Syracuse, besides being so often plundered by the barbarous hands of its conquerors, has likewise seen earthquakes destroy and swallow up its noblest ruins. The greatest catastrophes, of this kind, occurred in 1100, 1542, 1693, and 1735. It was from the midst of these ruins that there was extracted, eighteen years ago, a fragment of a statue of Venus, which I have carefully designed and which Mr. Osterwald will, doubtless, have engraved, as one of the most precious relics of the art of sculpture. The Museum of Syracuse contains also a statue of Æsculapius, smaller than life, in a fine style, which was discovered in 1803, and a bust of Timoleon. There was formerly upon the zocle of this bust, the following inscription.

EXTINCTORI TYRANNIDES.

A governor of Syracuse, in 1618, caused this inscription to be erased. The hero was avenged; expressions of admiration, in all languages, covered the zocle of his bust. The homage of the universe has replaced this great name. The museum of Syracuse contains also a multitude of epitaphs, of Greek inscriptions, chiefly collected in the catacombs. The only thing that can serve as an indemnity for not knowing Abbé Capodieci, director of this establishment, is the reading of his work on the antiquities, of his country.

Leaving Syracuse I unfortunately embarked on board a speronara for Catania. The air was like a furnace; the sirocco, it was hoped, would bring me thither in a few hours, and we should spare ourselves the fatigue of travelling forty-two miles on mules. Forgetting how ill the sea agrees with me, I yielded to these considerations. At eight o'clock in the evening we had scarcely left the port, and laid ourselves down on the deck of our vessel, when the wind changed to the *gregale* (or Greek wind). The crew affirmed that the wind was faint and would cease at midnight, and that they could use their oars; the contrary happened, and at daybreak we were only three miles from Syracuse. The sea being high, the crew tired, and all of us very sick, we took refuge in a little port called *la Tonnara*. I sent to Syracuse for horses, they brought me mules and a litter. I was very unwilling to get into this singular vehicle, which I, however, immediately found very convenient. My mules were very steady; they were guided by a man on horseback; another on foot either checked them or encouraged them, by varied but continued cries. This animated monologue consisted of reproaches and praises. The bad faith, the avidity of my sailors, almost hindered me from quitting la

Tonnara, where I had some difficulty in landing, because the
officer of health was not at his post.   An ecclesiastic, who happened to be on shore, took upon him to read our license at a distance of fifteen paces, and to convince himself that we did not
come from Tunis.   He interposed his authority, and very kindly
delivered me from the importunities of my sailors, by fixing the
price of the passage.   A love of contention and dispute is the
basis of the character of the Sicilians, whose cupidity has made
me a thousand times regret the Greeks, the Hebrews, and the
Arabs.   If you are obliged to take money out of your pocket, to
shake it in your hand, a group of persons, with whom you have no
business, is formed, presses and torments you, and devours with
greedy eyes the money which it cannot obtain.

Troubled with this melancholy thought, I recollected, in spite
of myself, that this island was long in a state of slavery, and I
was sorry to find in some of the inhabitants, signs of the chains
borne by their fathers.   Nothing is more intolerable than the
praises, the extempore admiration, and the continual attentions
with which you are persecuted in Sicily.   Twenty persons at
once press forward that nothing may strike against you, to assist
you in going down a staircase, to drive away a fly from the collar
of your coat, or a dog which happens to be in your path.   As
Madame de Sevigné pretended that the language of the learned
ladies of her time drove her to rudeness, so the obsequiousness of
this people inspired me with a liking for all surly countenances;
it would have been among them that I should have endeavoured
to recognise the descendants of Agathocles and Timoleon.

The path pompously called the road of Catania, is so rocky and
impracticable, that, in order to avoid it, the people cross immense
fields covered with thistles.   Sometimes following the course of
little streams, you pass under olive and pomegranate trees, mixed
with oaks and entwined with large wild vines.   The hand of man
is no where observed, and this ancient country assumes the aspect
of a virgin and unknown land.   This desert, covered with the
thorny solanum, the turpentine tree, mallows ten feet high, agnus
castus, and oleander, brought us to a wood of olives which occupies a vast hill.   From the summit of this place you perceive the
whole outline of Mount Etna, its principal eruptions marked upon
its sides, Messina, Taormina, Catania, the sea and the mountains
of Calabria.   We descended to Agnoni, a poor place belonging to
the prince of Palagonia.   After halting an hour we proceeded on
our journey to Catania.   When night set in the whole coast was
covered with fireworks.   They were celebrating the festival of
Corpus Christi, and we perceived at a distance the fireworks of
Catania.   We reached that city at nine o'clock in the evening.
In consequence of a severe earthquake two years ago, it has been

necessary to prop up the principal edifices; beams cross the streets and spoil the effect of the finest monuments.

Lava destroyed Catania in 1669; a dreadful earthquake completed its ruin in 1673; nineteen thousand of its inhabitants were the victims of this last disaster. They had at last begun to rebuild it on a larger and more splendid scale; but the works which were going on with ardour, have been suspended by the late shocks, which have done great injury to almost all the public monuments. Catania is supposed to contain about sixty thousand inhabitants. Though its silk manufactures cannot bear a comparison with those of Lyons, they are nevertheless one of the most successful branches of Sicilian commerce. Catania exports also leather, wool, necklaces of yellow amber, corn, sulphur, and wine in considerable quantities; agriculture is even more neglected here than in the rest of Sicily. The olives, left to themselves, are never pruned; and these trees, which are high and tufted, produce but little fruit. The wine is ill made; the corn is choked by weeds. If you endeavour to make the Sicilians sensible of the numerous inconveniences of such negligence, they first thank you, and then add, " What do I know of it; and of what use is it ?" Then nothing is properly done. The smith hammers the iron sitting in the most convenient posture that he can devise; the bricklayer, lying on a scaffold, slowly places an ill-baked brick, which becomes dust the day after: it is only for the priests that they work a little better, because hell is at hand for him who should not properly finish a door, or should neglect a roof.

St. Agatha reigns at Catania, though the last earthquake did not respect her church. A new one has been quickly built at a great expense. The portal of this monument is in a bad taste; but it is enriched with columns of granite which graced the Proscenium of the ancient theatre. In this edifice, which, however, has a degree of grandeur, I saw a detestable painting in fresco, representing the moment of the catastrophe of 1693, where all the religious communities being obliged to fly before the lava, hastily embarked; but what may be true, and was not sufficiently heroic to be authenticated, is, that the bishop was the first to quit the shore, giving it his benediction.

The itinerary of the prince of Biscari, enriches Catania, his native country, with a number of monuments which I had the simplicity to look for; among others a temple of Ceres, which is but a pretty little rotunda, by no means deserving that pompous name. Few persons are more credulous than antiquaries; they believe, as an article of faith, the most vague tradition. The smallest piece of marble is thus transformed into an important temple. We must, however, be just to the inhabitants of Catania, and thank them for the efforts they have made to discover the monuments of their former magnificence. This conduct ought to excite emulation in us, who so lightly call barbarians, the people who neglect such researches. Do we not leave in profound oblivion the city of Arles, the soil of which contains treasures which chance alone has hitherto brought to light? Do we not neglect an easy excavation, the success of which is almost certain, and that in the middle of the second city in the kingdom, Lyons, on the very banks of the Saone?

However this may be, the Catanians call by the name of Odéon, an edifice, the small dimension of which may indeed give reason to believe that it was intended for choragic exercises. Near it was a theatre as spacious as that of Taormina, cased with white marble, and all the remains of which bear evidence of its having been erected in the finest era of the arts. This monument is not entirely cleared, the exterior porticos are still inclosed in the lava, so that the upper part of them serves as the basis of several palaces. An entrance has, however, been made into the interior, and the circular galleries that led to the amphitheatre completely cleared.

Some workmen lately digging a well, found vaults and works which promise the discovery of the great circus of Catania. The enormous expense that this enterprise would require, has caused it to be given up. This circus, according to several writers, was 1900 feet in length, and 390 in breadth; termes, statues, columns, decorated the *spina*. The authors of the middle ages say that two obelisks of granite were also admired in it, one surmounted by a silver crescent, the other by a globe of glass. The statues of Ceres, Cybele, and Victory, that of the Earth by Mamurius, were reflected in two immense canals, called the Nile and the Euripus. Swans, the emblems of poetry, swam in these waters, which diversified one of the most sumptuous and most renowned gardens in the world. As for the amphitheatre, almost all the materials were carried away in the twelfth and thirteenth centuries, to be employed in the erection of edifices which are no more.

The grandson of prince B*** has inherited from his ancestors, who were distinguished citizens and patrons of learning in Sicily, a museum which would do honour to a sovereign. The finest ornament of this gallery is, without contradiction, a marble Torso of Jupiter, found by the grandfather of the present prince, in the excavations of the theatre of Catania. We saw in the same palaces a fine collection of costumes, beginning with the eleventh century and ending with the farthingales and hoops of our grandmothers.

As for the cameos and medals, they are not to be seen any more than the prince himself. A disappointed passion, a marriage in some measure forced upon him, have, it is said, disgusted him with the world, though he is only forty years of age, and has a handsome person. The prince's father and grandfather opened their palace to a select society, to travellers and artists, and frequently undertook great and useful works, which benefitted their country. The splendour of their mode of life, compared with the dulness of that of prince B. makes his countrymen too angry for us to believe all the ill they say of him. The fact is, that he has a large fortune, the application of which is not known, and that the care of his horses is the only thing that can divert him from the society of his intendants, &c. I must add, that, without having seen prince B., I found in him great politeness and extreme complaisance, and that the letters by which he did me the honour of answering me, are those of a very obliging and well-bred man.

With the exception of some houses, or rather some persons, especially signors Gioëni, Recupero, Gemmelaro, the Sicilian nobles visit but little, and never meet for fêtes or grand dinners. The gates of their palaces are hermetically closed, and though they are far from being deficient in good sense and education, they generally place their confidence in a confessor and an agent, who manage all their affairs. They sometimes take pleasure in the intimacy of a barber, who dresses the ladies' hair, shaves the master, and makes up their party of *calabresella* in the evening. This amusing and important personage then relates the current news of the town, the quarrels of the brotherhoods of penitents, or the rencontres between the processions. He arranges with the confessor the marriages of the daughters of the family, the investment of money, and protects the intrigues of the heir. The least haughty of the Sicilian noblemen go regularly every day and sit a couple of hours in the shop of their grocer or draper, to repeat eternal complaints of an innovation in the administration, of the establishment of the new code, or the imposition of a stamp duty on paper. The principal amusements of the ladies are when some poor young women of very noble birth and very melancholy, take the veil. On these occasions the church of the monastery is hung with drapery, a sermon is preached, and the friends and relations are invited for four days together, to eat sweetmeats in the parlour of the convent. The ignorance of these good nuns is such, that it cost me a great deal of trouble to persuade them that the French are Christians. Out of politeness they pretended to believe me, but they were far from being convinced.

The slender remains of the order of Malta are confined to a convent in Catania. These successors of the heroes of Saint Jean d'Acre, of Rhodes, and Malta, have returned to monastic simplicity. A venerable old man, the commander de Rechignevoisin, of the tongue of France, had the complaisance to shew me the crown and dagger, used at the installation of Paul I., as Grand Master of the Order of Malta. These, with the sword of d'Aubusson, compose the whole of their treasures. *Sic transit gloria mundi.* Hopes are held out to them that they will obtain an island in the Adriatic sea; but this age has destroyed much, and it establishes nothing. I even think that the isle of Lissa has been proposed to them; the difficulty will be to settle, to build a church, an hospital, forts, and vessels. All interests are changed; the Christian States have concluded treaties with the Porte, and even with the regencies of Tunis and Algiers.

An old grand bailiff, lieutenant of the Grand Master, drives about in a chariot, on which the arms of the order are painted: he might be taken for a contemporary of La Valette, or l'Ile Adam, whose virtues he inherits.

MOUNT ETNA.

I should now have come to that part of my travels, the description of which would be the most difficult, if I pretended to speak of Etna in a manner worthy of it. Celebrated by Pindar and Virgil, described by Thucydides and Strabo, explained by Spallanzani and Dolomieu, it has been the subject of so many admirable pictures, that I am too sensible of the impossibility of adding a single feature.

After having said like Rezzonico, when contemplating Etna: *Ed appena ardiva d'alzar gli occhi per guardarlo, vinto dall' orrida maestà colla quale giganteggia sul piano.* I humble myself before this phenomenon, the inconceivable majesty of which eludes the efforts of the greatest masters. I therefore only give an exact Journal of the employment of two days in Sicily.

Etna has long been considered as the wonder of Nature. Plato and Adrian ascended to the summit of this volcano. Empedocles, the Agrigentine, perished there 400 years before our era. Among the writers who described this mountain, are Bembo, Fazelli, Filoteo in the 16th century; Borelli, Bottone, Carrera, in the 17th; and Massa, Biscari, Ferrara, in the 18th. The base of Etna is sixty leagues in circumference; its height according to Dolomieu, is 10,080 feet; according to Needham 10,032; according to Saussure, 10,283; lastly, according to Ferrara, 10,198. Etna is not a single mountain, but a collection of volcanoes. A hundred craters, some extinct, others still smoking, surround this colossus, 180,000 inhabitants live upon it. Three regions divide Etna: *regione piedimonta*; this comprehends vineyards and rich harvests; *regione nemorosu*; covered with woods, *regione deserta;* covered with snow and ashes.

History has preserved the memory of seventy-seven eruptions of Mount Etna; eleven of which took place before the Christian era. Caligula, terrified by that of the year 44, of our era, fled from Catania, where he was, to Messina; Charlemagne was in Sicily at the time of the eruption in 812. Though there is a difference of opinion respecting the year of the eruption in the 12th century, one of the most terrible upon record, the most general opinion fixes the date of this disastrous event in 1183. John Agnello, bishop of Catania, his clergy, a multitude of people, were then buried under the ruins of the cathedral. Fifteen thousand persons perished, and every thing was overthrown.

The eruption of 1537 was accompanied by earthquakes, which destroyed Messina, and desolated part of Calabria. That of 1669 was announced by a darkness like that of an eclipse. The village of Nicolosi disappeared, an abyss four leagues in length, and five or six in breadth, suddenly opened; its depth was incalculable. Seven villages were swallowed up; a river of lava rose over the walls of Catania, and overthrew the finest edifices. The circumference of the principal crater of Etna then acquired an extent of nearly six leagues. The losses occasioned by this disaster were estimated at forty millions of francs.

The naturalist Bonelli, who was an eye witness of this phenomon, calculates that the volcanic substances ejected from the crater, might compose a cubic mass of 83,838,750 geometrical paces. The torrent of fire was five leagues in length, one and a quarter in breadth, and a hundred feet in depth. The eruption of 1693 destroyed 59,000 people in Sicily. The sea at the moment of the earthquake, rose to an immense height, and broke against the shore, overturning and carrying away on its passage the most solid monuments. Lastly, the eruptions of 1799 and 1800 may be considered as the longest and the most terrible. The shocks of the earthquake were continued; the shower of fire laid waste all the environs of Etna, which launched to a distance burning scoriæ of enormous weight.

The eruptions of 1809, 1811, and 1819, opened a crater of seven hundred and eighty four feet in circumference. A new Etna appeared upon *Monte Rosso*; twenty mouths threw out stones and ashes, and covered all the valley of Lingua-grossa.

We hired mules at Catania, and, provided with brandy, rum, and some provisions, we took the road to Nicolosi, where Mr. Gemmelaro, of Catania, possesses a pretty country house. I had reason to praise the reception given me by Mr. Gemmelaro. Reaching Nicolosi at eight in the morning, a pretty easy ascent took me to Gravina, Mascalcia, and Torre Griffo; three charming villages, situated in the most beautiful country in the world; where cultivation is at once the most easy, and the most neglected. Being received with much hospitality by Don Gemmelaro, we enjoyed from his terrace the prospect of this new Eden ; we saw, on all sides, pines, orange-trees, and poplars, entwined with vines and ivy.

Provided with a guide, named Antonio Mazzara, whom I recommend to travellers, because he is endowed with exemplary patience and civility, we left Nicolosi. You pass below Monte Rosso, which was produced in the eruption of 1696, and which having itself become a formidable volcano, destroyed two years ago the village of Tafarana. The people while assembled in the church of the village, were crushed by the fall of the roof. A man, who was listening to the sermon, stood on the stone of a vault, it gave way, and he was found alive in the sepulchre. We walked in lapillo, or black sand, across lavas three centuries old ; we next proceeded to the woody region, where we find verdure and a rural valley, and after having advanced four miles into this forest, we reach the *grotta delle Capre,* called likewise, *grotta de' Inglesi.* We lighted a good fire because the air was already cooler. We also took out our sketch books, but what can the vain efforts of the pencil do before so many wonders ? Our guides fetched us some snow, which greatly improved the Syracusan wine ; and, after a refreshing sleep, we set out at eleven o'clock in the evening. The night was gloomy, and our mules accordingly took their own way. These animals, which are safe and indefatigable, did not stop till they had gone four hours. The cold was become so sharp that our feet and arms were stiff when we alighted near the tower of the Philosopher. Mr. Gemmelaro, and some English officers, have had a small house built on this spot, where we did not lie down, because the snow, which surrounded it, rendered it still excessively damp. From this place, where we drank some rum and laid aside our great coats, we set out on foot to ascend the great cone. To reach its base you must cross a space of about a mile, covered with lava of the most singular form ; we were obliged to leap from point to point, to slip, to tear our hands, to get up again, to do the same a few steps further on. At last, however, we reached the mountain of ashes. Here a new kind of torment begins ; it is necessary to ascend almost perpendicularly in a whitish ash, where you plunge up to your knees at every step. This ash is strewed with scoriæ, enormous pumice stones, coated with sulphur, by which you attempt in vain to support yourself, for lying loose they often give way, and you lose the ground which you gained with so much labour.

I had scarcely got half way, and I already began to be discouraged. The rarefaction of the air rendered respiration difficult ; farther on this oppression was extreme ; it affected one of our companions so much that he fainted. We recovered him, and collecting all our strength, in half an hour reached the highest summit of the crater. I had never in my life suffered such fatigue. Strong shoes, thick gloves, all had vanished; I arrived barefooted and my hands cruelly torn. My first impression was to feel myself, like one in sickness, weakened and troubled, by the terrors of a fevered brain. The dawn of day whitened the horizon, and the first beam of light produced most singular effects upon the clouds, which rolled at our feet; they were driven towards us like immense phantoms; we might have fancied ourselves in communication with the heavens, where strange visions seemed to be preparing: I wished to look into the bottom of the crater; a sulphurous stifling smoke made me draw back; I then tried to sit down on the reverse, but this yellow friable crust was burning hot. Placed on one of the most elevated spots on the globe, we only waited for the departure of the clouds to enjoy a sublime sight. The sun dispelled the vapours of the morning, and the light broke upon us all at once, with dazzling splendour. Sicily formed but a small part of the foreground of this picture. On one side the eye penetrate into the abyss; on the other, in an azure space intersected by stripes of gold, it discovered Calabria, Africa, Malta, and the sea of Syracuse. The shadow of Etna was projected over Sicily, and extended from Paterno to the plains of Enna.

The wind changed, and I was able to look towards the volcano. Its immense crater, which appeared to me to be more than a league in circuit, is divided into three parts by the needle of a rock, the base of which forms the divisions. This rock rises from the crater like a Gothic spire; its colour is reddish, sometimes of a bituminous black, and the crust, which shines on certain parts, seems to me to resemble that of the aerolites : in other places this rock appeared like the interior of the crater, of an ash colour, with transverse stripes of pure sulphur. We were placed on the edge of the perpendicular rock; the descent appeared to me to be so rapid to the place where the great shaft becomes perpendicular, that it would have been impossible to descend into it without the melancholy certainty of being hurried into the gulf. The depth of this part of the tunnel may be from six to seven hundred feet.*

If Dante did not visit Sicily, if he did not ascend Mount Etna, which we may be allowed to doubt, since he several times went to Naples, his genius divined its terrible effects. His description of

---

* An Englishman had the rashness, a few years ago, to have himself let down by ropes into the crater ; he made too late the signal to draw him up ; his guides did so, but this new Empedocles was suffocated ;—all endeavours to restore him to life were fruitless.

Hell is the most faithful picture of Etna. Dante is the only guide worthy to conduct us through this labyrinth of valleys to the entrance of this mysterious abyss.

On our left was the last volcano, opened at the foot of the great cone ; its orifice, of a bright yellow, had thrown out all the lava which covered the valley *de' Bovi.* The black scoriæ produced by forty other volcanoes, marked the domain of the destroyers of the finest coast in the world. We descended with caution to the tower of the Philosopher, of which only a few stones remain ; it may be supposed that it was once an ancient oratory, a small temple erected to the infernal divinities, and afterwards, perhaps, a tower for observation ; and we proceeded, on foot, as far as *la Grotta delle Capre*, walking rapidly in the ashes and *lapillo*, and crossing the red ravines and the lava, which covered this gloomy desert. Mounting our mules we entered the *regione nemorosa*, which appeared to us to be an Arcadia, and soon returned to Nicolosi and Catania.

My mind had been struck by the greatest contrasts. In fact, when my wearied eyes would no longer look steadily on the clouds which exhaled from the bowels of the earth, they were relieved by expatiating in the immensity of the heavens and the seas. On one side the obscurity of the crater was dispelled only for a few seconds by gusts of livid smoke ; on the other, the sun rose in all its splendour, and reflected on the Calabrian sea a thousand brilliant colours. I breathed an icy air while the ashes burnt my feet. At last, the deleterious smell of all the most powerful volcanic substances warned me that I was upon the limits of the empire of man, and at the commencement of the domain of death.

Etna, surrounded by volcanoes, has poured forth rivers of lava which have flowed into the sea, hollowing out deep vallies in their course. The space which the torrents have traversed may give an idea of chaos : some of these rivers of lava retain the form of a cascade ; others that of a sea, the waves of which had been fixed and hardened in the midst of a storm. Some craters are surrounded by vegetation and flowers, like a garland on a coffin. A wreath of clouds covers the top of Etna, while the sky above, and the sea around it, are dazzling with light. This coast makes constant efforts to conceal, under verdure, the traces of the torrents of fire which incessantly ravage it. A thoughtless people inhabit and love this wonderful country ; they dance to the noise of the thunders of the volcano, and place the cradle of their children on the still smoking ashes, which buried the dwellings of their fathers.

When I was again at Catania, I felt a more lively sense of the comforts of my situation, because, during this fatiguing excursion, I had been constantly surrounded with scenes of suffering. The inhabitants of the foot of Etna are in want of water; they are obliged to go a great distance to procure it, and even then it is very bad: women, burnt by the sun, emaciated by labour, and privations of every kind, go barefoot, carrying only a large pitcher on their heads; we meet long files of them, following paths hollowed in the lava, and encumbered with rolling or pointed stones. Profound melancholy is impressed on their countenances; they have suffered yesterday, and to-morrow will bring with it the same wants, the same difficulties, the same uncertainty whether they shall be able to bring back some drops of water to their dwellings.

The water flows drop by drop into the marble fountains of Catania: the aqueducts are not repaired; the convents have cisterns; the intendants take their *gelati* and *granati*, and give themselves but little trouble to quench the thirst of the Sicilian people.

I shall only just mention the places by which I passed to Castro Giovanni, the ancient Enna. Some think that Paterno was founded on the site of the ancient city of Inessa, of which hardly any thing remains; some mosaics are the only indication of the ground occupied by the ancient city. Others think, that Paterno was Hybla Major, the name of which is claimed by many towns. The inhabitants have great quantities of bees, which feed on the most odoriferous thyme; the honey of this country appeared to me preferable to that of Mount Hymettus. Cortina, where they shew a very picturesque grotto, receives the water of a river, which there sinks into the ground, and re-appears at a distance of eighty toises. Aderno, *Hadranum*, has no remains of a temple that was once famous. Near it are modern ruins, an aqueduct began by Prince Biscari, was to unite two mountains, composed of two stories, like the Pont du Gard, it was about a hundred and thirty feet high; it is now neglected and abandoned, and in ten years little of it will remain. Centorbi, *Centuripæ*, was opulent. We now find none of its engraved stones, which attested its luxury and the excellence of its artists. *Argyrium* has entirely disappeared, nothing remains of this native city of Diodorus but the remembrance, and some medals. I obtained two very fine ones, one represents the head of Hercules, and the other that of Jupiter, both in perfect preservation. *Assorus* has nothing to excite curiosity; the Chrysus is but a petty brook. *Aidunum* no longer exists, and *Plutia*, now called Piazza, is far from meriting its ancient name of *Opulentissima*. Mr. Feghen, the English Consul, had undertaken important excavations in this place. Porticoes have lately been found there, and columns with the figures 12, 13, 14. There is every reason to suppose, that it was the palestra, and, perhaps, the most important one in Sicily. I passed through the little town of Mazarino, the birth-place of the family of Cardinal Mazarin.

Enna, now Castro Giovanni, was founded by Ennos, eighty years after Syracuse, and afterwards named by the Romans *Castrum Ennæ*. Its temple of Ceres no longer exists. Antiquities are often found here, which must be obtained from the hands of the peasants. The elegant bronze lamp, formerly placed in a sepulchre, now lights the cottage of the shepherd of *Enna*. The celebrated bridge of Capitarso, built in 1553, is really in a bold style, but does not merit the reputation it has in Sicily.

Returning to Catania by Metto, Bronte, Randazzo, and Lingua-grossa, we were too fatigued to visit the eastern side of Ætna, the wood of Santa-Venera, and *Castagno dei cento cavalli*, which has been seen by every body, and described so many times.

The country between Catania and *Iaci reale*, belongs to the domain of fable and the higher poetry. A landscape-painter might spend months at *Iaci reale* and the environs; it is situated upon the eminence, and communicates with its little port by a road hewn in the rock, supported by walls, built in the manner of arcades; the laurel, the cypress, and the aloe, form groups above the ruins, overshadow little chapels, and shew, between the intervals, the picturesque buildings and ancient towers of Iaci. A little lower is the sea, which is remarkably transparent. The painter continuing his way will meet with the sublime horrors of those torrents of black and frightful scoria, which Etna pours into the sea. A luxuriant vegetation every where covers the banks of these infernal rivers; they have destroyed ancient bridges, and have formed high masses before mountains which stopped their course. Upon these mountains of an irregular form, stand Saracen castles and crenated walls, the barbarous style of which makes a striking contrast with the elegance of the aqueducts that cross the valley.

We arrived at Giardini overpowered by the heat of the day: this hamlet, situated at the foot of the mountain of Taormina, and on the very sea-beach, is inhabited only by fishermen. A priest has just opened a very neat inn there. We went up the next day to Taormina, the theatre of which was placed on a high mountain projecting into the sea. The art, the taste, the magnificence of the ancients, were combined in this spot, where they erected a theatre, the remains of which still compose the finest sight in the world. Placed upon the highest seats, you perceive, through the porticos which adorn the stage, Etna, the ancient port of Venus, the shore on which stood the altar of Apollo, Iaci, Leontini, Syracuse, and the boundless sea. If this ruin in its present state moves and elevates the soul, what must it have been when, at the back of the same theatre, you might see the lava of the volcano threaten the shore, and its fires light the stage, while the mind and the eyes were struck at once, the latter by the storms of the ocean, the former by the griefs of Electra and the misfortunes of the Atrides ! Thus the prodigies of nature and of art appeared to have met on this promontory. Where could the Cyclops of Euripides be better represented ? since Etna emitting clouds of smoke appeared at the back of the stage. In Iphigenia in Aulis, the sea and ships were seen through the principal gate.

It is easy to shew that the theatre of Taormina was cased with marble. This theatre has some resemblance to that of Saguntum ; but this monument of the Spanish city could never be compared to the beautiful theatre of Taormina, which might contain from about twenty-five to thirty thousand persons.

Ruins of battlements and embrasures, prove that this place served as a fortress, perhaps at the time when the Saracen were masters of Sicily. This theatre has been the scene of feigned combats, and of bloody battles. At present it re-echoes only the sounds of the flute, or the songs of the shepherd.

Among the Sicilian songs several are impressed with a martial character, which proves their antiquity. The popular romances of Selinuntium, Sciàcca, Castro Giovanni, remind us of the feudal wars of the houses of Luni and Perollo. The Sicilians have forgotten the Verses of Stésichorus and Theocritus, as the Greeks have lost the lyre of Pindar and Timotheus. It will be difficult to discover what musical instruments were used in Sicily some ages ago: the use of the guitar is of recent date, and the peasants of the interior of the island remain faithful to the bagpipe and a very simple flute. In the north of Europe the national songs are melancholy ; all appear to be inspired by unhappy love ; by a melancholy recollection, or the fear of a more unhappy futurity : thus the first song of the man of the north was a complaint. The popular songs of Sicily, on the other hand, are impressed with the stamp of gaiety, which is indicative of its ancient prosperity, the riches of its cities, and the fertility of its fields. The authors of national songs are almost always unknown. The verses of Simonelli,[*] Levanti, Meli, and Bertolini, are not known to these islanders.

The frontispiece of this work will give an idea of a dance which I saw performed one evening in the theatre of Taormina. Large tombs placed at the bottom of the valley in the *Necropolis* of Taormina, resemble those on the Appian Way.

The small village of Mola is situated above the modern Taormina. These remains, as well as those of a crenated fortress, which crowns a work of still greater elevation, seem as if they had been the models for the bold pencil of Salvator Rosa.

Like all the little towns in Sicily, Taormina is dirty, ill paved, and with streets so narrow that two persons can scarcely walk abreast. This city has always been an important military post; consequently, we find at every step Greek ruins, Roman walls, and Saracen towers: the cactus, briers, and ivy, overgrow these useless works, while pines and palms gracefully wave above the ruins. An inscription, cut in the stone of a house, built in the Florentine style, and the handsomest at Taormina, might lead us to believe that it was inhabited by John of Arragon, after his army had been defeated by the French. In the church, situated in the square of Taormina, there are several Greek inscriptions; among others the following:

ΟΔΑΜΟΣ ΤΟΝ ΤΑΙΡΟΜΕΝΤΑΝ
ΟΛΤΜΠΙΝ ΟΛΥΜΠΙΟΣ ΜΕΣΤΟΝ
ΝΙΚΑΣΑΝΤΑ ΠΤΘΙΑ ΚΕΛΗΤΙ
ΤΕΛΕΙΟΙ.

I will add, for the satisfaction of my readers, and on the authority of a friend profoundly versed in this branch of learning, a more correct copy of the inscription, as it may be supposed to have stood originally:

Ο ΛΑΜΟΣ ΤΩΝ ΤΑΤΡΟΜΕΝΙΤΩΝ.
ΟΛΤΜΠΙΟΝ ΟΛΥΜΠΙΟΤ ΜΕΣΤΟΝ
ΝΙΚΑΣΑΝΤΑ ΠΤΘΙΑ ΚΕΛΗΤΙ
ΤΕΛΕΙΩΙ.

Populus Tauromenitarum (honorat) Olympium Mestum Olympii filium victorem in Pythiis, equo desultorio adulto.

The distance from Giardini to Messina is thirty miles. We had to go two leagues, sometimes climbing over the summit of rocks, sometimes passing through the sea water over shoals. The traveller is confined between a lofty mountain and deep waters, the dark colour of which shews him the abyss to which he is so near. All this is fatiguing, and might be very dangerous if the mules were not the safest animals in the world. We had to descend the rocks of Scaletta, the old towers of which hung over the way, to avoid the road which is impassable; and sometimes sliding, sometimes leaping, and holding by branches, to reach the sea-beach, which we did not leave till we arrived at Messina. This journey was extremely fatiguing, but the beauty of the prospect which lay before us indemnified us; we perceived the picturesque hills of Pelorus, the villages of Galati, Lardaria, and Camari; the sight of the

coasts of Reggio consoled us for having to traverse the beds of
torrents now dried up, and to pass under marble rocks heated
by the sun, when we descried the steeples and towers of Messina.

MESSINA.

No place in Sicily has fewer traces of antiquity than Messina, the monuments of which are boasted by Cicero, and
whence Verres carried off the statue of Cupid by Praxiteles.
There is nothing to point out the site of the temple of Hercules, and the palace of Caïus-Heius : it is thought, however,
that the church of Saint George is on the site of the temple of
Jupiter, and that that of Saint Philip of Argyre is built of the
ruins of the temple of Pollux.

Civil wars, pestilence, earthquakes, have many times swept
away the inhabitants of Messina, who amounted to a hundred
thousand at the beginning of the last century, and are now reduced to forty thousand, including twelve thousand monks or
priests. The number of the latter augments in a remarkable
progression ; I have been assured of this fact by the principal
magistrates of the country. The law of entails fills the nun-
neries and seminaries. None of the seven or eight brothers of
a prince is permitted to carry on trade or to follow the profession of the bar, and very few of them enter the army. Of his
numerous sisters only one or two marry, and the rest are devoted to the cloister.

In the port, which is the largest and safest in the world, I
counted hardly ten small vessels, which were unable to dispose
of the cargoes they had on board. The admirable situation of
the port of Messina ought to make it the natural entrepôt of all
the commerce of Greece the most advantageous place of exchange between the inhabitants of the east and west, yet it is
almost deserted. Since the disaster of 1783 the city has been
rebuilt, but nothing has been finished. A great part of the
houses have but one story ; many people live in pretty conve-
venient barracks : all has the appearance of being temporary.
Messina owes to this mixture of monuments overthrown, and
of palaces just begun, the most singular appearance. The
streets, of which *la strada Ferdinanda* and *el Corso* are the most
remarkable, are generally quiet and almost deserted ; its innumerable churches are filled, with a few exceptions, with indifferent pictures. Lastly, its theatre would be hardly worthy to
receive the Buratini of Rome. The steeple and the upper part
of the façade of the cathedral have fallen : what remains of
this edifice, which was built by count Roger, is in a fine Gothic

style; the columns which decorate the interior must have belonged to an ancient temple. This church is called Madona della Lettera. According to an ancient tradition, the Holy Virgin wrote a letter to the people of Messina, sending with it a lock of her hair, but neither the one nor the other are shewn.

Never were more miserable bronze statues seen than those which decorate the public squares of Messina. I would make an exception in favour of that of Don John of Austria, but the hero of Lepanto is very stiff, and has a very small head. As to the equestrian statue of Charles III., and the pedestrian statue of the present king, they are caricatures in bronze. The author will never be accused of flattery. King Ferdinand looks like a butcher; the artist has very unskilfully exaggerated the feature which has procured this monarch the name of *Nasone,* instead of giving his countenance the expression of goodness which marks it.

I saw the procession which takes place every year to celebrate the entry of Cardinal Ruffo, at the head of his Calabrese army. An immense file of monks, each holding by the hand two little children of five or six years old, dressed in a monk's habit, opened the procession, and preceded eight robust lay-brothers, who carried a large statue of Saint Anthony. The monks chatted with the ladies who were in the windows; the latter often talked upon their fingers, which, as I have already observed, they do in Sicily with great quickness. We meet too often in the streets of Messina, men habited in the coarse dress of penitents; this costume, which is generally dirty, suffers only the eyes to be visible; they carry a death's-head, and impudently hold it to you in the name of the souls in purgatory. I often saw twenty in a day, and every time this hideous figure, this sepulchral cry, made me feel new horror.

The gloom of the inhabitants of Messina forms a singular contrast with its charming situation. It is always a priest who governs in the families of the rich; he engages the servants he likes, discharges those that displease him, and shuts the door against every body: thus Messina appeared to me less sociable than Tripoli and Tunis. If you go to your banker, or the consul of your nation, his wife, his daughter, his sister, his maid servants, all fly.

The fête known by the name of *la Vara* is a very interesting time for the people of Messina. They have represented and put in action the dream of a monk, who, whether convinced or not, succeeded in convincing others, that one night, that of the Assumption, he had seen the Virgin, transported by angels.

surrounded by the thrones, the seraphim, and the dominations, and thus reaching the Eternal, amidst the concerts of the archangels and the cherubim. Devotion seized upon this dream, an [ambulating theatre was contrived and drawn about the streets. The fête of *la Vara* takes place every year, on the 15th of August. Platforms are supported by masts, a hundred feet in height, and the platforms are fifty in circumference; this enormous machine is upon a stage furnished with wheels and drawn by more than six hundred persons. In the lower story you see the Virgin, surrounded by the twelve Apostles; it is a young woman lying on a death-bed. The upper story is occupied by the sun, moon, and stars, which, by means of cylinder wheels, move at once in different directions. Silver gauze, tinsel, azure-coloured veils, and glass, hide the timber work, and imitate the firmament and the clouds. Poor little children, mute with terror, or uttering piercing cries, roll round with their legs in the air and their heads downwards: most of them in a fainting state, are very bad representatives of the celestial spirits. A young woman, still more unfortunate than they, is held upon the outstretched hands of a man, who represents the Eternal Father, eighty feet from the ground, and on the outside of the machine. Iron bars, ingeniously concealed beneath the draperies of brocade, alone prevent the fall of these two persons; the one of whom is generally chosen from among the most robust porters of Messina, and the other from among the handsomest young women of that city. All the members of the government, the tribunals, the monks, the brotherhoods, follow or precede this moving spectacle, which the population receives with exclamations of frantic joy. The young woman, who acquitted herself very well in the part of the Virgin, was charming; accordingly she obtained, by the collection made next day, a decent portion; but the porter was said not to be so fortunate.

A mixture of paganism and christianity has also given birth to the fête of Zancle and Rhea. The inhabitants of Messina believe that the Kronos of the Greeks, the Saturn of the Latins, was their founder. They have converted Zancle to the Christian faith; Rhea has been baptised. Hence it comes that they still carry about, and always on the 15th of August, two figures forty feet high, mounted on wooden horses. The costume of Zancle was not very different from that of the brave Perce foret; the mantle of Rhea, which does not resemble the costume of any age, sweeps the streets of Messina. Musicians follow the procession. The windows and balconies are filled with ladies in full dress, who make the air resound with exclamations of joy, the cathedral is illuminated; lastly, five or six hundred bells ring without ceasing. All this gives but a feeble idea of the appearance of Messina, and the transport of its inhabitants during the four days of the fête of *la Vara.*

It was on the 5th of February, 1783, that a subterraneous noise, followed by a slight oscillation, announced the earth-quake which destroyed Messina and Calabria. The shocks continued to increase during several days; but the most terrible was that of the 28th of March. The appearance of Calabria was entirely changed by it. In 1638 a similar catas-trophe had destroyed two hundred towns and villages, and nineteen thousand persons. The earthquake of 1783, over-threw the palace and the cottage, followed man every where, left him without an asylum, and it seemed as if the earth was going to sink in; the rivers were dried up, lakes succeeded to plains, and forty thousand people were buried under heaps of ruins. The inhabitants of Scylla had assembled on the beach, all succeeded in embarking; but at the very moment, a part of Mont Bacci fell into the sea, and the unfortunate fleet was swallowed up by the mere recoiling of the waves. It is thought that twelve hundred individuals were the victims of this melan-choly catastrophe.

Some persons miraculously escaped death; among these was the mother of the present Vice-Consul of France, who remained buried fifteen days under the ruins. Her hand passed between some beams, and was recognized by the maid-servant, by a ring upon her finger: she was extricated from the rubbish, and was safely delivered a short time afterwards, of the son who told me the history: she is still living.

We may believe that Calabria and Sicily were formerly united. Eschylus, Diodorus, Strabo, and Pliny, affirm it. Rhegium, now called Reggio, in Greek signifies *to rend*, the bare inspection of the place favours the idea that, as at Calais and Dover, Gibraltar and Ceuta, some great convulsion has separated the two countries by forming a strait. When I went to Reggio, the passage, as-sisted by the current, took only an hour and a half. This town is covered with ruins, and by the materials intended for re-build-ing it. Orange-trees grow without culture in the plains of Reg-gio; and, before the Saracens were driven from Italy, all the avenues of the place were embellished with groves of palm-trees. The Christians, whom this beautiful tree, it does not ap-pear why, put in mind of Mahometanism, cut down almost all the palms on this coast.

Before I leave Sicily, which appears to me to retain too little remembrance of what it was, to become for a long time what it ought to be, I think it proper to say a few words on the Sicilian character, though I fear, indeed, that I shall be refuted by the events which have just desolated the island. The heroic conduct of the Greeks has sufficiently proved to me, that I have not received the gift of prophecy, and I am therefore further than ever from believing my judgment infallible. A recent traveller has spoken with ill-humour of every thing he met with in Sicily, and would wish to change it all at once. It is not to be doubted, that there are great abuses in Sicily; but would that country become the happiest in the world, if, to please a discontented stranger, it changed at once its priests, its convents, and barons, for high roads, inns, and numerous journals? What we may be allowed to desire is, that power and experience combining gradually to enlighten the people respecting their true interests, may pay more attention in Sicily to the happiness of the inhabitants, that distress may be more regularly relieved, that humanity may preside in the management of the hospitals, and that enlightened justice may provide for the salubrity of the prisons and bagnios. Had the traveller we speak of had time to study the causes of what so greatly shocks him, to appreciate the influence of the climate, that of religion and education, on the Sicilian manners? Has he been able to trace to the source, the rivalry of the provinces, the hatred which divides the cities? Has he considered, without partiality, the ascendant of the priests, the pride of the nobles, the egotism of the merchants, the prejudices of the farmer, in short, every thing that he paints in such gloomy and discouraging colours?—I shall, therefore, only say what struck me in the principal features of the Sicilian character. The first, and doubtless the most honourable, is their love of their country. Their attachment to their native soil always revived their courage after the numerous disasters of which they were the victims. This sentiment gives them strength to vanquish all obstacles; it fecundates the lava, fertilises the ashes, and builds a city on the ruins of that which has just been swallowed up. The Sicilian, agitated by a personal passion, or carried away by the torrent of national vengeance, becomes gloomy, inexorable, terrible. He is no longer that man who, for a few pence, anticipated your wishes, and submitted to your slightest wishes; he is a tiger thirsting for carnage. A longing for independence heats his blood, and hatred of foreigners becomes his ruling passion: such was the Sicilian during the massacre of the vespers, such he still is, superstitious, undisciplined, distrustful, and untamable. His patriotism, well directed, might render him capable of the greatest efforts. He, of all the Italians, would most impatiently support a foreign yoke. It is to him particularly that we may apply the fine verse of Alfieri:

Schiavi siamo si, ma schiavi ognor frementi.

The Neapolitan character is completely different; there is reason to believe that a struggle upon equal terms between these two people would be advantageous to the Sicilians. The heaviest chains will never check the Neapolitan gaiety. This frivolous people would be content with making songs upon its slavery, and ridiculing its masters. The Sicilian, on the other hand, can endure hunger and thirst; he cherishes for a long time the plan of a remote vengeance; but he will never betray hospitality, or forget a benefit.

The period of the Lower Empire which humbled Rome, and degraded the other people of Italy, roused the Sicilians from all the habits of effeminacy and slavery. Renovated and invigorated by perpetual wars, they learned to love and defend their country. In short, we cannot deny to these two nations the precious endowments of genius, understanding, taste, and sagacity; but a sort of austere, lofty pride will always render the Sicilian more capable of great crimes, of sublime discoveries, noble writings, and heroic actions.

Meantime I learnt that all Calabria was in commotion, and finding that more serious troubles might render my retreat difficult, and perhaps impossible; I embarked at Messina for Naples on board a brig employed as a packet. The violence of the current and contrary winds greatly impeded our progress, and a storm arising we were obliged to put back to Milazzo in Sicily. The wind abating, we again sailed, but had scarcely got sight of Stromboli when fresh storms rose, and tossed us in a terrible manner for three days. At length we entered the gulf of Policastro in Calabria. This town still bears the marks of the severity with which it, as well as some neighbouring towns, were treated under the government of Joachim, who had pardoned them several successive revolts. Never did a more savage population inhabit a more delicious country. Groves of olive and almond trees come down to the sea shore; beautiful streams fall from the mountains. Thick forests rise like an amphitheatre to the summits of the mountain of Volgaria, one of the highest in Calabria. Some villages perched like the eyries of birds of prey, are suspended to perpendicular rocks. We travelled on mules from Policastro, and after passing a bad night, reached the plains where the rich Pæstum formerly stood. The inhabitants of Pæstum are sallow, sickly, and malicious. Why is man gloomy and poor when Nature lavishes on him all her treasures? Why do thorns now cover those fields, formerly divided by hedges of rose-trees, which blossomed twice a year?

I was extremely happy to meet again with a high road, and the marks of wheels: I had seen nothing of the kind in Sicily.

Salerno appeared to me a delightful place, and I staid there two days. It was at that time in great agitation between the revolutionary movement, and the splendor of its processions. They offered to the Holy Virgin the colours of the Carbonari, whose costume and threatening appearance cast a gloom over this fine landscape. I met, however, two hundred penitents carrying in procession a statue of St. John the Baptist, gilt, covered with precious stones, and saluted by all the muskets and *pétards* of the Calabrese.

Being arrived at Naples, I here conclude the task which I had prescribed myself. The Abbé Minichini, and Lieutenant Morelli, entered the city almost at the same time with me, at the head of the armed bands of the Capitanata and the other neighbouring provinces.

VIEW OF THE EVENTS WHICH TOOK PLACE IN SICILY, IN 1820.

The revolt broke out in Sicily just as I was quitting Messina. Before I speak of this coast it is indispensable to go farther back, and to point out the facts which may have been the cause, or the pretext. I will add a view of the population of Sicily, as well as of the state of its clergy, and their influence on the barons and the people.

According to the census made in 1812, of the population of Sicily, it amounted to about one million eight hundred thousand souls; and the taxes, besides the local imposts, according to the last act of parliament of 1815, was estimated at the sum of 5,700,000 Neapolitan ducats.

An ancient and generally received prejudice, long made it believed that King Roger divided Sicily into three equal portions, the first of which he assigned to the clergy, known by the name of *braccio ecclesiastico,* the ecclesiastical class, the second to the nobility, *braccio militaire* or *baronale,* the military or noble class; and the third to himself. This pretended division, contrary to all the principles of society, never existed in Sicily. Three or four convents, the Benedictines of Catania, Monréale, and Saint Martin, possessed considerable revenues, the rest of the clergy were hardly above want. The bishops of Monréale, Palermo, Catania; the chapters of Catania, Girgenti, and some abbeys, alone enjoyed all the riches of this order. The present king united with the crown domains the bishopric of Monréale, which had a revenue of 90,000 Sicilian crowns, and assigned to the bishop a revenue of 8000 piasters. He gave to Prince Leopold the abbey of Magione, which produced about 60,000 crowns. The other estates of the clergy have had a tax of 10 per cent laid on them.

The number of priests, monks, &c. in Sicily, may be now estimated at fifteen thousand. The convents of the women are so numerous, that people do not hesitate to affirm, that they contain about twelve thousand nuns.

The king of Naples twice took refuge in Sicily, namely, in 1799 and 1800. His first stay was only for some months, and the second about ten years. Sicily was less enriched the second time by the presence of the court, than by that of the English, who expended a great deal of money in that island. The king necessarily spent there a part of the subsidies paid him by England, which amounted then to 120,000 pounds sterling. Commerce and agriculture flourished, the farmers grew rich, and the value of the land was nearly doubled.

Sicily, which since the peace has been left to itself, experiences the embarrassments and the distress which have threatened it since 1750. At present, the competition with the wheat of Odessa is entirely to the disadvantage of the island, as well as the balance of trade. Some foreigners have formed great establishments there; but these are only advantageous to the proprietors, who spend elsewhere their large profits. The people cultivate the ground for others, and cultivate it ill. The entire want of high-roads renders the interior of the island unsafe, and commerce impossible. The Sicilians have already paid five times over, the sum which would be necessary to make every where as fine roads as those of which we saw some specimens in Palermo and other parts of the country.

Sicily, under the dominion of the kings of Aragon, had a parliament which, in the last century, assembled three times in the year. This parliament was composed of three orders, the clergy, nobility, and the *braccio dommiale*, and was definitively subject to the will of the king; but it had preserved, with the right of remonstrating, that of voting or consenting to and apportioning the taxes. The nobility and clergy made the taxes bear upon the people; but the representatives of the latter took advantage of the wants of the barons, to make stipulations in their favour, and obtained commissions advantageous to their communes.

The military chamber was composed of the great barons and vassals of the crown; in process of time all land-owners, who could form upon their estates a village of forty houses, were added. The same individual had one or more votes, according as he possessed one or more villages of forty houses. The perogatives attached to the members of the military chamber were transmitted, by inheritance, from father to son, according to the right of primogeniture.

The ecclesiastical chamber comprised all the bishops, prelates, and abbots holding commanderies; the suppression of an office was attended with the loss of the right of sitting in the chamber.

The third chamber was composed of all the representatives of the corporate cities and of the domains: the delegates were elected by the senate or the municipal council of each borough.

In 1810 the Queen, who had the preponderance in the council, wanting money to carry on the war with the French, who were at that time masters of Naples, attempted, without the consent of the parliament, to levy a new duty of one per cent. upon all articles of commerce, *(ogni contrattazione.)* It has been supposed, that this idea was suggested to the queen by Chevalier de Medicis. The parliament complained loudly: the king threatened; the parliament refused the tax, and were supported by the nation. The court exiled five of the principal barons, namely, the princes Iaci, Villafranca, Belmonte, Castelporto, and the duke of Angio. This act of authority induced the parliament to desire the interference of England. Sir William Bentinck, the British commissioner, went to Sicily, and was nominated by the king generalissimo of the kingdom; he liberated the five barons, composed a ministry of them, and, under the protection of Great Britain, he convoked, in 1812, a new parliament, divided, as in England, into an upper and a lower house. The king and queen, retiring to their palace of Ficuzza, nominated the hereditary prince vicar of the kingdom, and approved of the new constitution; but, notwithstanding the entreaties and threats of Sir William Bentinck, the king rejected with much firmness a proposal that was made to him to abdicate. The constitution, however, was carried into execution, and Sicily enjoyed, under the protection of the English, an order of things, obtained without bloodshed, and without violent commotion.

It may have been believed that the queen, indignant at the conduct of the English, secretly negotiated with France; but it would be impossible to adduce the smallest proof of this fact. Scarcely had this princess gone to Vienna, by way of Constantinople, when Medicis and Ascoli were exiled by the English, and the king, in a manner, confined and guarded by them at Ficuzza.

The face of things soon changed; the fall of Napoleon led to new political combinations. The king immediately took advantage of it, resumed his power, sanctioned the constitution of 1812, and the prince royal resigned the regency. The period of the hundred days, the treaty of Paris, the overthrow of Joachim, replaced the king on the throne of Naples. Before he set out for that city, and, after having obtained a gratuitous gift of

100,000 ounces, he cashiered the parliament which had just voted it, and annulled the constitution, by a decree, dated Messina, on board the vessel which was to convey him to Naples.

The Sicilians protested, and appealed in vain to the guarantee of England, which abandoned them, blaming and disavowing a little the conduct of Sir William Bentinck. On the 8th of December, 1816, the king assumed the title of Ferdinand I. and declared Sicily a province of the kingdom of Naples. This island then lost its privileges, its laws, and its ancient flag. The code Napoleon was adapted, as well as it could be, to the Sicilian manners, and the country was subject, for the first time, to the conscription, and the stamp duties.

It cannot be doubted that these measures irritated the people of Sicily and augmented their hatred of the Neapolitan dominion. The distress arising from the accumulation of provisions added to the general discontent. We may, therefore, in some measure, excuse the sedition which broke out in Sicily, the signal for which was given by the kingdom of Naples, to the prosperity of which this island thought it had been sacrificed. The Sicilians saw their efforts forgotten and their fidelity overlooked; it was easy to persuade them that silence and submission could only make their situation worse. This high spirited and exasperated people was thus placed between distress and revolt.

The first troubles broke out in the town of San Cataldo, where the register of the stamp paper had been burnt by the people. At Girgenti and Calta Nisetta the conscripts were rescued from the hands of the soldiers. The Bagaria, near the capital, became the theatre of the most sanguinary scenes between the people and the Neopolitan troops. Thus every thing indicated, that in the state of fermentation which prevailed at Palermo and the rest of the kingdom, the slightest spark would produce a great conflagration. Such was the situation of Sicily on the 1st of July, 1820.

Meantime the revolt broke out at Naples, on the 2d of the same month: some troops who deserted on *Monte Forte* joined the Carbonari of the two provinces of Salerno and Avellino. Soon this armed force increased so much that, on the 6th of July, the king was obliged to grant the Spanish constitution. The new provisional government of Naples, either from want of firmness or of foresight, or from the habit of considering Sicily as a necessary appendage to that kingdom, dispatched no person, sent no information to Palermo of what had happened at Naples, and the revolt was not known there till the 15th of July; about the middle of that day a small English vessel made the people of Palermo acquainted with the change that had taken place in the monarchy, and even the colours of the rebellion. This news was received and published in the midst of the bustle occasioned by the crowd collected to celebrate the festival of Saint Rosalia. Four hundred soldiers of the regiment of the guards rushed into the Cassaro, wearing the colours of the *Carbonari ;* the people joined them, crying, " Long live the Constitutional King," and all passed with a degree of unanimity and moderation. On the evening of the 15th General Church, an Englishman, in the service of Naples, indignant at the insubordination of the troops, met a soldier with a ribbon of the *Carbonari,* he tore it off and ordered him under arrest. His comrades collected and were going to seize General Church ; he took flight, and General Coglitore received a wound in the arm in saving this officer from the popular fury. General Church succeeded in taking refuge with Lieutenant-general Naselli, who facilitated his escape. The people resolving to avenge the insult offered to the soldier, proceeded to the house of General Church, seized his furniture and burnt it in the public square with remarkable disinterestedness. On the 16th of July they also burnt the furniture of the public gaming-house and that of the minister Ferreri, who had long been a subject of suspicion to the Sicilian nation.

All was tranquil till noon ; the Palermitans then learnt that the troops were assembling in the barracks with hostile intentions. They proceeded to the Lieutenant-General to know what orders he had given. Naselli was confused and in fear for his safety : the people asking for arms he yielded, and gave up the arsenal of Castel a Marc. The citizens armed themselves and went out without committing any excesses. Meantime a regiment of cavalry, of which Prince Campofranco, a Sicilian, was colonel, was drawn up in order of battle towards the gate Felice. It is not known from whom this officer had orders to charge the people in the street of Cassero. The colonel said in his defence, that three hundred insurgents having come from the Bagaria to open the prisons and liberate the criminals he thought it his duty to remedy this disorder by making a powerful diversion. Other persons affirmed that the order came from Naselli himself. This regiment killed or wounded between three and four hundred persons, but it was partly destroyed either by the populace, who came from the adjoining streets, or by the citizens, who fired on the soldiers from the windows and balconies. At length the garrison and the rest of the regiment were obliged to take refuge at the Bagari. Naselli determined to embark in the packet boat, which was in the roads protected by the castle, on board of which he had caused his furniture to be removed five days before. This project was executed, and the governor abandoned his post and retired to Naples.

The people after having made themselves masters of the fort, looked, during the 17th, for Prince Cattolico, who had given orders to fire upon them; they found him at la Bagaria, where they killed him; Prince Iaci and Captain Lanza suffered the same fate, because they had spiked two cannons which the insurgents were dragging after them. It is afflicting to be obliged to say that there were seen in the ranks of the vilest populace and by the side of felons, nobles, priests, and even nuns, who took part in the sedition. On the 18th of July the troops were disarmed, and the officers confined in a house by themselves. Meantime, by a sort of justice which marked out only the leaders to the popular fury, Neopolitans or foreigners had nothing to fear either for their lives or for their property; and after five or six days' confinement they were at liberty to return to their country with their families and their effects. A Junto of government was elected at Palermo; it endeavoured to re-establish order, which it did with pretty good success till the 28th of July. A deputation left Palermo on the 2nd of August and proceeded to Naples to demand of the king the independence of Sicily, and to renew, at the feet of the throne, the oath of fidelity.

At Naples, however, secret hopes were entertained to divide Sicily against itself, by declaring Messina the capital of the island. It is necessary to state that the population of Messina is reported to be entirely devoted to the English, and to have been jealous of the preponderance of Palermo.

The Neopolitan government thought that the principal of the Sicilian barons had organized and directed the troubles of Palermo of the 16th and 17th of July; they were even loudly accused of having cried " *The constitution of* 1812 *for ever*;" thus exciting the people to demand the chambers of peers and of commons. It was added, that the Sicilian barons excused their revolt under the specious pretext that the king had sworn to and sanctioned the constitution of 1812, and that the Neapolitan influence had alone deprived them of that benefit.

However this be, the example of Spain influenced the minds of the people, and plunged them into that abyss of misfortune from which wisdom and firmness have hitherto been able to give them but trifling relief. It may be said in defence of the Sicilian barons, that their renunciation of the right of the peerage immediately followed the news of the acceptance of the Spanish constitution. Thus the question could not be embarrassed by the claims of the nobility, who never separated themselves from the rest of the nation, and only seconded, with all their power, the ancient and constant aversion of the Sicilians to the Neapolitans.

Don Diego Naselli, a Sicilian noble, then sixty years old, was not calculated to govern Sicily in a moment of revolution. His whole conduct bears the stamp of weakness and irresolution; but he does not merit the odious reproaches which have been lavished upon him. His greatest fault, which may be considered as the cause of all the events which followed, was to arm the people, for from that time no barrier could stop the torrent ; and certainly the state of Europe for the last thirty years held up to this governor, great and terrible lessons, which were lost to him and to Sicily.

The first ebullitions of this insurrection, might certainly have been checked by great firmness and strict justice, perhaps too there ought to have been more frankness and promptitude in communicating the news from Naples. Such in short was the revolution of Palermo, the explosion of which was determined and rendered more terrible by the ignorance of the people, and the timid silence of the government.

We will conclude this sketch of the events of which Sicily has been the theatre. The Prince of Villafranca arrived from Naples at Palermo on the 24th of July. He was borne in triumph by the people, and immediately invested with the office of president of the junta. Two Neapolitan frigates and two brigantines, were refused entrance into the port, which came to solicit the liberty of the Neapolitan soldiers who had been imprisoned since the 16th and 17th of July. This demand was rejected. The junta of Palermo addressed a circular to all the Sicilian Municipalities. Messina, always the rival of Palermo, remained attached to the Neapolitan interests. The opposition of Calta Nisetta was punished by the Palermitans in a most cruel manner. The towns of Cefalu, Bisacguino, Carini, Calta, Gidone, Ficarra, Aidone, Licata, Marsalla, Traina, Mistrello, hastened to nominate representatives to the Palermitan junta. This junta, being invested with the national authority, organized the military force, collected patriotic gifts, and endeavoured to introduce a sort of regularity in the collection of the taxes ; it made changes in the magistracy, enrolled the citizens, and declared that all persons in office were a part of the military force.

While all this was passing in Sicily, the deputation sent to Naples received an answer, calculated to allay the ferment in the people's minds, and the Prince, vicar general, soon chose Don Florestan Pépé to treat with the Palermitan junta. The deputation returning from Naples to Palermo on the 8th of September, announced to the Sicilians, that the independence of the island would be granted by his Neapolitan Majesty, provided it was proved that this independence was the wish of the greater part of the people. Thus the king of Naples would have governed two nations, independent of each other, under different constitutions.

General Pépé landed at Milazzo on the 15th of September,

at the head of about four thousand men; he refused to treat with eight deputies of the junta and manifested his intention of marching to Palermo. That city prepared to endure a siege. The wiser part of the inhabitants were sensible of the danger of entrusting the defence of a capital to a populace more disposed to pillage than to combat. The president of the junta and seven other members set out for Termini, and endeavoured to regulate with Pépé the conditions of a capitulation. A violent storm prevented the deputation from returning by sea to Palermo, to make the city acquainted with the terms of the treaty. The people of Palermo assembled tumultuously, and the approach of the troops of General Pépé was considered as an act of treachery in the junta, which was suspected of intending to deliver up all the leaders and supporters of the events of the 16th and 17th of July. Soon all the posts of the civic guard were assailed, the authority of the junta entirely disregarded, and the palace of Villafranca broken into and plundered.

The arrival of the troops of Pépé at the gates of Palermo, obliged these undisciplined bands to think only of their own defence; they advanced furiously towards the Neapolitan troops, attacked them at all points, and compelled Pépé to retreat. The Neapolitan fleet had not been able to support the land army, because the fortress and the gun-boats at Palermo, kept up upon it, for four days, a continual fire, and so well directed that it was forced to withdraw from the coast.

The situation of Pépé became the more critical, as the attacks of the Palermitans was supported by insurrections in the little towns in the neighbourhood, which incessantly harassed his troops during the night. A reinforcement of a thousand men that was coming to him from Trapani, was routed at Monréale. These reverses induced the Neapolitan General to send a flag of truce to Palermo. Major Cianciulli, who was entrusted with this mission, found the city a prey to the most dreadful anarchy. The prince of Paterno, who is much beloved by the Sicilians, then took upon him the direction of affairs. After several conferences, a treaty signed on board the English sloop, the *Razor*, rendered General Pépé master of the city, and guaranted to the Sicilians the execution of several conditions, stipulated within the limits of his full powers. Palermo opened its gates, Pépé occupied the forts, and placed the Prince of Paterno at the head of a provisional junta, consolidated public order in the city and the neighbouring valleys, disarmed the people, and appointed General Campana governor of Palermo. As soon as the parliament of Naples was informed of these events, it declared null and void the military convention which General Pépé and the prince of Paterno had just concluded. The annulling of the treaty caused the highest discontent in Sicily. Florestan Pépé was recalled, the Neapolitan parliament sent General Coletta in his stead : this general set out for Palermo with a fresh reinforcement of troops, and adopted the severest measures against all classes of citizens. A great deal of property was sequestrated, and the imposition of a contribution of 90,000 ounces reduced Sicily to despair.

The Neapolitan parliament declared Messina the capital of Sicily, but this measure only increased the spirit of opposition and rivalry which existed between Messina, Catania, and Girgenti on one side, and Palermo and all the rest of Sicily on the other. The disorder increased with the weakness and the irresolution of the Neapolitan government. Placed out of the pale of the law of nations, by the congress of Laybach, preparing with activity to defend its own territories, the Neapolitan parliament abandoned Sicily to the effect of its own convulsions. Anarchy was at its height in this beautiful country, when the Austrians made themselves masters of Naples, occupied the kingdom, and, under the command of General Walmoden, landed at Palermo on the 31st of May, 1821 ; to the number of six thousand men. A second expedition, landing at Messina, was distributed over the eastern coast of Sicily.

Bands accustomed to disorder, and formed of all the felons, who by means of the last troubles have succeeded in breaking their chains, and escaping from the bagnios in which they were confined, have taken refuge in the most desert parts of the country, pursuit is made after these banditti, but a precipitate flight removes them far from the place where it was expected to surprise them, and they re-appear some where else. There is no internal safety in Sicily, and every thing is provisional. A decree of the king of Naples has, however, restored the seat of government to Palermo. A supreme council is to govern that country, but at present it reigns only over hatred, ashes, and profound misery.

ON THE POPULAR TRADITIONS RELATIVE TO THE FORMER EXISTENCE OF GIANTS IN SICILY.

The belief in the existence of giants, and the discovery of gigantic bones, have been so general in Sicily, that my readers will probably peruse with pleasure the opinion of d'Orville on this subject, as expressed in his work on Sicily.

"Many writers, almost all Sicilian, speak of tombs and bones of giants which exist, especially in the ports of this island. The Sicilians still give credit to these reveries. Desirous of acquiring certain information respecting so wonderful a subject, I resolved to do my utmost to discover somewhere the remains of these sons of the earth, to convince myself that such exist in Sicily or elsewhere; I have not been able to find any; my careful and persevering researches have been in vain. After having maturely considered, I have come to the conclusion, that what authors have written, and what has been told us respecting this prodigious race of men, must be placed in the class of fables. In fact, I have seen a great number of bones and ribs of large fish, whales, and other animals, which were preserved here, and which people in their ignorance take for the bones of giants.—The least degree of education would suffice to demonstrate the absurdity of these popular tales.

"These vast tombs, these caverns hollowed in the rock, were almost always formed to receive several bodies. These Sarcophagi, larger than the human body, such as are every where discovered, were not intended for one person. There may have been, and in fact there were, various reasons, why coffins exceeded by some feet the human stature. Often vain pride caused the erection of tombs of an enormous size. Princes, kings, emperors, even after their death have had more spacious abodes assigned to them than the human body requires. It is to be remarked, that it was also customary to bury several things together; this made it necessary to increase the dimensions of the Sarcophagus. In the most remote times, not long since among us, and even now among some people, animals, especially horses, have been buried with men, which rendered larger tombs necessary. I can quote an unexceptionable testimony to the truth of this assertion. In 1555, there was found at Utrecht, in a church dedicated to the Virgin, the tomb of Gisbert, Lord of Goye, who had been buried with his arms, and his horse, as was shewn by the remains of arms and horses' bones. Of this fact, which is well proved, I was lately assured by Peter Haming, author of a Flemish poem. This and other similar examples are a sufficient answer to all that has been said on the vast dimensions of some tombs, and to the inferences that may have been drawn from them. These tales of giants having been rejected even by Sicilians, among others by Carausius, should not seem to deserve that we should spend much time in refuting them. However, as it is difficult to efface superstitious ideas, when they have once taken root in the mind, and as enlightened people do not regret the marvellous when it is offered them by such writers as Fazelli, who

often calls himself an eye-witness, it is he that I shall endeavour to confute. I will readily leave to Thomas Fazelli the
reputation of an honest man, and I will acknowledge him to be
a writer who loves the truth; but whether it be the fault of
the age which was not yet cleared from the darkness of barbarism, or the error of a weak mind, it will be easy for me by
numerous arguments to demonstrate to the impartial and enlightened reader, that Fazelli was himself possessed by the
most superstitious credulity. I desire no other proof of this
than the stories he tells of the river Alpheus, the fountain
Arethusa, the enchantments of the demons, and the miracles
of Saint Philip d'Argyre. I pass in silence all these tales which
in the end would excite ill humour.

"Let us examine more closely his conjectures respecting
the giants. To make them inhabitants of Sicily, he takes his
examples from the most remote antiquity. He goes back to the
fabulous times, and places in the rank of incontestable truths,
the seventy cubits of the corpse of Antæus, however, Hyllus,
the son of Hercules, surpassed Antæus,

"*Quantùm lenta solent inter viburna cupressi.*"
(Vir. Ecloe. 1. v. 26.)

"Philostratus (Heroïc. p. 671.) reports, and Fazelli believes,
that the corpse of Hyllus, nine acres in height, was buried in
Phrygia. Now, as the acre contains a hundred and twenty
feet, we have here a skeleton measuring a thousand and eighty
feet. It would be almost equal in dimensions to Og, respecting whom the rabbis have related so many fables; in whose
skull, they affirmed, a huntsman wandered three days, and
had great difficulty in finding his way out. The credulity of
Philostratus does not excuse Fazelli. The former might, perhaps, be either explained or excused, for he does not say nine
acres, but nine *orgyies*; so that, according to him, the stature
of Hyllus was only eighteen feet.

"Let us return to the giants of Sicily,—Fazelli says, that it
is proved, to any one that is neither mad nor blind, that it is
in the nature of things that giants should have inhabited Sicily.
He adds: ' In 1343, the curiosity of the inhabitants of Eryx,
excited by the account of several individuals, induced them to
take arms, and march to a cavern of Mount Eryx. They found
there a human body of very large stature, in a sitting posture,
with the left-hand resting on a club, resembling the mast of a
ship. As soon as it was touched, the outside of this stick
crumbled into dust; it covered a club of lead. The body
also fell into dust, with the exception of three teeth of astonishing size, and of the front part of the skull, which was large

enough to contain several Sicilian hogsheads.   The opinion of
the learned was, that the body was that of Eryx, and the cavern still bears the name of that giant.   These molar teeth
were still seen in my time in the church of the Annunciation,
hanging by an iron wire to the feet of a crucifix ; afterwards
the inhabitants made a present of them to the Pope.'

" We must regret the leaden club ; antiquarians would easily have determined the truth of the fact by the nature of the
metal.   But as the club was, doubtless, soon melted, and the
teeth have disappeared, we are allowed to doubt the truth,
stated to have occurred long before the time when Fazelli
wrote.

" John Boccacio, (General. deor. lib. iv. cap. 68,) who lived
at a time nearer this epoch, relates the same thing.   He af-
firms, that the height of the giant was two hundred cubits.   I
shall take the liberty of raising some doubts on the opinion
of these learned gentlemen, who will have it, that Eryx was
buried in this place.   I shall not regard this new method of
burying, which represents a man seated, holding a club in his
right-hand ; but I beg them to read Virgil with me, where he
relates how Entellus, a disciple of Eryx in boxing, refused to
fight on account of his age, throws, however, into the Arena
two cestuses of enormous weight, which Eryx was accustomed
to use in his combats.   Dares, who was to fight with Entellus,
was more astonished than all the rest, and refuses these arms ;
then Entellus boasting says, ' It is with these two cestuses
that Eryx combated the great Alcides, and I use them myself.'
If Entellus had used the cestuses of Eryx, their size might
have been nearly in the same proportion ; but it was not so ;
for the son of Anchises brought cestuses of the same size, and
fastened them to the hands of both.   Unless, therefore, we
choose to place Dares among the giants, it is not possible that
his adversary and he should have used cestuses of equal size.
Entellus was taller ; but, according to the narrative of Virgil,
he did not much exceed others in strength.   It is said, that
this Eryx combated with Hercules ; but the same poet gives
us to understand, that the arms of the demigod were also
heavier.

" To judge by the accounts of the poets and the productions
of the statuaries, it does not appear that Hercules had extraordinary strength and stature, unless Omphale was also of
gigantic stature.   If we admit that Hercules was a giant, how
could he have fitted the skin of the Nemæan lion to his
armour, unless there were giants also among the lions?   In
what labyrinths do the defenders of the race of giants lose
themselves !

"But let us go to the other traditions of Fazelli; for that of the giant of Mount Eryx seemed fabulous even to the learned Jerome Maggi, who yet endeavours to prove that giants really did exist.—(Miscell. sive. var. lect. lib. 1, cap. 4.) The following is Fazelli's second proof : ' In the year 1516, a report was spread at Mazarino, that a dead body had been found upwards of twenty cubits in height. Count Braccio-forte and his wife Emelia were confounded at the sight of a prodigious body, and of a head as large as a hogshead. At this sight Emelia, seized with horror and almost dead with fright, miscarried. Unskilful persons having afterwards touched the body too violently, it crumbled into dust ; only the teeth were preserved, each weighing five ounces.' How shall we assign such a disproportion in the structure of this race of giants ? It is true it was after an interval of thirty years, in 1546, that this history was related to Fazelli, near Calta Nisetta, by Antoine de Moncade, count of Adrani, or rather by his sister Emelia. We have therefore to depend on the testimony of a woman ; and may we not suspect her of weakness or superstition ? A picture was in the house of Emelia representing this singular event in her life.

"Fazelli relates in the third place, that every day a quantity of large bones are extracted from tombs at Milazzo, between Lentini and Syracuse. But these bones doubtless belong to animals, and these sepulchres have formerly been quarries which, perhaps, were afterwards employed to bury the dead. I have in vain sought with the greatest care on the spot. Some inhabitants of Hyccara and Palermo attest a fourth example of Fazelli who, among other rarities, possessed a monstrous shoulder blade, but was he sufficiently versed in osteology to distinguish a human shoulder from that of an animal such as a horse or an ox ?

"The fifth testimony is thus reported : ' In the year 1547, Paolo Lentini accidentally found, in a field at Palermo, a human corpse of gigantic size; its height was eighteen cubits ; all the limbs were detached. Paolo having touched them with too little care, all, except the jaw, crumbled into dust.' So that nothing remains of this pretended discovery which made a great noise at the time.

"But it is fit we should know what Mario Valguarnera, a Sicilian, thought and published (Antiq. Panorm. p. 219) of this narrative of Fazelli. If he is not altogether free from superstition he is at least more reasonable. Thus, after having said he had filled, in a cave, four handkerchiefs with giant's bones, he adds, ' though this cave is every where so covered with giant's bones that it would be easy to bring away a very great quantity, yet the oldness of the soil and the humidity arising from the waters which filtrate through it every where, have corroded and consumed these bones, so that they crumble at the slightest touch; they are, besides, so attached to the earth that we cannot obtain them except by piece-meal, and with the earth itself.' I, therefore, never could understand how, in the time of Fazelli (a hundred and fifty years before), the body of this giant, which was not inclosed in any particular monument, could be in such a state of preservation, that it was possible to measure it. Most certainly, as soon as we got sight of a bone, we spared no pains to procure it entire. I am, therefore, persuaded that Fazelli did not measure the body, and that he only presumed the length of it from the size of the two molar teeth.

"I am, however, surprised that, after having found in his own country this proof of the uncertainty of the existence of giants, Valguarnera, who is distinguished above all the writers on Sicily, by the profoundness of his judgment and erudition, should have related things so little worthy of credit.

Let us add some more of Fazelli's testimonies. " In the year 1548, says he, George Adorno, of Genoa, having gone from Syracuse at the head of some armed men, entered a cavern to look for ancient gold medals. Having forced the entrance of this grotto, he descended and penetrated into a deep cavern, where he found a human body of the length of twenty cubits."

" But if medals have been found in these caverns must we not suppose that, in the time of the Greeks and Romans, these places were appropriated to the purpose of interring the dead? In fact, there still exists, in the environs of Syracuse and near the suburb Achradine, a great number of very spacious catacombs which I have visited, after many others observers. Fazelli adds, that ' almost the whole body crumbled into ashes.

" The rest of his narrative furnishes no proofs that are more convincing than those which I have already quoted. But to return to this cavern, it was doubtless one of those catacombs, the whole of which is, in general, hewn in the rock. Besides, he says nothing of the breadth and depth of the steps of the staircase, from the measure of which more solid arguments might have been drawn, than from some teeth or imperfect fragments.

" After the death of the governor of the citadel of Calatafimi," says Fazelli, " in 1550, some peasants, who were digging his grave, perceived a chest containing a human body, measuring about twenty-two cubits.

" This giant, therefore, would have been only thirty-three feet high, which is not very imposing after we have had others so much more extraordinary; but it is worthy of remark, that the ancient race of the Cyclops, the first inhabitants of Sicily, should

have put their dead into chests : though, as Homer tells us, Poly-
phemus while alive was contented to live in a cavern of Etna.

" The peasants broke these bones, of which no trace is left, any
more than of other similar discoveries. A story of the same nature
is of the year 1552. ' Some masons discovered by chance several
giants' tombs inclosed in freestone ; they found in them dead
bodies, most of which were above eight cubits in height.'

" We know not what became of this precious discovery. But I
stop and think I have sufficiently proved that the assertions of
Fazelli and Valguarnera are not supported by any well authenticated fact.

" After so many researches, so many discoveries of which there
were such numerous witnesses, there is not the slightest visible
proof remaining of all that they have said ; and I think we may
safely place in the rank of fables all that other authors may have
written about the first inhabitants of Sicily."

THE BENEDICTINES AT CATANIA.

In the museum of Prince B***, there are specimens of the
lavas of Mount Etna ; their number and the order in which they
are placed, enables us to study their nature.

Rezzonico says, " The lava of Etna, when reduced to powder,
show a grey surface. Brydone was mistaken in supposing that
they differed but little from each, and were not worthy to be
compared with the beautiful productions of Vesuvius. Dolomieu
justly observed, that Etna and the volcanoes of the Lipari
Islands carry to their summits the porphyry and granite, on which
they rest, and the chain of porphyry begins here, and extends
under Stromboli."

There are likewise some specimens of the mines of Sicily,
which evidently prove the abundance of metals in the island ;
but the working of them would be so expensive, that it has been
necessary to give up many attempts that have been made without
advantage. Leanti relates, that some coins were struck in 1734,
of silver, taken from the mines of Sicily. They have the effigy
of the Emperor Charles VI., who was then sovereign of the
island, with this Latin epigraph : *Ex visceribus meis.* Charles
II. wished also to work the Sicilian mines. That prince employed Saxon labourers, who are well skilled in this kind of
work ; but there was a want of wood ; and the expense exceeding
the profit, the enterprise was again abandoned.

I think it may interest the reader to extract a passage from
the work of Count Rezzonico, relative to a curious bas relief,
supposed to be Egyptian, which is in the collection of Prince

B***, without, however, meaning to answer for the correctness of the opinion given by that elegant, learned, and sensible writer:

"Un basso rilievo altresì mi fù presentato d'oscurissime allusioni, ed abile a rintuzzare gli sforzi di qualunque erudito, che non siasi iniziato nell' esoteriche dottrine cosmologiche, e nell' astrusa teogonia de' popoli primitivi a me nota per le recenti scoperte fattesi nel Bengala e i samscretici misteri disvelati dagli accademici di Calcutte. Vedisi una donna spremere il latte dalle sue vizze pope, ed irrigarne il labbro ottangolare di un' arca, che in se contiene molti animali e varie teste di fanciulli, che animati dalla prolifica rugiada emergono dall' imo fondo; intorno alle pareti è scolpita una pompa egizia funebre in minutissime figure. Escono dal labbro alcuni fanciulli, che porgono mano ad altri molti, da' quali è sostenuto il cadavero d' un grosso bue colle zampe alzate verso il cielo, e pare che tentino di gittarlo in quel vaso. Or chi non vede quì effigiata la natura, il cahos, e le tre potenze di creare, mantenere e distruggere, ossia l'indica *Trimurti?* Imperochè il bue morto dinota evidentemente la distruzione; e l'atto e lo sforzo de' genj per gittarne il cadavero nel gran vaso si è il circolo perpetuo della morte alla vita, che mantiene eterne le cose, avvegnachè pajano a' nostri debili sensi annichilate e distrutte. A togliere poi ogni dubbio della mia spiegazione basta osservare, come feci io stesso alla seconda volta, dietro la natura le ali manifeste dell' incubazione, e queste formate in modo, che figurano eziandio le natatoje de' pesci, e sono coperte di squame fin là d' ond' escono le penne ritorte all' inù della chioccia, e così tutto evvi egregiamente espresso il cosmologico pensiero degli Sciti e degli Egiziani."

LETTER FROM THE VIRGIN MARY TO THE INHABITANTS OF MESSINA.

The following is the Latin translation of this letter, such as it is engraved behind the high altar:

Epistola, juxta antiquam et piam traditionem, VIRGINIS MARIÆ ad Messanenses.

Maria Virgo, Joachim filia, humilis ancilla Dei, Christi Jesu crucifixi mater, ex tribu Juda, stirpe David, Messanensibus omnibus salutem et Dei Patris omnipotentis benedictionem.

Vos omnes fide magnâ legatos ac nuncios per publicum

documentum ad nos misisse constat : filium nostrum Dei Genitum Deum er hominem esse fatemini, et in cœlum post suam resurtectionem ascendisse, Pauli apostoli electi prædicatione mediante viam veritatis agnoscentes, ob quod vos et ipsam civitatem benedicimus, cujus perpetuam protectricem nos esse volumus. Ex Hierosolymis, anno filii nostri xLII, ind. I, nonas junii, lunâ xxvii feriâ v.

BULL OF POPE BENEDICT XIII. RELATIVE TO THE LETTER OF THE HOLY VIRGIN.

His holiness, Benedict XIII, granted an indulgence of a hundred days to any of the faithful, so often as he devoutly recites the following prayer :

Ave, filia Dei Patris, quæ Messanenses in filios elegisti.

Ave, mater Dei Filii, quæ Messanenses matenè exaudisti.

Ave, sponsa Spiritûs, sancti, quæ Messanenses veritatis spiritui despondisti.

Ave, templum S. S. Trinitatis, unde Messanenses per sacram epitolam benedixisti.

My readers may consult on this subject the works of P. Belli and Dominique Argananzio, called, " Pompe festive celebrate dalla nobile ed esemplare città di Messina, nell' anno 1659, per la solemnità della sagratissima lettera scrittale dalla suprema imperatrice degli angeli Maria. Messina, 1659.

On the subject of this letter Rezzonico says,

" I shall say little of the Greek image of the virgin and of her letter to the people of Messina. The learned Monsignor Grano informed me that that image was revered long before Costantino Lascari landed in that port ; and as it stood upon a leggio, (reading desk) it was vulgarly called the Madonna de Leggio ; and in corrupt language, del Letterio; since in barbarous Latin it was written Lectorium. The cunning Greek took occasion from this corrupted and ill-understood word to invent the letter, which he pretended to have discovered among the parchments in the archives of Messina, it having been translated by the Apostle St. Paul from the original Hebrew into Greek : and with this falsehood he deceived the city of Messina ; and the Greek had an honourable salary, with the obligation however of giving instructions in his language. He afterwards made a present to the city of his extensive library, which went to Spain.   This ingenious Greek likewise discovered other documents, such as relative to the assistance given by the people of Messina to Honorius, which is equally fabulous.   On the Greek table was H ΠΟΡΓΟ ΕΠΗΚΟΟΣ, and above was the usual monogram $\frac{\Omega}{MP}$ $\frac{\Omega}{OY}$ that is *Madre di Dio, sollecita ascolatrice.*

St. Paul was at Reggio and not at Messina, according to the Acts of the apostles ; and was elected apostle forty-three years after the birth of Christ, according to the best chronologists. Lastly, the diplomatic style, and still more the date, the feria, and the indiction, accuse of manifest falsehood and ignorance the knavish grammarian, who ought to have known that Dionysius Essegno was the inventor of the vulgar era, and that this was not received by the Church till the eighth century. The people cannot be enlightened, but men of learning at Messina, for there are such, laugh at the stories, and English travellers ought not to ridicule the credulity which has always been the inheritance of the unlearned mob, and which I have seen triumph in their own highly civilized island, and in London itself, as it does elsewhere, both in the mob, and even in classes above them."   (Rezzonico, Viaggio della Sicilia, tom. vi. p. 88.)

THE END.

G. Sidney, Printer,
Northumberland Street, Strand.

RUSSIAN MISSIONS

INTO THE

INTERIOR OF ASIA;

I.
NAZAROFF'S EXPEDITION TO KOKAND.
II.
EVERSMANN AND JAKOVLEW'S ACCOUNT OF BUCHARIA.
III.
CAPT. MOURAVIEW'S EMBASSY TO TURKOMANIA AND CHIVA.

Translated from the German.

LONDON:

PRINTED FOR SIR RICHARD PHILLIPS AND Co.

BRIDE-COURT, BRIDGE-STREET.

1823.

G. SIDNEY, Printer,
Northumberland Street, Strand.

INTRODUCTION.

Russia appears, by its geographical position, to be, of all the states of the Continent, that which is the best calculated to serve as an entrepôt for Europe and Asia. On the one hand, rivers and canals unite the Baltic with the Caspian Sea, and make Nischnei-Novogorod and Astrachan great markets, where commerce would become of great importance, if its safety were insured on the roads which it is obliged to follow; on the other hand, the ports of the Black Sea are open to the mercantile fleets which trade to the Levant. Yet, notwithstanding the advantages of this position, it has hitherto been impossible to surmount all the obstacles to the progress of commerce, arising from the unsocial character of the Asiatic tribes, bordering upon Russia. The difference in manners, religion, and civilization, between the Europeans and the Orientals, or the consequences of a distrustful and suspicious policy, have caused the people of Asia to remain in a state of separation, which, while it gives them security, leaves commerce without a sufficient guarantee, to enable it to follow a regular course.

Caravans have long been accustomed to go from Bucharia to Orenburg and Astrachan, and this last town has a commercial intercourse with the Turcomans; but the routes which these caravans take, pass across *Steppes* infested by the invasions of the Kirghis; and the expeditions from Manghichlak to Astrachan are neither constant nor regular.

The Russian government has, of late years, taken various measures to give more solidity to its commercial relations with the countries in the interior of Asia, near its own frontiers ; efforts have been made to conciliate the independent tribes ; and various missions have been sent, an account of which will be found in the following pages.

The first is a short extract from an account of an expedition to Kokand, in the years 1813-14, by Mr. Philip Nazaroff, interpreter to the Siberian Corps employed in the expedition.

The second is the account of an embassy to Bucharia in 1820 1821, at the head of which was Mr. Negri, Counsellor of State : described under the title of a " Journey from Orenburg to Bucharia," by Dr. Eversmann, physician to the Embassy, in which we have inserted several interesting extracts from the letters of Mr. P. L. Jakovlew, secretary to the embassy.

The third is the narrative of a Journey to Turcomania and Chiva, by Captain Mouraview, who was sent on a mission to those countries in 1819-20.

RUSSIAN MISSIONS

INTO

THE INTERIOR OF ASIA.

No. I.

EXPEDITION TO THE COUNTRY OF KOKAND IN THE YEARS 1813 AND 1814. BY PHILIP NAZAROFF, INTERPRETER TO THE SIBERIAN CORPS EMPLOYED IN THE EXPEDITION.

THIS account, which as we are informed has never been translated from the original Russian, does not, it must be owned, give so much information as might have been expected, concerning this interesting part of Asia, the seat and centre of the barbarian grandeur of Timour, and of Gengis Khan, his predecessor; yet it affords some little insight into the strength and character of the Tartar hordes, who now roam over a small, but favourite portion of that once magnificent and boundless empire, and an analysis of it seems to be a very proper introduction to the accounts of the subsequent missions into the adjacent countries.

The Sultan of Kokand, at the time of this expedition, was a young man of twenty-four years of age, named Valliami, (more properly Uaelnahmi) of a warlike and enterprising character, who had subjected to his dominion, various Tartar tribes dispersed on those immense plains, called, by the Arabs, Mawn-el-nahar, which contain the once celebrated cities of Bokhara, Balk, and Samarcand, a tract of country remarkable for its fertility and beauty. This central part of Asia is bounded on the north by the Algydim Zano mountains, on the west by the Belur Tag, on the south by the Hindoo Koo and Pamar mountains, and on the west by the river Jihon, and the Lake (or Sea) of Aral.

The occasion of the present mission was as follows: a deputation had been sent, in 1812, from the Sultan, or Khan, of Kokand to the court of Petersburgh; which, on its return, halted at the fortress of Petropaulousk, (marked St. Peter in the charts), on the river Ishim : the principal person caught a fever and died ; the next in rank was a most depraved character, and frequented the company of profligate women, in whose society he formed an acquaintance with an exiled Russian soldier.   This man, with a view of getting possession of the Tartar's money, enticed him one day to the Ishim to bathe, and, availing himself of the opportunity, murdered him, and threw his body into the river.   These untoward circumstances induced the Russian Commandant of the fortress to accompany the remaining part of the deputation with an escort, in order to obviate any unfavourable interpretation that might be put by the Khan on the unfortunate end of his two envoys.

Mr. Nazaroff, being well acquainted with the language of the Kokans, offered his services, and was dispatched by the commandant, in May, 1813, with credentials and presents in the name of the Emperor, under the protection of a party of Cossacks ; and, at the same time, an opportunity was taken of sending a caravan, or a company of traders, to endeavour to open a commercial intercourse with the people.   Having crossed the Steppe of Ishim they entered upon the possessions of the northern Kirghis ; whom Mr. Nazaroff describes as consisting of three hordes, over each of which is a Khan ; each horde is divided into other portions, over each of which is a Sultaun ; and these are again subdivided into separate companies, placed each under the controul of a Bia, or Elder. Both the general government and that of the hordes are very cruel : their religion is that of Mahomet, and their laws are founded on the precepts of the Koran.

The Kirghis are excellent horsemen ; even children of four or five years old are able to manage a horse with great dexterity, and the women are not less expert than the men.   Their horses are of the Arabian breed, fifteen or sixteen hands high, and in their predatory excursions will hold out for several days at the rate of an hundred miles a day.   The hordes are honest and faithful to their word among themselves, but make no scruple of plundering their neighbours.   Nocturnal excursions to drive off cattle are very common ; and the women, on such occasions, armed with clubs and lances, take as active a share in any combat that may ensue as the men.

Marriages are contracted by the parents while the parties are infants ; and such contracts are held sacred.   At the marriageable age, which is very early, the young people have free access to each other.   They have a tent set apart from the rest of the horde, to which the bride is brought every night for a fortnight before the marriage, and left alone with the bridegroom ; but such, says Mr. Nazaroff, " is the native

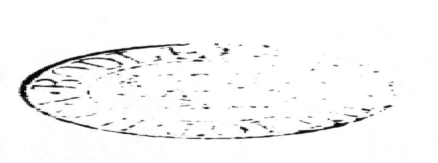

modesty implanted in the breasts of these people, that no indecent or improper liberty is ever taken by the young man." On the day appointed for the nuptials the relations meet, the mollah receives the declaration of the parties, unites their hands, and invokes a blessing and a numerous offspring ; barrenness being, according to their estimation, little short of disgrace.

Mr. Nazaroff and his party stopped at a place called *Tur-Aigrah*, in Turkistan, near which was a lake about thirty miles in circumference, called *Kitchubai-Tchurkar*. On a sloping bank of this lake they observed an extensive burying ground, containing a multitude of square wooden tombs, some marked with spears, as a memorial of the good horsemanship of the deceased, and others with the figures of hawks, as a sign of their skill in fowling. To this burying-ground the rich Tartars bring their deceased relations from every part of the territory of the Kirgis. In the winter months, when the country is covered with snow, and no food is to be had for their cattle, they suspend the bodies, swaddled in thick felt, from the branches of trees, and in spring collect and carry them to the sanctified cemetery. " Crossing the deserts of Tartary," says Mr. Nazaroff, " in the winter months, one frequently meets with these dismal objects covered with hoar frost, and dangling, in all directions, to the chilling blast.

The borders of this lake are the resort of various wandering tribes, who barter their horses, camels, and sheep, with the caravans for clothing and other articles of necessity and luxury. While Mr. Nazaroff remained in this place, one of the horde was condemned to suffer death. A halter was immediately thrown round the neck of the offender, the end of which was fastened to the tail of a horse, which, being mounted by a Tartar, set off at full trot, and continued galloping round the encampment till the life of the unfortunate criminal was terminated. " Having inquired into the cause of so excruciating and dreadful a punishment, I was surprised (he says) to learn that the sufferer's offence was that of stealing two sheep, whilst those who condemned him were at the very moment, under pretence of private quarrels with the neighbouring tribes, carrying off whole herds of cattle, and requiring ransom for their restitution.

The farther they advanced through Turkistan, now a part of Kokand, the more fixed the population appeared ; the tents of the Tartars were exchanged for houses of stone, and fields cultivated with grain, among which towns and villages were interspersed, were seen on every side. Every thing now wore the appearance of improved civilization. They had now reached the territory of Tash-Kand, which is watered by the Sir and its numerous branches. The Khan sent his officers to demand the usual duties from the caravan, at the same time inviting them, in the most friendly manner, into the town of that name. He advised Mr. Nazaroff to proceed with his Cossacks alone to Kokand; not succeeding in this, he detained the caravan with a part of the Cossacks, at Tash-Kand, but graciously permitted the mission to set forward with the remainder of the escort (about twenty), which they did without guides, confiding in the local knowledge of the Kokaners whom they had brought with them from Russia.

With the utmost difficulty they succeeded in crossing the river *Tchirtchik*, on account of the rapidity of the stream, and the large stones which it rolled down with it. This is one of the numerous torrents which fall from the high mountain called Kindertau, a prolongation of the Belur Tag, and which swell the Sir or Sihon. Mr. Nazaroff says, that the roaring of this turbulent stream may be heard at the distance of 15 wersts, and that it is so tremendous, that even the beasts of prey dare not approach it. The valleys of this range of mountains are inhabited, it appears, by little hordes of savage or uncivilized Persians of the East, who are called the Men of the Mountains.

Proceeding southerly, the mission passed the Khojund and the Sur-Daria, and arrived at the city of Khokand, the capital of Kokania, situated in the centre of those interminable plains, where Gengis-Khan was in the habit of assembling a general council of all the khans, governors, and military chiefs of his extensive empire; and where, we are told, were once assembled 500 ambassadors from the conquered countries only. It was here that the magnificent feast was given by Timour on the marriage of his six grandsons; where, according to Gibbon, following the statement of Sherefeddin, " the plain was spread with pyramids of meat, and vases of every kind of liquor, to which thousands of guests were courteously invited;" where " pearls and rubies were showered on the heads of the brides and bridegrooms, and contemptuously abandoned to their attendants;" where " a general indulgence was proclaimed, every law relaxed, every pleasure was allowed, the people was free, the sovereign was idle."

On arriving at the gates of Kokand, the Cossacks dressed themselves in full uniform, and the whole cavalcade entered the city, marched by the palace, and were lodged in a garden with one small pavilion in it. Two tents were immediately pitched for the cossacks, and one for Mr. Nazaroff and his companion Beziuzikoff; the Kokaners were taken away, and a guard of, fifteen men placed over the Russians, with orders not to suffer them to leave the garden.

During the night they had a visit from the vizier, who demanded what their object was in coming to Kokand? They replied to bring home the Kokaners; to explain the unfortunate circumstances of the death of the two envoys; and to open a commercial intercourse with the country. The vizier then told them that provisions for themselves and their cattle should daily be sent to them, and without explaining himself further, departed. The garden, while the Europeans were confined there, was crowded with spectators, who stood gazing from morning to night. This continued for eleven days, when the hour was announced for delivering the credentials and presents to the Khan. This short period of confinement showed the degree of respect deemed necessary for the Russians, the delay being in the ratio of the estimation in which the envoys are held.

The distance of the garden from the palace of the Khan, was about fifteen wersts, the whole of which was lined with cavalry. The two Russian envoys mounted their horses, but the cossacks, four of whom, attended by a corporal, carried the box which contained the imperial presents and credentials, marched on foot in two columns. Before they reached the outer wall of the palace, Mr. Nazaroff and his friend were ordered to dismount, and were detained about half an hour, when the gate was opened, and Mr. N. alone was conducted through a court-yard, at the extremity of which the Khan was pointed out to him at a window. In proceeding towards the royal presence he was told that he must pay the same marks of respect as were observed to his own sovereign, upon which he took off his hat, made a bow, and put it on again. The Khan was seated on a lofty throne, placed on an elevated platform covered with carpets, and the viziers and principal grandees of the court, were ranged on each side of him. Mr. Nazaroff was told to put the credentials on his head, and holding them with both hands, a common ceremony in the east, (dictated probably by precaution,) was brought to the foot of the throne. Here he was desired to fall upon one knee, upon which the Khan took the credentials from his head, and gave them to one of his viziers; he then stretched out his hand, which Mr. Nazaroff took in both of his, after which he was led by two of the ministers to the door, always keeping his face towards the throne. There were present on this solemn occasion ambassadors from China, Bucharia, and from the various surrounding petty states, for all of whom a dinner was prepared, consisting of coloured rice and horse-flesh, and this being finished the Russians returned in procession to their garden.

Soon after this interview, it was announced by the secretary of the Khan that the detachment would be sent back to Russia in the course of three days; but that Mr. Nazaroff must remain there till the following spring, when the caravan and certain deputies would be sent by the Khan to enquire more particularly into the real cause of the death of his two ambassadors. Mr. Nazaroff now began to suspect that he was a prisoner, and he was in fact removed in a few days from the garden, and lodged with his corporal and four cossacks in the castle of the governor, with a guard over him. He remained here twelve days, at the end of which he was brought before the great men of the court, and asked what compensation he meant to offer for the murder of the Khan's ambassadors. If our envoy was startled by such an abrupt question he was not much relieved when he was told that three alternatives would be submitted to him,---to pay the money demanded by the relations of the deceased---embrace the religion of Mahomet---or be suspended from a gibbet, to which they pointed at the same time. " I replied thus," says Mr. Nazaroff,---" to pay an adequate sum is quite out of my power; to betray my faith and my sovereign, I am not prepared; and as to death I am not afraid to meet it; well knowing that my sovereign will fully avenge any insults that may be offered to my person." " Finding" he continues, " that I boldly replied to their questions, I was ordered back to my prison; and from this moment the governor of the castle treated me with the greatest kindness; but he shortly after told me that the Khan had determined to send me into exile.

Accordingly, an invitation was one day brought for Mr. Nazaroff to attend the Khan on a hunting party, to a place called Margliand, about 250 wersts from Kokand. Two carriages were prepared to transport him and his Cossacks, accompanied by an officer and two drivers. After having passed through a great number of villages they entered a very extensive desert. Thinking this a good place to come to some explanation with the officer, " I rushed upon him," says Mr. Nazaroff, " with my sabre drawn, and desired him, if he regarded his life, to tell me whither he was ordered to convey us." He answered trembling that he had secret orders to convey us to the fortress of *Jarmazan,* on the frontier of Persia; but that if I preferred it he would take us to Margliand, distant about 50 wersts." Mr. Nazaroff preferred the latter, and in two days they arrived at that place, where lodgings were ordered for them by the governor, who behaved with great kindness.

Here they were kept for three months, when, by the intercession of the Vice-Khan, they obtained permission to return by a very pleasant and populous route to Kokand, from which they were sent to Tash-Kund, where the deputies of the Khan to the Emperor of Russia joined them. It was in consequence of this Mission that the Emperor Alexander resolved to send an embassy to Bucharia, the account of which follows in the next chapter.

The people of Kokand speak the Turkish language with the greatest purity, and are far advanced in civilization. The strictest probity prevails among them. Whoever is convicted of imposition is immediately stripped of all his clothes, without respect to person, scourged with whips through all the streets, and compelled to proclaim himself aloud to be a cheat. Their law-suits are carried on without any records of the proceedings. The priests are their judges, who in large assemblies, at which the commander-in-chief presides, hear causes and pass sentence. Treachery and usury are punished with death. The property of a person executed falls to the public treasury; his wives and grown up daughters are given in marriage to common soldiers. For theft one or both hands are lopped off, according to the value of the thing stolen; immediately after the execution of the sentence, the stumps of the arms are dipped in boiling oil, and the thief is then suffered to depart, as incapable of further mischief. A murderer is given up to the relations of the person murdered, who are at liberty either to kill him or sell him. Adulteresses are buried in the earth up to the breast, and then stoned to death by the people.

No. II.

EMBASSY TO BUCHARIA BY DR. EVERSMANN, PHYSICIAN, AND MR. JAKOVLEW, SECRETARY TO THE EMBASSY.

AFTER various fêtes we left Orenburg on the 10th of October, 1820. Our caravan consisted of 500 camels, about 230 Cossacks, as many infantry, and two cannons. As the Kirghis are very distrustful of Russia, it was difficult to persuade them to furnish camels, and it was only by the prudent conduct and wise measures of General Essen, Governor of Orenburg, that they were prevailed upon.

A good camel carries, on a long journey, sixteen poods, (one pood thirty-six pounds English,) and can travel from forty to fifty wersts in a day. The pace is very slow in comparison with its size, even slower than that of an indifferent horse, or about seven or eight wersts in an hour.

When a caravan is to be assembled a negotiation is commenced with the rich Kirghis about the price; when this is settled they endeavour to collect, in the Steppe, as many camels as their credit and their fortune permit; they partly supply their own camels, and partly hire them of the poorer Kirghis. Every owner of camels in a caravan is obliged, not only to attend and take care of them, and collect them when the caravan sets out, but to load and unload, and guide them, so that the owner of the goods has no trouble; for this purpose the owner of the camels hires a certain number of drivers, according to the number of the animals; a good driver generally having the care of eight or twelve camels. When the camels are loaded, all those belonging to one driver are fastened together, one behind the other, by a rope, only the first is guided by the driver, who either goes on foot or rides upon a horse, ass, cow, or ox, sometimes on the camel itself, which he manages with a halter. Travelling with the caravan is, indeed, fatiguing, but a good constitution is soon accustomed to it; at first its novelty pleased me, but I afterwards found the endless Steppe extremely tiresome till I was gradually used to it; and the rambling life under tents even became agreeable to me. When a caravan stops, in the evening, the first thing is to set up the tents, taking care (as at court) to see from what quarter the wind blows; to open the roof of the tent on the opposite side, that the smoke may have free egress. Then tea, the chief beverage of the Asiatics, is quickly drunk out of large cups, a frugal supper is prepared, and the weary traveller reposes on skins, spread on the ground, without needing to invoke Morpheus to his aid.

The leader of our caravan was named Jamantschibai, an old Kirghis, who rode before; after him came the vanguard of Cossacks, then camels, soldiers, cannon, &c. till the rear guard closed the procession. Cossacks rode at some distance, on both sides, in order to have early knowledge of any hostile attack.

Early in the morning of the day of our departure the caravan preceded us; only the officers of the embassy remained behind to enjoy a few hours more on the cultivated soil of their native country, till at length the departing day obliged us to mount our horses. We rode rapidly through the gates, and over the wretched bridge across the Ural, and were now on Asiatic ground, and had before us the boundless

Steppe of the free Kirghis. Three wersts from the Ural, in the Steppe, is the bartering place, a large space surrounded with stone shops, where the Asiatics and Russians annually exchange their goods ; we left it on the right and proceeding to the south-east, overtook our caravan, which was encamped twenty-one wersts and a half from the town, on the little river Berganka, which falls into the Ural about eight wersts further. The Berganka, or as the Kirghis call it, Darataldi, like almost all the little rivers of the desert, consists of deep holes, or pools, united by narrow and shallow currents, and in a dry season, or when the sources have but little water, they cease to flow, and only the pools with putrid water remain. The cause of the scarcity of water in the desert is, undoubtedly, to be looked for in the entire want of wood. On the Berganka are the old copper mines already mentioned by Pallas, which are now entirely abandoned, being too poor to pay the trouble and expense of working them.

On the 11th of October we halted, because the Kirghis wished to make several purchases at Orenburg ; we left our camp the next day, crossed the Berganka three wersts further, and continued our journey to the south-east, through an undulating country overgrown with dry grass.

On the 26th we encamped near Bitlissu, i. e. lousy water, where there are some small pools, the corrupt water of which well deserves the name. Just after sunset, we saw a ball of fire fall from the sky, which, as it approached the earth, increased considerably and rapidly in size. The Kirghis told us the phenomenon is often seen in the desert, and, without troubling their heads further about the matter, they call it Tängri-Fermani, i. e. command of God. In general the Kirghis, like all other followers of the mechanical worship of the Koran, are little disposed to reflection : thus, if you ask them if it will be fine weather to-morrow, they always answer " God knows ;" if you ask them how many days' journey it is to any place, they reply, " God knows," though they have passed the same way fifty or a hundred times : to obtain an answer to your question you must reverse it and ask, " the last time you made this journey how many days did it take you."

On the 13th of October, at sunrise, we left Bitlissu, and soon reached a small spring river, called Kundissu, i. e. Blood water, from the numerous leeches in it, which fasten on those who bathe in it. On our way we killed many foxes of the desert, which are so numerous that a great trade is carried on with their skins in the Russian frontier towns, as also in Bucharia, Taschkand, Turkestan, &c. In size and colour they resemble the common fox, only that their ears and the lower part of their feet are black.

Continuing our road through the desert, which offered but little variety, we came to an eminence where there were many ancient graves ; they consisted of longish heaps of stone, which were mostly lower in the middle. These graves are said to belong to the Kirghis, but, to judge by the appearance of the stones, overgrown with lichens, this can hardly be possible, as the Kirghis have not inhabited those parts above two hundred and sixty years.

On the 16th of October, at sunset, we continued our journey, at first parallel with the little river Usunburta, which lay on our right, and afterwards, went further and further from it. The country here, as well as near our camp the night before, was a little more mountainous, or rather the undulating hills were higher. After travelling about twenty-one wersts we reached an eminence visible at a considerable distance ; there is here a hill, consisting of sand, sunk in the middle, and measuring about 150 paces in circumference, which is evidently a work of human hands ; around it were several smaller hills of stones, like those I have mentioned before. When I asked the leader of our caravan, he told me that a Tartar prince was buried under the great hill ; that each individual of his people had carried the corner of his garment full of earth, and thus they had formed the hill ; and his sons lay round him. The eminence upon which these graves are must be pretty considerable, as the prospect from it is extensive ; it was a general custom with the Tartars, as it is still with the Kirghis, to bury their dead in the highest places ; all the graves which we saw in the sequel confirmed this.

After going thirty-five wersts and a half we encamped near a little wood, a great rarity in this barren desert ; the trees, which are pretty high, are alders mixed with poplars and willows, that are not so high. The last day's journey rather fatigued us, we therefore broke up the following morning later than usual. We crossed two small rivers, consisting, at present, of single pools ; they both join and fall into the Ilek, the course of which we could discern by the trees growing on its banks. It flowed, with many windings, on our right hand till we reached it, after travelling about twenty-eight wersts. Upon the banks of this river, in a spot overgrown with trees, and very agreeable for this desert, we met with the Auls of the Sultan Arungasi, who afterwards accompanied us from that place to the Jan-Darja. An Aul signifies, among the Kirghis, several tents, (Kibit) standing together ; Aul in the Tartar language means a village.

Arungasi was just employed in passing sentence of life and death; at first, it was said, that he would do us the honour of having the criminal, who had stolen some horses, put to death in our presence; but afterwards his life was spared, because the Sultan hoped by this clemency to obtain the protection of Heaven to the Jan-Darja. But the culprit did not entirely escape punishment; I was witness of it, and will here describe it. The delinquent, with his hands tied upon his back, almost naked, and his face blackened with charcoal, was driven round the tents; if he did not run fast enough, those who rode after him struck him with their whips. He was then compelled to go a second time round the tents, a rope being put into his mouth, which was fastened to the tail of a horse, on which a man rode before him, while another horseman behind him urged him on, and so he was driven a second time round the camp. After this he was upbraided with his crime, and forced to confess that he had well deserved his punishment. This being done, his horse's throat was cut, instead of his own, and each of the Kirghis cut off a piece of the still palpitating flesh, to make himself a delicate supper; not a morsel of the horse remained. The whole execution passed, of course, amidst the loudest cries and noise. I will here add some of the Sultan's laws, which, as far as I know, compose his whole code.

1st. He who steals any cattle, a camel, horse, sheep, &c. is punished with death: in general his head is cut off with a knife.

2d. A murderer must pay a certain value in sheep; from 500 to 2000 sheep, according to his wealth; if he cannot pay this sum he suffers death.

3d. To hinder horses from running away, three of their legs are tied together with a thong, contrived for that purpose; if a person steals such a thong, both his ears are cut off.

4th. Other trifling faults, quarrels, affrays, &c. are punished by flogging.

The delinquent, who is to suffer death, is placed bound on the ground; then he must repeat aloud certain prayers prescribed by the Koran; if he does not know them, which is almost always the case, they are repeated to him by a Mollah, and he must say them after him; when this is done they cry, " it is done," and the executioner, who is any person that may be chosen, performs his office.

On the 18th of October we again halted for the day. Arungasi, who had before presented us with an ox and several sheep, waited on the ambassador early the following morning, but the ambassador, on account of his situation, could not return his visit. The fine weather invited us to walk on the banks of the Ilek, a pretty river about 60 paces broad. A great number of shell-fish live in its sandy bed, but with all my pains I could find only five different species. We found the little ponds or lakes to abound in fish, but only of three kinds, namely, the pike, the carp, and the white fish. The water of these ponds was rather salt. The Sultan Arungasi having still some affairs to settle, set out some days later than we did, who continued our journey on the 19th. We went at first up the Ilek, which was on our right hand, for about four wersts ; when we crossed it, and left it pretty far to the left, till we reached it again, at sun-set, having gone 31 wersts. On the left side of the river, there is a long row of pretty high hills, which are only ancient graves.

The Ilek is bordered in its whole course with trees and shrubs, especially the silver poplar, the black poplar, the aspen, and several species of willow; it is the last river beyond the Russian frontiers, the banks of which are bordered with trees ;---farther to the south, the face of Nature becomes more and more melancholy, till it attains the highest degree of sterility, in Bucharia itself, as we shall see in the sequel.---After proceeding 28 wersts we encamped on a small spring rivulet, which consisted at present only of separate pools : it falls into the Ilek, and is called Tambutak, from the sepulchre of a Tartar Prince, close by, which consists of a square of brick, about 15 feet in breadth, eight in length, and 10 feet in height ; it is hollow within ; the walls are about four feet and a half thick ; the bricks on the outside are burnt, those on the inside only dried clay. A square hole is left on each side. Besides this sepulchre, we met with many graves like those we had already seen.

From Tambutak we came the following day across the Batbakli, i. e. moory ; it falls into the Buschtamag, or five throats, because five streams there join, which contribute to form the Ilek. After travelling 30 wersts, we encamped on a pond called Suukssu, or cold water, where, as far as the eye could reach, nothing but the desolate Steppe was to be seen. So far we had always fine weather ;---the night temperature was only a few degrees below zero, by day the sun afforded an agreeable warmth : but the sky now became gloomy, the cold disagreeable, and in the evening the thermometer being at 8 degrees of Reaumur, below zero, we had a fall of snow.

On the 23rd of October we left the Suukssu, where we had halted one day. The sky had cleared up during the night, and in the morning early it was very cold ; even in the day it was from 10° to 12° of Reaumur. After going 16 wersts, we passéd a pretty considerable rivulet, Issanbai, i. e. rich in health; and some wersts farther, a second, called like that we passed on the 21st, Batbakli: both come from the south, and fall into the Ilek. After 35 wersts we encamped near a small river, Talaschbai, i. e. rich in quarrels: 16 wersts from this, we passed, on our left hand, a small river, called Karagandi, from a low shrub called Karagan, which abounds there. On its banks are numerous petrifactions, especially of shells. The rivulet was hard frozen, and we took ice with us to our resting place for the night, which we reached after travelling 32 wersts, and halted in a large plain, quite overgrown with Artemisia, which afforded excellent fodder for the horses and camels: the latter eat with great avidity the dry stalks of that plant.

From Orenburg to this place we had in general ascended, as the course of the rivers which we passed evidently shews. Our journey on this last day was constantly ascending, and at length pretty rapidly, till we reached the highest point, a few wersts from the place where we encamped for the night. Here there is an extensive level, which has the name of Bussaga, i. e. the threshold, because at the highest point, it determines the course of the rivers, and not as if you came into a different country, for it is as desolate on the one side as on the other. The country all around is a sterile clay, in which no grass grows, but only two kinds of Artemisia, and several lichens. The 25th of October we saw on our right many elevated graves or tumuli, overgrown with grass, and some wersts farther, on an eminence, several graves marked out by stones: on many stood an irregular red stone, with various characters on it, which probably signify no more than the words of the Koran, Lah-illah-illalah (i. e. besides the one God, there is no God,) and prove that those graves are not very old, but of Mahometan origin. The characters were of the same age as the erection of these stones, as might be seen by the lichens, which spread over the characters as well as on the rest of the stone. Between these tumuli there was another square brick building, as I have before described, but it was still more dilapidated; another similar one had stood near it, of which nothing remains but the foundation of the walls. The stones of the sepulchres, as well as the bricks, were all covered with lichens.

When we came to the little river Iaman-Tirmissu, which was frozen over, I crossed the ice, at a place where the right bank was about 60 feet high, to look for petrifactions, when suddenly something precipitated itself from above, and fell upon the ice, not far from me. In my first surprise I thought it was a man, but it was a Saiga (Antelope Saiga) which probably had been chased by dogs, and in the rapidity of its flight had not perceived the precipice ; it was dashed to pieces by the fall ; it was a female, brown above and white below, with a very short white tail. The Saiga lives in the Kirghis steppe, in herds, like all antelopes : in spring and autumn, when it is a dry season, and the burning sun has destroyed all the grass in the steppe, it often comes in herds over the river Ural, to the Russian territory, and commits great ravages, especially in the corn-fields. It is found in the whole Kirghis steppe, to the country about Bucharia, where, as well as another antelope, which lives in the mountains near Samarkand, it is often tamed by the Bucharians, and runs about in the court-yards of those who are rich.

Continuing our journey through the same description of country, we halted, on the 31st of October, at the little river Kurwandschur, about three wersts from an eminence, on which there is an ancient burying-ground, where, as the Kirghis believe, Kalmucks were buried ; they relate that a hundred years or more ago, they did not know whether Mahometans or Infidels were buried there ; it was therefore resolved to open some of the graves, where they found skeletons of men sitting on horseback, and many articles of silver, such as sabres, stirrups, &c. ; women were also found, whose necklaces, consisting of pearls and precious stones, were put into their mouths. The sepulchres consisted of heaps of stones, lower in the middle, like some I have mentioned before. It may be believed that the Kirghis really opened the graves, not to look for treasures, but to discover whether Mahometans of former ages were buried there ; for such places are sacred in their eyes, and the only spots where they now bury their dead ; wherever there is a Tartar sepulchre, Kirghis graves are seen all round it.

On the 2d of November, we made a long day's journey, and did not reach, till half-past eight in the evening, our intended resting place, lake *Karakul*, that is black lake, or *Chodsakul*, from a rich Kirghis, of the name of Chodsa, who is buried there. The Kurwandschur, which lay a little to our left, on our day's journey, falls into this lake. On the 3d, we halted upon the Karakul, which was distinguished by some marshes and a great quantity of reeds ; to judge by appearances, it must be very extensive in the spring. The Kirghis say that it takes a day to ride round it.

The next day, at some distance from the Kuraka, we came to several lakes, which we left on our right. These lakes are probably all connected in the spring, and form the great Karakul. After passing them we went some wersts over a flat

Steppe, and reached the sandy desert of *Uluburssuk*, i. e. the great Burssuk. Properly speaking, it cannot be called a desert, for the vegetation is more diversified than in the rest of the Steppe : we found there several shrubs and plants, an acacia, astragalus, and some other plants ; there was particularly a great quantity of reeds, with the roots of which the sand, in many places, is interwoven in all directions, and which prove that the whole tract has but lately arisen from Lake Aral.

The country itself consists of sand hills ; it is quicksand, and it is surprising that the plants can live in it ; it would, indeed, be impossible, did not nature strive to overcome, by instinct, every obstacle which she lays in her own way ; thus, for instance, the roots, which in other soils are but small, ran for five, ten, or more paces under the sand, partly to bring sufficient nourishment to these plants, in the dry and parched soil ; partly not to be left wholly bare by the sand, which is easily carried away by the wind.

After going thirty wersts we had crossed the sandy desert, which extends to lake Aral, and encamped at the east end of it, near a little lake surrounded with fountains, the superfluous water of which flows into it. About three wersts before we came to the place, we saw, in the desert, a large bare spot, consisting of white bitter salt, of a considerable depth. Such places are very common in the Steppe ; they are salt lakes dried up, most of which are filled with water in the spring. The journey through the deep sand had fatigued our horses so much that we were obliged to halt again the next day, which gave me an opportunity to examine the surrounding country. The lake was quite dried up, and its bright surface, which I had taken for ice the day before, was composed of that bitter salt. There was similar lakes in the neighbourhood, one of which, instead of the bitter salt, contains beautiful sea salt; this lake was also dried up, the surface of pure salt about two inches and a half thick : under this it was mixed with earth.

On the 8th of November, after travelling ten wersts, we reached an eminence, from which we could overlook the country before us to a great distance ; it consisted of many large and small, even, sandy bare spots, which had a dazzling white appearance from the efflorescence of the bitter salt upon the surface, so that at a distance, where the whiteness is not so dazzling, they look like water ; between these salt spots there were patches of sand, which were scantily covered with the usual plants of the Steppe ; but upon the salt there was not a trace of vegetation.

On the 10th of November we rested for a day near several

springs with sweet water, called *Saribulak,* which enabled me to examine the surrounding country. Three wersts to the north a high bank (above 200 feet high) extends from west to east ; before this bank, and connected with it, are many equally high and bare hills, to which the rain and the influence of the weather have given singular shapes ; they consist of marle, which in many places is so soft that it forms a sandy clay. In this clay there is an innumerable quantity of univalve and bivalve shells in pretty good preservation, also bones of glires, vertebræ and teeth of fish, and bones and skulls of the common horse, (and not of the wild horse, as the Ural Cossacks, to whom I showed these skulls, and who were able to judge, unanimously affirmed.) Among the univalves two kinds of murex were particularly well preserved ; of the bivalve Cardium two small species were in such an amazing quantity that they formed nearly the whole mass. There were also two kinds of turbinates, and many worm shells.

These hills, as I have said, have very picturesque forms, the whole together having the appearance of a ruined castle, with watch towers built before it. The leader of our caravan affirmed that, only sixty years ago, lake Aral extended to this place, though its nearest bank is now sixty wersts distant. It is therefore probable, that all the shells found here are still living in that lake. A well, which the Kirghis had dug early in the morning, contained good water, only it had again a strong smell and taste of hydrogen gas.

On the evening of the 14th we reached a sandy desert called Sapak-kum, in which we proceeded for six wersts with great difficulty ; the high and loose sand hills were very troublesome to our caravan ; in the evening we encamped on a bay of the Aral, the smaller creeks of which spread far around. None of these creeks were frozen, though the water in them was much shallower than in the bay which we left in the morning, which was covered with ice four inches thick. The sand of the Sapak-kum is mixed with innumerable shells of the same kind as those which lie on the banks of the Aral; it is not however to be understood that lake Aral overflows this tract ; on the contrary, it is well known that a few years ago it was entirely under water, and the traveller evidently sees that it is of the very latest formation : that this Steppe is not overflowed in the spring by the water of the Aral, is evident from its being the resort of numberless kinds of mice, which would not frequent a country that was inundated a part of the year, when they must naturally perish. The subterraneous dwellings of these mice are often very troublesome to the traveller, the ground being frequently so undermined that the horse is in danger of breaking his legs, from its giving way at every step.   The next day (November 15th) we had six wersts further to go through the sand of the Sapak-kum, which was bounded, on its eastern edge, by dried up salt ponds ; in one place there was fine sea-salt, and under it lay a firm compact bitter salt, which turned the edge of the hatchets with which the sea salt was hewn. Twenty one wersts further on we came to a great lake of fresh water, which is connected with the Sir Darja ; it is called the bay of the Sir.   It was hard frozen all over ; in fact, we had for the last week an extraordinary degree of cold for that country, from fifteen degrees to eighteen degrees of Reaumur.   An uncommonly large species of *mya* lay on its banks, and another bivalve shell in great abundance.   Going on, till we had travelled twenty-five wersts and a half, we rode round this bay and encamped on the south side of it.

Our caravan halted here two days, to make an excursion to the mouth of the Sir.   We set out early the next morning, accompanied by forty Cossacks, rode northwards, about the bay, the longest extent of which is, from N. E. to S. W. and proceeded along its bank for about 35 wersts, till we reached its junction with the Sir, and then 15 wersts on the right bank of that river, to the place where it falls into Lake Aral.   Along the Sir are many small lakes, formed by its overflowings, and some of them are still connected with it.   The banks of these lakes, and particularly those of the great bay, are almost every where covered with reeds to a considerable extent, which grow three times the height of a man, and even more ; on the mouth of the Sir, they are so abundant, and the banks of the Aral are so thickly covered with them, that we could not properly see the lake itself ; as far as the eye could reach, the western horizon was bounded with reeds, and we had no time to look out for an eminence.   These reedy plots are inhabited by many very poor Kirghis, who subsist by agriculture and fishing.   Having been plundered of every thing in the preceding spring by the people of Chiwa, they had at that time but very few cattle, which are fed on young reeds. Their huts, which are made of reeds, are chiefly in the midst of the plots, in order to be protected against wind and weather. The reed is every thing to these people ; it serves them for fuel, affords materials for buildings, food for the cattle, and by burning the stubble, they obtain an excellent manure, which makes the grass grow with great luxuriance.   The corn-fields, which are always near the water, consist of several small sunk spots, separated from each other by little dams.

The above bay of the Sir may be about 25 or 30 wersts long in a straight line ; its breadth differs considerably.   The bay as well as the Sir were hard frozen ; the fishermen say that it is about forty feet deep, and has a pretty strong current, so that it requires in each boat three men to row against the stream : but if we consider their wretched boats, which are constructed in a very singular and curious manner, we must wonder that they can go against the stream at all ; they are flat-bottomed, with perpendicular sides, are pretty large, and consist entirely of little pieces of wood, from two to three, at the utmost four feet in length, and from three to four inches thick, which are fastened together with wooden pegs, there is no iron in the whole boat, and as the pieces of wood of which it consists are irregular and crooked, it is no wonder that one man is always employed in baling out the water.   Yet such a boat is a great treasure to a Kirghis of this part, because the wood is fetched many hundred wersts from Turkestan.   It serves them not only in fishing, but in summer also, to convey the caravans over the river, from which they derive great profit ; most of the boats are so large, that from four to six camels, not loaded, can be carried over at once, and for every camel, they charge 17 ells of a coarse Bucharian cotton stuff ; they will not take money : the price is certainly high, but the labour is considerable.

In this desert country, there is no wood whatever ; nor, except the reeds upon the banks, any grass or other forage, for the cattle.   Here and there are a few stunted shrubs.   We passed the night at the north of the Sir, and continued our journey back at sun-rise, and joined our caravan soon after sun-set, having ridden nine hours without stopping.   I was very cold, and some snow fell.   On our arrival we learnt that the caravan of Bucharians, coming from Orenburg, would soon overtake us.

On the 18th of November, we left the bay of *Kamuschli.* One road lay over undulating argillaceous sand ; on the left there were many steep ledges, often rising like terraces one above the other, which were probably the former banks of lake Aral.   Three wersts before we reached our night's quarters, we ascended an eminence called Akürāk (white duck).   To the south-east of our camp we saw two hills, on which there were many decayed sepulchres of the Kirghis ; that on the right hand is called *Kutbai,* and that on the left *Sutbai,* from two distinguished Kirghis buried there.   The next day, soon after we set out, we passed between Kutbai and Sutbai, and left, on the S.W. another hill, upon which there was also a large sepulchre and many inconsiderable graves of the Kirghis.   I will give a short description of this one Kirghis monument, which will suit all the rest, which are very frequent in the S. W. desert, particularly beyond the Sir; it consists of a round building, with a vaulted cupola, with a small pillar on the top, in front a projecting entrance with a Gothic arch, and about it four pillars, united with the building, which are a little higher than the break where the cupola begins. They are built for the most part of bricks, sometimes also of rough stones. All these monuments are very new, and built by the Bucharians, whom the Kirghis pay for their trouble, either with sheep or corn; the Kirghis are used to perform their devotions at these places. The whole, however, is a miserable work, and I mention it only because people in Europe form notions of such things very different from the reality. The graves of the poorer Kirghis in the southern desert, where there are no stones, consist of a sloping roof of clay rather lower behind than in front.

On the 20th of November, we halted on the right bank of the Sir, uncertain how we should cross it; it was only partially frozen, yet horses and unloaded camels passed backwards and forwards. The weather became more mild, and there was no prospect that the ice would become firmer; we therefore hastened to get the open places next the bank, filled up with reeds, and on the following day, the artillery and loaded waggons were conveyed over the river without accident; the rest of the caravan followed on the 22d of November. Our passage was very fortunate; one camel, indeed, fell through the ice, but was saved as well as the burthen. In two hours our caravan was on the opposite side; we were followed by that of the Bucharians, which had overtaken us two days before, and had brought us news that the caravans of Chiwa, from Orenburg, had been entirely plundered by the Kirghis.

The breadth of the river in this place was nearly 800 feet; the banks were not every where steep, but in many places flat, and no where much above the level of the water; nay, in many places, at a distance from the river, the land was certainly below it. On both banks, for several wersts together, there is a boundless tract of reeds, which serves as a retreat for wild boars and tigers; the former are very numerous. - There is no appearance of woods or shrubs, such as one is used to see upon the banks of rivers; the Sir creeps slowly and sluggishly through the reedy marshes, to the great pool, the Lake Aral. Ravens, crows, and magpies, collected in great numbers in our camp; they were so starved in this desolate country, that these birds, which are otherwise so shy, ventured within four or five steps of persons who were eating, and en deavoured, by a desperate leap, to carry off a piece of meat; they followed us on our route, alighted upon the camels, and tried to steal the meat out of the bags.

On the left side of the Sir we went three wersts up the stream, as far as Karatubä, a sandy eminence and a burying place of the Kirghis; then leaving it a little on the left, we encamped near a small lake, having gone only about nine wersts through high reeds. Many deep graves and the traditions of the Kirghis indicate that the place was formerly inhabited; the old town of Jankend stood about one day's journey farther up the stream; on the right side of the Sir, were many sherds of broken vessels, and bricks, glazed with different colours, point out the spot.

On the following day we travelled through the same uniform Steppe, and on the 24th reached the Kuwan-Darja, a small river only twenty-five or thirty paces broad, and in some parts pretty deep in comparison with its breadth; the water is fine and clear; and the banks by no means so thickly grown with reeds as those of the Sir. On the 27th and 28th we ascended the Kuwan, and encamped in a large plain covered with reeds, which was full of herds of swine: our Cossacks killed eleven of these animals. On the 29th, when we halted in the above plain, we nearly came to blows with our Kirghis guides, who already pronouncing their watchword *alatsch*, hastened from all sides with their arms, but order was soon restored by the infantry, which marched to the spot, and by the interference of the elder and more reasonable Kirghis.

On the 30th of November we entirely left the Kuwan, and took the shortest course to the Jan-Darja. The way was through reeds and then over sandy hills, till having gone thirty wersts we encamped in an agreeable spot, but without water. The trees, which we had before met with in the Steppe, but only as shrubs, are called by the Kirghis and Bucharians, Saxaul, and attain there the height of twelve or fourteen feet, the wood is very solid and heavier than water, but cannot be worked in any manner, being extremely brittle; it has the peculiarity of burning nearly without smoke, for which reason it is highly prized by the Kirghis; the coals are remarkably heavy, and burn for a long time under the ashes. This tree is of the class of those which have the male and female flowers perfectly separate, the former consists of a bunch of stamina, without calix or corolla; the latter, on the contrary, is pretty large and consists of five petals. There are considerable woods of this Saxaul, which are very pleasant, and in summer, when this tree is in flower, those spots must be very romantic, compared with the other parts of the Steppe.

On the 1st of December we had a pleasant journey through woods of Saxaul, which was very agreeable to us who had for a long time seen nothing but sand. To our left we saw the ruins of an ancient town or fortress, which were very much decayed. In one of the buildings, which was the largest, about four fathoms high, there were still two windows, in the Gothic style, the whole was of unburnt bricks, four or five inches thick, mixed here and there with some that were burnt. As far as we could see, it had consisted of three walled inclosures, one within the other; here and there, in the line of the walls, were the ruins of the buildings. For a great distance around there were numerous fragments of broken pots, not glazed. These ruins, which were probably a fortress, are called by the Kirghis, *Kutschuck*, who affirm that they are of Tartar origin: but no reliance can be placed on their assertions; they ascribe every thing in the desert, of which they do not know the origin, to the Tartars, who lived there immediately before them.

After travelling thirty-four wersts we suddenly came out of the Saxaul wood, and saw the former bed of the Jan-Darja before us. We halted here the next day to provide ourselves with water for five days' journey through the sandy desert, which is called the Kisilkund. For this purpose we filled all our leather bottles with water, and the sacks with ice.

Nothing remained of the Jan-Darja but its ancient bed, in which there were here and there small pools of corrupt water, which had a smell of sulphurous hydrogen gas. It is said not to be very long since this river ceased to flow, and that it was nearly equal to the Sir-Darja. " Ah," said our caravan leader, a pious Mahometan, with tears in his eyes, " when I was here seven years ago, what a fine river was this ! God has reduced it every year, till it is now quite dried up."

On the 3d of December, well stocked with water and ice, we continued our journey ; we traversed the bed of the Jan-Darja almost perpendicularly, and then proceeded through an extensive and almost bare plain, the soil of which is a barren clay, which even after we had gone thirty-three wersts to our encampment for the night, stretched out as far as the eye could see. In this plain were many ruins of ancient towns and sepulchres, which are filled with quicksand ; if the Kirghis are questioned respecting the names and number of these ruins, they say, " who can name all the towns that formerly stood there." Probably this country was, formerly, as populous as Bucharia now is ; and was watered by the Jan-Darja, as Bucharia is by the Kuan and Wafkan.

On the 4th, in order to make our day's journey longer, we

set out at four in the morning : travelling in the dark was new
to us, and gave us much pleasure ; the setting moon and the
fire of our camp, which was visible at a great distance, had
a striking effect.   Having gone some wersts through the above
plain, we came into the actual Kisilkum, that is, red sand.
This desert has the same appearance as the former ; an ocean
of sand with little hills, which, in some places, formed small
chains ; the sand is not so deep ; that is, it is firmer.

The Bucharians say, that many attempts have been made,
and in different places, to dig wells, but always without success : others again say, that water might be found, but that it
is not done in order to be more secure against the robberies of
the Chivans, who cannot remain so long in places where there
is no water, to watch for the caravans.   We travelled that day
forty-two wersts by four o'clock in the afternoon, and the
next day forty-four wersts.

On the road we met several Kirghis coming from Bucharia ;
they brought us news that four thousand Chivans were wait
ing for us at Bukan, (the next well) with hostile intentions.
We, therefore, immediately sent a Tartar to inquire into the truth
of this report.   He joined us the next day, at the end of the
desert, informing us that he had not met with any signs of
an enemy.   The report of the Kirghis was, however, not
quite false, for a week afterwards the second half of the Bucharian caravans, coming from Orenburg, was plundered and
entirely destroyed ; the caravans from Orsk and Troizk, which
followed it, turned back.

On the 6th we set out at three in the morning, and after
thirty-five wersts the way turned to the right, towards the
well of Bukan, and at forty wersts we reached the end of the
Kisilkum ; we rode six wersts further and encamped there,
about fifteen wersts to the east of the well Bukan, in an undulating sandy desert, where two kinds of artemisia afforded
some fodder for our cattle.   The plain through which we passed is a clayey sand ; it is nearly surrounded by the Kisilkum
mountains, at least, on the north, west, and south.

On the 8th we halted at Juskuduk, or the hundred wells,
which is no exaggeration, there being in fact an amazing
number of wells near that place ; but most of them are decayed, and appear only as corrupt stinking pools ; one alone
is in perfectly good condition, and contains good water sufficient
to supply a whole caravan ; it is lined with brick work, is
about seven feet in diameter, and, to the surface of the water,
about nine feet deep ; the water is said to be between three
and four feet deep.

On the 12th of December we set out, at five in the morning ; the sky was cloudy, but the moon afforded us light. Our road led us through the plain in which we had encamped, so that the low mountains were on our right and left, at first nearer, then more distant, and, at last, the plain extended so far that only higher mountains were visible, particularly on the right, at a great distance. At the end of thirty-seven wersts a new country suddenly appeared to us ; we looked down from an eminence into an extensive plain, which was surrounded by low hills ; in the middle of which we were astonished to see a little wood of mulberry tree ; and there we took up our lodging for the night. In the middle of this wood is a small eminence, at the foot of which, under the shelter of the far-spreading roots of a mulberry trees, there is a little fine clear reservoir of water, on the sandy bottom of which a number of little springs bubble up, and make the water appear as if it boiled. The water is lukewarm, and seems, therefore, to be cold in summer and warm in winter ; it smells like gunpowder, the taste indicates sulphurous hydrogen gas. The stone next the spring is compact feldspar, the rest of the place is compact limestone, and to this stone the spring probably owes its origin. The earth, close to the spring, is black and slimy, and has the same qualities as the water by which it has probably been deposited. In the neighbourhood are similar springs, with the same qualities, the waters of which join with the first, and so form the origin of a brook, which is said to flow into the Amu-Darja. The grove with the spring is considered as sacred by the Mahometans, and no one ventures to do the least injury to the trees ; under the hill, they say, a saint of the name of Kara-ata, (black father) is buried, whence the place is called by that name. For this reason many ceremonies are performed there. All travellers who arrive there, wash and say their prayers : the sick make pilgrimages to this place, and offer sacrifice ; a part of every thing that the patient eats, is laid down near the spring ; old clothes and rags are then laid aside and offered ; the various rags being tied to the trees (this is in general the way in which the Mahometans offer to their saints, and in Bucharia itself the trees, in the sacred places, are hung with rags ; and at the rocks lie little heaps of fruit and corn.) If many of the patients recover, as they say, it is probably owing to the water ; but the neighbouring burying-ground, where there are pretty many graves, seems to prove also that numbers die.

At Karaata we met with six Bucharian soldiers, who keep guard at this place, which is the most northern frontier of Bucharia, but they are chiefly placed there to accompany mer-

chants, who, arrive there with their goods, to the city of
Bucharia, that there may be no fraud in the payment of the
customs.

On the 13th, we travelled 38½ wersts to our encampment,
near which many springs issued from the grey limestone ; they
are called Agetma, and contain the same kind of water as the
spring of Karaata. Not far from this place are many hundred
small clay hills, with various low shrubs growing on them ;
they appear to be the remains of the country, which was
formerly higher, but washed away by inundations ; among
them is one larger hill, which is an artificial mound, and still
serves to overlook the country, for there is the second Bucharian
frontier post, which likewise consists of six men. It is said
that a fort formerly stood there : many bricks lying around
seem to prove this.

On our arrival at Agetma, we met fourteen camels, laden
with fruit and bread, and fodder for our horses, which had
been sent to the embassy, by the Khan of Bucharia ; as well as
30 Bucharian soldiers to receive the embassy.

On the 14th of December we halted at Agetma. The plain
is there very extensive, like the plain near Karaata ; it seems to
have been a lake, for the hills which surround it have every appearance of having been formerly washed by the water : the
next steep bank that I visited was about 400 feet high ; it
consists in general, as well as the surrounding country, of
lime-stone. From this high bank I could see, at a distance
to the east, a lofty mountain, called Nura-tau, which we had
seen for two or three days before ; its summit, which is said
to be about 100 wersts distant, rose above the horizon ; and we
also saw many lower mountains. The little river Wafkand,
which waters Bucharia, rises on the Nura-tau.

Leaving Agetma on the 15th, we crossed the plain and afterwards several hills, beyond which we came to one of the most
dreary deserts that we had met with on our whole journey : there
was hardly a trace of vegetation ; however, the sand was not
so deep and the road not so bad, as on former occasions : we
found in some places a firm clay bottom under the sand ; and
about our encampment, where ruins of a fortress or entrench-
ment were still to be seen, there were evident marks of former cultivation, which agrees with the tradition, that this
part was formerly inhabited, and that the quicksand annually
encroaches on that side, upon the grounds of the Bucharians.
The next day we set out at six o'clock, and soon came to a
well, which is lined with wood and two fathoms deep. Near
it is a row of five dwellings for travellers or guards, all built of
clay.

Many persons, induced by curiosity, came from the neighbouring villages to meet us ; and after going some wersts we at length saw the promised land, in the horizon beyond the desert. At a short distance before the country seats, which are called villages, 200 Bucharian horsemen came to meet us, drew up in two lines, and let the embassy go between them. We then passed through some estates destroyed by quicksand, and came to the camp of the Kusbegi (prime minister), who had come from Bucharia to receive the embassy. His camp consisted of many party-coloured tents, and his retinue of 500 men. From there we went about three wersts between estates which had suffered more or less.

The quicksand, as we have already said, annually encroaches on the cultivated land. We are told that five years before, a piece of ground, planted with vines and melons, was entirely covered with the sand, and when the wind carried away the sand two years afterwards, the fruits were said to be perfectly well preserved, and in the finest condition.

On the following day, the 17th of December, we travelled only eighteen wersts, partly because the crowds of people hindered us, and partly because the roads were too bad to allow us to go faster. We proceeded without interruption, between country seats, till, at the end of sixteen wersts, we reached Wafkand, a small town, which may be about three wersts in circumference ; it is surrounded with a wall of clay, of which almost all the buildings consists, and may be known by a tower built of bricks, which is about sixteen or twenty fathoms high, broader at the top than at the base, and smallest in the middle. We left this town on our right hand, passing close under its walls : at the southern side of it we crossed a large canal, or arm of the Wafkand, and encamped two wersts beyond it, among country seats.

A Bucharian country seat (called in the Tartar Aul, and in the Persian Sachra) consists of a square, surrounded by a high clay wall, in which the dwellings are situated ; but as they are lower than the wall which encloses them, they cannot be seen on the outside. The lands lie round this square, and can be laid under water at pleasure by means of numerous canals.

On the 18th of December our road still lay between country seats, till close to the city of Bucharia. After riding about fourteen wersts we arrived at the river Wafkan, which further below spreads into a lake, and is called Karakul, or the black lake. At the place where we crossed it, over a stone bridge, it is about thirty paces broad, and not deep.

After we had gone twenty-five wersts the embassy encamped three wersts from Bucharia, and I went through the city gate as a merchant, and took up my lodging in the Tartar caravansary.

And so ended our tedious journey, which had taken two months and nine days.

GEOLOGICAL RETROSPECT.

WHEN I look back upon the extensive and desolate tract which we have traversed, I must consider the greatest part of the desert to be a production of modern times ; the barren soil, without any mould, the naked sterile banks of the rivers, the many salt ponds in the Steppe, the former banks of lake Aral, which are still very distinguishable, and which I have observed above an hundred wersts distant from the present borders of the lake, indicate this ; the ruins of the city of Jankend, which, according to old maps, stood close to the junction of the Sir with lake Aral, are now four days' journey distant from it.   To judge by the rapidity with which lake Aral is said still to diminish from year to year, it certainly cannot be much above a thousand years since this lake was united with the Caspian Sea, for they are separated by a flat desert Steppe, like that which we have passed through ; and it is well known that the Caspian Sea diminishes as well as lake Aral : tracts of country at the junction of the Ural with the Caspian Sea, which formerly could not be passed at all, or only for a short time in the year, are now dried up, &c. : I am even inclined to go farther, and to affirm, that at a time not further back than the commencement of our era, the Caspian Sea was connected with the gulf of Finland, with the Baltic.   It is evident that the Caspian Sea, at the time of Pliny, extended very far to the north, because that naturalist considered that connexion still to exist.   The geologist who has seen the whole, will not find this conjecture so improbable as it may at first appear ; for instance, what kind of rocks are between Orenburg, Astrachan, and Moscow, far and near, to the right and left ?—chiefly lime-stone of the latest formation, with petrifactions of all kinds, and sand-stone, both with horizontal strata ;—beyond Moscow, to the north, is the same, as far as the Walda mountain, which extends from the west, and formerly, perhaps, was a cape, and however, is nothing but a very insignificant and low Flötz lime-stone mountain.   What is between the Walda mountain and Petersburgh ? nothing but a sandy clay marsh land, which is impassable, except by means of logs of wood, laid down to form a road, and the rocks of which consist of foliated lime-stone, of late formation, likewise with horizontal strata, extending below St.

Petersburg, westwards to Esthonia and Livonia; and northwards, joining immediately to the granite of Finland; these countries, Esthonia and Livonia, likewise consist only of marshes, where the traveller, unacquainted with the road, is even now in danger of sinking into the bogs. Lastly, what is Prussia? a sandy desert, which human industry has cultivated. We have already seen that lake Aral, and the Caspian Sea, retire into narrower limits; but that the Baltic, namely, the Gulf of Finland, has retired, is proved, partly by the nature of the country round St. Petersburgh, and especially by the circumstance, that workmen digging in the ground, near the little town of Preussuisch-Holland, found a stone wharf, in which the iron rings, used for mooring vessels, were still fixed. This fact is known to the inhabitants of the town, and mentioned in its chronicles; it is true, I did not read it myself, for want of time, though it was offered me to read, when I passed through the town.*

All the mountains and ridges of the Kirghis Steppe, through which we travelled, are only low, inconsiderable, naked eminences, which I have not always ventured to call mountains, but hills; they resemble each other, and their external and internal appearance, is every where the same. The Mugosarki mountains, are, undoubtedly, the Trap formation of the northern Ural mountains, which become flatter at Werg-Uralsk; they stretch almost direct from north to south, and reach their visible end, at the shores of Lake Aral.

The Ildertau---Kapkata---Pütpüldück---Susses Kara chains, are all connected together, and probably belong to the lofty Nuratau, which is to the north-east; the formation of which, I however cannot state. These are the five chains of mountains which form the skeleton of the Steppe through which we passed; they are all low, rocky, naked, and bare, and all belong to the transition and Flötz-trap formation. The flat, or undulating Steppe, lying between them, is partly of the Flötz formation, and partly alluvious land.

It is an important circumstance, that the Sir-Darja has changed its course; about thirteen days' journey from lake Aral, it divides into two branches; the northern, which is now the main stream, is justly considered as the continuation of the river; the lower is the Kurvan-Darja, which, at present, has but little water, but is said, never to have been considerable, as is evident from its narrow bed: from this branch, about

---

* Mr. Counsellor Von Pansner, assures us, that a precisely similar circumstance happened in a place in Livonia; and it is a well-known fact, that the gulf has become much shallower about Cronstadt, since the first survey made by Peter the Great.

a day's journey below the first division, issues the third arm
of the Sir, the Jan-Darja, which is said formerly to have been
the main stream, as its bed, which still remains, plainly proves;
but it has been dried up for some years. This circumstance
perfectly corresponds with the fact, that the Amu-Darja (Oxus,)
which undoubtedly once flowed into the Caspian, and the ancient
bed of which is said to be very discernible, has changed its
course, and now flows into lake Aral. The fertility of the
Kirghis desert decreases, the further you go from the Russian
frontier, to Bucharia itself, and, in general, is at the lowest,
between lake Aral and Bucharia; there a single Carex, is almost the only fodder for horses, and in some places an Artemisia; and for camels, the *Ferula persica.*

Extracts of Letters from Mr. Jakovlew, Secretary to the Embassy.

December 16th.

After having gone 17 wersts, we arrived at the village of
Djigabachi. We received notice yesterday that our interview with the Bucharian vizier would take place to-day. At
the distance of five wersts from the village, two hundred horsemen came to meet us; they were mounted on the finest horses that can be conceived. The inhabitants of the neighbouring
village had come in great numbers to see the Russians. Some
were on horseback, some on camels, some on foot, and some
on donkeys. The crowd was so great that they obstructed
our passage, and we were obliged to halt at every step. But
the jessaouls, or police-officers, armed with large sticks, without
mercy began to strike men, camels, horses, and asses; their
blows fell like hail on the Bucharians, who were very eager to
see us; on all sides, turbans flew in the air, shewing the
shaved heads of all these musselmen. It was in the midst of
this throng, accompanied by drums beating, and with the aid
of the constant exertions of the jessaouls, that we reached the
place where the vizier expected us.

Some persons appeared to conduct us; the ambassador,
captains Tsiolkovski and Meyendorf, lieutenants Volkhovski
and Timofeiev, doctor Pander, the two interpreters, and myself,
escorted by fifty Cossacks, advanced towards the place where
the vizier was to receive us. We perceived tents striped with
different colours; the largest was the audience chamber.
Necessity obliged us to alight, for it was not possible to advance a step on horseback. Bucharian foot-soldiers, under
arms, were drawn up on each side, they made a singular appearance, being men of different ages, old and young, dressed

in robes of different colours ; some had caps, others turbans, or only drawers ; some had boots, others none at all, all held their matchlocks in both hands. They have but two words of command, " rise" and " sit down ;" they never pronounce the word fire, because the matchlocks cannot fire, and because the Bucharians have in fact no infantry. Before our arrival, the Khan had caused all the matchlocks to be collected ; they got together 200 : and the Khan desired all persons to announce themselves, who desired to hold a matchlock, when the Russian embassy should come to visit him. Thus was formed this terrible Bucharian infantry, through which our procession passed to wait upon the vizier.

He received us sitting, and had on his right hand four counsellors in the same posture. The ambassador placed himself opposite to him ; we were desired to do the same, and though with our dress nothing could be more disagreeable than to sit on the ground, we were obliged to comply ; we took our places opposite the four counsellors. Then began the ceremonies, congratulations, and compliments : the servants of the vizier now appeared, and set before each of us a dish, in which there were pistachios, dried raisins, manna, and a sugar-loaf.

The vizier is a man of about forty-five years of age, he speaks with ease, and a degree of emphasis : he has a particular manner of turning his eyes, and shrugging his shoulders. In about half an hour the four counsellors retired ; we did the same ; the ambassador remained alone with the vizier.

I had never seen such a throng, and so mixed a crowd : Bucharians, Chivans, Afghans, Kirghis, Hindoos, our Cossacks, the soldiers, Baschkirs, altogether formed a very striking sight. The weather was very fine, as clear and warm as in the month of July.

In about an hour the ambassador came out of the tent : we re-mounted our horses, and proceeded on our journey : it was four wersts from the tent of the vizier to the place where our Kibitki (tents) were already set up : we were told we were near the village, " there is the village," said a Bucharian, " but it is a fort."---" That is the same, it is a village." In fact it was one. When I entered it in the afternoon, I perceived that it consisted of four crenated walls built of brick, dried in the sun, with only two openings, a gate and a postern, and not a single window in the walls. Such is the outside of a Bucharian village. There is not the least appearance to indicate that there are any living beings behind those rude walls. If you enter by the postern, you perceive in the opposite wall, the gate, to which you go through a street, so narrow that a loaded camel can hardly pass through it.   On the two sides of this street you see only walls, as high as those on the outside, crenated in the same manner, and doors to the right and left : there are entrances to the houses, and you see in them the horses, camels, and asses, of the Bucharians.   In every court there is a cistern and a well.   The rooms have no windows, so that the doors are always obliged to be open.   They have no notion of ovens, but they have in each room a hole, in which they put hot coals ; over this hole they place a table covered with a thick carpet.   The Bucharian sits down by the table, puts his feet under the carpet, and says he is warm. This carpet is the only ornament in the rooms.

Wapkand, 17th December.

The next day we proceeded on our journey.   The crowd of people was the same, and the merciless jessaouls were equally active with their long canes.   After we had passed through the town of Wapkand, we encamped at a short distance from its walls.

The Bucharians continued to-day, as they had done before, to crowd round us till late in the night ; nothing could keep them at a distance, even the jessaouls at length gave it up. It was quite an amusement for us to see an innumerable multitude, which accompanied us from place to place, and when we stopped to encamp, ranged themselves round us, and remained sitting till night, without uttering a word.   Our visit will be an era in the history of Bucharia.   It is affirmed that the inhabitants of Wapkand hired a horse for two or three ducats, to see the Russians ; and they got beat by the jessaouls into the bargain.   In the afternoon a Bucharian, who was a pupil of some Indian jugglers, appeared.   He had a monkey whose tricks filled the whole multitude with admiration.   We too went out of our tents.   The monkey was really extraordinary.   None of us, not even Mr. Pander, the naturalist, had ever seen one like it.   The Bucharian suddenly threw four knives into the air, the monkey caught one in each of his paws, held them fast, and walked, putting the points on the ground.   He danced, saluted the company, and played as many tricks as a Russian bear.

On the following day, the 18th, we went five wersts beyond Wapkand, to the banks of the Sir-Icherchan, which we passed over a bridge of boats, bearing the name of Mikhter-Kassim, who built it : we went twenty-five wersts to Basartche : the jessaoul bachi, chief of the Khan's guard, came at the head of twenty horsemen to receive us, five miles before we reached the village.

Basartche, which is two wersts distant from Bucharia, belongs to the vizier; this village likewise resembles a fort; the interior is divided into courts and gardens. Our baggage remained there during our stay at Bucharia.

For four days together our soldiers, our cossacks, and ourselves, were in full uniform. In this interval the drums beat the general march, which gave infinite pleasure to the Bucharians, and especially to the jessaouls. They were continually begging the officers to order the drums to beat: we were almost tempted to think that it was to have an opportunity to exercise their canes, for at the first stroke of the drum the people rushed in a body towards the soldiers; the jessaouls, in their turn, fell upon the people, and their canes were in constant motion.

The road from Kagatan to Basartche, being continually intersected by canals, it cost much trouble to get the artillery over the wretched bridges which serve to cross them.

n.

ENTRY OF THE RUSSIAN EMBASSY INTO BUCHARIA.

20th December.

THE negotiations relative to the entry of the embassy into the capital are finished. To day the Khan has sent a letter to the ambassador, in which he accepts the proposals made by the latter.

As soon as the dispatch was received, the Russian embassy left Basartche, in the following order; thirty Ural Cossacks, with an officer; the Mollah Bourkhanbei Pansad-Bachi, Asad-Khan Da-Bachi, and twelve jessaouls; fourteen persons carrying presents; the Ambassador, at his right hand the Secretary to the Legation, holding in his hand the Emperor's letter; the Officers of the Staff of the Guard; Doctor Pander, and the Counsellor Chapochnikow; the Interpreters; the Gentlemen of the Suite; a hundred and fifty foot soldiers, commanded by M. Tsilkovski, captain of the guard; lastly, a hundred and fifty Cossacks of the Ural and of Orenburg, with their jessaouls.

I need not say that the crowd was prodigious; in the town it was still worse; the throng of spectators, of all ranks and ages, and both sexes, filled the streets in such a manner that we were obliged to stand still at every step. At last we reached the palace. The procession ranged itself outside of the square; we alighted near the great gate, and entered the palace. After we had crossed three courts full of Bucharians seated, and holding in their hands matchlocks and falconets, the persons bearing the presents, and thirty infantry, without muskets, remained in the last court; we entered into the audience chamber, the ambassador having first given to the Bourkhan-Bei a list of the presents, then taking the emperor's letter from the hands of the secretary, he advanced.

The apartment was very large, a handsome Persian carpet covered the floor, the Khan was seated on a raised platform; he was dressed in a stuff resembling a shawl, had a rich dagger at his girdle, and a black aigrette in his turban, the vizier was standing at his right, his two sons at his left hand; on each side the officers of the Khan, dressed in silk, were ranged along the walls. The ambassador saluted him : " welcome," said the Khan, " approach." The ambassador remained standing at a considerable distance from the prince, and delivered the following speech in the Persian language.

" The Emperor of Russia, my most gracious master expresses to your highness his sentiments of affection and esteem, and desiring to consolidate commerce, the source of the riches of the subjects of the two states, he has sent me as his ambassador to your highness. The contents of the Emperor's letter, will make your highness acquainted with the intentions of my sovereign towards a monarch, celebrated for his many and brilliant qualities, and the founder of the prosperity of his people. I shall esteem myself perfectly happy, if while I fulfil the orders of my sovereign, I can obtain the favour of your highness.

" His Majesty likewise sends to your highness, as a testimony of his friendship, some presents, which are the produce of the countries subject to his dominion."

The ambassador after he had finished speaking, kissed the letter of the Emperor, raised it above his head, delivered it to the vizier, and sat down again.

The Khan took the letter, and opened it; and after having read it aloud, said that he was happy to see that the wishes of the Emperor of Russia agreed with his own, and that for the advantage of the two states, it was proper that caravans should go frequently from Bucharia to Russia, and from Russia to Bucharia.

Then the ambassador presented us to the Khan. The prince put several questions to us respecting our journey, and the country of the ambassador, and enquired of him whether he had long inhabited Russia, &c.

At last he desired to see the thirty soldiers, who were in the court-yard; and they were introduced to him.

The ambassador bowed a second time and retired.

When we reached the house prepared for the embassy, the escort, and the baggage returned to Basartche.

THE CITY OF BUCHARIA,

Is rather longer than it is broad, and its longest diameter may be from three to four wersts; it is surrounded by a clay wall, from three to four fathoms high, with a breast-work, and embrasures.

The streets are very narrow; for a European particularly so: in the narrowest two people can hardly pass, and in the broader ones, a loaded camel touches the houses on both sides.

The dwelling houses are neatly built of clay, some rich persons have them partly of brick, of one or two stories, but not higher; the entrance to the street is through a very small door, so that when you walk through the street you see only clay walls on each side. The houses, without exception, have flat roofs; they have no windows whatever, and the rooms are lighted only by doors, which look into the court-yard.

The palace of the Khan, (called Aerk) lies on a clay hill 60 feet high, which is an artificial work; it takes almost half an hour to walk round it; the lower half is, at least externally, of bricks, the upper half clay: it is steep, only on one side there is a path leading obliquely to the residence of the Khan, which is built of bricks of different colours, glazed, with inscriptions. The other part of this mound is built up with clay huts standing close together, in which live the Khan's servants, women, &c. At the entrance of the palace are two high towers, built in the usual style of this country, at the top almost as broad, and even broader than below, and smallest at about two-thirds of their height. There are many such towers in the city; they are in general a distinction of a city, and considered as ornaments; they are used to proclaim from the summit the hour of prayer: the highest of them is particularly used to throw down from the top of it persons who are detected in illicit connexions of every kind, or who are found intoxicated; whereas other criminals, sentenced to death, after having had their throats cut, are hung up in the square before the Khan's palace, which is called Registan, where they remain three days. This Registan is the only open place in the whole city of Bucharia; even this is very small, and filled up with shops and butcher's shambles; in the midst of these shops stands the gallows, which is seldom vacant, for not only Bucharian criminals are hung on it, but the heads of their enemies are exposed there in the oriental fashion.

The town is intersected by many canals, which are called Rud; whereas those out of the city, which water the fields, are called Arik. These canals supply with water many ponds lined with hewn stones; this water, which serves the inhabitants for drinking and other uses, is drained off, twice every month, and fresh water let in.

It is said that Bucharia contains 360 mosques, and 285 schools, in which there are three hundred teachers. The mosques and schools very much resemble each other; they are large and lofty brick buildings, having within, after the manner of convents, a large court (all the houses have such a court,) in front is a large and handsome gateway leading from the street. These mosques and schools have their estates; each of them has a steward, appointed by the Khan, and the teachers are paid out of the revenue. The estate consists chiefly of lands, or of caravansaries, of which there are many in the city; a caravansary consists of many stone booths, built close to each other, so as to form a square, which serves both to load and unload the camels, and to let them remain there, if necessary, for some days. Almost a third part of the city is composed of these caravansaries, market places, and booths; a market is not, as with us, a large open place, but a narrow street, with shops on both sides; there is a continual crowd, bustle, and disputing; in every shop you hear crying, " ah if you are a Musselman you must let me have the article for this price," the seller exclaims, " if you are a Musselman how can you ask such a thing?" Many Bucharians live all their lives in such a shop, without having any other dwelling.

Most of these shops remain open the whole week, others, on the contrary, only twice a week, namely, the jewel market and the slave market. In the jewel market they sell rough, polished, and also set stones. They chiefly consist of turquoise, rubies, violet fluorspar, polished cornelian, and calcedony; the lapis lazuli is seldom polished here, but almost always used as a colour for painting rooms, &c. The turquoise is brought rough from Persia and polished here. The polished cornelian and calcedony are said to be brought from Arabia, through Persia; they are polished in the form of seals and as beads; they are of excellent quality, and very cheap; the mode of selling them is by weighing them in a scale against pure silver; if any person should think this dear, as it at first seems to be, he will be convinced of his error if he makes a trial, by putting both into a scale. The lapis lazuli and the violet fluorspar come from Badakschan, by way of Kokand;

the latter is enormously dear : in its rough state, as it comes from Badakschan, it is called Isilan, and when it is polished here it is called finussa ; the pood (thirty-six pounds) of lapis-lazuli costs, in its rough state, from twenty to forty Dutch ducats, according as more or less of the mass of the rock is attached to it ; but the pure washed powder, as it is used for painting rooms, costs from two hundred to three hundred ducats and upwards. The ruby is called, in Persian, Sailan, and in the Tartar language, Jachet. There is, likewise, here a very dear precious stone, called lahl, which I take to be spinel ;* it is rose colour, and fully agrees in its internal properties, hardness, and lustre, with the sapphire, which is also sometimes sold here. The prices of these stones are low, it is true, when compared with those of Europe, but the stones of a larger size are seldom perfect.

Besides these, many other polished stones, partly of the above-mentioned kind, are brought here for sale, which are found not far distant, in a place called Kamuschkand : whenever a high wind has blown, and disturbed the sand, these stones are found, and many other things, as amulets, in various shapes, gold, silver, and copper coins, &c. which belong to very different periods ; partly to the Mahometan period after Mahomet, with Arabic and Persian inscriptions ; partly to the time of the Greeks, with Greek inscriptions, and partly to a more ancient period, with inscriptions in a language with which I am unacquainted. The stones which are without an inscription, are either round or oval, convex above or angular ; but they are all cut concave below, as if they had served to receive hair and the like ; or they are adorned with inscriptions in characters unknown to me, with idols, dragons, quadrupeds, birds, &c. and have probably served as amulets ; all these figures however are not raised, but engraved.

The slave market is also twice a week ; persons of all nations and both sexes are sold there, except genuine Mahometans ; but especially the Persians, who as followers of Ali, are considered as the greatest heretics ; and by far the majority of the slaves here, that is, many many thousands, are Persians, who are most of them carried off and brought here for sale by the Truchmenians, who, make inscursions into the Persian provinces. The labour of agriculture, in Bucharia, is performed exclusively by Persian slaves.

When a merchant arrives, he puts up at some caravansary,

---

* This conjecture of the author is certainly well founded, as appears evident from the description of the Laal, or Lahl, given in the Persian treatise on precious stones, by Mahommed Ben Mansur.

where he hires one or two shops, according as he can afford it ; here he has his goods, carries on his business, sleeps, dresses his wretched meals, and sometimes lives twenty or thirty years, in such a miserable hole, according to circumstances ; that is, he either takes a journey every year and fetches a fresh stock of goods, or he remains stationary several years, and his countrymen or partners make the journey for him. Thus in the Indian caravansary, there are many Indians who have lived there above thirty years. The individuals of these several nations generally keep as much as possible together. Several caravansarys have a second story, each booth or shop having a small room over it, which serves as a kitchen or sitting room. Such a one I myself occupy, the close damp shops being intolerable to those who are not accustomed to them.

The caravans come from all parts of Asia.

1. From various frontier places of Russia, as Troizk, Orsk, Orenburg, and from Astrachan, by way of Chiva ; they bring English and Russian goods, such as cloth, calicos, silk and cotton handkerchiefs, &c. brass, copper, iron, hardware, &c. The traders are, in general, Bucharians, Russian Tartars, and Armenians, from Astrachan, who take back Bucharian productions, especially silk and cotton, both raw and wrought, Cachmere and Persian shawls, indigo, Chinese wares, &c.

2. From Persia, Medsched, and Herat, there come annually only a few, (about 500) camels to Bucharia, bringing chiefly Persian silk and cotton manufactures, shawls, stuffs, &c. They take in return, partly Russian goods, especially silks and cottons, and a great quantity of raw cotton. The traders are Bucharians and Persians.

3. From Kokand, Kashkar, and Tashkend. The principal articles imported from Kashkar, are Chinese wares and tea. The caravans on their return take almost all kinds of articles of trade ; especially all kinds of furs, gold thread and lace, real coral beads, cloth, printed calicos, &c. From Kokan and Taschkand the chief articles of importation are white calicos, which are printed here, besides these, silks, raw silk and cotton. The caravans on their return to Kokand and Taschkand, take the calicos which are printed here, and a few silks, besides taking for Kaschkan the things mentioned above. The merchants here are Kokaners and Bucharians, (Russian) Tartars, and Armenians. The caravan goes from here to Kokand, through Orutuba (the last Bucharian city) and Chosand, (first Kokandian town) in from fifteen to eighteen days, and from thence in twenty to twenty-two days to Kaschkar.

4. From Cashmere and Caboul, Cachmere shawls, printed Indian calicos, which are much better than those of this

place, Indian silks, embroidered with gold, of a particular quality, and indigo, (here called nil) are brought. From Cachmere 40,000 shawls are said to be annually exported, but of these only 3000 come to Bucharia. The returning mer-chants, who mostly consist of Afghans and Indians, (few Bucharians) take from here particularly, Dutch Ducats, which come from Russia.

The Afghans are all Mahometans, but do not shave their heads ; they are fiery, hot, quarrelsome, and have a constant and unbiassed love for their country. The Indians consider the cow with religious veneration, and worship it ; they cannot think or conceive any crime more dreadful than to kill a cow; and often when they see a piece of cow's flesh they begin to weep ; they use the urine for all manner of purposes, mixing it in all their food ; and as they are about three hundred, and have only one sacred cow, they are obliged to be very sparing, so that frequently only a few drops of urine are mixed with a pailful of water. They paint their countenances, chiefly the forehead over the nose, and the ears, in various figures and colours ; this is probably intended as a charm, the colours being mixed up with the urine of the sacred cow. These Indians, notwithstanding their silly religion, are however a virtuous, good-natured, polite people, and by no means inferior in honesty to us orthodox christians, and to the Mahometans, who far exceed us in religious zeal, and are ready to sacrifice their lives for the truth. The Afghans, it is true, think themselves far superior to them on account of their true religion, but they esteem them on account of their probity and good-nature. The Indians, besides praying before the cow, likewise pay their adoration to the rising sun.

THE SOVEREIGNS OF BUCHARIA.

To come to the reigning Khan I will begin some generations back ; but I cannot exactly state the era or length of the reigns ; I here give the genealogy, as I had it from a mollah, in Bucharia.

Schaibani Chan left a son and heir, Abaidula Chan, who was succeeded by his son, Isskander Chan, who left two sons, Abdula Chan and Dschani Muhamed Chan ; the first succeeded him in the government, and is said to have erected the first regular caravansary, about a hundred years ago ; he left five sons, Din Muhamed, Baki Muhamed, Uali Muhamed, Imam-kuli, and Nadir Machmed Chan : Din Muhamed inherited the throne; he was succeeded by his son Abdul Asis Chan, who also left two sons, Subhankuli and Abaidula Chan; Subhankuli Chan inherited the throne, and was followed by his son Abulfais Chan. This Abulfais was murdered by the Usbeck Rachim Bi; and his son Abdul Mumin Chan, an infant between eight and twelve years of age, was placed on the throne; he enjoyed his dignity however only two or three months; for having once cut a water melon in two with a sabre, in the presence of his mother, and she asking him the reason, he said, I do not cut a melon, I cut off the head of Rachim Bi. The latter hearing this, did not feel himself at his ease, and therefore murdered him also. He had now liberty to do as he pleased, he married the sister of the murdered Abdul Mumin Chan, and so intruded himself into the royal family. He and the Usbeck Daniel Atalik, governed the kingdom, but, for appearance sake, placed on the throne an individual of the royal family of weak intellects, named Abdul Gasi Chan, and then did as they pleased. Rachim Bi died two years and a half after he had murdered Abdul Mumin: Daniel Atalik died some time after him, leaving a brave son, Schamerad Uälnahmi, who married the widow of Rachim Bi, (sister of Abdul Mumin Chan,) and thus likewise introduced himself into the royal family. The weak Abdul at length dying, Schamerad Uälnahmi ascended the throne; by the widow of Rachim Bi he had a son, the present sovereign, Emir Haider Khan, who ascended the throne, twenty-two years ago, on his father's death; he is a man of above forty years of age, indulging to excess in wine and sexual pleasures of all kinds. He is besides a devotee and bigoted Musselman, in the highest degree, and quite unfit for the business of government; his sole occupation is with religious exercises; he has daily a thousand scholars whom he instructs in the Koran. He has four sons, the eldest is Saidmir Abulhassan Chan; the second Bahadir Chan; and the third Umer Chan; the fourth is not known to me. The eldest, who is called also Tourou Khan, i. e. Crown Prince, has a wife of the family of Dschudat; the founder of this family lived 130 years ago, under the reign of Abdulah Khan. He was reputed a great saint, for which reason the Khan once sent to him, and asked him what was the best thing in this world, to which he replied, eating, drinking, and, in general, all sensual enjoyments, on which the Khan left him with indignation and contempt. Some time after this the Khan was affected with indigestion, and to such a degree that all the physians failed in curing it, whereupon Dschudat, the saint, came to him and asked him whether he was now of his opinion: the Khan answered in the affirmative and begged him to relieve him ; Dschudat immediately began to pass both his hands over the Khan's body, repeating certain prayers ; the patient feeling himself relieved, made the saint a present of an estate, and begged him to proceed in his operation ; continuing to give more estates, in proportion as he felt the benefit of it ; by which Dschudat became so rich, that a great part of the city which bears his name, now belongs to his family. It is reported that the wife of the Crown Prince brought to her husband sixteen poods of ducats as a portion : an enormous sum for this country ; perhaps, however, it is an Oriental hyperbole.

The royal family, the reigning Khan and his sons exeepted, live together in country-seats near Wafkand, and in case the Khan should die without leaving a son, one of the family is chosen, and placed upon the throne, as was the case with Abulgasi-Khan.

The royal treasury is supplied partly by taxes, (consisting of corn) which the cities of Bucharia are obliged to deliver every year ; partly from the toll which the caravans pay on their arrival, and especially from the many estates belonging to the Khan. The inhabitants of Bucharia, as being the capital, pay no taxes, except the Jews.

THE INHABITANTS OF BUCHARIA,

Consist of Tadschiks, Usbecks, and Jews. The Tadschiks, are the original inhabitants ; the Usbecks afterwards made themselves masters of the country, and constitute in some measure the class of the nobility ; they fill all employments, civil and military, the Tadschiks being only merchants. The word *Usbeck* literally translated means *own master*, from *Us* own or self, and *Beck*, master, lord, or nobleman. They are said to have received the name from the prophet Mahomet, because the Usbecks while they yet inhabited the south-west part of Russia, once sent troops to his assistance, when he was hard pressed by his enemies ;---it is said that they came too late, but for their good will the prophet made them all Usbecks. Be this as it may, the statement that a hundred Usbecks first adopted the Mahometan religion, and that this is the origin of the name, meaning a hundred lords, is false, for a hundred is *Jus*, and therefore, it ought to be Jusbeck.

In the city, the Usbecks are said to be to the Tadschiks as one to three, in the surrounding village, estates, &c. the proportion is said to be exactly contrary.

The language of the Usbecks is a corruption of the Tartar,

which is called Türki, so that the Tartars can understand it, but it is much mixed with Persian words. The Tadschiks speak Persian, and this is the most common language, for when an Usbeck speaks with a Tadschik, they speak Persian.

These Mahometans are perhaps one of the most common, and basest nations on the face of the earth; commerce and religion have extinguished in them every spark of honour and honesty; when they have said their prayers five times a day, as prescribed by the Koran, every thing is lawful. For a few pence, a Bucharian is capable of betraying his father and his brother; nothing is sacred in his eyes but gold. In the midst of the most violent quarrels, if the hour of prayer comes, they suddenly leave off, say their prayers, and after this they begin with the same heat as when they left off.

The Jews, the third nation residing in Bucharia, are allowed to live in but one quarter of the city, because they are much despised by the Mahometans; they all speak Persian, and but few among them understand Türki. The Tadschiks and Usbecks pay no tribute to the Khan, but the Jews, as soon as they have attained the sixteenth year, must pay for permission to reside, from one to four Tanga a month, according to their riches. The number of these Jews registered as paying the tax, is 1200. They have the perfect jewish countenance, although they are in other respects handsome and well made. They have no historical books, and only know by tradition, that about 1000 years ago, they came hither from Persia; they obtain their religious books from Constantinople, and when opportunity offers, from Russia. Their chief means of subsistence is dyeing silk and cotton, which is almost exclusively in their hands: the richer Jews likewise carry on wholesale trade. Farther to the east, for example in Kokand, Tashkand, Badakschand, Kaschkar, there are no Jews; only in Samarkand some few families, who have removed from Bucharia. They are much oppressed here, and have difficulty in maintaining their religion. That a Mahometan may not salute them from mistaking them for people of his own religion, they are compelled to wear, by way of distinction, particular black caps, and to bind their garments with a cord, instead of a long and narrow silk sash as is usual; nay they are not even permitted to ride on horseback; they shave their heads like the Mahometans, but leave a long lock on each side. All these three nations have very fair complexions; they are almost as fair as those of the northern Europeans, especially in their youth; the countenances of older persons are in general, but not always, more or less sun-burnt.

Here too the Mahomedan Religion, permitting Polygamy,

and considering woman as a slave, that is, bought and sold, has produced a great corruption of morals ; I could relate incredible facts, were I not withheld by shame.   Certainly there is no country, not even Constantinople, where unhallowed propensities are so common as here ; nor is any secret made of it : the Khan himself, besides his Harem, has in his palace forty or fifty other degraded beings, though he severely punishes such crimes in others.   If the Persians have beautiful amatory poetry, the Bucharian has no notion of refined sentiments, and though all the works of the Persian poets are known here, the Bucharian thinks only of sensual pleasures.   Not content with these excesses, all the horrors and abominations of Sodom and Gomorrah are here practised, and even the frequency and severity of the punishment inflicted, are unavailing to deter them from the commission of these enormities.

THE COUNTRY AROUND BUCHARIA,

Like the whole of the Kirghis Steppe, is in itself very unfruitful and salt.   The soil of the cultivated part is a firm clay, where the bitter white salt, which I have before mentioned, effloresces and covers the earth with a white crust, which very strongly reflects the rays of the sun.   This cultivated clayey soil is entirely surrounded by deserts of pure quicksand, which is annually driven further from the north, covering more and more the fine cultivated lands ; and no human power is able to check it.   At a considerable distance from the cultivated parts, the ruins of ancient plantations are seen in the desert ; in many places the sand has been blown away again, and we there see the same clayey soil as in the cultivated parts, which shews that this soil extends horizontally under the desert. Though this saline clay, upon which hardly any wild plants can thrive, is in the highest degree unfruitful, yet Bucharia is a large and beautiful garden, where all the fruits of France and Spain come to perfection.   This fertility is entirely owing to the astonishing heat, and the excellent mode of irrigation ; the fields and gardens are almost the whole year under water, which is effected by means of many large and small canals. The water is conducted by means of principal canals from the higher country, far to the north, near the mountain Nuratua, from the rivers Wafkand and Kuan, which rise there, so that the canals lie higher than the land.   The fields are all separated from each other by low dams, like those which I have described on the Sir Darja, only on a much larger scale, so that each single field may at pleasure be laid under water, which can be again drained off into canals that lie lower ; which serves both to give the necessary moisture, and also to dissolve the salt which continually rises to the surface. Such fields and gardens, with the dwellings belonging to them, are called villages (Aul, Sachra ;) and all the country round Bucharia is cultivated in this manner, particularly on the road by which we came ; and then southwards to the town of Karakul and the lake of the same name, which is an extension of the river Wapkand, and was formerly united to the Amu Darja, (Oxus) and particularly from here to Samarcand, and from thence to Oratuba, the most easterly town in Bucharia, which is a distance of eleven days' journey ; where you travel, almost without interruption, through such villages and some towns. One part of these villages is principally inhabited by Arabs, who were sent here in A. D. 699, by the Caliph Valid, with his General Kotahiba, to induce this nation to adopt the Mahometan religion ; they still speak Arabic among themselves.

If the rivers Wafkan and Kuan bring down sufficient water the whole year, Bucharia has a productive season ; but as they are very inconsiderable rivers, there is often a scarcity of water in summer, which causes a failure of the crops. Whether the water will be abundant or scarce, depends on the quantity of snow which has fallen on the Nuratua mountains ; hence there is an ancient custom, that he who brings to Bucharia the first news that snow is fallen on the Nuratua, receives from the Khan a present of a silk chalat. A chalat is a kind of loose robe, which, with a pair of drawers, constitutes the whole dress of the Bucharians.

The fruits, &c. cultivated in Bucharia, consist, as far as I have learnt, of a particular kind of millet, a large species of peas, a short, thick turnip, apples, quinces, pears, plums, cherries, apricots, peaches, almonds, figs, dates, pomegranates, pistachio nuts, walnuts, and many kinds of grapes, among which there is one species which has no seed in it, and many sorts of melon. Many kinds of seeds for seasoning and for medicine, also many ornamental plants, are cultivated here ; but I cannot specify them, having been here only a short time, and in winter. The above juicy fruits may, for the most part, be had fresh and at moderate prices, till February and March ; the markets are supplied with melons the whole year.

The principal, or rather the only domestic animals of the Bucharians are the camel, the horse, the ass, the mule, the cow ; the Kirghis and Arabian sheep are not so common. There are three kinds of camel : first, the Bactrian camel, with two bunches and long hair ; second, the dromedary, with one bunch, and the same long hair with the preceding; thirdly, another camel with one bunch, here called Luk, which is larger than the two others, and has short, curly, dark brown wool. The dromedaries are more esteemed than the camels, being in general stronger. The Bucharian horse is well known to be one of the finest races in the world; it is tall, slender, and extremely spirited; it rears, and springs, and dances continually in the most graceful manner, if I may so express myself; it has a very peculiar pace, something between an amble and a gallop; its hair is very short, smooth, and glossy.

Bucharia seems to be the native country of the ass, for the number of these animals is inconceivably great. They are of almost all colours, black, white, brown, grey, &c. which seems to prove that they have been much longer domesticated here than in other countries. Mules are also common and much dearer than asses.

Very few sheep are kept in Bucharia, because fodder is very dear; but the Kirghis drive in flocks from the Steppe as many as are wanted. There are also but few cows, because the inhabitants are not fond of milk diet, and drink their tea without milk.

Storks build here in the towers of the city; they go away in autumn, and come again at the end of February. Here too they are held sacred, so far at least that nobody will injure them. There are two kinds of swallows, one is the *Hirundo rustica,* and the other a species unknown to me. The first arrives in the beginning of March. The Afghans assure me that the storks and swallows come here by way of Kabul, and take from eight to twelve days in their flight hither; they likewise told me that they winter in Hindostan.

The Tarantula is seldom or never found close to the city of Bucharia; but is frequent further to the east, about Samarcand, and Oratūbä, particularly on small hills. Their venom is mortal: the only remedy known here, is to read aloud without interruption, certain verses or sacred books before the patient, making him breathe violently; if he becomes fainting and exhausted by this exertion, they leave off a few minutes, and then begin again. They affirm that in this manner the patient breathes out the poison. If this does not avail, death is said to be inevitable.

Scorpions are frequent about Bucharia, and the Kirghis Steppe, south of the Jan and Sir-Darja; their sting is seldom or never mortal; a person who had been stung coming to me, I made him rub the place with oil, and the next day the pain was nearly gone. They have particular exorcisms, which they pronounce on going to bed, if they are afraid of scorpions;

the effect of which is said to be, that the scorpions in the chinks, or holes of the chamber, are unable to move.

In general there are very few insects in Bucharia; the reason is evident, partly because the cultivated country is under water, the greater part of the year, and partly because the uncultivated country is almost without vegetation.

PHYSICIANS, MEDICINES, AND DISEASES.

PHYSICIANS are very numerous; almost every learned man is more or less a physician, because he has read medical books. Their practice is evidently the pure Brunonian system : they divide all diseases into hot and cold, as also the medicines and food. If a sick person comes to them, they first determine whether the disease is hot or cold; if it is hot they prescribe cold medicines, if cold, hot; in the same manner they order the diet, on which they lay great stress. In their books all kinds of medicines and food are divided into hot and cold, and in this they go so far that, for instance, the pulp of grapes is cold, the seed warm ; bread alone is neutral. Of course they distinguish various degrees of heat and cold, i. e. very hot, very cold, almost neutral, &c. The physician, however, does not prescribe the medicine, but when a patient consults him, and he has determined for instance, that the disease is hot, he writes down on a slip of paper, a list of cold medicines ; the patient pays for this paper a Tanga, goes with it to the druggists, and buys any one of the medicines on the list; if this does him no good, he tries another, and so on. Their surgical knowledge is almost confined to bleeding. They have a great opinion of feeling the pulse, and though not one of them has any notion of it, they affirm that a good physician can discover, by the pulse, every disease, either local or general ; many persons came daily to me, and would have me discover by their pulse if they had a wound, for example, in the foot or elsewhere. The same opinion prevails among the Kirghis, and probably among all nations out of Europe.

Beggars are so numerous and so insolent, that one has to quarrel with them all the day ; their various cries, consisting of wishes, prayers of the Koran, and benedictions, are at first amusing, but one soon gets tired of it. One of them often stands in a cross-way, and howls out his prayers in every direction, so that I at first thought murder had been committed ; but the Mahometan is affected by it, and purchases a blessing, for a Pul (the smallest brass coin) : the beggar takes him by the hand, and shakes him with such violence, that the dislocation of the shoulder might be apprehended ; he then takes him by the breast, and shakes him with the same violence, and then repeating some prayers, tells him all that heaven shall bestow upon him. I saw a Bucharian moved even to tears : all this is done in the public streets, when hundreds crowd round, for a Pul from him who receives the blessing ; unless other spectators, moved by the beggar's speech, give him something more.

In your room, in the caravansary, you have not a moment's peace for these beggars ; and many, if they receive a refusal before they enter, force their way in, and demand alms, asking " if you have no god ?" To this question I sometimes answered " no ;" and as this had never happened to them before, they left me with disgust. In the streets they often hold one fast, saying, " give me money !"

The Khan is a zealous Mahometan, favours them, and gives them abundant alms, instead of giving them work, as they do in other countries ; thrice a year there is a grand distribution of alms, all the beggars meet, and the Khan having the bags of money by his side, gives each of them three or four Tanga. This of course increases their number. It is said that there are beggars who are very rich, and yet beg in the streets for a Pul.

There is an establishment called Fatahabad, for poor blind people, where they are maintained at the expense of the Khan ; it is said to be very full ; notwithstanding which, there are innumerable blind beggars in the streets.

Another kind of beggary, which is rather more genteel, is the following : a poor author copies prayers in verse, or moral sentences out of some books, and learns them by heart, or he compiles them himself out of different books ; he then comes in the evening, with many copies, to a caravansary, or into the street, and bawls them out, where he finds amateurs, who, for a few Puls, buy some copies of these fine verses. Such beggars as are unable to walk, sit down in the streets and beg alms ; they try every art to obtain money ; they often pretend to have convulsions and fits, and sometimes as if they were in the agonies of death ; indeed, they very often die of hunger and misery.

Wine and Brandy are consumed in great quantities in Bucharia, the manufacturers of these are the Jews, and one Armenian, who has the chief sale. These people are permitted to make as much as they please for themselves, and also to get intoxicated in their own houses ; but they dare not leave their houses intoxicated, nor sell any wine, otherwise the

Khan does with them as he pleases. Thus, for instance, five years ago the principal physician here, a Jew, who became rather intoxicated on the marriage of his son, fell a victim to this law; for the Khan had him hanged. Yet, notwithstanding this law, the Khan does as he pleases: not long ago, he had the houses of all the Jews searched to see whether they had a stock of wine; and if any was found, the owners were beaten in the most dreadful manner in their houses; but the richest of them was confined in a tower on bread and water, and daily beaten, and was told that he should recover his freedom, if he would give the Khan his stone house, which was valued at 800 Bucharian ducats. But as the Jews in Bucharia, as well as in other countries, consider riches as the greatest good, he had not yet consented when we were there. Yet the Khan drinks to excess, and after him the superior Usbecks, whose houses the police officers do not venture to search, and to whom the Khan does not think it expedient to shew his authority in this respect. These noblemen all receive their wine from the above-mentioned Armenian, who is, indeed, protected by them, but yet is in a critical situation. When the Khan had the houses of the Jews searched, he ordered the Armenian to quit the kingdom in three days. The order was indeed afterwards revoked, but the Armenian was still afraid that as soon as the embassy departed, his life would be in danger, and therefore resolved to leave Bucharia at the same time, till the Kusbegi himself at length assured him that he had nothing to fear, and begged him to remain. I may observe, that the Armenians, though they are Greek Christians, are more esteemed, or rather less despised, by the Mahometans, than all the other nations, and this was the reason why the Armenian was asked to stop; the Khan thinking it beneath him to buy his wine of the Jews.

Other poor devils, who may happen on any occasion to indulge in wine, must often pay dear for it, for the police officers, who are always on the watch, almost daily detect some in the streets, coming from the Armenian or the Jews, with a bottle concealed under their clothes. They are dragged to the police office, severely beaten, and sometimes even punished with death, if they have been before detected.

The wine which is made here is far more intoxicating than any European wine; it is made of the ripest grapes; in general the grapes here have a degree of sweetness, such as I never tasted in any other country.

Brandy is also made of grapes, but only of the ripest, or of raisins, and then rectified. It is made of the strength of rum, is colourless, and in my opinion has a disagreeable smell and taste. It gives me the head-ache, and a determination of blood to the head.

The particulars which I have communicated in the preceding pages, were written down clandestinely at Bucharia, during the night, with the intention (as I thought, to travel farther,) of sending my notes to the University of Berlin by the returning embassy. Partly for this reason, and partly because in those countries it is always dangerous to ask a question, or to take a walk, except on commercial business, I must request the indulgence of my readers. After three months' stay at Bucharia, I was ready to set out with another caravan to Kaschkar, when I learned, by a singular chance, that a Bucharian, with whom I had become acquainted at Orenburg, had denounced me as a Russian spy, and that the Khan had hired persons to attack and murder me on my road, as soon as I should leave Bucharia. As this news was certain, I was obliged, in order to save my life, to return with the embassy.

SOME ACCOUNT OF BUCHARIA, FROM MR. JAKOVLEW'S LETTERS.

THE kingdom of Bucharia is bounded on the North by a part of the Kirghis Steppe, Kokand, and Aderkand: on the East by Naimatchin and Badakhchan; on the South by Anderab, Balk, and Ankoa; on the West by a part of the Kirghis Steppe and Chiva. The length of this country, from the town of Ouratup to Sareksa, is estimated at thirty days' journey with camels, in a straight line; its breadth from Bucharia to Old Balk, twenty days' journey.

The population of Bucharia is estimated at three millions of souls: but as no census is taken, it cannot be stated exactly. The capital is Samarcand, but the Sovereign resides at Bucharia. Chakh-roud is a suburb of this city. The kingdom is divided into seven Tumans, or Governments, each of which has a civil governor.

Samarcand, the capital, is situated on the river Kouanderia, which has its source in lake Pandjikand or Taran. This river traverses Bucharia, and falls into lake Karakul; innumerable canals are filled from it, which water the towns and villages; it is navigable, but navigation is not in use in this country: they content themselves with floating down the Kouan-deria, the wood which is cut on the banks of the Pandjikand. Samarcand is a pretty well-built city; it has several stone-houses, but the greater number are of earth. It has 250 mosques, and forty schools, the professors in which are priests, and read lectures on the Mahometan law, and the Arabic language. This city contains 150,000 inhabitants. There are three caravansaries for the merchants who arrive from the interior, and from the other towns of Bucharia. Samarcand is governed by the Delvet-by, who is at the head of the administration, both civil and military. The garrison consists of 3000 horse.

The religion of Bucharia is Islamism. There are mosques in all the towns, and even in the ports and villages. The Mollahs celebrate divine service, and instruct the children in the Koran. The rich people send their children to the schools at Samarcand or Bucharia, where they finish their education. Bucharia is at present governed by the Khan Mir Haïdar. In 1821, he was about forty-five years of age: his authority is unlimited and hereditary. His eldest son, Tourou Khan, the heir to the crown, is twenty-three years old. He was Commander-in-chief of the Army, but has ceased to be so, and lives with his father. The principal public functionaries about the Khan's person are six in number, the Kissoubeghi, or Grand Vizier, makes known and executes the will of the Khan; he enjoys all his confidence: Nias Bekbei, is the chief of the army, for whom the Khan has great esteem. Raasbek-da-Akha is likewise a general, he is related to the Khan: Mouknistan-Divaa Sarkhar fills an office like that of Grand Marshal of the household, and is the most important person about the palace. Moursa Saadik is the first secretary of state: Moursa-Dja'far-Mouchraf is the grand treasurer, he pays the salaries of the civil and military officers. The assembly of these officers, at which twenty other honorary officers are invited to attend, forms the council of the Khan, of which the Kissoubeghi is president, and which directs the most important affairs, such as declarations of war, treaties of peace, and other similar subjects.

The Kazy-Kalam is at the head of the ecclesiastical order, and besides this is judge in civil affairs; his decisions are executed like those of the Khan; he can pass sentence of death, but whoever is not satisfied with his sentence, can appeal to the Khan through the Kissoubeghi. After having examined the case, he reverses the decree of the Kazy-Kalam, if he finds it unjust, and according to the importance of the affair, either deposes him, or contents himself with only reprimanding him. The former very rarely occurs. Every day after sun-set, the Kazy-Kalam informs the Khan of all the causes he has decided during the day. The Grand Mufti is the second person in the order of the priests; he is at the same time the adjunct of the Kazy-Kalam to hear complaints and petitions. He quotes the decisions of the Koran, and shews who is right or wrong, but the Kazy-Kalam decides. The Kazy Ourdas form the third class of the priesthood; there are two in Bucharia and Samarcand, and one in each of the other great towns. They have under them the inferior muftis, and they are in the same relation to them as the Kazy-Kalam to the mufti. To guard the person of the Khan and the Palace, there is a kind of troops under the command of the second Oudaïtchi-Bachi, he is always about the Khan, and accompanies him in all his journeys through his kingdom.

The envoys who come from adjacent countries, are maintained at the expense of the Bucharian government; they enjoy full liberty in the city. The military force of the kingdom is estimated at 300,000 men, consisting of a well-organized cavalry, besides artillery and some infantry. The Kissoubeghi is the generalissimo of the armies; but, except at Bucharia, he does not personally concern himself about them. He has under him several generals, who, in time of war, have full powers to act, but on the other hand, they are responsible. In case of ill success, they not unfrequently lose their head. The Khan sometimes commands his army in person. When he is absent from Bucharia, the Kissoubeghi directs the administration, but sends him daily a report of what occurs.

After the ecclesiastics rank the merchants. Every Bucharian carries on commerce, more or less, according to his abilities. Civil and military officers, and even the persons about the Khan's person, are merchants; they have clerks and agents, and by their means export goods beyond the frontiers. The villagers are labourers and gardeners, gather the harvest, dig canals, &c. The inhabitants of towns are more inclined to follow mechanical arts and professions. They weave and dye calicos, and spin cotton and silk; this is particularly the occupation of the women. The latter, agreeably to the Mussulman law, do not appear in public, being slaves to their husbands; they are entirely devoted to domestic labour, and the education of their children. Their husbands, though pretty active out of doors, indulge in idleness at home. Having, in their wives and concubines, faithful and obedient servants to their will, they remain sitting without doing any thing, and singing hymns from the Koran : these consider themselves as pious men : others pass their time in amusing themselves. Their games are chess, cockal, &c. they frequently play for large sums. Many of them are very fond of spirituous liquors, which the Jews sell to them in great quantities. However, as the Koran forbids the use of fermented liquors and games of chance, and as government severely punishes these infractions of the law, they do not indulge in such excesses except privately. The Turcomans, Usbecks, and Jews pay a personal tax. The tenants of the crown lands give a third of the produce to government, and keep two-thirds for themselves. The lands are taken from the idle, and from those who are unable to cultivate their fields. The Turcomans live between Serakhs, Marv, and Djardja, on the Amou Deria ; the number of tents of these nomades, is estimated at 90,000, which gives a population of 900,000. They furnish 50,000 warriors to Bucharia. It is now about twenty years since that people began to accustom themselves to a settled abode. Several of them already have houses, and apply themselves to agriculture and the tending of cattle. At present they are not much acquainted with the mechanical arts. Their flocks are very considerable, they have excellent horses, and they pay as a tax, one sheep out of forty.

The Jews are not numerous, except at Bucharia and Samarcand, in these two cities they occupy 8000 houses ; the population is supposed to amount to 40,000. They live separate from the Bucharians, though in the full enjoyment of their liberties. Every man pays a tax of one tanga a month. The produce belongs personally to the Khan ; he employs it for the maintenance of his court. The Jews perform their worship in their synagogues, without any restrictions ; they carry on commerce, follow different trades, manufacture silk stuffs, and are distinguished as goldsmiths, tinkers, and smiths ; they are however despised. Some of them are very rich, but do not enjoy more rights or more respect than the others ; it is only on extraordinary occasions that they are admitted to the Khan. They are not permitted to ride on horseback in the city, nor are they allowed to wear either shawls or silk garments. The Jews alone have the permission to make wine and brandy ; they drink these liquors themselves, and sell them in secret to the Bucharians, by which they make large profits.

The climate of Bucharia, generally cold, is temperate in the northern parts. Spring commences very early, in the beginning of March every thing is in flower. The heat of summer is the more violent as it seldom rains, which obliges the inhabitants to water their fields by canals from the Kouan Deria and the other rivers. In autumn the rains are pretty frequent. The winter is not very severe, it lasts only three mouths ; but little snow falls, and the thermometer is seldom more than ten degrees below zero.

The soil is generally clayey and sandy; there are many gardens; nature amply repays the labour of the cultivator. Every thing that can satisfy his appetite, and even his fancy, grows without difficulty. The Sorgho constitutes the principal food of the inhabitants, from the Khan to the poorest of his subjects. This grain produces such abundant crops that large quantities are exported. Grapes and other fruits are equally common. They are dried partly for home consumption, and partly to be sent to Russia. They cultivate much cotton, which forms the principal article of the commerce of this country. They spin or weave it, or send it raw to Russia. The greater part of the goods sent to Russia are calicos. The country does not produce much silk, for this reason, they procure it from Persia. There are no considerable manufactories in Bucharia. Individuals manufacture at home, according to their means. A proprietor sometimes employs twenty labourers, but never more. They manufacture all kinds of cotton, the most of which are dyed of mixed colours, an operation which is partly performed by other artizans. They also manufacture silk and cotton stuffs, for all kinds of clothing.

They breed great numbers of cattle in this country. The Arab, or broad-tailed sheep, are very common. The lambs of this race being in great request in China and Turkey, great numbers are sent to those countries; many also go to Russia. The best lambs are those which are called premature. Horned cattle are not numerous, but only sufficient for the people. The race of horses, called Bucharian horses, is also pretty common : the Truchmenian horses are the most esteemed, they are called *argamaks,* and are often sent as presents to the court of Russia. Between Bucharia and Samarcaud there is a species of horse called Karabair, but greatly inferior to the Argamaks.

Wood is very scarce; there are no forests except on the Pandjikand. No mines of iron, copper, gold, or silver, have been discovered; all these metals come from Russia, either raw or wrought. Bucharia has coins of gold, silver, and copper. The gold coin is the achraf, a fourth part heavier than the Dutch ducat; it is coined at Bucharia, and is called by the name of the sovereign. The tanga, the silver coin, is the twentieth part of a ducat. The pouli-siah is the copper coin ; fifty make a tanga. The Bucharians trade with all the adjacent countries ; government demands of the Russians the fifth part of the value of their merchandize, according to valuation ; but if they are brought by a Mahometan subject of Russia, only one ducat on forty; as but very few of our christian merchants go to Bucharia, the produce of this tax is not considerable. They receive from China a pretty large quantity of tea, silver in bars, silk stuffs, rhubarb, and porcelaine. They send to that country beaver and other skins, coral, velvet, furs, great numbers of Arabian lambs, cloth, plates of gold and silver. The commerce with the Chinese is carried on in the towns of Kachgar, Akssa, Jarkand, Ili, and Khotan, which are adjacent to Bucharia, the entrance to the Chinese empire being prohibited to foreigners on this side also. The inhabitants of these places profess Mahometanism, and frequent all the cities of Bucharia. The duties of custom are, on each side, one ducat on forty of the value, paid either in kind or in money. The Bucharians receive from Hindostan, Afghanistan and Cashmere, indigo, many shawls, muslins of different sorts, chintzes, veils, Indian stuff for clothing, and sugar in powder; they give in exchange cochineal, gold or silver plates, coral, gold thread, cotton, long robes, cloth, velvet, Argamak horses, and Dutch ducats and crowns. They send their goods to all these countries, and visit every part of them without hindrance; however, they pay a duty in each, which increases the price of their goods. The Indians and Afghans, on their side, are allowed to come to Bucharia without any obstacle. They pay one ducat in forty.

They procure from Persia, silks, shawls of Kerman wool, which serve as girdles for the soldiers, beautiful Persian carpets, silks embroidered in gold, and plain silks; girdles wrought in gold, are brought from Ispahan, for the great and rich people, also turquoises, sugar in powder and loaves, pepper, ginger, and all kinds of spices. They send in return cotton, cloth, cochineal, gold thread, copper, and velvets. The inhabitants of these two states go backwards and forwards without any obstacle. The former pay one ducat in twenty, the latter only one in forty.

The produce and manufactures of Kokan are the same as those of Persia. The Kokaners require no import duty from the Bucharians; the latter, on the contrary, levy a tax of one ducat in forty, on the goods of their neighbours. The commerce with Chiva is not considerable, the produce of the two countries being nearly similar. The Bucharians receive from Chiva, silks, dried fruits, melons and apples, for which they send in return spun cotton, colours, &c. The import duties are reciprocally one ducat in forty.

The Kirghis–Kaïssak lead their numerous flocks into Bucharia, and on the frontiers of Russia; they sell and exchange great numbers of sheep and cows, as well as articles of their own manufactures, such as coarse and light felt, camlet, camels' hair, raw hides, and furs of wild animals :—they take from

Bucharia long robes, woollen cloths, sargho, &c. The Kirghis pay the same duties as other Mahometans. The duties are levied in the frontier towns as well as in Bucharia and Samarcand, by officers who are under the Kissoubeghi. The receipt amounts to 47,000 Bucharian ducats, and, according to the accounts of the inhabitants, the Khan spends it entirely in the relief of the poor.

The Khan rises every day before the sun; after having finished his ablutions, he prays for an hour in the mosque of the court, in the presence of the principal officers of state and the ecclesiastical dignitaries; upon which he sends the public functionaries to fulfil the duties of their office, and then with his courtiers and mollahs goes to the Khanaka, which is a great hall, where he takes his seat and sends for persons of different classes, particularly literati and young men of the first distinction. After this conference he reads in the Koran for two hours, and then goes to the audience chamber, where the Kissoubeghi, the Kazi, Ourda, the Oudaïtche bachi, the moukchajan, the chigaoul, and other officers are waiting for him. First they pay their respects to the Khan; when this ceremony is over, all those who have a right squat down, those who do not enjoy this privilege retire when they have saluted the Khan. Each public officer then makes a report on the affairs of his department and obtains decisions. Those which cannot be decided in this council are referred by the Khan to the Kissoubeghi. Individuals who have requests to present are also admitted and receive a speedy answer. This business lasts two or three hours. The Khan then returns to the mosque; when he leaves it he retires to his private apartments, to which the Kissoubeghi attends him; after some time he goes to the dining room, where five or six of his relations sit down to table with him. After the repast he reads the Koran for half an hour and says his prayers; then he retires to his cabinet, where it is said he attends only to his private affairs. At five o'clock in the afternoon he repeats a short prayer, which is succeeded by the time for recreation; he converses with his favourites, drinks tea, and eats dainties; and, after sun-set, the Kazy Kalam reports to him the cases decided during the day. When the Khan has heard them he sups, sometimes in the audience chamber with his favourites, and sometimes in the interior apartments with his women. After supper he retires to the chamber of her with whom he intends to pass the night, or he returns to his apartment and takes one of his concubines. During the night he rises to make his ablutions, after which he says his prayers, and retires again.

The Khan seldom goes out of his palace; when he shews

himself to the people in the city, it is always in great state, accompanied by two oudaitchi-bachi, and his guard, and preceded by mikharam-jessaouls, or officers on horseback, who in a loud voice announce the approach of the sovereign. This prince is dressed in the same manner as the Bucharians who come to Russia, except that his attire is more costly. He wears a robe made of shawl or silk, enriched with gold and precious stones ; he proceeds at a slow pace, on a beautiful Turcoman horse, magnificently caparisoned. Whoever is on the road, either on foot or on horseback, must, as soon as he hears the voice of the mikharam-jessaouls, stop, dismount, and wait with his arms folded, till the Khan passes, when he is to exclaim : " Assalâm alikom !" (God bless you !) A Salam Agassi who immediately precedes the sovereign, replies with a loud voice. " Ou alikom salâm !" (God be with you.) In summer, the Khan goes sometimes to his gardens near the capital, where he passes his time with his women and his favourites.

He has four wives, and a great number of concubines. The wife to whom he is most attached, is Khanakma, the daughter of Seït Bii, Governor of Issar ; the one who holds the second rank in his affections, is the daughter of Moumin Khan, who was sent as Ambassador to Saint Petersburgh, in 1820.

Mir Haïder Khan is of the race of Genghis Khan, for the sovereign cannot be taken out of any other family. He was twenty-five years old when he ascended the throne, and by his equity, his rigorous observance of the laws, and his goodness, has made himself universally beloved by his subjects ; he lives in a regular manner, strictly adheres to the principles he has adopted, and maintains peace with his neighbours. If any one disturbs the public tranquillity he has him punished with the cruelty which characterizes the Asiatics. His subjects love him, and his neighbours esteem and fear him. Though the Khan of Chiva is also a sovereign prince, and has troops, still he is subject to the influence of the sovereign of Bucharia, who has more than once humbled his pride, and obliged him to fulfil his obligations. A striking instance occurred on occasion of the plundering of the caravans. The Bucharian merchants suffered no less than the Russians, by the conduct of the Kirghis, who encouraged by the people of Chiva pillaged them ; but they always obtained full and prompt satisfaction, through the interference of their respective governments. The Kirghis, themselves, a ferocious and untameable people, and who recognize no law of nations, fear the Bucharians ; I mean, however, to speak only of those who live a wandering life on the frontiers of Bucharia. On the south-west of this country are the cities of Marv and Serakhs, belonging to Persia. The continual disputes of the Bucharians with this kingdom, led to a war, in which the former made themselves masters of those two cities ; this conquest was facilitated by the assistance of the Turcomans, who lead a roving life on the banks of the Amou Deria ; it took place under the reign of Mir Manzoum, the father of the present sovereign. The Khan has a garrison there ; a great number of the inhabitants have been removed to towns in the interior of Bucharia.

Mir Manzoum Khan had three brothers ; Oumour Kchou Bii who was commander-in-chief, and two others who lived in retirement., Mir Manzoum had also three sons : Mir Haïdar, the present Khan, who, during the lifetime of his father, was governor of Kartch ; the two others were governors of Marv and Samarcand. Outkar, the father of the present Vizier, a sensible and active man, devoted to his prince, was Kissoubeghi, before the death of Mir Manzoum. This prince being dangerously ill, and all hopes of his recovery being lost, Outkar, who desired that the throne should fall to Mir Haïdar, the eldest son, as the lawful heir, sent an express to Kartch, desiring him to come with an army to Bucharia, as soon as possible. Meantime the Khan died. To avoid an insurrection, Outkar concealed the death of the monarch, even from his nearest relations. According to law, the public functionaries must come every morning, to pay their respects to the Khan. Outkar dismissed them three days in the name of the prince. People began to conceive suspicions, for this had never happened before : on the evening of the third day, Outkar summoned the most considerable persons in the state, to assemble the next morning in the audience chamber. When they were assembled, and each had taken his place, Outkar coming from the interior apartments of the palace, entered the hall, and placing himself before the throne, declared aloud that the Khan's will was, that before they learnt the subject of their convocation, they should lay aside their sabres and daggers. When this order had been executed, Outkar told them that the Khan ordered them to go home, and return again the next day to hear an extraordinary communication. They were then convinced that the Khan was no more ; but being disarmed and surrounded by soldiers, they dared not to undertake any thing, and separated. A report was immediately spread in the town, that the Khan was dead, and that the Vizier intended to usurp the throne, and that he ought to be prevented ; but nobody ventured to undertake any thing. The Khan's brother, Oumour, considering himself as the lawful heir, resolved to act; being generalissimo, he assembled all the commanders of the armies, communicated to them his suspicions of the Vizier, declared his right to the throne, proposed marching to the palace with his troops, and demand of Outkar to be admitted into the presence of the Khan; and, in case of refusal, to enter by force. Several generals approved of his proposals, others on the contrary, opposed it: saying, that such conduct, would be a manifest violation of the law, and an act of unpardonable rashness. These arguments did not dissuade Oumour; he went to the palace with his partizans, entered it, desired to see Outkar, and called upon him to conduct him into the Khan's presence. The Vizier kept him back, represented to him that he violated the obedience he owed to the monarch, in attempting, with a handful of rebels, to disturb the peace of the Khan and of the people; and declared to him, that if he did not disperse his band and go home, he would repel him by force. Oumour, in spite of his remonstrances, persisted. Then Outkar, turning to the soldiers, cried with a threatening voice, " I order you, in the name of the Khan and in mine, as your supreme chief, to retire immediately, otherwise, I declare you rebels, and will have you fired at." Some confusion appeared among the followers of Oumour; all his people abandoned him, and he fled to the province of Kata-Kourgan, the inhabitants of which took him under their protection. Meantime, the people, by Outkar's order, pillaged his house and all that he possessed. The same day, at midnight, Mir Haïdar arrived from Kartch with his army, and was received by Outkar, as his Sovereign. The following morning, the most important persons in the state were convoked in the audience chamber, where they were informed of the death of Mir Manzoum; and that, according to the laws, Mir Haïdar, his eldest son, was to ascend the throne. The new Khan, in the presence of the whole assembly, took the solemn oath, to govern with equity, to make the laws respected, and to love his subjects. All the persons present took the oath of allegiance.

The following day the deceased Khan was buried with all the honours due to his rank. After Mir Haïdar had ascended the throne, he sent to Katakourgan for his uncle; the inhabitants refused to deliver him up. A general was sent with five thousand men to seize him by force. After a resistance of two days, the inhabitants were obliged to open their gates, and deliver up Oumour to the general, who immediately caused his head to be cut off, and sent it to the new Khan. This barbarous act is called by the Bucharians justice.

Mir Haïdar's brothers, who, as we have said above, commanded in Marv and Samarcand, incurred the disgrace of their brother, and were obliged to fly beyond the frontier.

No. III.

JOURNEY TO TURCOMANIA AND CHIVA, BY CAPTAIN MOURAVIEW.

General Jermolow, governor of Georgia, having conceived the plan of sending an expedition to the east coast of the Caspian sea, in order to establish a friendly intercourse between the Turcomans and the Russians, wished to form upon the coast, an establishment where the Russian merchant vessels might anchor and land their goods without danger.

In the year 1813, Mr. Rtichtchew, general of infantry, and commander-in-chief of Georgia, sent to Turcomania John Mouratow, an Armenian merchant of Derbend, who carrying on trade at Astrabad, had correspondents in those countries. Mouratow communicated the proposals of General Rtichtchew to Sultan-Khan, who commanded a party of Turcomans, and who hoping that he might one day become the legitimate chief of the Turcomans, who at that time did not acknowledge any master, received with joy the promise of protection given him by general Rtichtchew; he sent him a deputation composed of persons the most respected for their age and character. They were commissioned first to ask that Russia would cast an eye of pity on the Turcomans, whom the Persians had severely chastised for the robberies they had committed.

These envoys, among whom was Kiat-aga, whom I shall have frequent occasion to mention in the course of my narrative, did not reach General Rtichtchew at the camp of Gulistan, till he had just concluded a peace with Hussein-Khan, plenipotentiary of the court of Persia. The latter knowing how dangerous the Turcomans, supported by the Russians, might be to his country, required that our government should have no connexion with that people. General Rtichtchew consented to this, and dismissed the deputies loaded with presents. The Turcomans much vexed at this disappointment, and feeling themselves unable to resist Persia, submitted to that power, and gave hostages. Those who would not submit, went to settle upon the bay of Balkan, where they were secure from the power of the Persians, others went to Chiva, where they were welcomed by Khan Mohamed-Rahim, the declared enemy of the dynasty of Kadjar, which fills the throne of Persia. Sultan-Khan also went to Chiva, where he fixed his residence.

General Jermolow wishing to renew the attempt to form a connexion with the Turcomans, gave the commission to Major Ponomarew, commanding the district of Elizabethpol, I received orders, as an officer of the staff, to visit with him, the eastern courts of the Caspian sea, and to go to Chiva to negotiate with the Khan, and to describe that country. Such were the reasons for my journey to the coasts of the Caspian sea, and to Chiva.

General Jermolow having delivered to us the papers relative to our mission, set out on the 17th of June, 1819, for the Caucasus, where military operations rendered his presence necessary. The Armenian Mourotow, was to attend us, to act as interpreter.

On the 18th I left Tiflis, with captain Rennenkampf, and joined Major Ponomarew, at Soganloughi. On the evening of the 20th, we arrived at Elizabethpol, a pretty town on the Ganginka. We remained here till the 1st of July.

On the 2nd we passed the Kur at Minghit-chaour, upon a raft. We had hitherto passed only naked Steppes, crossed here and there by saline marshes; but the country now assumed a different appearance. The banks of the Kur are adorned on both sides by woods and gardens, on the left bank are lofty mountains, while on the right you have a view over an immense cultivated plain, in which are the ruins of an ancient city called Arevcha.

On the 3d we were at New Chamakhi. On the 4th, we began to ascend the steep mountains which separate it from the old town. From the summit of the mountain I beheld the vast and rich plain that extended behind us. Armenian villages were grouped on the summit, and in the ravines of the chain : the labours of the harvest, in which the inhabitants were engaged, gave animation to the scene.

We entered Bakou on the 6th. From an eminence in front of the town we saw the fortress, the city, the sea, and the vessels. The town is surrounded by a double wall, flanked with towers, with battlements and cannon. The environs are mountainous and naked, both water and wood are scarce; it is not well situated. The streets are narrow, with high buildings, but pretty clean. The population is numerous, the bazaar well supplied, and the caravansaries in good order. Bakou carries on a considerable commerce with Astrachan.

The vessels being ready for us, we embarked thirty soldiers of the garrison, with an officer; Major Ponomarew took Mr. Polétaew for his secretary.

Our two vessels were the *Kasan*, of 18 guns, commanded by G. G. Bassarghin; and the *Saint Policarpe*, a merchant ship, with part of our escort, and our cargo ; commanded by lieutenant A. F. Ostolopow.

On the evening of the 8th we embarked and set sail. We soon passed by the ruins of a great caravansary, which is partly under water, and half a werst from the shore; its towers still rise above the waves. It is not known how and when this edifice was swallowed up by the sea ; it was probably occasioned by an earthquake. The environs merit particular attention, as well on account of the inflammable earth which is impregnated with naphta, as of the great number of ruins which are extremely interesting in an historical point of view.

On the morning of the 20th we landed on the isle of Sara, which is in the form of a crescent, and eight wersts long ; the soil consists of a layer of shells.

The *Saint Policarpe* had arrived at Sara three days before us ; having taken in water she sailed to Lenkoran, a fort which is situated fifteen wersts from Sara, to take in wood.

On the 24th we weighed anchor. We had intended to land at Cape Sérébrénoï, none of our sailors knew it, or any other part of the coast.

On the 28th we perceived the coast of Turcomania and a cape, which we took for the Beloï, or Akh-tépé. We cast anchor seven wersts from the coast, and by the help of a telescope, perceived on shore some Turcoman tents ; we resolved to land the next day to examine the country, and to employ our interpreter to communicate with the inhabitants.

On the 29th I embarked with the interpreter and four other persons in a boat, rowed by twelve men armed with a twelve pounder carronade, and two falconets, having on board six marines ; we took biscuits, and water for one day only. As soon as we landed I discovered, by my telescope, that the supposed cape, or Beloï-Bougor, was a mountain, which is probably connected with some chain ; it appeared to me to be ten wersts distant ; that we were separated from it by an arm of the sea ; and that we were in an island.

I had at first intended to proceed to the north to look for a creek, where the Turcomans hide their flat-bottomed boats, but the information given me by Mr. Dobytchew, a subaltern officer of the marines, and a sailor, induced me to look for a creek towards the south, on the side of Astrabad ; I expected besides to meet with a river ; I, therefore, went along the coast with four sailors and Petrovitch, our interpreter, while Lieutenant Jourçff took the same direction with the boat. We had attempted to dig a well, but the water was brackish. After having gone fifteen wersts along the coast, and following the track of camels, horsemen, &c. we perceived on the other

side of the bushes a long pole with a flag fastened to the end
of it. This signal leading me to suppose that there was a
Turcoman boat in the neighbourhood, I was going to pass
through the bushes, when I discovered that great quantities of
branches had been piled upon a heap of sand, and a long pole
with a flag set up. Being thus disappointed, after having
walked all the day over a burning sand, I resolved, at three in
the afternoon, to return on board the corvette, leaving Petrovitch on shore to look for a Turcoman camp. On a sudden a
violent gust of wind obliged us to land again and pass the
night on shore. This stormy weather made me uneasy, as I
feared it might last several days; we had neither provisions
nor water, and might besides be suddenly attacked by the
Turcomans. To be able to defend ourselves we brought the
two falconets on shore, and encamped upon two hills. The
sand incommoded us much, filling our eyes and ears. We
lighted a large fire that the corvette might know where we
were. Two wells were dug, but the water was too salt to
drink. Petrovitch joined us in the evening, he had not met
with any body. Notwithstanding our fatigue and thirst, the
lieutenant and myself were obliged to watch by turns through
the night. Our situation became every moment more disagreeable, the bad weather continued, our provisons were consumed, the torment of thirst began to be so insupportable that
several of our people dipped the remainder of their biscuits
in the sea water. To put an end to our deplorable situation,
I resolved to proceed in the Steppe towards a hill which was
visible at a distance, and hoped to find there a camp, or at least
sweet water; I was going to set out, when we observed that our
boat was near sinking. We immediately rushed through the
waves, threw the carronade overboard, and with much difficulty succeeded in drawing the boat on shore. I then advanced into the Steppe, with a subaltern officer, Petrovitch,
four marines, and two men with pickaxes; after a fatiguing
march of four wersts, in deep sand, we suddenly sunk up to
our knees in black mud, in the midst of a dried up salt lake.
We were obliged to turn back; two other attempts to find
sweet water by digging wells having failed, I resolved to make
use of a method which I had heard spoken of in Persia, which
consisted in firing a musket into the well, to hasten the appearance of water; in fact it did appear more rapidly than
usual, but it was nevertheless salt. Returning to the coast,
without the hope of finding water, I resigned myself and sat
down on the sea-shore, waiting till it should grow calm. Its
waves at length subsided, and in the evening we resolved to
lighten the boat and send it to the corvette.

It set out when the moon rose; I had written to Mr. Ponomarew, to send us some provisions; I told him also that, in case of any accident, we would proceed to Astrabad by land. The boat, which returned to us on the 31st in the morning, brought us provisions for only one single meal; Mr. Ponomarew begged me to return on board. The sea permitted us to return in two or three hours.

On Sunday, the 31st of August, during divine service, we were told that three Turcoman boats had been seen near the coast; in fact, we perceived ten going under full sail, towards the north. We hailed them, and fired the carronade loaded with powder only; but not understanding this signal, the vessels spread all their sails; we then fired two shots, which did not reach them. It was necessary, therefore, to launch a boat, which had on board several armed men and Petrovitch. The boat had much trouble to overtake them; the last of the Turcoman vessels, seeing itself on the point of being taken, ran on shore: there were on board five men and three women, who fled into the bushes. Our people landed, and Petrovitch laid hold of a Turcoman, and told him that our intentions were peaceable; the others, at length, determined to come forward and ask us for mercy. We again told them they had nothing to fear, and let them go, except Devlet-Ali, the master of the boat, a man of about sixty years of age. Notwithstanding all our testimonies of friendship, he was sorrowful, and seeing himself our prisoner, expressed fear.

The camp of these Turcomans, placed between the two hills which I have mentioned above, is called *Hassan Kouli;* it was the residence of Kiat Aga, who in 1803 had been deputed to general Kitchtchew. The flocks of these Turcomans feed on the pastures in the neighbourhood of Serebrenoï-Bougor: notwithstanding the distance of that pasture, they have chosen this place for their camp, on account of the facility of having their boats, which are the source of all their welfare: they obtain fresh water at the river Gurghen-Tchaï, the mouth of which is near Serebrenoï-Bougor; it flows about half a day's march from the camp, and a day's journey from Astrabad: in the interval is another little river, the Kodja Nefes.

Devlet-Ali spoke to me of the ruins of towns, which are found in Turcomania; among others, near Serebrenoï-Bougor, the foundation of which is attributed to Alexander the Great.

Sultan Khan, surnamed Djadoukiar, of whom Petrovitch had often spoken to us, had taken refuge in Chiva, after the peace concluded between Russia and Persia, in 1813. According to the account which I received from Devlet-Ali, the Turcomans do not recognize one single chief; they are divided into tribes, each governed by an elder. He named only five, though he told me that they were more numerous. He assured me that the Chivans lived in great friendship, and had frequent intercourse with his tribe; he pretended, that in fifteen days, one might go from their camp to Chiva. We could not obtain any other information from this man, who appeared to be very uneasy among strangers, and begged us to set him on shore, promising to send Kiat-Aga to us.

We, therefore, cast anchor opposite the place at which he said his camp was, but the shoals obliged us to stop before we were within sight of land. In the evening, Mr. Ponomarew resolved to land Devlet-Ali, and to wait opposite to Serebrenoï-Bougor for his return with Kiat. We hoped to lay in a stock of water at this cape, and by keeping nearer to the shore, to be better able to communicate with the Turcomans, and to choose a favourable situation, for our intended establishment.

During the night, we twice saw the sky reddened by fire. Devlet-Ali informed us, that it was occasioned by the reflection from the burning of the dry grass in the Steppe.

Having weighed anchor on the 3d of August, we reached Serebrenoï at seven in the morning. The *Saint Policarp* had arrived there three days before. Lieutenant Ostolopow, who commanded her, came in the corvette with Nazar Mughen, the elder of the camp, situated near this point. He was a man of agreeable appearance: but his character did not correspond with it. We learned that the village of which he was chief, contained as many as two hundred tents of the Turcomans, having fixed abodes.. They cultivate the ground, and seem to enjoy a certain degree of welfare. We received Nazar Mughen well; he promised to conduct Petrovitch to Kiat-Aga, who was gone to a fair in the Persian territory. Kiat is an important person among the Turcomans, many chiefs or elders obey him, that is to say, when they please to obey, for they say that *God alone is their chief, and that they are sworn enemies to the Persians.*

We were soon visited by ten Turcomans, whom we received, as well as possible, and treated with pillaw. When we spoke of sending Petrovitch to Kiat-Aga, Nazar Merghen, who had at first promised to take him there for three ducats, demanded five, and then ten. Mr. Ponomarew, at length losing patience, sent them all away, except Nazar Merghen, who did not become more complying. Devlet-Ali consented to what we desired, for a present of small value, which, however, excited the envy of Nazar, who received two gun flints and a pound of powder; in the evening, Petrovitch set out with his guide. From the apparent simplicity of the Turcomans, one would not be led to suppose that they were so fond of money.

Cape Serebrenoï is not very high. The Turcomans say, that upon its summit are the ruins of an ancient city, to which they give the name Guchim Tépé. According to my observation, the cape is situated in 37° 5′ 22″ North latitude.

On the 4th of August I went on board of the Saint Policarp, and then got into a boat with Mr. Ostolopow, to ascend and examine the Gurghen Tchai, the mouth of which is three wersts to the south of Cape Sérébrenoi. The boat of the Saint Policarp followed me with ten soldiers, two swivels, and one cannon. Our boat was obliged to stop on account of the shallows : the sailors hauled it along the coast ; we then took one of the country boats, a kind of proa, made of a trunk of a tree hollowed out, which our people hauled in the same manner to the mouth of the river. The banks are low, marshy, and inundated to a considerable distance ; its current is slow and choaked with reeds, a yard and a half high : though low in summer it was now quite dry. When we had gone about two wersts up it, we were near to a Turcoman camp. At some distance from this place there is a ford, which the inhabitants pass to go to Astrabad. Cape Serebrenoi was plainly to be discerned from this point. Three wersts from the ford I met with some Turcomans, with whom I conversed for about two hours ; they invited me to their aul, or village ; but I deferred my visit to another day. They expressed to me the unanimous wish of their countrymen to see the Russians rebuild the fort, near Cape Serebrenoï, which had been destroyed. " We will take vengeance of the Persians for their robberies," said they, " the heads of our Turcomans want brains, we would have rebuilt the fort but we do not understand it ; when we make a general call to arms, we assemble above 10,000 men, and we beat the Persians ; five years ago we cut to pieces three Sardars, (military chiefs) near this place, and we took from them great numbers of cattle." " Should you like to have cannon from us?" said I. They seemed delighted at this offer. They said they had frequent intercourse with Chiva, and that a company of half a dozen men might go thither without danger. They made a pompous description of Chiva, and said that the Khan who governed that state possessed great treasures.

These Turcomans cultivate the ground and possess numerous flocks. They understand how to make gunpowder, and are in want only of manufactured goods. Fifteen wersts from the little river, on the side of Astrabad, there is a forest, from which the Turcomans affirm, that timber for ship-building might be obtained. They had seen Petrovitch the day before going to Kiat-aga, in a boat with Devlet Ali, and two men of their village. After two hours' conversation with them I re-embarked in the evening to return to the corvette.

On the 6th of August, very early in the morning, the Saint Policarpe sent a boat on shore to fetch Nazar Merghen and the principal persons of his village ; it returned about dinner time with only one elder, named Devlet-Ali-Khan, whom Nazar Merghen had requested us not to send for, doubtless in hopes of receiving the presents intended for him. The Khan told us that he had not come sooner, not to trangress the custom which forbids a Khan to make a visit without having been invited ; this was only a pretext ; the truth was, that having been raised to the rank of Khan by the Persians, he was afraid of offending them by communicating with us. Devlet-Ali-Khan has more understanding than most of his country-men ; he had served under Aga-Mahomet-Khan, and then in plunder of Tiflis in 1792. He has since left Feth-Ali-Shah, and has been raised to the dignity of elder in his own country. He did not give us any more information than the rest, and seemed better inclined towards the Persians than to the Russians. He named the principal chiefs or elders, including himself ; they were Kiat-aga of the village of Hassan-Kouli ; Tagan Koulidj-Khan and Tepé Mirza-Khan, of the village Gheréi ; Kodjum-Kolibai and Tagan-Kazi of the nomades of the river Atrek.

The Atrek flows two miles to the north of the Gurghen. The villages are situated on the sides of the two rivers. On the banks of the latter are the ruins of towns and fortifications. Mr. Ponomarew wrote letters to call together all the persons I have just named, and after having presented to the Khan a piece of damask, he gave them to him to forward to their destination : Nazar-Merghen, who remained as a hostage on board the corvette, told us that, according to Devlet-Ali-Khan, the Turcomans were in great alarm because they expected that many Russian vessels, loaded with troops and cannon, would come to their coasts the following autumn. The same day Petrovitch returned with Kiat aga. This chief shewed at first some mistrust ; when Mr. Ponomarew made him ac-quainted with the designs of our government, he entered into a long discussion, and concluded by saying, " If your inten-tions are sincere I am again ready to serve you ; but you will more easily succeed if you go to the 'Tcheleks, where I have relations ; the coast there would afford you a more convenient situation for your intended establishment, and you will not be above fifteen days' journey from Chiva ; there too you will find the people of Sultan Khan, with whom I will send your envoy to Chiva. I am also ready to conduct you to the Tcheleks."

I soon landed near Serebrenoï Bougor, and visited Devlet-Ali-Khan in his village ; I then saw that what we had taken for a little hill was the wall of a large building, and that the sand of the Steppe accumulating against the eastern side gave it the appearance of a sand hill, upon which the inhabitants had cultivated a little field. Between this wall and the sea there are many other ruins.. It is more than half a werst from this place to the village ; I left outside of the village an escort of a dozen men, whom I had brought with me, and repaired to the Khan, who gave me a very good reception. A great crowd had assembled round his tent ; I also saw his wife. They offered me curdled camels' milk and bread, and begged me to let my escort enter the village. Mirza Khan, one of the chiefs to whom Mr. Ponomarew had sent letters of invitation, had already arrived there ; he came to see me at the tent, and wished to accompany me when I returned on board ; he afterwards changed his intentions, saying he would wait for the arrival of the three other chiefs who had been summoned. The Khan begged me to shew him the manner in which our soldiers fire their muskets. " We have heard from our old men, said he, that the Russians are so well exercised that when a man stamps his foot, three hundred do it at the same time, and we should be very glad to see it." I made our people exercise and fire, which seemed to please and surprise them greatly.

The tents of the Turcomans are made like those of the nomade Turks in Georgia; the Turcoman women do not veil their faces ; they have pleasing features ; their dress consists of coloured pantaloons and a large red chemise ; their head-dress is composed of a kind of cap which, for its height, might be compared to those worn by the women of Canchois in Normandy. These caps are ornamented with gold or silver, according to the fortune of the husband. The hair is divided over the forehead, and fastened in a long braid behind.

On the morning of the 7th, I returned to Sérébrénoï-Bougor with workmen, provided with pickaxes and shovels, in the hope, that by digging, I might find some medal which would acquaint me with the antiquity of these ruins. To divert the attention of the Turcomans, I landed some soldiers, who, preceded by a drummer, went to exercise in the village, while I undertook my researches. I cannot yet say any thing positive on the ruins of Sérébrénoï-Bougor ; it is the outer wall of a great building or fort, on the east side of which, a sand hill has accumulated ; but I found tombs in this wall, in which I discovered human bones ; bodies had been buried there in the Turcoman fashion, that is to say, placed on the side, with the head turned towards the east. I suppose that these skeletons are of a later date than the ruins. The wall may be about a hundred toises in length, and at the utmost, two in height ; it is built of burnt bricks of a good quality. Seventy toises from this wall, on the side of the sea, we saw a promontory which did not appear to us formed by nature ; in some places, I found walls of houses, round towers, and little places paved very regularly with large bricks, half an arsheen square. This place is entirely covered with the fragments of bricks, even into the sea, to the distance of thirty or forty toises. To my great surprise, these remains did not look like ruins ; the walls are all on a level with the horizon, which made me believe that they belonged to buildings which had been swallowed up by an earthquake, like the caravansary in the road of Bakou, and that I had been walking on the terraces or roofs of houses. The inhabitants have often found gold and silver coins ; they affirm that this fort was built by the Russians, who formerly commanded on this coast. I made the workmen dig in the inside of one of the towers, where I found only fragments of earthen-ware and glass, a square bottle of which we found the neck and the upper part, which was quite different from the bottles of the same kind in Russia. I would have continued to dig to the foundation of the tower, had not the workmen been overpowered by the heat.

Reading the voyage made in 1782 by the Russian squadron of Count Voinovitch to Astrabad, and on the east coast of the Caspian sea, I found that the description of Sérébrénoï-Bougor, did not agree with what I had seen, it being there called an island. In fact, Kiat and the other Turcomans, told me that it really had been an island, and had not been joined to the continent above four or five years.

Very early in the morning of the 11th, I landed with Kiat to survey Cape Sérébrénoï ; Kiat told me that our people who were going to look for water, ought to be on their guard, and not disperse, because the Persians had gained some inhabitants of other villages, who were disposed to hide themselves in the reeds, to fire at us.---The heat was oppressive ; my survey being finished at one o'clock, I returned to the village to repose. Devlet-Ali-Khan and Nazar Merghen, received us hospitably.

On the 17th, Kiat, Devlet-Ali-Khan, and Kodjam-Kouly

Bey, assembled on board the corvette ; but Mirza Khan, and Tagam-Kolidj Khan, did not come ; they had sent their people to beg us to wait for them, because they wished to choose a more favourable opportunity to escape the suspicions of the Persians, who were watching them. Mr. Ponomarew, however, began the negotiation without them ; he proposed to the three chiefs, to send Kiat as Ambassador to General Jermolow, giving him full powers in writing. They joyfully agreed to our proposal, and promised to procure the consent of all the other chiefs, even of the kazy or priest, the most eminent in dignity, and whom they consider as the prince of the tribe of Jomoud. Kiat hoped to succeed in obtaining their assent in about four days. We, therefore, resolved to send him ashore, and to go by sea to Hassan Kouli, to await his return, and then to the bay of Krasnovodsk, which is in the Balkan, to induce the elders there to consent also to our proposal, and then prepare for my departure for Chiva.

The dignity of Khan is not hereditary among the Turcomans ; they are nominated by Persia ; sometimes the people obey them for their personal qualities, and sometimes for their conduct. They employ slaves whom they purchase, or prisoners of war, to cultivate their fields.---The dignity of Akh-Sakhal, (white beard,) or elder, is conferred by the people ; it seems to be superior to that of Khan, and to be retained in the family, when, after the death of the person invested with it, his relations are entitled by their conduct to the general esteem.

On the 24th we went on shore, and after having bid adieu to Devlet-Ali-Khan, who for the fourth time offered us a horse which we refused, because we could not carry it away. I returned to the corvette with Kolidj-Bek, and a relation of Kiat, to whom we made some presents. He told us that the Turcomans established in the neighbourhood of Persia, obey that power, but that those who reside on the borders of the Atrek, and farther north, do not acknowledge its dominion. Having landed Kiat's relation, we ordered him to proceed directly to Hassan Kouli, and inform Kiat of our speedy arrival.

The Turcomans have not that austerity and uprightness of character which distinguish the tribes of the Caucasus ; in the midst of poverty, these people are strangers to the laws of hospitality ; they are so greedy after money, that there is nothing, however mean, to which they will not submit, for the smallest recompense. They speak a Turkish dialect, resembling that in use in Kazan. It is only their Mollahs that have some education ; they are of the sect of Omar, and scrupulously fulfil every thing relating to the external practice of their religion and prayers ; they have no distinct idea of the dogmas. They are tall, broad shouldered, have short beards, their physiognomy resembles that of the Kalmucks ; and they dress like the Persians.

When we arrived opposite the coast of Hassan Kouli, the water was so shallow that we were obliged to stop at so great a distance from the land, that we could not see it with the naked eye ; with the aid of the telescope, we descried several boats. According to my observations, the latitude of this place is 37° 27′ 51″ north. On the 27th, Mr. Ponomarew went on shore with me. Kiat had come to meet us, accompanied by all the inhabitants of the village ; they had prepared for our reception a tent with carpets. There are a hundred and fifty tents at Hassan-Kouli. This village received its name from the ancestors of the Turcomans, who have been long settled on this coast. It was formerly an island, but is now joined on the north side to the continent, and forms a peninsula, separated from it on the east, by a bay six wersts broad, and twelve long. Kiat endeavoured to divert us by the sight of Turcoman games. They shot at a mark, both with a musket and the bow, wrestled, and run races : the prizes were awarded by Mr. Ponomarew, and the inhabitants seemed very eager for them. Their arms are clumsy and ill kept ; their powder is of the worst quality, and they did not display much address. Many of these people are pretty well clothed, and lead rather an idle life, from which it may be inferred, that they derive great profit from the only kind of trade which they follow, which consists in taking naptha and salt to Persia. They also manufacture carpets of good quality ; they are indifferently skilled in various arts, their goldsmiths strike coins, which serve as ornaments for the women ; they have two-stringed instruments resembling a Russian guitar. The peninsula supplies them with nothing but water-melons. The produce of their fishery has for sometime past decreased one-half ; in winter they chace the swan, from which they procure a considerable quantity of down. Numbers of wood-cocks are always to be seen on their coast ; the animals which frequent the Steppes and the borders of the Atrek, are the wolf, the fox, antelopes, wild boars, jackals, &c. The winds which blow almost constantly from the sea, render communication with the coast difficult.

The chiefs of the village of Hassan-Kouli, are divided into two parties, of which that of Kiat is the strongest. Though the writing we had drawn up was subscribed by most of the chiefs, Mr. Ponomarew insisted on having the general consent of all the Turcomans, to the sending of Kiat as ambassador to our government; he therefore called together all the elders in the presence of Kazi and Kiat, and in this assembly, which was held on the 29th of August, his nomination was unanimously confirmed. On the 30th, the wind having abated, we went on board the corvette in the evening, accompanied by Kiat, who would not have any person share his labours, or rather participate in the presents and the confidence which he expected from us. We weighed anchor on the 31st, but the wind being unfavourable, we made little progress. I obtained, however, from Kiat, various information respecting the several tribes and their chiefs, which may be of use in future intercourse with this country. On the 2d of September, we came in sight of the isle of Naptha, which is pretty accurately described in the account of the expedition of Count Voinovitch, and its position well marked on the map. The isle of Dervich, which was at that time on the south-west of the isle of Naptha, was united to it 15 years ago by an earthquake. In the afternoon we landed with Mr. Ponomarew, near the village, on the south-coast of the isle of Naptha. It contained only 15 tents. The inhabitants have a trade in Naptha and in salt, (which last they procure from a lake,) with the Turcomans from Hassan-Kouli or Sérébrenoi-Bongor. The springs of Naptha are on the other side of the mountains, where some families live; there are 100 families in the island; there are only four wells, the water of which is fit to drink, though salt. There are also some pastures in the interior of the island, but their only cattle are camels and sheep; they have no wood for fuel but brush-wood; the winters are said to be very severe. Some of the inhabitants still recollect Count Voinovitch; one of them had even preserved a writing given by him, which he promised to bring and show to us at Krasnovodsk, to which place we were going. Our voyage was however very tedious, on account of contrary winds and calms, so that though we sailed early in the morning of the 3d, it was not till the 10th, in the forenoon, that we anchored in the bay of Krasnovodsk, in three fathoms water, one werst and a half from the shore, and from mount Oog. Nomade camps are on several parts of the coast, where there are wells with fresh water, as well as at cape Krasnovodsk. This bay is not dangerous for vessels, and of all the places we had visited, this would certainly be the most suitable for an establishment. As soon as we arrived, Kiat was put on shore to find a person who should accompany me in my journey to Chiva. On the 11th, we landed in a place, where a well, hewn in the rock, furnishes excellent water. The mountains near the coast are steep, and strewn with rocks of a friable stone.   On the 14th, we assembled all the principal chiefs of the bay of Balkan, on board the corvette, where they passed the whole day.   I went on shore ; an entertainment had been prepared for the elders, to whom Kiat made proposals to dispose them in our favour.   The guide whom they had recommended, refused to accompany me.   Kiat sent for another, who arrived on the 15th.   Kiat again assembled all the elders on board the corvette ; by way of signing, they dipped their fingers into the ink, and applied them to the paper.   Moulla Kaïb ratified their consent.   The presents were then distributed.   During this time, I agreed with Seïd the guide, who wished to set out for Chiva on the 21st, or according to their manner of reckoning, on the 12th of the month Zylkhidje.   He engaged to take me to Chiva and back again for forty ducats, the half to be paid in advance. The Saint Polycarpe, which was to bring us provisions, had not yet arrived ; it was thought that she had sprung a leak, and was obliged to return to Sara, and as we could not remain without provisions, we resolved to send the corvette to Bakou ; on my return from Chiva, I intended to winter on the coast.

I went on shore on the 17th, to purchase a horse, they brought me one which was little, old, and miserable, and not worth above thirty francs, and which, far from carrying me as far as Chiva, would not have borne two days' journey; they asked me more than ten times its value.   I declined the bargain, and resolved to use a camel.

JOURNEY TO CHIVA AND RESIDENCE THERE.

I passed the 17th of September in making preparations for my journey to Chiva ; I had two letters for the Khan, one from general Jermolow, and another from major Ponomarew ; which expressed the desire of the Russian government, to establish regular caravans between Chiva and the Caspian sea.

The 18th in the evening, every thing was ready for my departure ; we received good news from the Saint Policarpe, which induced us to give up our first plan ; we immediately sent back the boat, and desired lieutenant Ostolopow, to go as soon as possible to Krasnovodsk.   In the evening I landed with our chaplain, lieutenant Linitskoï, and midshipman Jourieff, and passed the night in two Kibitkas, belonging to an old Turcoman.

I undertook this journey without much hopes of returning; however, I made myself easy by reflecting that I had already advanced one step towards the accomplishment of the dangerous duty which I had undertaken.

I left the coast on the 19th. My guide Seïd, lived in a camp near the well of Soudji-Kubil ; he had sent me four camels by one of his relations ; I procured two horses, and in this manner, we entered the Steppe. I had with me only Petrovitch, the interpreter, and one soldier who waited on me. I was, however, armed with a good pistol, a gun, a large sword, and a dagger, which I never laid aside during the journey. Petrovitch was a very obliging man, much attached to me, and besides, of a lively disposition : he often amused me by his pleasantries when I was inclined to despond.

Kiat and Tagan-Nias, accompanied me only as far as Sendovoï-Ob. Having ascended the lofty rocks, which form the bank of the bay of Balkan, I had a view over the immense Steppe, which I was about to cross. It is in some places sandy, in others sprinkled with bushes. Though there is no grass in these dry and naked plains, yet there are herds of camels and sheep, which browze on the bushes which are scattered here and there. The Turcomans are idle and careless, and subsist on camels' milk and corn, which they buy at Astrabad or Chiva. Their only profession is robbery, they carry off Persians at Astrabad, and sell them for a very high price at Chiva.

I was very well received in the camp of Seïd, which was twenty-eight wersts from our anchoring place, Krasnovodsk. I left on one side some inconsiderable eminences, which are a branch of the Balkan mountains, and towards evening, arrived at Ob Seïd, the habitation of the Turcomans of the family of Kelte.

These tribes are spread through the whole Steppe, almost from the Caspian Sea to the frontiers of Chiva. They are subdivided into an infinite number of branches, each of which elects an elder, who is obeyed, or to speak more properly, esteemed, for his old age, his intrepidity in robbery, or his riches.

I have since learned that the elder of the tribe of Kelte, a friend of Hekim-Ali-Bey, elder of the tribe of Kirindjik, whose brother had offered to conduct me for a hundred ducats, an exorbitant price, which I refused to give, had persuaded Seïd not to accompany me. Seïd, who had given me his word, resisted every persuasion and resolved to remain with me. This conduct, so different from the general avidity and cunning of the Turcomans, was an effect of the influence of Kiat, who had persuaded him to set out with me, by making him hope that if my journey succeeded he would easily obtain what he wished from the Russian government. Seïd was perhaps the best of the Turcomans that I was acquainted with ; though unpolished and of confined understanding, he was faithful, resolute, and brave, and famous for his robberies in Persia.

I found the Turcomans of this village more mild in their manners than those on the coast.

I set out from Soudji-kabil on the 21st of September; mounted on an enormous camel, I had great difficulty in keeping my seat when it rose. My caravan was composed of seventeen of these animals, and belonged to four Turcomans, who had engaged to serve me as guides; they were going to buy corn at Chiva. Seïd was the oldest of the four.

After travelling twenty wersts we stopped about noon for an hour, after which we joined a caravan commanded by Hekim-Ali-Bey. As we proceeded our company was increased by persons from the camps, near which we passed, so that on the third day after entering the Steppe, we had with us two hundred camels and forty men; all going to buy corn at Chiva.

The quarrel between Hekim-Ali-Bey and Seïd affected me; each of the caravans travelled apart, and, in the evening, each formed a separate camp. My people were well armed; which probably prevented Hekim from attacking and plundering us. He never condescended to salute me; sitting before the fire with his companions he abused us; I succeeded however in disposing several of the people of his caravan in my favour, by offering them tea, of which the Turcomans are very fond. Perhaps Hekim shunned me because he was afraid that if he conversed with me the Khan of Chiva might receive him ill; whatever was the motive of his conduct, I was constantly on my guard, and, during the sixteen days that our journey continued, never laid down my arms.

I passed this time very uncomfortably; the rough pace of the camel did not fatigue me so much as an invincible ennui. I was absolutely without society, having nobody to talk with. The heat was very oppressive. The view of the Steppe was no way calculated to amuse me; it was the image of death, or rather of desolation, after a convulsion of nature; neither quadruped nor bird was to be seen; no verdure, no plant refreshed the sight, only at long intervals we met with spots where some miserable bushes grow with difficulty. In the midst of this frightful desert my thoughts dwelt upon my native country, from which I was so distant, and from which I feared that an eternal slavery might separate me for ever.

I wore the Turcoman dress, and had taken the Turkish name of Moura-Bek; this precaution was very useful to me, for though I was known to all the people belonging to the caravan, yet when we met with strangers I avoided their idle questions by passing for a Turcoman of the tribe of Djafar-Bey.

We had proceeded in an easterly direction. In the night there was an eclipse of the moon, which lasted for above an hour, and greatly disturbed the Turcomans; they asked me the reason of this phenomenon, assuring me that the moon was never eclipsed except on the death of a sovereign or of an elder; they added that this eclipse probably announced that I should have a bad reception at Chiva. As it was of consequence to me to remove this notion; I endeavoured to explain to them the motions of the celestial bodies, which eclipsed each other at certain periods. They did not understand me, and appeared to consider deeply; at length they said, " you are indeed an ambassador, an extraordinary man, since you know not only what is done upon the earth, but also what passes in the heavens." I completed their astonishment by telling them which part of the moon would first become visible.

We continued our journey on the 22d, at one o'clock in the morning; it was very cold, and the dew fell in abundance. After a march of twenty-four wersts we arrived, at day break, at the wells of Suili, where there were about twenty Turcoman tents. These wells are fifteen toises deep, the water is not good.

Nea rthis place is a great burying ground; the tomb-stones, which are pretty large, appear to me to be limestone; there is sculpture on some of them, which is not the work of the Turcomans. The inhabitants say that this burying ground is very ancient.

On the 23d we set out at midnight, and an hour before sunrise, having gone eighteen wersts, we reached the wells of Demour-djem, which are in a cavity, the bottom of which is level, and is supposed to be the bed of an ancient lake.

After having passed near forty-eight hours without closing my eyes, I alighted from my camel. Overwhelmed with fatigue, I fell into a profound sleep while they were watering our animals, which took about an hour. The afflicting thoughts which possessed me during the day, represented themselves to my imagination. I dreamt that I was bidding an eternal adieu to my eldest brother, and that I was going to certain destruction and frightful captivity.---When I awoke, I was surrounded by women and children, who crowded about me and examined me with great attention. The transition was so rapid that I could hardly recollect myself, but the voice of Seïd, calling to me to rise quicker, put me in mind, that I was in the hands of the Turcomans; and, perhaps, on the eve of that captivity, which had just troubled me in my dream.

The bottom of the ancient lake has not a single bush; we halted six wersts from Demour-djem. During the whole journey, we had not met with a blade of grass; the camels endured hunger as well as thirst; they fed on little branches, and whatever they found in the Steppe. As we had some days' journey to go, without any hope of finding water, our guides had filled their skins at the wells of Demour-djem.

During the whole way which we had just passed, was through the dried-up bottom of a lake. It is remarkable, that the water found here should be of such different qualities; a well of sweet water is often close to another of salt. There are some wells 250 feet deep; they are lined with timber; the inhabitants cannot tell by whom they were dug.

Five wersts to the left of the road is a great lake, which the Turcomans call Kouli-Deria, or Adji-Kouyoussi. It extends to the north and south, to the length of ten miles, and joins the bay of Karabogaz. This lake does not appear to be known to geographers, and the bay of Karabogaz, (in which the inhabitants pretend is an unfathomable abyss,) has not been visited by our navigators. Though the Turcomans coast without danger a part of the shore, when they go to fish for seals, they have never dared to venture to the farther part of the Kouli-Deria, of which they speak with a kind of mysterious apprehension.

" What necessity," said they, " is there to venture upon this lake ; all living creatures avoid it, the animals of the Steppe are afraid to drink its water, which is excessively bitter, and causes death ; even the fish keep at a distance from it." They pretend that the waters of the Caspian sea are swallowed up in this lake, because they rush with extraordinary rapidity into the bay of Karabogaz. It is very easy to perceive the diminution of the Kouli-Deria, the ancient bank of which is distinguished at a little distance in the Steppe; the northern banks are steep. According to a popular tradition, the birds which fly over this lake fall down, blinded by the pestilential vapours which rise from it.

We set out on the 24th at sun-rise; and after travelling thirty wersts, stopped near the summit of the chain of the mountain Sare-Baba, which extends to the north and south. We had began to ascend the Sare-Baba, which had been long in sight ; when we were half way, the ascent was pretty gentle but very long. On halting in the evening, we were tormented by a high wind, which enveloped us in clouds of sand, and by a cold air, which we felt the more, as it was with great difficulty that we collected some branches to make a fire.

At midnight we set out again, and soon descended the

mountains, which are pretty steep on this side. On the summit of this chain rises the Kyr, a hill where there is always a high wind, and on which is a monument in honour of Er-Sare-Baba, founder of the Turcoman tribe. The Turcomans relate, that Er-Sare-Baba, lived in a very remote period, and was revered for his virtues, and his numerous children ; that he desired to be buried on the top of these mountains, near the road, that the passengers might pray for him ; this chain is called by his name. The monument which is raised for him, consists of a pole, on which are hung rags of various colours, and round it they have heaped stones, stag's horns, &c. These offerings are deposited here by all the Turcomans, of whatever tribe they may be, who pass near this place, and none of them dare touch the tomb, for fear of profaning it ; near it are traces of an ancient burying-ground.

As we descended the heights, the climate changed ; we left the region of wind and cold ; and entered into a mild and calm atmosphere. We walked over a moveable sand, in which some bushes grew.

At three in the morning, on the 25th, after going twenty-five wersts, we arrived at Touer, where there are six wells of good water ; the soil is so barren, that we did not see the least verdure, nor even a bush.

Near these wells is a stone monument, pretty well built ; and raised in honour of Djafar-Bey, one of the ancestors of the Jomouds : he has given his name to the most courageous and the most numerous branch ; it counts 2000 tents, and has assumed a certain superiority over the others. Scïd, who belonged to this tribe, affected airs with the Turcomans of other tribes. From Touer are two roads to Chiva. The shortest is liable to two objections ; the first is the want of fresh water, the other, the proximity of the camps of the tribe of Téké, which is always at variance with its neighbours, and the most addicted to pillage.

The second road turns to the left in a north-east direction ; it is two days' journey longer than the first, and is equally destitute of water, but is less dangerous ; nevertheless, Scïd loaded his gun, and advised me to do the same. We halted after travelling forty wersts,---Hekim-Ali-Bey continued to behave to me with much rudeness ; disregarding the dangers to which we were exposed, he would never wait for us, that we might travel together ; it is true, I had not asked him, and to judge by his manners, I could not have depended upon him in case of an attack. I encamped at some distance, and every night took the necessary precautions, making a kind of rampart with my baggage, and never quitting my arms. Some people of his caravan, once advised me to join them, for the sake of safety. I replied, that they might join my caravan if they were afraid ; they left me without adding a word. One of Hekim's companions, who was very fond of tea, came and joined me with sixteen camels, and one clerk : he followed me during the whole journey, in hopes of receiving rich presents ; which I did not think proper to bestow.

The country which we traversed on the 25th was a little hilly; after proceeding twenty-three wersts we reached, on the 26th, before day break, the well of Dirin, which is in a deep valley and lined with stone ; though the water was putrid and salt we were obliged to fill our bottles with it, because we were going to enter a steppe which was entirely arid. The valley of Dirin has very steep sides, and presents the traces of a river, which formerly flowed from north to south ; it is the ancient bed of the Amou-Deria, which is now dry.

Hekim-Ali-Bey having met my caravan here, gave me for the first time a good reception. " My sincerity," said he, " is not on my lips, like that of the people who surround you, but it is in my heart." I turned away without answering. Several persons' expressed their desire to go before me to Chiva, to announce my arrival to the Chan ; but, knowing their perfidy, I declined their offers.

On the 26th we travelled the whole day, and on the 27th before sun-rise halted, after having gone fifty-one wersts. We met a small caravan coming from Chiva, and I gave to the Turcoman Mahomet Nias, who was with it, a letter for Mr. Ponomarew ; in which I informed him of my safety, and begged him to seize the son of Hekim-Ali-Bey if any accident should happen to me.

On the 27th we travelled thirty-one wersts, and on the 28th and 29th one hundred and twenty-eight wersts, and halted at the wells of Bech-Dichik, the water of which is excellent. I was much rejoiced that they had chosen this place to pass the night. During the ten days that we had been travelling I had hardly enjoyed any repose ; being unable, like the Turcomans, to sleep on my camel ; if I happened to drop into a slumber it was at the risk of falling off. At this place I was able to sleep comfortably, and had time to change my clothes, which were full of sand and dust, I had excellent water to refresh myself, make tea, and dress some food ; I besides pleased myself with the reflection that I had passed two-thirds of this troublesome journey.

The whole way which we passed was covered with moving sand ; before us the prospect extended to a distance, over a steep bank almost perpendicular to the horizon, and intersected with large fissures ; my companions assured me that it was the shore of an ancient sea, of which I shall have occasion to speak.   Ten wersts from the wells, we had met with the bed of a great river, now dry, above an hundred toises broad, and about fifteen deep.   The banks are very steep, and, as well as the bottom, covered with brambles ; its direction is from north east to south-west ; the steepness and looseness of the banks hindering us from crossing it, we were forced to turn to the left, and follow the course of this ancient river, among little hills of sands heaped up by the wind ; their height was about two toises.   Having gone seven wersts along the bank, we found a place where we could descend into it, and stopped at the wells of Bech-Dichik, near a great caravan.   From thence I saw the coasts of this ancient sea ; it was at two wersts distance, and extended in a direction parallel to the bed of the ancient river.

As in becoming dry in the midst of this steppe it has retained its form, I frequently met with the sinuosities, which perfectly resemble those of a river, and I concluded it was the bed of the ancient Amou-Deria, which the Emperor Peter the Great caused to be looked for with so much care.

On my return from Chiva, Kiat told me, that though the mouth of the river was obstructed with sand, it was still to be distinguished, and that on the coast of the sea a small house had been built of beams placed horizontally, in the Russian fashion. The oldest inhabitants have no account of the erection of this building ; it inspires them with a kind of veneration and superstitious fear, which contributes to its present preservation.   It is not surprising that such a cabin should have stood so long in such a dry climate.   If it was built by the Russians, it must have been since the time when Peter the Great sent an expedition to look for the gold sand ; the present inhabitants of the sides of the Balkan have no tradition on the subject, probably because other Turcoman tribes lived there at the time that the cabin was built.

In the places which have not been covered with the sand, the bed of the Amou-Deria offers a soil entirely different from any other in the Steppe ; in some parts there is grass and even trees, and very good water is found in it ; at the wells of Sare-Kamych it rises over the brim and forms a brook, which flows at the bottom of the dried up river ; close to it is another well, the water of which is salt.   At the place which we had chosen for our encampment, there were six excellent wells. On the road from this place to the real frontiers of the state of Chiva, there is a considerable quantity of brush-wood.

On our arrival I was much surprise to see Hekim-Ali-Bey

and his brother come to meet me, unyoke my camels, and take off the bales. Hekim coming up to me, excused himself for his conduct on the journey, and protested his desire to repair it, and to do me all the service in his power. While I received his assurances with indulgence, and offered him tea, I did not place the more confidence in him, and during the night was more on my guard than ever. The sudden change might be explained by supposing that, if he had really formed any hostile projects, now that he saw that he was unable to execute them, and that I was on the point of arriving at Chiva, he thought it would be most advantageous to pretend an attachment to me, because it appeared probable that the Khan would receive me well, and that then I should be able to do him some service. This supposition was confirmed by the fact, that he had learned from the caravans we had met, that the report of the speedy arrival of a Russian embassy had been spread at Chiva, and that it was said there that Mahomet Rahim expected me with great impatience to receive four bales of ducats, which it was supposed the Akh-Padishach, or white Czar, had sent him. The news of my approaching arrival had been brought to that town by Turcomans from the Gurghen and the Atrek, who, when we were in their neighbourhood, had learned that I had made inquiries respecting the road to Chiva, and suspected my intentions, which in fact I had not endeavoured to conceal.

On the 30th, at day break, we set out and did not stop till sunset, after going 25 wersts. This day's march was very agreeable. Having passed to the other side of the ancient bed of the Amou-Deria, we followed its direction at a short distance, for the space of three wersts, leaving to our left the great steep bank, which the Turcomans regard as that of a sea. We lost sight of it in the distance. Its appearance was every where very uniform, its height might be about 20 toises. The part of the Steppe situated above was as even as that below, on which we travelled. We were much amused by an echo which repeated several syllables many times over. The road turned to the right, and we perceived on the bank five openings, regularly hewn, which appeared to be the entrance of a dwelling. So strange an object amongst so ignorant a people, necessarily gave rise to some fables. In fact, my guides informed me that it was known to their whole tribe, that these five openings led to a vast palace which, from the most remote antiquity, had been the residence of a Czar, with a numerous family, great treasures, and daughters of extraordinary beauty. Some curious persons having been so bold as to enter these subterrancous recesses, had been stopped by an invisible power and died.

Though their accounts differed from each other, I would not pass this enchanted spot without visiting the old Czar, to judge of the beauty of his daughters, or without entering a caravan which might have been the retreat of banditti. I therefore went with one of my Turcomans towards these ancient habitations ; they are at little more than half the height of the bank ; immediately below these openings is a projection which forms a kind of esplanade, about a hundred fathoms long : the ground was of a very light earth, which crumbled under our feet ; I however climbed up, to pass by a narrow crevice between the bank and a rock, which had become loose. Above my head a stone of enormous size was suspended, which seemed to need but a slight shock to crush me under its weight ; I was obliged to get through a narrow interval which this stone left, in order to reach the projection, whence it seemed easy to get to the caverns. My Turcoman walked before ; he penetrated without difficulty into the narrow passage, but when he got further, he found it impossible to proceed, because the projection was interrupted for the length of two toises ; if we could have crossed this break we might easily have entered the caverns, which are only a few steps further. We might have surmounted this difficulty, by the means of ropes, but the caravan was already at a very great distance, and I was obliged, though very unwillingly, to hasten to overtake it. It may be presumed, that the real entrance of the cave had been at the place where I was, and that it had been purposely closed by rolling a piece of rock before it, which almost entirely covered it.

I do not know what to think of this steep bank, which the Turcomans say was once a sea-coast ; the appearance of the country renders this assertion probable ; at least if it is not the coast of a sea now dried up, it may be reasonably supposed to have been the shore of an immense lake, the extent of which cannot be overlooked from one point.*

Before sun-rise on the 2d of October, we met with a numerous caravan of Turcomans of the tribe of Igdyr. It consisted of 200 men and 1000 camels. As they went along, they were very noisy,

---

* According to the system of Buffon, Pallas, and others, these may have been the ancient banks of the Caspian sea, when it was united with lake Aral ; the saline nature of the Steppe and of its waters, support this hypothesis. This system agrees with that of Strabo and Eratosthenes, who relate that in remote ages, the Black sea, the Caspian, lake Aral, and the Palus Neotis, formed one sea.— *Note of the Translator.*

laughing and singing, and rejoiced at having left Chiva, and having made advantageous purchases of corn. Meeting this caravan where the passage was confined between bushes, we were obliged to stop till it had passed ; they perceived by Petrovitch's cap that he was not a Turcoman.

They looked at us with curiosity, and asked our Turcomans what people we were, " They are Russian prisoners," replied they ; " this year one of their vessels stranded on our coast, and we took three of them, whom we are going to sell at Chiva."

" That is right, (replied the Igdyr, with a ferocious smile,) take and sell those cursed infidels ; we have just sold three of them for a good price, at Chiva."

On the 3d we met several caravans with corn, from Chiva, from which we learnt that the Khan had just imposed upon the Turcomans a tax of eight francs for every camel which should arrive. The Turcomans refusing to submit to this tribute, and demanding that it should be revoked, the Khan had ordered the caravans which had arrived to be detained, promising to go to the fortress of Akh-Saraï to receive their elders, listen to their demands, and accept their presents: they added, that in spite of this, several caravans had already fled, and that probably we should meet at Akh-Saraï with the Khan, whom they supposed to have already left Chiva. This news gave me pleasure, because it seemed to indicate the speedy conclusion of my mission. I even prepared the speech which I should make at my first interview with the Khan ; I gave it to Petrovitch, and ordered him to learn it by heart : I greatly deceived myself !

Since we left our halting place the day before, we found roads crossing in all directions, which led to villages or camps in Chiva. The whole caravan of Hekim-Ali-Bey had dispersed, to buy corn ; we remained alone upon the road. This place is exposed to frequent robberies ; nobody, however, approached us. I was glad to see the marks of wheels, and felt great consolation at being again in an inhabited country, being far from thinking of the bad treatment which I received.

On the 3d we discovered, in the distance, a thick mist, which covered all the horizon. I looked in vain for the appearance of the sun ; and perceived at length that what I had taken for mist was a cloud of sand, which continued, without interruption, the whole day. I was obliged to cross it ; we halted ten wersts beyond the canal. My ears, eyes, nose, mouth, and hair were full of sand, and my face was excoriated by the violence of this whirlwind.

Our camels turned away from the wind ; the sand was so

thick that we could not distinguish objects at a small distance. Two hours before sun-set, Seïd made the caravan stop, and alighted to look for shelter in some tents which he perceived. He returned in an hour, and had much trouble to find us again ; he conducted us to these tents, which belonged to Turcomans of the race of Kyryk ; Atan- Niaz-Morghen, their elder, was there.

Of all the Turcomans I ever knew, this was the one I most esteemed. After having settled in the country of Chiva, he had entered into the service of the Khan, as a partisan ; he went every week to pay his respects to the prince, and had but very lately returned when I arrived at his tent. He received me with a kindness which shewed him to be an honest and disinterested man, and took all imaginable pains to procure me rest. He killed his best sheep for me, gave me water to wash, had my food dressed, and sent away all the curious people who assembled to see me.

He told me that the news of my arrival had already reached the Khan, and he advised me not to send a messenger to Chiva, but to go directly to that town, to repair, according to their custom, to the palace of the Khan, announcing myself as his guest, and as an ambassador ; he added, that by conducting myself in this manner, I should certainly be well received. I could not persuade myself that so abrupt an arrival could please the Khan, and thanking my host for his well-meant advice, resolved to act differently. He presented to me his four sons, who were very handsome men ; they showed their horses and long guns, which they had received from the Khan. Atan-Niaz-Merghen was going shortly to send his second son to Astrabad, at the head of thirty men, who had united to go on a plundering expedition.

My worthy host accompanied me on the 4th to the distance of 12 wersts from his residence. There was nothing to mark the road in the steppe we had to pass, except to go between two canals, Dach-goous, and Akh-Saria ; this tract is covered with little hills : the whirlwinds not having ceased, the sand incommoded us more than the day before, and our host himself missed the way. As the wind abated I saw on both sides the ruins of forts and edifices ; the whole tract which I had passed was strewed with pieces of brick and other fragments. At length, after having gone 24 wersts towards the south-east, we perceived, in the evening, the canal Akh-Saraï, near which were many tents, well-cultivated fields, and even trees. We had wished to reach a village where Seïd's relations lived, but were forced to give it up, and to stop at a poor Turcoman hamlet. The inhabitants were a tribe from the confines of

Bucharia. They surrounded and tired me with questions: I thought I had found an excellent means to get rid of them, by frightening them with the name Mohamed-Rahim-Khan, whose guest I said I was. Disregarding this, they refused me admittance, and said they did not know Mohamed-Rahim-Khan: then I raised my voice, on which they immediately retired, and forming a circle at some distance, began conversing together. When I had made my preparations to bivouac in the midst of their tents, one of them came up to me, and offered his habitation, saying he had already cleaned it. I accepted the invitation, and having entered a miserable hut, I began to act as master, and instantly drove out a number of curious people who tired me with their questions. My old host, who had a Chinese countenance, did not know what sort of people he had to do with, and seemed very much surprised when I offered him some tea, instead of turning him and his daughters out of the room. The great number of curious people who came to see me, induced me to order my Turcomans to keep a good watch during the night.

On the 5th, after going 10 wersts by the side of a canal, we arrived at two villages where Seïd's relations lived.

The farther we advanced along the canal, the more culti-vated lands we discovered. The fields covered with rich harvests, struck me by their contrast with those I had passed the day before. I had never seen, even in the heart of Ger-many, fields cultivated with so much care as those of Chiva. All the houses were surrounded with canals crossed by little bridges. I walked in beautiful meadows, in the midst of fruit trees. Numerous birds animated with their song these fine orchards. The tents and the houses of clay, scattered in this enchanting spot, presented the most agreeable prospect, and I rejoiced at having arrived in such a delicious country. I asked my guides why they did not also apply to agriculture, and come and fix their abode in the territory of Chiva, since their own country was not fertile.

" Ambassador," replied they ; " we are the masters ; these are our workmen ; they fear their chief, and we fear none but God."

I was very well received by Seïd's relations, who gave me a small room, which was rather dirty and 'dark : while I was dressing, several elders assembled to congratulate me ; I ad-mitted the principal ones, and having conversed with them, went out to see the others : all received me in the most friend-ly manner. I sent one of the Turcomans to Chiva, to carry the news of my arrival to the Khan, who had not yet quitted the town ; and sent the other for the same purpose to one of the officers of the Khan, who commands the neighbouring fortress of Akh-Serai.

I was very much displeased with the language of the Tur-comans, respecting me, " The Russian ambassador," said they " must be a man out of the common way, since he knows how to read, and at all the wells where we stopped, he marked their depth ; he has also noted the distance from one halting place to another." All this came to the Khan's ears, as we shall soon see, and gave occasion to the sentence of death, which was passed upon me, for they took me to be a spy.

Berdi-Khan, a Turcoman elder, who came from Chiva, called to see me. In 1812, being in the Persian service, he was wounded, and taken prisoner by the Russians. Having served two years under General Lissanevitch, he returned to his own country, and took refuge at Chiva.

After having received from him some information about the Khan, I wanted to go that evening to Chiva, which was only forty wersts distant, but Seïd absolutely refused to yield to my desire. I was angry, and scolded ; he consented to send for horses, but he most likely ordered his messenger, at the same time, not to procure any. I fancy he wanted to detain me, in order to force me, in some measure, to make presents to his relations, or to do a service to the elders, who had brought caravans, and hoped, by joining my suite, that they should get their camels into Chiva without paying duty. They endeavoured to make me understand them, but I seemed not to comprehend their meaning.

The want of horses, obliged me to stop the whole day in this place. I took a walk, followed by a crowd of people. A Turcoman, very well dressed, who served in the Khan's troops, while he was talking with me, began to examine the buttons of my riding coat, to see if they were really silver ; wishing to get rid of him, I asked him if the silver of Chiva, was the same colour as ours ? All who heard me, began to laugh. The Turcoman stepped back, and putting his hand to the hilt of his sword, answered, " Mr. Ambassador, we Tur-" comans are a rude and unpolished nation, we are pardoned " for things of this kind, but we are esteemed for our courage, " and for our swords, which are always at the service of the " Khan." " They will also be at the service of our white " Czar ;" replied I, " as soon as I have succeeded in the " establishment of peace between the two countries." These words appeased him.

I retired to rest rather late, and was already asleep, when I was abruptly informed of the arrival of an officer from Mohamed-Rahim-Khan. Abdoulla, a young man of good ap-

pearance, accompanied by a person advanced in years, entered.
They sat down by my bed side ; the young man inquired in the
name of the Khan, the cause of my coming, and the intentions of my government ; I answered, that I would tell the
Khan himself, or any other person whom he should name ; that
besides, I was the bearer of papers, the contents of which
were unknown to me.   I shewed Abdoulla a sealed letter, and
requested him to convey my answer to the Khan.   " It is
surprising," continued he, " that Ambassadors from the white
Czar should have arrived from different sides ; we have at
Chiva four of these envoys, and it seems that you are likewise
from that Czar."   I endeavoured to persuade him that they
could not be ambassadors, and that they must be deserters,
who had assumed the title ; that they ought to be arrested,
and that if they were impostors, I would have them bound,
and sent back to Russia.   I afterwards learnt that they were
four Nogaïs, who brought a letter to the Khan.   " Are you
used to take tea," asked Abdoulla, " if you are, you may
make some for me."---" We take it in the day time," replied
I, " and as I am unwell and fatigued by my journey, you will
oblige me by leaving me to take some rest, adieu."   He left
me, and I afterwards learnt that he was son of an officer of
the highest rank, who had been in the Khan's service, that
Mohamed had not given him any commission to me, and that
he was brought merely by his curiosity.

The same day, I learned that two Russians, having heard of
the arrival of a corvette on the coast of Turcomania, had fled
the day before my arrival at Akh-Sarai, to try to reach the
sea side, that they had left wives and children, and had been
retaken soon after.   The Chivans have many Russian prisoners,
who are sold to them by the Kirghis, who take them on the
line of Orenburg : they have also Persian and Curd slaves,
whom the Turcomans bring there in great numbers.   They
treat these unhappy people with great rigour.   On the least
suspicion of their intending to escape, they are cruelly
punished, and if they find them transgressing in this respect
for the second time, they nail them by the ear to their door,
and leave them in that dreadful situation for three days ; those
who do not sink under this punishment, continue to vegetate
in the most frightful slavery.

On the 6th, in the morning, some hired horses were brought
me ; but having been invited a moment before they arrived, to
breakfast with one of the elders, I lost two hours, which gave
quite a different turn to my affairs ; for I should have arrived
at Chiva the same day, and the Khan, surprised at my sudden
arrival, would probably have received me well and speedily

dismissed me. I had scarcely gone eight wersts when I met a horseman in full gallop, who came to request me, in the Khan's name, to stop, and wait the arrival of two officers, who had been dispatched to me the night before from Chiva. They soon arrived, attended by four men on horseback : the eldest, who might be about sixty, was a man of low stature, with a long grey beard, and the countenance of a monkey ; he stammered a little, and every word shewed the maliciousness of his character, and his eagerness for money. His name was At-Tchapar-Alla-Verdi. His companion was a robust and a very large man, with a little beard ; he had a noble and frank countenance, which his language did not belie, and with which all his conduct corresponded. His name was Ech-Nezer, and he might be about 30 years of age ; his rank was that of Jous-Bachi, or centurion, which does not mean the commander of a hundred men, but officers to whom the Khan in time of war gives the command of corps of troops, different in number. I learned afterwards, that At-Tchapar was of Astrabad, and of Persian origin ; he had been carried into slavery in his youth, had embraced the law of Suily, and had married. His son, Khodjach-Mehhrem, had rendered the Khan great services in a battle, had become his favourite, and soon was placed at the head of the board of customs ; he afterwards gained the entire confidence of the Khan, and endeavoured to make the fortunes of his father and brothers. The Khan gave many estates and canals to Khodjach Mehhrem, who having increased his property by large acquisitions, was become one of the three richest and most distinguished persons in the country of Chiva. As he had commercial dealings with Astrachan, he had asked the Khan to let him lodge me in his house till my fate was decided. It was probably to receive the presents, in case my affairs turned out well, or to do the Khan the pleasure of strangling me in case this service had been agreeable to his master.

It was probably for this reason that At-Tchapar signified to me the Khan's order to follow him to his estate, Il Gheldi, where every thing was prepared for my reception. We travelled 18 wersts, through a beautiful and populous country, with the exception of a sandy tract between two canals. The weather, which was very serene, permitted me to see. at a great distance, a small fort with a little garden ; this was the fort of Il Gheldi, forming a square, flanked by four towers, the walls built of clay and stones, about three toises and a half high, and twenty-five long. It belonged to Khodjach Mehhrem. At Chiva most rich persons have similar forts, but without embrasures. In the interior they have a small reservoir, some houses, chambers, magazines, and mills, and reserve a place for their cattle. The custom of fortifying houses originates in the troubles which occur on the death of their prince, and generally end in civil war. Even in times of peace the Turcomans frequently pillage the Chivans. These forts contain provisions; each family is at all times able to resist the attacks of a little troop of Turcomans. There were at Il Gheldi about sixty inhabitants, part of them occupied the chambers and others were in tents, placed in the court-yard; they had their wives with them. In the wall opposite the gate there was a tower with a small door leading to the garden, which contained a small muddy reservoir, and a few trees and vines of a good quality. This garden was surrounded by a wall, about ten feet high, against the outside of which the house of a mollah and a mosque were built.

When I arrived at Il Gheldi, I saw Khodjach Mehhrem's brother; he was a young man of prepossessing appearance, and a mild and amiable character. During the first days, my hosts treated me with remarkable attention, Seïd Nezer, bringing me the compliments of the Khan and his elder brother, brought me a tea-kettle, and some sugar and tea; they dressed pillau for me, presented me with several kinds of fruits, and lodged me in a separate room. As the weather was hot, this chamber, though dark, appeared to me supportable, because it was so cool and neat. I walked from time to time in the court-yard, and now and then in the garden. There were sentinels at all the outlets: I at first took them for a guard of honour, but I soon discovered that I was a prisoner. The four Turcomans who accompanied me, received permission to go and see their friends. I had been assured that the Khan would send for me the day after my arrival; but it was already the 7th of October, and nobody appeared. Jakoub, the third son of At-Tchapar, who came that day from Chiva, told me that the Khan would certainly send for me the day following.

On the 8th of October, I received a visit from a certain Jakoub Bey, who spoke a little Russian. He had formerly been a merchant at Astracan; after having dissipated his fortune, he returned to Chiva, and obtained an employment in the custom-house. He came from the Khan to ask who I was, the purpose of my coming, my instructions, and also to demand my papers, that he might give them to the Khan. I refused them positively, saying that I was sent to the Khan alone, and if he would not see me, he had only to send me back; however, added I, you may tell the Khan that I have to deliver presents and two letters, one from the Governor of the country between the Caspian and Black Sea, and the other from Major Ponomarew, who governs one of the provinces under our Sardar. Jakoub Bey rose angrily and left me.

One of my Turcomans had heard that the Khan had left Chiva, and that he would give me audience in a fort near Il Gheldi. I communicated this information to my guards, At-Tchapar, and Jous Bachi, who assured me it was false. I learnt, however, the same evening, that when Jakoub Bey came to see me, the Khan had already left Chiva to go on a hunting party to a Steppe twelve days' journey off. Meantime I was every day treated with more rudeness, and my food diminished; they ceased to give me tea, or wood to dress my meals; they even forbid me to buy provisions, but they afterwards relaxed in this point, because At-Tchapar, who took this upon himself, kept part of the money for himself. I was watched with more strictness, and prohibited from leaving my room, even for a moment, without two guards; they placed sentinels at my door with orders to admit nobody: a man slept across the threshold of the door, so that it was not possible to pass without waking him. My Turcomans learnt from people who frequented the bazar, that after my arrival the Khan had called a council, composed of the first persons in the state, that the debates had been very long, but that the result was not known. A few days after, I learnt from some Turcoman friends of my guides, one of whom was in the service of the Khan, that Mahomet Rahim, having been informed that I had taken notes on the road, considered me as a spy, and said to the council; " The Turcomans who brought him should not have let him enter my dominions; but they ought to have killed him and delivered his presents to me. Since he is come we can do nothing; I desire to know the opinion of the Kazi. ' He is a miscreant,' replied the latter, ' and ought to be carried into the fields and buried alive.' I thought you had more understanding than myself, said the Khan, but I perceive you have none at all. If I kill him, his master, the white Czar, will come next year and carry off the women of my harem; it is better I should receive him, and then send him back; meantime let him remain in prison till I learn from him what brings him here. As for you, withdraw."

In this council some imagined I had come to treat for the ransom of the Russian prisoners; others, that I wished to obtain satisfaction because ten years before two of our vessels had been burnt in the Bay of Balkan, by Turcomans of the tribe of Ata, who after having been expelled from the coasts by the Jomouds, submitted to Mahomet Rahim. Some even thought that the object of my mission was to demand satisfaction for the death of Prince Bekevitch, who was murdered in the year 1717.

They also said that our fleet had approached the coasts of the Turcomans ; that the foundations of a great fort had been laid and it was already half built, and that knowing the route, I should return to Chiva in the following year, at the head of an army. Some of the members of the council fancied that our commander-in-chief, being at war with the Persians, wished to engage the Khan of Chiva to afford him assistance. They even pretended that the Russians had already taken the fort of Akh Kala, near Astrabad. But if their opinions on the motive of my journey were different, they almost all concurred that I ought to be sent to punishment, or be put to death secretly, or be kept in slavery. The Khan himself was much alarmed at my arrival ; but his fears of our government hindered him from putting me to death publicly, however much he was disposed to do it. For this reason he determined to keep me in prison till he had made further inquiries, and had thought of a better means to accomplish his design. They sent persons to sound me respecting the intentions of my government ; but I took care to let nothing transpire. What I heard of the deliberations of the council and the secret designs of the Khan, of course alarmed me ; at first I did not credit it, but the truth of it was fully confirmed by subsequent circumstances.

In this situation I hesitated whether I should submit patiently or attempt to make my escape. However, I determined to resign myself, and as they had left me my arms, I resolved to have them ready, being resolved to sell my life dearly if I should be suddenly attacked. Fortunately I had for my consolation Pope's translation of the Iliad. Every morning I went into the garden to read it, and sometimes forgot my misfortunes.

Thus the time passed on. I perceived indications of the approach of winter. The mornings were cooler, the leaves began to wither and fall from the trees, and reminded me that even if my affairs should end happily, I should in all probability be obliged to give up the idea of returning to my own country, there being every reason to believe that the frost would oblige the corvette to depart and leave me to my fate, in the midst of a ferocious people. My captivity lasted forty-eight days.

I was visited at Il Gheldi by a child, ten years of age, the son of Kodjach Mehhrem, a favourite of the Khan, who liked to play at chess with him ; his father sent me word that he should soon come and see me. I had been so often deceived that I would not believe this messenger. I had always thought that among those who surrounded me, I might induce some to bring me from time to time certain news from Chiva. Having assembled them all and offered what I had to give, I tried to discover which of them I might induce to serve me; not one ventured to speak, for fear of being denounced by one of the witnesses of our conversation. I then thought of a poor Bucharian, named Bey Mahomet, who had left his country seventeen years before to go to Mecca; he remained in this fort, where he gained his livelihood by making girdles. I gave him a pair of scissars, he came secretly to me and gave me all the information he could obtain; though not important, he did me great service, by acquainting me with a dispute which had arisen between Jous Bachi and At-Tchapar on my account. I found that Jous Bachi, a worthy man, was my real keeper, and had been ordered to watch me most strictly. Having invited him one day to come to me, he had been seized with fear and endeavoured to avoid an interview alone. At-Tchapar never let him enter my room without following him immediately, lest I should make him some presents. When I perceived this jealousy I asked At-Tchapar to visit me, and though I had already given him some cloth, I now presented him with some linen, desiring him not to mention it to any body, but particularly not to Jous Bachi. The old rogue concealed the linen under his robe, and fled like a robber, hid his booty and sat down close to Jous Bachi as if nothing had happened. I took the first opportunity of telling this story to Jous Bachi, who laughed heartily at it; in truth, he despised At-Tchapar and all his family. Having succeeded in gaining the confidence of Jous Bachi, I took him alone into the garden, where I had the consolation to hear from him, that though the day was not fixed, he expected every hour that I should be sent for; that when the Khan returned he would probably not go to the chace again, because the people said that he was afraid of the Russian ambassador, not knowing what answer to make him, and fled into the Steppe.

My Turcomans seeing the bad state of my affairs, became less respectful; they sought to avoid me for fear of sharing my fate. When they went to the bazar the people surrounded them, and asked what day was fixed for my execution; they were even asked one day whether the ambassador had not been strangled the night before. The elders advised them to fly, both on account of the danger they might incur in remaining with me, and partly because the Khan was very angry at their not having yet paid the tribute he had imposed on the caravans. Seïd too grew insolent; and upon one occasion, when I reprimanded him, he rose, and said " Adieu, Mourad Bey: I have served you till this day, but if you choose to treat me in such a manner, I shall leave you." He again said

" Adieu !" and went out.   I called him back : he looked as if he expected some apology from me, but I said,—" Seïd, depart: you see my unfortunate situation ; it is possible you may share my fate.   Return to your family, and tell Kiat-Aga, who ordered you to accompany me, that you have abandoned me : but learn, also, that as long as I have these arms, I fear neither you nor any man : Adieu ! do not return."   This reply confounded him ; he sat down, reflected, shed tears, asked my pardon, and vowed that he never would forsake me, but share my fate ;   I was reconciled to him.

At-Tchapar had seven Russian prisoners, one of whom, named David, lived at Il Gheldi.   He had been made prisoner at the age of 14, and had been sixteen years in slavery.   He had served several masters, and though he had adopted the manners and customs of the Chivans, he refused to change his religion.   Having one day met Petrovich, he desired him to ask me to try to take him home with me.   I endeavoured to see him, but had very few opportunities.   I asked him to enquire of the Russians who came from Chiva, what passed there, and what was said of me.   His accounts, as well as those of sixteen Persian slaves at Il Gheldi, confirmed the truth of the reports of the deliberations of the Council.   Having been some time without seeing David, I found means to let him know that I wished to see him in the night ; though it was forbidden, under pain of death, to hold communication with me, he came at midnight, and told me what I had already heard from the Turcomans ; he also gave me much information respecting the situation of the Russian prisoners, and I dismissed him with the present of a ducat.

The prisoners are chiefly taken by the Kirghis on the line of Orenburg ; they sell them at Chiva, and it is said there are as many in Bucharia as in Chiva.   The number of Russian slaves at Chiva is estimated at 3000, and that of the Persians at 30,000.   The Chivans force the Persians to renounce their Faith, but they do not compel the Russians.   David assured me that they had a separate room, where they placed the images of their Saints, and that they go there at night to say their prayers.   Their masters allowing them to walk about during the two great festivals, they take the opportunity to meet, and get intoxicated with the brandy which they distil from the fruit of the country ; these festivals generally end in some murder.

· Though the masters have a right to kill their slaves, they seldom exercise it, not to lose a 'labourer ; to punish them they put out an eye, or cut off one of their ears.   One day At-Tchapar was going, in my presence, to cut off one of David's ears, because, on his way to Chiva, he had stabbed, with a knife, a Persian slave, with whom he had a quarrel. He began by striking him across the face with his whip, and afterwards seizing his knife, he desired Sergum to throw David down, that he might the more easily execute his intention. His clerk, Ouzbek Mahomet Aga, prevented him. I took care not to interfere, and retired for fear I should injure poor David. The following night he came to me and said,—" Sir, you have seen how I was beaten ; that dog was going to cut off my ear ; yesterday evening his son gave me 500 blows with his whip; but towards these dogs it is necessary to behave in this manner, that is to say, boldly ; though they have beaten me, they are afraid of me ; you should see how they all run away from me when I am drunk !"

On the 20th of October, we were visited by Seïd Nazar, of Ourghendi, who came to see me several times. I do not know whether he suspected me of intending to escape ; but when I asked him if the Khan would soon return, he replied vehemently, " do you think of escaping ? venture to make the trial, and you will see what will be done with you." These words vexed me much, but that he might not discover the intention I really entertained of flying, I answered, that he was mistaken, and that an Ambassador never took flight, because his Sovereign was answerable for his inviolability. This circumstance made me suspect that they had some idea of my project ; I went into the garden to examine the walls, and found that a ladder had been removed, upon which I had placed much reliance. I complained to Jous Bachi, of the rude language of Seïd Nazar, adding, that to begin with At-Tchapar, an old man, whose grey beard ought to inspire respect, the whole family appeared to me contemptible. " Certainly, replied Jous Bachi, his beard proves nothing, for goats too have long beards."

On the 21st of October, I received a visit from Hekim-Ali-Bey, who assured me of his attachment, and told me that he was preparing to fly from Chiva with his caravan. " The eyes of the Khan are full of blood said he ; formerly every one had access to him ; at present, he wont listen to any body, demands of us enormous duties for the caravans which arrive, and in this manner, he shuts us entirely from Chiva, has us hung, impaled, &c."

In fact, the Khan frequently punishes Turcomans who inhabit his dominions, for thefts or other crimes ; it is the only means by which he has succeeded in establishing tranquillity in his kingdom. Five Turcomans were hanged while I was there.

Hekim-Ali-Bey asked me for a letter to major Ponomarew; being afraid of trusting him with one, I gave him a medal of Julius Cæsar, which he was to deliver to father Timothy, chaplain of the corvette, begging him to place, in my name, a taper before an image. "This is customary with us," said I, "however, do not suppose that I mean to make a secret of it, on the contrary, you may tell it to whom you please." Every body on board the corvette knew that I possessed this medal, and I sent it that they might know that I was still alive. "Forget what has passed," said Hekim-Ali-Bey, rising; "and at your return, do not say, that I have treated you with Turcoman unpoliteness." However rigorously the Turcomans were forbidden to come to me, they always found means to speak to me; I wished to see some of them, but the greater part only disturbed me.

At length, the Khan returned from his hunting party on the 23d, and every body then gave me hopes, that he would soon send for me. Five days, however, passed, and I was still watched with the same strictness; when seeing that I had no means to escape from this cruel slavery, I had recourse to threats; I therefore repeatedly addressed my keepers, desiring them to tell the Khan in my name, that winter was at hand, that the corvette was in danger of being frozen in, and of perishing in the bay of Balkan, because it could not set sail without me. I added, that if it met with any accident, the Khan would be answerable to the emperor of Russia. None of my keepers would charge himself with this message to the Khan. Three of my Turcomans, perceiving that my affairs went on badly, began to refuse to obey me, one of them even demanded his discharge. I gave it him, and left him to repent as well as Seïd.

On the 31st, I sent for At-Tchapar and Jous-Bachi, that they might inform me of the Khan's intentions; I again begged them to acquaint him with the situation of the corvette, and of the responsibility which he would incur; they persuaded me to have patience for one day, to wait the arrival of Khodjach-Mehhrem, whom they expected every hour. Their irresolution made me think of sending Petrovitch or Seïd to Chiva, but they would not permit it.

On the 4th of November, I learnt from a Turcoman, that Jomoud-Nias-Batyr, had come from Krasnovodsk, and had arrived at Chiva, and had brought two letters from major Ponomarew, one for the Khan, and the other for me. On the 6th, at day break, I secretly sent Koultchi to look for Nias-Batyr, and to demand my letter; he came himself the next day, bringing me the compliments of the Khan, and delivered me by his order, the letter from major Ponomarew. Nias-Batyr told me that the Khan had expressed much pleasure at seeing him. "Mahomet-Rahim," continued Nias, " has been deceived by some Turcomans, who assured him that the Russians were building a fort on the coast; I have undeceived him, and as a mark of his favourable disposition towards you, he has ordered me to deliver this letter personally, and to request you to have patience, because he has resolved to send for you shortly. All on board the corvette are well, they amuse themselves, and are waiting for you. I am come to be your deliverer, for without me you might have passed all your life in this fortress." He added much more, and though I had not much confidence in him, I treated him as well as I could, and on that day, my old friend At-Tchapar took more pains, and spent more money for me, than he had done in a whole week.

The letter from major Ponomarew contained nothing important; he hoped I should be back by the 8th of November. I made a considerable present to Nias-Batyr, telling him that as I did not wish to conceal any thing from the Khan, I requested him to deliver my letter to him, that he might read it. Nias-Batyr vowed that the Khan would certainly send for me in two days. He passed the night with me.

Though I had no reason to give full credit to Nias, yet, from the weakness which induces the unfortunate to catch at the slightest hope, all this news filled me with joy, and the following day I invited all the relations of my Turcomans. I bought two sheep and millet, and had large dishes of pillau prepared, to regale my hosts as well as I could. I did not forget the inhabitants of the fortress, and joy entered, for the first time, into this gloomy abode. The famished slaves and Turcomans greedily devoured the portions given them. The entertainment being over, I let Nias-Batyr go, putting him in mind that he had promised to give me constant information.

Koutchi, who had been sent to Chiva to look for Nias-Batyr, returned in the evening. He had seen some Turcomans hung, and was in great terror. On the evening of the 9th, Nias came back; he had met the Khan at Maï-Djenghil, where he was gone on a hunting party, which was to last two days. He again protested his attachment, and set out on the 10th for Chiva.

However, I did not receive any messages from the Khan. David informed me that the Prince was making preparations for my reception, and that he had even ordered garments which were intended for presents; he added, that there would be in my room a door, secured by a lock, behind which a Russian would be stationed to listen ; and lastly, that I should be sent away with honor.   Being unable to believe all this news, I entreated Jous-Bachi to tell me whether I was to pass the winter at Chiva, or whether I should be sent home, that I might take my measures accordingly.   "Not to deceive you," said he, I will frankly own that I know nothing about it ; yet I think you may expect very shortly to receive the invitation you desire."   I repeated to him my constant request, that he would go himself to the Khan, and represent to him the dangerous situation of the corvette.   "If nobody comes from Chiva between this and to-morrow, I will certainly go," said he.   Three days passed, yet he did not set out.   I represented to him that he had nothing to fear, since, according to the report of Nias-Batyr, the Khan was perfectly well-disposed towards me, and that, besides, the blame of such a step could fall only upon me.   "You have chosen to deceive yourself," said he, "and I have not thought proper to undeceive you by blackening a man whom you have thought worthy of your confidence ; I will now tell you, that Nias-Batyr is a rogue without any conscience."   These accusations seemed probable, because Nias not only did not send me any intelligence, as he had promised, but even tried to cheat me in purchases which he had undertaken to make for me.

At length on the 14th, Jous-Bachi, who for some reason unknown to me, violently quarrelled with At-Tchapar, came and told me that he was immediately going to Chiva, in order to inform the Khan of the shameful manner in which I was treated, and of the situation of the corvette.   He added, that without regarding the danger which he might incur himself, he was resolved to declare to the Khan, in my name, that if the vessel suffered any injury, he would be responsible to the Emperor of Russia ; and that if he was resolved to keep me he had better send away the corvette.   The Khan was to set out again in three days for the Steppes, where he intended to hunt for three months ; he had already sent his hunting apparatus and his tents.   "If I succeed you will see me again to-morrow afternoon," said he.   He did not, however, return at the time appointed, I was therefore persuaded that he had been punished for the boldness of his declaration, or that my affairs had taken a bad turn, and I again returned to my old plan of escaping.   I had never made any overtures on the subject except to Petrovitch, fearing to trust Seïd.   However, as it was absolutely necessary for him to be in the secret, I sent for him, and after some conversation contrived to bring him to make me the proposal of escape: I at first pretended to disapprove this design, and then to yield to his arguments; so that we had only to provide means for the execution.

Having concerted our measures, Seïd left me on the morning of the 16th, to make some necessary purchases, after which he was to return, and then go in the evening to his village to provide horses, with which he was to wait for me under the walls of the fort. Meantime, I and Petrovitch examined the fort and garden, to find the best method of escaping from it. Noon passed, and I had seen neither Jous-Bachi nor Seïd; plunged in melancholy reflections, I sat down in a corner, waiting the decision of my fate, when Seïd arrived, and sat down by me; and being questioned as to the cause of his delay, said, " that he had considered that man was governed by destiny, and that if we took flight, destiny would punish us for having disobeyed it." I was angry, and asked him whether he had purchased what was necessary? " I have bought nothing, (said he,) there is your money." I had given him ten ducats, which he had exchanged for silver, and had brought me back the value of eight ducats, saying that the rest had served to pay the agio.

Perceiving myself entirely at the mercy of Seïd, I remained lost in thought, not knowing what to determine. My affliction moved Seïd, who begged my pardon, weeping like a child, assuring me that he would prepare every thing necessary for our flight the next day. All at once Koultchi came running in with the news that Jous-Bachi was arrived. The latter entered, and joyfully congratulated me, saying, " The Khan desires to see you; we shall go to him to-morrow morning: he was angry that I had quitted my post, but when I detailed all the particulars, when I spoke to him of the situation of the corvette, and of the inevitable responsibility to which he exposed himself in thus detaining an ambassador, he has resolved to send for you, and to receive you in a becoming manner." I thanked Jous-Bachi, and made him a present by way of acknowledgement; and the evening after receiving this good news was the gayest of the forty-eight I spent at Il Gheldi. My Turcomans were again respectful; the rude, insupportable At-Tchapar became extremely civil, and had even the meanness to ask me not to tell any body of my bad fare during the time I lived at his house.

During the night I sent to a neighbouring village to hire some horses; the report of the good intentions of the Khan towards me, spread so rapidly, that on the following morning, a crowd assembled to congratulate me, attracted by the hope of receiving some present, or of joining my suite, and

feasting upon pillau and tea, all the time I should be at
Chiva.   Before I left Il Gheldi, I ordered Petrovitch to distribute some money among the inhabitants, and particularly to
give a piece to each of the servants or slaves, who had endeavoured to do me service.

. The distance to Chiva was thirty-five wersts, in a north-
easterly direction, across two sandy steppes, intersected by
canals, on the sides of which were large villages and gardens.
The water is conducted to them with so much skill that at
one place I saw a canal over which a bridge passed, supporting
another canal, and this again had a bridge across it, over
which we passed.   At five wersts from Chiva, the eye ranges
over an infinite number of gardens with narrow lanes between them, sprinkled with forts, which are the residence of
the wealthy inhabitants.   The view of the town is very agreeable; above the high wall which surrounds it, the vast domes
of the mosques rise, surmounted by golden balls, and painted
of an azure colour, which forms an agreeable contrast with the
verdure of the gardens.   When we came to a place where the
road was crossed by a narrow canal with a very handsome
bridge over it, I found numerous groups of people attracted
by curiosity; they accompanied me as far as the habitation
prepared for me; and when I entered the narrow streets of
Chiva, the crowd became so considerable, that it was impossible to pass through it; the people stifled themselves,
and fell under the feet of our horses.   Jous Bachi was obliged
to use force in order to make a passage for us; it was with
deep affliction that among the spectators, who were attracted
by mere curiosity, I recognzied some unhappy Russians, who
took off their caps, and begged me in a low voice to save them.

After going about half a werst through the narrow streets,
we at length stopped before a house, the outside of which had
a pretty good appearance.   Jous-Bachi introduced me into a
court-yard very clean and paved; this led to the apartments,
one of the largest of which was assigned to me, and a smaller
one to the Turcomans.   My chamber was very well furnished,
in the Oriental style, with magnificent carpets; a vain advantage which was no indemnity for the insupportable cold.   As
the crowd had followed me as far as my residence, Jous-Bachi
drove them away, and went to announce my arrival to the
Khan.   During his absence the people again collected, so that
quarrels arose at the door, and the passage across the court-
yard was completely obstructed.   The Khan's servants, who
had been placed to maintain order, could not drive away this
immense crowd.   Jous Bachi, as soon as he returned, rid me
of them by employing force.   The gates and all the avenues

were secured by good locks ; nobody was left with me except my guards, who did not dare to enter my room without being desired.

Jous-Bachi congratulated me in the name of the Khan on my arrival, and informed me that I was the guest of Mekhter Aga Joussouf, first vizier to the Khan. Soon afterwards, they gave me a cook, and besides what was prepared for my table at home, the vizier sent me enormous dishes of all kinds of food, besides sugar, tea, and fruits. The politeness with which they treated me was not natural to this people ; but in the midst of this parade, which lasted five days, they did not cease for a moment to keep a strict watch over me.

On the evening of my arrival, Khodjach-Mehhrem came to see me for the first time. He was a crafty man, but very agreeable in his manners : we had an hour's conversation, which passed in reciprocal compliments ; among other things he asked me to permit him to apply to the Khan for the favour of being entrusted with all the affairs of the embassy. I replied that I had not the right to prescribe their duty to the officers of the Khan. He succeeded in settling every thing the same evening, and came to let me know that the Khan had honoured him with this employment ; he then asked me in his name for the letters and presents I had brought for him ; but I would not consent till Jous-Bachi had assured me of the truth of it. However, I gave him only the letters ; in the course of the night he came to ask for the presents. I did not think this unseasonable, when I found that the Khan slept during the day-time, and attended to his affairs during the night. Jous-Bachi advised me to seal up what I sent, lest Khodjach and his brethren at the custom-house might appropriate the most valuable articles to themselves. I placed upon a plateau, cloth, damask, and other things, and having wrapped them up in a piece of linen, gave them to Khodjach, who was followed by his people, and carried them away in a mysterious manner. I ordered Petrovitch to accompany him. Two hours already passed, and the latter not returning, I began to fear that he had met with some accident, when he suddenly entered with a great noise, dressed from head to foot like an Usbeck. Throwing off the great cap which formed part of his costume, and the kaftan in which he was muffled up, he swore that he would never again execute such a commission ; he told me that he had been left to wait in a passage, and that at last Khodjach had come and taken off the dress he wore, and in the name of the Khan gave him another, and dismissed him. The next day, At-Tchapar, Khodjach's father, desired him to return the dress. Mekhta Aga, the president of the council, asked for the plateaus which had been borrowed to put the presents on : I told Jous-Bachi to return them. He answered me that the owner would never see them again, for that the Khan was a powerful man, and never returned any thing that once fell into his hands.

Among the presents there was a plateau, with ten pounds of lead, an equal quantity of powder, and ten gun flints. The Khan spent the whole night in examining what had been sent. He was astonished at the weight of this plateau; when he lifted it up, he asked Jous-Bachi, if it did not contain the ducats which he expected; he immediately unsealed the linen envelope, and was greatly disconcerted at not finding what he expected. It seems that the meaning of the presents upon the plateau, was explained by them in the following manner; two sugar loaves placed with the lead and powder, signified according to them, propositions of pure and kind friendship, and in case the Khan did not consent to it, the powder and lead were equivalent to a declaration of war.

The Khan would not yet receive me ; on the 18th, I intended to send some presents to his elder brother, Koutli-Mourad-Inakh. I was told that I could not do it without the express permission of the Khan ; Jous-Bachi obtained it for me, and in the night, I charged Petrovitch to carry him some cloth, damask, sugar, and other trifles. Petrovitch was not admitted into the presence of this personage, but he sent him five tilla in gold. Among the presents I had sent him, there was a small dressing case, which contained a tin box, with a piece of black soap in it. Inakh, in examining all the articles one after the other, saw this piece of soap, which excited his suspicions, because he could not conceive what it might be. He asked his physician, who knew no more about it than himself; they sent to me to ask what it was ; having forgotten what the case contained, I begged them to send it me for a moment, that I might explain it to them : this they refused to do, and when I desired that they would only shew me the single article which embarrassed them, they would still not consent. " Do not expect to see any thing again, said Jous-Bachi, our Inakh is as tenacious as the Khan ; what he once has he never returns ; but I fancy it is a piece of soap, and I will make him easy."

The same evening, I recollected that there were ten glasses which I had forgotten to send to the Khan ; I therefore begged Jous-Bachi to carry them to him, and to make an apology in my name for having omitted them. " That is of no consequence," said he, " our Khan takes every thing, the only difficulty is to get something from him. Glass is very rare among ns; I am sure they will please him, but you must not send ten, because that number among us, is considered unlucky; it will be sufficient to send nine." He immediately left me with the glasses; he returned after midnight, and told me that the Khan had been very much satisfied, that he examined them all one after another exclaiming, " What a pity that they were not sent me when I drank brandy." He had formerly drank it habitually, but had since given it up as well as smoking, which he also prohibited to his subjects, under penalty of having the mouth slit open as far as the ears. This prohibition is not always strictly observed: the Khan knows that several persons about him smoke, and he pretends not to perceive it.---Most of the Chivans, instead of tobacco, smoke hemp; it is very unwholesome, and causes those who are not accustomed to it, to faint.

Among the presents sent to the Khan, there was one of the glass vases through which the Persians make the smoke of their pipe pass. The Khan very much astonished, asked Jous-Bachi, what it was; the latter, who did not dare to tell him, told him that it was a vase to keep vinegar in, of which the Khan is very fond. A burning glass which I had much surprised the Chivans. Several came to me merely to see it; they pretended that glass could not possess so marvellous a quality, and that it must be rock crystal.

As I was closely guarded, and nobody ventured to come and see me without permission, I recollected that while at Il Gheldi, David had told me that, when I should come to Chiva, a Russian would be placed at one of the doors in my room, to listen to my conversation. On examining my apartment, I really found this door; it was locked; it was easy to perceive that somebody was stationed on the other side. I sat down purposely near the door, and conversed in a loud voice, with my interpreter, in Russian, on the military qualities of Mahomet-Rahim-Khan, his strength, the superiority of the people of Chiva, over the Persians, &c.---I was listened to for three days, and my discourses were faithfully reported to the prince. During this time, notwithstanding the attentions paid me, the time hung heavily on my hands, because I was not at liberty; and I feared that the Khan would set out for the hunting party which was to last three months, and for which I knew every preparation had been made.

The first minister and my keepers carried their attention so far that, seeing my ennui, they brought to me one Molla Seide, a man about forty years of age, witty, and as amiable as an European; I never met any person who played chess so well. Molla Seide lived upon the presents of the first officers of

Chiva, with whom he spent the evening playing chess, reading, reciting verses extempore, and telling stories. He was versed in the Arabian, Persian, and Turkish languages; expressed himself in a very clear and agreeable manner; was acquainted with the ancient history of the east, recited with animation passages from it, which he mingled with extracts from the best poets. He told me jokingly, that he had a country-house which he had not entered for fourteen years, and that during this time he had always passed the night at the house of some one of the most distinguished inhabitants of Chiva; complaining of the present times, he thought the Khan excessively severe, because he had prohibited the use of brandy and hemp for smoking. He remained with me till two o'clock in the morning.

On the evening of the 20th of November, Khodjach sent Seïd Nézer to inform me that I was expected by the Khan. I dressed myself in full uniform, retaining the Chivan cap; but lest some of the Russians about the Khan should recognise the branch of the service to which I belonged, I took off my embroidered collar and put on one of plain scarlet. Jous-Bachi told me that according to their customs I could not retain my sabre in the presence of the Khan; however, as I was resolved to keep it, I begged him to let the Khan know. "You will spoil every thing by that," said he; "the Khan is at present in a good humour, I will rather tell him that you do not wear a sabre, but a large knife," (instead of a sabre I had a large Tcherkessan dagger.) He left me and soon returned, saying, that the Khan had told him to request me to come without arms, merely not to break through their customs. I consented to take this request into consideration, in order to terminate my mission as soon as possible.

Jous-Bachi and the officers of my guard opened the procession; some jessaouls, with long canes, kept back the people who crowded about us, the roofs were covered with spectators; I again heard the complaints of some of my countrymen, who were mingled in the crowd. In this manner I walked about a quarter of a werst through narrow streets to the gate of the Khan's palace, where I was left till he was informed of my arrival; soon afterwards I was invited to enter. The gateway is built with bricks and in good taste; I was first introduced into a small sanded court, surrounded by dirty clay walls, round which sixty-three Kirghis envoys were sitting, who had come to pay their respects to the Khan; they were to go away after having taken part in an entertainment, and each received a piece of coarse cloth to make a kaftan.

The second court, a little smaller than the first, contained the Khan's arsenal; there are seven cannons upon their carriages, resembling ours; they were placed one upon the other in very bad order, the wheels were broken; I was particularly desired to notice them. I entered the third court where the council assembles, and then into a passage, at the entrance of which were some of the Khan's servants; it was covered with reeds, the walls were of clay, the ground dirty and uneven; I went down a few steps into the fourth court, which is much larger than the other three, but dirtier; plants climbed up the walls; in the middle of it was the Khan's tent.

While I was going down some steps I saw a man come towards me in a dirty garment, whom, by his slit nostrils, I recognized to be a criminal escaped from Siberia; he got hold of my scarf behind, and wanted to lead me. It immediately occurred to me that I had been deceived and brought to this place, not to be presented to the Khan, but to be put to death, and that this was the reason they had disarmed me, under pretence of their customs. I turned round angrily and asked him, why he had laid hold of my scarf; he instantly drew back with a threatening posture; Jous-Bachi approached me, saying, that according to their customs an ambassador ought to be led into the presence of the Khan. The Russian again advanced, but not venturing to take hold of the scarf, he walked behind me holding up his hand.

I stopped before the tent where the Khan was seated, dressed in a robe made of the red cloth with which I had presented him, fastened over the breast with a silver clasp. He wore a turban with a white band, and sat without moving, upon a Korassan carpet. At the entrance of the tent Khodjach Mehhrem was on the one side, and on the other Jossouf Mekhter Aga, an old man, whom I saw for the first time. The Khan, though rather corpulent, has an agreeable appearance. They say that he is six feet and a half high, and that his horse cannot carry him for more than two hours together; his beard is thin and of a light colour; he has a pleasing voice, and speaks with purity, ease, and a certain degree of dignity. Standing before him I saluted him without taking off my cap, and not to infringe their customs, I waited till he had spoken. In a few minutes one of the persons nearest him made the following prayer: " God preserve this state for the advantage and glory of its sovereign." The Khan then passed his hand over his beard, as well as the two persons who were present at the audience. Jous-Bachi kept at some distance; the prince then addressed me, saying, welcome. He then added, " Ambassador, why are you come, and what have you to ask me ?" I replied; " The very happy Russian Commander-in-Chief of the country situated between the Black and Caspian Sea, having under his government Tiflis, Ganja, Georgia, Karabag, Chouchia, Moukhia, Cheki, Chirwan, Bakou, Kouba, Lezghistan, Derbend, Astracan, Caucasus, Lenkoran, Salian, and all the forts and states taken by the imperial arms from the Kadjares, (Persians) has sent me to your highness to testify his respect, and present to you a letter written in a favourable moment.

The Khan. I have read his letter.

The Ambassador. He has also intrusted to me some presents for your Highness, which I have already had the happiness of delivering. I am also ordered to converse with you upon some other subjects, and wait for your decision to speak of them ; when do you consent to hear me ? now, or at another time ?

The Khan. Speak now.

The Ambassador. Our Commander-in-Chief desiring to form an intimate friendship with your Highness, would be happy to have frequent correspondence with you. For this purpose it will be necessary to consolidate the commerce between our people and your's, and to make it advantageous to both. Your caravans going to Manghichlak, have to travel thirty days through a steppe destitute of water ; and the obstacles which occur on this road are the cause that our commercial intercourse has hitherto been inconsiderable. The Commander-in-chief would wish that these caravans should come to the port of Krasnovodsk, situate in the bay of Balkan ; this new route is no more than seventeen days' journey, and your merchants will always find at Krasnovodsk ships from Astracan, with the merchandize and other things sought for by your people.

The Khan. Though the road by Manghichlak is in truth much longer than that by Krasnovodsk, the people of Manghichlak are submissive to me ; the Jomouds of the coast living at Astrabad chiefly obey the Kadjares, and consequently my caravans would run the risk of being plundered by those hordes ; I cannot, therefore, consent to this change.

The Ambassador. When you are our ally, your enemies will be ours. I afterwards added, " The glory of your Highness's arms is well known to me ; but what do you order me to reply to our Commander-in-chief, who desires your friendship ? he begs you through me to send him a confidential person who may assure you of his friendly intentions. Immediately on my return to my country, I shall be sent to His Majesty the Emperor, to give an account of the reception you have given me, and deliver your Highness's answer.

The Khan. I shall send with you some good men, such as are desired, and give them a letter for the Commander-in-Chief; I am myself desirous to see a true and indissoluble friendship established between us. Farewell!

I accordingly bowed and retired. I was conducted back to the third court, followed by Khodjach and Mekhter-Aga, and several dishes with sugar and fruit were brought to me; during the half hour that I remained here, Mekhter Aga asked me for information respecting the relations between Russia and Persia, and of the state of our forces in Georgia. I replied that we had there an army of about 60,000 regular troops, and that besides we could raise among the inhabitants as many corps of cavalry as we pleased, composed of the best partizans. Jous-Bachi rejoined us, followed by a man carrying a robe of cloth of gold which the Khan gave me; when I had put it on they girded me with a rich scarf of cloth of gold of India, in which they placed a dagger with a silver sheath; they then muffled me up in a kind of surplice, with short sleeves of cloth of gold of Russia. They exchanged my cap for a worse, of which the Khan made me a present, and then again conducted me to his tent. The same ceremony was observed; the Khan ordered every thing I had said before to be repeated, and he made the same answers. " Khan," continued I, " tell me how I have merited the kindness which you have shewn me ? I should esteem myself happy if I could return to you next year to assure you of the friendship of our Commander-in-Chief." " You will return if you are sent," answered he; " you will place my ambassadors entirely at the disposal of the Commander-in-Chief; if he pleases he may even send them to the Emperor."

I crossed the courts to return to the outer gate, where they had ready for me a beautiful grey horse of the Turcoman breed. They set me upon it, and my Turcomans ranged themselves on both sides to lead it by the bridle; two placed themselves at the stirrups. There was so great a crowd, that Petrovitch, who was on foot, could not follow me. While I was speaking to the Khan, I had affected to elevate my voice, and to shew great assurance; it seemed strange to those who surrounded him, who were accustomed to slavery and meanness; and they looked at me with an air of displeasure during the whole audience. The crowd accompanied me as far as my residence. Khodjach arrived with some robes of cloth for my people. Seïd was very much displeased at their giving him a red dress of coarse cloth like that of his companions; he had a great mind to refuse it, but he had not the courage. Khodjach communicated the different commissions which the

Khan had given him for me. He told me that Mahomet had a cannon-founder, who had come from Constantinople, and that within these few days he had ordered him to cast a seventy-pounder.

There too they informed me that I was free, and that I might return; they took all my domestics from me; when left alone I was surrounded by such a crowd of curious people that, but for the assistance of Jous-Bachi, I should have had much trouble in getting rid of them. It would even have been difficult for me to leave Chiva without his aid, as I had neither horses, nor anything that I wanted. This want of horses obliged me to pass another night at Chiva, very well pleased at the happy termination of my mission. After my return from the Khan, I sent to ask his permission to make presents to the three most distinguished persons in the country; namely, Mekhter-Aga, and Kouch Bey, who was absent from the capital, and Khodjach Mehhrem. I sent each of them a piece of cloth, some silks, and a watch. Notwithstanding all my endeavours, I could not see Sultan-Khan, who in 1813 had reconciled three Turcoman tribes, to make them act against Persia.

As for the rest of the presents, I requested Jous-Bachi to distribute them according to the importance of the persons who received them. In the distribution which he made, he forgot a glass smoking vessel, for which he had an extreme desire; he told me to pull my cap over my eyes, and to think of the person who was most deserving of this present; of course it could be no other than himself. At-Tchapar also tormented me to obtain something; I gave him a small remnant of cloth. He seemed greatly dissatisfied, and went away in anger, and did not shew himself again. I learnt that Khodjach Mehhrem had presented to the Khan enormous bills for my board at Il Gheldi; they amounted to thirty-two francs daily; his father, At-Tchapar, also demanded sixteen francs daily.

RETURN.

I HAD intended to leave Chiva on the 21st of November, very early in the morning, for Il Gheldi, where I was to wait for the arrival of the ambassadors appointed by the Khan; they were Jous-Bachi, Ech Nezer, and Jakoub Bey, whom I have already mentioned. This man could read and write, was very crafty, and somewhat malicious. But I was detained at

Chiva till dinner-time, by the ambassadors, who had received orders from the Khan to entertain me, and they regaled me with some bad cold pillau. During this time Jous-Bachi went to the bazaar to make different purchases for me ; at length, all being ready, and the horses saddled, I recollected that the lock of my two-barrelled gun was out of repair, and begged them to bring me a gun-smith ; a young man with a fair complexion, and handsome countenance, and dressed in a turban, came to me. His physiognomy immediately betrayed his origin. I asked him in Russian if he spoke that language ? No, replied he in Turkish, and taking the lock continued the conversation, sometimes in Persian, and sometimes in Turkish ; he had very easy manners, and after having examined what was the matter with the lock, he ran home with the gun. I learnt from others that his father, who was a Russian, had been taken prisoner, and sold at Chiva. Having embraced the Mahometan faith, he married a Persian slave, and they had this son, who had studied with so much success, that he had been raised to the dignity of Mollah ; he was able to support his parents by his labour, and had even redeemed them from captivity. I was just setting out, when the young man returned out of breath with my gun, but very indifferently mended, and some dozens of eggs and white loaves ; I gave him a ducat, and spoke to him no more in Russian for fear of embarrassing him ; I gave the gun to Jous-Bachi, begging him to examine it, and if he found it in a bad condition, to have it repaired and brought to me at Il Gheldi.

A Russian bringing me a horse, uttered in a low voice abuse of the Chivans on account of the difficulties they made to procure me horses. Going through Chiva, I saw in several places, some of my unhappy countrymen in separate groups, they saluted me, calling me their deliverer. One of them for a long time walked close to my horse, and on my turning to him, he said " Accept, Sir, the assurance of my profoundest respect, and when you return to your country, do not forget your unhappy countrymen." This man seemed to be above the lower class. As I was leaving the city, the people collecting in a crowd ; I ordered my interpreter to throw among them two handsful of small coin ; this produced disputes, of which we availed ourselves to proceed.

To my great regret, Petrovitch perceived at ten wersts from Il Gheldi that he had lost a little purse containing 300 ducats, with which I had intrusted him ; he wept bitterly, and appeared overwhelmed with despair ; I had much trouble in learning the cause of his affliction. Very fortunately Seïd found this purse ; Petrovitch seizing it with transport, shed tears of joy; I was no less pleased than he, for it would have been impossible for us to reach the corvette, if we had not sufficient money to pay the expense of the journey.---Seïd begged Jous-Bachi to obtain from the Khan an order, not to pay the duty for seventeen camels; I attempted in vain to dissuade him from making this request, and I was obliged to tell Jous-Bachi not to meddle in an affair of this kind: nevertheless, the Khan exempted Seïd and his companions from the duty on camels; I afterwards gave him money to buy grain.

I arrived at Il Gheldi at 11 o'clock at night, in a severe frost. David came a good way to meet me; and the Bucharian Moulla-Bey-Mohamed, and in general, all the inhabitants of the fort, rejoiced at the happy issue of my affairs, and congratulated me on my return. The good reception given me by the Khan, had raised me in the general estimation; the persons whom curiosity brought to see me, retired without hesitation as soon as I chose to dismiss them. My Turcomans had become very docile, and had acquired a degree of politeness, with which my visitors had reason to be contented. I was particularly satisfied with Aboul Hussein, and Koultchi, whom I had promised to take to the commander-in-chief, as ambassadors from the Turcomans. As it froze hard, I provided myself with sheep-skin cloaks, coverings for the legs, and large Chivan boots; and a Kirghis cap to wear at night. I bought mutton and millet, and some small Russian horses, which are common at Chiva. I put my arms in order, except my double-barreled gun, which the Russian at Chiva had spoiled: it, however, did me a great service. It was brought to me at Il Gheldi, three or four days after my return from Chiva. As I was setting out, I was going to load it; one of the barrels would not let the air pass when I blew into it; I ordered it to be cleaned, and a paper rolled up, was taken out; I opened it when I was alone, and read as follows:

"Most noble Sir, we take the liberty to inform you, that there are in this country 3000 Russian prisoners, who have to endure hunger, cold, and the insupportable labour imposed on them, as well as all kinds of insults: take pity on our unhappy situation, and lay it before His Majesty the emperor. Give a poor prisoner cause, eternally to pray to God for you."

It would be difficult to describe what I felt in reading this note; it made me the more sensible of the gratitude which I owed to Providence, for having delivered me from the danger; but, at the same time, my head was oppressed at the idea of leaving my unhappy countrymen in a rigorous captivity, without my being able to afford them any assistance. I resolved that as soon as I returned, I would do every thing to deliver them. This duty I have performed; our government has been made acquainted with the existence of these unhappy men, and will, doubtless, take all the necessary means to afford them deliverance. David brought to me another of my unfortunate countrymen, an old man, named Joseph Melnikow, who had been thirty years a captive. He was the son of a soldier, and was made prisoner by the Kirghis a week after his marriage; they sold him at Chiva. By working during the night and saving a part of his allowance, he had been able to make up the sum which his master required for his ransom; but the latter took his money, and instead of restoring him to liberty, sold him. " My parents too," continued the old man, shedding tears, " had saved some money, and sent it by a caravan, but the money was sent back, and my liberty refused; I am tortured, beaten, compelled to labour incessantly, and I know not when I shall be delivered from these ferocious beasts. I pray every night to our Saviour Christ; we are all Russians: we consider you as our deliverer, and pray to God for you. For two years more we will bear our sufferings, and pray for you in our hearts in expectation of your return: if you do not come back, several of us will unite, and venture into the Steppes of the Kirghis; if God pleases that we should die, be it so; but we will not fall alive into the hands of our persecutors."

Melnikow spoke the Russian very badly, mixing with it many Turkish words. The voice and miserable appearance of this old man, made such an impression on me, that I could not think of him without a sensation of melancholy.

On the 26th of November, Jous-Bachi arrived at Il Gheldi, but Jakoub-Bey had remained at Ourghendy, for some private business.——I left Il Gheldi on the 27th; all the inhabitants of the fortress, young and old, bade me farewell in the most affecting manner.——We were to stop the first night, twelve wersts from the fort, at a Turcoman camp, and lodge in the tents of one Aman, a friend of Seïd's, who having some connexions at the court of the Khan, had been able privately to inform me of what passed there; but he was a great rogue, and had so cheated me in the purchases he had made for me, that I had been obliged to turn him away. However, before my departure, Seïd had brought him to me to ask pardon. The hope of receiving some presents, made them wish me to pass the night with them. I was so happy to be on my way back, that I could not sleep the whole night, but passed it in conversation with a Turcoman, above eighty years of age, who had been famous in his youth for his robberies, and was respected in his old age for the prudent counsel which he gave.

His conversation, in fact, shewed him to be a judicious, experienced, and sensible man.

Our caravan had left Aman on the 28th of November, at noon, and, after proceeding twenty wersts, arrived in the evening at the canals of Bouz-Ghemen, which are the last in the country. In our passage through the desert country that followed, we saw, on the 29th and 30th of November and 1st of December, a great quantity of ruins ; and on the 2d arrived at the ruined fort of Chakh-Senem, after which we saw no more ruins. With great difficulty we found the little reservoir formed by the frozen snow of which I have spoken ; it was not above two feet deep, twelve broad, and thirty long. We immediately set to work, while some looked for wood, others dug out lumps of the frozen snow with their daggers, and melted them to make tea. The cold was very severe during our journey; on the 4th, about noon, we reached Akh-Nabal ; the whole road as far as Touer was strewed with the carcasses of horses and camels, which had sunk under fatigue and been abandoned by the caravans that had preceded us.

On the 11th I was delighted at meeting the son of Kiat Aga, who had been sent to meet me ; and on the 12th we reached the camp of Seid ; on the 13th I descried the corvette, and hoisting my hat on a pole as a signal, two boats soon came on shore. I immediately went on board, where Mr. Ponomarew was delighted to see me, and all on board expressed their joy. We learned on the 16th from Petrovich, the arrival of the caravan at the camp of Seid. The Chivan ambassadors came the next day : on the 18th we set sail, and arrived on the 24th in the road of Bakou. On the 6th of January, 1820, we received orders from General Jermolow to go and meet him at Derbend ; we arrived there on the 15th ; on the 17th we presented to him the ambassadors of Chiva, and those of the Turcomans on the 21st.

The General ordered us to take the ambassadors to Tiflis and wait there for his further directions. We arrived there the 24th of February, and General Jermolow came there unexpectedly on the 23d of March. On the 4th of April the ambassadors were presented to him, and on the 22d I delivered them letters for Mohamed Rahim Khan, in which I expressed my gratitude for the attention that he had shewn to me, and informed him that I was going immediately, by order of the commander-in-chief, to give an account to his majesty the Emperor of the amicable relations that had been established between the two countries.

FINIS.

G. SIDNEY, Printer, Northumberland Street, Strand.

A

VOYAGE

ROUND THE WORLD,

BETWEEN THE

YEARS 1816—1819.

BY M. CAMILLE DE ROQUEFEUIL,

IN THE SHIP LE BORDELAIS.

LONDON:

PRINTED FOR SIR RICHARD PHILLIPS AND Co.

BRIDE-COURT, BRIDGE-STREET.

1823.

D. SIDNEY and Co. Printers,
Northumberland Street, Strand.

VOYAGE

ROUND THE WORLD,

Between the Years 1816—19.

THE maritime commerce of France, almost annihilated by the revolution, by the wars, and the errors which have survived it, was, at the time of the second restoration, confined within very narrow limits; and to aggravate its distress, an enormous quantity of ready money was periodically taken from us, comformably to the late treaties. Under such circumstances, it was certainly undertaking an enterprize useful to France, to seek new markets for the national industry; to attempt, by means of our own produce, to revive and to maintain our commercial relations with a country, whose productions Europe has not been able to obtain, till these latter times, without sacrificing a considerable portion of the precious metals which are supplied by the New World.

M. Balguerie, jun. of Bourdeaux, a merchant, whose fortune and honour have withstood the vicissitudes of the revolution, has acquired a double claim to the esteem and gratitude of the public, by fitting out alone, at a great expense, an expedition to the South Sea and to the North-west Coast of America. His object was, to procure those articles which are in request in China, where they were to be sold, and the produce converted into merchandize of that country which is consumed in France, and with which our markets might thus be supplied, without the exportation of money, and by a useful employment of the produce of our soil, and of the French manufactures.

Being at Bourdeaux in 1816, a superior officer of the navy, under whom I have had the honour to serve, had the kindness to recommend me to M. Balguerie, as qualified to direct his intended operation. As there was little appearance of my being able to gratify, on board the King's ships, my love of a sea-faring life, and as a voyage round the world had always been a favourite project with me, the proposal made to me could not fail to be agreeable. But I did not accept it, without stating to M. Balguerie, that my commercial knowledge was limited to those general notions which it is agreeable to have, respecting whatever is connected with the interest of one's native country.

The Bordelais, a three-masted vessel, of 200 tons burden, was fitted out in the summer, and nothing was neglected to render her fit for the voyage. She was provided with spare stores for two years; with a long boat, as large as could be put on board, two whale boats, one in pieces, and a jolly boat; she had two cannons (four pounders), six carronades (eight-pounders), a sufficient quantity of arms, of all kinds, for the crew and for the boats. Besides the usual nautical instruments, we had an excellent chronometer by Breguet. Vice Admiral Rosily had the kindness to send me several maps and books, among which were, the chart of the northwest coast of America, and Vancouver's Voyage. Our crew consisted of thirty-four men, including the officers, who were Messrs. Foucault, lieutenant in the navy, Briole, and Salis, and the surgeon, M. Vimont. We had also on board a foreign seaman, whose name was Sicpky, who was acquainted with some parts of the Great Ocean.

The Bordelais unmoored from Bourdeaux on the 11th of October, 1816, I joined her at Pauillac on the 16th; and on the 19th, in the morning, the wind being favourable, and with the appearance of continuing, I prepared to put to sea.

Our voyage, during the remainder of the year, offers nothing out of the usual course of such expeditions. On the 1st of January, 1817, at noon, we were in 50° 13′ south latitude, forty leagues from the coast of Patagonia, and thirty-five from the Falkland Islands. The day was beautiful, and I never saw, in any climate, one that excelled it, in the purity of the atmosphere and the mildness of the temperature. The sea, calm as a pond, was scarcely ruffled by a gentle breeze from the north-east, which enabled us to make three or four knots an hour, amidst shoals of phocæ, and flocks of penguins and albatrosses, which came close under the bowsprit. The thermometer was at 16° above zero. The neighbourhood of the Falkland Islands reminding me, that France once had a settlement there, which promised a considerable increase, I wished that it would again occupy those islands, which, it is true, would not furnish any rich produce, but where many hands might be employed in their cultivation. This colony would be useful to our fisheries; it might serve also as a place of deportation, and would afford a vent to our superabundant population. Spain, which is on the point of being excluded from South America, could have no interest in preventing us : and even the power which embraces the world with its colonies and squadrons, could hardly look with a jealous eye on the occupation of this desolate coast.

On the 3d, at nine in the morning, we descried Terra del Fuego to the south, six leagues distance. Approaching the coast, I recognized it to be the part between Capes St. Ines and St. Paul. The coast, in this part, is of unequal height, and bordered by hills, many of which have their feet in the sea, which breaks on divers parts. The interior is very mountainous ; the highest summits were covered with snow, which was lying also in some valleys, though others had a tolerably fine vegetation. We saw no appearance of detached rocks or shoals. I continued to run along the coast at the distance of three or four leagues. It blew fresh from the west; the sea was high and hollow; we sailed rapidly before the wind, at the rate of seven miles, by the log. At three o'clock, the weather, which was gloomy, cleared up, and we saw ahead considerable tracts, covered with pyramidal mountains, the singular indentations of which had the most savage appearance. They extended on the starboard, and blended with those which we saw ahead. This land seemed to form an immense bay, terminated to the west by a low point, near which we were, and beyond which it stretched out in the distance. Believing that I had not run above a dozen leagues since noon, I could not make my supposed position agree with the bearings and distance of these new discoveries, which I could not have failed to recognize as Staten Land, had I not believed myself ten leagues too far off to see it. I was relieved from this uncertainty at four o'clock, when this distant land, detaching itself from that which we had ahead, left a passage open, which could be no other than Strait Lemaire.

I cannot attribute, to any other cause than the influence of currents, the error in which I was, for some time, respecting my position, for I cannot have committed so considerable a one in my observation at noon. Saving the comparatively insignificant error in the bearings, I reckon, from my observations, that we had made eighteen leagues in four hours ; of which, I attribute eight to the currents, having made only ten by the log. This difference, extraordinary as it may appear at first, will not astonish those who know what rapidity currents may acquire, when the force of the tide is augmented by a fresh wind, along an extent of forty leagues of a coast without any considerable projection. Though the weather was gloomy, I resolved to attempt passing Strait Lemaire during the night, in which we did not succeed quite so soon as was expected, the wind having failed in the middle of the night. On the west coast, we saw several fires, which the natives had lighted, as they usually do when they see a vessel; but none of their boats appeared. We saw but one whale in the Strait, which La Peyrouse saw covered with them. At five o'clock, we were out of Strait Lemaire, and steered to double Cape Horn.

From this time the weather was variable, and very stormy, so that we incurred great danger, and suffered much hardship. The sea ran extremely high, and frequently covered the ship, so that, with this, and the frequent rain and thick fogs, it was impossible to dry our clothes for several days together. Happily, our vessel proved to be a most excellent one, and had less lee-way than any I ever knew. During this rough weather, as the currents continually set towards Terra del Fuego, I always tacked so as to keep as far from it as possible; yet, notwithstanding this precaution, the currents, and repeated bringing to, made us come twenty-eight leagues to leeward of Cape Noir, and twenty-four leagues of Cape Pilares. On the 22d, we doubled the parallel of this promontory, which is the western extremity of Strait Magellan, having thus gone round Terra del Fuego, on the eighteenth day since we made land at Cape Ines, and the sixteenth after quitting Strait Lemaire.

At present, almost all vessels bound to the South Sea, pass to the east of the Falkland Islands and Staten Land, without approaching them. When, at this latitude, they meet with westerly winds, which are so common on these seas, they run to the south, as far as 60°, or thereabouts; there they find variations, which permit them to go to the north-west. Without pretending to blame the practice adopted by most navigators, I will observe, that by passing through Strait Lemaire, you are immediately twenty leagues further west than those who go round Staten Land, an advantage which is not without importance in seas, where the great difficulty is, to proceed in that direction. If you find it difficult to clear the passage, and do not choose to wait under the shelter of Terra del Fuego for the favourable winds, which are the most common, the worst that can happen is, to double Cape Saint John, the eastern extremity of Staten Land, which requires only a few hours.

The navigation round the Magellanic countries has long since been practised at all seasons; and if it is more fatiguing for the crew in winter than in summer, on account of the cold, and the long nights, we have the advantage of more frequent easterly winds, and of longer duration, than in summer. On the whole, this passage does not present any difficulties which a good vessel need fear to overcome. It is astonishing, that the disasters of the squadrons of Anson and Pizarro should not have sufficed to give credit to a contrary opinion in the middle of the last century, when we recollect, that at its commencement, during the war of the Spanish succession, numbers of our vessels annually doubled Cape Horn. It is still more surprising, when we compare the state of nautical science at that time, with what it was in the age of Columbus, De Gama, and Magellan. We may add, that the important progress it has since made, has freed modern navigation from so many dangers, and given it so many means to overcome the difficulties which still remain, that, in this respect, as well as in the importance of their discoveries, no parallel can be drawn between the Argonauts of the fifteenth and sixteenth centuries, and the most celebrated navigators of modern times, not excepting even Cook himself.

The weather became more favourable as we proceeded towards the north, and we were able to open the hatchways to air and dry the ship, and perform other necessary operations. The hope of being soon in port, made us the more easily forget the hardships we had suffered, as they had not affected the health of the crew: thanks to the constant attention paid to this point! It is true, the crews of the English and American whalers, which neglect most precautions, except cleanliness, and consume three times as much salt provisions as we do, are robust and healthy, but they consist of men inured to fatigue, which was not the case with my crew.

On the 1st of February, at noon, we descried the coast of Chili, and at seven o'clock were within two leagues of port Saint Antonio. We had a pretty strong south wind, and the fear of the currents induced me to put out to sea, that we might not be carried to the leeward of Valparaiso, from which we were only ten leagues distant. However, we did not observe any current, and the wind suddenly falling to a dead calm, and being afterwards very unsteady and variable, with a thick mist, it was not till the 5th that we got in sight of Valparaiso. At four o'clock, in the afternoon of that day, a vessel, under Spanish colours, came on board, with the director of the customs, the port captain, and the pilot. At a quarter past five, we anchored before Valparaiso, three months and seventeen days after our departure from the Gironde. Having fired a salute of twenty-one guns, which the fort returned with eleven, I landed with the ship's papers, and some letters of recommendation. Don José de Villegas, captain of a frigate, and governor of Valparaiso, received me in a most handsome manner, not only authorizing me to provide for the wants of the ship, but also promising to afford me every facility that depended on him.

On the 6th, the San Sacramento, a large merchantman, sailed for Lima, with exiles, many of whom were ecclesiastics and monks. Don Villegas forwarded to Saint Jago a packet, containing a letter I had written to Don Marco del Ponte, president and governor-general, who had been prisoner of war in France, and one from M. Blandin, of Bourdeaux, at whose house this general had lived, during part of the time that he was a prisoner. I was presented to the principal officers, and the most distinguished private individuals among the European Spaniards and Creoles. I had occasion to perceive, in the course of my visits, that the spirit of revolutions had not forgotten this country. The movement which has already changed part of South America, had extended as far as Chili. After having raised the standard of independence, this country had been subdued, in 1814, by General Osorio ; but the revolutionary ferment still existed, and the spirit of party, which excludes moderation, and often justice, still prevailed on both sides. I also remarked, with very different sentiments, that, notwithstanding the evils which an unjust aggression had brought upon their country, the Spaniards, far from considering the French as enemies, had resumed towards us those sentiments of good will, which are natural to two nations united by the tacit, but indestructible bond of common interest.

I was dining with M. de Villegas, at the house of a merchant, when he received a packet, the reading of which sensibly affected him. A corps of troops from Buenos Ayres had passed the Andes, and obtained some successes, which, without being decisive, greatly alarmed the company, which consisted of European Spaniards. They did not dissemble how much they apprehended that the enemy would be joined by a great number of mal-contents, hitherto kept down by fear, but who only waited for a favourable time to throw off, for the second time, the dominion of the mother country. Mr. Villegas, alone, did not participate in the general consternation ; but all his efforts to inspire confidence, by shewing the great resources which the government had at its disposal, made little impression upon men who were already struck with terror.

On the 17th, a Spanish transport arrived at Chili with recruits. The governor obliged me to deliver to him the muskets which were on board the Bordelais ; however, I delivered to him only the half, and I had the strongest assurances from him, that those which he took should be either restored or replaced, if the resources of the arsenal of Saint Jago permitted it; otherwise, they were to be paid for at an advantageous price, respecting which I would not make any stipulation, that I might be more at liberty to claim the restitution of them.

Besides the cargo destined for the North-West Coast, the Bordelais had a considerable assortment of merchandize, suitable for South America. This secondary, but important, branch of our operation, was, like the principal, but a trial, to open new channels for the produce of the French manufactures. Meantime, the news daily received from the interior, announced the progress of the troops of Buenos Ayres; detachments of which, sent to different points, made the country rise wherever they appeared. These accounts only increased the uneasiness of the Spaniards, and of the small number of Creoles attached to them. The passage of the mountains, by the insurgents, had not been known twenty-four hours, and they were already preparing for flight. The officers of the government were the first to embark their property, with a scandalous haste; their families, and some even of themselves slept on board, to be prepared at all events. These movements, added to the reports which were spread of the progress of the insurrection, inflamed the heads of some indifferent characters among the crew, who had embarked only in the hope, excited by absurd reports, believed by the rabble at Bordeaux, that the ship was to cruize as a privateer. The measures which I had taken, betimes suppressed these dangerous notions, without my being obliged to act with the severity with which I had threatened the ill-disposed. While this was passing, I received, on the 10th, a satisfactory answer from the captain-general, to my letter of the 5th, but, in the existing circumstances, I did not think fit to avail myself of the permission he granted me, to repair to San Jago. The joy of the Creoles, and the despondency of the Spaniards, made me expect no advantage to the latter, in the issue of the contest; I therefore wrote to thank the captain-general for his kindness, and to inform him, that I was preparing to continue my voyage: I added, that I expected, with confidence, that the arms taken from me would be replaced, or their value paid me; and in case neither could be done in Chili, I trusted that his excellency would send me the necessary papers, to receive the arms in Peru, or a sufficient indemnity for them.

All was pretty quiet the two next days, and some reports were spread of advantages gained by the royal troops; but this illusion was destroyed in the evening of the 12th, by the arrival of several fugitives, who brought news of the complete defeat of the royalists, who, on the 13th, began to arrive in bodies, mostly without commanders, and without order; the officers generally preceding their soldiers. Every one endeavoured to get on board the ships in the roads, where nothing was prepared to receive the troops. On the 14th, I sent Mr. Briole, in the morning, to settle our little account, and, if possible, procure some fresh provisions; but that officer found the city in the most dreadful confusion; the inhabitants, emboldened by the terror of those whom they considered as their oppressors, had seized upon the government and batteries, the cannon of which were spiked. One of their detachments, of forty or fifty men, concealed by the angle of the lower battery of the fort, surprised the fugitives, who, arriving a few at a time, could not fail to fall into their hands, and were immediately taken to prison. In the midst of this confusion, Mr. Briole could not return without some difficulty, and even danger. Pressed by the disbanded soldiers who assailed the boat, he was obliged to abandon part of the provisions which he had procured, and some musket-shots were fired at his boat, which, however, wounded nobody. On the way, Mr. Briole put on board a Spanish boat, the few unhappy persons whom he had been able to put into his own vessel, and returned on board at seven o'clock. Brigadier Atero sent to me, from on board the Britannia, where he had taken refuge, to ask for our boats, for the conveyance of troops. I had already promised them to Mr. de Villegas, who had come to concert measures with me; but the report of Mr. Briole, confirmed by the presence, in the Roads, of the officers, whose superintendence might have accelerated the embarkation, by preserving order, made me conceive, that it would be imprudent to employ our people. The whole difficulty of the operation arose from the precipitation and pusillanimity of the fugitives. It might have been conducted with perfect order and tranquillity, if, instead of being in a hurry to evacuate all the posts, and to send out the transports, they had kept possession of the works which command the city, to hold the inhabitants in awe. The Britannia alone, which had twenty guns, if properly stationed between Valparaiso and Almendral, would have removed all apprehensions of an attack from the enemy, till his artillery should arrive. Besides, the victorious troops were still at a distance, and the Spaniards were harassed only by a small number of citizens, whose boldness arose from the terror of their enemies.

Having no reason to delay my departure, I sailed at nine o'clock, and steered for Calloa.

The sudden revolution which took place in Chili, during our short stay, was, perhaps, less occasioned by the troops of

Buenos Ayres, than by the spirit of discontent which pervaded all classes, and which broke out as soon as they appeared. A vanguard, entirely composed of cavalry, crossed the Andes in the beginning of February, and sent out parties to different points, where the insurrection immediately broke out. In order to keep the people in check, the Spaniards sent detachments, which arrived too late, or were too weak. A corps, left to guard the defiles, could not stop the passage of the main body of the army of Buenos Ayres, commanded by Don Jose San Martin, who, including his vanguard, had under him about four thousand eight hundred men, well equipped, and chiefly cavalry : this army was accompanied by mules, which the soldiers mounted in the difficult roads and mountains. Pressed on all sides, the Spaniards, all whose corps united would have amounted to nearly the same number, rendered their situation still worse, by dividing the troops which they had remaining, to cover the capital. Twelve hundred men, with some pieces of cannon, stationed at Chacabuco, twelve leagues beyond St. Jago, were attacked, on the 12th, by San Martin, at the head of his principal forces, and entirely defeated, after five hours most obstinate resistance. The battalion of the regiment of Talavera, which had the greatest share in the success of General Osorio, perished entirely, with the exception of five officers and eighteen soldiers. The loss of the insurgents was also very considerable. The Spanish troops, who, to the number of a thousand men, at length marched from St. Jago, with the artillery, commanded by the captain-general in person, to reinforce those who were engaged with the enemy, learnt, from the fugitives, the news of the disaster, at some leagues distance from the field of battle. This only inflamed the ardour of the soldiers, who loudly demanded to march against the enemy. Instead of taking advantage of their enthusiasm, the time was lost in deliberating. The loss just sustained, and the recent insurrection of several towns in the interior, induced the general to retreat. This measure had a fatal influence on the minds of the soldiers : the fugitives, who would have rallied behind the troops, if they had found them marching forwards, communicated their own fears to them, and drew them along in the rout, the consequences of which were complete and decisive. St. Jago was evacuated with the greatest precipitation ; and the crowd of fugitives hastened to Valparaiso, where they caused that confusion, which prevailed at the embarkation.

When the transports, loaded with these melancholy remains, left Valparaiso, the fate of the captain-general was not known. It was not till the next month that it was known in Peru, that he had been taken prisoner, in attempting to reach Port St. Antonio, where he hoped to find means of escaping. Of his whole government, nothing remained to Spain of all the continent, except Baldivia, and the peninsula of Talcaguana, near Conception. The isle of Chiloe remained faithful.

Our passage from Valparaiso to Callao was not distinguished by any thing remarkable, except the facility with which it was effected, till we made the coast of Peru. On the 26th, at ten o'clock in the morning, we descried the isle of St. Lorenzo, which closes the bay of Callao to the west. At two o'clock, a canoe, with two Indians on board, came to us, and sold us some fine fish, at a moderate price.

After having taken the opinion of the two Oydors, whom I had brought from Chili, I permitted one of our passengers to go on shore in this boat, upon the express condition, that he should observe the most profound secresy with respect to the affairs of Chili.

Like almost the whole coast of Peru, this part is generally arid, and with no vegetation or culture, but at great intervals. It is in these Oases the beautiful appearance of which indicates great fertility, that the habitations are situated. Two leagues to the south of the port, a boat came out to inquire who we were, and the state of the crew's health. The Spanish passengers embarked, with their effects, on board this boat. I delivered to Mr. Pereyra, a letter for the Viceroy, in which, after having stated the reasons which induced me to go to Lima, I asked his protection, and permission to pay my respects to him at his residence. Don Fernando Camunez, captain of the port, came on board with Don Primo Ribera, lieutenant-colonel of the regiment of the Infant Don Carlos. The latter had just been detached to Callao, with a battalion of his regiment, to prevent the movements which the news brought might excite among the prisoners at Fort Real Felipe, and awe the discontented by a display of force. This was a consequence of the indiscretion of our passenger, who, notwithstanding the most solemn promises, had proclaimed the revolution in Chili.

The lieutenant spoke French with facility, having been long a prisoner of war. The good treatment which he had received in France, had inspired him with esteem for our nation, which he took pleasure in showing.

The next day, I went early to visit the port-captain, who introduced me to Don Antonio Baraco, captain of the navy. I was received in the most affable manner by this officer, who had served in the combined army during the American war, and had been acquainted with several officers of the French navy. He did me the honor to come on board, accompanied with a numerous suite.

In the evening, the Santo Sacramento and the Santo Christo arrived from Valparaiso. The distress that had been experienced by the latter, which was crowded with fugitives, excited compassion and alarm for the unfortunate persons crowded together in the other transports, which were equally destitute, and were exposed for a longer time.

The viceroy returned a favourable answer to my letter, and gave me an invitation to Lima.

On the 1st of March, I set out for Lima, with one of my passengers, in a cabriolet of the country, drawn by two horses, and driven by a postillion. From Callao to the city of Lima, which is full two leagues distant, there is a causeway, almost in a straight line, which is nowhere more than three feet above the level of the ground.

On going from Callao, you see to the right the village of Bellavista, and shortly after, on the left, a large plot of reeds, which is a retreat for robbers. On the same side, at a place called Legue, half way to Lima, there is a small church, and a public house, both objects of regard to the postillions, who never fail to make the sign of the cross before the one, and to stop at the second to drink some brandy. The Capuchins, to whom the church belongs, take advantage of the halt of travellers, to come and ask their charity, in the name of *nuestra Senora de la Legua.* So far, there is scarcely any trace of cultivation, but after having passed La Legua, the road is bordered with trees, which, a mile further, form, on each side of the road, a verdant avenue. Two miles from Lima, the road, as far as the gate, forms a beautiful avenue, and promenades, furnished with benches : two small canals maintain an agreeable coolness, and fertilize gardens, the beauty of which is less due to art than to nature. This avenue is interrupted by several circular places. It ends at the Callao gate, which, notwithstanding the defects of its architecture, has a striking appearance, from its solidity, and agrees well with the rest of the picture. The interior of the city forms a disagreeable contrast with the exterior. On entering the gate, you have before you a square, or, rather, a large vacant place, covered with black dust, a foot deep, and surrounded by clay walls, belonging to stables, and abandoned inclosures, where they deposit filth, which rises, in a heap, above these wretched constructions. This place is a rectangle, four or five hundred paces in length. Its appearance indicates rather a ruined village, than the entrance to an opulent capital. The houses are at the other extremity. The streets, which are long, straight, and cross each other at right angles, have a pleasing effect from their regularity, which is counteracted by their want of cleanliness and the monotonous exterior of the houses, which have but few windows to be seen.

I went to the house of Don Martinez Teron, a friend of Mr. Pereyra, who, with his family, received me in the kindest manner.

In the evening I went with Mr. Pereyra to pay my respects to the viceroy, who gave me the most flattering reception, and thanked me for the manner in which I had behaved to the two Oydors and the other subjects of his Catholic Majesty, whom I had received on board. His Excellency conversed with me upon the news from Europe, and especially from Chili, which country he intended to re-conquer as soon as he should have received from Spain the re-inforcements which he expected. He invited me to dine with him the next day.

Mr. Pereyra also introduced me to the Archbishop Don B. M. de Las Heras, a venerable and most pious prelate, to Don Torribio Aubal, secretary-general, and many other persons of distinction.

The next day I paid several visits, among others to the Commandant of the Marine, and to Don Fedro Abadia, agent to the Philippine company, who by his place and personal credit had great influence upon foreign commerce. I then went to the palace, where I was presented to the vice-queen. At dinner the conversation turned upon the affairs of Chili. Among the guests was General Mariano Osorio who had subdued that country in 1814, and had been Captain-General till the arrival of his successor, whom the ministry at Madrid had appointed.

The good offices of Messieurs Pereyra and Caspe having already inclined him to favour me, the Viceroy listened kindly to my request, to be allowed to dispose of part of the cargo suitable for the consumption of the country, on condition of converting the produce of the sale into merchandize of Peru. This favour, which had never before been granted to any vessel which had come without license from the Spanish ministry, seemed to insure the accomplishment of the hopes which Mr. Abadia had inspired me with. But several circumstances concurred to disappoint my expectations. The arrival of an American vessel in only ninety-three days, with three hundred tons of European merchandize, the importation of which was secured by a license from Madrid ; the approaching arrival of several Spaniards, announced by a vessel from Jamaica ; and lastly, the effect of the bad news which we had brought, caused a progressive decline, and I was obliged to accept terms, the advantages of which were absorbed by expenses, charges, and enormous duties.

By means of the papers with which I was provided I easily got the government to recognize the justice of my claims, on account of the arms which I had been obliged to give up at Valparaiso. Unhappily the arsenal was too ill provided to replace them, and I could only obtain thirty muskets ; the remainder was paid for upon a liberal estimate made on view of those which we still had. As the payment of our goods was not to be made till the expiration of two months, according to the invariable custom of Lima, I thought of employing the ship to advantage on some voyage which might be made in that time. After much consideration I thought to go and purchase corn on the coast to the north of Callao, which being very productive, cargoes of wheat and rice might be obtained in the ports of Saint Pedro and Trusillo, at 40 per cent. below the price at Lima, but I was obliged to give up this plan because the chamber of commerce strongly opposed granting such a favour of commerce to a foreigner. It is as extraordinary as certain that a branch, which would be so advantageous to the capital and to the provinces, was yet to be created, and did not employ a single coasting vessel. This shews the imperfect state of navigation and commercial intercourse between the several ports of Peru, and of the blind jealousy of the commerce of Lima towards strangers. I obtained from the equity of the Viceroy liberty to export the money which I had received in payment for the arms. Being obliged to convert into goods the produce of the sale, I laid it out chiefly in copper, which is almost the only article fit to take to China, where it generally meets with a ready and advantageous sale. I took also some articles of exchange for California and the north-west coast of America. The greater part consisted of provisions, which if they could not be disposed of in the way of trade, would be a resource for the crew in the course of the voyage, which I foresaw would extend beyond the time fixed in France, and the means with which we were supplied.

As I had learned from the reports of the whalers, and a journal of Captain Porter, of the American frigate Essex, that sandal wood, which is much esteemed in China, might be obtained in the Marquesas Islands, I procured a certain quantity of whale teeth, which are much sought for by the natives of that archipelago, which I determined to visit during the bad season, if I could not employ my time better.

During the time I was necessarily detained at Lima, I endeavoured to acquire some knowledge of the country and the inhabitants, and made some excursions in the neighbourhood.

On the 7th I visited the suburb of Malumbo, on the left of the river Rimac, which communicates with the town by a bridge of the same name; it is of hewn stone, and though old does not seem to have suffered by earthquakes. The bed of the river is of an irregular breadth; it fills only one part of it, dividing into several branches which form a great number of stony islets, some of which are covered with verdure. This defect, adding to the nakedness of the left bank, renders the view of the river, near Malumbo, disagreeable. The river on this side forms a pleasing contrast with the other: above the suburb it is bordered by immense avenues of gigantic orange-trees, forming promenades, which only want a little care to make them all that can be wished. In this part the bank is lined with masonry, to hinder the river from undermining the soil at the time of the high water, caused by the melting of the snow.

On the 8th the American ship, Sidney, anchored at Callao. She had come in only ninety-three days from Baltimore. On the 11th I went to Callao with Mr. Espinosa, a merchant. Having learned on board that a whaler had some barrels of biscuits to spare, I procured some in exchange for brandy. There was at that time an immense concourse of strangers in Callao, composed of emigrants from Chili, and inhabitants of Lima, besides those who were there on our arrival for the purpose of sea-bathing. In this season many rich families of the capital come and reside in this port; though the want of every ordinary convenience makes it insupportable to men like us accustomed to European comforts.

The environs, which are destitute of shade and almost of verdure, do not offer any kind of compensation except the sea baths, for which it is indebted to nature; Callao has nothing to attract its numerous visitors, but there is a freedom of social intercourse which forms a contrast with the mode of life at Lima. The women, who in that city never appear abroad otherwise than enveloped in the saya and the manta, here go abroad in the European fashion and in hats, a dress which very much becomes them. They have frequent assemblies, in which the etiquette of the capital gives way to pleasure.

I returned to Lima on the 12th with Mr. Espinosa, who confirmed what I had already heard of the robbers and their well known retreat, where they are never disturbed; consequently, no one travels during the night. But a few years ago several carriages having ventured to set out from Callao an hour after sunset, were stopped and plundered, though they went together. I returned to Callao on the 14th.

On the 24th I received an invitation from General Osorio to visit the arsenal. It is situated near the ramparts of the city on the south side. It contains a manufactory of arms and a foundry, where they cast cannon of the caliber of twenty-four pounders. This establishment seemed to be kept in good order: the extraordinary demand upon it during the intestine war, had stripped it of arms of all kinds. The general assured me that the muskets made there cost seventy piastres a piece. General Osorio was fond of his profession ; he had a military library, chiefly composed of the works of our authors. He had the confidence of his troops, and appeared to enjoy the favour of the Viceroy.*

On the 27th the Veloz Passagera corvette, and the Vezuela brig, having under their convoy three transports with troops and ammunition, sailed for Talcaguana. This post had already served General Osorio as a place of arms in 1814, and was, with Valdivia, all that the Spaniards had left in Chili.

The Flying Fish, Captain Fitch, an American vessel fitted out for the seal fishery, left the port to continue its voyage. He was going to visit several detachments that he had left on different parts of the coast and adjacent isles, to collect the produce of their fishery, to take away his people from the places already exhausted, and to leave detachments in other stations. This branch of maritime industry, besides the expense of the ship and the provisions, requires only instruments of little value, without expense for the crew, because each individual has a share. It has been a source of riches to many English and American ship owners. Within these last thirty years the latter in particular have been extremely active and successful in this fishery, as well as that of sea lions, the blubber and teeth of which are highly valued. Hence these species are greatly diminished in number. The seals in particular are not numerous, except in places lately discovered. Sometimes the finding of a rock makes the fortune of the happy discoverer. Such is the spirit of enterprize and the activity of these mariners, who are inured to danger and fatigue, that an American has been known to leave a detachment of his crew at the Falkland Islands, to double Cape Horn, ascend to the north, leave a second detachment on the rocks before St. Francisco, in California, 2500 leagues from the other, then repass the Cape with some men, collect his detachments on both coasts and purchase in China with the produce of their fishery, a cargo for the United States. Several captains

---

* After the disasters of the second expedition to Chili in 1818, General Osorio set out for Spain, but died of the yellow fever at the Havannah.

of whalers have also made these voyages. I observed on board
the vessels, of both these nations, employed in the different
expeditions, activity, order, and economy, and the double talent of turning every thing to account, and of supplying the
want of every thing. The skill of their carpenters also attracted my attention.

In the evening of the 30th, which was Palm-Sunday, the
procession of the boriquito (or ass) was celebrated ; this is a
grotesque and ridiculous ceremony, unworthy of the Castilian
gravity, and especially of the dignity of our religion : it attracted,
as may be expected, an immense concourse of people, both
from the city and its environs. Returning from Callao in the
evening, I found the road crowded with a cavalcade of negroes,
and people of colour riding full gallop and uttering cries of
joy. The eagerness of this multitude, the singularity of their
dresses, and the harness of the horses, formed a picturesque
scene which was obscured by a cloud of dust. Many women,
who were equally intrepid with the men, took part in this
procession.

On Easter-Eve the public joy began to show itself, a multitude of persons of all ranks filled the squares and principal
streets of Lima. The great square in particular, was filled
with Spaniards, Peruvians, mulattos, and negroes. The tents,
booths, and tables, which had been set out, were occupied till
a late hour, chiefly by the lowest classes of the people. I was
surprised at the silence which prevailed on this occasion, for
except the explosion of a few crackers, our village feasts would
have been much more noisy. Now and then I heard some
monotononous songs, and cries proceeding from negro slaves.

The Spaniards who, in Europe, are remarkable for their
sobriety, have not communicated this virtue to the races subdued, or carried by them to the New World ; on the contrary,
the posterity of the conquerors, whom fortune has confounded
in the mass of the population, are no less intemperate than
the Indians ; there are, even women who are not exempt
from this vice, which is so odious in their sex. In the emotion excited by strong liquors, they passionately indulge in
lascivious dances, till, their strength being exhausted, they fall
from a state of intoxication into that of insensibility, which
is no less disgusting.

The festival of Easter was celebrated with much pomp, and
the public diversions, suspended during Lent, were resumed.
In the evening, the theatre was opened. I cannot say much in
favour of the performance, or of the performers. The inside
of the theatre is neatly fitted up, and would look pretty if it
were better lighted ; except the box of the viceroy, and some

others, the whole resembles our theatres of the second rank. The behaviour of the audience of Lima might serve as a model to those of many other places. They have, however, one custom, which is very repugnant to our notions; as soon as the curtain is let down, the noise of flint and steel is heard on all sides, and every mouth, even the most delicate, is furnished with a segar, and the theatre is filled with a cloud of smoke, so that you cannot see from one side to the other.

On the 21st, the first bull-fight put the whole city in commotion. I calculated that the amphitheatre might contain about 10,000 persons. Cock-fighting is also much in vogue at Lima.

I made an excursion on horseback, with several persons, to the village of Miraflores, situated near the sea, about three leagues to the south of Lima. The road is covered with the finest dust, which is extremely inconvenient. The ground, as in the whole country, is level from the coast to the foot of the mountains, the parallel chain of which seldom extends its branches to the sea. The soil is so fertile that the slightest cultivation makes it produce with the luxuriance peculiar to the equinoctial regions. There is a rich plantation of olives, the oil of which is esteemed to be nearly equal to that of Spain. In the neighbourhood of the city there are many ruins, of the times of the ancient Peruvians: their extent and elevation sufficiently prove the greatness of that nation, and most of them still retain an air of magnificence. Two or three appear to have belonged to aqueducts. It is well known that those people had the art of conducting water from the mountains to great distances; and that, by means of this system of irrigation, agriculture was carried among them to much higher perfection than it is now in the same country.

Several parts of the coast are strewed with ruins; the most remarkable are situated opposite to the little islands, called Pachacumacs. In this part, for which the Indians had a superstitious veneration, are the remains of a vast temple, dedicated to the sun. All these buildings, as well as the more modern ones, are of unburnt bricks. These frail edifices, which, under another climate, would have been destroyed by the inclemency of the seasons, still cover Peru, after the lapse of many ages, and attest, at once, the singular mildness of the climate, and the industry of its ancient inhabitants.

There are many good-looking houses at Miraflores, but as most of them belong to inhabitants of the capital, several of them were not inhabited, which gave the village a deserted appearance: the gardens, which, however, I only saw as I passed, appeared to me much inferior to their reputation

The coast, which is about half a league distant, is steep, and about 150 feet high. From this high coast is an extensive view over the sea, whose calm surface blends with the distant horizon; to the right and left, a bold and steep coast, forming an immense crescent; the Moro Solar, isle Saint Lorenzo, the rocks of Palominos, and the pretty village of Lurin, were the most striking objects in this fine picture, which the sun just then illumined with its last rays. The impression caused by the sight of a grand prospect, the splendour of the Peruvian sun, the ruins of the temples, all contributed to call to mind a mild and unfortunate people, who formerly came to behold, from this coast, with profound feelings of religion, the immersion of the sun into the ocean.

The Zephir, an English whaler, arrived at Callao on the 10th of May. It had lost, near Pisco, its captain and three men, who were killed by a whale, which dashed their boat to pieces. This vessel announced the appearance of insurgent privateers, but this report, as well as several others of the same sort, during our stay, was not confirmed.

While we were at Lima, two Russian ships, the Kutusoff and the Suwaroff, belonging to the American company, arrived at Callao. I had the good fortune to become acquainted with captain Hagemeister, who commanded them. This distinguished officer shewed a sincere desire to serve me. To the information which he gave me respecting the north-west coast, and, in particular, the settlements of his nation, he added a letter to Mr. Baranoff, the governor, in case he himself should not be there. What he told me of those countries led me to expect but little success in that quarter, on account of the bad selection of our goods intended for exchange, but this was the principal object of our expedition, from which I was not at liberty to depart.

Having, at length, settled all my affairs at the custom-house, so that I could continue my voyage, I paid my visits, to take leave of the persons from whom I had received so many civilities. Being obliged to leave one of my men at the hospital, I placed in the hands of the superintendent, the sum required for every patient who is left there. This man, unfortunately, had both his hands mutilated, when discharging a cannon, at an entertainment which I gave on board the ship, to several of our Spanish friends. Besides being deprived of this man, five others had deserted, and our officer, Mr. Salis, being in an ill state of health, I had consented that he should remain behind; he was to return to Bourdeaux on board an English ship. I gave him letters to Mr. Balguerie, to my family, and some friends, besides some from the officers, and several of the crew. As soon as he had left us, which was about nine o'clock in the morning, of the 29th of May, we set sail.

Before we quit the coast of Peru, I will communicate some remarks on the country in general, and on the capital in particular.

Peru would offer an immense market to our commerce, if it were free ; but, even as we found it, in 1817, the consumption of our manufactures was considerable. Those which are most saleable, and profitable, are silks, linen, cloth, wine, and fashionable articles. The exports are, cocoa, copper, Peruvian bark, common and Vigonia wools, and Chinchilla skins. Cochineal might become an important article of commerce, if attention were paid to it, but when we were at Lima there was not a pound in the market.

Spain was far from deriving from Peru all the commercial advantages which so rich a colony might have procured it. The productions of the mother country imported into this country were, wine, oils, some kinds of silk, and other articles of less consequenc. The remainder of the cargoes was derived from foreign countries.

The population of the city of Lima and its environs is eighty thousand souls, of which I do not think that the European Spaniards are above a twentieth part ; the number of white Creoles is much more considerable ; that of the African slaves may be equal to both the others ; they are generally treated with mildness : the situation of those in the country is more unfortunate, as I have been assured. The remainder of the inhabitants is composed of people of colour of all shades, a mixture of Spanish, African, and Peruvian races.

The hatred which the Creoles shewed against the Spaniards so far back as the time of Frezier, has increased with the progress of the population. The events which followed the invasion of Spain by Napoleon, the steps taken by the Cortes, and the system of the present government, have given a new impulse to this sentiment, which is almost general among the Creoles. The example of the provinces of the La Plata, and the late events in Chili, have increased their desire for independence and the hope of gratifying it. To judge by the happy condition of the people of Lima, which I was assured the provinces enjoy in an equal degree, this restlessness of mind cannot be, in the multitude, any thing more than the effect of that desire of innovation (others call it melioration) which has spread over the world during these last thirty years ; and of the insinuations of the higher classes, whose self-love and ambition are offended by the preference which the government shews to Europeans, though it sometimes confides important offices to Creoles. Men to whom fortune, travels, and some knowledge not common among their countrymen, give a degree of superiority, fancy themselves equal to the management of the most important affairs, are angry at not being called to the administration of their country, and employ every means to hasten the change which will put an end to their obscurity, by establishing their independence. It is to be feared that it would for a long time be a fatal present to a country, where the rights and the duties of the citizen are generally unknown; where superstition and effeminacy, enemies to patriotism, prevent public spirit from expanding, and where the puerile love of distinction and the lust of power would be most frequently combined with inability to use it for the public good. The circumstances of the times would probably cause a republican government to be erected, and the manners are monarchical.

Among the principal establishments at Lima are the following.

The University of Saint Mark, founded by Charles V., in 1553.

The Orphan School, founded in 1654, which has been much improved since its first establishment.

The churches, which are numerous, are decorated with a degree of splendour, which can be only attributed to the abundance of the precious metals in Peru. Gold and silver are the principal ornaments, and jewels heighten the splendour of these holy edifices.

Unhappily at Lima, as elsewhere, the progress of civilization is accompanied by extravagance and luxury, and their dangerous consequences.

The women are very expensive in their dress, and have a particular taste for pearls, the whiteness of which forms an agreeable contrast with the deep carnation of their complexion, and the brilliant black of their hair. The Peruvian women are, in general, handsome or pretty; but these advantages lose their charms by a licentiousness, of which there are few examples among other civilized nations; a well-educated man cannot hear their common conversation without blushing. They are very proud of handsome arms and small feet: with this view, the girls are accustomed, from the tenderest age, to wear very tight shoes. They prefer dancing to all other amusements. Luxury, at Lima, extends only to the toilette: for the houses, the outsides of which are agreeable, shew in the inside neither taste nor splendour. The extreme love of shew which animates the women, and from which even the men are not exempt, might have fatal consequences if families did not find in commerce, means to meet the excessive e pense which vanity occasions. The merchant is so much esteemed at Lima, that the nobles engage in commerce without thinking it any disgrace to their rank ; this is not the least remarkable trait in the character of the Peruvians.

When we set sail from Callao I steered N. N. W. passed near the rocks, called by the Spaniards *Formigas* and *Firello-nes*, and passed the Galapagos Islands, which I intended to double on the south, and to cross their latitude at a great distance to the west, so as not to fear the calms, which at this season are frequent in this Archipelago, and to the east of it as far as the coast of Peru. On the 8th, at one o'clock in the afternoon, we descried the south side of Albemarle Island, but we did not touch at any of these islands. From the Galapagos I steered N.W. ¼ W. with the intention of keeping beyond the extreme limits of the W. and N.W. winds, which in this season, called winter, prevail on the coast of Mexico. Mr. Von Humboldt, who has visited these seas, assures us that they are not perceived above 150 leagues from the shore. Rome confines them within a zone of seventy leagues. One of the best pilots at Lima, who had made the voyage from Peru to California, had told me that it was proper to come in sight of Socoro, and thence ascend the coast. After such authorities I could no: fear being hindered by these winds while I held a course which was generally more than 200 leagues from land, and did not approach it within 150 leagues, except at one point. Yet the winds turned to the W. and N.W. in 6° north latitude and 100° west longitude ; when I was above 200 leagues from the coast of Guatimala.

My hopes of a fine passage to the coast of California were wholly disappointed ; we had contrary and variable winds during the whole of July, the currents took us out of our course, and nothing occurred to break the monotony of this tiresome voyage. We did not see twenty birds during the whole month, and still fewer fish ; whole weeks passed without seeing a living creature, so that we might have fancied ourselves alone in the creation. The appearance of a flying fish was an extraordinary occurrence. The month of August did not begin with better auspices ; however, on the 3d we had some indications of the neighbourhood of land, and on the 5th, at two o'clock in the afternoon, we descried the coast of California. At five o'clock we perceived the port of St. Francisco, and soon after the fort, on the south east point of the entrance ; we hoisted our colours and fired a gun, the fort did the same, hoisting the Spanish colours. The vessel entered rapidly with the tide ; at six o'clock we passed under the fort ; the officer hail -

ed the ship, and we answered that she came from Lima. We run into this basin, proceeding to the bay of Hyerba-Buena, where Vancouver first anchored. Just as we dropped anchor the ship touched the bottom, but without the slighest shock, as the ground was soft, and the next tide set us afloat again.

Two officers who had hailed us on the coast came on board in the boat, their names were Don Gabriel Moriaga, (sub-lieutenant of cavalry, governor par interim of the Presidio,) and Don Manuel Gomez, lieutenant of artillery. These gentlemen were equally pleased and astonished to see us. No French vessel had ever before entered their port. They remained about an hour on board, partook of a little collation, and conversed with us in the most cordial manner. They did not appear to trouble themselves about politics, and had no knowledge of what was passing in Chili. They told us that Mexico was almost entirely pacified; I learnt that there were but few furs in the country, an American, who left Monterey a fortnight before, having taken away the whole stock. Don Gabriel obligingly granted me permission to provide myself with the articles which I was in need of, and invited me to the Presidio. The next day he sent horses for me and the surgeon. We rode four or five miles through a very uneven country, the horses gallopping all the way, and entered the Presidio through the principal gate, where there is a guard. We alighted at the house of Don Gabriel, who, as well as his wife, received us with great politeness. Don Gabriel advised me to come and anchor at the Presidio, which I declined doing till I had seen the watering place; Don Manuel offered to accompany me to it. I found it inconvenient because it is some distance from the sea. Returning to Don Gabriel I met the father Ramon Abello, superior of the mission, whom I intended to visit. He congratulated me on my happy arrival, offered me whatever his mission could afford, and said that he should be happy to see me there.

The road from the Presidio to the mission is over sand-hills, which produce only a coarse vegetation, ferns, stunted trees, pines, oaks, hollies, &c. This part was still more arid than the neighbourhood of our anchoring place. The mission is situated in an irregular valley between the hills on the north, and a small arm of the sea on the south. The soil seems much more fertile than at the Presidio, and the temperature is sensibly milder. The church is kept in good order, and handsomely decorated; the sacred utensils and the pictures are the work of Mexican artists, and exceed in richness and taste, what is generally seen of this kind in most of the towns of the second and third rank in France and Germany: it may contain from

5 to 600 persons. There is not a single seat in it : the whole does credit to the piety and taste of the fathers : the Magazines well stored with corn, pease, &c. the looms, in which cloth for the habits of the Indians is woven, and the work-rooms, though not what might be desired, shew the industry and activity of these worthy men.

On going to pay another visit to the Presidio I met on the way Don Louis Arguello, the governor, who used me very kindly, and promised to contribute all in his power to fulfil the object of my visit : I had some conversation with him on the interior of California and the Indians who inhabit it. He had ascended the San Sacramento to about fifty leagues from its mouth, and assured me that he had always found from seven to eight fathoms water. The breadth of this river is very unequal, being two or three miles in some places, and not more than as many cables' lengths in others. In the rainy season it often overflows and covers the low country, on both sides, to the distance of three or four leagues from its mouth. This part, which is marshy and full of lagoons, is inhabited by Indians, who subsist upon fish. The interior is extremely fertile, the vine grows spontaneously, and though the grape is of inferior quality, for want of cultivation, Don Louis thought that brandy might be obtained from it. Maize hardly requires any attention. The savages, notwithstanding the inferiority of their arms, resist the parties which the Spaniards send at long intervals. If they are informed of their approach they abandon the villages, which are almost always found deserted, or occupied only by a few old people, who have not strength to fly. They lie in ambush and endeavour to surprize their enemy. In these incursions, the object of which generally is to look for natives who have deserted from the missions, it is very seldom that the Spaniards lose anybody, their jackets of buffalo's hide being a sufficient defence against the arrows of the savages.

After the accounts of La Peyrouse and Vancouver, and the complaints which the officers themselves made about the absolute want of workmen, I was surprised at seeing, in their houses, tables and benches of pretty good workmanship. On inquiring whence they obtained this furniture, Don Louis told me that they were the work of one of the Kodiaks, who had been taken prisoner while hunting the otter. Thus in an establishment formed forty years ago by Spain, a savage from the Russian possessions was the most skilful workman. I obtained some information respecting the singular incursion made by the Kodiaks, in the years 1809, 1810, and 1811. These intrepid fishermen came from Bodega, (where, as the Spaniards say, the Russians have several hundred of them), in divisions of thirty or forty boats, each with two men. They entered, keeping along the north coast of the inlet; when they had once got in they were masters òf this gulf, in which the Spaniards had not a single boat. The otters, which till then had nothing to fear but the attacks of the Indians of the country, were now pursued by the most intrepid and experienced enemy; it was estimated that about 8000 were destroyed in the three years that they repeated their incursions. The confidence with which the Kodiaks were inspired by the Spaniards having no boats, having made them imprudent, some of them were surprised upon the coast, where they went to refresh themselves, while the islands offered them a secure retreat against the Spanish horsemen. At length, upon the representation of Don Louis, some boats were built. They are four in number, manned with Indians, and so heavy and ill equipped that, I have no doubt, the Kodiaks might continue their fishery with success if the present governor of the Russian establishment thought proper.

On the 10th, with most of the officers of the crew, I attended divine service at the Presidio, which was performed in a great hall, till the church, which had been burnt, should be rebuilt; this chapel, which was white washed and neatly kept, had an altar in pretty good taste, some pictures, and benches on the sides. Besides ourselves there were present about forty men, almost all military, and about a hundred women and children, all neatly dressed, and behaving with much decorum. After the service two children sung in a correct and agreeable manner, an invocation, each verse of which was repeated in chorus by the congregation. Father Ramon, who had officiated, invited us, as well as Don Louis, to dine at the mission. The repast, which was neatly served up, was composed of a small number of plain and substantial dishes, well dressed in the Spanish manner. The bread, meat, and vegetables were the produce of the mission, and of good quality. The conversation turned chiefly on the terrible decrease of the native race in the missions of the two Californias. They agreed that it was almost entirely extinct in old California; and for this reason the number of the missions was reduced from seven to two; it was also confessed that in the new province, which is more fertile, and was always more populous, there was not a single mission, where the births were equal to the deaths.

On the 12th we completed our store of wood and water, and delivered the articles which I was to leave in the country. The difficulty of disposing elsewhere of several of our goods, and the facility of obtaining provisions here, made me determine to come back ; and we were to receive at our next visit, the payment of the balance which would be due to us above the price of provisions furnished, and the otter skins which had been delivered to us. Don Louis and Father Ramon promised to reserve for me all the furs which they should be able to obtain.

Having taken leave of our kind friends, we set sail at five o'clock on the morning of the 14th of August ; and, having met with nothing particular, came in sight of the coast of America, a few leagues to the west of the entrance of Nootka, on the 1st of September, at four o'clock in the morning. The following morning we saw several boats ; two of them with seven Indians came along side, but were afraid to come on board. They told us that Macouina was still alive, and pressed us to enter, assuring us that we should find a great number of otter skins : one of the boats had two, which we obtained.

In the afternoon the breeze, though faint, gave me hopes of entering ; for this purpose I spread all the sail, keeping three miles from the coast, on account of the shoals marked upon the charts ; we saw none of them, only some breakers on the shore. At three o'clock the wind freshened and brought up a thick fog which covered the coast ; as I could not venture into the entrance under such circumstances, I cast anchor on the north side of Point Breakers. The fog continuing with calms, or unfavourable wind, it was not till the 5th that we were able to get into the entrance, which it is rather difficult to discover. The scattered trees on the west point are the best guides, their small number in this part contrasting with the thicket on the other side.

At five o'clock we ran into the entrance, and, as soon as we were in, the wind, which was already faint, entirely died away, and it was only by the help of the boats that we got into Friendly Cove, where we anchored at half past six, in ten fathoms water. In the night the officers kept watch, as at sea, the boarding nets were fixed, the guns loaded, and part of the arms placed on deck.

On the 6th, we got out several articles that we thought the most proper to exchange with the natives : they came in great numbers, and remained a good while in their boats, alongside. Our traffic began by the acquisition of four pretty fine otter-skins ; we procured, also, a quantity of very fine salmon, and some other fish. The advanced season had caused the village to be almost deserted ; the great chief, Macouina, as well as the majority of the population, were at Tachès, his winter residence. On the 7th, Macouina came from Tachès, and remained some time alongside in a small boat, full of salmon: there was no ceremony that announced the presence of their chief, but the natives having pointed him out to me, I invited him to come on board; he got on deck with great activity, for his age, and immediately gave me his hand, with a mixture of confidence and dignity. I received him as well as I was able; I offered him a collation, to which he did honour, and a present, which he accepted with no less satisfaction: notwithstanding his incognito, he was saluted with seven guns, an honour which flattered him greatly, though it made him stop his ears.

Macouina, on his arrival, had made me a present of the salmon in his boat; after having received my present, he gave me three small otter skins, which I likewise accepted as a present, but he immediately asked for the payment. He left me at three o'clock, with many protestations of friendship, and promised soon to return. An inferior chief, named Noak, with whom we had already become acquainted, participated in our liberality, on account of his usefulness as an interpreter.

Soon after the departure of Macouina, a boat came from Clayoquot, a district in the dominion of Wicananich, a powerful chief, of whom Vancouver speaks. The Indians on board wore white blankets, or cloaks of blue cloth; they had three or four guns, in good condition, and appeared superior in activity, strength, and understanding to those of Nootka; they were besides more cleanly. We understood that they invited us to visit them, and offered to pilot the ship.

The presence of our vessel in Friendly Cove had augmented the number of the inhabitants, and the return of the chief, who promised to remain during the ship's stay, would render it still more considerable. Though nothing in their conduct had lessened the confidence which their apparent weakness inspired, I added to the defensive measures already in force, some new regulations, which I thought the best adapted to repel a surprize, the only species of attack from those people which is dangerous, and which they always employ against vessels.

Macouina came on board on the 9th, at seven o'clock: instead of the train with which we expected to see him surrounded, he had with him only Noak, two other persons whom we had seen before, and whom our people called his ministers, and two of his children, one of whom was his eldest son, named Macoula, who did not appear to possess the intelligence and activity of his father. A great number of boats came. Many of the natives endeavoured to come on board; but the interpreter himself having given an intimation of their propensity to steal, I had the boarding nets put up, to secure us from their rapacity. This operation having alarmed Macouina, I had the net removed on one side, on which he made an animated address to his subjects, on the conduct they ought to observe towards us.

I went with Macouina to the village, where there were only five or six habitable huts remaining ; of the others, only the uprights were left, the planks which covered them having been conveyed into the interior, to serve for their winter habitations, according to the custom of all the Indians of the north-west coast : the planks which remained were three feet broad. The most remarkable house was that of the chief, of which only the skeleton remained. . The tree which formed the ridge-piece was seventy-six feet long, thirty-nine inches and a half in diameter at the large end, and seventeen at the smaller ; it was supported by two enormous pieces, sculptured, representing, on the inside, gigantic figures of the most hideous forms.

I saw the spot where Meares had built his boat and his house. Noak gave me an account of the death of Canicum, who was killed by Martines, whom he had bitterly reproached, calling him a robber, on account of the plundering of a hut by his people. Except this officer, the natives speak well of the Spaniards, and have adopted many words of their language.

A large boat of Wicananich having come alongside, Macouina appeared extremely angry at its coming into his port, and made a violent speech upon the subject ; but after he had finished, I saw him laugh aside at the fictitious part which he had just acted.

After dinner, I visited the watering-place, situated at the north point, and as I returned I went into a hut, which proved to be that of Omacteachloa, son of Canicum, who is so much celebrated by Meares : his dwelling was in a wretched condition, small, and half open, but rather less dirty than the others. He was not there, but I saw his two wives, one of whom, who was blind of one eye, and very talkative, spoke a little English : she begged me to spit upon her child's head, because it had got the head-ache. She took care to inform me, that her husband was the next chief to Macouina, and that the chiefs alone had a right to two wives. In the evening, Omacteachloa himself came on board, with all his family ; I gave a hatchet to the chief, and looking glasses to his wives.

A party of the natives left the village on the morning of the 10th, and set out for Tachès : this change of habitation is made with surprising expedition, by means of boats, with which every family is provided. In less time than an European traveller wants to pack up his portmanteau, the Indian takes down his hut, conveys into his boats the planks that cover it, and the two or three trunks which contain his riches, and the dried fish which compose his stock of provisions ; the others, containing their train oil, the instruments for fishing, and the chase, he embarks with his wife, children, and his dogs, and on the same day erects a new house at 10 or 12 leagues from that which he left in the morning : they choose calm and dry weather for these family expeditions.

As the Indians leave the uprights standing, they rebuild their huts as quickly as they take them down.

On the 11th Macouina arrived at six o'clock, accompanied by his son and Omacteachloa ; they made me a present of two pretty fine skins, but which had been worn. At table he made a long speech, but it was thrown away upon us, as the interpreter was absent : I only understood that we were the subjects of it, and the tone of his voice made me think he spoke favourably of us. Noak arrived when we had finished dinner, after which I made Macouina a present in return for his : he seemed but moderately satisfied, because there was no cloth in it, though otherwise it was considerable, and soon after he asked for some cloth : knowing that I should have to begin again at every visit, I endeavoured to put him off to the next time, but he made me understand that he should not come back again. I gave him 2 ells of blue cloth ; he demanded some for his son, and I gave him the same quantity. He then wanted some balls, and pretended that his son ought to partake of my presents, because he was proprietor of one of the skins which I had received. Not content with having received, for nothing, powder, balls, coffee, rice, &c. he importuned me for a bottle of brandy, which I gave him to get rid of him. In short, Macouina shewed himself in this visit an importunate and insatiable beggar, as Vancouver describes him, and not the generous prince that Meares would make him. I was very much inclined to dismiss this begging potentate, rather than yield to his importunate demands ; but the hopes of deriving some advantage from him next season, induced me to send him away satisfied. At last he departed for Tachès, after having made me promise to return, and engaged to keep his furs for me.

Immediately after his departure, I went on shore with the carpenter to look for spars. The difficulty was to find trees small enough. Having followed a path which led a little from the sea, I suddenly came to a lagoon of fresh water, divided into several branches, and every where bordered by trees and underwood. The wild vine is met with at every step, as well as a beautiful shrub, which bears berries of an agreeable taste, of which the natives consume a great quantity. Having left the path to return to the strand, I entered a thick wood, and arrived first at a small and rocky point, a mile from the entrance. Hitherto we had seen only pines, here we found some firs, which had no fault but that of being too large for us. However, we met with some that suited us.

I questioned Noak when he returned on board respecting the furs, and the vessels that are employed in the trade: he told me that the English formerly had a house, that the Spaniards had a larger one, but that both were abandoned. He added, that thirty months before, (he held up three times, the fingers of both hands,) an English vessel had come into the cove, the captain of which had a wooden leg, and that he stopped only three days: that before that, and after the departure of the English and Spaniards, only two vessels had entered the Bay, one English, the other American; that they had anchored at Mawina; that at present, and for a long time since, his countrymen sent the furs to Naspaté, (at the western extremity of the island,) where they exchanged them for handsomer blankets than ours. He told me also that the fishery lasted six months; that it had been finished two months, and would consequently begin again in four months, and he assured me that they would reserve the skins for me, if they were certain I would come back for them, which I positively engaged to do. Other accounts confirmed most of the statements of Noak on the sea otter fishery, and the present state of the communications of foreign vessels with these people.

On the 12th I went with Noak to examine the west side of the Bay, which I ascended 8 or 9 miles to the north, near to Mawina. About a mile at the most from Friendly Cove, there is another smaller one, which affords excellent anchorage at three fathoms at low water, and a carecning place which is entirely closed: the natives call this cove by the name of Outza.

From this point to the north, the coast forms the western side of a channel a league long and a mile broad, closed on the east by a chain of three woody islets, called Hinasohous. From the northern point of the largest, which is the middle one, a kind of ledge extends, composed of a mass of rocks, in which there is a break, five fathoms broad, and twenty long, which serves as a communication to a beautiful lake, that extends several miles into the country. During the tides this passage becomes a sluice, through which the waters rush with great noise and rapidity. It was now high water; being warned of the danger by these circumstances, as well as by Noak, we kept close to the shore, where the current was weak. We

easily reached the summit of the coast, which is about forty
feet high, and when we got to the opposite side, saw at
our feet a magnificent basin, as smooth as a mirror, sometimes extending between verdant hills, covered with gigantic
frees, and sometimes bounded by high naked banks. This
scene of wild and tranquil nature was animated only by some
salmon sporting on the surface of the water, and by an eagle
which hovered above us. I regretted my inability to explore
this little mediterranean. On our return we met several
boats of the natives, from whom we received only testimonies
of kindness.

On the 13th, the fishermen came late, but at eleven o'clock
they arrived in great numbers, and we were surrounded with
boats the rest of the day; among others, there was one from
Clayoquot, on board which was a chief of some importance,
who had a cloak of two otters'-skins, which he offered to sell.
He was admitted on board, and regaled with biscuit and treacle.
He exceeded his countrymen in the tediousness with which
he bargained; having baffled the talents of Eyssautier, our
principal agent in these negotiations, he disappeared, and was
strongly suspected of having carried off the iron helm of the
long boat. He soon returned, but without his cloak, and protested his innocence, and, as we had no proof against him, we
were obliged to take his word, but I sent him away, because
he had not fulfilled his engagement. This man was better
made, and more robust, than those of Nootka; his physiognomy bespoke more vivacity, understanding, and cunning.

The next day some families returned to their habitations,
and two huts were already built at six o'clock in the morning.
Numerous boats came, but no more furs than the day before.
Among the women who came on board, there were two girls,
who were tolerably pretty, and not so dirty as the others; a
sailor having spoken to one of them, was violently reprimanded
by her mother.

Having gone to the outer coast to take the elevation, I was
accompanied by three young men, who, without incommoding
me, followed me every where. Returning on board, I took
with me two of them, whose countenances spoke in their
favour. When evening came, we had some difficulty in getting
rid of our new friends, who wished to pass the night on board.
They did not go away till we had promised them presents for
the next day, and till they had given us a specimen of their
dancing and music. Their singing was simple, and not disagreeable, but interrupted by frightful cries; the couplets
very short, and the words of the ritornello sonorous: *Hellé
yalla hé, hellé yalla hellé.* Not understanding them, I thought

they had borrowed them from the Lascars, on board some vessel from India, but the explanations which they gave me of their own accord, confirmed us, that these songs were in honour of their country, of which they speak with enthusiasm. The eldest assured us, that Macouina said *wacoch* to the sun.

I went ashore early on the 15th, with ten men, to convey, from the forest to the beach, the trees which had been cut by our carpenters. Eachtel, a nephew of Macouina, joined us with another man ; both took great pains to gain my favor, by assisting us in our labour, and by shewing me various species of berries of an acid, and pretty agreeable taste, which abound in this place ; one of them resembles a currant in its form and taste, though the berries grow single. These two Indians understood the use of the lever, and managed it very adroitly. Eachtel gave me to understand, that it was by this means the great stones were raised, which are employed in building the huts of Macouina.

After making some observations, I returned on board with my two companions ; they eat and drank with tolerable propriety, and though rather awkward with their knives and forks, it was plain that they were not unacquainted with the use of those instruments. After dinner, Eachtel shewed a small round box, which served him as a dressing case. It contained a comb, some necklaces and ear-rings, a mirror, some down to serve as powder, and several little bags, with black, white, and a red dust, resembling black lead. Few of the natives go from home without these articles, for, with all their dirt and ugliness, they are inconceivably vain. When our guest was going away, I observed that his boat was new, and very well made, and expressed a wish to purchase it : he manifested his readiness to part with it for about four yards of cloth, to which I added a mirror ; but our Indian, who had hitherto shewn so much frankness in his dealings with us, endeavoured to carry off one of the three paddles. I expressed my dissatisfaction at this conduct, and the wife of the chief, who was present, also reproached him for it.

Mr. Vimont found some human bones, which, with other indications, led us to imagine that they were the remains of a repast of Cannibals. In the course of the following day, (16th of September) several boats came with families, going to take up their winter quarters at Tachès. Some of these boats were very large ; one, which was very well made, had fourteen persons on board. The chief to whom it belonged, was received on board, at the recommendation of Omachteachloa, who had given us a fine salmon. This chief was well made and robust ; he had a much thicker beard than the other

Indians; he was a man of about thirty years of age, a relation of Macouina, and his deputy in a village on the coast of Clayoquot. He appeared to be much respected by the other chiefs, and shewed a frank and decided character in his intercourse with us. We purchased of him four otters' skins and one bear's skin.

Omacteachloa and Machoalick passed the day on board, and were very gay during the repast. I gave each a present, and they endeavoured to express their gratitude and friendship towards me. I thought this would be a good opportunity to find out the secret respecting the bones which our surgeon had seen. I therefore went with him to the spot, and questioned Machoalick, who confirmed our conjecture, that this place, some hundred paces in the forest, behind the abode of the chief, was consecrated to festivities; but I obtained no positive information on the principal point; he either could not or would not understand, whenever we asked how his countrymen treated their prisoners, and whether they eat human flesh. The bones, he said, belonged to bodies unburied by the bears, which often disturbed the graves. They inter their dead any where, and have no fixed burying ground. This place was destined to the repasts which followed the whale fishery; a large trunk in the wood served as a drum, on which Macouina beat time, and accompanied himself when singing. Machoalick entered into details on the subject, which we could not fully comprehend, and which related to the ceremonies used by the natives before and after this undertaking, which is of so much importance to them. The chief, before he distributes their portions to the guests, acts a kind of pantomime, during which he frequently imitates the blowing of the whale. Machoalick doubtless alluded to some formal act of invocation when he emphatically repeated, that Macouina said *wacoch* to the sun; I know not whether it was the idea of an abominable repast, suggested by the accounts of Meares, which had possessed my mind, and cast a gloom over all this scene, but I shuddered during this recital, made at the beginning of the night in a dark and desert place, by an enthusiastic savage, who made furious gestures, imitating the motions and cries of his chief, when he cut up a sea monster that he had killed with his harpoon.

The next day I made an excursion in the whale boat to examine the east side of the entrance, towards the south. After having crossed it I came into a cove, to the east of Friendly Cove, at the foot of a mountain. The only remarkable thing here is a steep rock, which forms a natural arcade, under which I landed. The sea at high water rises beyond it, and covers a pretty beach, not more than 100 feet in circumference. The arch may be about 20 feet deep, 13 or 14 high, and 10 broad. We breakfasted on biscuits and brandy, and some enormous muscles which we found on the rocks ; we had also strawberries and raspberries. The wind rising, I determined to return on board, where I hastened the preparations to get under sail, which we did at one o'clock in the afternoon.

During our short stay at Nootka, the Indians gave us no cause for alarm. We took in with the greatest facility our supplies of wood and water, and the provisions which the country affords ; but, unfortunately, the furs are much scarcer than they formerly were, so that we had only procured twenty sea-otter skins. Most of the families that still inhabited Friendly Cove left it the same day that we did, and the two or three that still remained with Omacteachloa, intended to follow them to Tachès, as soon as we should have left their district. To the little I have said of making land at Nootka, I will add, that Point Breakers, at the extremity of a slip of low land, is a good guide, all the east of the coast being high land, especially to the west. The general aspect of the country is also a good guide ; the mountains which surround the bay have angular summits, cut in strange forms, as well as several peaks, among which we may observe that of Tachès, which resembles a steeple. To the west the profiles of the mountains are more regular, and generally rounded.

On the 18th of September, at 5 o'clock in the morning, we were off the entrance of Nootka and Point Breakers. A boat from behind the point came alongside ; there were nine Indians, only two of whom were allowed to come on board. They recognize Macouina for their supreme chief. They were in general better made, more lively, and less dirty than the inhabitants of Nootka. They sung, beating time with their paddles, while one of them standing, executed a kind of pantomime, mixed with gesticulations and attitudes, sometimes ferocious, and sometimes grotesque. They tried to persuade me to anchor in their port, which they shewed us, where they promised we should have many otter skins ; but I invited them to bring them on board.

On the following day I kept near the coast, in hopes that some boats should come out with furs, as I had asked them ; I wished also to examine this part of the coast. I was disappointed in both : I was not, however, much surprised at not seeing the Indians, as I could imagine, from what I had heard and seen at Nootka, that their stock of furs was exhausted at this time of the year. I determined, therefore, to proceed to

Nitinat, or Berkeley-Sound, not in the hope of better success, but to collect information for the following year.

On the 20th we made the land, distant three or four leagues, N.N.E. At 3 o'clock I steered N.E. to pass between the group of islets on the west, and that on the east; but on approaching, I perceived from the mast-head that the further part of this channel, which is wide at its entrance, was full of breakers. I resolved to try the passage between the east coast and the group, which appeared to be safer, though less open. Though the sky was clear, and the moon bright, I would not venture into this labyrinth, respecting which I had no guide but Vancouver's map, which, in this part, does not appear to me to be very correct, and which, besides, is on too small a scale to steer by. As for Meares' plan, it no more resembled the entrance I had before me than that of the Ganges. The depth, (sixty-four fathoms,) being too great to allow me to anchor, I bore off: a calm soon followed.

The state of the weather was such, for the three following days, that it was not till the 24th that we got into the channel, between the continent on the east, and the islands on the west. We put out the long-boat, and a whale-boat; and Mr. Foucault was sent to seek for an anchoring place towards the north, while the vessel proceeded in the channel with a faint breeze.

Several boats approached, but the natives would not come alongside till the arrival of a chief, who came on board without shewing any distrust.

At six o'clock Mr. Foucault returned after having found on the east side, two arms of the sea near each other. He entered the largest, which afforded good anchorage, but the depth was great at the entrance. After several other trials, in which we were in considerable danger, being obliged to cut our cable and losing our best whale boat, we could find no better anchorage than in the smallest of the two arms which Mr. Foucault found the day before, where the vessel was moored on the 25th in nine fathoms water.

Notwithstanding the rain, we were visited by many Indians, among whom was Nanat, a distinguished chief, who came on board alone. He gave us an otter skin as a present, in the same manner as Macouina. For some succeeding days nothing remarkable happened. We employed five days, but to no purpose, in dragging for our cable and anchor, but on the 5th of October, though the loss was very disagreeable, I resolved to give up the search, as the lateness of the season and ill health of the crew made it a duty to leave these shores and pass the winter in a milder climate. I employed part of the 5th in examining the passages which lead to the channel between the islands, though all appears clear in the chart which Vancouver gives of them after the Spaniards, several are impracticable, either on account of sand banks which obstruct the entrance, or because they are too narrow; as for the special plan which Meares gives of Berkeley-Sound, it appears to me to be made according to his own fancy.

The Indians on the Nitinat shore are generally better made and more cleanly than those of Nootka; they seem more active, and have more expressive countenances; but, in some respects, they are more remote from civilization, having less communication with strangers; they have a more savage look, are more inclined to theft, and more importunate in demanding presents. However they never showed any hostile intentions either on board or towards the boats; which, it is true, were always armed when they were sent to any distance, and on board the net was always put up before the number of Indians became considerable. Of all the means of defence which the Bordelais possessed, there was none which they dreaded so much as a black mastiff dog, which we brought from Peru. We saw several men and a greater number of women, whose complexion differed from white only by a tinge of pale yellow. Some young people, of both sexes, had a colour, and many children would have been thought pretty in Europe. The greater number of the Indians have black hair, the remainder a light red, all wear the hair long, and the women comb it carefully and divide it over the middle of the forehead. Both sexes dress the same as in Nootka, with this difference, that the women wear under their other garments a kind of apron of bark, not woven but only fastened to a girdle. We saw many well-made women with good arms, but, in general, very ugly hands. On the whole they are better looking than the women of Nootka, though there is something harsher in their countenances, chiefly owing to their narrow foreheads, which are wrinkled at an early age. We saw only three or four who in Europe would have any pretensions to beauty. One of them was the wife of Cia, who had received us hospitably; another the wife of a great chief, was almost white; she had large black eyes, regular features, a fine countenance, and much propriety and dignity in her manners. The women and girls appeared as modest as those of Nootka, and still more reserved.

We observed here the same hierarchy and the same subordination as at Nootka. Nanat appeared to be the grand chief; he exercised his authority with more arrogance than Macouina; we frequently saw him behave harshly to Cia, and a part of the presents which we had made the latter, passed into the hands of his superior.

As far as I could understand, the natives call by the names of Anachtchitl and Oheia the district which surrounds their bay; at least it is certain that the name of Nitinat belongs to no part of it, but to a village which is situated far to the southeast, towards the strait of Fuca. They give the name Tchaxa, or rather Tchacktza, to Port Desire, (Port Désiré,) and the district which surrounds it. We had given this name beforehand to the anchoring place, the discovery of which interested us so nearly. This port, into which the natives told us no vessel had ever before entered, is situated two leagues from the passage, on the east side of the bay, and, and as there is every reason to believe, on the great island Quadra, of Vancouver. The only mark is a steep hillock, destitute of trees but covered with a beautiful verdure, which is on the sea side, some cables' length to the south, and which has the appearance of a ruined fortification. Being surrounded in the interior by trees which command it, it is not very easily to be distinguished. Even the entrance of the canal of Tchachtza, which is only ten fathoms broad, and surrounded by lofty trees, could only be seen when very near, if it were not preceded by a cove less open than deep, but which has too much water to anchor with a single cable. In this recess was our port, as well as another arm of the sea, more spacious but less sheltered and obstructed in the inside by rocks and shoals.

Before I left these coasts the Indians solicited me to return the next year, but I would not bind myself to pay a second visit to this port, which the otters have long since nearly forsaken.

We got out to sea on the 7th of October, but the wind failing we were soon obliged to come to an anchor. Shortly afterwards a man, who was nearly white, came on board; there was something in his manners and address which indicated a higher degree of civilization. When he came alongside he asked, in English, with a kind of politeness, to be admitted; I took him down into my cabin and offered him treacle, biscuit, and wine. He behaved with much propriety, without asking for any thing. He spoke English better than any other Indian, so as to make himself well understood, notwithstanding his bad pronunciation. His name was Swanimilich, and he lived at Tchinouk, behind Cape Flattery, as he gave me to understand, whence he had come to fish. He assured me that there was at that place four Americans, who were left by a vessel from New York. He named three very distinctly, Messrs. Clark, Lewis, and Kean. They had a house of their own, in which they were to pass the winter : he told me that several ships came every year, and mentioned an English vessel, called the Ocean. I never was able to ascertain the truth of these facts, of which the Americans, whom I have seen since, had no knowledge.

After what I had heard from the Spaniards, it was my intention to go to the Russian settlement of Bodega. I came in sight of it on the 13th, but fogs and calms hindered me from anchoring off the port, till two days after. A boat with two Kodiaks immediately came out to us. From their manners and dress they looked more like European sailors, than like savages, whose name is hardly known in Europe. One of them spoke tolerable Spanish : he was among those who had been taken while hunting otters in Port St. Francisco, whence he had found means to escape. After giving them some breakfast, I went on shore with the one who spoke Spanish.

I found that only small vessels can enter the port, which is obstructed by a bar, where the depth is only one fathom and a half at low water. I understood that the Russian settlement was some leagues further north, at the mouth of a small river, which the Russians call Slavinska Koss, in latitude 38° 30', on a part of the coast where there is no anchorage. Mr. Koskoff, the governor of the settlement, had just departed for St. Francisco, on board the company's ship the Kutusoff. This account made me abandon the hope which had brought me to this place ; I, therefore, returned on board, at noon, and continued my voyage for St. Francisco, where we arrived on the 16th, and found the Kutusoff at anchor, off the Presidio. I immediately landed, and met, on the beach, Don L. Arguello, who, as well as the other officers, received me as an old acquaintance, and expressed much pleasure at our return.

The very next day we began our labours. I went to the Presidio, and the mission, to take measures for a regular supply of bread, meat, and vegetables ; a wholesome and restorative diet being necessary for the crew, six of whom were on the sick list, and the others more or less affected by our expedition to the North-West Coast. I likewise thought of laying in provisions for the continuation of our voyage, which seemed likely to be of much longer duration than was at first imagined.

The 19th being the anniversary of our departure from France, all work was suspended. I went to the Presidio, with the officers and crew, to attend divine service. The men had double rations for dinner. On the 21st, some parties were sent on shore to commence their labours, but, on their return, in the evening, we found that two of the men, named Paris and Ostein, had deserted. I immediately went with Mr.

Briole in search of them, but not meeting with any horses, we were obliged to give up the pursuit, our deserters being mounted. On the 28th and 29th, as we found that our sick recovered very slowly, I took advantage of the offer made by the fathers of the mission, and sent four of the sick to their infirmary, where Mr. Vimont attended them every day.

It was now that I had the first information of a plot, formed during our stay at Nitinat, to carry off the ship, after getting rid of the officers. Ostein, one of the two deserters, had been the author of it, but he found so few of the men wicked enough to commit such a dreadful crime, that he was obliged to give up his project. Circumstances not permitting me to investigate this affair, without injury to my employers, I thought it best to dissemble, and retain for the success of the expedition, men who had no claim to mercy.

The progress of our labours was considerably impeded by the numbers of our sick, so that this delay, and the duty of allowing time for the recovery of the patients, caused our stay at St. Francisco to be twice as long as I had intended. On the 11th, the Kutusoff sailed for New-Archangel.

On the 14th, our boatswain, Charles Renom, fell a victim to his disorder, notwithstanding the care of Mr. Vimont, and the attention he received at the mission, where all our sick were treated with the greatest kindness. He was buried the following day, and I attended his funeral, with two officers and six men. Renom was universally regretted, and his loss sincerely affected the crew.

On the 17th, Paris and Ostein were arrested by the soldiers, and brought on board, where they were put in irons. On the 19th, at noon, we unmoored ; at three o'clock, the officers of the Presidio, who had come on board to take leave, returned on shore. In the night, the ship was rid of Ostein : his removal gave general satisfaction to the crew.

On the 20th of November we sailed from St. Francisco, for the Marquesas Islands, and, on the 22d of December, came in sight of the most eastern of the group, discovered by Mendana. We first saw Hatouhougou, (Hood Island, of Cook,) and, shortly after, Ohevahoa, (the Dominique, of Mendana,) and some land, which appeared detached from it, unless it is connected with the great island by some low land, and which can be no other than St. Pedro.

On the 23d, at four o'clock in the morning, I approached Raouga, and Hatouhougou appeared to the east-south-east. We sailed along the south of the first of these islands, at five miles distance. It seemed to us not very woody, but there are some fine groups of trees in the villages, which lie between very steep hills.   At nine o'clock, we saw, successively, the islands of Nukahiva to the west, and Rahopou to the south-south-west; we steered towards the former, and made every preparation to come to an anchor.   In Comptroller's Bay we sailed along the coast, at the distance of a mile, doubling the little isle of Tahia-Hoy, which forms the eastern point of Port Anna Maria of Hergest; we perceived at the farther part of this fine anchoring place, a three-masted vessel, which immediately hoisted the American colours.   We had hoisted ours on the coast.   We tacked, to reach the anchoring place.   At half-past four o'clock, a whale-boat came, rowed by the natives, which had on board an American, from the United States, of the name of Ross, who had resided several years in this country, where he acted as agent for the vessels which came for sanders-wood.   He offered me his services, as well as that of Captain Cornelius Sowle, of the Resource, of New York, which we saw at anchor.   After having given me some general information, Mr. Ross took leave, promising to give my thanks to Captain Sowle, and to assure him, that I should be happy to render him any service.   Soon after, the captain himself came, and repeated his obliging offers.   At eight o'clock, we anchored in eleven fathoms, on a bottom of fine gray sand, five cables from the shore.   While I was conversing with Captain Sowle, who explained the reasons which had induced him to exclude the women from his ship, one of my people came to inform me, that about fifty of them had got on board my vessel, having swam to it, and entered by means of the ends of ropes hanging down.   Notwithstanding the prudent advice of Mr. Sowle, I did not think fit to drive them away; and, besides, I should not have known what means to adopt to expel such an enemy, who was already in possession of the deck.

On the 24th, I visited the old chief Keatanouï, surnamed Porter, who, in this country, where there is no acknowledged authority, enjoyed all the respect that affection and esteem can give.

I found this good old man under a shed, on the sea-shore, on a platform, covered with large pebbles.   He made me sit down by him, on a mat, and seemed delighted at the arrival of a ship from the country of good muskets; for he knew France only as the place where those brought by Captain Sowle had been manufactured.   What I told him of the quantity of arms, powder, &c. that we had on board, gave him great satisfaction.   The old chief having had some cocoa-nuts brought to refresh me, we conversed, by the aid of an English sailor, who had lived several years in the island.   We were soon surrounded by natives. Some women came under the shed, a greater number of men sat down on the platform, or remained standing around. The men were of a superior stature to most Europeans, and excelled them no less in the perfection of their forms. Except a girdle, they had no clothes on, unless we consider as such the tattooing, which covers the bodies of the adults. The women, in general, are about as tall as the French women, very graceful, well made, and have agreeable and regular features. Taïa, the daughter of the chief, was remarkable for an agreeable figure, pretty countenance, and mild looks. The colour of their skin is a tint of bright citron. With the exception of the oil, with which they rub the skin, the women, as well as the men, were remarkable for their cleanliness. Their dress is composed of a girdle, descending to the knees, and a mantle fastened over the left shoulder; both are of a stuff made of bark, as well as a kind of cap, which covers the hair, and very much becomes them.

Christmas-Day was a holiday. Captain Sowle dined on board. The original object of his expedition had been the seal fishery, but some delays in fitting him out, having hindered him from sailing in time, for the season of 1816, his owners had given him some muskets, to exchange for sanders wood, till the time for the fishery came. He had collected about sixty tons of wood during five months' stay in this Archipelago. He was on the point of departing to follow the principal object of his voyage. What I learnt from him, confirming the information I had already received, on the advantage of visiting the islands to the windward, where it is easy to obtain, at a small expense, articles which may be exchanged at Nukahiva, I resolved on making this excursion, as soon as I could have the company of Mr. Ross.

The Resource sailed, on the 27th, for China, where she was to dispose of her sanders-wood, before she went to the fishery. Captain Sowle took charge of a packet for France, and a letter for Manilla, both of which he was to leave at Macao.

The departure of the Resource leaving Mr. Ross at liberty, I was not willing to put off my visit to the windward islands any longer. We sailed the next day, having on board, besides Mr. Ross, five natives his boatmen, and two Englishmen, who had lived for some time in these islands, and had asked me for a passage, with the intention of making some purchases. At two o'clock, on the morning of the 30th, we doubled the eastern extremity of Rahopou, and steered for Ohevahoa, which we saw in the east, at day break. Shortly after, we saw Taouhata (Santa Christana) to the south east. Intending first to visit Ohevahoa, which is the most fertile island in the Archipelago, I steered so as to pass into the channel, which separates it from Tahouhata, to reach the anchorage of Taogou, (the Ontario of the Americans) which Ross pointed out as the most favourable for our plan. As soon as we had anchored, the vessel was surrounded by natives, principally from the west part, both in boats and swimming. I went with Mr. Ross into the whale-boat, visited the village of Taon, at the bottom of a large bay, to the west of Port Ontario. Only three months before, a boat belonging to the Flying Fish, which we had seen at Callao, had been taken by the natives of this place. The unhappy crew had atoned for their imprudence with their lives, and their corpses had become the prey of their assassins. Ross, who two years before had resided several weeks at this village, did not think fit to trust himself to his ancient hosts, and we rested on our oars within musket shot of the shore, which was soon covered with Indians of both sexes. Several swam round the boats ; most of them were women and girls, who, though not so handsome as those of Nukahiva, were, however, very pretty, and I could not imagine that such agreeable countenances could belong to Cannibals. The men, whom curiosity, or, perhaps, some criminal motive, drew round us, were equal, in their stature and appearance, to those of Nukahiva, but their limbs were more vigorous, and their countenances more savage ; their skin was of a darker colour, and they were more tattooed. As they could not supply us with either sanders wood or hogs, we staid but a very short time.

At six o'clock we went in the whale boat of Ross, accompanied with the long boat, to the creek of Atouona, which is separated from the port only by a slip of land, which closes it on the north-west side ; the Indians expected us there with several lots of sanders wood, of which we soon obtained nine quintals for as many pounds of powder. The boat returned at seven o'clock. In order to keep up a good understanding it had been necessary to admit some young girls, who had expressed a desire to become acquainted with our people.

The same regulations were observed during the night as on the north-west coast, except that the nets were not put up : the proas, with outriggers, used by these islanders, and their awkwardness in managing them, giving us no reason to fear their boarding us.

On the 1st of January, 1818, our boats went in the morning to Atouona, and brought eight or nine hundred pounds of sanders wood and several hogs.

I set out early on the 2d with Mr. Ross, in his whale boat, to visit the creeks to the east of the port. The long-boat accompanied us, carrying muskets and other things for traffic.

At 7 o'clock we reached the little creek Hanahehe, where we cast anchor. The valley seems to extend into the interior and is sprinkled with houses down to the beach; few Indians however were assembled. Some of both sexes swam to our boats. Ross negotiated with them, but after waiting three hours for the hogs they promised, we proceeded to Hanamate. This creek affords better shelter than the first; however they are of no importance on account of the proximity of Port Ontario, which is preferable in every respect. Our expedition was not fruitless, for we got thirty hogs, part of which had been brought from Hanahehe; we paid three muskets for the whole. We visited Hanamaté again the next day, but though Mr. Ross had taken measures the day before to prevent all delay, it was a long time before we could collect the cargo, which was again composed of hogs; Mr. Ross went on shore with his friend to remove some difficulties. Seeing many women and children on the beach, I determined to follow him; I was soon surrounded by women, who were in general taller and more robust than those of Nukahiva; but they were not so well made, and had less pleasing countenances.

Ross returned after a short absence and declared I had acted imprudently, notwithstanding the security which the proximity of the armed boat afforded. A young American named Charles Person, a native of Boston, who had lived several months with an old chief, the father of Ross's friend, had come to Hanamaté to see the latter; I invited him on board, hoping to obtain some information from him; he greatly praised his hosts, but it must be confessed that he possessed nothing that could tempt them. The next day I again went ashore with Ross expecting to find wood and provisions which had been promised us. Considering the bad condition of the only light boat which we had left, I desired to obtain the whale boat of the Flying Fish, which the Indians had drawn on shore after they had murdered the crew. The boats were soon surrounded by Indians of both sexes, who swam to them, most of them were young women, who sported like Nereids, diving and swimming in all kinds of attitudes; and never failed to ask a recompense for the amusement they had afforded us; a piece of biscuit contented them. The old acquaintances of Ross had also come to visit him, and bring him proofs of their regard. They invited him to go on shore, but their friendly outside concealed perfidious designs. One of Mr. Ross's boatmen, who had gone to examine the state of the whale boat which I wanted to purchase, brought word that the Indians had hidden some arms in a spot covered by the rocks, and that without doubt they would have turned them against us, had we acceded to their treacherous invitation. We quitted these cannibals without having attained the object of our visit.

On the 5th we took the usual precautions at night. The sky was very cloudy and dark, and heavy rain fell almost without intermission. At half past one in the morning the dog barked furiously; soon after we perceived that the head-fast of the long-boat had been cut; another was immediately fixed, and double vigilance exerted. At a quarter past two both head-fasts were cut at the same time, under the very eyes of the watch, whose attention, excited by the first attempt, was particularly directed towards the boat. But the darkness prevented them from seeing any thing but the motion of the boat; it was still near enough for them to leap in and secure it. The crew was immediately on the alert. I had some musket shots fired upon both banks, though the most profound silence prevailed. The long-boat was instantly put out to examine the ropes. We had already found that the small bower cable was cut. We continued to keep good watch till day-break; two men remained in the boat, which was moored alongside. As soon as we could see the buoy of the bower anchor, we immediately took it on board.

Our short stay had procured us, besides some vegetables, 4000 lb. of sanders wood, and above 80 hogs. Having accomplished my chief object, I would not prolong my stay among these perfidious savages, but resolved to return to Taïa Hoy, without touching at the other islands of the south of this archipelago, which are all inhabited by tribes as treacherous as those of Oiswahoa; besides, the sanders wood is inferior to that of Nukahiva.

While we were preparing for our departure, an old chief whom we had seen several times, with some other Indians, brought us some hundred weight of sanders wood, and some hogs. In order to discover the authors of the hostile attempt which had been made upon us, I pretended to believe that he was concerned in it, though his now coming was a proof of his innocence. The old man evinced, at this accusation, a degree of terror which it would be more difficult to describe than to account for. He protested his innocence, and said that the people of Atouna had been guilty of the crime, in which he could not have taken any part, as he belonged to a hostile and distant valley. This assertion was confirmed by the other Indians. On their departure, all seemed to think themselves happy in not having felt the effects of our vengeance; perhaps it was from their fear of reprisals, that we obtained for a pistol, the articles which they had brought. At one o'clock we sailed from the port of Taogou, and at nine, being to leeward of Hanamaté, and pretty near shore, Mr. Ross landed his young fellow-countryman.   On our return to Taïa Hoy, we immediately set about the operations which the damage the vessel had sustained had rendered necessary.   During the first few days after our return, we obtained some thousand pounds of wood in exchange for hogs.   But this traffic was of short duration : the time of the great solemnities, when there is an enormous consumption of these animals, was still some months distant.

The weather, which since our return had been generally rainy and windy, being pretty fine, I went on the 11th with Mr. Ross to Hacahouy, two leagues to the west.   The Americans call this place Louis Bay, after the first of their captains who entered it, though he had been preceded by the celebrated captain Krusenstern, who denominated it Tchitchakoff, a name which will probably never be pronounced by any inhabitant of the Marquesas.   We came out by the passage within the rocks on the west, which is not practicable except for boats ; we passed before the creek of Chaoutoupa, separated from this port by a slip of land.   At the farther end are some huts, and scattered groups of cocoa and bread-fruit trees. From that place to Hacahouy the coast is steep and bold, above a hundred feet high, with hardly an interval where it is possible to land.   In the same manner as to the east of Taïa Hoy, there are often parallel strata of various colours, and volcanic rocks, some of which rise to the height of the coast. While sailing past, it is impossible to avoid remarking one situated about half way.   The perpetual breaking of the sea, has formed a deep cavern, in which the waves, dashing with prodigious force, produce a detonation like that of a large piece of artillery ; while part of the waters issuing through a vent which the waves have made in the vault of the cavern, rises to a considerable height, where it disperses in spray. This double phenomenon induced our people to give this rock the name of the Whale.

The creek of Hacahouy terminates, to the south, a valley which we traversed in the opposite direction for more than a league.   To the west and east it is confined by two ramparts of rock, which, on the sea-shore, and for more than half a league inland, narrow it to three or four hundred toises at the most.   The mountain on the east side afterwards declines, and taking a bend, permits the valley to extend towards the northeast.   The other is joined to the south with the steep coast, and stretches inland towards the north.   Both of them rise far above the tallest trees in the valley.   A considerable stream, which runs between the village and the mountain on the east, gives extraordinary fertility to this happy valley. All the ground which is not occupied by the numerous huts of the natives, is entirely covered with various plants, cocoas, bread-fruit trees, banians, and other large tropical trees. Some produce food, which is equally agreeable and salutary ; others furnish materials for building, or for the few clothes which custom and vanity, rather than the climate, render necessary to the inhabitants. Lastly, they afford a cool shade, which is the most agreeable retreat during the long heats.

The Indians of both sexes are no less favoured than those of Taïa Hoy. I remarked a greater proportion of individuals of colossal stature, and, in general, they were of a stouter make. The complexion of the women seemed to me to approach nearer to the white, than that of their neighbours, a difference which may be accounted for by the almost continued shade which covers the valley. Though Ross assured me that these people were not so good as those in our port, and that we must not trust them, we were every where received in the most satisfactory manner. In many huts which we visited, in search of sanders-wood, they offered us excellent cocoa-nuts. Going alone into one of the best-looking huts, I found two young women, the handsomest I saw in that part of the world. Their curiosity, and that of their female neighbours, by whom I was soon surrounded, being excited by my dress and complexion, I had some difficulty in escaping from the minute investigation which they were disposed to make. Before we departed, we made a collation of the provisions we had brought on shore, and the fruits of the country, in a little hut on the sea-side, under a delicious shade. It was occupied by a widow and her daughter, by whom we were received in the most affable manner.

Two double canoes from Ohévahoa arrived on the 14th, which did not enter till they had cruised for some time, and announced their arrival by blowing large shells, which produce a sound similar to our bagpipes. They were hauled upon the beach with much ceremony, and great rejoicings, by the inhabitants of the neighbouring valleys, who came in great numbers, dressed in their finest style. During the day, these strangers, to the number of about forty, brought us, besides some pieces of cloth, gourds, and other productions of their country, a poem, in honour of the eldest son of the young chief, the grandson of Keatanoui Porter, and other effusions of their poetical genius, which they sung to monotonous airs, something resembling our church music. On the 25th, we saw a great number of women come from the different valleys, who repaired to the hut of an old chief, named Pahou-

tehe, and, by strangers, called the elephant, on account of his
enormous size.   I learned from Ross, that this extraordinary
concourse of women was on account of the desperate situation of his wife, to whom they were going to celebrate the
mournful ceremonies, of which I shall speak in the sequel.

Early in the morning of the 9th of February, I went on
shore with Partarieux and Ross, to make an excursion to the
highest of the mountains, which close the valleys on the north-
east of the port.   We were much fatigued by climbing up the
steep path which leads to the summit.   In this excursion, I
had occasion to admire the agility with which the natives
passed the most dangerous places.   Though often loaded with
fifty or sixty pounds of sanders-wood, they advanced much
more lightiy than we who carried nothing.   Happily, the
bushes and reeds which border the precipices, render the passage less dangerous.   Half way up the mountain there is a
spring of delicious water, near which we breakfasted.   Some
of the natives, whom we met, were very courteous and obliging.   When we reached the summit, which commands a view
of the coast and the interior, the most beautiful prospect presented itself to the view.   To the east, we saw Comptroller's
Bay, the great valley of the Taïpis, that of the Happas, whose
huts we saw; the first one, the other two leagues distant.   On
this side, there is a road not so bad as that by which we had
ascended, though still very steep.   This was the way that
Captain Porter passed, when marching against the Taïpis, and
where the natives of Taïa Hoy, his allies, brought up a cannon; an enterprize that must have been as difficult to these
savages, as the passage of Mount Saint Bernard to our armies.

The strangers from Ohevahoa departed on the 16th for their
own country.   They had derived good profits from their merchandize, but more from the productions of their muse, which
had obtained for them the most hospitable reception, and
numerous presents from the amateurs, who frequented their
courts.   These representations were very often repeated, particularly at the commencement of their visit.   The multitude
of both sexes, who came from the most distant valleys, and
met early in the morning, made me conjecture that the fête
was announced beforehand, and the time and place appointed.
The latter was always one of those enclosures, which are in
all the villages, in the form of a rectangle, from three to four
hundred feet long, and about a quarter as much in breadth,
surrounded by a parapet breast high, ten feet thick, faced and
covered with large pebbles, and sometimes with flags, hewn
out of a very soft stone.   There is often a row of trees on the
inside, not far from the parapet, and on the outside there are

always several avenues, which form agreeable promenades, the coolness of which enhances the advantages of these amphitheatres. The musicians assemble at one of the ends, where they squat down. The principal person of the band, or the poet himself, sings, first alone, each couplet, which is immediately repeated by the others in chorus. Some accompany themselves by clapping their hands, others holding the left fore arm crossed upon the breast, strike with the right hand both the breast and the external part of the arm at the joint. They strike so hard that each blow produces a very loud sound, and they sometimes bruise themselves so as to take the skin from the arm. They likewise have large tamtams (a kind of drum) the only instrument I saw among them. When they reach the place where the concert is to be held, most of the amateurs lay their presents at the feet of the musicians. Both sexes always put on their finest and most valuable ornaments. All their new things are kept for these occasions, when they appear to be dressed with the most studied neatness; but the stranger is disagreeably undeceived when he becomes sensible, on going near them, that they have been very liberal in the use of train oil.

Up to the middle of the month we had procured only 10,000 pounds of sanders wood; but little remaining in the valleys about the port, I thought of procuring some at Hacahouy; for which district I set off early in the morning of the 17th with one whale-boat, accompanied by Mr. Ross in his. We had an agreeable and speedy passage, and were well received by the friends of Ross, especially by a chief who had visited us on board, who was no less remarkable for his stature, seven feet high, than for the perfect proportion of every part of his colossal person. We extended our researches for above two leagues in the interior, and went into about twenty huts, the proprietors of which had sanders wood. Most of these huts were built on the right bank of a pretty stream, through which we waded. We took a breakfast of cocoa and biscuit in the habitation of a friend of Ross. Returning we chose another way, and visited the huts which we had not yet seen. We passed again by that of the colossal chief, who had prepared for us a meal, consisting of bread-fruit and cocoa nuts mixed together and formed into a paste, on which Ross's boatmen regaled.

We afterwards returned to the sea side, where I commenced a bargain for sanders wood. On this occasion an act of inconsiderate confidence on my part had nearly been followed by fatal consequences. One of the owners of the sanders wood had come with me in the whale boat, to see the powder which I offered him for his wood : after having concluded the bargain, I thought I might agree to his request, to take his powder on shore, and the more so as the wood was on the beach ready to be embarked : when Ross saw the powder in the hands of the Indian, he openly expressed his opinion of my imprudence ; in fact, when about half of the wood was embarked, the Indian, under the pretence that he had not been sufficiently paid, refused to deliver the rest. He was seated near a heap of wood, holding in his hand a kind of club. The thoughts which agitated him gave to his countenance an expression of ferocity, which it was as difficult to mistake as to see without shuddering. After having strongly represented to him through Ross, the injustice of his claims ; judging by his silence and his countenance that stronger arguments were necessary, I called to the whale-boat to approach, and the men to have their arms ready, but not to make use of them without orders. I immediately returned to the Indian, and knocking the club out of his hand with a billet of wood, with which I had armed myself, I demanded his *ultimatum.* He made no answer, but his gloomy silence and ferocious look indicated that he was agitated by the most violent passion. While he was divided between the temptation of cupidity and the fear of being punished, his father, who was present, fearing the consequences of his obstinacy, and seeing me resolved to maintain by force the justice of my right, took a handful of wood and threw it into the boat. His example was followed by several other savages, and in an instant the wood was embarked. I congratulated myself on having succeeded without coming to extremities ; but the Indian, enraged at not having been able to derive any advantage from my imprudence, meditated a cruel revenge. After having carried the powder home he returned armed with a club, of the height of a man, and thick in proportion, such as the natives often use as a staff, and, while I was walking on the beach, not fearing any evil, came behind me, holding the club with both hands, and had already raised it over my head, when his father darted forward in time to seize his arm, and to lead him away. I did not learn this fact till Ross told it me as we were returning ; the noise made by the Indians on the beach hindered me from attending to what passed behind me. This man, whom Ross described as one of the most wicked and dangerous in these islands, was one of the very few who had two wives. These were the two handsome and remarkably fair persons, whom I have before-mentioned ; and whatever might be the violence of his passion, it is certain, at least, that jealousy had no part in his resentment towards me.

I had much reason to acknowledge on this occasion the good offices of Jahouhania, priest of one of the valleys near Hacahoui. We had been for some time acquainted; he had visited me on board, and asked me to change names with him; he was afterwards known by the name of Roké, as the islanders could not pronounce my name, I had reason to suppose that this was not a step dictated by vanity or interest in this man, who had every appearance of a good character. My friend afterwards visited me from time to time, and brought me some presents; among others, a beautiful fan of that country: he never failed to make me remark the exhausted state of the bottle of brandy which he had received before.

We made three other expeditions to Hacahoui, which produced about eleven thousand pounds of sanders-wood, generally larger than that of Taïa-Hoy. All passed very peaceably in our intercourse with the natives; we always treated upon the strand, within reach of the boats. I never omitted these precautions after the advice of Ross, who told me no strangers had ever been so far into the valley of Hacahoui as I had.

On the 25th we had on board four hundred and twenty quintals of sanders wood, which took up above eighty tons of our room, and, together with our other goods, filled the vessel in such a manner that we were obliged to store part of it in the lockers, and even to leave some upon deck.

The repairs, necessary to enable the ship to go to sea, were retarded by the bad weather, towards the end of the month, so that notwithstanding my desire to reach the north-west coast as soon as possible, we were not ready before the 27th.

Mr. Siepki, our third officer, was landed at his request, and on the certificate of Mr. Vimont, that his health, which had been bad from the beginning of the voyage, was such that he could not proceed without danger; I then settled with Ross, with whose services I had been satisfied.

We weighed anchor at half past nine on the 28th of February.

The Marquesas are a good port for vessels, which, after having doubled Cape Horn, may have occasion to visit some parts of Australasia; for whalers which visit the great southern ocean, and for vessels going to the north-west coast, which may not be able, for urgent reasons, to go to the Sandwich islands, which are in every respect preferable; lastly, the Marquesas are the natural port where those ships may stop to refresh, which are bound from the ports of South America to China, and of those which, sailing from the north-west coast, double Cape Horn.

Notwithstanding the facilities which the port of Taïa-Hoy

affords for taking in wood and water, and the confidence
which the peaceful conduct of the natives up to this present
time naturally inspires, that of Taogou in Oevahoa seems to
be preferable, especially for those navigators whose only motive for putting in here is to obtain refreshments.   The cascade
on the north-west side, and the little wood surrounding it,
will supply them with wood and water, with this advantage,
that the vessel, when moored athwart the watering-place, will
have its parties under the protection of the musketry, in case
of an attack by the Indians.   Besides, a watch at the mast
head might observe all their motions, the country being absolutely naked in that part, with the exception of the little wood,
the trees of which do not stand very close together.   It would
be proper to keep on board, till the departure of the vessel,
some daughters of the chiefs, who are as ready to visit strangers as those of the inferior classes.   The boats, well armed,
and under the direction of a prudent officer, may go into the
creeks on the east side, and collect refreshments.   Besides
the hogs, which may be procured in any number, at the rate
of ten for a musket, this isle produces sugar-canes, potatoes,
gourds, bananas, small oranges, the pulp of which is red,
and several kinds of fruit, besides the bread-fruit, which, with
the cocoa, is the chief food of the inhabitants.   There is also
a kind of nut called *ahi,* and the *ty,* a root, the juice of which
is of the same quality, and almost as abundant as that of the
sugar-cane, and which, baked under the ashes, is an agreeable
and wholesome food.   Vessels moored on the coast will probably receive from the natives, as we did, a quantity of these
articles, which it is not possible to procure from Nukahiva,
where, except some cocoa nuts, nothing is to be had but wood
and water.   If the object of visiting the Marquesas is to get
sanders wood, putting in at Oevahoa will still be of use,
though the wood is of inferior quality, and many articles
may be obtained there which can be disposed of to advantage
at Nukahiva.

This last island produces the best sanders wood in the Archipelago.   Captain Rogers, an American, was the first who
took any, as an article of commerce, after having discovered
this precious wood when passing near a fire, by the smell proceeding from some pieces which the Indians had thrown into
it. In 1810 he procured above 260 tons in exchange for goods,
the primitive worth of which was about 1000 piastres, composed of hatchets and other utensils, and some whale's teeth
which happened to be on board, one of which was then worth
three or four tons.   He sold his cargo in China, at the rate of
20 piastres per pickel, and returned for a second cargo, with

the value of 3000 piastres in articles of exchange. This time he had ivory, which he fashioned on board into the form of whale's teeth, not having been able to procure them in sufficient quantities. This fraud produced him a large profit; but the natives soon discovered it, and cannot now be deceived by it. A few weeks were then sufficient to obtain a cargo, which was sure to be sold with advantage, both on account of the quality and size of the wood. Now all is changed; the exportation of nearly 1800 tons has almost exhausted the resources of this little island; the small quantity of sanders wood which is still in the interior, is crooked, stunted, and very small, most of the pieces not exceeding two inches in diameter. From the results of the researches of Capt. Sowle, and our own experience, no more than 10 or 12 tons of sanders wood can be collected in a month. With some comparatively trifling exceptions, the natives take nothing in exchange but muskets, powder, or other ammunition. These articles must retain their value on account of the continued state of hostility in which the natives live. Whale's teeth are not valued, unless they are of the enormous size of three fingers' breadth in diameter. The teeth of the black fish and seals are also of some value when they are strong and well sorted. Hatchets, and some other utensils are in request, but iron, in general, is not much esteemed. Handkerchiefs, blue and white linen, are in fashion, chiefly among the women. They have also the usual predilection of their sex for looking-glasses. Plumes of feathers, especially red ones, are much sought after.

All these articles, however, are only accessaries in the traffic, the basis of which is arms and powder. The comparative value of these articles with respect to sanders wood has declined; a musket some time ago was worth a ton of wood. The following are the terms on which we concluded our bargains. For one musket, 500 lbs. of sandal wood; for two pounds and a quarter of powder, 200 lbs.; for a hatchet, 45 lbs.; a whale's tooth, 200 lbs. Of these last we disposed only of the finest, and there were none of a large size among those which we had received at Callao.

There is reason to distrust the whites who are met with in these islands, most of them are deserted sailors, who have all the vices of civilization, though without the advantages of education. Notwithstanding their small number, they do not a little contribute to make the Indians lose the good qualities, which still distinguished them at the close of the last century, according to the reports of navigators of that period. I make an exception in favour of Ross, who was sent to these islands by Mr. Wilcock, consul of the United States at Canton, to facilitate the traffic in sanders wood, to the vessels of his nation.

According to the accounts of Mr. Ross, the natives, only a very few years ago, were still such as they are represented by Quiros, Marchand, &c. Their moral character has since greatly changed, for it is incontestable, that mildness and humanity were the basis of their character, before their intercourse with the Europeans. Ross, who had better opportunity of knowing them than any other, does them this justice. But a few years have made a deplorable change in all the island. Even at Wahitou, the sons of those whom the sight of the blood of their countrymen had not induced to any excesses towards the imprudent strangers whom they might consider as his assassins, perfidiously seized, in 1815, an American boat, the crew of which they massacred and devoured; for, notwithstanding the mildness of their manners, the inhabitants have long been cannibals. They are, certainly, the finest race of men I have ever seen, as well for their lofty stature and fine figures, as for their personal strength. None are ever deformed. I observed among them some marked differences in the colour of the skin, the features of the face, and the hair; but those who were so distinguished were not sufficiently numerous to give reason to suppose that there are two races. Some were a pale black, others are less tanned than many natives of Provence. The women are of the ordinary stature, pretty, and very well made; they are inclining to plumpness, their countenances lively and agreeable, and they have most beautiful teeth. There are some whose complexion would not be thought dark in the south of France, and they take the greatest care to preserve it; they never go out of doors during the great heat, and if they are obliged to expose themselves, they shade themselves from the sun with their fan, and the stuff in which they envelope themselves. Though I am an admirer of them, I cannot agree with Quiros, when he gives them the preference to the beauties of Lima, who, to the perfection of form, add the charm of more delicate features, and a more intelligent physiognomy. However, the portrait which our French navigators give of them is not too highly flattered.

The men generally wear a piece of stuff, extracted from the bark of a kind of mulberry-tree, which they wrap several times round the waist. Some of the islanders, but they are the petits-maîtres of the country, wear a piece of cloth, in the manner of a mantle, like the women. In cool mornings, some wrap themselves up in the mats, which they sleep on. They shave the head from the middle of the forehead to the nape of the neck, and, on each side of this stripe, which is about an inch broad, they wear the hair tied up in a kind of bow, and the ends floating on their shoulders. On great occasions, they adorn their heads with a diadem of feathers, of cock's tail, or other birds. At Oevahoa we saw a chief with a diadem of tortoise-shell, incrusted with ivory and mother-of-pearl, in pretty good taste.

The dress of the women, consists of a girdle coming down to the knee, and a large piece of stuff, with which they cover their shoulders, and which falls rather lower ; but they use it only when they go out of their huts, for at home they lay it aside. On extraordinary occasions they use a very fine handkerchief, of which they make a cap, that sits close to the head, and hides the hair. The corners, which are turned back, form a kind of bow, which completes this very becoming head-dress. Few of them have long hair ; almost all have it cut short, even with the shoulders. They often wear necklaces made of little bunches of flowers, small cucumbers, &c. They have also, for particular occasions, necklaces of seals'-teeth, and ear-rings made of whale's-teeth. The largest are the handsomest; there are some above two inches in diameter, but those usually worn are not above half that size. Glass beads and bugles are out of fashion. Some women hang round their necks ivory, shells, and coral of various shapes, often in the form of a large tooth.

The men have beards like the Europeans, but they never preserve them entire. Some wear mustachios, some only a few scattered hairs, but most pull them out.

Among other singularities of these people, a man is not allowed to wear, or even to take up, any part of a woman's dress, or the mat upon which she sleeps. No individual of either sex is permitted to sit down upon a pillow, which the women alone have the privilege of using. They believe that a violation of these customs is punished by disease or death. They have a kind of superstitious respect for the hair of the head ; I saw a woman carefully pick up and swallow some, which she perceived on the ground : Ross told me it was their custom. They do not like strangers to touch their children's hair. When friends meet they touch noses, but this is a testimony of friendship which is very rarely given, and I received this mark of kindness only from my friend Roké. I saw very few persons who were tattooed, according to a regular design ; it should seem that, in the face especially, they avoid symmetry, and like contrast. It is seldom that both hands are tattooed, and still more seldom that they are both done in the same manner. The women, in general, tattoo only the hands

and feet, but there are some that have a circle on the lobe of
the ear, in the middle of which is the hole for the ear-ring.
Many women are also marked with a kind of epaulette, or they
have on the arms or thigh the figure of a lizard or a fish.
Some Americans informed me, that they had seen at Magdalen
Island, a woman of lofty stature, who was tattooed from head
to foot, like the men.   Those whose tattooing is of the same
pattern, or alike in the principal features, such as a particular
mark upon the nose, over the eyes, &c., form a kind of association or fraternity, and assist each other in time of need,
like our freemasons ; the choice of the tattooing is, therefore, an important affair. .

These islanders seldom resist the temptation which the
sight of any valuable article excites in them, and it is, therefore, very dangerous to expose them to it.   The young women
whom we received on board, and not only those of the lower
classes, but even those of the highest rank, made no scruple
of committing thefts, even after having received presents, with
which they seemed quite satisfied.   Among other things, they
one day carried off my hat, with two or three books, which
had been put in to stretch it : they were fond of taking books,
for the sake of the paper, of which the natives make car-
tridges.   In general, it is now very imprudent to venture on
shore any where, except at Taïa-Hoy (Port Anna-Maria), and,
even there, the islanders always steal when they have an opportunity, but, at least, they use no violence.   They do not
think stealing dishonourable ; and this action, which is infamous amongst us, fixes no disgrace upon the individual who
has committed it, unless he is caught in the fact ; he is then
looked upon as a bungler, and that is all.   If the lawful proprietor finds his property in the hands of the thief, or elsewhere, he has not the right to take it back, and he can only
recover it by clandestinely taking it in his turn.   What is still
more surprising than this want of police, is, that quarrels very
seldom ensue ; and the people have naturally so much mildness in their character, that murders never happen on these
occasions.   According to the testimony of Ross, and what I
saw myself, no chief has sufficient authority to cause stolen
goods to be restored.   The only means is, to arrest the robber,
or one of his relations, or even one of the chiefs ; and the
restitution of the property is to be ascribed to the attachment
borne them, and not to their authority.

I must say, to the praise of these islanders, that assassination
is equally unknown among them, unless it be inspired by the
spirit of vengeance, or of party, which brings it within the
class of homicides, authorized by the law of nations, in a

country where every one has the right to make war on his
neighbour. On the other hand, it must be confessed, that, for
some time past, there is not an island, the inhabitants of which
have not been guilty of the greatest excesses towards strangers. The introduction of fire-arms, lessening their fear of the
whites, and their ideas of their superiority, has produced an
unfortunate change in their manners; and, when their interest is concerned, they do not hesitate to murder a stranger.
The inhabitants of Taïa-Hoy are an honourable exception to
this remark, though several murders have been committed
there; but, if the natives have sometimes laid aside the natural mildness of their character, they have been impelled to it
by revolting conduct, or by perfidious insinuations. We ourselves have traversed these valleys, carrying with us articles
highly valued by them; we shewed them openly, without experiencing any trouble or running any danger: it is to be understood, however, that they steal every thing that is not well
secured.

Except at Carnicobar, in the Bay of Bengal, I have no where
seen a picture of happiness comparable to that which this
country exhibited. Nature lavishes on its fortunate inhabitants every thing that is necessary; and what is no less happy,
she has given to their country no fictitious riches, none of those
precious productions which are sought after by civilized nations, and which often bring misfortune upon the country
where they are to be found. Their habitations are surrounded
by cocoa and bread-fruit trees, which require no attention,
and which afford wholesome, abundant, and agreeable food,
while the trunk, bark, and leaves supply them with materials
for their clothing and habitations. The Marquesas being
much more healthy than the Nicobar Islands, their productions
more rich and more various, their inhabitants would, doubtless, be more happy, if they did not diminish their domestic
felicity, by licentiousness of manners and propensity to theft.
This vice, which is not repressed by any fears of authority, induces them to steal the fruit, which does not grow high
enough to be safe from their rapacity. Their mutual distrust
of each other prevents them from applying to the easy cultivation of several wholesome vegetables, which grow in abundance in other islands, where there is a better police. It leads
them to use the precaution of gathering the bananas before
they are ripe, and even before they are full grown.

The only inhabited parts are those which are provided with
cocoa and bread-fruit trees. These plantations are almost
always due to nature, the natives seldom taking the trouble to
plant these precious trees, in places where they do not grow

spontaneously. The lands are private property : the chiefs have considerable estates. They generally reside on the sea-shore, and let out the lands situated in the upper part of the valleys, for a small rent, paid in the produce of the soil. The will of the two parties alone determines the duration of the lease. The proprietors, as may naturally be supposed, have much influence over the farmers, who may be considered as their vassals ; but this voluntary vassalage is an interchange of good offices between the chief and his farmers. This is the principal source of the authority of the chiefs, for, otherwise, they have no influence in their valleys and in their tribes, except such as bodily or moral qualities confer among equals. But there is, in reality, no public authority ; no one owes an account of his actions to any person whatever ; and he who in any manner injures another, has no fear, except from the person injured, or from his friends. Men possessing but little land, are often seen to enjoy more respect and influence than some chiefs ; for instance, Ross's friend, Agomohiti. The chiefs have no ornament, or mark of distinction, except in the manner of wearing the hair. They do not adopt the custom of dividing the hair, and shaving the head in the manner before described, but only fasten it in a knot behind ; nor is even this distinction exclusively reserved for them, for I saw some who, though not chiefs, had preserved their hair entire.

The property of the land is not always secure to the posses-sors ; it sometimes happens, that the strong seizes on the property of the weak ; a powerful relation on that of an infant heir. I was witness to the difference excited by the unjust claims of an uncle upon the estate of his nephew, son of the deceased protector of Ross. A kind of family council had been held early in the morning, which, however, decided no-thing. We arrived shortly after it broke up. Besides the relations and friends, the inhabitants of that part of the valley had assembled in divers groups ; almost all were armed with their large clubs ; some had lances of a hard wood. They disputed, and reproached each other at times, the dispute grew warm, so that it appeared they were going to come to blows ; but the whole passed over without bloodshed. The only blows given were by an aunt of the child, to one of his cousins ; the latter had the worst of it : it was all over in a moment. This woman, who was young, and of tall stature, supported, as well as her sister, the interest of her nephew ; both acted their part very well in the midst of this confusion, and did not seem to be out of their place. When the quarrel was at the highest, several of the competitors were seen to beat down the bushes with their clubs, as if to try the strength of their arms, or to clear the field of battle. Some men and many women were spectators, and remained, for the most part, at a little distance. None of them, however, manifested any fear, in case the parties should come to blows. The protectors of the infant being the greater number, his adversary appeared to relax from a part of his pretensions. But, some days after, having taken measures from which he expected more success, he returned to the estates of his nephew. This new attempt was not more successful than the preceding : Ross having collected in the night, without the usurper's knowledge, the partisans of his friend's son, the uncle did not venture to try the chance of arms, and he was again driven from the land, of which he now demanded only a part. His unjust projects having completely failed on this side, he turned against one of his brothers, older than himself, and blind, who, after having seconded him in his attempt against their nephew, not being so well supported as the child, was obliged to take refuge in a corner of his estate, and abandon the rest to his younger brother. It may be observed, that Keatonouï Porter, though first chief, took no part in these quarrels. The relations or friends of the parties interested alone interfered. In the wars between the tribes, the prisoners, without distinction of age or sex, are put to death, and eaten, except those whom the priest thinks fit to consecrate to the gods, and who are buried, after they are put to death. Neither women nor children are ever present at these horrible repasts ; this privilege is preserved for warriors, and young men who are already tattooed. In the civil wars between one valley and another, or between two families of the same tribe, the prisoners are not eaten. I have been convinced, by my own observation, that the children are not only spared, but may pass in entire safety over the lands, and before the door of the enemies of their father.

At the time of the great fêtes, all hostilities are suspended, during the preparation, and for three days after their celebration ; even enemies are well received ; and to cross the whole country they have only to say that they are going to the fête of such and such a valley : they are hospitably treated ; they share in the entertainments and the diversions, together with the people of the tribe who pays the expense. They usually go away in the night of the third day ; those, however, who are detained for some hours beyond the time, are spared. The inhabitants of Taïa-Hoy treated those of the other villages as enemies ; they killed and eat all those who landed on their coast. It is but a few years since this state of permanent hostility has ceased to exist : humanity owes this obligation to the old chief Keatonouï. At present they are at war only with Rahouga. The inhabitants of this isle are divided into two tribes, between which the greatest animosity exists. Nukahiva takes part in their quarrels. The Hapas being the allies of one tribe, and the Havans of the other, they make expeditions, which are always injurious to the island. Each party carries away the hogs, and the produce of the harvest, belonging to his adversary, cuts down the cocoa and bread-fruit trees, in a word, commits all kinds of ravages.

Captain Porter, after having ravaged the country of the Taïpis, had obliged them to make peace with those of Taïa-Hoy, who were inclined not to take arms again. But when the fear of seeing the Essex return had vanished, the Taïpis, who still harboured resentment, re-commenced hostilities, by killing a priest who had come among them without fearing any harm. Now the greatest animosity appears to exist between the two tribes. I did not learn that any important expedition had been made against the Taïpis, but small detachments sometimes pass the mountains, advance secretly into the thinly inhabited valleys, and carry off the unfortunate individuals whom they can surprise. They spare neither age nor sex; nothing can save the victim from death, or hinder him from being devoured by his enemies. The priests alone can claim him in the name of their *Etouas*, or gods. In general this kind of consecration cannot save the life of the prisoner, only he is not eaten, but buried near the huts where the Fetiches are interred. I was told, as a fact without a parallel, that a young girl had been preserved by a priest, who, after having kept her some time with him, sent her to her own country.

Though these islanders have their priests, I could not discover among them any worship, or any idea of a Supreme Being. The Fetiches, which might at first be taken for idols, are thrown carelessly about the huts, and no kind of veneration is shewn them. All that I could discover relative to their belief, is, that the chiefs, and generally all those who have been renowned in this life for their strength, or any other quality of body or mind, enjoy the same advantages in another life.

The canoes are taboo for the women, who are forbidden to enter them when afloat, and even to touch them when they are hauled on shore. The taboo extends to the mats, outriggers, &c. of their boats, though these things are often placed in huts, or put under a shed. I was assured that this taboo is in force through the whole Archipelago. From Marchand's account it seems not to have been adopted at Taouhata, in his time. It may have been introduced since, for it frequently has a temporary and local existence. These interdictions take place at the will of the priests; but, to become general in a tribe, the proposal they make must be adopted by the chiefs. A priest declares that he has communicated with one of his brethren, or with a chief, who is deceased, and become an etoua in the other world, on account of the rank which he filled in life. This spirit has announced to him, that the effects of his anger would fall upon every individual who should eat of a hog having a particular mark; or any woman who should touch any article belonging to the men. The animal, or the article pointed out, becomes prohibited. These people have the good sense to leave to their etouas the care of revenging themselves, and of punishing those who infringe the taboo. Hence, it often happens, that a sickness, or any misfortune which happens to an individual, who does not scrupulously observe the taboos, is considered as a punishment from the divinity.

Many of these islanders die of old age, almost without having experienced any of the infirmities with which it is frequently accompanied among civilized people. They are, in general, carried off by a consumption, which slowly undermines them without pain, till the approach of their last moments. They employ no means to delay it, and do not seem to lose by it; at least, they have the advantage not to torment themselves in vain. I saw several individuals attacked with this disorder. They take to their couch, and expect the conclusion, almost without ever quitting their hut, and, at least, with apparent tranquillity; their relations are eager to provide for their wants. When the disease has made some progress, they begin to prepare for the funeral, and the coffin; this is a large piece of the trunk of a cocoa-tree, hollowed out, in which the deceased is exposed, without being covered up. The hut, also, in which the body is to be deposited, is begun; it is usually adjoining to that which is inhabited by the family. All these preparations are made under the eyes of the patient, to whom they announce his approaching dissolution. These arrangements, the sight of which would be painful to us, are considered by these islanders as proofs of the attachment of their relatives, and certainly do not excite any painful sensations in them, for I have seen several, on such occasions, who did not seem at all affected by these mournful cares. I have also seen some men working at their own coffins, though they did not seem likely to want them soon.

At the approach of death, all the arms in the house are discharged; the relations and friends of the same sex as the deceased assemble round him. If he is a person of importance on his own account, or belonging to a great family, all

persons of a certain rank come together. I witnessed, at
Nukahiva, one of the scenes of grief; these person who was the
object of it, was the wife of the old chief Pahoutehe, surnamed the Elephant ; for more than a year she had been labouring under a consumption, which seemed likely to carry her
off very soon. Forty or fifty women had assembled in the
house, in the middle of which they had placed the patient,
who generally occupied a small separate apartment at one end.
All were clothed in white linen, dressed in their finest ornaments, and, especially, with perfect cleanliness, the use of oil
and saffron being prohibited in these mournful ceremonies.
Her husband holding her right hand, and one of her sons the
left, they rubbed them gently, warmed them between their
own, and bathed them with their tears. There was a certain
concord in their lamentations ; all the female mourners did
not employ the same expressions, but they spoke in the same
tone, and terminated their verses simultaneously, with cries
and groans in cadence, which stifled their voice. This exercise being the more fatiguing, because it was a constrained
action in most of them, the performers were relieved from
time to time, and went on one side to recover from the fatigue
which this restraint had imposed upon them. Except the
hired mourners, the rest of the assembly seemed to be but
little affected ; they chatted, and even laughed, as they would
have done any where else, only making less noise. This co-
medy was repeated two successive days, and each time lasted
five hours. On the third day, the patient had recovered a part
of her strength, and, at the time of my departure, which was
above six weeks after, she still struggled with the disease,
which, in these countries, at least, has never medicine for its
auxiliary.

The language of these islanders is soft, harmonious, flexible,
and easy to be pronounced. The great number of vowels of
which it is composed, gives it this advantage, which, however,
is common to the people who live between the tropics.

The inhabitants of Rahopou have the advantage above all
the other islands, of not having been troubled, for a long time,
by intestine wars. I know not whether it is to their own prudence that they owe the charms of peace : at least, it is certain,
that by virtue of a taboo, which has been long in force, the
exportation of sanders-wood is forbidden. This regulation,
the natural effect of which is, to hinder the introduction of
fire-arms, with which navigators inundate the other islands,
is a proof how much this religious interdict, the only legisla-
tion of the South Sea islanders, might contribute to their welfare, in the hands of wise depositaries, who, instead of the

frivolous and ridiculous use, often made of it, should know how to employ it with address, for the interest and welfare of their fellow countrymen.

But if the inhabitants of Rahopou are peaceable towards each other, they are cruel to foreign prisoners whom chance throws in their hands. The English brig, the Matilda, Captain Fowler, being at anchor off this island, was plundered in the month of April, 1815. Five natives of the Society Islands who had been taken on board as sailors, had deserted a few days before and joined the natives. Taking advantage of a dark night and a high wind blowing towards the shore, they cut the cables which held the ship; the sea being very high, it was thrown upon the coast, and filled with water. When the natives saw that it was impossible to set it afloat again, they resolved to massacre all the crew, which seems to be the general custom of the islands of this Archipelago, when bad weather or any accident causes a foreign vessel to strand upon their coast. Captain Fowler had happily acquired the friendship of the chief named Nouhatou, who presided in the kind of tribunal which was to decide the fate of these unfortunate sailors. He permitted without difficulty the plunder of the Matilda, but would not consent to the massacre of the crew. These unfortunate men perceived by the few expressions which they were able to comprehend and the gesticulations that were made, that their lives depended on the issue of the debate of which they were the subject. Several chiefs, but of inferior quality, strongly opposed Nouchatou; it was only by the most ardent solicitation that he could save this unfortunate crew from the fury of the barbarians. It is even related that seeing all his prayers and arguments fail of making an impression on the assembly, he took a rope, and placing it round his own neck and that of his son, ordered a chief, who was nearest to him, to strangle them both : " that I may not see," said he, " during my life, so infamous an action; and that I and my son may not be accused of sanctioning by our presence the death of men who had never done us any harm." So magnanimous an action excited the surprize and admiration of the savages, who remained a moment petrified with astonishment, and then cried out unanimously, chief, chief, let the strangers live, we will keep our chief. The lives of the unfortunate Englishmen were saved, but the vessel was totally pillaged.

Having sailed from Nukahiva, on the 28th of February, we passed the following morning by the Island of Heheaou, which Ross had told me was occupied by a little colony from Nukahiva. These people not finding themselves comfortable at home, (the northern part of the island) gave to an American, a certain quantity of sanders wood to take them to an island, with which he pretended to be acquainted, and of which he doubtless gave them a picture very different from the rock on which he left them. Their new abode produces only some cocoa trees, but they also find some resource in fishing. Though they have indeed enough to keep them alive, they begged the captain of a ship which touched there, to carry them back to Nukahiva; but he had just come from it, and the situation of these islands, to the leeward of the Archipelago, and still more the want of wood to build boats, will prevent these unfortunate Indians from returning to their happy island, which they had the imprudence to leave.

From this time nothing remarkable occurred till our arrival in the roads of New Archangel, where we cast anchor on the 5th of April. Mr. Heigemeister, captain of the Kutusoff, had just taken the command of that place, which is the principal settlement of the Russians in this part of the world belonging to the North West Company. In my first interview with him he gave me proofs that the kindness he had already expressed towards me at Lima and Saint Francisco, was not cooled now that he was able to shew it in an effectual manner. He promised to afford me all the assistance towards repairing the unsuccessful commencement of our expedition, which he could command without prejudice to the interests entrusted to him.

We concluded together an agreement to undertake the sea otter fishery on our joint account. The principal stipulations were that the company should furnish us with thirty baidares, each manned by two Kodiak hunters, the whole under the direction of two agents ; that the produce of the chace should be equally divided, and that 200 piasters should be paid, as an indemnity for each hunter who should lose his life in an attack from the Indians. This arrangement seemed to me the more advantageous, as the experience I had acquired the preceding year allowed me but small hopes of success in trafficing for furs with the Indians in exchange for our goods, which were badly chosen ; and as the contingency, in which I was bound to an indemnity, had been for several years of rare occurrence. We were also authorized to place, free of expense, in the company's warehouses, the sanders wood and other things which could be of no use during the expedition.

My departure for port Saint Paul, in the island of Kodiak, where we were to take the hunters on board, was retarded by the necessity of examing the copper sheathing, which was decayed. On the 21st I went to visit an Indian establishment in one of the little islands, five or six miles to the north-west of New Archangel. I made this excursion in a baidare for three persons, which was given me by order of Mr. Heigemeister. One of the Kodiaks who accompanied me had been some time a prisoner among the Spaniards at Saint Francisco, and spoke the language tolerably. His residence at that place had given him a certain predilection for the country and its inhabitants, which is very natural if we compare the rude climate, and the laborious life of the Kodiaks in their own islands, and the other Russian settlements, with the temperature of California, and the happy *far niente* which sheds its influence, more or less, upon every thing connected with the Spaniards.

We entered a cove which is almost wholly closed by an island, on which is situated an Indian village, consisting of about twenty wooden huts. The landing place being inconvenient, the Indians, whom the sight of the baidare had drawn together, to the number of fifty, lifted up the boat before I could get out of it, and amidst loud cries, carried me to the hut of their Chief who received me with hospitality, and ordered slices of some kind of fat to be brought, which I tasted, and to my great astonishment found eatable. He then presented me with two kinds of fruit pies, one of a pretty agreeable taste resembling currants, the other mixed with rancid fat which was execrable. They were served in china plates with knife and fork complete, and all tolerably neat. After he had consulted with his wife, the Chief presented me with four small white martens' skins, though he saw clearly from the trifling presents I had made him that I had but little to give him in return. There were about a hundred Indians in his hut who behaved with great propriety. The women seem to be treated with great respect by the natives.

All our preparations being completed by the 1st of May, we made ready to put to sea with the first breeze. Petrowsky, the agent of the company, who was to direct the sea-otter fishery, came on board with the pilot and a passenger for Kodiak. Mr. Heigemeister came on board to take leave, and I gave him a packet for France, which he promised to send by the sloop which he was going to dispatch for Ochotsk. Our voyage was sufficiently favourable, and we anchored in port St. Paul on the 12th. The next day I went on shore to see the chief of the establishment and Governor of the island, Mr. Patarotch, who had the title of superintendaht. He received me very kindly, congratulated me on my arrival, through the medium of an American who spoke Russian, communicated the orders which he had received in our favour, and expressed himself ready to do all that depended upon him to dispatch the baidares without delay, and to do any thing else that was agreeable to me. The baidares were ready in consequence of the orders previously given by the governor general. Nothing was wanting but to collect them, which would require only a few days. The two following days were employed in landing the goods embarked at Sitka for this establishment.

During the remainder of the month we performed the necessary operations for our expedition, got on board a sufficient store of dry fish, train oil and tobacco, for the Kodiaks, and also trunks to contain the furs. The carpenters made a spare deck in the hold, and every thing was got ready to receive the baidares as soon as they should be dry enough to be put on board, which the rainy weather had not yet allowed. We began to get them on board on the 29th, and were obliged to put them through one of the windows. Twenty-two, which with some difficulty could be got between decks, were disposed of in the most convenient manner. On the 30th, most of the Kodiaks belonging to the expedition brought on board their lances, darts, and other apparatus for the fishery. I called the crew together and prescribed the conduct they ought to observe towards these peaceable but rather irritable people. I prohibited all intercourse except such as the service required, all purchasing of effects, arms, &c. upon any pretence whatever. We received a swivel, ten muskets, &c. for the expedition, and set sail on the 1st of June.

Being unacquainted with the Russian language and that of the natives, I could gather but little information respecting Kodiak. The population is considerably diminished, since it is under the dominion of the Russians, being reduced to twelve or fifteen thousand souls. I was convinced by my own inspection that the villages are thinly scattered, and that the islands before the port, formerly occupied by a numerous population, have now only three small villages. This diminution is particularly ascribed to the ravages of the small pox. This scourge had probably been checked sometime since by the vaccine. The company employs in its civil and mercantile administration, and in magazines, about thirty Russians, and twice as many creoles, children of women of the country.

The Russian company has the most absolute monopoly at Kodiak, as well as in all the Russian possessions in this part of the world. The measures which it takes to secure this monopoly, added to the submission and the character of the natives, oppose such great obstacles to smuggling, and allow so little hope of profit, that it is not likely to be attempted. Under a less exclusive system, fire-arms, powder, and other ammunition, coarse woollens and cottons, and the most common carpenters' tools, would meet with an advantageous sale. One might obtain in exchange otter skins, and other valuable furs which the Kodiaks, if they were free, would dispose of to strangers, as the Indians on the north west coast do, rather than deliver them to the Russians at the price fixed by the company. The Kodiaks are not allowed to have fire-arms in their possession, though they are taught the use of them, and intrusted with them, as a loan, to enable them to defend themselves against the continental Indians.

On the 7th I was not able to take the latitude ; but at noon I made myself twenty leagues west half south of Cape Adding-ton, on Prince of Wales' Island, and at half past seven in the evening we saw land to the north-east half north, and at ten saw the little eastern point of Coronation Island, which is the most easterly of the Hazy Islands. Being at the northern limit of the tract appointed for the otter fishery, I endeavoured to find an anchoring place, which might serve as a station. I steered so as to pass to the south-west of two islets, which are very remarkable, notwithstanding the diminutiveness of their size, on account of their detached position from the labyrinth of breakers, rocks, and islets which line the bottom of the gulf between Cape Addington and the Hazy Islands. We had no sign of the five rocks which Vancouver places to the south of the point of Warren Island, though we were within a league of the position which the chart assigns them. I am far from opposing my remarks to those of a navigator and geographer, who is remarkable for his exactness ; it is possible that the view of these rocks was concealed from us, though the weather was then very clear. At two o'clock I left, two miles to the east, the two islets, which are the north-west extremity of this dangerous Archipelago, and which I shall call Les Balises, and steered towards another island near the south coast of the gulf, and separated from the group. Off the east point of this detached islet we were observed by three Indian canoes, which remained beyond musket shot, with every mark of distrust, much more evident than that of the Indians in the south. At length one of these canoes approached us, and an Indian, who spoke some words of English, came on board. He was from Kaïgarny, a place much frequented by the Americans ; he informed me that the brig Brutus, captain Nye, was at Haniga, some leagues to the north, and offered to conduct me thither. I preferred an anchorage which he point-ed out in a cove on the north-west part of Prince of Wales' Island. After having reconnoitred it we anchored there, at half past six, in twenty fathoms. We took, for the night, the precautions usual on the south part of the coast.

As soon as the ship was moored, I conferred, through the

medium of Petrowsky, who spoke a little English, with the chiefs of the expedition. It was agreed that they should go out the following day to reconnoitre. The Indians had left us, and, according to their custom, bivouaked during the night on 'he sea coast. I had permitted the one from Kaigarny to sleep on board, hoping to derive some advantage from him. He had expressed much curiosity to know who we were, for our flag was unknown to him; and the sight of the Kodiaks and their boat giving him reason to take us for Russians, it cost us some trouble to undeceive him, and to convince him that we were Frenchmen, a name which he knew only from our muskets, brought by the Americans, the superiority of which they appreciated.

On the 9th the long-boat was dispatched, under Mr. Foucault, with eight baidares, which had on board the chiefs of the expedition, both Russians and Kodiaks, who went to examine the great entrance to the east of our anchoring place. Mr. Foucault went several leagues along the coast, without seeing any traces of population. He met with spacious bays, and an arm of the sea which extends farther than the eye can reach, to the south. Though the weather was fine, the strong breeze from the north was unfavourable to us, as the otters seldom shew themselves when the sea is agitated; we saw only two, but the Kodiaks thought that they frequented this part of the coast, and that it deserved to be tried.

The following day the twenty-nine baidares, each armed with a pair of pistols and two daggers, sailed to begin the fishery. I escorted them in the long-boat, but though we proceeded a considerable distance, and the Kodiaks dispersed among the winding channels of a group of islands, only a single otter was found. During our absence, four canoes of the natives had come alongside, from which nothing could be obtained but some fish, two beavers' skins, and some otters' tails. The Indian from Kaigarny having been surprised at the window of the great cabin, talking to his countrymen, was driven out, and left the ship with anger and resentment painted on his ferocious countenance. On the return of the hunters, the Company's agent solicited me to let them bivouac on shore, near their boats, which, from the nature of the materials employed in their construction, cannot remain long in the water without spoiling. These considerations, added to the confidence which I thought I could repose in a man who had that of his superiors, and who, in six years' residence, must have become acquainted with the country, and the genius of the inhabitants, induced me to agree to his proposal. From that time the Kodiaks passed the night on shore, under the protection of a guard, commanded by an officer. They also remained there during the day, if the weather was not favour- able to the fishery, which was frequently the case. The otters appeared only in small numbers; our hunters had obtained only twenty-one skins. During the same time we had received ten in exchange from the natives. At our arrival we had found only five or six of these savages, who are always wandering about in the fine season. Afterwards about thirty appeared, of both sexes and divers ages, and their numbers afterwards varied. On the 17th, in the morning, more Indians appeared than on the preceding days, with a pretty considerable quan- tity of furs. They retired, as usual, at noon, to take their repast, promising to return to barter the rest of the furs, of which they had not yet disposed. None of them, however, returned in the evening. The following day only a single canoe appeared, which landed at the back of the cove, without stopping at the ship. This sudden disappearance of the natives, after the promise they had made the day before, exciting my suspicions, I resolved to recall the Kodiaks, who were in their bivouac, the weather not having permitted them to go out: but not supposing there was any thing to fear from the Indians during the day, the camp being within musket shot of the ship, I deferred the execution of my intention till the even- ing. Meantime I went on shore to visit the environs of the camp, where I generally made an excursion about 5 o'clock. I intended also to watch for the hour of high water, the moon being full. I immediately sent back the little whale-boat; some Kodiaks took this opportunity to return on board. Per- ceiving that the tide was already very high, I put off, till the hour of high water, my intended excursion about the camp, and walked towards the bottom of the cove, along the beach, watching the tide. After going two or three hundred steps, I crossed an Indian, who stopped a moment, stepping aside to make way for me, and said, smiling, some words which I did not understand, and could only reply by nodding my head. A stick appeared to be the only weapon he had. A few minutes after my attention was roused by a musket shot on the side of the camp, which I thought at first must have been fired by the Kodiaks who had that morning practised firing with pistols, but this first shot was immediately followed by a discharge, after which the fire, though less constant, was continued with some briskness. Judging then it must be an attack of the Indians, my first impulse was to turn towards the camp, but seeing the Kodiaks fly without resistance, I thought that my pre- sence could be of no use, and that I had only to provide for my personal safety, which the encounter I had just had rendered more precarious. I called the boat which had put me on shore, and had not yet reached the ship, but in the confusion I was not heard. After having waved a handkerchief to make myself observed by the ship, for it was dangerous by calling, to let the savages know where I was, I undressed by the bushes, which lined the beach. Some moments after, having again waved my handkerchief, I threw myself into the sea, with my watch between my teeth.

Meantime, the ship fired upon the Indians, and sent out the long boat, which, having first steered towards the camp, turned aside on perceiving me, and reached me when I was still near the shore. It was immediately received by a very brisk fire, which it returned with its blunderbusses and muskets. As it came up, I made an ineffectual attempt to get into the boat, in which I perceived that several men were wounded. Not choosing to detain the boat under the fire made upon it by the Indians, who had come up in great numbers, under cover of the bushes, which I had just quitted, and not seeing, in this part, any Kodiak to assist, I ordered Mr. Partarieux, who commanded the boat, to stand off, without losing time to take me in. I kept by the side of the boat, which rowed off, firing towards the camp; it afterwards took me on board, and I found four men wounded of the seven who composed the crew. Two were wounded but slightly; but most of the ammunition was consumed, and the boat was incumbered with casks. Under these circumstances, I did not think fit to return into the fire, and I made it steer towards the ship, which we reached at half past one. It continued to fire towards the places from which the fire of the natives came, who kept themselves constantly under cover from the wood, by means of which they had approached within pistol-shot, without being perceived, and had suddenly attacked the Kodiaks, who had thought themselves perfectly secure. The two whale-boats being ready when I arrived on board, I dispatched them under the orders of Mr. Foucault, to take in such of these unfortunate people as might have been able to escape the fury of the first attack, either by throwing themselves into the boats, or by concealing themselves in cavities of the rocks, which line the beach. Mr. Briole took out of several bai-dares, which were full of water, being pierced with shots, seven men, of whom four were wounded, and one dead. The great whale-boat having gone to take in a Kodiak, who was seen among the rocks to the north of the camp, saved seven others, who crept successively out of the same hole, where, under other circumstances, three men would hardly have found room. Our boats went to take the fugitives on the shore itself, or at a very small distance from it, as it were, under the muskets of the Indians. Though supported by the fire of the ship, I regard it as an effect of Providence that they experienced no loss. This success amidst the disasters of this day, was owing to the devotedness and coolness of the officers in fulfilling a duty equally sacred and dangerous, and to the conduct of some brave men who voluntarily accompanied them.

At three o'clock the long boat, under Mr. Foucault, and a whale boat, under Mr. Partarieux, rowed along the coast at a small distance, to pick up the Kodiaks who might have saved themselves on this side, but they returned at four without having seen any. Meantime the Indians fired at intervals on the ship, which immediately discharged its cannon towards that part of the shore from which the firing came. Some of them came singly about the baidares to plunder, but retired on the first musket shot. Their presence was not very alarming, but the certainty that they were concealed in a position where every thing was in their favour, did not allow us to go on shore to take away the baidares and bury the dead. As for the wounded, besides the natural cruelty of the savages, the sight of the ground but too clearly proved that none of them were alive. Before night the deck was cleared of every thing that might hinder the working of the guns, and the long boat was completely equipped. During the whole night five or six guns were fired every hour to keep off the savages. They returned only one musket-shot at half past ten.

On the morning of the 19th some natives still showed themselves, both about the baidares and at the back of the cove. The long boat and a whale boat were sent under the command of Mr. Foucault, accompanied by the second agent. They ascended the west side as far as the point; the agent called from time to time, in the Kodiak language, in order to draw from their retreat those who might have found refuge in this part; but no voice answered to the call, which must have made the fugitives come forward if any had existed. Mr. Foucault saw at a great distance, three canoes which seemed to come from the entrance and to steer to the north-west; he returned on board at three o'clock. As every thing indicated that the main body of the Indians had retired, Mr. Foucault was again sent, at six o'clock, to bring back the baidares. All means was taken to secure his retreat in case of attack, and to prevent surprise. He did not go on shore till he had reconnoitred all the environs of the landing place. Our boats brought back eighteen baidares. Some arms were also collected, and nineteen Kodiaks were counted dead in the camp or on the shore at a small distance. They had all been killed by musket-shot; most of whom had been struck by several balls, which must have been fired point blank. Some pistols being found discharged, proved that some of these unfortunate people had defended themselves; among these, according to the report of the fugitives, was the interpreter, a young Creole of a very lively and intelligent disposition, who, after having fired his pistol, seized a pike, when he received a ball in his breast. Of forty-seven Kodiaks who were in the camp at the moment of attack, twenty were killed, twenty-five escaped by swimming or were picked up by our boats, which made forty-five whose fate was known. There remained only two whose fate was doubtful, probably they were drowned, for one of the baidares had upset, and the barbarity with which the Indians had killed the women did not admit of the supposition that they had been made prisoners. Of twenty-five who escaped twelve were wounded, most of them very seriously.

Mr. Foucault was sent on shore on the 21st with four men, under the protection of the long boat, to bury the unfortunate victims of the ferocity of the Indians. The Kodiaks would not go to perform this pious duty to the remains of their fellow countrymen; they did not appear to be at all affected at their death, and behaved on this occasion with the most disgusting insensibility. A young man who had the misfortune to lose his father and brother, did not shed a tear nor shew any signs of grief. These people have a degree of obduracy such as I never met with elsewhere; they seem to reserve for the chace and fishery, all the intelligence and vivacity that nature has given them.

Wishing to recover the baidares and arms which were still wanting, I went in the whale boat to make an excursion in the cove. I landed first near the camp, where there remained only some pikes and a few articles of little importance, belonging to the Kodiaks. I saw in the wood, a hundred and fifty paces from the shore, the dead body of an Indian, which had been discovered the day before, and which I recognized to be one of those who had most frequently visited us on board. He still had on a waistcoat and trowsers which he had received from us, and over them a blue great coat. His countrymen had seated him under a tree, with his back towards the sea; except the upper part of the head he was entirely covered with moss, in which they had stuck a branch which rose over his head. I then went to the bottom of the cove, where on the south-west, we saw the remains of two extinguished fires, and found near them, under a tree, a baidare for three persons, in good condition. I went up the beach with some men as far as the camp, but without discovering any other object of our search. I was astonished at finding on the place where I had undressed on the 18th, the trowsers, and other effects, which I had left there. Of the thirty baidares belonging to the expedition, only one was wanting, which the Indians might easily have concealed.

I landed a second time on the east side, with two men, in the little whale boat, under the pretence of seeing the wood, which had been cut before the affair, but, in fact, to dispel the panic terror which had seized some of my sailors, at the distant report of two musket-shots. Convinced that a longer stay would be equally useless to the interests of the expedition, and those of humanity, I resolved to quit this fatal spot as soon as the wind would allow, intending to go to New Archangel, to replace the arms of the hunters, lost on the 18th, repair the baidares, and land the wounded. The next day we weighed anchor early, and tacked several times to get out, but without making any progress, notwithstanding the aid of the boats, as the breeze was very faint, and at nine o'clock I was obliged to anchor in nine fathoms, only half a cable's length from the watering place; I had the sheet anchor carried out to the north-west, with a hundred fathoms of line, to relieve us from this bad position, where the Indians might alarm us with advantage, under cover of the wood, which we had in the rear; at the same time, we took measures to receive them. Three canoes had appeared at day-break, near the island, at the entrance, and after having remained for some time on the watch, landed near the eastern point, from which some Indians came to the camp, along the sea-shore. With horror we saw them disinter their victims, to plunder them of their miserable spoils. We fired some cannon-shot at them, which they returned, by firing their muskets at the boats, which carried out the warp. We set sail at four o'clock, and at length quitted this fatal cove, directing our course to New Archangel.

Desiring to ascertain the disposition of the Kodiaks, who, since the catastrophe of the 18th, appeared struck with terror, I proposed to the agent, to send some baidares to make an excursion, in sight of the ship, after we had come to an anchor, on the 24th, not far from Les Balises, upon the breakers of which we were nearly carried by the current, our Kodiaks gave a proof of good will, or of submission, on this occasion. Of ten baidares, only four were found in good condition, and departed, under the escort of the great whale boat, steering north-west, towards the Coronation Island. I set sail at nine o'clock; the signal for rallying was hoisted, and our hunters returned at half past eleven. They had taken a large otter, the liver of which we eat, and found it very good.

On the following morning, one of the Kodiaks, wounded on the 18th, died.

At three o'clock in the afternoon of the 26th, we doubled the island, which forms the south-east extremity of Sitka, and entered the bay, which was covered with a thick fog. We fired two guns as a signal for a pilot, who came on board at seven o'clock. I sent the governor a parcel, with an account of the catastrophe of the 18th. About an hour after, the boat belonging to the port arrived; it was armed, as well as the whole crew, the natives having killed two Russians, in the very sight of the settlement. We anchored at nine o'clock, in eight fathoms. I immediately went to the governor, whom I found much affected at our common misfortune, but still full of kindness, and inclined to do every thing to enable us to repair our losses. His good will was manifested by the proposal he made me, to join the hunting party, which he had just sent out, with all the baidares I could equip, if the Kodiaks would consent to go out again. I did not hesitate to accept this offer, which, considering the chances of success that long experience had given to the Russians, made me conceive the hope of making good, by the produce of the chace, the indemnity to which I was bound for the Kodiaks who were killed, and to do it with less danger than if it were reduced to our own resources.

Mr. Heigemeister spoke to me of the hostility of the Indians, who seldom let the fine season pass, without giving reasons for alarm. The great quantity of berries which they find in the woods, and the abundance of fresh water fish, securing them an easy subsistence, they are enabled to employ, in the gratification of their malevolence, the time which, in other seasons, they are obliged to devote to procuring food. The surgeon of the Kutusoff came, on the 27th, to fetch the wounded Kodiaks, eleven in number, and conveyed them on shore. The baidares were sent to the arsenal to be repaired. It was my intention to go out the next day; the baidares were ready, and the Kodiaks, persuaded by Mr. Heigemeister, were disposed to go on this new expedition to try their fortune with their countrymen.

In the morning, Mr. Foucault informed me, that the crew expressed some repugnance to go out again with the baidares. When I went on deck, sometime after, the greater part declared their opinions, through the medium of the armourer; the sailors grounded their refusal on the fact, that the kind of service, which the protection of the baidares required, was not mentioned in the engagement signed by the crew, and that the men who might be disabled had nothing to expect from the owners. I thought it my duty to employ persuasion, and the impression which the few words I addressed to them, seemed to make, induced me to hope I should prevail upon them, I was however astonished to see among them those on whom I principally depended, and who had given proofs of zeal on the 18th. My hopes were not realized; the motives of duty, honour, and even interest, which I urged in the manner best calculated to stimulate them, could not encourage these people who were struck with terror. Symptoms of this weakness had appeared at Kowalt, even after the affair. This disposition of their minds had been increased by the state of alarm in which we had found the Russian colony, in consequence of the murder of two Russians, who had been killed by some Indians in sight of the colony, and by the exaggerated accounts given by some officers of the strength and former success of these savages. The means of persuasion having failed, and it being quite out of the question to undertake a service which would continue some months, with persons ill disposed towards it, I yielded to necessity, renounced the execution of the project concerted with the governor, and resolved to employ immediately the only resource which I had left, namely, to visit the straits and trade with the ill-assorted cargo that I had still to dispose of.

July 2d the Kutusoff sailed for California with Mr. Heigemeister, leaving Mr. Yanovsky as his deputy: his intention was to procure a cargo of corn, and probably to make some final arrangements with the Spanish government. I intended to sail as soon as the pilot, who was also on board the Kutusoff, should return: he did not come back till the following day, and we had the mortification of being detained by contrary winds and calms till one o'clock in the morning of the 6th of July, when we got out with a slight breeze. The pilot left us as soon as we were beyond the shoals, and at eleven o'clock we doubled Woodhouse Point. It was my intention to double Cape Tchirikoff, sailing along the west coast of King George's Island. I proposed to visit the Straits to the east of that island, where furs are abundant, after having conferred with Captain Young, of the Company's brig the Finland, who convoyed an expedition that had lately sailed, from whom I hoped to obtain useful information.

At day-break on the 8th, the south-east part of Admiralty Island, and the entrance of Frederick's Sound, were in sight to the north, but very indistinctly on account of the mist. The north part of the eastern coast of Christian Sound being clear, I had approached it, that the current might be more favourable; for in this strait, as well as in Chatham Strait, of which it is only the prolongation, the flood sets north, and has more strength on the east side, and the ebb sits south and is stronger on the west side. At nine o'clock we saw several baidares to the north, under Gardener Point of Admiralty Island; some of them came up to us. The Kodiaks told us that the main body of the squadron to which they belonged, was in Frederick's Sound, and that the Finland and a schooner were in Port Cambden. I took on board a Kodiak who knew their anchorage, and desiring to see Captain Young, I entered the sound, and perceived the Finland under sail; the wind being very faint I got into the great whale boat to go on board the brig, which I overtook off port Cambden. Captain Young gave me but vague information respecting the trade of this country; he had not been fortunate in his fishery, his seventy baidares had taken only four hundred otters. The expedition which he commanded, had not been attacked by the Indians. Those of Kekh appeared only once to the number of thirty-seven, in two large canoes; but the Kodiaks, though distant from their escort, rendered bold by a long residence in this country, had remained firm, and awed the Indians, who intimidated at seeing the baidares form a circle round them, contented themselves with proposing that they should exchange hostages. The Kodiaks having referred the decision of the affair to the commander of the expedition, the Indians retired without committing any hostilities. At five o'clock in the afternoon I returned on board with Captain Young, and the three vessels proceeded to leave the Sound. I steered for Chatham Strait, which I entered with a slight breeze from the south. At day-break on the 9th we fired a gun and hoisted American colours, these being the best known by the savages of this coast. At six o'clock we saw a canoe coming from the west coast; we lay to for it to come up to us; after some hesitation one of the Indians came on board, where he remained half an hour, examining every thing with the greatest attention, with all the signs of distrust usual among these people. He had nothing to dispose of and appeared to come only to reconnoitre. Till we met this canoe we had seen, for thirty leagues along the coast, on both sides of the straits, nothing which indicated that the country was inhabited. I approached the east coast, where I knew the village of Houts-nau is situated. In the middle of the channel we were visited by two canoes, one of them was recognized to be the same which had visited us this morning. He had a pretty fine otter skin to sell, which we obtained in exchange for powder. They soon after quitted us, and another canoe, coming from Houts-nau, came along side. An Indian, of a ferocious countenance, but dressed with a degree of pomp, came on board. He said he was a chief of Houtsnau, and had made several cruises on the coast, with the Americans. He seemed to be intelligent, and to have a knowledge of the trade and navigation of the Straits. Thinking that he might be useful to us, I gave him the permission which he had desired, to remain on board. He immediately sent away his boat, and made me a present of an otter skin, and a beaver skin ; in return for which I gave him, also as a present, some powder, and a sword which had attracted his attention.

Though we were soon in a convenient situation to receive the boats of the natives, and several appeared, only one came alongside, and that had nothing but fish. As this confirmed the assertion of Youtchkitau, that there would be no traffic if the ship did not come to anchor, Mr. Foucault was therefore sent to examine the anchorage in Hood-bay, which was pointed out by the Indian who accompanied him, but he returned at noon, without having found one, the pilot having conducted him into the cove before the village of Houtsnau, where the depth was too great. The wind being faint, and the sea calm, as many as eleven canoes came out, one of them manned with thirteen men, another with seven, and the others with a smaller number, most of them armed with muskets. This sight revived the fears of our cowards, whom the presence of several women and children ought to have encouraged, if fear could reason ; besides, the boarding-net was fixed up, and every precaution taken before the number of canoes was considerable. Some Indians were admitted on board, and among them one of the principal chiefs of this country, named Katahanack, and his son. Most of the canoes had brought furs, but the natural distrust of these people being increased by the reserve of our crew, they did not offer them for exchange. I retained my position to the leeward of Houtsnau during the night, not choosing to sacrifice, to the panic terrors of my crew, the advantages which it afforded for the trade.

On the 11th the canoes came at 10 o'clock, but in small numbers, and with few skins. The Indians repeated their intreaties to bring the ship to an anchor, pretending, that at a distance from shore, the slightest agitation in the sea incommoded their canoes alongside, which was, indeed, evidently true. Mr. Foucault was therefore sent, at 6 o'clock in the evening, to look for an anchoring place in Hood Bay, where he found one that was tolerable, in which we cast anchor the next morning. The ship was soon surrounded by canoes ; our traffic went on briskly, and was not interrupted by any attempt on the part of the Indians, whose behaviour afforded no serious subject for complaint. None were admitted on board except those who had furs to dispose of, and some chiefs who dined with us. I was satisfied with the conduct of Youtchkítau, who on several occasions informed us of the measures which it would be proper to take. Some changes in the wind brought us into a position before the village of Houtsnau. While we were there, the Indians hoisted a white flag, and the Russian merchant flag, on a palissade, which appeared to be a defensive work. We replied to this civility by hoisting our colours. I was going to fire a gun, but Youtchkitau assured me that it would cause alarm. We kept our position during the night, and at half past five in the morning arrived at Houtsnau. The sea being calm, and all the circumstances favourable, several canoes came out, with which we carried on a lively trade, in the most amicable manner.

These two days had procured us forty-five otter skins, besides other furs of less value. The greater part was paid for in powder, at the rate of 12 lbs. for one otter skin. Here, as at Nootka, the Indians found our woollen goods very bad : as for the muskets, there were some among those of the French manufacture which suited them, but they would not take the Spanish muskets at any price. At this rate the powder which we had remaining would not be sufficient to procure more than about two hundred otter skins. Youtchkitau having assured me that in Cross Sound, and in Lynn Channel, I should find furs as cheap again as at Houtsnau, I resolved, by his advice, to visit that part. We entered Cross Sound at three o'clock in the afternoon of the 14th. Youtchkitau telling me of an anchoring place on the north-east side of King George's Island, I steered towards it ; but as we approached he appeared uncertain, and spoke of the rocks in the vicinity. We were therefore obliged to seek another place, in which we did not succeed that day. On the day following, our Indian pointed out a passage between an island which he said was Kitghaka, and a little island to the north-west, which would lead to the anchoring place ; but, before we entered it, he frankly confessed that the fog had led him into an error, and that this passage was too shallow. He then pointed out what he stated to be the true channel, which we were unable to reach, having fallen to leward. After dinner I sent Mr. Briole, with Youtchkitau, in the whale-boat, to examine the anchoring place, which we so much desired to reach. Mr. Briole found it very indifferent, and too near the coast, and I therefore determined to quit this narrow channel, where we had tacked to no purpose the whole day, and to fall to leeward of the islands, where we had plenty of room. The crew, which had been on deck ever since four o'clock in the morning, till nine in the evening, was at length able to take a little rest. The night passed in manœuvring to keep the ship at a distance from the islands to the east of Kitghaka, towards which it was carried by the ebb, of which I could not take advantage, for want of local knowledge. I had no information respecting this part, except that given by Vancouver, who represents it as a labyrinth.

On the 16th, at day-break, the tide was at the highest, and soon turned. At five, we fired a gun to announce our arrival to the neighbouring Indians. At two o'clock, a canoe from the south, in which were two men and one woman, came along side of us, but crossing, it was overset by the whale-boat, in which the three Indians saved themselves. The whale-boat was sent out to pick up the canoe and its effects. In the evening, a young deer swam by the ship, and was picked up by the whale-boat; it was without a wound, and must have been a very short time in the water. The flesh of this animal was found excellent at the officers' table, and refused by the crew, to whom I offered a part; they said it was an animal that died of itself. This deer had probably leaped, when flying from some enemy, from the top of the steep rocks, which border this coast, the rudest I ever saw. We likewise saw a humming-bird, which fluttered some time round the ship. We afterwards proceeded to an anchorage, which had been pointed out by the Indians belonging to the canoe, who quitted us after they had repaired their vessel : I presented the shipwrecked old woman with a grey blanket and a small looking-glass, which had to reflect the most hideous countenance ever worn by a human creature.

At five o'clock, in the morning of the 17th, two miles from the east of the island of Kitghaka, I dispatched Mr. Partarieux to reconnoitre the anchorage pointed out to us, which he, in fact, found to the south-east. We steered towards it, but the breeze having gradually fallen into a calm, we were carried to the south by the current, and were obliged to cast anchor, at ten o'clock, in twenty-eight fathoms, at less than a cable's length from the shore; however, a breeze springing up, we were enabled to weigh, and anchor in a better place towards the north-west point, two cables and a half from shore.

In the afternoon of the following day, several canoes came with furs, which seemed to give much pleasure to Youtchkitau, who was quite ashamed since our entrance into the canal, where he had shewn himself such a bad pilot. At three o'clock, a handsome canoe, with fifteen men on board, came alongside. Recognizing Katahanack and his son, I invited them to come on board, and they dined with us. The arrival of these persons, and the reception I gave them, seemed to displease Youtchkitau ; but he soon assumed the most friendly manner, conversed with them, and listened with much attention to a story they told him, at the conclusion of which he broke out into execrations against the inhabitants of Ako. Soon after, a large boat entered the bay by the eastern point. The chief and his son immediately embarked in theirs, prepared their muskets, of which they had, in a trunk, more than enough for all their men, and went to meet the new comers, who advanced singing. When they came within a short distance, they hailed the strange boat, which stopped, and that of Katahanack immediately went alongside. The people in the two vessels took their arms, they disputed violently for a moment, one of the strangers was struck, and fell. His companions immediately yielded. Katahanack's people carried off skins and muskets, and retired with precipitation through the channel between the two islands. The canoe which had been plundered came along side : it belonged to Ako, and had on board fifteen men, and one woman, who steered. The wounded man, who had been struck on the forehead with a dagger, by the young chief, was dressed by Mr. Vimont. I made a present to him and to the woman. Youtchkitau gave every sign of lively indignation, when he saw the conduct of his countrymen ; it appeared to us, that he had been deceived by them. Some hours after, he himself shewed as much avidity. The possessor of a mantle of elk's-hide, refusing to let him have it at his own price, he asked my permission to take it by force, a proposal which I rejected with contempt.

Several canoes came out on the 19th, but fearing that they might be plundered by the pirate Kutahanack, they brought only furs of small value, except one otter-skin. This disappointment destroyed the hopes which had induced me to visit this part, and I determined to leave the canal, and return to Chatham Strait, which I had reason to regret my having quitted.

The bay to which the Indians gave the name of Koutikikakoa, and to which, before I knew it, I had given the name of Balguerie, is formed by the two islands Kit and Kaka, the coasts of which form an arc, cut into two by a channel of less than a quarter of a league. This bay is a central position, where, under circumstances less unfavourable than those in which we were placed, furs may be received from Lynn Channel, and the northern coast of Admiralty Island. Wood and water may be procured at a small distance from the shore ; but here, as well as on the whole coast, it is advisable to proceed to these operations as soon as you arrive, not to give the Indians time to contrive a surprize.

We sailed on the 20th, at eleven o'clock, and passed between the two islands, on which we perceived ruins of habitations, with an abandoned palisade. The wind was contrary on the 21st, and we made but little progress. A canoe came from Admiralty Island, which had only some small and indifferent skins to dispose of. What gave me still less pleasure was, the news of the arrival of a brig, which the Indians had seen to the south. We entered Chatham Strait, and though the wind had fallen in the night, we were, at six in the morning, opposite to the village Houtsnau. We perceived the port towards the north, and, near the village, a brig, which fired a gun, and hoisted the flag of the United States; we hoisted ours.

A great number of Indians, with furs, came on the 22d, but we had no dealings with them, the only article which they demanded being powder, and I would not give the same quantity as I had done before, Youtchkitau having given me to understand, that the rate was too high, and might be reduced, by giving, instead, hatchets, and other iron instruments, of which we had an abundance. The Indians quitted us before noon: I hoped they would come back, and proposed to relax in my pretensions, rather than do nothing, but my expectations were not realized. There remained alongside only the canoe of Youtchkitau, who had brought one of his wives, his son, an infant, and three of his brothers. I gave some trifles to his wife and child; Youtchkitau, after having long conversed with his brothers, informed me of his design to return home, in order to put a stop to the disorders which had been committed by strangers, and which could not be prevented by his wives. He made a long speech on this occasion, in which I clearly saw his bad faith, his covetousness, and effrontery in asking. He left me at six o'clock, taking, besides what I had given him before, a little assortment, composed principally of hardware, but not a double-barrelled gun, which for some days had been the object of his desire, and the theme of his importunities. In order to conquer my resistance, he acted, at the moment of his departure, the part of a wounded person : he pretended to have had a fall, and uttered lamentable cries, saying that he had fallen upon old wounds, with which he was, in fact, covered.

Meantime, the brig had left the port, and advanced towards us. We found that this vessel had sailed from Boston twelve months before; it was called the Brutus, and was commanded by Captain Nye, who offered to accompany me to the port, if it was my intention to anchor there. Hoping to obtain information, I went on board of her, with Mr. Vimont. Captain Nye received me very kindly, and was surprised to find in these seas, a vessel without a pilot, especially coming out of Lynn Channel, which was the most dangerous on these coasts. "You have, doubtless, visited these coasts before, in one of our ships," said he. I replied in the negative. "But you have some officer who knows them." "None." "How do you manage then? How do you manage yourself? I have made three voyages to the coast as an officer, before I commanded." "One of your countrymen first navigated these seas without a guide, and I do the same."

We agreed to anchor in the south port, at the bottom of Hood Bay, and to share the produce of the trade, as long as we should remain together. In the morning of the 23d, the Brutus sent her second officer to pilot us: she then took the lead and we followed, along the south side of Hood Bay. At eleven o'clock, we entered the port called Tchastichl by the Indians, and Suddart Harbour by the Americans. But few canoes visited the two ships, with furs of land animals only. I passed the afternoon with Captain Nye, who was indisposed. We chiefly conversed on the navigation of these coasts. He had just gone round Admiralty Island, and had got only a single fur.

Captain Nye having resolved not to protract his stay in this place, sent me four beaver-skins, being the half of the produce of his traffic; ours had been still more insignificant: he received in exchange some hard-ware. As he was still indisposed, I went to see him before his departure. He gave me a series of American papers, down to the month of October, 1817. We gave each other some provisions, of which neither of us had an abundance, and made some trifling exchanges.

In order to put an end to a competition, which, notwithstanding the insignificance of our resources, could not but be injurious to him, Captain Nye proposed to me, to let him have the remaining part of our cargo. Though experience had proved the impossibility of turning to account a cargo so ill sorted, I gave up all idea of an arrangement, when I learnt that he was only authorized to give me in exchange skins of land-animals. He advised me to go to Sitka, where I should find Captain Davis, who had a share in several vessels, and had more extensive powers than he had.

In order to strengthen the crew, which had still many sick, I engaged two young men of the Sandwich Islands, out of four that were on board the Brutus.

We were shortly afterwards visited by Youtchkitau, who

brought on board two skins, of which he made me a present. He made me a long speech, from which I understood, that he announced a great supply of furs for the next day. But this information did not prove to be true ; the few boats that came had nothing but fish and small skins ; and Smed, a chief whom I had known at Sitka, told me, that the majority of the Indians had gone to the otter fishery, and would not return for several days. This news destroying all the hopes of the success which I had expected, after the departure of the brig, I resolved, in expectation of the return of the Indians, to go and try my fortune in Frederick Sound, where Captain Nye had made me hope to find Indians of the Kekh tribe.

. The weather for several days was variable, and, on the whole, unfavourable, and it was not till the 29th, in the morning, that we reached the entrance of Port Cambden : we fired two guns to acquaint the Indians of our arrival. At one o'clock, nothing appearing, we sent Mr. Foucault to look for an anchorage under the islet, at the west extremity of the port. At three o'clock, a canoe arrived, and, soon after, another came from between the islands, which, without coming alongside, appeared to make enquiry of the first. Mr. Foucault returned, having found an anchorage, where we indeed cast anchor, at five o'clock, in thirty-five fathoms water, in a spacious cove, formed by a number of little islands. Several canoes came, but as most of them, like that in the morning, came to reconnoitre, we had but few skins. One canoe, in the morning, left us soon, to make a report to the chief, named 'Tachahanak, who had sent it, of whom the natives spoke to us, as a person of importance. The others did not quit us till nine o'clock, and passed the night on the neighbouring islands. The next day some canoes visited us, but they had only a few furs ; and the Indians, who had more need of clothing than of ammunition, found, like all the others, that our woollen goods were good for nothing, though care had been taken to make mantles of blue cloth, with trimmings and buttons. Meeting several canoes, I returned on board sooner than I had intended, for I had not much confidence in the natives of this district. It was they who, at the beginning of the establishment of New Archangel, had surprised a large party of hunters at Macartney Point. Out of three hundred hunters, nearly two hundred were killed or taken, the remainder wandered a long time in the woods, only a part were able to return to the colony, the rest perished, or were made slaves. During my stay upon this coast, one of these unfortunate persons, was brought back by an American, who had ransomed him from the savages.

. Tachahanak, one of the principal chiefs of the country whom

I impatiently expected, visited me on the 31st, in a handsome canoe manned by six rowers, with his two wives, a child, and his brother, whom we had seen in the morning. This personage made me a present of five skins, but what I offered him in exchange for his generosity was not to his taste, and, notwithstanding the collation he took, and the presents I made to his wives, we had some trouble to come to an agreement ; for not finding on board the articles that would have suited him, he wanted every thing we had. These two-brothers had an agreeable physiognomy, with a certain behaviour and comparative cleanliness, which took from them a part of the savage rudeness which characterizes the Indians of the north. They were dressed entirely in the European fashion, except shoes. The two women were also tolerably neat.

We quitted this place on the 1st of August, it being my intention to return to Houtsnau, where I hoped to obtain without a competitor, the produce of the fishery, which the Indians must have collected during my absence. It was on the morning of the 3d that we entered port Suddart, where we were visited by our old friend Youtchkitau. He gave me a long account, which I could not understand, of the war between Katahanak and the people of Ako, of a brig anchored at Kutzetll, in Cross-Sound, and, lastly, of the bad success of the fishery. After having spoken of the scarcity of furs at Houtsnau, he told me, that many might be had if I would pay for them at the old rate, which I did not hesitate to promise. I was surprised to find him in this place with his wives, where he had encamped for some reason unknown to me. The canoes which came on the 5th were not richer than those that came on the preceding day ; which had nothing to offer but fish and the skins of land animals. Smed came in the evening, accompanied by another chief, in a manner which gave us some hope. He first presented me with two beaver skins, but he fancied this generosity authorized him to make exorbitant demands. He was not more moderate in treating for his friend, who had three skins, of which we could procure only one for powder, at the current rate Smed, however, generally behaved with propriety, and I permitted him to remain on board. Of all the Indians of this coast none had so much mildness in his countenance and manners : he was very intelligent, and appeared to be perfectly acquainted with the channels of the north part. I learnt, however, from him, that but few otter skins could be procured in this season of the year ; that they would begin to come in December, and would be abundant in February. After this information, and what I saw myself, I resolved to quit this place as soon as possible. The only skin which I received this time was the sixtieth collected in the strait, or, more properly, at Houtsnau.

We left port Suddart on the morning of the 7th of August, but the winds were remarkably contrary, so that we did not reach Christian Sound till the evening of the 9th, and anchored the following day in the outward port of Iknou. Early in the morning of the next day we fired two guns to call the Indians together, but though the weather was pretty fine only one canoe appeared, which had nothing but fish. The officers found on the north-west coast a little cultivated spot, where there were still some potatoes. This discovery confirming my opinion of the recent passage of Captain Nye, who had spoken to me of this garden, induced me to resolve to make no longer stay in this place, where there was nothing more to glean, and, considering the little chance of success that remained on this coast, I determined to sail to New Archangel, where, from what Captain Nye had told me, I expected to meet with Captain Davis, and to treat with him about the exchange of the rest of our cargo for furs.

We were off Woodhouse Point early on the morning of the 18th, but fogs, high winds, and calms, having detained us three days, I left the ship at the entrance, and went in the great whale boat to New Archangel. They had not yet heard of Captain Davis, whose delay caused some uneasiness. After dining with Mr. Yanovsky I went with him on board the Kamschatka frigate, which had arrived shortly before, and was commanded by Captain Golownin, who was not on board. I was received in the most obliging manner by Mr. Moraview, the first lieutenant. When we returned on shore we saw Mr. Golownin at the house of Mr. Yanovsky; he received me with equal kindness; his interesting and instructive conversation made the hours pass unperceived, and when I rose to take my leave, it being too late to go on board my own ship, I accompanied Mr. Patouchkin on board the Okritie, a vessel belonging to the company, which he commanded. The morning being foggy I did not reach my ship till eleven o'clock, and we immediately got ready to stand out to sea. At ten o'clock at night, under Cape Engano, we perceived a fire at a small distance, and immediately heard a musket shot. Supposing that it was a vessel in danger, I steered towards it with a light at the bowsprit. On approaching I perceived a brig, which, when we were near enough to hail, proved to be his Britannic Majesty's brig the Colombia, which had sailed from Europe, in 1817. It fell astern while we were speaking; at midnight it again approached us, and half an hour after fired two musket shots to which we did not reply. We lay to and the captain called to me that he was coming on board; which he did immediately after. He declined looking at the ship's papers, saying that he came as a friend, and merely to obtain some information. I communicated to him all that I knew of that coast, the Russian settlements, &c. He appeared to be much interested in the change of the governor of New Archangel, which place he was going to visit. He had left Europe in a state of profound peace: he informed me of the restoration of the Colombia to the Americans, and told me of the departure of the Uranie for a voyage of discovery, without being able to tell me the name of the commander. This captain, whose name was Robson, spoke in a very loose and unconnected manner, and had nothing of the officer in his dress and manners. He went away at three o'clock in the morning, after having had a severe fall upon deck. My fruitless visit to Sitka having again caused me to lose several days, I determined to proceed directly to the entrance of Peres, and to confine myself to some parts of the coasts which it washes, and to Nootka to endeavour to exchange the rest of my cargo for furs. At nine o'clock in the evening we descried Forester's Island, situated to the north-west of the entrance. We steered into the entrance of Peres the next morning, keeping to the north side, along which we steered to Cape Muzon. When we doubled it I had a gun fired and the American flag hoisted, under which the vessel appeared at the opening of Port Cordova, which the Indians call Kaïgarny.

Having learnt from the Americans and Russians that the inhabitants of this district had taken most share in the affair of the 18th of June, I formed the project of seizing the first that should come on board, and making them pay a ransom in furs, as a just indemnity for the losses which the perfidy of these Indians had caused us. With this intention, I had made various changes, in order to disguise the ship, had it painted differently, &c. After having doubled the Cape, I steered towards a village, at the back of a little cove, the first on ascending the west side of the port. A canoe came out with five Indians on board, who, after having observed us at a distance, came within hail, and asked us whence the ship came, its name, that of the captain, &c. To all these questions I gave answers calculated to inspire them with confidence, and asked them to give me a pilot to conduct us to the anchoring place; but instead of coming near they rowed away, and reached the coast. Conceiving that any other attempt of this kind would be fruitless, and the want of time and of local knowledge not permitting me to endeavour to inflict on them the punishment which they merited, I stood off, and directed my course to

Port Estrada, on the north coast of Queen Charlotte's Island, of which we came in sight at five o'clock in the afternoon. The country, in this part, forms a striking contrast with that of the north, or rather with all that I saw on the north-west coast. It is low, especially on the sea-side, rising almost insensibly towards the interior, where it rises into moderate hills, the rounded summits and gentle declivities of which had none of those steep rocks, and rugged indentations which are so frequent elsewhere. The foliage of the woods appeared to me to be of a less gloomy tint, and the whole scene much less rude.

The outline of this coast, which Vancouver has given after the Spaniards, seems to be very correct, and I had no difficulty to distinguish the port which I sought, from Port Masseredo, and several other inlets which were in view at the same time, in the west. Perceiving four canoes, three of which were under sail, we took in the studding sails, to enable them to come up to us. They however passed, without coming along-side, and the day being too far advanced to think of entering a channel which I heard to be dangerous, we stood off.

Early on the 26th we entered the port, or rather arm of the sea, at Massett, under the guidance of an Indian named Tayan, who came in a canoe to meet us. He made us steer towards the south-east part. At eight o'clock we passed the south-east point, and soon after, being opposite to a large village, we were surrounded by canoes. At nine o'clock, being within seven or eight miles of the point, we cast anchor. Several canoes came alongside on the 27th, with furs, of which we obtained only two, because the Indians, who desired woollen goods in exchange, found ours of a bad quality.

In the morning it blew hard from the south-east, and we dragged our anchor, and were obliged to moor again. The movement of the anchor made the natives, several of whose canoes were alongside, suppose that we were going to sail. I endeavoured to make them understand that I had no such intention; but in spite of my assurances, the fore-top stay-sail having been hoisted, they threw themselves into their canoes with so much precipitation, that they left behind them three skins, for which they had not yet been paid. In spite of all our endeavours to undeceive them, they went on shore on the south side. At two o'clock in the afternoon a canoe came alongside to reconnoitre. Being encouraged by our promises, and especially by seeing the small bower anchor dropped, they called to their countrymen, and a great number of canoes came round us. Those who had left their furs in the morning did not fail to ask for payment, and seemed agreeably surpri-

sed at receiving it. They had but few furs, and in their intercourse with us, proved to be the most covetous of all the
Indians with whom we had dealt on this coast.

Several canoes came on the 28th, but they had but few otter
skins ; they attributed this scarcity to the visits they had already received from the Americans. We obtained a pretty canoe
for an indifferent double-barrelled gun. Here, as well as at
other anchoring places, we procured a sufficient quantity of
fish, and, for the first time on the north part of the coast,
water-fowl which had not a fishy taste.

The Indians gave us no cause of alarm. They are the finest
men on the north-west coast ; they seem better fed, stronger,
and much cleaner than the others. In their persons, and in
every thing belonging to them, there is an appearance of opulence and comparative cleanliness, superior to all that we had
before observed. As far as we could judge, the huts composing the four villages, on the two sides of the entrance, are
better built, and in better order, than those of the north.
There is something picturesque in the whole appearance of
this large village ; it is particularly remarkable for the monstrous and colossal figures which decorate the houses of the
principal inhabitants, and the wide gaping mouths of which
serve as a door. Ascending the arm of the sea, there is, on
the north side, above the largest village, a fort, the parapet of
which is covered with beautiful turf, and surrounded by a palisade in good condition, which gives it the appearance of the
out-works of our fortresses. This district, and the whole
north side of Queen Charlotte's Island, is beyond comparison
the finest that we saw in this part of America. The Indians
were informed not only of the affair at Kowalt, but also of our
appearance at Kaigarny, a boat of that tribe, which was their
ally, came to inform them of it. This circumstance, and the
recent quarrel with the Brutus, explained the terror of those
who had quitted us so suddenly the day before. They disap-
proved of the conduct of those of Kaigarny, or at least endeavoured to persuade us so.

My intention was to get under weigh the 29th, with the ebb,
but the fog prevented me. We hoisted three flags, to dry
them ; the sight of these obtained us a visit from a dozen canoes, of which only two had come before. Itemtchou the
head chief of Masset came in a handsome canoe, accompanied
by his three wives. His face is long, a little morose and savage,
and has something of the Swiss character. A zig-zag red line on
his forehead, was continued to part of his nose. He wore, by
way of a mantle, a white blanket, with a blue stripe at the extremities, open before, and fastened by a cord : his hat was in

the form of a truncated cone, in the Chinese fashion. He would not come on board, till we had promised that au officer should remain as a hostage in his boat. We received him in the best manner, and made some presents, both to him and to his wives. We conversed by means of an Indian of Skitigats, named Intchortge.* Having asked the name of the chief, telling him my own, he thought I wanted to change names with him, which, among these people, is the most inviolable pledge of friendship. He eagerly acceded to this proposal, which seemed to flatter him. The exchange was made, not-withstanding the difficulty the chief found in pronouncing his new name, which, to oblige him, I softened into Roki ; we made each other some presents, and parted good friends. In endeavouring to quit this place, our movements were so counteracted by contrary currents, that the ship ran aground close in shore. We had had not less than eleven fathoms water, a cable's length from the shore, not ten minutes before we ran aground. We had then only eight feet before, and twelve under the mizen-chain-wales.

We immediately proceeded to take the best steps in this disagreeable situation, but it having been necessary to take down the nets, the Indians who accompanied us to trade, gradually got on board in such numbers that they became at least equal to that of our crew. Though the few arms, and the numbers of women and children in the canoes, did not indicate any thing hostile on their part, any more than their conduct, these pacific appearances might change in a moment. But in the circumstances in which we were placed, it was less dangerous to act with confidence, than to shew a distrust, which, by letting them see our critical situation, might induce them to take advantage of it, to attack us. Besides, I was made easy by the presence of my friend Itemtchou, who had come on board shortly after we had run aground, without requiring a hostage. He endeavoured to make me easy respecting the situation of the ship, and especially with regard to his personal sentiments in our favour, on which he said I might entirely depend, in consequence of the friendship which united us. I expressed to him the entire confidence

---

* Intchortge was well made, of fine stature ; his complexion was slightly tan-ned, and his countenance entirely European, except the eyes, which, in all the natives of the north-west coast that I saw, have always something savage in them. He piqued himself not only on speaking English well, but also on his polished manners ; of which he endeavoured to persuade us by saying, frequently, " *Me all the sames Boston gentleman.*" These Indians, who have no intercourse except with the vessels from Boston, conceive that city to be the capital of the civilized world.

which I placed in his inclinations towards us, as well as in the pacific disposition of his subjects; but, at the same time, I gave him to understand, that the great number of men which covered the deck, and the quantity of canoes which surrounded the ship, without making us uneasy, hindered us greatly in the measures which it was necessary for us to take to get the ship afloat. He made no answer to this indirect solicitation, but, a moment after, when we were going to carry out an anchor, he took leave of us. After he had left the ship, he spoke some words in a loud voice, and, in about five minutes, there did not remain a single canoe alongside, and not a single man on board, except the interpreter. This Indian told me, that he stayed only with the permission of his chief, and also begged mine, which I readily gave him. This man, whose English I understood, was very intelligent, and well acquainted with this country. Continuing our operations during the night, we got the vessel afloat again before noon, on the 30th. My friend Itemtchou came back in the morning, like a man certain of being welcome, and expressed much joy at our success. I gave him, besides several trifles, a double-barrelled gun. This man has a feeling heart, and this, perhaps, prevented all hostile attacks from his subjects. We bargained for some more otter-skins, and weighed anchor soon after.

On the 31st, in the afternoon, the weather being very fine, we passed, at a distance of four or five miles, round Point Invisible, which cannot be more properly named. The tongue of low and sandy land which terminates it, seemed to me to extend farther than Vancouver marks it after the Spaniards. To the north of the woody part, its small elevation, its white sands, and its scarcely sensible inclination, give its appearance something indefinite, even in clear weather, and must render it very dangerous during the fogs, which are very frequent in these seas. In doubling the point, we found that the ebb set into the channel, between Queen Charlotte's and Pitt's Islands. We steered towards this strait, which we entered at half-past four o'clock, Invisible Point being to the west of us.

This evening was singularly beautiful; the atmosphere was pure, the sky without a cloud, the sea calm, the temperature mild. The coasts which bound this beautiful channel were visible on each side; those of Queen Charlotte's Island, which begin to rise at a small distance from Invisible Point, and soon form steep mountains, were near enough for us to distinguish those parts of the rock which were bare, from those that were woody. For several hours the most extraordinary and magnificent sight was presented to our view. For an extent of about two leagues, their outlines, accurately marked on the blue sky behind, represented a series of buildings, some of which seemed to be in a perfect state of preservation, and others in ruins; some resembled Greek monuments, others gothic works, and others, from their gigantic size, resembled Egyptian edifices. We could distinguish immense fortresses some antique, with lofty towers, others resembling our modern fortifications. Some rocks, which were only irregular masses, were frequently mingled with these visionary monuments of human industry, which seemed ranged in perfect order, forming not only entire buildings, but, even parts of large cities. This singular view, equally remarkable for its grandeur, as for the forms of the masses, must be attributed, I suppose, to the arrangement of the rocks, which crown the heights of this part of Queen Charlotte's Island, as well as most of the mountains of these countries. I must say that, though several had already attracted our attention in other places, none approached the regularity and grandeur which in this part excited our admiration. We were able to observe them several hours, and the night alone concealed them from our view; their forms not having undergone any sensible alteration, except what was naturally produced by the progressive motion of the ship. This circumstance induces me to believe, that it cannot be attributed to clouds, which, indeed, would be hardly less extraordinary. The sublimity of the scene, heightened by the splendour of the setting sun, filled our hearts with a religious emotion, and it is indelibly impressed on my memory.

I would willingly have touched at Skitigats, one of the principal Indian villages, of which the Captain of the Brutus and Intchortge had spoken to me, but it would have cost me more time than I could spare.

On the 1st of September we went down the channel, with a good north-west wind, keeping in the middle, for fear of the currents, respecting which I had no information, Vancouver, my only guide, not having explored these parts. It is laid down in his atlas only after the Spanish surveys, and drawn in a particular manner, which seems intended to indicate that it has not been so perfectly explored as the other coasts.

We tacked early to approach Queen Charlotte's islands, the lofty coast of which forms several inlets. The current had no sensible influence; I fired a gun and hoisted a flag at the main-mast to attract the natives. We were in 52° 46'; the land ahead five or six miles distant. We had to leeward a point from which some smoke arose; it formed the southern extremity of a spacious entrance strewed with little islands.

We kept to windward to enter another more to the north, where the two Sandwich islanders, whom I had from captain Nye, assured me that he had traded. The natives delayed, and I was close to the point where the fire appeared, when we saw a canoe come from the bay to the north. One of the five Indians in it came on board without any fear, and according to custom, invited us to anchor at Skitansnana, a village which was already known to me, both by the report of Captain Nye, and the information I had received at Masset. This Indian had several otter skins; he showed us one, of very middling quality, for which he asked four blankets. He seemed to disapprove those we showed him, as well as all our woollen goods. Two other canoes visited us, which produced four otter skins and several small furs; the natives probably had others in the trunks on board their canoes. All entertained the same opinion as the first, of our goods, and would only have woollens, and not powder which we offered them. They readily exchanged their small skins for tin utensils, and some articles of hard ware. But it was with great difficulty that we obtained the bad fur of the first that came, and it was impossible to have any others. We had again the sorrow to see valuable furs escape us, the acquisition of which was the principal object of the expedition, for want of suitable objects to exchange. It not being my intention to make any stay in this place, and the wind being favourable to proceed to the south, I took advantage of it to sail to Nootka, intending to touch on the way at Nouhiti or at Naspaté the western point of the same island, if the weather should permit.

The natives of Skitansnana are evidently inferior to those of Masset, as well in stature as in strength and energy. They seemed not to be so well fed, and were far from having that appearance of comfort, abundance, and cleanliness, which distinguishes their neighbours. There is also a marked difference in the district which they inhabit: though it may be less rude than the coasts of the more northern islands, it is more mountainous, entirely covered with trees, which I conceive to be resinous from the gloomy colour of their foliage. Circumstances not being favourable to examine the anchorages at the extremities of the island of Quadra and Vancouver, I resolved to steer directly for Nootka, off which we arrived two days after. On the 5th several canoes appeared and immediately came along side. The boarding nets were fixed not so much to guard against the hostility of the Indians, as to secure ourselves from the importunities of these good people, who by their reiterated cries of wacoch (friend,) shewed great joy at our return. The crew having dined, the long boat proceeded to tow the ship into the harbour, assisted by sixteen canoes, which came with great readiness to meet us, and offered their services in the most friendly manner. At 11 o'clock the Bordelais anchored in Friendly Cove in eight fathoms and a half. Each of the Indians in the canoes which towed us received a small fishing hook : they were much satisfied with this recompense. This second entrance was effected on the anniversary of the first.

At noon Macouina came without attendants ; he appeared very happy to see us again, but he soon expressed how much he was mortified at not being able to satisfy us with respect to the principal object that brought us hither, after the loss which he had just experienced. He then related, with all the marks of grief and indignation, that an American three-masted vessel having entered the cove, he went on board, with his son, at the desire of the captain, who was lame. That after having been received with apparent cordiality, and entertained at the captain's table, they had been seized and bound, by his orders : that to recover his liberty, and that of his son, he had been obliged to give a great quantity of furs, which had exhausted his store ; he added, that this vessel had sailed ten days before, and had been at Naspaté. Notwithstanding the improbabilities of this story, I did not shew any doubt respecting its truth. The ingenuity with which the chief explained, by signs, the terms which we could not understand, and the singular quickness of Eyssautier in comprehending the language of these savages, induced me to believe that I was not mistaken respecting the substance of his narrative, which the old chief delivered in a persuasive and impressive manner. I replied, that though deceived in the hope of finding furs, I was nevertheless his friend ; that I was obliged to him for the reception which he, as well as his people, had given us on our first visit, and, lastly, that the confidence with which he had come on board, immediately on my return, was very agreeable to me. We fired a salute of seven guns, and I added to this honor a present with which he was no less pleased. I gave some articles of less value to his son, Macoula, who had arrived a little after him, in a boat laden with fish for the ship. I let the chief know, that furs being the principal object of my visit, I should depart in two days, if no furs came ; but that if any were brought, I should remain four or five. I begged him to let the subjects of Wicananich come with him. He not only acceded to this request, but promised to send his son to acquaint his neighbours with our arrival, and induce them to bring us their furs. He also readily undertook to procure us a spar for the top-mast, and to have wood cut for us. I wished

to take advantage of the convenience of this station, to take
in as much wood and water as possible, and I was glad to
employ these savages in work on shore, for notwithstanding
their peaceable conduct, and the testimonies of their chief's
good will, I did not like to send my people from the ship.
Macouina went ashore at half past two, and we soon after saw
him leave the cove in a small canoe. The Indians soon brought
wood, morels, and more fish than we could consume; we gave
them in exchange fish hooks, medals, &c. As the disposition
of the natives was so satisfactory, the long boat was sent for
water as soon as the ship was moored.

At half past six Macouina came on board, towing the spar
which he had chosen very judiciously, according to the directions given him. I presented him with a musket, and he
seemed delighted with this mark of my satisfaction. Notwithstanding the pacific conduct of the Indians we took the
usual precautions during the night. The long boat continued
to take in water, which being in small quantities for want of
rain, caused this service to go on slowly. The cooper and the
steward were employed in gathering the young shoots of the
fir, of which beer was made the same evening. The spar
which we had received from Macouina was landed on the
beach near the village, and the carpenters were employed in
squaring it, which they completed in the course of the day.
The Indians brought us great numbers of fish and fire wood.
We had their canoes continually alongside, their conduct was
always peaceable, and we had nothing to complain of but their
poverty. They were not able to furnish us with more than
three small otter skins, which we purchased, as well as some
furs of land animals.

Macouina and his son breakfasted with us, after which the
latter left us to signify our arrival to Wicananich. We were
also visited by their wives, with several little children. Some
presents were made to these ladies, who at our first visit did
not come on board. At half past two, at Macouina's request,
I went on shore with him. He took me to his house,
where I was received by his numerous family and some persons of consequence, with repeated cries of wacoch! wacoch!
These exclamations were frequently uttered in chorus during
the very animated discourse of the old chief, of which I understood rather by his attitudes than his words, only the expressions of his affections for us; and it seemed to me also to
contain some imprecations against the Americans. This part
of his speech seemed to be listened to with indifference by his
auditors, and in his own manner there was an air of affectation.
These circumstances favoured the suspicions which I had con-

ceived of Macouina's story, that what he related of the perfidy of the American captain was a mere fiction, to excuse
himself for breaking the promise he had made the year before, to
reserve all his furs for me. However, the poverty which appeared in the abode of this chief, and the dress of his subjects,
seemed to attest the truth of his statement. In his hut I saw
but one musket, which was the one I had given him the day
before. It is true, we might suppose that he had already removed the great part of his riches to his winter residence at
Tachès. After his discourse he eat some boiled fish, and then
took from a trunk a goblet and a bottle containing a little
brandy, and giving me to understand that it was the remainder
of what I had presented him last year, invited me to drink. After this visit I went to look at our carpenters, and then took a
walk in the village, where the inhabitants of both sexes expressed their joy at our return. I remarked the same want of
European articles which had already struck me in the Indians
that came on board. Very few had any blankets, and these
were so dirty that it is evident they were not the produce of
the trade of the year. The village which had been found entirely
abandoned at the same time the last year, was nearly deserted
at our second visit.

During my walk Macoula returned much disappointed at
having been obliged to give up his embassy, on account
of the very high sea which he had met with out of the port.
I returned to Macouina's hut, and this time prolonged my
visit to examine his spacious dwelling, which we had found
uninhabited and even stript the year before. It was seventy-
four feet long, thirty-six broad, and about thirteen high to
the top, and was divided into only three compartments. The
partitions, which did not go up to the roof, formed two
apartments to the right and left of the principal door, which
was made in the middle of the long side opposite the port.
These chambers, between which was a passage, took up nearly half the depth of the house. Along three sides there was
a platform raised a few inches, covered with mats, serving for
sleeping places. Trunks were placed on the sides, and enormous bottles, formed of the entire skin of a seal, and containing train oil, were suspended to the walls and the timber of
the roof. Several of these immense vessels were ornamented
with strange paintings. Macouina inhabited the apartment
on the left, and his son that on the right. Each had its fire
place in the middle; the roof over it being open to let out the
smoke. I remarked more cleanliness in the apartment of
Macoula, which, indeed, was less frequented and less encumbered than that of his father. This young chief had a wife,

whose countenance was pretty agreeable, and one child; on his return from his fatiguing and fruitless embassy, she presented him with something to eat; these very slight attentions and some cold caresses seemed to us, under such circumstances, but faint marks of attachment between a young couple who had hardly been married a year. I was but little surprised at it, being accustomed to the manners of these men, in whom a precarious existence and a state of constant hostility with all the creation, tend to develope the hateful passions rather than mild affections. The other half of the house, in which there were only mats and some fishing implements, and household utensils, was the habitations of the slaves. Two colossal and monstrous figures already mentioned, were the principal decorations of this Indian dwelling.

I returned on board with Macouina and his son, where I was visited by Omacteachloa, who said he had come on purpose from Tachès, to see his good friends, the French. The evening passed in conversing, in the most friendly manner, whether it was, that our conduct had gained the good will of the Indians, or that their own interest made them put on the appearance. As, among other subjects, I spoke of the possibility of another visit to Nootka, the old chief expressed a lively wish that we would return, and form a permanent establishment, as the Spaniards had formerly done. He was also extremely desirous to keep Eyssautier till my return: his happy character, joined to a singular facility in comprehending their language and signs, gained him the favour of all the savages, with whom he was our natural interpreter. Macouina begged me to leave him behind, and endeavoured to gain him by the assurance of his constant friendship, by the offer of a wife of a family of distinction, of his own choice, and the promise to let him share with him in the noble labours of the whale fishery, and the pursuit of sea-otters. Nothing seemed to him more seducing, and more calculated to shake the resolution of our young companion, than the picture which he gave him of the delightful repose he would enjoy during the bad season, or rather the absolute idleness in which he would be able to indulge, and which he expressed in a manner not to be mistaken, by folding his arms, and pretending to go to sleep. He then explained, in a very intelligible manner, that he had concluded a treaty with the Spaniards, which he made us understand by signs, had been put in writing; that by this convention he had ceded to them a piece of ground, on the coast of the bay, in return for a quantity of iron instruments, woollens, &c., which they delivered to him at stated periods; that they lived together on the most friendly footing.

(the Spaniards occupying one part of the cove and the Indians the other) ; that they had built large houses, and erected batteries upon the little Islands at the entrance ; that their presence was very advantageous to him, well as on account of the useful things which he received from them, as the terror they inspired into his enemies. He expressed great regret at their departure, spoke in high terms of the commanders, Quadra, Alava, and Fidalgo, and gave to all the Spaniards in general, except to Martinez, praises, which seemed to be assented to by Omacteachloa himself, who, in his hatred to the murderer of his father, did not include his countrymen, who had had no share in his crime.

Macouina spoke also in praise of Vancouver, Broughton, and the English captains who frequented Nootka at the same time. He mentioned, among others, Meares, who, he said, had built a small house, in a place which he pointed out to me, in the western extremity of the village. I took this opportunity to obtain, at the fountain-head, information on a subject which has become interesting, on account of the quarrel to which it gave rise. The result of my enquiry was, that Meares's house had been built with the permission of Macouina, but that there had not been any act of cession or treaty between them. These, then, are the buildings erected by Meares, and his rights to districts and portions of land, rights which England pretends were transferred to it by Meares, who went from Macao to America, under the Portuguese flag, without any public character whatever. Such was the subject of the quarrel, which was on the point of kindling a war between the three great maritime powers, in 1790, and for which France alone fitted out forty-five ships of the line. The chiefs left us at seven o'clock, and were soon followed by the canoes which were alongside of us. A few minutes after, a small canoe with a single Indian approached softly, and with the greatest precaution. This poor fellow, who shewed much fear lest Macouina should be acquainted with his visit, could hardly be persuaded to come on board, and approach the candle, under pretence of remaining incognito ; but the cause of all this mystery was, that he had the skin of a land otter to dispose of, which he hoped to pass off in the dark for a sea otter. We had obtained only one fine skin during the whole day.

On the 8th, the weather being fine, Macoula again set out on his mission to Wicananich. In the night of the 9th, a shoal of herrings came to seek an asylum on our coast, having been chased by a whale, which pursued them to the very bottom of the cove, within a small distance of the land, where the shallowness of the water placed his prey in security. The innumerable quantity of herrings rendering this asylum insufficient, the whale attacked those which remained exposed; struck with terror at his approach they leaped out of the water, with a noise like that produced by a short wave in breaking; a small number of these unhappy fugitives hid themselves under the sides of the ship, and, when the whale approached, we saw them, according to the position of their terrible enemy, pass from one side to the other, with a rapidity which, notwithstanding the phosphorescent streak which they left behind, scarcely allowed the eye to follow their motions.

Some Indians from the interior brought a few furs : but the small quantity they produced did not allow me to hope that sufficient would come to authorize me to prolong my stay, especially as we could not expect that Wicananich would send any. A young man who said he was the son of that chief, had come on board at day break, and had told Eyssautier that no furs would come from his father as long as we remained at this anchorage : but that we should receive some as soon as the vessel should appear upon his coast. This young chief spoke with animosity of Macouina, but seeing Omacteachloa, who was probably sent to watch him, he leaped into his canoe, notwithstanding the endeavours made to persuade him to stay, and went away without seeing me. Upon this I resolved to depart the next day, and sail for California, after having sailed along the coast of Clayoquot to communicate with the canoes of the west side. Thus we learnt, that notwithstanding the diplomatic talent of Macoula, he had failed in his negotiation, which did not astonish me, as I knew that the alliance between these two families, by the marriage of Wicananich, with one of the daughters of Macouina, had not extinguished their rivalship.

Besides the large stock of wood and water, collected without exposing or fatiguing our people, and which would save us much trouble at Saint Francisco, where these things are not to be obtained without difficulty, we had also procured from the natives a great quantity of mats, which would be very useful to us in California to make wheat sacks. Lastly we had obtained here, wholesome and abundant food, consisting of game, fish, and vegetables : of which we took with us sufficient for several days. All this did not cost us above 50 francs, in fishhooks, knives, and trifles, of which we had a great deal more remaining than we could employ. We had also made some casks of good beer : but we had the misfortune to lose the best in the fermentation. These advantages were some compensation for the little success in trading, which increased our stock by only eleven large skins.

On the 11th in the morning every preparation was made to put to sea. Macouina and Omacteachloa did not fail to partake of our dinner, according to their custom: the conversation was animated and very friendly: it was chiefly on our return, which our guests seemed much to desire; they asked us many questions on the subject, which I answered, as much as possible to keep up their hopes without flattering them too much. Macouina made the fairest promises, to induce me to realize them. They took an affectionate leave of us: I gave each of them a present.

It was near six o'clock when we weighed the last anchor; but the wind soon failing, I made the canoes that were still alongside take the tow-rope, and called to the people on shore to send some others; eight or ten soon came, conducted by the old chief in person. With the assistance of our friends, we succeeded in our object, and a breeze from the south-east springing up, the canoes cast off the tow-rope, at our desire. To reward this service, which had been performed with all the zeal of friendship, I gave Macouina a little present, and delivered him a sufficient number of knives to distribute among his people, who had assisted us. We took a last farewell, drinking a glass of brandy together; the old chief and his companions withdrew, crying out *wacoch! wacoch!* as an expression of their wishes for our happy voyage. These manifestations of friendship, so far from our country, surrounded by the gloomy scenes of savage nature, made, I must confess, a deep impression upon my heart, and I should have been sorry not to believe in the sincerity of the sentiments which they expressed.

Soon after ten o'clock we saw a canoe under sail, coming from Point Breakers. It came up to us, and one of the six Indians that composed the crew came on board; this man told us a long story; speaking very loud and quick, like him whom we had seen there the year before, he gave us to understand that the subjects of Wicananich were particularly in want of blankets, and that an American brig had been at anchor two days in one of the ports. Though I was tempted to believe that this was only a trick of Macouina, to make me give up my intention of communicating with his rival, this information made me refrain from exploring the coast of Clayoquot, and the more readily as the weather hardly allowed us to hope that the canoes would come out to trade. As I would not risk the loss of time by going to anchor in the ports of Wicananich, whom I had strong reason to distrust, I resolved to proceed directly to California. Among other powerful motives, the business which I had to settle at St. Francisco, the provisions which it was necessary to replace, the wheat which we had to procure, to fulfil our engagement with the Russians, made it necessary for me to reach that port as soon as possible, as I had to return to New Archangel before the bad season was too far advanced. I thought, however, to touch at New Albion, to the north of Cape Mendorino, if circumstances were favourable.

The numerous ships that have visited Nootka, since the time of Cook, leave little to be said respecting the country and its inhabitants. The government is, in many respects, patriarchal, the chief *(Tahi,)* not only exercising the functions of Prince and Pontiff, but in some manner acting, likewise, as the father of a family. There is no intermediate class between the patricians, *tahis-kalati,* (brothers of the Tahis,) and slaves, *(Mitschlmis,)* among whom are included all those that are not brothers of the chief, or his relations to the third degree, and likewise prisoners of war, and their descendants. We did not learn that there were any of these slaves at Nootka, peace having prevailed for a long time.

They adore a beneficent God, the creator and preserver of all things ; but at the same time they believe in, and abhor, a malevolent divinity, the author of war, death, &c. To obtain the favour of the former, the chief subjects himself to long fasts, and observes the strictest chastity from the new to the full moon. He chaunts hymns in chorus with his family, in praise of the protector, (Kouautzl,) burns train-oil, and throws feathers in the air by way of returning thanks.

They affirm that God, intending to propagate the human race, first created a woman, whom he placed in the flowery groves of Youcouast, (Nootka,) where he had already placed dogs without tails, stags without horns, and birds without wings. In the midst of this company she felt herself alone, and did nothing but weep night and day. Kouautzl being at length moved by her tears, she one day saw a canoe of the brightest copper, full of young persons, who rowed with paddles of the same metal. In the midst of the astonishment which was excited in the solitary woman, by this singular sight, one of the handsome strangers landed on the earth, and announced to her that it was the Almighty himself who had the goodness to visit her retreat, and bestow on her the society for which she longed. At these words the tears of the woman increased, and a humour issued from her nose, some drops of which, on her sneezing, fell on the sand. Kouautzl having commanded her to look that way, she perceived to her great astonishment, a little child, whose body was just formed. The God ordered her to put him in a shell, proportioned to his size, and not to fail to place him in larger ones. The Creator then embarked again; but not without conferring benefits on the animals, for immediately after, the stag had horns, the dog a tail, and the birds wings, with which they soon took flight. The infant grew in size and strength, and was successively transferred to larger shells, till he began to walk. He soon arrived at adolescence, and became the husband of the woman; the chiefs descend from his eldest son, and the rest of the people from his other children.

Their era commences with the arrival of Kouautzl.

They are extremely afraid of Mattoch, a fantastic being, dwelling in the mountains, whom they believe to be a hideous and ferocious monster, covered with black hair, having a human head, with an enormous mouth, furnished with teeth longer and more formidable than those of the bear, and both his hands and feet armed like that animal. The thunder of his voice throws down those who hear it, and he tears in pieces all that have the misfortune to fall in his power. The people of Nootka believe in the immortality of the soul, and that after death it only changes its mode of existence, but with this difference that the souls of their chiefs and of their relations, go and join those of their ancestors residing with Konautzl, and those of the mistchimis into an inferior Elysium, called Pin Paula. The former preside over the thunder and rain, by means of which they manifest their displeasure or good will. They are so proud of their dignity that they are persuaded that if any misfortune happens to a chief, the rain is nothing more than the tears shed by his ancestors from the grief they feel at it. The chiefs, who indulge in luxury and gluttony, or who neglect the worship of the divinity, share in the other world the fate of the mistchimis.

If a degree of felicity, inferior to that of the chiefs, falls to the lot of the common people in the next world, on the other hand, they can better enjoy pleasure in this life, being excused from the abstinence and religious exercises which the chiefs are obliged strictly to observe. The death of a chief is mourned for four months, and the women as a testimony of their grief cut off their hair within a few inches of the head. His body is carried to the summit of a mountain, where it is deposited enveloped in otter skins, in a bier which is suspended to a tree. The chiefs of allied tribes attend the funeral; like most savages, they make incisions on their body as a sign of affliction. On the decease of a chief, as well as of a near relation, some of their particular friends go daily for a certain time to visit his mortal remains, around which they sing hymns expressive of their grief, being convinced that they are

by the soul which hovers about the body till its entire dissolution.   The mistchimis are buried in the ground to be nearer
to the abode, which they are to inhabit with Piu Paula, where
they experience no other privation than that of being separated from their old masters, without any hope of ever attain-
ing the perfect felicity which they enjoy.

The Indians call by the name of tché-ha the shed which
serves as the burying place of the great chiefs of Nootka only.
At the entrance of the shed there are five rows of wooden
statues, rudely carved, extending to the other extremity, where
there is a kind of cabinet decorated with human skulls.   Several of these statues wear the distinctive features of a man,
and even have natural hair.   A gallery of human bones marks
the limits of the shed.   Opposite the entrance there are eight
large whales made of wood, placed in a line, on the back of
each, skulls are symmetrically arranged.   On a lake near the
burying place there is a canoe which is generally strewed with
eagle's feathers.   The interment of the chiefs is performed by
burying their bodies under the shed, eight feet deep : after a
certain time they take them up again, to take off the head,
which is then placed on the back of a whale, in memory of the
skill of the deceased in throwing the harpoon : lastly, they set
up his statue, as a monument to his honour, and to shew that
no other is to be buried in that spot.

None but chiefs have a right to enter this cemetry, and
Macouina had those put to death who he knew had entered it.
He often went there in the night, or early in the morning, before any person in the village was up, to salute the manes of
his ancestors, and to implore the sun, as his god, to render him
happy in the other world.   When Macouina catches a whale
he goes in the night to the shed to render homage to the sun
for the success of the day, and to offer to his ancestors a part
of his prey.   After the conclusion of this ceremony, he presides at the distribution of this whale, which he shares among
all his vassals.   He then ordains a grand fête, which is held in
a small wood behind the village, and where he addresses the
sun aloud, in the presence of all the people.   The diversions
at this fête consist in eating whale's flesh, in dancing to the
sound of a large empty trunk, and in making all kinds of con-
tortions, and above all a great deal of noise.   After these rejoicings Macouina carves a rude figure of a whale in wood,
which he places before the shed in memory of his offering.

The great chiefs of Nootka, their wives, and children to the
age of twelve years only, may be interred in this shed.   As
for other individuals of all classes, they are laid out without
any covering, in the small wood behind the village.   The

natives have the greatest veneration for Macouina; they imagine that he is a relation of the sun, and every time he goes to the shed it is to confer with him; they also believe that the great chiefs return when they please, and that the canoe which is opposite the shed serves them to cross the lake every night; for that is the time, say they, that they return to walk in the village. The notion of these savages that the prince who governs them, will one day be able to command the elements from the abode of the blessed, to which he is to be admitted, inspires them with a profound veneration for a person who will partake in the attributes of the divinity. However, we did not see any thing servile in the homage paid by the people to the chiefs. The dignity of Tahi descends from father to son. It devolved upon Macouina, in the year 1778, when his father was killed by the Tahumasses, a nation inhabiting the other side of the island: his successor avenged his death in a terrible manner.

From the accounts of the English and Spaniards, as well as what we saw ourselves, it seems that there are always at Nootka three principal chiefs, who exercise great authority over the people as delegates of the Tahi, to whom they are entirely subject. At the time of our visit these deputies were Omacteachloa, the son of Canicum; Machoalick, and Noak. Both the Tahi, and Subaltern Chiefs, when age renders them incapable of exercising their functions, often abdicate in favour of their son, if they are able to take their place. The descendants of the collateral relations of the Tahi, who form the body of patricians, lose this privilege in the third generation, and descend into the class of the common people. These miserable chiefs, of hungry and half naked tribes, the dirty inhabitants of smoky huts, are as proud of their illustrious origin as the first potentates of the civilized world. Their wives and daughters share their pride. The rank of persons of this sex is determined by that of their father and mother.

At Nootka, and on all the north-west coast, polygamy is in custom among the Tahis and nobles, who consider it as a mark of wealth and greatness. In fact, they cannot obtain a girl in marriage without giving the parents furs, canoes, European clothing, muskets, &c. they are therefore a source of riches to their fathers if they are at all well looking. The poor Mitschimis who can dispose of but a small part of the fruit of their labours, are seldom able to go to such an expense; the most fortunate are those to whom the Tahi gives a wife for their services; the majority live in a melancholy celibacy. Though the women are bought in this manner, they are treated with much mildness by their husbands; who require from them only the household cares and labours which are suitable to their sex. According to various creditable accounts, the women exercise a decided supremacy over the other sex: in some tribes of the north, they have been seen to use the men in the most cruel manner. It is certain that in those parts the matrons assist in their deliberations. It is almost always one of them that commands the war canoes. The destruction of the first Russian establishment at Sitka, was resolved upon in consequence of the complaints of the women of the neighbouring tribes, who were incensed at the contempt of the mistress of the Governor. Among other affronts, this woman, a Creole of Kodiak, had spit in the wooden ornament in the lower lip of the wife of a chief; they told the men that if they had not courage to fight the Russians, they would go and attack the fort themselves.

At Nootka, and I believe along the whole coast, the nuptial ceremonies are confined to an entertainment. The women marry about the same age as in Europe. When a chief has a son, he shuts himself up for a time in his hut without looking at the sun or sea, for fear of drawing upon himself the anger of Kouautzl, who causes his death as well as that of the infant. At the end of a month the father gives him a name before the assembled chiefs, to whom he gives an entertainment and presents. The son of a chief, as he enters the different changes of life, successively takes a new name, which is always significant or allegorical. The same change is made for a girl when she is grown up. This change is accompanied with much ceremony if she is the daughter of a great chief; it is accompanied by games, in which prizes are given to the conquerors. The Tahi then taking her to a loom tells her, that now she is become a woman she must attend to the duties of her sex. From that time she no more quits her father's house, renounces dancing, singing, and all the amusements of childhood, applies to the various works suitable to women, and observes an exemplary reserve in her behaviour.

The conduct of the inhabitants of Nootka induces us to believe, that they are the tribe, on the whole north-west coast, an intercourse with whom is the least dangerous to navigators; it must also be confessed, that it is one of the weakest, and the poorest, we have hitherto seen. However, the comparative mildness of the manners of these savages, gives reason to presume, that the sense of their inferiority is not the only cause of their moderation. They are but little addicted to theft, the general vice of savages. Their population does not seem to have been diminished since the arrival of the navigators who visited them.

On the whole, the people of Nootka are but little favoured by nature; they are dirty and idle, and, at present, poor and week, but they are generally pretty intelligent, and have a lively imagination. They have much mildness and docility in their character, are inclined to good, and sensible to kindness. The chiefs, though always ready to ask, are not destitute of generous sentiments. They are good hearted, and the best people on the whole north-west coast; they may be dealt with on a more confidential footing, and from whom navigators can the most easily obtain a supply of their wants.

The weather, on the 13th, was extremely fine, and the sky remarkably clear; but, on the 14th, a mist in the horizon, in the east, indicated the neighbourhood of the land, along which we sailed. A wood-pigeon, exhausted with fatigue, lighted on the rigging, and was taken. Nothing particular happened the two or three following days; but on the 17th, at seven o'clock in the morning, a gentle breeze sprung up from south-south-east, and soon after we descried the land, at a great distance, in the north-east, which was indistinctly seen the whole morning, extending from east-south-east to north. At six o'clock we took the bearings, the last points, as well as the summits, being hid by the clouds. We saw several fires on the low land nearest to us. One of these extended for a great space to the north-east, and was seen several hours. At midnight we spread all our sails, and steered southward, parallel to the coast, which, in all this part, is of equal height, pretty regular, and generally woody. At six o'clock, after having gone twenty-two miles, we had, to the south-south-east, a point, which I judged to be Cape Mendocino. At half past seven, we suddenly discovered, to the south-south-east, a considerable fire on Cape Mendocino; this fire covered the greater part of the hill, from the sea-shore to the summit, and it appeared to extend to the other side. Impelled by a fresh breeze, it made a rapid progress. This mountain of fire, its summit crowned with immense clouds of smoke, the sea shining with the reflection, which every wave mutiplied, the rocks scattered round the promontory, and the second hill clothed with various tints, this prospect, in the gloom of night, was of the most majestic description, and filled the soul with exalted ideas.

Accurate inquiries at Saint Francisco, convinced me that this fire which, at a distance, might have been mistaken for a volcano, must be ascribed to the Indians, as well as other less considerable, and more distant ones, which we saw that and the preceding nights. The natives, at this season, set fire to the grass, to dry the pods of a grain which they use for food, to render it more easy to gather. It was, doubtless, this circumstance, which was unknown to our illustrious La Peyrouse, and that was the cause of his error, when seeing a great fire on Cape Mendocino, about the same time of the year, he thought it was a volcano. The wind being very faint, we did not make any rapid progress, and it was not till the 20th that we arrived at Saint Francisco. We passed close to the point on which the fort stands, which presented a scene of animation for that country, and very agreeable to us. All the Presidio had come out; we distinguished the governor Arguello, and our other friends, who welcomed us with attitudes of congratulation. They hailed the ship as it passed the fort, we answered that she came from Nootka. At six o'clock we cast anchor near the Presidio, in seven fathoms. I immediately went on shore, where I was received as an old friend, by Don Louis and the other officers.

The next day, I immediately set about two things, which would have obliged me to go back to California, even if I had not had occasion to go there, to receive the price of the goods, which I had left there at my two preceding visits. Our salt meat and vegetables were almost entirely consumed, and it was indispensable to lay in a stock to serve us, till we reached China. It was also of great importance to me, to procure produce from the country, to fulfil the engagements which we had contracted with the governor of New Archangel; and, secondly, to be able to pay, in the least burthensome manner possible, the debt contracted in consequence of the affair of the 18th of June. A tent was erected near the landing place, as a workshop for the cooper, and for other necessary operations.

After having made arrangements with Don Louis, I repaired to the mission, to agree for the daily supply of bread, and fresh vegetables, and to consider of means for obtaining from the missions situated upon the port, wheat, tallow, and pulse. Father Ramon was at Saint Raphael, a new establishment, formed on the northern coast; I found only his colleague, Father Vincente Oliva, who, not having the power of his superior, to treat upon business, could only confirm my hopes of the inclination of the mission to supply me with any part of their produce that I might desire. Father Vincente merely engaged to send me the daily supply of provision, and the salt necessary for pickling our stores.

A courier was dispatched to Montouy the same day, to give notice of our arrival. On the 25th, Don Louis having sent me word that the courier had arrived with the orders of the governor concerning us, I went to the Presidio, where he communicated to me the dispatch, containing the orders which the governor gave respecting us. They were, that the Bordelais, which was upon an expedition wholly commercial, should be subject to the prohibitory regulations lately published: that it should not be permitted to remain in the port longer than was necessary to supply its most urgent wants : that it should not be allowed to have any communications, except for this purpose, and that only on the beach. The same courier brought news of the arrival of the Russian frigate, the Kamt-schatka, and the return of the Kutusoff, which she had met going out; the latter had sailed again. On the 22d, the Columbia brig, with which we had communicated off Sitka, arrived at Montouy.

The most positive information leaving me no doubt that, in adopting towards us measures so different from the treatment which we had before received, the hateful insinuations of the captains of Peruvian privateers had been listened to; one of them having expressed his blind jealousy while we were at Callao; I resolved to go to Montouy, to do away the effects of these calumnies. But Don Louis, to whom I was obliged to apply for permission, and the means to take the journey, assured me that he was not authorized to grant my request, and that I had only to write to the governor. My letter to Don Pablo Vicentes Sola, governor of Upper California, was to the following effect, "that after the hospitable reception which I had till then met with, in the various ports of Spanish America at which I touched, and particularly in the ports of his government, I could not ascribe the rigorous treatment which I had now met with, to any thing but false reports; my conduct having been unexceptionable, could not have caused such a change. As I was certain of removing, if I could have the honour of seeing him, the unfavorable impression which he might have received, I begged him to allow me to go to Montouy. If he should not think proper to grant me this favour, I requested him to make strict enquiries into the facts, which might have been imputed to me, and even to have an examination on board the ship. That if the result was favourable to me, as I was assured it would be, I begged him to allow me a fortnight to re-victual, and, especially, to lay in a stock of salt provisions. I likewise asked permission to land some sick, on whose health the air of the country could not fail to have the most salutary effect, and their presence need not cause any uneasiness, as they had no contagious disorder." I also acquainted the governor with the engagements that I had entered into with the governor of the Russian settlements, and begged him to enable me to fulfil them. I, at the same time, wrote to Captain Golownen, to acquaint him of my situation, and to ask his good offices, to ensure the success of an operation which would be useful to the colonies of his own nation.

These dispatches were sent on the 26th, with those of Don Louis, who consented, till he received new orders, to mitigate the rigour of the restrictions imposed upon us. The answer of the governor, Don Pablo de Sola, came on the 28th; it was conceived in very polite, but very vague terms. I thought it tolerably satisfactory, though all my requests were not explicitly granted. He consented to my taking in provisions, but he did not clearly express himself respecting the articles which I desired to take in as a cargo. I also received a letter from Captain Golownin, who had had the kindness to speak in my favour to the Governor, from whom he had not obtained a more precise answer than I had received. He gave me very prudent advice respecting my intention of taking corn to New Archangel; this advice was founded on the abundant supply which those establishments would receive from the Kutusoff, which had five hundred tons on board, and might have induced me to renounce my intentions, if my arrangements with Mr. Heigemeister had not been both a sufficient guarantee on his side, and an indispensable obligation on mine. He told me that the Columbia, which at its arrival had asked his protection, met with the same difficulties at Montouy, as I had met with at Saint Francisco. Captain Golownin informing me of his approaching departure for Russia, obligingly offered to take charge of my packets for France.

Don Louis sent a circular letter to the three missions, desiring them to send their corn on board. This circular was drawn up in such terms as shewed rather that it came from him than from the superior authority, the consequence of which was, that the Father Superior did not consider this as sufficient authority, and would not suffer the corn to be sent. However, he wrote immediately to the Governor in the most urgent terms, requesting him to give permission for the exportation of the corn which was no less advantageous for the country than ourselves. The commandant, both the military and the colonial came on board to provide themselves with such articles as they wanted, especially woollens and all kinds of clothing, all supplies from New Spain having ceased for some years in consequence of the troubles. The courier sent by the Father Superior to Montouy, returned on the 9th with dispatches entirely satisfactory. He immediately informed the missions that they might send the corn which they had to dispose of.

On the 10th another courier arrived from Montouy bringing dispatches in which the governor stated that an American brig which had arrived at San Barbara from the Sandwich islands, affirmed it had left there two vessels of Buenos Ayres, carrying thirty-two, and twenty-four guns : which were to make an attack upon California. In consequence of this notice Don Louis took such defensive measures as his small resources permitted to repel an attack.*

The health of the crew had sensibly improved : one of the three sick, whom we had sent to the mission on our arrival, and several others who had been subsequently attacked, were entirely recovered ; but two were unable to undertake another voyage to the North, and I therefore consented to leave them behind, and paid them their wages that they might have some resource in a strange country. The superiors of the mission promised to pay them every attention till they were recovered, and I gave him a letter to the governor, thanking him for the regulations which he had ordered out of humanity for our sick, begging him to continue his protection, and when opportunity offered, put them in a way to go to Europe. On the 17th I went to the mission to settle our accounts, to take leave of the superior, and to see our sick men once more. I encouraged them by informing them of the favourable disposition of the Governor of the Missionaries, through which they would find means to return to France when their health permitted. I exhorted them to behave in a manner worthy the kindness shewn them, and honourable to the nation to which they belonged. I gave each of them a certificate of my satisfaction with their conduct and services.

I likewise settled with Don Louis his private account and the duties both on the articles embarked as a cargo, and on the goods imported by way of payment. These latter were taxed at seven and a half per cent. on the sale price ; the corn fifteen per cent, and the tallow sixteen per cent. on the value. The total produce of the sale on our three visits was 6226 piasters, that of the purchases, provisions, and duties, included 6356 piasters, being an overplus of 130 piasters which was paid in specie.

All the preparations for our departure being concluded, I took leave of Don Louis and his Lieutenant, who came to partake of the last dinner that we should have in their country. About five in the afternoon our friends took leave with the most cordial expressions of friendship and good will on both sides. The wind being very weak and contrary, the high lands to the north of Port San Francisco were still in sight at six o'clock in the evening of the 19th.

---

* This attack was made soon after our departure, upon Montouy and the Southern presidios which were conquered without much resistance. San Francisco was not disturbed.

On the 20th of October, at two o'clock in the morning, we set sail from St. Francisco for New Archangel. In the course of our voyage we experienced a very violent storm, which did considerable damage to our vessel; we however arrived without any serious accident at Sitka, on the 9th of November. The following morning I waited upon Mr. Heigemeister, the governor, and Mr. Yanowsky, to whom he had delegated his powers, because he was shortly going to set sail for Europe. These gentlemen made no difficulty to receive, according to our agreement, the corn which I had brought, though the Kutusoff had taken a cargo on board at California. During the month that we remained at Sitka, we made the necessary repairs to our ship, after landing our corn. We then re-embarked our sanders wood, which we had deposited in the warehouses, and took in our stock of wood and water. On the 7th of December, the Kutusoff set sail, to return to Europe, by way of the Cape of Good Hope. I went to take leave of Captain Heigemeister, from whom I had experienced much kindness.

On the 12th of December all our labours being finished, we landed the remainder of the goods which Mr. Yanowsky had accepted in payment of the balance due from us to the Company. By means of these goods, which we could not possibly have got rid of in China, and the provisions from California, we had but a very small sum to pay in specie, both for the indemnity due for the Kodiaks killed at Kowalt, and for the articles of various kinds which we had been supplied with. Among these were a cable and anchor, a boat, some spars, cordage, sail-cloth, &c. We did not get clear of the Bay till 9 o'clock the following morning, when we experienced an extraordinary change in the temperature, for we were scarcely a league out at sea when the thermometer, which had been at 4° below zero, in the port, rose to 4° above it. At sun-set we finally quitted the north-west coast of America, which we had explored during ten months, with more danger and fatigue than I had ever endured at sea.

The experience we had in these ten months fully confirmed what our predecessors have observed of the great diminution of the otters on the north-west coast, especially about the Strait of Fuca, and the island of Quadra, or Vancouver. Farther to the north the otters are more numerous, and it is even affirmed that the race is not sensibly diminished. According to every account, all the coasts both of the continent and the islands situated to the north of the 51st degree, are more frequented by the otters than those to the south. The Indian tribes, from whom the furs are to be purchased, being weak,

and scattered for the most. part without fixed abodes, the difficulty of meeting with them on the immense extent of coast
over which they roam, is one of the principal obstacles that
navigators meet with in their traffic on these coasts.

For the first two days after we left Sitka we had a very
strong east wind, but met with no remarkable occurrence on
the whole voyage to Owhyee, where we cast anchor off the
village where Tameamea resided, on the ninth of January,
1819.

The wind was so unfavourable that it took us three days to
go to Woahoo, and after we had employed five days in embarking the water and provisions, and some sanders wood, we
were detained seven days longer by south winds and calms.
The chagrin caused by this delay was something alleviated by
the kindness of three American gentlemen, Messrs. Davis and
Meck, owner and captain of the Eagle, of Boston, and Mr.
Pigot, of the Fouster, who had lately arrived from Kamtschat-
ka. Taking leave again of Woahoo, on the 26th of January,
I steered southwards, to the eighteenth degree, intending to
keep in that latitude till we reached the Mariana Islands.

On the 24th we came in sight of Assumption and Agrigan.
The summit of the former was constantly hidden by a small
cloud, or white vapour, from which flakes, which soon disappeared, every moment detached themselves. I think it can
only be the smoke of some subterraneous fire. Early in the
morning of the 7th of March, we were only a few miles from
the northernmost of the Bachees islands, and on the 9th came
in sight of the coast of China. On the 11th we cast anchor
off Macao, to which I immediately went to procure a pilot, to
conduct us to Wampou. The ship did not anchor in the roads
till the following day, which, for the inhabitants of that town,
was the 13th of March. We advanced our reckoning a day
accordingly. I returned on board with the pilot, and on the
17th, in the afternoon, we anchored at Wampou, alongside the
Indienne of Nantes.

The delays which we had experienced, both in America and
the Sandwich Islands, had an unfavourable influence upon our
operations in China, where we did not arrive till the latter end
of the season. The difficulties which obstruct business at this
late period of the year, were increased by the extraordinary
number of Americans, who, having preceded us, had caused
the value of imported goods to fall, and had exhausted, or
raised the price of, the produce of the country.

I endeavoured to avail myself of the smallness of my ship,
and the insignificance of its cargo to be excused from the
enormous duties imposed upon our ve ,sels, at a time when all

those which came to China were of large burden, and to have it treated like the Americans coming from the north-west coast ; notwithstanding the absurdity of assimilating the Bordelais to a Company's ship, the Chinese alleging the established custom, rejected my application : the only advantage I obtained was a reduction of 700 piastres in the payment to the Comprador, the best part of which, as well as other similar expenses, turns to the advantage of the authorities.

We left Wampou on the 23rd of April and cast anchor before Macao on the 25th. I passed the following day in that town to dispatch my packets for France, and to take in wine and some medicines. On the 27th we sailed in company with the Indienne.

Before I quit China I must acknowledge the kind reception given me by factors and merchants of the several European Nations. I shall not continue my narrative any further as the interest attached to the expedition of the Bordelais till its arrival in China does not extend to the voyage home, which could add nothing to the knowledge that we have already acquired by two centuries of constant intercourse. I shall content myself with saying that leaving Macao on the 17th of April, we stopped from the 1st to the 17th of July at the isle of France to repair a leak, doubled the cape on the 13th of August, and having been delayed by unfavourable winds in the voyage to the Azores, the Bordelais was obliged to ask a supply of provisions from three different vessels, and did not make the coast of Oleron till the 19th of November. She entered the Gironde on the 21st, and thus completed her voyage round the World in 37 months and two days, having been 22 months and 6 days under sail.

FINIS.

D. Sidney and Co. Printers, Northumberland Street, Strand.

INDEX

TO VOL. IX.

———

Check Out More Titles From HardPress Classics Series In this collection we are offering thousands of classic and hard to find books. This series spans a vast array of subjects – so you are bound to find something of interest to enjoy reading and learning about.

Subjects:
Architecture
Art
Biography & Autobiography
Body, Mind &Spirit
Children & Young Adult
Dramas
Education
Fiction
History
Language Arts & Disciplines
Law
Literary Collections
Music
Poetry
Psychology
Science
…and many more.

Visit us at www.hardpress.net

CPSIA information can be obtained
at www.ICGtesting.com
Printed in the USA
BVHW071036150819
555975BV00016B/1216/P